AFRICA'S GOLD COAST THROUGH PORTUGUESE SOURCES

Fontes Historiae Africanae/Sources of African History is an international editing and publication project initiated in 1962 to organise a series of critical editions of the sources for the history of sub-Saharan Africa (i.e. Africa south of the Mediterranean lands), under the general auspices of the Union Académique Internationale. In 1973 the British Academy established a British committee to publish volumes in the series. Since 1997, the volumes issued by the British Academy's Committee have been published in the **New Series**.

FONTES HISTORIAE AFRICANAE
SOURCES OF AFRICAN HISTORY
22

AFRICA'S GOLD COAST THROUGH PORTUGUESE SOURCES

1469–1680

EDITED BY

KWASI KONADU

Published for THE BRITISH ACADEMY
by OXFORD UNIVERSITY PRESS

Oxford University Press, Great Clarendon Street, Oxford OX2 6DP

© The British Academy 2022
Database right The British Academy (maker)

First edition published 2022

British Library Cataloguing in Publication Data
Data available

Library of Congress Cataloging in Publication Data
Data available

Typeset by Newgen Publishing UK
Printed in Great Britain by
TJ Books Ltd, Padstow, Cornwall

ISBN Hardback 978-0-19-726706-6
ISBN Digital ebook (epub) 978-0-19-288471-8

To the memory of the African lives recorded in these documents

CONTENTS

Contents

GLOSSARY

Adail: a military commander.

Aguardente: literally, 'burning water' or 'fire-water.' Brandy or any distilled beverage.

Alabarda: literally, 'halberd.'

Albarda: a jacket, and a pack saddle.

Alçada: a kind of itinerant tribunal.

Alcaidaria: the office of *Alcaide*, the governor of a fortified village or a fortress.

Alcaide-mor (or chief *Alcaide*): the governor of a fortified village or a fortress.

Aldeia: a settlement ranging in size between a town (*vila*) and a hamlet (*lugar, povoação*).

Aldea do torço: Akatakyi, also known as 'Komenda.'

Aldea das duas partes: literally, 'village of two parts,' referring to the area divided by the Benya River, creating a peninsula on which the São Jorge da Mina fortress was built in 1482 and an adjacent village called Adena.

Algália: the glandular secretion produced by the civet, used for making perfumes.

Aljaravia: a type of tunic, with short wide sleeves and hood. This 'dressing gown' was made in Morocco, purchased by Portuguese merchants, and sold or exchanged on the Mina (Gold) Coast.

Almadia: a canoe or, more generally, a small boat, such as a ship's boat or cutter.

Almafega (also written *almáfega* or *almárfega*): a coarse, light-colored woolen cloth, which was used, among other things, for sacks and to wear during mourning.

Almoxarifado: the office of the *Almoxarife* (collector of the royal rents and duties) or the district under his jurisdiction. The *Almoxarife* was also responsible for guarding, distributing, and inventorying goods.

Almude: a measure of volume, which varied geographically, between approximately 15 and 25 liters.

Alqueire: during the fifteenth and seventeenth centuries, roughly equivalent to 10–13 liters.

Apontador: literally, a 'pointer,' that is, someone who took note of absences and other matters related to the attendance at formal occasions, such as an election.

Arame: a type of red-colored copper, from which, when mixed with calamine, brass is made.

Armação: outfit; in some cases, probably a ship with its cargo and crew.

Armazém: 'a structure (both material and social) combining the concepts of a warehouse and a fitting-out base'; 'warehouse' is thus only a partial translation.[1]

Arrátel: a unit of weight, equivalent to approximately 0.460 kilograms.

Arrecadação: the term has perhaps as its closest equivalent in English 'bill (of exchange).' According to context, it may be translated as 'bill' or, more frequently, as 'receipt.'

Arribar: to make an unscheduled call at a port; to make port, or to divert a ship from its course (possibly by boarding it).

Arroba: a unit of weight, equivalent to approximately 14.5 kilograms.

Assentamento: literally, 'settlement,' a given amount of money paid by the King to members of the Royal Household and other noblemen.

Atabaque: a tall, wooden, hand-drum.

Audiência: literally, 'Audience'; the place where a magistrate listens to the parties in public.

Auto-da-fé: literally, 'trial of faith.' A ceremony for the punishment of convicted heretics, operated by the Portuguese Tribunals of the Inquisition.

Bacharel: holder of a first degree from the university.

Balão: a fast vessel, like the brigantine.

Banda: 'two strips of cotton one or two palms wide' which 'the [Africans used] for covering themselves.'[2]

Bar (sing.): unit of mass, the equivalent of 16 to 21 *arrobas*, or a quarter of one *quintal*.

Barça: a kind of basket or cover for bottles and other glass vessels.

Barca: a small boat, such as a ship's boat or cutter.

Barinel: a vessel, probably propelled by both oars and sails, which was heavier and shorter than the caravel.[3]

Barrete: a kind of brimless cap, usually made of wool.

Batel: a small boat, such as a ship's boat or cutter.

Batelada: the maximum cargo carried by a *batel* (i.e. a small boat, such as a ship's boat).

Beatilha (cf. English *Bettille*): a fine muslin. The Portuguese purchased significant quantities of *beatilhas,* some of a striped variety, others dyed red, and still others embellished with flowered embroidery.

Benesses: the income received by a parish priest from weddings, funerals and baptisms.

---

[1] See P.E.H. Hair, 'Portuguese Documents on Africa and Some Problems of Translation,' *History in Africa* 27 (2000): 95.

[2] António Brásio, ed., *Monumenta Missionaria Africana. Africa Occidental* (Lisbon: Agência Geral do Ultramar, Divisão de Publicações e Biblioteca, 1952–88), 3: 89–113.

[3] See also George Robert Schwarz, 'The History and Development of Caravels '(Master's Thesis, Texas A&M University, May 2008).

Bentinho: diminutive form of *bento*, i.e. 'blessed,' meaning a small scapulary.

Berço: a small breech-loading cannon, in the same category as the falcon but of a smaller caliber, probably the equivalent of the falconet.

Bergantim: two-masted vessels (the same as *fragatim*).

Besta: usually refers to beasts of burden such as mules.

Bilharda: a children's game played with sticks with tapered ends, like tip-cat.

Biscoito: a kind of hard bread, especially designed to last longer; also known in English as 'pilot biscuit,' 'ship's biscuit,' 'sea biscuit' or 'hardtack.'

Boçal: 'ignorant of the Portuguese language'; frequently used to mean 'newly-arrived enslaved person' who had not yet learned Portuguese.

Bolinar: to sail with the bowlines hauled or to sail close to the wind.

Bolo: a mass of dough, usually round, which is cooked in an oven.

Bombardeiro: an early form of cannon which fired stone balls (or cannonballs), or the person who bombards.

Bordão: a kind of palm tree, with a sweet sap, from which the *maluvo*, a fermented beverage, is made.

Borzeguins: knee high boots.

Braga: short and loose shorts.

Brocatilho: an inferior sort of brocade.

Bruxaria: witchcraft. See also *feitiço/feiticaria*.

Bueta: a box or a small box; a coffer.

Búzio: species of cowry found in West Africa and the Indian Ocean and used as currency.

Cabaia: a kind of tunic, low-cut, closed in front and open at the sides, of mid-leg length, which was originally made from a certain type of light silk called *cabaia*.

Cabeceira: literally, 'head' as in 'head of the bed/table'; the title given to someone who governs over others, as a leader of a group, thus the 'headman.' *Cabeça* was also used for a ruler or chief minister.

Cabo: the person who is the head; also, in some contexts, the same as 'corporal.'

Calabrete: a thinner mooring line or hawser; probably the same as 'warp.'

Calico: general term the English applied to all Indian cottons; the name is derived from Calicut in Malabar, southern India. Originally, *calico* was a specific variety of Indian cotton cloth.

Canada: from the Low Latin *cannata*, ancient measure of capacity of 4 *quartilhos*; the *quartilho* was the fourth part of the *canada*, equivalent today to half a liter. The *canada* was thus equivalent to 2 liters.

Capitão de mar e guerra ('captain of sea and war'): the official holding the command of the largest ships, such as men-of-war.

Capitão-mor ('captain-major'): title of Portuguese military commanders but referring also to the office of governor at a fortified post on behalf of its territorial ruler and to the representative of the Portuguese King in overseas territories.

Carapuça: a kind of flexible, conical cap.

Caravela (caravel): small-sized vessel with crew of 20 to 30 people.

Caravelão: a ship similar to the caravel, though smaller.

Caroço: possibly the same as 'nut.'

Carreira: see *Navio de carreira*.

Casa: literally, 'house'; an organized body.

Casa de Guiné: the Guinea agency, responsible for contracts and trade with West Africa in Lisbon.

Casa da Índia: the 'India House' in Lisbon, at which goods arriving from Asia were unloaded and auctioned, and duties collected.

Casa Real: royal household.

Casas de Lisboa (also known as *Sete Casas* ['Seven Houses']): these were specialized in the collection of the *sisa*, a tax imposed on certain kinds of products.

Caudel (or *chaudel*; pl. *caudéis/chaudéis*): a kind of calico used for bedcovers.

Cavaleiro fidalgo (or knight *fidalgo*): a rank of the nobility.

Cavaleiro mercador: literally, 'gentleman merchant,' i.e. a nobleman who traded in goods.

Chantre: Precentor.

Chatim: trafficker, dishonest trader.

Clérigo de missa: an ordained cleric, able to celebrate Mass, as opposed to *clérigo de evangelho* (deacon) and *clérigo de epístola* (subdeacon).

Com salva: that is, with the proviso (for example, that the original document, or a first copy, had been lost), an equivalent of 'second copy.'

Comarca: Portuguese territorial and judicial subdivision of a state or region.

Comarcãos: the inhabitants of a *comarca* (a territorial subdivision, in which justice is administered by a magistrate named *Corregedor*).

Comenda: a grant, usually in the form of a piece of land, bestowed on clergymen and knights of military orders. This term was likely used on the Mina (Gold) Coast for a 'piece of land' known locally at Akatakyi, but for which the Portuguese called 'Komenda.'

Con registro de Su Majestad [Spanish]: i.e. carrying goods which were previously registered in the port of loading, so that duties be paid for them.

Condestável: either a commander of artillery or a keeper of a fortress.

Côngrua: unlike the English 'congrua,' the contribution of parishioners to the sustenance of the parish priest.

Conselho Ultramarino ('Overseas Council'): directorate of the maritime empire in Lisbon.

Consulado: like the *alfândega*, a customs house, but one where export duties were paid.

Consulta: denotes both the action of inquiring, discussing or issuing opinions, and the paper where the results of that action are recorded.

Contador: an official of the Exchequer, who assisted the Overseers of the Exchequer (Vedores da Fazenda).

Conto: one million.

Contrariedade: the counter-argument presented by the defendant's attorney to the prosecutor's charges.

Contrato de São Tomé: a monopoly of trade in São Tomé and adjacent areas rented out by the Crown to private persons.[4]

Coronheiro: 'stocker' or 'finisher,' the one who made and finished the stocks and other wooden parts of the gun.

Corregedor: a royal official, a kind of magistrate, responsible for administering justice in each of the Portuguese territorial subdivision known as *comarcas*.

Correição: the district over which the *Corregedor* has jurisdiction; the visit of a *Corregedor* to administer justice in the places of his jurisdiction.

Cortes: the Portuguese parliamentary body, where the three estates of the realm were represented.

Costume: in trial documents, a witness is asked 'the customary questions' regarding any enmity existing between himself and the accused.

Criollo [Spanish]: a word used to designate a person born in the overseas Spanish territories, whose specific meaning depends on the context.

Cruzado: Portuguese coin worth approximately 360 *réis* in the sixteenth century and 400 *réis* in the seventeenth century.

Denúncias: denunciations; accusations.

Deputado: literally, 'deputy.' The term used for the members of the *Mesa da Consciência* as well as of other bodies.

Desembargador: a judge of a higher court; an appellate judge.

Desembargo: the equivalent of the Supreme Court of Justice.

Despacho: can refer both to the act of approving documents and to the approval itself.

Disciplina: both the scourge used as mortification of the flesh, and 'spiritual/ penitential discipline' in a wider sense.

Dobra: gold coin minted in Morocco and Castile. Monetary reform in Portugal led to the minting of *escudos* in 1435–6 with a parity with the *dobra*, which was also the official currency of São Tomé and Príncipe.

Dobrão: old Portuguese gold coin, worth 24,000 *reis*.

Dom ('lord'): title of Portuguese nobility, from Latin *dominus*, but also used in the Portuguese records for some African political leaders and their male kin. This title is abbreviated as D, as in D. Henrique. The feminine form is Dona.

Donatário ('donatary' or 'beneficiary'): the title given to someone granted a piece of land of considerable extent in the overseas territories, to populate, explore and administer on behalf of the Portuguese King.

---

[4] See Maria Inês Côrtes de Oliveira, 'Quem eram os 'negros da Guiné'? A origem dos africanos na Bahia,' *Afro-Ásia* 19–20 (1997): 44.

Ducat: a Spanish money equivalent to 11 Spanish *reals* of 34 *maravedís* each. During the sixteenth and seventeenth centuries, 10 Spanish *ducats* equaled 11 Portuguese *cruzados*. Each *cruzado* was worth 400 *réis* or Spanish *reals*. For most of this period, 2.5 and 3.0 guilders (Dutch currency) equaled one *cruzado*.

Durázio: as an adjective, 'with a hard and thick skin and/or flesh'; as a noun, whether a kind of peach (*pêssego-durázio*) and or a type of olive, which bears as a name the feminine form (*durázia*).

E.R.M.: an abbreviation for '*Espera receber mercê*,' i.e. 'Hopes to be granted the [requested] favor.'

Edict of faith: pronounced by inquisitors on arriving in a town, giving people 30 days to come forward and confess their lack of orthodoxy or denounce the failings of others.

Embala: from Umbundu *ombala*, an important, or main, locality; a large village where the *soba*, an indigenous leader, lives.[5]

Encomienda [Spanish]: either the granting of the dignity of *Comendador*, together with the lands and rents ascribed to it, or the right to exploit indigenous labor, a system characteristic of the Spanish colonization of the Americas.

Escarlata (from the Persian *scarlat*: red fabric): fine crimson but not as fine as carmine.

Escopetero: literally 'one who fires an *escopeta*,' i.e. a 'blunderbuss' or 'fowling piece.'

Escrivão da Descarrega: Scribe of the Unloading.

Esquadrão prolongado ('elongated pike square'): a military formation, usually of three aligned squares.

Estação (da missa): a pause made during mass, just after the reading of the Gospels or immediately before the 'Lavabo' (the ritual washing of the hands during the mass), to explain the text which was read (homily) or to give certain information to the audience. The address made by the Priest to the faithful (from the Latin *statio*).

Estado: the average height of a man.

Estado da Índia (Portuguese 'State of India'): The Portuguese empire in Asia, comprising in the sixteenth and seventeenth centuries a small number of enclaves along the Indian Ocean littoral of East Africa, from Mozambique to Melaka, and in the Indonesian Archipelago and East Asia. *Estado da India* also refers to the administration of the Portuguese viceroys of India in Goa and other royal officials serving in Asia.

Familiar: spy of the Inquisition in towns and villages expected to keep an eye on behavior and help with arrests and manhunts.

Farragoulo: a short-sleeved hooded cloak with mantle.

---

[5] See, for instance, Teresa Manuela Camacha José da Costa, 'Umbundismos no Portugês de Angola: Proposta de um Dicionário de Umbundismos' (PhD thesis, Universidade Nova de Lisboa, 2015), 14.

Febres: coins below the stipulated weight (from the French *faibles*).

Feitiço/Feiticaria: literally, 'magic' or 'sorcery,' applying to 'fetishes' and to European witchcraft. A range of objects and practices integral to African spirituality were equated (falsely) with Iberian notions of sorcery and witchcraft. English 'fetish' derives from the Dutch/English pidgin *'fetisso,'* which itself derives from Portuguese *feitiço* and Latin *facticius*. Notions of 'fetish' and 'fetishism' on the Mina (Gold) Coast date to the late seventeenth and eighteenth century.[6]

Feitor: factor or royal trading agent, modeled after Venetian functionaries of the Levantine trade.

Feitoria: the institution of the royal factor, or the self-governing communities of foreign merchants residing in European, African and Asian cities. In certain cases, *feitoria* may also refer to office-holding in the Factory, which entitled its possessor to a portion of the profits or of the goods traded there.

Feitoria da Roupa Velha: the establishment in charge of preparing and legally selling the old clothing of the ships' crews and the King.

Fidalgo (*filho de algo*, 'a son of somebody'): aristocrat or member of the upper nobility, corresponding to Spanish *hidalgo*.

Fiel: an assistant of the Treasurer, charged with watching over weights and measures.

Forçado: a term usually applied to 'galley-slaves' but also to those forced to work as captives without receiving any payment.

Fufu: skirt, dress.

Fusta: a vessel similar to the galley, though smaller.

Galinha do mato: literally, 'helmeted guineafowl.'

Gandar: a kind of coarse cotton cloth, exported from India to Africa.

Gottdorim: a common, coarse cotton cloth of northwestern India; one of several cottons the English termed 'Guinea cloth.'

Grã: the same as 'carmine,' a crimson pigment derived from cochineal insects.

Guarda-Roupa: a royal official, equivalent to an official of the English Royal Wardrobe.

Homenagem (or *menagem*): the same as 'homage,' that is, a ceremony where a vassal pledged submission to a lord.

Infante: title of Portuguese princes.

Joris (cf. English *joories*): plain white cotton cloth of Sindh roughly equivalent to the *baftas* of Gujarat.

Juiz dos Feitos do Rei: an office like that of Judge of the King's Bench, but with somewhat narrower jurisdiction. He judged cases regarding the King as concerns rights pertaining to the Crown.

---

[6] See Roger Sansi-Roca, 'The Fetish in the Lusophone Atlantic,' in *Cultures of the Lusophone Black Atlantic: Studies of the Americas*, eds. N. P. Naro, R. Sansi-Roca, D. H. Treece (New York: Palgrave, 2007); William Pietz, 'The Problem of the Fetish, I,' *RES: Anthropology and Esthetics* 9 (1985): 5–17; idem, 'The Problem of the Fetish, II: The Origin of the Fetish,' *RES: Anthropology and Esthetics* 13 (1987): 23–45; idem, 'The Problem of the Fetish, IIIa: Bosman's Guinea and the Enlightenment Theory of Fetichism,' *RES: Anthropology and Esthetics* 16 (1988): 106–23.

Junta de Fazenda: literally, 'Exchequer's Commission.'

Junta Governativa: Governing Board.

Justo: gold coin of the reign of Dom João II (r. 1481–1495), of 22 karats, weighing 121 grains or 38 marks. It was worth 380 *reais brancos*. Its name derived from the first word of the motto written on the reverse: *Justus ut palma florebit*, a motto which encircled the image of the King seated on the throne. On the obverse it bore the coat-of-arms of Portugal (already reformed) and around it the name of the monarch and his titles.[7]

Ladino: the term *ladino*, as opposed to *boçal*, refers to a category of 'slaves' (or Africans) who have assimilated elements of Portuguese culture and language, and it is sometimes used in the sense of 'smart' as opposed to 'stupid.'

Lambel (pl., *lambéis*): striped woolen cloth, usually used to cover benches and tables, which, in the commerce of Guinea, was exchanged for gold. An imported, narrow striped woolen cloth from North Africa in high demand.

Laqueca: a glossy orange-red stone from Asia; probably the same as 'red coral stone,' mainly used for earrings.

Légua: the Portuguese league varied from about 5.5 to 6.0 meters.

Lençaria: a term generically applied to any kind of wool or cotton fabric, though usually a woven material of linen or cotton.

Libra: a unit of weight equivalent to 12 to 16 ounces, but also a unit of currency.

Licenciado: holder of a university qualification higher than that of a *Bacharel*, usually someone qualified to exercise a profession (law, medicine, etc.).

Livro da carga: book of lading.

Livro da/de armação: the book where all the transactions, together with the ship's costs, were noted down by the scribe who travelled on board the ship (thus distinct from the logbook); another, less precise, alternative might be 'ship's book.'[8]

Livro dos pontos: literally, 'book of notes.'

Malagueta: either 'malagueta pepper,' a kind of *Capsicum*, or, originally, 'melegueta pepper,' commonly known as grains of paradise or Guinea pepper and a species of the *Zingiberaceae*.

Manguito: literally, small sleeves used to protect or adorn the wrists, and thus a probable corruption of *maniquete*, the name given to the ornamental fabric or lace which is used as trimming in the alb's sleeves.[9]

Manilha: copper or brass rings, like bracelets or anklets, worn on the wrists and ankles but, more importantly, used as trade currency in western Africa.

---

[7] Cf. *Grande Enciclopédia Portuguesa e Brasileira* (Lisboa: Editorial Enciclopédia, 1936-60), 14: 421.

[8] See José Virgílio Amaro Pissarra, 'Livros de armação,' in *Navegações Portuguesas* (Lisboa: Instituto Camões, 2002-2006), at http://cvc.instituto-camoes.pt/navegaport/c13.html. For an alternative and approximate English translation of '*livro de armação*' ('book of cargo'), see Joshua Montefiore, *Commercial Dictionary: Containing the Present State of Mercantile Law, Practice, and Custom...* (London: Printed for the Author, 1803), under 'Book of Cargo or Loading.'

[9] For the English equivalent, 'cuffs,' see *Thesaurus: Vocabulário de Objectos do Culto Católico...* (Lisboa: Universidade Católica Portuguesa / Fundação da Casa de Bragança, 2004), 178.

Mantaz: a sort of cloth which comes from Cambaya.

Mantimento de conduto: this specific term, instead of the more generic *mantimento,* appears to have been used specifically for the 'food allowance' of some officials.

Marlota: a short cloak of North African origin.

Marmelada: the traditional jam or sugared quarters made from quince (*marmelo*, in Portuguese).

Matamingo/matamungo (cf. *miçanga/masanga*): a term of possibly Kikongo or Kimbundu origin meaning small glass beads.

Meirinho: official of justice, similar to a bailiff, who carries out arrests and other judicial warrants.

Mesa: a board, i.e. an organized body of officials, or the table at which official meetings were held. In specific cases, the assembly of the inquisitorial judges of the first instance, as opposed to the *Conselho Geral* (which judged the appeals).

Mesa da Consciência e Ordens: literally, 'Board of the [King's] Conscience and of the [Military] Orders'; it was created in 1532, the military orders' affairs having been incorporated into the *Mesa* by the middle of the century.

Mestre de Campo: a former military rank, equivalent today to that of Colonel.

Mestre-Sala: master of ceremonies.

Moço da câmara: the equivalent of 'chamberlain,' an official of the Royal Household who attended on the King (or some other member of the royal family) in his chambers.

Moço de estrebaria: an official of the Royal Household who served under the orders of the *Estribeiro-mor*, the equivalent of the 'Equerry.'

Moço do monte: a nobleman and royal official who served under the orders of the *Monteiro-mor* (chief *Monteiro*), the main official in charge of the hunting grounds and of the hunts attended by the King on royal grounds.

Moço fidalgo: one of the lowest ranks of the aristocracy.

Moio: unit of mass (and length), which varied over time. It was divided into sixty *alqueires*—the *alqueire* being the equivalent to roughly 10 to 13 liters.

Monção ('monsoon'): by extension, also the period of the year most favorable for sailing to certain places.

Morgado: in Portugal, the first-born male descendant who inherited a family's entailed property, according to the institution of the *morgadio*.

Nau: the name generally given to large vessels.

Nau de estado: possibly a ship used by the state representatives, or else a ceremonial one.

Naval: a thick linen fabric from which boys' clothes were made.[10]

Navio de carreira: this term was normally used for ships travelling (regularly?) between Portugal and its outposts overseas. The modern equivalent would be 'liner.'

---

[10] See Rafael Bluteau, *Supplemento ao Vocabulario Portuguez, e Latino...* (Lisboa: Na Patriarcal Oficina da Música,1728), 69.

Navio: a common term to designate any kind of large vessel.

Oficial: skilled workman rather than laborer.

Ordenações (Ordinances): the Portuguese General Law.

Ouvidor: a local magistrate.

Padrão: literally, 'standard'; monumental pillar laying claim to the lands 'discovered' by the Portuguese. This stone pillar surmounted by a cross and the arms of Portugal were placed on prominent sites along the African coast to aid navigation and establish claims to Portuguese sovereignty.

Padrasto: an elevation overlooking a town or fortress.

Padroado: literally, 'Patronage'; an arrangement between the Holy See and the kings of Portugal (and Spain) for the coordination and promotion of evangelization in the newly-discovered territories, by which the administration of local churches was delegated to the monarchs.

Panaria: though the dictionary meaning of *panaria* is 'granary,' it seems that in Portuguese overseas territories *panaria* also carried the meaning of 'cloth' (as a collective noun).[11]

Paragem: the latitude at which a ship cruises, while awaiting others or the enemy, or at which it anchors and can be made ready to sail at any time.

Párea: ruler used to measure the volume of casks.

Patacão: copper coin from the time of D. João III (r. 1521–1557).

Pau branco: or 'whitewood'; whether some type of a less valuable timber, as in English, or a specific type of wood coming from trees endemic to Brazil, the Azores, or Madeira and Canary Islands.

Pau vermelho / Brasil: Brazilwood, a leguminous plant used in dyeing.

Peça: as a military concept, a 'piece of ordnance,' that is, a mounted gun, or a cannon.

Pelote: a popular kind of garment with wide armholes, which could also be translated as 'cloak' or 'robe.'

Peloteiro: a maker of pellets.

Pelourada: a shot with an iron bullet.

Peso: the name given in numismatics to a certain kind of metallic pieces used in the past to ascertain the legal value of the coin, or Spanish coin, the same as *duro*, equivalent to five *pesetas* (beginning in the twentieth century). *Peso* is also a unit of mass corresponding to 4 *arráteis*, i.e. 64 ounces. One *arrátel* was equivalent to 459 grams.

Pimento: species of the genus *capsicum*, though probably (hot or mild) 'bell peppers.'

Pipa: like the cask, larger than the standard barrel (or the Portuguese *barril*); one *pipa* has a capacity of about 500 liters.

---

[11] See, for example, António Carreira, *Panaria Cabo-Verdiana Guineense: Aspectos históricos e sócio-económicos* (Lisboa: Museu de Etnologia do Ultramar/Junta de Investigações do Ultramar, 1968).

Presidio: name given to any Portuguese settlement where there was a garrison of soldiers.

Processo: trial or trial dossier.

Procurador: lawyer; legal advisor (cf. *promotor*).

Provedor dos Almazéns: Provider of the Depot; the *almazém* (or *armazém*) was, like the 'depot,' a place where military equipment and supplies were stored, though it could also have a broader meaning of 'warehouse' or 'storehouse.'

Quartel: money falling due every three months.

Quarto: a nautical term used to describe a period into which a day aboard a ship, together with the assignment of duties to the crew, is divided.

Quintal: unit of mass, equivalent to one hundred kilograms.

Quinto: a tax on goods of 20 percent, or the royal fifth. Refers also to the percentage due to the Crown of any booty taken by force of arms.

Real (pl. *réis*): Portuguese coin and basic unit of currency. The *real branco* was coin of silver and copper first launched in 1415 and then reckoned to the worth 35 *libras*.

Regaço: literally, 'lap,' thus probably the cloth which is wore on the lap by a bishop when sitting during some religious ceremonies.

Regimento: official instructions or directives drawn up to govern the conduct of office holders and military and naval commanders.

Relação: generally, the King's Court of Appeal.

Repartição: a colonial administrative division.

Reposteiro: an official of the Portuguese Royal Household, equivalent to an officer of the English Royal Wardrobe, responsible for drawing the curtains and for laying the cushion on which the King (as well as other members of the Royal Family) kneels.

Requeredor da Alfândega: Solicitor of the Customs House.

Resgate: literally, 'ransom' or 'redeem'; the term was used more generally to designate the broader exchange of goods for precious metals and enslaved peoples, but also to places of commerce along the Guinea coast or up one of its rivers. Depending on the context, and whenever the verbal form is used, *resgatar* is translated herein as 'to exchange or trade.'[12]

Responso: prayer (for the dead).

Retrós: 'silk thread' or 'sowing silk.'

Rochoada: an assemblage of rocks, a small fortress.

Roupa Velha: the old cloth of the ships' crews and the King which were sold legally. One of the main officers of the Factory (*Feitoria*) of São Jorge da Mina was the *Feitor da Roupa Velha* ('Factor of the Old Cloth'), the official responsible for these sales.

---

[12] For a discussion on the meaning and translation of the term *resgate*, see Hair, 'Portuguese Documents on Africa,' 96–97.

Roupas pretas: a specific category of eastern fabrics.[13]

S.C.R. Majestade [Spanish]: the abbreviation for *Sacra Católica Real Majestade*, Portuguese version of a title used by the Spanish monarchs from the sixteenth century onwards.

Sainho: a specific kind of women's dress.

Santa Casa da Misericórdia: literally, 'Holy House of Mercy,' a charitable organization of royal foundation caring for the sick and poor.

Sapa: trenching shovel.

Sargento-mor: a general Infantry officer, high in the army's hierarchy.

Sé: both the church and the official seat and jurisdiction of a bishop.

Secreto: a part of the Inquisition building, where files, books and other documents were kept in secret.

Seirão: a kind of basket or pannier.

Serralheiro: someone who is also a locksmith performing similar work with metal.

Sesmaria: Portuguese medieval system of granting lands, later exported to the colonies, according to which the grantee was obliged to make them productive.

Sharif: Sixteenth century Portuguese sources for the Mina (Gold) Coast use the term *xarife/xerife*, derived from the Arabic *sharīf*, a title of respect and nobility. The use of Arabic or Arabic-derived terms comes of a long history of Arabic's influence on the Portuguese language. On the Mina (Gold) Coast, the *xarife/sharīf* was usually the chief advisor or representative of local polities in contact with São Jorge da Mina.

Tafecira (cf. English *tapseels*). One of two cottons (mixed with silk) of India that commanded premium prices in Asian and European markets.

Taxa: a fixed value (with the generic meaning of fixed 'payment').

Tenes aljaravia (see '*aljaravia*'): reference to the provenance (Tenes in the Kingdom of Tlemcen) of the type or pattern of the fabric used.

Terçado: a kind of short broad sword.[14]

Terço: a type of military administrative unit (*tercio* in Castilian/Spanish).

Termo: the countryside around a village or city.

Terno: in the Catholic church, complete paraments (a three-piece parament set), that is, chasuble and two dalmatics. Also, a three-piece suit: trousers, jacket and waistcoat.

Tirar/Tomar (a) residência: the act of examining an official regarding his conduct in office; literally, 'to take (the) residence.'

---

[13] See Nigel Tattersfield, *The Forgotten Trade: Comprising the Log of the* Daniel and Henry *of 1700 and Accounts of the Slave Trade from the Minor Ports of England, 1698-1725* (London: Pimlico, 1998), ch.7.

[14] See Antonio Luiz M. C. Costa, *Armas Brancas: Lanças, espadas, maças e flechas: Como lutar sem pólvora da pré-história ao século XXI* (São Paulo: Editora Draco, 2015).

Vagante dos providos: according to this system, appointment by the King to an office did not take place when necessary, as when its previous holder finished his period of service, but when there was a need to grant a favor to someone. Those appointed 'in vacancy' could only serve their offices when those appointed before them had served out their term.[15]

Vara: unit of length equivalent to 1.10 meters.

Vedor da Fazenda: official charged with the administration of the Royal Patrimony and the Exchequer.

Vintena: literally, 'the twentieth part'; a fixed payment.

Vizinho: a term usually referred to resident members in a community or resident householders, and, by extension, to households. It can also mean, when referring to outsiders, 'neighbor.'

Voto: literally, 'vote'; that is, a member (of a Council) entitled to vote.

Zabra: a type of vessel used in trade, especially typical of the Cantabrian sea.

---

[15] See Ana Teresa Hilário, 'Capitães das fortalezas do Índico no tempo do Conselho da Índia: Continuidades e rupturas da vertente social do Estado da Índia,' *Revista de História da Sociedade e da Cultura* 17 (2017): 81.

MAPS

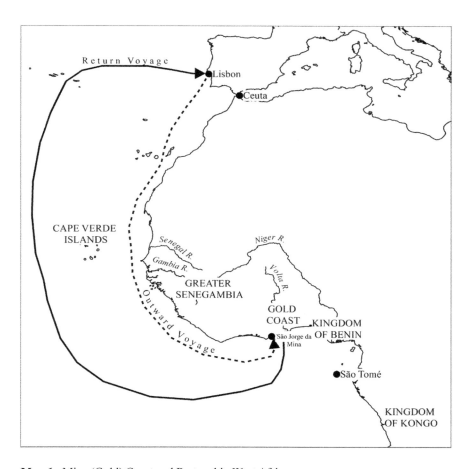

Map 1. Mina (Gold) Coast and Portugal in West Africa.

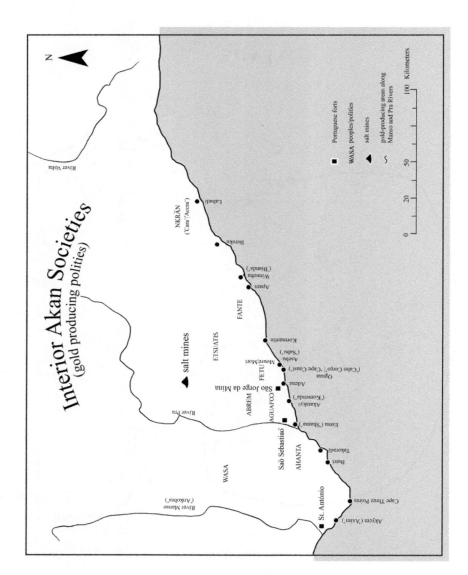

Map 2. Mina (Gold) Coast.

ABBREVIATIONS

ANTT	Arquivo Nacional da Torre do Tombo
AV	Archivio Segreto Vaticano
BADE	Biblioteca e Arquivo Distrital de Évora
BNL	Biblioteca Nacional de Lisboa
BSGL	Biblioteca da Sociedade de Geografia de Lisboa
CA	Colecção de Alcobaça (BNL)
CC	Corpo Cronológico (ANTT)
CM	Cartas Missivas (ANTT)
Epistolae Mixtae	*Epistolae mixtae ex variis Europae locis ab anno 1537 ad 1556 scriptae*
Gav.	Gavetas (ANTT)
MHSI	Monumenta historica Societatis Iesu
MM	Miscelâneas Manuscritas
MMA	*Monumenta Missionaria Africana*
PMA	*Portugaliae Monumenta Africana*
caixa (cx.)	box
cap.	chapter
cf.	compare or check out
doc.	document
fl.	folio
liv.	book
maço (mç.)	bundle
ms.	manuscript
número (n.)	number

INTRODUCTION

While conducting archival research on the fifteenth and sixteenth century history between the Mina (Gold) Coast and Portugal between 2012 and 2016, and by reading hundreds of known and newly discovered documents, I realized these sources in English translation could be of great benefit to students, scholars, professionals, and general readers with an avid interest in early modern African, Atlantic, and world history. The present volume contains 201 'Portuguese' sources written in Latin, Italian, French, Castilian (Spanish), and Portuguese, the vast majority of which appear in English translation for the first time (thirty-one of these sources appear on the *Fontes Historiae Africana* (FHA) website rather than in the volume due to space limitations). These sources add to the handful of existing translated manuscripts, but particularly illuminate the late fifteenth to seventeenth century relations between the Portuguese empire and the Mina (Gold) Coast and offer comparative materials for other European interlocutors— e.g. Spanish, French, English, and Dutch—garrisoned on the coast or offshore in their vessels. Over that concentrated period, and especially where no other European-supplied records exist, these uncomprehending Portuguese outsiders archived the local ideas, personalities, polities, and cultural forms animating the Mina (Gold) Coast as well as African-Portuguese relations. This introduction provides some historical background to place those relations in perspective, but also pays homage to the scholars whose earlier works created a starting point for this volume, while assessing their value and limitations and what separates the present volume from previous attempts to make accessible a large corpus of Portuguese sources for the history of Africa's Mina (Gold) Coast.

Historical Background[1]

The historic encounter and subsequent relations between West Africa's Mina (Gold) Coast and Portugal sit within a wider, long-standing transcontinental gold trade.

---

[1] Readers will find in this historical background in-text references to specific documents in the volume, indicated by parentheses and document number in bold, e.g. (**Doc. 21**).

Indeed, the purity and valuation of West African gold since the first millennium CE made it highly prized in the Mediterranean world economy, connecting western and central Eurasia and Saharan-savanna Africa. Since 1200 CE, the shiny metal remained a predominant commodity and currency desired by Christian European kingdoms, Islamic states from North Africa to Asia, and as far west as imperial China. Portugal sat on the southwestern tip of Europe and the western extreme of the Mediterranean Sea, and it too desired West Africa gold in the fifteenth century, during the rise of West Africa's Songhay empire and the decline of imperial Mali. Rather than depend on intermediaries connected to the gold-producing areas under these empires, the economically backward and small-sized Portugal plowed African waters for direct access to the sources of West African gold.[2]

One of the more compelling trios of early empires in world history were Wagadu, ancient Mali, and Songhay, nestled in the West African Sahel-savanna ecotone.[3] Their expansion, prestige, and power rested on controlling not only the source of West African gold but the routes on which the yellow metal was traveled and traded. An added feature was trafficking captive people through Muslim brokers who used trade networks, connecting forest-savanna lands with Sahelian empires and Saharan oases, on which gold and captives traveled to Europe, Mediterranean lands, and further. With the decline of Wagadu and the rise of imperial Mali in the thirteenth century, lands to its south became primary sources for captives and gold. Still, the fourteenth and fifteenth century was a crucial moment in the Africa-Eurasian world economy. Mamlūk Egypt and Malian deterioration, linked to political and climatic factors, led to the former folding under the Ottoman empire and Songhay eclipsing imperial Mali. On the margins of these climatic and political cycles were the forest regions of gold to the south. These never came under the control of any Sahelian-savanna empire, but traded gold, kola, and more with them. The Mina (Gold) Coast was one such region, having gone global through its shiny metal across terrestrial trade routes, and soon this would continue throughout the Atlantic seaboard.[4]

---

[2] Ray Kea, 'The Mediterranean and Africa,' in *A Companion to Mediterranean History*, eds. Peregrine Horden and Sharon Kinoshita (West Sussex: Wiley Blackwell, 2014), 425–9, 433–6; Joseph E Inikori, 'Africa and the Globalization Process: Western Africa, 1450–1850,' *Journal of Global History* 2, no. 1 (2007): 69–86; Ian Blanchard, *Mining, Metallurgy, and Minting in the Middle Ages*, vols. 2–3 (Stuttgart: F. Steiner, 2001).

[3] I follow Michal Tymowski's critique of 'empire' in African historiography and use 'early empire' instead. See Michal Tymowski, 'Use of the Term 'Empire' in Historical Research on Africa: A Comparative Approach,' *Afrika Zamani* 11–12 (2003–2004): 18–26. For a recent study of these Sahelian-savanna early empires, especially in the context of gold and long-distance trade, see Michael A. Gomez, African *Dominion: A New History of Empire in Early and Medieval West Africa* (Princeton: Princeton University Press, 2018), but also Hadrien Collet, 'Landmark Empires: Searching for Medieval Empires and Imperial Tradition in Historiographies of West Africa,' *The Journal of African History* 61, no. 3 (2020): 341–57.

[4] For an overview of trans-Saharan trade, see Ralph A. Austen, *Trans-Saharan Africa in World History* (New York: Oxford University Press, 2010); Ghislaine Lydon, *On Trans-Saharan Trails: Islamic Law, Trade Networks, and Cross-Cultural Exchange in Nineteenth-Century Western Africa* (New York: Cambridge University Press, 2009). On Mali's decline and Songhay's rise, see Gomez, *African Dominion*.

Large agrarian settlements in the forest and on its southern and northern edges populated the Mina (Gold) Coast region by 1000 CE, when the kingdoms of Wagadu and Gao reached their apogee. Working in iron and gold, trading the shiny metal, utilizing a stone-iron-metals monetary system of local origin yet adapted to trans-regional trade, sprawling trading towns connected societies of the deciduous forest and settled the exchange rates which prepped them for increases in world trade and the demand for West African gold. Between 1125 and 1250, West African gold reigned supreme, and a distinctive Africa-European market structure emerged in the bi-metallic exchange of African gold for European silver. Medieval European gold mining only reached maturity with the first major gold mine in Serbia around 1250. By that time, coins of pure West African gold were already being minted in Morocco, Tunisia, and Egypt and flowed through northwest Africa to the Iberian and Italian peninsulas. Traders from the Italian peninsula exchanged goods for gold. Florentine banking operations in Tunis in 1250 facilitated wool and woven fabrics trade with Tunisia through Genoa and Genoese merchants. Genoese and Florentine merchant-bankers invested in mining and minting and traded with West Africa for its gold.

Why West African gold? Europeans sought this gold because of its purity; from it, high-quality coins or objects could be produced without refining. And late medieval Europe had virtually a universal concern for the purity of gold. Out of this period came a Mina (Gold) Coast region once in the shadow of Wagadu, Mali, and Songhay, and from the economic backwater of southwestern Europe came Portugal and its maritime empire, sustained by Mina gold. Their paths thus crossed on the Mina (Gold) Coast.[5]

The Portuguese seaborne empire can be traced to the capture of the North African caravan terminus and seaport of Ceuta, on the coast of Morocco, in 1415. Under crown authority, the 'empire,' a sprawling network of coastal enclaves and fortified trading posts along the shores of Africa, Brazil, and Asia, grew throughout the sixteenth century.[6] Though Ceuta did not successfully lead to the conquest of Morocco and, by extension, the crusade against Islam, the Portuguese occupied several towns and built fortresses on Morocco's Atlantic coast. Off the Atlantic coast of Mauritania, a factory on the island of Arguim was established in 1445. However, the Arguim factory, which became a fort in 1461, failed to

---

[5] Blanchard, *Mining, Metallurgy, and Minting*, 2: 738, 740–741, 747; Lauren Jacobi, 'Reconsidering the World-System: The Agency and Material Geography of Gold,' in *The Globalization of Renaissance Art*, Daniel Savoy, ed. (Leiden: Brill, 2017), 144, 146, 151; David. J. Mattingly et al., eds, *Trade in the Ancient Sahara and Beyond: Trans-Saharan Archaeology* (New York: Cambridge University Press, 2017).

[6] See, for instance, A. R. Disney, *A History of Portugal and the Portuguese Empire, Vol. 1: From Beginnings to 1807* (New York: Cambridge University Press, 2009); A. J. R. Russell-Wood, *The Portuguese Empire, 1415-1808: A World on the Move* (Baltimore: The Johns Hopkins University Press, 1998); Bailey W. Diffie and George D. Winius, *Foundations of the Portuguese Empire, 1415-1580* (Minneapolis: University of Minnesota Press, 1977); Charles R. Boxer, *The Portuguese Seaborne Empire, 1415-1825* (New York: A. A. Knopf, 1969).

divert the gold trade to West African producers and North African consumers and merchants, who exchanged gold for merchandise from Italian traders who had a factory in Ceuta. Nor did Arguim evolve into a Portuguese center for gold trafficking. Rather, Arguim became a base for Portuguese trade, slaving, and other incursions into surrounding regions. Severely impacted by the Bubonic plague and subsequent outbreaks but no longer under Islamic control, reports of fabled West African lands of gold encouraged a Portugal determined to locate these sources—all during Europe's great bullion famine of precious metals.[7]

A partnership between the Portuguese crown and Italian merchants and shipowners, besides the latter's settlement of Atlantic islands, targeted West African gold. The pursuit of gold and the ideological fervor of the crusades paved the way for reaching the region dubbed 'Mina,' shorthand for *Costa da Mina*—Coast of the Mine.[8] In November 1469, Portuguese ruler Afonso V, nicknamed 'the African,' leased the Guiné trade to Lisbon merchant Fernão Gomes. This commerce with West Africa took place from coastal Morocco to present-day Sierra Leone, which navigators Pedro de Sintra and Soeiro da Costa had reached in 1461–2. Sintra and Costa ventured, according to chronicler and later Mina official João de Barros, as far as the 'Soeiro River' between Cape Palmas and Cape Three Points, near Akyem ('Axim'). Gomes and his associates plowed a hundred miles south of Sierra Leone each year of their five-year lease at 200,000 *reis* per year (**Doc. 1**). The contract between the king and Gomes forbade the latter from trading in lands near the Cape Verde islands, but Gomes secured the trade of Arguim from prince Dom João for several years at 100,000 *reis* per year. In January 1471, through João de Santarém and Pedro Escobar, Gomes' expedition 'discovered the trade of gold in the place we today call the Mina.' This locale was 'a village called Samá' (Esma; 'Shama'), the site of initial gold trading, and then at a place 'called by our people Aldeia das Duas Parte [village of two parts].' This village, called Adena by its peoples, lay adjacent to the future site of São Jorge da Mina.[9] A 1471 map of the region demarcated the newly labeled *Costa da Mina* from *Cabo das Tres Pontas* (Cape Three Points), passing *A Mina do Ouro* ('mine

[7] John Day, 'The Great Bullion Famine of the Fifteenth Century,' *Past & Present* 79 (1978): 3–54; cf. Vitorino Magalhães Godinho, *Os Descobrimentos e a Economia Mundial*, 4 vols., 2nd edition (Lisboa: Editorial Presença, 1981–3). On the bubonic plague, see Monica H. Green, 'The Four Black Deaths,' *The American Historical Review* 125, no. 5 (2020): 1601–31, and her citations for a review of the most recent literature.

[8] See Vitorino Magalhães Godinho, *Documentos sobre a Expansão Portuguesa*, 3 vols. (Lisbon: Edições Cosmos, 1956).

[9] João de Barros, *Da Asia de João de Barros e de Diogo do Couto*, Década I, liv. II, cap. II, pp. 141–51; G. R. Crone, ed. and trans., *The Voyages of Cadamosto and Other Documents on Western Africa in the Second Half of the Fifteenth Century* (London: Hakluyt Society, 1937), 109; James D. La Fleur, *Fusion Foodways of Africa's Gold Coast in the Atlantic Era* (Leiden: Brill, 2012), 62. Pilots Martim Fernandes and Alvaro Esteves also accompanied the captains. See António Brásio, ed., *Monumenta Missionaria Africana. Africa Occidental* (Lisbon: Agência Geral do Ultramar, Divisão de Publicações e Biblioteca, 1952–88), 6: 436–43 (specific reference on 438). Henceforth, 'MMA.'

of gold'; Esma) and *Aldea de Duas Partes* ('village of two parts'; Adena), and terminating at the *Rio da Volta* (Volta River).[10]

Famed court chronicler João de Barros wrote of the Gomes expedition as discovering 'the traffic of gold at the place we now call the Mina.' Barros's contemporaries considered the Mina (Gold) Coast the most significant 'discovery' in the oceanic exploration of the West African coast. Gomes's expedition ended a hiatus in exploratory voyages since Prince Henrique's death in 1460 and ushered in a new era for western Europe, with Portugal leading the uncharted way. But this newfound goldmine became embroiled in succession disputes between Portugal and Castile (Spain), which spilled over into the earliest of international sea battles, triggered by Gomes reaching the new world of the Mina (Gold) Coast. Fernão Gomes made a huge fortune with which he helped the king in Ceuta and in the conquest of North African towns such as Alcazar and Tangier. The king knighted Gomes and, when his lease ended in 1474, having reached an area just pass Gabon, he was given a new title—Fernão Gomes da Mina—and coat of arms, which João de Barros described as 'a crested shield with a field in silver and three black men's heads, each of them with three gold rings on their ears and noses, and a necklace on their necks, and "Mina" as a surname, in remembrance of its discovery.'[11]

Within a decade after Gomes and his agents reached the real 'rivers of gold,' no less than 50 Portuguese and 20 Spanish ships embarked for the Mina (Gold) Coast. Safeguarding this goldmine required a treaty, and one was concluded with Spain in 1479. The treaty targeted Portugal's exclusive right and access to western Africa. Still, the bullseye was the Mina (Gold) Coast, and military commander Diogo Azambuja was dispatched to defend those concessions by arms or negotiations.

The 'Guinea trade,' as the Portuguese called the commerce with western Africa, revolved around the axes of gold and captives, and so intra-European exchanges often became conflictual. Seville merchants often plundered Portuguese caravels traveling from West Africa with gold and captives. Portuguese crown agents abroad, risking life and limb, were rewarded in the currency of gold and captives. Soeiro Mendes, *alcaide-mor* of the Arguim fortress, received lifelong annual pensions of 12 enslaved Africans or the same value in gold. The incoming flow of captives and gold enriched the crown and aristocracy, bolstering crown revenue and embroidering the bonds between commerce and professions of faith. Gold came to matter more than the rhetoric of saving souls. As the gold trade grew, the more the crown and ruling elites asserted their 'spiritual rights in the lands of Guinea.'[12] Commerce and Christian theology reified and found receptivity in each

---

[10] A. Fontoura da Costa, *Uma Carta Náutica Portuguesa, Anonima, de circa 1471* (Lisbon: Agência Gêral das Colónias, 1940), 61. Cape Three Points was known for canoe making.

[11] Barros, *Da Asia de João de Barros*, Dec. 1, bk. 2, ch. 2.

[12] Luís de Albuquerque, Maria Emília Madeira Santos, and Maria Luísa Esteves, eds., *Portugaliae Monumenta Africana*, vol. 3 (Lisboa: Comissão Nacional para as Comemorações dos Decobrimentos Portugueses, 2000), 1: 29–30, 33, 36-37, 144. Henceforth, PMA.

other. The gold trade and the Mina (Gold) Coast accelerated their bond, and yet the need to safeguard Portugal's empire on the Mina (Gold) Coast was immediate.

If the 1479 treaty made Portugal the sole European force on the Mina (Gold) Coast, the Treaty of Tordesillas, which divided their conception of the known world between Portugal and Spain, left Atlantic Africa and the Indian Ocean to Portugal. Insufficient as all agreements were, a fortified Portuguese base was erected on the Mina (Gold) Coast as the ultimate deterrent to European competitors. That base was São Jorge da Mina, a marvel that decorated early modern European maps. The São Jorge da Mina fortress was built on a rocky peninsula adjacent to Adena. This fortress was the first permanent European base of operation on the west African mainland. São Jorge da Mina was constructed to securely store goods related to the gold trade and safeguard Portugal's trade monopoly against its own nationals engaging in private trade as well as European competitors—initially the Spaniards, and later the French, English, and Dutch—throughout the sixteenth century.[13] São Jorge da Mina was soon the center of Portuguese activity on the Mina (Gold) Coast, with trading posts under its authority at Akyem ('Axim') and Esma ('Shama') in the second and third decades of the sixteenth century and a transient trade site at Nkrãn ('Cara'; 'Accra') to the east, never materializing into a stable post (**Doc. 7**).

São Jorge da Mina was also the center of the gold trade under Portuguese royal monopoly, and more broadly of Portuguese commerce, missionary work, and Atlantic slaving between Greater Senegambia and West Central Africa. This included a regional trade nexus involving Benin, São Tomé, the Kingdom of Kongo, and the Mina (Gold) Coast. The most explicit edifice representing a European presence in Africa and one that dominated late fifteenth and sixteenth century accounts of African-European commerce was the São Jorge da Mina fortress. The Vallard Atlas (ca. 1540s) illustrated the literal and symbolic importance of the Mina (Gold) Coast with a gigantic image of São Jorge da Mina, but also underscored its international status as a symbol of Portuguese claim to sovereignty over, and its relative monopoly of, the seaport trade of western Africa.

João II had his eyes on the Mina (Gold) Coast since Fernão Gomes's expeditions returned with gold that filled the coffers of imperial Portugal. João II knew from the conflicts he inherited—with Castile and other Europeans—that Portuguese claims in West Africa had to be defended. Building São Jorge da Mina in 1482–3 was necessarily an act of building an empire. Through it, the way to Atlantic Africa and into the Indian Ocean was paved. São Jorge Da Mina's initial completion around 1482–3 signaled an expansion of the trade in gold and captives that enriched Portugal but also the growth of the empire. 'Through this fortress,' navigator and later Mina captain Duarte Pereira wrote, 'trade so greatly increased by the favor of

---

[13] On rivalry between these European nations on the mid-fifteenth century Mina (Gold) Coast, see A. Teixeira da Mota and P. E. H. Hair, *East of Mina: Afro-European Relations on the Gold Coast in the 1550s and 1560s: An Essay with Supporting Documents* (Madison: University of Wisconsin, African Studies Program, 1988), 81.

our Lord that 170,000 dobrões of good fine gold.' At current gold prices, 170,000 *dobrões* would be worth over $73,600,000.[14] All this wealth coveted by so few led to corruption, theft, and a purging of the Portuguese nobility. Wealth of this magnitude also guided the creation of new legal slave codes, further refining how the Portuguese understood themselves as an empire, viewing sources of this prosperity as religious and racial undesirables yet economic necessities. Through Portugal and its cascading effect on Europe, the soil of expansion was plowed, sowed with seeds of captives, commodities, and gold. While the Portuguese felt secure inside the São Jorge da Mina fortress, they least expected their greatest threat would come from the peoples whose land laid pregnant with gold.[15]

Though Portuguese spheres of relative control on the Mina (Gold) Coast were limited to Akyem ('Axim') and São Jorge da Mina, the São Jorge da Mina 'town' and the African polities with whom it collaborated formed the first permanent European trading 'state' and 'keystone of Portuguese hegemony in the south Atlantic area.'[16] São Jorge da Mina became a model for subsequent fortified settlements and to expand the Portuguese empire—and other Europeans who followed their lead—in Africa, Asia, and the Americas. Between 1480 and 1540, the Mina gold trade doubled Portugal's public revenue in the first twenty years and remained significant in the Portuguese economy in the next three decades (**Doc. 9**). More specifically, Mina gold provided Portugal purchasing power for trade in Asia, functioned as collateral for loans, helped to purchase German silver to stabilize its economy in 1489 and luxuries for the nobility, and paid for armies and fleets, including some transatlantic voyages.[17]

In 1510, while the Portuguese established an imperial foothold on the coasts of India and in its spice trade, the biggest threat to Portuguese claims to a trade monopoly over the Mina (Gold) Coast came from an African merchant named João Serrão. In concert with the ruler of the neighboring polity of Fetu, he orchestrated a revolt to oust the Portuguese from the entire Mina (Gold) Coast. Although eventually exiled to São Tomé, João Serrão returned to his homeland and resumed this thorny role in the Portuguese's side. Serrão represented the political force and figures of his homeland, and his relations with Portugal's representatives on the Mina

---

[14] The calculations are mine, based on current gold prices (as of October 2021) and Portuguese valuations (using *dobrões*) around the time Pereira wrote, roughly 1498–1503. See ANTT, *Contos do Reino e Casa, Núcleo Antigo* 928. Transcribed in PMA, 3: 92–99.

[15] ANTT, Chancelaria de D. João II, liv. 13, f. 90v; liv. 16, f. 65; PMA, 1: 270–86; Andrés Bernández, *Memorias del Reinado de los Reyes Católicos*, ed. Manuel Gómez-Moreno and Juan de Mata Carriazo (Madrid: Real Academia de la Historia, 1962), chap. 6; Barros, *Asia*, bk. 3, ch. 1; A. C. De C. M. Saunders, *A Social History of Black Slaves and Freedmen in Portugal, 1441-1555* (New York: Cambridge University Press, 1982), 113–33; Nicolas von Popplau, *Reisebeschreibung Niclas von Popplau, Ritters, bürtig von Breslau*, ed. Piotr Radzikowski (Kraków: Trans-Krak, 1998), 78; Francis M. Rogers, *The Obedience of a King of Portugal* (Minneapolis: University of Minnesota Press, 1958), 47; John W. Blake, *Europeans in West Africa, 1450-1560* (London: The Hakluyt Society, 1941–2), 1: 208.

[16] John Vogt, *Portuguese Rule on the Gold Coast, 1469-1682* (Athens: University of Georgia Press, 1979), 91.

[17] Vogt, *Portuguese Rule*, 91–92.

(Gold) Coast were a microcosm of a global, macro-portrait. When Africans, like Serrão, entertained Portugal's officials and exiled criminals, entering into trade and other agreements with them, the Portuguese king had the power to decide whom to protect and supply with arms or whom to oppose. These agreements were invitations to intervene in local politics. By the time the king's directives reached Serrão's land, the intended effect faded into the ether. Agents tasked with executing imperial orders were not powerless, but they were surely dependent, and local merchants of royal pedigree like Serrão knew this. Indeed, he exploited it. His continual presence exposed the underbelly of the empire, to the extent the next two captain-governors of São Jorge da Mina until 1522, Fernão da Correia and Duarte Pacheco Pereira, pursued a policy of appeasement with indigenous polities and their powerful figures.[18]

João Serrão secured a place between the Portuguese and his land, gaining personal insight into the relative strength and weakness of their position at São Jorge da Mina, their fortified headquarters. And then something shifted on the horizon. At the captain's table where João Serrão and the captain dined and negotiated, Serrão brokered an alliance with a local ruler, both of whom wanted little to do with the strangers (**Docs. 17–18, 21**). Indeed, they wanted to oust the Portuguese from the entire coast! A decade or two earlier, when there was an upsurge in trade irregularities, especially in gold monopolized by the crown, hinterland Mina (Gold) Coast polities staged their own monopoly of access to foreign goods and brokers for inland-supplied gold. This was also the coming of age of João Serrão. On Portugal's balance sheet, gold from the Mina (Gold) Coast was a lifeline, shoring up hospitals and grocery stores in Lisbon, pensions for servants of the empire, paying off debt and enabling the purchase of silver, and feeding an imperial patchwork of forts and factories in Antwerp, Morocco, and Goa. Portugal's newfound prosperity did not go unnoticed. French, Spanish, and Scottish pirates raided Portuguese caravels, some conveying Mina (Gold) Coast treasure, at times with the aid of Portuguese pilots who had coveted navigational knowledge.[19] In the Gulf of Guinea, where São Jorge da Mina doubled as a major hub and clearing house, the regional spice trade ran through the fortress city as well as the regional triangular trade in enslaved peoples. Men like Serrão and his partnership with local rulers threatened the Portuguese empire and any European who dared establish a foreign presence on their land. Eventually, Serrão's alliance fell apart, he disappeared from the records, and the coast returned to calm (**Docs. 27–28**). A letter from King João III then arrived, telling the captain to do all he could so the partnering villagers of Adena do not leave. If they leave, there would be no gold. And if there was no gold, perhaps no empire.[20]

---

[18] ANTT, Corpo Cronológico (CC), parte (pt.) 1, maço (mç.) 9, no. 61, fols. 1–3, 2 September 1510. See also PMA, 5: 709–12.

[19] See, for instance, **Docs. 105, 111, 113, 126, 154**, in this volume as well as PMA, 5: 558–60, 615–8.

[20] ANTT, CC, pt. 1, mç. 9, no. 61, fols. 2r-2v; CC, pt. 1, mç. 9, no. 60, fol. 3r.

In 1523, King João III wrote a scathing letter to captain-governor Afonso de Albuquerque to protect Adena villagers (**Docs. 67–68**).[21] Albuquerque, though certainly cruel, was much less competent than his namesake Afonso de Albuquerque (c. 1453–1515), who forged an empire in the Indian Ocean. With the inland gold merchants unable to come to the fortress, the gold trade was lost. The finest gold which Portugal and Europe coveted originated from the richest mines deep inland. The king's admonishment came during the peak of gold exports to Portugal, revealing how precious this gold was for the full extension of the empire, but how precarious its source and relations were with its producers. João III could not afford to lose the Mina (Gold) Coast, for his long reign, which oversaw Portuguese sea power in the Indian Ocean, colonization of northeastern Brazil, establishment of the Society of Jesus and an Inquisition, owed something to the boon in gold during the 1520s and 1530s.

The 1530s were the start of a downward slope for the gold trade through São Jorge da Mina with a definitive turning point in the 1540s and 1550s.[22] In the early 1530s, João III wrote to his exchequer about the gold trade, wishing gold imports had remained as they were under Estêvão da Gama. The son of Vasco da Gama, Estêvão served as captain-governor from 1529 to the early 1530s before following the footsteps of his father and other captain-governors in assuming the governorship of the Portuguese State in India in 1540 (**Doc. 74**). By then, attempts to control European piracy and commerce on the Mina (Gold) Coast affected the crown's bottom line. The end of the 1540s was capped by a blistering report by the São Jorge da Mina vicar, complaining of the unchristian conduct of Portuguese residents, blaming especially African women, one of whom was dispatched to the Inquisition in Lisbon, for the 'Sodom and Gomorrah' environment (**Docs. 99, 102**). But even the vicar called attention to the French and Dutch pirates on the coast (**Doc 105**). During these decades, European competition on the Mina (Gold) Coast increased. To undermine his European competitors, King João III banned all European imports to São Jorge da Mina as well as captives and glass or coral beads from Benin.[23] Threats to Portuguese claims of Christian authority and commercial monopoly shook their foundations on the Mina (Gold) Coast.

At the height of the Portuguese empire (ca. 1550–80), and having made impressive gains in Brazil, Council of State member Jorge da Silva and his supporters argued for the importation of Portuguese colonists and the colonization of the Mina (Gold) Coast, while an anonymous report of 1572 also advocated the development of plantations and 'many sugar mills' along the Mina (Gold)

---

[21] MMA vol. 1, doc. 136, pp. 451–52; Jeremiah D. M. Ford, ed., *Letters of John III, King of Portugal 1521-1557* (Cambridge, MA: Harvard University Press, 1931), 3–4. Cf. Malyn Newitt, ed., *The Portuguese in West Africa, 1415-1670: A Documentary History* (New York: Cambridge University Press, 2010), 96–97.

[22] See João Cordeiro Pereira, *Le Troc de l'or à Mina Pendant les Règnes du roi Jean III et du roi Sébastien* (Paris: Fondation Calouste Gulbenkian/Centre Culturel Portugais, 1990).

[23] Vogt, *Portuguese Rule*, 98–99; Pereira, *Le Troc de l'or à Mina*, 189.

Coast as part of a broader colonization scheme (**Docs. 121–22**).[24] On the eve of placing the northeast coast of Brazil under a nominal colonial scheme, rank-and-file Portuguese personnel at São Jorge da Mina and members of the Council of State in Lisbon argued for the colonization of the Mina (Gold) Coast, extolling its many benefits. It was a time of flux in the empire, and its teenage sovereign finally acquiesced to a century-long push for free trade. In the 1570s, the crown abandoned its trade monopoly on the Mina (Gold) Coast; instead, this commerce was handed over to a consortium of merchants (**Doc. 124**). Merchants, members of the king's council, and ordinary functionaries felt this moment was an opportunity to seize. And so, numerous proposals came before the king (**Doc. 123**) in the early 1570s, when the grandson and successor of João III, Sebastião, ruled Portugal. Sebastião's reign began when he was three, and the matter of the Mina (Gold) Coast came before him as a late teenager or in his early twenties. Whatever the effects of disease, psychosis, or misogyny claimed for Sebastião, the detailed reports from São Jorge da Mina and the parliamentary case urging its colonization did not achieve the desired effects on the young king. Instead of pursuing colonization, news of newly discovered gold mines on the Mina (Gold) Coast, its agricultural bounty, and its imagined prospect for Christendom, Sebastião decided to crusade against Islamic Morocco, allying (ironically enough) with the Muslim claimant to the Moroccan throne. This decision proved fatal for Sebastião, because he died in Morocco, and for the Portuguese empire. Sebastião died at the hands of Muslims in the region where the empire began in 1415, and it would fall under the control of Spain through Sebastião's uncle Filipe I (Philip I). The Iberian empires were then governed separately, but under Spain's global empire.

Soon after plans to colonize the Mina (Gold) Coast failed to materialize, the Portuguese still sought to project an air of dominance. Despite this attempt, Portuguese threats and cannon fire did little to change their waning presence or the calculus on the ground. Africans attacked and destroyed the Portuguese trading post at Nkrãn ('Accra'), killing the Portuguese residents and any hopes of accessing gold traded there. The French and the Dutch were no longer timid traders and opportunistic pirates. They were direct competitors, enabled by coastal and inland Africans who ignored Portuguese injunctions, but certainly heard their coast-wide complaint about 'the pirates who control all that coast and its commerce' (**Docs. 125–26, 132**). The Viceroy of Portugal and officials debated solutions, including allowing Portuguese subjects to trade freely on the Mina (Gold) Coast. Still, these lacked enough support, most notably the backing of Filipe II, who was more concerned about his Spanish empire. The internal struggles amongst the high nobility and clergy in Portugal, the same schisms that arose after the defeat of Sebastião's army in Morocco and which allowed for Filipe I's invasion and ascension to the throne in 1580, prevailed again. Kingless at home and devoid of African support abroad, Portugal was left to concede its

---

[24] Vogt, *Portuguese Rule*, 122–23; Brásio, *MMA*, 3: 89–113 Mota and Hair, *East of Mina*, 81.

empire's presence on the Mina (Gold) Coast, though not without a half-century-long fight with the Dutch. The Mina (Gold) Coast's relevance diminished while Portugal came under Spanish rule (ca. 1580–1640), yet the Portuguese kept a presence on the coast decades after losing—and failing to regain—their trading posts to the Dutch.[25]

It is not farfetched to believe, as contemporary Portuguese citizens and later historians did, that Sebastião's death on African soil was a harbinger of things to come. Perhaps this view is shortsighted. Sebastião's youth and decision-making at critical junctures in the empire were unexceptional because his predecessor, João III, also inherited the throne as a teenager and reigned for more than three decades, earning him the nickname, 'colonizer.' João III came to power in the decade when gold from the Mina (Gold) Coast peaked and when French, Dutch, and English pirates were a mere nuisance in the African region that attracted the most European empires. Thus, following Sebastião's death, Spain claimed a wounded Portugal. Although Portuguese merchants won some concessions by supplying captives needed in Spain's American colonies and who would also settle there, Portugal lost by inheriting Spain's enemies. Enemies who, especially the Dutch, seized Portuguese strongholds from the Mina (Gold) Coast to Malacca, upending its empire (**Docs. 167, 169, 174, 180**).

Before meeting their decline, the African headquarters for the Dutch, like their predecessor, was the Mina (Gold) Coast. But Dutch, British, Danish, and other European staying power on the Mina (Gold) Coast hinged on degrees of African partnership and support. As much as Europeans competed on the 350-mile Mina (Gold) Coast littoral, Africans connected to various polities and migrant groups vied for political and commercial supremacy against each other as they did with the Europeans. These entanglements prompted a new era in which it was not sea power which made maritime empires that mattered, but their relation to the land of gold. Although gold remained valuable, it was the seizure of African bodies to feed transoceanic commerce and colonies across the seas that matched or surpassed the shiny metal. The Mina (Gold) Coast became globalized through the trade of its gold; it did so again through the trade in captives that populated imperial colonies in the Americas.

Global wars among empires, culminating in the Dutch ousting of Portugal's empire from the Mina (Gold) Coast, set the stage for a Dutch presence in the region (**Docs. 182, 190–91, 194**). That presence, however, competed with the British, as both made the Mina (Gold) Coast the West African headquarters for their new seaborne empires, concentrating on gold and captives. By the second half of the seventeenth century, European chartered companies (Dutch, Danish, English, Swedish, and Brandenburg) had set up trading stations—castles, forts, and lodges—in the port towns along the Mina (Gold) Coast seaboard. An

---

[25] See, for instance, Filipa Ribeiro da Silva, *Dutch and Portuguese in Western Africa: Empires, Merchants and the Atlantic System, 1580-1674* (Leiden: Brill, 2011).

abundance of superior quality gold had attracted European merchant capital to the Mina (Gold) Coast since the late fifteenth century; this did not change in the centuries thereafter. The total West African gold exports between 1471 and 1500 amounted to an estimated 17 tons, and a substantial share likely came from mines in the Mina (Gold) Coast's Pra-Ofin-Birim basin. This gold helped finance the Portuguese crown's most expensive ventures, namely the opening of a Cape of Good Hope route around the southern tip of Africa to the Asian trade. In the seventeenth century, Mina (Gold) Coast exports in gold were again subsidizing Dutch and English trading companies' operations with 'rich Guinea gold' to India and Southeast Asia.

Akan merchants from the Mina (Gold) Coast were crucial actors in the movement of gold bullion in the world economy, supplying European trading stations with two-thirds of the annual gold exported from the region.[26] By 1700, gold and luxury items, and goods from the Americas, Asia, Europe, and Africa were integrated into a single global circuit of pricing and commodity flows, reminiscent of Africa-Eurasian trade.[27] Portugal effectively cut its losses and claim to the Mina (Gold) Coast. Although there is little or any extant Portuguese documentation for the 1670s–80s, when they occupied Christiansborg, Nkrãn, and a trading post at Anashan, their limited and fading trade presence paralleled the rise of the Dutch and English, who fought for European supremacy on the rebranded 'Gold Coast.'[28]

Earlier Work on Portuguese Sources for the Mina (Gold) Coast

Since the last century, historians of Africa and of Portugal's principal commercial base in West Africa have almost unanimously lamented the dearth of sources for the Mina (Gold) Coast during the sixteenth century, much less the nearly 'complete absence of primary sources,' one historian pronounced, 'for the period of the fifteenth century.'[29] To buttress this state of archival affairs, historians have equally clung to the fire and flooding of the 1755 earthquake in Lisbon, which destroyed the castle of São Jorge and the royal archives.[30] They have, in the main, concluded there is no need to search further or there is little to be discovered.

[26] See, for instance, Ray Kea, 'The Local and the Global: Historiographical Reflections on West Africa in the Atlantic Age,' in *Power and Landscape in Atlantic West Africa: Archaeological Perspectives*, eds. J. Cameron Monroe and Akinwumi Ogundiran (New York: Cambridge University Press, 2011), 339–75.
[27] Joseph E. Inikori, 'Africa and the Globalization Process: Western Africa, 1450–1850,' *Journal of Global History* 2, no. 1 (2007): 63–86.
[28] On the (waning) Portuguese presence in the latter seventeenth century, especially from an English point of view, see Robin Law, ed., *The English in West Africa, 1681-1699: The local correspondence of the Royal African Company of England, 3 parts* (Oxford: Oxford University Press, 1997–2007).
[29] Vogt, *Portuguese Rule*, x.
[30] For factors other than the earthquake for the state of the archival records, see Ivana Elbl, 'Archival Evidence of the Portuguese Expansion in Africa, 1440–1521,' in Lawrence J. McCrank, ed., *Discovery in the Archives of Spain and Portugal: Quincentenary essays, 1492-1992* (New York: Haworth Press, 1994), 339–40, 346, 351.

This helps explain the widespread reliance on translations by the likes of John W. Blake, Avelino Teixeira da Mota, and P. E. H. Hair, and on collections of transcribed Portuguese materials by António Brásio and others.[31] For instance, John Vogt's exhaustive search in the Portuguese archives revealed a reliance on the 1755 earthquake or on scant translations was premature. But even Vogt, for the thousands of documents he claimed to have uncovered in his 'long search,' produced by his own admission a 'work [that was] admittedly European and imperialist in its scope and organization. It was not my intent,' he explained, 'to attempt a complete account of the history and development of the structure of African society and life on the Gold Coast during the period under discussion.'[32] This approach severely undermined Vogt's avowed 'attempt to emphasize the vital central role which the post of São Jorge da Mina played in effecting trade and Portuguese authority within the region of Mina ... [during] the height of the gold trade between Mina and Portugal,' for there was no equal attempt to explicate the African side of the story.[33] The present volume seeks to address this imbalance by not only providing a rich set of documents in English translation for the early modern history of the Mina (Gold) Coast, but also the history of Portugal and its global empire and the formation of the so-called Atlantic world.

The Portuguese produced the earliest Western European written records for the western African coast. Since they began their overseas colonial experience in this region—an experience that influenced later activities in Brazil and Asia—the recorded interactions and observations made on the Mina (Gold) Coast are significant in the early history of European expansion. The foundation of African-European relations was laid during the period from the 1440s to the 1550s when the Portuguese in western Africa had little substantial competition from other Europeans. In the next century, the Mina (Gold) Coast trade remained vital to the Portuguese crown and so too did São Jorge da Mina as the principal base for Portuguese gold trading by sea. For the 200-year history between the Mina (Gold) Coast and Portugal, there are only two general histories—one in English, the other in French.[34] For the historian, the main body of surviving records is preserved in the Portuguese language and in either archives in Portugal or in published collections that mainly consist of transcriptions.

---

[31] For a recent collection of Portuguese documents in English translation, see Malyn Newitt, ed., *The Portuguese in West Africa, 1415-1670: A Documentary History* (New York: Cambridge University Press, 2010). The title and the documents therein are misleading. The bulk of the documents focus on West Central Africa—the Kingdom of Kongo, Ndongo (Angola), and Portuguese colonial holdings in Angola, Benguela, and the outlying islands—rather than on West Africa proper. The volume contains only two documents related to the Mina (Gold) Coast.

[32] Vogt, *Portuguese Rule*, xi.

[33] Vogt, *Portuguese Rule*, x-xi. For much of the fifteenth and sixteenth century, the Mina (Gold) Coast stretched from Cape Three Points to the Volta River—essentially, the 'Gold Coast' found in later European sources. For a 1471 map showing the Portuguese view of the coast, see da Costa, *Uma Carta Nautica Portuguesa*, 61.

[34] For a broad overview, see Antonio da Silva Rego, 'Ghana and the Portuguese: A Synthetical Survey of Relations,' *Ultramar* I, no. 4 (1973): 7–27.

Though Portugal's national archive, the Arquivo Nacional da Torre do Tombo/Instituto dos Arquivos Nacionais (IAN/TT), has begun to digitize its vast collections, beginning with the earliest extant documents, those for the 1440s to 1650s remain largely in late-medieval Portuguese handwriting. Fifteenth-to-sixteenth century royal scribes and clerks used no consistent rule in transcribing dictation and wrote in difficult, highly abbreviated handwriting. An example of the painstaking work of transcription and comparison of manuscripts, which is the methodology that underpins this volume, involved an inquisition trial (**Doc. 99**) written in a terrible Gothic hand by multiple scribes and where there was no published transcription to compare. The process was slow and careful, and for this and other difficult texts, I consulted professional paleographers in Lisbon to ensure mechanical aspects of transcription and translation also captured the nuances of speech during the period.[35] Other examples include Mina captain Manuel de Góis's letter to King Manuel about trade irregularities at São Jorge da Mina (**Doc. 21**), where there was a published transcription but a comparison with the original, a fragmented document (archived as 'fragmentos') revealed gaps in the transcriptions because the original was damaged or illegible in certain parts. There was also another fragmented and undated document (**Doc. 32**), in which evidence from individuals named in the document and prior knowledge of their biographies—alongside deciphering some opaque passages—led to being able to date it to 1512–13. The unstable state of the orthography did not help inherent problems of interpretation. This situation, as I soon learned, demanded two fundamental skill sets—careful paleographic transcription and accurate translation into modern Portuguese, and then English. Efforts to do both by scholars in Portugal and historians of Africa began in the 1960s, though Portuguese archivists and editors have been transcribing records concerning the Portuguese in Africa since the nineteenth century.[36]

This volume extends the pioneering work of John W. Blake, A. F. C. Ryder, P. E. H. Hair, Avelino Teixeira da Mota, António Brásio, John Vogt, Joseph Bato'ora Ballong-Wen-Mewuda, and others. Blake's two-volume collection of English translations was certainly useful until the 1970s, but the collection is now dated, contains errors, and only covered West Africa up until the 1550s.[37] Published in the early 1940s, Blake's volumes relied heavily on transcripts from printed Portuguese collections (e.g. Visconde de Santarém's *Quadro elementar das relações politicas e diplomaticas de Portugal*), some unpublished IAN/TT materials, and from Jeremiah Ford's transcribed letters of João III's reign

---

[35] I am greatly indebted to Angela Miranda for all her help with transcription and translation, and for all our discussions about Portugal's history and language as well as the many questions I posed, some related to documents in this volume.

[36] See, for instance, the nineteenth century multivolume work by Visconde de Santarém, *Quadro elementar das relações politicas e diplomaticas de Portugal* ... (Paris: J. P. Aillaud, 1842–76), whose volumes 3 and 15 have diplomatic records with bearing on the Mina (Gold) Coast.

[37] Blake, *Europeans in West Africa*.

(ca. 1521–1557).[38] By the 1960s, A. F. C. Ryder's English language guide to the Portuguese archives listed many West African materials, some of which were noted in Santarém's volumes and some of which appear in full in Brásio's volumes.[39] Brásio compiled, transcribed, and published a vast collection of archival materials; although this collection remains a staple among scholars and will remain more relevant than Ryder's guide, the volumes are not all-encompassing— for instance, they do not include some materials cited in Ryder and published in Hair and da Mota's collaborative work.[40] P. E. H. Hair and Avelino Teixeira da Mota translated several (shorter) archival materials, but focused largely on (longer) Iberian manuscripts. Hair alone has underscored that the fifteenth and sixteenth century history of the Mina (Gold) Coast has received far less attention than subsequent periods, but has also shown the significance of that period by publishing several deeply contextualized studies with sources in translation.[41] Indeed, as Ryder argued some time ago, the surviving fifteenth and sixteenth century 'material is a fair sample of the lost whole, so that ... the general impression which may be gained from careful study is probably accurate.'[42]

Though John Vogt was neither a compiler nor editor of Portuguese source materials for West Africa, in his *Portuguese Rule on the Gold Coast*, he claimed to have made the most exhaustive search in Portuguese and related archives in Europe. Vogt indeed cites many documents in the IAN/TT, but the majority are listed in Ryder's guide and a significant number were published in either Blake's or Brásio's collections.[43] Vogt's 15-year sojourn in mainly Portuguese archives netted him some three thousand documents on the Mina (Gold) Coast, but the results, as Vogt admits, was an 'imperial history' that said little about the Africans or the wider history of the Mina (Gold) Coast region. More recently but in stride with Vogt's study, Joseph Bato'ora Ballong-Wen-Mewuda's two-volume *São Jorge da Mina* focuses principally on the fortress rather than the histories of the African polities in the hinterland or interior with whom the fortress interacted,

---

[38] Papers of Professor Paul Hair, University of Liverpool, Special Collections and Archives, GB141 HAI/1/1/4, item 8, 'Sources for English and French Voyages to Guinea in the Mid Sixteenth Century,' p. 1. See also Santarém, *Quadro*, especially volume 15 on Anglo-Portuguese relations; Jeremiah D. M. Ford, ed., *The Letters of John III, King of Portugal, 1521-1557* (Cambridge, MA: Harvard University Press, 1931). The 372 transcribed letters from João III were addressed primarily to de Ataíde, who was instrumental in the plan to colonize Brazil, and to a few other ambassadors to European courts.

[39] A. F. C. Ryder, *Material for West Africa History in Portuguese Archives* (London: The Athlone Press, 1965).

[40] Da Mota gave Hair about 12 unpublished and transcribed documents for the Mina (Gold) Coast, which are not found in Brasio's volumes, and some were published in English translation in da Mota and Hair, *East of Mina*, 59–91.

[41] For the Mina (Gold) Coast, see, for instance, P. E. H. Hair, *East of Mina*; idem, *The Founding of the Castelo de São Jorge da Mina: An Analysis of Sources* (Madison: African Studies Program, University of Wisconsin, 1994); idem, 'The Early Sources on Guinea,' *History in Africa* 21 (1994): 87–126.

[42] Ryder, *Material*, 3.

[43] Papers of Professor Paul Hair, University of Liverpool, Special Collections and Archives, GB141 HAI/1/1/4, item 8, 'Sources for English and French Voyages to Guinea in the Mid Sixteenth Century,' p. 1.

and surprisingly ignored the work of Blake and Vogt, among others.[44] Though Wen-Mewuda uncovered few new documents, the principal sources on which his study relied, and limited to the period until 1566, were published as transcripts in volume two's appendix.[45] Though many of these sources are known and published, the problem for English-speaking scholars is these materials remain in Portuguese, much like Brásio's collections.

Africa's Gold Coast Through Portuguese Sources accomplishes two goals vital to African and world history and the specific histories of the Mina (Gold) Coast and Portugal: covering the period 1469 to 1680, it make one of the largest caches of published and archival Portuguese documents related to the Mina (Gold) Coast available in English translation, and includes a diverse and ample range of chronologically deep sources that elucidate the histories of Portugal, the Mina (Gold) Coast, and a nascent 'Atlantic World.' More precisely, *Africa's Gold Coast Through Portuguese Sources* contains translated documents that cover the widest possible extent of the Portuguese presence on the Mina (Gold) Coast but does so in a way that builds upon previous efforts, especially the 'Guinea Text Project' Avelino Teixeira da Mota and P. E. H. Hair initiated.

In 1969, P. E. H. Hair and his team at the University of Liverpool and Avelino Teixeira da Mota and his team at the Centro de Estudos de Cartografica Antiga (CECA) in Lisbon began to finalize what Hair then called a 'Project for the translation of Portuguese texts on Guinea.'[46] Hair created a working committee that would work on producing, jointly with da Mota and his team, 'multilingual edition[s] (Portuguese-French-English)' for the 'history of Guinea 1500–1700,' but given the lack of English editions he argued the 'need for English translations is therefore even greater.'[47] The Hair-led committee planned to work on the English translations, but to translate from the French translation (rather than the late-medieval Portuguese original) and from the French notes 'prepared by da Mota's team.'[48] By October 1969, the project had been renamed the 'Guinea Text Translation Project.' Given the green light to 'work from the French translations and check only against the Portuguese,' Hair could 'envisage a 5-year scheme' where '4–5 volumes published' would be realistic.[49] These would, however, be issued in a Portuguese-English series of texts parallel to the Portuguese-French texts published by a group of Portuguese and French scholars who began to

---

[44] Critical but missing among sources which would have enriched Wen-Mewuda's study was Ivana Elbl's unpublished thesis, 'The Portuguese Trade with West Africa, 1440-1521' (PhD diss., University of Toronto, 1986).

[45] J. Bato'ora Ballong-Wen-Mewuda, *São Jorge da Mina, 1482– 1637: La vie d'un Comptoir Portugais en Afrique Occidentale* (Lisbon: Fondation Calouste Gulbenkian, 1993), 2: 493–633.

[46] Papers of Professor Paul Hair, University of Liverpool, Special Collections and Archives, GB141 HAI/1/3/6/6, item 19, Memorandum from Dr. Hair to Mr. Lamb, Mr. Varley and Dr. Rowe, 10 September 1969, p. 1.

[47] Ibid., p. 1.

[48] Ibid., p. 2.

[49] Papers of Professor Paul Hair, University of Liverpool, Special Collections and Archives, GB141 HAI/1/3/6/6, item 26, Memorandum from P. E. H. Hair, 29 October 1969, p. 1.

edit bilingual editions of early Portuguese texts for western Guinea in Dakar and Bissau in the 1950s and 1960s. Raymond Mauny, Théodore Monod, and Avelino Teixeira da Mota constituted this Dakar-Bissau group, but da Mota's role was larger because he was also the joint editor (with Armando Cortesão) of the six-volume *Portugaliae Monumenta Cartographica*, and editor of what was then a new and ambitious series of carefully edited Guinea texts published in Portuguese-French and Portuguese-English. At the time of da Mota's death in April 1982, only André Donelha's *Descrição da Serra Leoa e dos Rios da Guiné e Cabo Verde* (1625) had been published in the series, with a two-volume edition planned for André Álvares de Almada's *Tratado Breve dos Rios do Guiné e Cabo Verde* (1594).[50]

Hair continued to translate several other works—all on western Guinea—for the project; some were published in abbreviated versions, and others as 'interim editions,' that is, minimal or no annotations and scholarly introductions.[51] These 'interim editions' included accounts by Álvares de Almada (1594), Fr. Manuel Álvares (1616), André de Faro (1664), and Lemos Coelho (1669).[52] Avelino Teixeira da Mota's library is housed in the Biblioteca Central da Marinha, while the CECA was expanded and incorporated into the Centro de Estudos de História e Cartografia Antiga under the direction of Luís de Albuquerque, who might be considered da Mota's successor. Albuquerque and his team of scholars have indeed made use of da Mota's vast documentary collections and have furthered da Mota's research, publishing five volumes of the *Portugaliae Monumenta Africana* (PMA). Naturally, many of the documents from earlier collections, especially Brásio's 22-volume *Monumenta Missionaria Africana*—a standard reference for scholars—have been reprinted in the early volumes of the PMA. The five volumes of the PMA cover the period from 1443 to 1510, contain primarily shorter but many unpublished archival materials in partially modernized transcription, little to any scholarly annotation, and brief document summaries in Portuguese, French, and English.[53] Hair completed much, if not all, the English summaries before his death in 2002.[54]

---

[50] P. E. H. Hair, 'The Teixeira da Mota Archives and the Guinea Texts Project,' *History in Africa* 10 (1983): 389.

[51] Ibid., p. 390–91. Hair shared a brief list of Avelino Teixeira da Mota's Africanist publications at the end of the article, but noted where a fuller bibliography could be found.

[52] Papers of Professor Paul Hair, University of Liverpool, Special Collections and Archives, GB141 HAI/1/1/4, item 1, P. E. H. Hair, 'The Guinea Texts Project: A further note,' 14 June 1987, p. 1. Several of these editions are available online through the University of Wisconsin-Madison Libraries, under the auspices of the Africana Digitization Project: http://digital.library.wisc.edu/1711.dl/AfricanStud ies.Africana.

[53] Hair noted one of the forthcoming volumes of the PMA would contain a cumulated index.

[54] For Hair's reflection on his role as translator of these summaries, see P. E. H. Hair, 'Portuguese Documents on Africa and Some Problems of Translation,' *History in Africa* 27 (2000): 91–97. In this article, Hair outlines the larger value of the PMA project, notes problems of translation, and includes a list of corrected errors in his translations for the PMA volumes.

The Nature of the Sources

Most of the surviving documents concerning Portuguese expansion in Africa are in the Arquivo Nacional da Torre do Tombo, renamed the Instituto dos Arquivos Nacionais in 2009. For the period 1440 to 1521, a recent survey of the IAN/TT found five of the 14 collections related to Africa account for 93 percent of the sources, and the most important collection of the five was the *Corpo Cronológico*, which contains almost half (41 percent) of the total materials.[55] A chronologically ordered, vast set of relatively short documents, the *Corpo Cronológico* was organized into three overlapping parts, constituting those documents retrieved or salvaged from the 1755 earthquake and fire that destroyed the Torre do Tombo.[56] The *Corpo Cronológico* documents relate to 'the daily operations of the agencies administering the Crown's African enterprise. Most are letters from Crown officials to the king and his letters and orders to them, as well as receipts, requisitions, or inventories.'[57] Other collections among the five, in order of importance, include the *Gavetas* ('drawers') consisting of single formal documents (e.g. treaties); the *Núcleo Antigo* ('old nucleus') containing registers and codices (e.g. law codes); the *Leitura Nova* ('new transcription') containing copies of documents and chancery materials; and the *Chancelarias* containing registers of royal chancery records. The *Corpo Cronológico* and *Núcleo Antigo* 'offer much more detail ... and enable historians to gain much deeper insight into the workings of the Portuguese enterprise in Africa.'[58]

The crown's approach to this enterprise and the importance of the Mina (Gold) Coast is revealed by the percentage of Portuguese documentation devoted to the region: 16 percent of IAN/TT records related to central crown agencies, and 70 percent of this concerned the *Casa da Mina e Guiné*, the main agency through which the crown administered its African enterprise, supplied overseas parts of empire, and marketed African goods. For the 25 percent of IAN/TT records related to African factories, the São Jorge da Mina and Akyem ('Axim') fortresses accounted for 41 percent and more than half of the 14 percent of IAN/TT records related to diplomacy focused on the Mina (Gold) Coast.[59] These statistics, of course, follow the history and patterns of Portuguese expansion, in the form of royal factories on the Mina (Gold) Coast and chartered settlement on São Tomé, followed by trading relations with West Central Africa and East Africa. The high level of diplomatic activity between the crown and the Mina (Gold) Coast

---

[55] Elbl, 'Archival Evidence,' 326, 330. For an earlier survey, which included archives beyond the IAN/TT, see Ryder, *Materials*.
[56] On the history and organization of the *Corpo Cronológico*, see Pedro A. de Azevedo and António Baião, *O Archivo da Torre do Tombo, sua historia, corpos que o compõem e organisação* (Lisboa: Annaes da Academia de Estudos Livres, 1905).
[57] Elbl, 'Archival Evidence,' 331.
[58] Elbl, 'Archival Evidence,' 336.
[59] Elbl, 'Archival Evidence,' 337–38, 344–45.

contrasts sharply with western Guinea and Benin, two regions with which the Portuguese frequented as much as the Mina (Gold) Coast, but which accounted for only five and six percent respectively of surviving diplomatic records.[60] Not surprisingly, the bulk of the records categorized as 'diplomatic' come from the *Corpo Cronológico*. Prior to 1521, western Africa and more specifically the Mina (Gold) Coast remained at the center of Portuguese activity and expansion, the latter with the single largest portion of the extant sources related to Africa. Though Ivana Elbl is correct, in that surviving documents remain 'relatively unexploited,' it may turn out that new evidence in the IAN/TT and other archives will do more than 'filling in details' and could open 'entirely unsuspected dimensions' in the study of Africa and Portugal.[61]

Africa's Gold Coast Through Portuguese Sources contains new and unpublished as well as extant documents found principally in Portuguese archives, more than half of which were transcribed in António Brásio's *Monumenta Missionaria Africana*. In addition, I have selected everything from documents in Italian archives to special collections at Harvard University to transcriptions in Ballong-Wen-Mewuda's second volume.[62] Along the way, I have had to retranslate documents found in John Blake's collection, and in the works of Paul Hair and Teixeira da Mota. Choosing a chronological order, that is the date(s) inscribed on a document that indicate when it was written or recorded, I selected archival documentation to map onto a timeline from 1469 to 1680, but also sparingly used excerpts from manuscript sources or narrative chronicles to flesh out that timeline.[63] The result is a selection of sources that add texture and some depth to our understanding of the cultural, political, and economic life on the Mina (Gold) Coast, since this documentation provides information on and identifies individual African traders and rulers, women and men, and Portuguese impressions of their lifeways. This corpus is thus an important source for indigenous West African history and African relations with the Portuguese and other European nations, empires, and chartered companies.

Though historians of the Mina (Gold) Coast are aware of the IAN/TT and Brásio's collection, there has surprisingly been little interest in exploiting these sources for the early modern history of the region. For those who have drawn attention to or used these records in any serious way, the list is a very small, though respectable one—Avelino Teixeira da Mota, P. E. H. Hair, John W. Blake,

---

[60] Elbl, 'Archival Evidence,' 346.

[61] Elbl, 'Archival Evidence,' 353–54.

[62] For a dated but still useful survey of Portuguese materials related to west Africa in Italian archives, see Robert Garfield, 'Sources for Portuguese West African History in the Vatican and Related Collections,' in Lawrence J. McCrank, ed., *Discovery in the Archives of Spain and Portugal: Quincentenary essays, 1492-1992* (New York: Haworth Press, 1994),

[63] I have not included many of the narrative chronicles which Paul Hair surveyed some time ago, precisely because many of these are their own standalone work—e.g. Duarte Pacheco Pereira's *Esmeraldo de situ*—or are widely available, such as the founding of the São Jorge da Mina fortress, in the collection of John Blake and Paul Hair's *The Founding of the Castelo de São Jorge da Mina*. See Paul E. H. Hair, 'The Early Sources on Guinea,' *History in Africa* 21 (1994): 87–125.

and John Vogt. Rather than probe the original materials, most scholars have simply been content to cite the spare and highly selective translations and analysis of those named or the handful of translations in the Furley Collection at the Balme Library, University of Ghana. Named after British colonial official John Talford Furley, the Furley Collection consists of handwritten notes, photocopies, and a typeset of primary sources in different European languages, though very little in terms of Portuguese sources not already known.[64] The consequence has been a dogmatic vision of the late fifteenth to early seventeenth century history of the Mina (Gold) Coast built on a handful of documents, and the occasional passing reference to the Portuguese and their documentation as if both were inconsequential.[65] This volume hopes to encourage more scholars and graduate students to research and write on the 'Portuguese period,' in much the same way historians Kwame Daaku, Ray Kea, Robin Law, and Ivor Wilks have fruitfully mined Dutch, Danish, and English records, respectively, for the seventeenth and eighteenth century Gold Coast.[66]

Though these historians and many others might know of some of the Portuguese sources in this volume, overall the Portuguese materials herein significantly revise their findings as well as 'standard' views of the late fifteenth

---

[64] There is a handwritten index by E. F. Collins and Albert van Dantzig for the Furley Collection. On the value and utility of the collection, see Albert van Dantzig, 'The Furley Collection. Its Value and Limitations for the Study of Ghana's History in European Sources for Sub-Saharan Africa before 1900: Use and Abuse,' *Paideuma* 33 (1987): 423–32.

[65] See, for instance, the early and even later writings of reputed historian Ivor Wilks, specifically his collection of essays, *Forests of Gold: Essays on the Akan and the Kingdom of Asante* (Athens: Ohio University Press, 1993). There has certainly been an overreliance on select and well-worn European travelogues in English translation. Ironically, these carefully annotated scholarly editions are used widely and even uncritically, especially among English-speaking scholars, but they also do not encourage more editions from a broader swath of scholars. As a leading figure in the scholarly preparation of European source materials for African history, Paul Hair lamented, 'many of the standard edited texts used by African historians ... urgently need re-editing.' This situation, not to mention the plagiarism, errors, and mishandling of African language terms in European-supplied texts, makes the need for translations from scholars who 'have a command of all the known sources on the locality [in question] over a long period' that much more important. See P. E. H. Hair, 'The Task Ahead: The Editing of Early European-Language Texts on Black Africa,' *Paideuma* 33 (1987): 38. For a brief history of editing texts for 'Black Africa,' see pages 31–35.

[66] On the seventeenth and eighteenth century Gold Coast, see, for instance, Robin Law, 'The 'Golden Age' in the History of the Pre-Colonial Gold Coast.' *Transactions of the Historical Society of Ghana* 17 (2015): 109–36; idem, "There's Nothing Grows in the West Indies but Will Grow Here': Dutch and English Projects of Plantation Agriculture on the Gold Coast, 1650s–1780s,' in *Commercial Agriculture, the Slave Trade and Slavery in Atlantic Africa*, eds. Robin Law et al. (London: Boydell & Brewer, 2013), 116–37; idem, 'The Government of Fante in the Seventeenth Century,' *The Journal of African History* 54, no. 1 (2013): 31–51; idem, 'Fante Expansion Reconsidered: Seventeenth-Century Origins,' *Transactions of the Historical Society of Ghana* 14 (2012): 41–78; idem, 'The Akani War of 1693–6,' *Transactions of the Historical Society of Ghana* 11 (2008): 89–111; idem, 'The Komenda Wars, 1694–1700: A Revised Narrative,' *History in Africa* 34 (2007): 133–68; Ivor Wilks, *Akwamu 1640–1750: A Study of the Rise and Fall of a West African Empire* (Trondheim: Norwegian University of Science and Technology, 2001); idem, *Forests of Gold*; Ray. A. Kea, *Settlements, Trade, and Politics in the Seventeenth Century Gold Coast* (Baltimore: The Johns Hopkins University Press, 1982); Kwame Yeboa Daaku, *Trade and Politics on the Gold Coast, 1600–1720: A Study of the African Reaction to European Trade* (London: The Clarendon Press, 1970).

to seventeenth century Mina (Gold) Coast. To be sure, these materials, whether newly found or translated or revised, point to new directions in Mina (Gold) Coast history. The 1499 inquest (**Doc. 7**), covering 1495–99, and Beatriz Gomes's manumission letter in 1499 (**Doc. 6**), reorients our understanding of slavery and European-led slaving, wherein São Jorge da Mina served from the very beginning as a slave depot and enslaving institutions. While Gomes's letter is the earliest known manumission granted for an enslaved person on the Mina (Gold) Coast and perhaps in early modern Africa, the inquest provides the fullest picture of Portuguese slaving and gold trading operations through São Jorge da Mina, with detailed profiles of all the Portuguese officials and residents, their activities, and relations with local rulers and merchants, including a female merchant recorded as Briolanja. These probing and unprecedented insights are extended decades later through detailed lists of Portuguese officials and residents (**Docs. 17–18, 25**), and enslaved and local African 'hostages' from ruling families (often a son), one of whom was the infamous African merchant João Serrão (**Docs. 27–28, 34**). Our knowledge is also advanced by the three Inquisition cases which exist for the Mina (Gold) Coast, all in the sixteenth century; two concern African women, while the other targeted an old, Portuguese captain of São Jorge da Mina.[67] One of the earliest and fullest of these cases appears in this volume (**Docs. 99, 105**) and involves an elderly African woman baptized Graça. Until now, scholars had not been aware of these inquisitional cases, nor an emissary to Rome (**Doc. 84**), or the scathing reports of vicars on everything from armed bandits to African women and cultural observations (**Docs. 105, 175**), and, more importantly, how they reorient our view of the Mina (Gold) Coast and its peoples.

The translated documents in this volume, and of which the above were a small sample size, bring closure to certain important debates and revise our view of taken-for-granted understandings, which have become accepted. First, the long-standing 'Big Bang' theory of fifteenth-sixteenth century Akan social and political transformation proposed by Ivor Wilks finds no support in those documents.[68] Second, the view of the Mina (Gold) Coast as balkanized and divided up into 'petty states' and various 'ethnicities' receives clarification in

---

[67] These cases can be found in ANTT, Tribunal do Santo Ofício, Inquisição de Lisboa, processos 01604, 11041, and 12431.

[68] Ivor Wilks, 'The State of the Akan and the Akan states: A Discursion,' *Cahiers d'Etudes Africaines* 22, 3–4 (1987-88), 232–35; idem, *Forests of Gold: Essays on the Akan and the Kingdom of Asante* (Athens: Ohio University Press, 1993), 41–90. Cf. Mariano Pavanello, 'Foragers or Cultivators? A Discussion of Wilks's 'Big Bang' Theory of Akan History,' *Journal of West African History* 1, no. 2 (2015): 1–26; Gérard Chouin, 'The 'Big Bang' Theory Reconsidered: Framing Early Ghanaian History,' *Transactions of the Historical Society of Ghana* 14 (2012): 13–40. Having not consulted nor engaged the Portuguese materials, Wilks was also misled by his own propositions concerning the early documentary history of the Mina (Gold) Coast. See Ivor Wilks, 'Wangara, Akan and Portuguese in the Fifteenth and Sixteenth Centuries. II. The Struggle for Trade,' *The Journal of African History* 23, no. 4 (1982): 463–72; Idem, 'Wangara, Akan and Portuguese in the Fifteenth and Sixteenth Centuries. 1. The Matter of Bitu,' *The Journal of African History* 23, no. 3 (1982): 333–49.

the extant documentation. The Portuguese were uncomprehending outsiders, often unable (lacking discernment) or unwilling (relying on African interpreters, rather than learning local languages) to distinguish the social and the political, assuming local 'kings' did not have a social position that tempered their political will or *different* polities ('states') with *different* language or culture groups. The Portuguese 'Acane(s)' referred neither to polity nor place but to people—Acane/Akani is *akanni*, 'I am an Akan person.' The plural is formed by adding the suffix *-fɔɔ*, as in 'eguafoɔ' or 'twifoɔ,' which is to say *aguafɔɔ* ('market people') and *twifɔɔ* ('Twi people').[69] These peoples settled in but cut across multiple lands and polities, and the most prominent had homes in the interior, hinterlands, and on the coast. And so the distinctions the Portuguese made between Akan societies, using size ('Big v. Small Akan'; **Doc. 114**) or language ('Portuguese v. Castilian Akan'; **Doc. 34**) resulted from incomprehension, not precise location or a grasp of people, places, and polities. Indeed, many accepted associations under the dubious rubric of 'toponyms' and 'ethnonyms' need serious revision, and the Portuguese materials—and the maps to this volume—are helpful in that direction.

These translations benefit not only scholars but also make the value and insights of the extant records accessible to students and the reading public. For the history of the Mina (Gold) Coast, the surviving records selected for translation add much to existing knowledge and inspire further study of the region's early documentary history. Historians use some 39 European travel accounts of Africa's Mina (Gold) Coast that describe events that occurred between 1470 and 1700. Chronologically, two accounts (one Spanish, one Portuguese) fall within the fifteenth century, four (one Spanish, one Portuguese, two English) within the sixteenth, and thirty-four (nine Dutch, nine German, seven French, four English, two Danish, one Spanish, one Portuguese) within the seventeenth century. A few of these accounts describe more than one locality, but even this is skewed toward specific areas: the majority focus on Adena, Oguaa ('Cape Coast'), and Nkrãn ('Accra'), followed by Moure/Mori, Akatakyi ('Komenda'), Cape Three Points, Assinie, Fetu, and Akyem ('Axim'). Between 1470 and 1550, the four extant travel accounts were written either in Portuguese or Spanish and all focused their

---

[69] See introduction to Kwasi Konadu and Clifford Campbell, eds., *The Ghana Reader: History, Culture, Politics* (Durham: Duke University Press, 2016); Kwasi Konadu, *Akan Pioneers: African Histories, Diasporic Experiences* (New York: Diasporic Africa Press, 2018); idem, *The Akan Diaspora in the Americas* (New York: Oxford University Press, 2012). Cf. On 'Akani,' see Daaku, *Trade and Politics*; Kea, *Settlements, Trade and Politics*; Albert van Dantzig, 'The Akanists: A West Africa Hansa,' in *West African Economic and Social History: Studies in Memory of Marion Johnson*, eds. David Henige and T.C. McCaskie (Madison: University of Wisconsin, African Studies Program, 1990). Cf. On 'Eguafo,' see Sam Spiers, 'The Eguafo Polity: Between the Traders and Raiders,' in *Power and Landscape in Atlantic West Africa: Archaeological Perspectives*, eds. J. Cameron Monroe and Akinwumi Ogundiran (New York: Cambridge University Press, 2012); Gérard Chouin, *Eguafo: Un Royaume Africain 'au coeur francois (1637-1688)* (Paris: Aftra, 1998). 'Etsi' is likely the Fante or European corruption of 'Twi'; on the former, see John Kofi Fynn, *Oral Traditions of Fante States* (Legon: Institute of African Studies, University of Ghana, 1974); idem, *Asante and its Neighbors 1700-1807* (London: Longman, 1971).

attention on São Jorge da Mina and the adjacent village of Adena.[70] Over the next 50 years there are two English accounts, both appearing in Richard Hakluyt's *Principal Navigations*, whereas in the period from 1601 to the 1670s, when the Portuguese had been effectively removed from the Mina (Gold) Coast, most of the accounts are in German or Dutch. The most notable is Pieter de Marees's *Beschrijvinghe ende historische verhael van het Gout Koninckrijck van Gunea*, published in 1602, and the well-known 1629 Dutch map that provides some ethnographic data.[71] The Portuguese sources in this volume allow us not only to plug the gaping chronological holes for the fifteenth and sixteenth century, but they also give us comparative materials through which to interpret the extant travel accounts, especially when they become more plentiful. These start in the early to mid-seventeenth century, by which time the Portuguese lost São Jorge da Mina in 1637 and Akyem ('Axim') in 1642 to the Dutch. Published collections of translated non-Portuguese documents related to the Mina (Gold) Coast thus date *after* 1650; Ole Justesen's edited two-volume set of Danish documents begins in 1657 and Albert van Dantzig's edited volume of Dutch documents begins in 1674.[72]

Though the records in *Africa's Gold Coast Through Portuguese Sources* have multiple uses, such as providing comparative materials against which such widely used accounts as that of Pieter de Marees can be evaluated, the extant records also suffer from certain limitations. The geographical and chronological scope of the records limit themselves to the Portuguese hub at São Jorge da Mina and

---

[70] See Martín Fernándes de Enciso, *Suma de geographia que trata de todas las partidas y provincias del mundo* (Seville: Jacobo Cronberger, 1519); João de Barros, *Da Asia de João de Barros e de Diogo do Couto* (Lisbon: Na Regia Officina Typografica, 1778); Duarte Pacheco Pereira, *Esmeraldo de Situ Orbis* (Lisbon: Imprensa Nacional, 1892); Hernando del Pulgar, *Crónica de los senores reyes católicos Don Fernando y Dona Isabel de Castilla y de Aragón*, ed., Juan de Mata Carriazo, 2 vols. (Madrid: Espasa-Calpe, 1943).

[71] The mid-sixteenth century accounts of William Towrson and Robert Gainsh appear in volume 6 of Richard Hakluyt's *The Principal Navigations, Voyages, Traffiques and Discoveries of the English Nation*, 12 vols. (Glasgow: James MacLehose & Sons, 1903–05); the Dutch accounts begin with Pieter de Marees, *Beschrijvinghe ende historische verhael van het Gout Koninckrijck van Gunea* (Amsterdam: Corn. Claesz, 1602), translated into English as *Description and Historical Account of the Gold Kingdom of Guinea (1602)*, eds. and trans., Albert van Dantzig and Adam Jones (New York: Oxford University Press, 1987), and continue with Dierick Ruiters's *Toortse der Zee-Vaert (1623)*, ed., S. P. l'Honoré Naber (The Hague: Martinus Nijhoff, 1913), the 1629 Dutch map in Algemeen Rijksarchief (Den Haag), Leupe-collectie 743 (map of the Gold Coast dated 25 December 1629), Jacob de *Lange's Demonomanie of Der Mooren Wonderheden …* (Amsterdam: Bartholomeus Schouwers, 1658), the *Vijf dagregisters van het kasteel São Jorge da Mina (Elmina) aan de Goutkust (1645-1647)*, ed., Klass Ratelband (The Hague: Martinus Nijhoff, 1953), and Olfert Dapper's *Naukeurige Beschrijvinge der Afrikaensche Gewesten* (Amsterdam: Jacob van Meurs, 1668). The accounts of several German-speaking travelers appear in Adam Jones, *German Sources for West African History 1599-1669* (Wiesbaden: Franz Steiner Verlag, 1983), while among the few French sources the standout is Nicolas Villault de Bellefond, *Relation des costes d'Afrique appelées Guinée* (Paris: D. Thierry, 1669).

[72] Ole Justesen, ed., *Danish Sources for the History of Ghana, 1657-1754*, 2 vols., trans. James Manley (Copenhagen: Det Kongelige Danske Videnskabernes Selskab, 2005); Albert van Dantzig, ed., *The Dutch and the Guinea Coast, 1674-1742: A Collection of Documents from the General State Archive at the Hague* (Accra: Ghana Academy of Arts and Sciences, 1978).

the Akyem ('Axim') factory, temporally beginning in the late fifteenth century and terminating around the 1670s, or certainly by 1680, though they maintain a greatly reduced presence east of São Jorge da Mina. But we also get more than the occasional regional insights about the movement of gold, goods, and people between the Mina (Gold) Coast, Benin, São Tomé and Príncipe, and the Kingdom of Kongo, besides reports from the hinterland and forest interior, maps, ship logs, visits from interior peoples to São Jorge da Mina, and inquisitional cases that brought alleged heretics to Lisbon to stand trial. A second yet unsurprising limitation is that Africans wrote none of the records, though evidence of their language, testimonies, and socio-political orders exists. Finally, we will never know what and how much was destroyed in the 1755 earthquake, but the continuous stream of surviving letters and reports for over a century and a half gives us a fair idea of the kinds of records the Mina (Gold) Coast might have once had. These limitations, however, underscore the caution scholars must exercise in their judicious use of these records—translated or in original form—and make the available recorded observations on African societies and their constituents that much more valuable.

Structure of Present Volume

The volume is chronological, beginning in 1469 and ending in 1680, with each document numbered in bold and bracketed atop, followed by a heading and an abstract of its contents and then the translation. The source(s) of each document is supplied by a footnote affixed to the heading, and any comparative primary or secondary materials, including transcriptions or translations or commentary by other scholars. The complexity of documents make some repetition across the voluminous footnotes necessary. Since the primary purpose of the volume is to make these 'Portuguese' materials accessible to English readers, annotations are minimal, and attempts to clarify and direct attention to relevant materials from, say, Brasio's collections, or other archival and even secondary sources. For the Brásio transcriptions and Blake's and da Mota and Hair's translations, these have not been reproduced since they are readily accessible to scholars. Overall, Brásio's readings of the original material and foliation are generally accurate, though necessary corrections and improvements on his readings were made by consulting the original sources. And as far as issues raised by word formation or punctuations Brásio inserted, these have been noted in the footnotes. Brásio's collection is cited using the acronym 'MMA,' followed by the volume and document number (e.g. MMA vol. 1, doc. 45), whereas reference to documents in Corpo Cronológico are cited using the acronym 'CC,' followed by the part, bundle, and document number (e.g. CC 1–2–45).

Though most of Brásio's material on the Mina (Gold) Coast derives from the IAN/TT and thus *Corpo Cronológico*, other materials came from additional Portuguese (e.g. Arquivo Histórico Ultramarino) and other European archives. So, for instance, Brásio found records I did not find at the IAN/TT, but Avelino

Teixeira da Mota found records Brásio overlooked, and I found records—in lieu of accessing da Mota's papers—from inquisitional trials (*processos*) and from *Corpo Cronológico* and *Núcleo Antigo* that both apparently did not. For these newly discovered and unpublished records, their archival citations are indicated in the translations and their paleographic transcriptions appear in the new Fontes Historiae Africanae/Sources of African History website (https://www.fonteshis toriaeafricanae.co.uk). Where annotations that clarify and direct attention to contemporary materials are made, including cross-references between relevant Portuguese sources, they are kept to modest proportions since the documents and not the footnotes are the primary focus. Viewed from this perspective, the translated documents challenge existing interpretations—around themes of history, politics, culture, religion/spirituality, and socio-economic life. I have included the 'proper' Akan/Twi names of peoples/peoples—with no attempt at precise locations, for the sources provide no such latitude—and indicate the 'original forms' in footnotes. The Portuguese attempted to record what they heard, in their language's sound system, and so they meant to record Akan (not 'Acane'), Wasa (not 'Assas'), Etsi/Atis (not 'Antis'), the Eguafoɔ or Akatakyi (not 'Acomane' or 'Komenda'), Ahanta (not 'Anta'), Labadi (not 'Labidan'), Fetu (not 'Afuto'), and so on.[73] Where uncertain and where the textual evidence or linguistic analysis is unsupportive, I have made no attempt at identification.[74]

The approach taken toward the English translations of records in late-medieval Portuguese, sometimes in a gothic handwriting, with several in partial or full Latin, Italian, Castilian (Spanish), and French, is simple and straightforward: keep as close to the original sources' meaning and tone but make it intelligible for readers in the twenty-first century. This does not mean the translations are modernized; it simply means there is a balance between the writer's meaning and readability, leaning more on the side of literal translation to keep to the original tone and prose as much as possible. More specifically, the current norms for Portuguese transcriptions were followed, where '[]' indicate problems in the paper or corrections where there was no preexisting transcription, and '[[]]' indicate corrections or erasures by the scribe. In the translations, paleographic notes are added when necessary for comprehension of the text or to indicate illegible words; erased words are indicated where necessary; and there was a preference for 'scribe' rather than 'notary', 'secretary', or 'registrar,' since the latter correspond to precise functions. In the translations, a question mark between brackets means the original text was obscure at that precise point. Finally, on numerals and names, the Roman rather than Arabic numerals are used, but first names are left unmodernized such as 'Pero' (now 'Pedro') or surnames such as 'Roiz,'

---

[73] On the history of Fetu, see Yann Deffontaine, *Guerre et Société au Royaume de Fetu (Efutu): Des débuts du commerce atlantique à la constitution de la Fédération Fanti: Ghana, Côte de l'or, 1471-1720* (Ibadan: IFRA, 1993).

[74] For instance, Ballong-Wen-Mewuda identified 'Ampia' with 'Ampeni' and 'Jamou' with 'Jabi/Yabi.' While I do not reject these, I am equally not convinced by their identification.

which can be transcribed as 'Rodrigues', but in fact both forms were equivalent and interchangeable. This volume uses the day-month-year date format (e.g. 21-6-1521 = 21 June 1521), set off in parentheses under the title of each document. And for matters concerning punctuation, capitalization, double consonants, headings, and grammar, the aim has been to keep the integrity of the text with the corresponding goal of accessibility and readability.

Acknowledgment

Mpaeɛ. Onyankopɔn, Asase Yaa, abosompɛm, nananom nsamanfoɔ, m'abusuafoɔ, meda mo ase bebree. Na monim sɛ meresua, momma menhu da biara. To Kyima (Ronnie), Abena, Sunkwa, and Afia, *monim sɛ ɔdɔ nyera fie kwan.* This project owes much to Angela Miranda, first and foremost. Thanks for all the help with my unending questions, shipping books from Portugal, putting me in touch with archivists, and more. Conversations with John Vogt, Clifford Campbell, Scot Brown, Amari Johnson, Kofi (Bright) Gyamfi, Roger Crowley, Trevor Getz, and Monique Bedaase have been tremendously helpful, even if indirectly. Malyn Newitt, Toby Green, Robin Law, and members of the *Fontes Historiae Africanae* committee welcomed the project, provided support and critical feedback, and helped to make the volume a better book. Finally, I thank you, the reader, for choosing this book. The usual disclaimers apply.

DOCUMENTS

1 Leasing of the Guinea Trade [1] (1469)

ABSTRACT – *Chronicler João de Barros explains how King Afonso V leased what was called the 'Guinea trade' in West Africa to Lisbon merchant Fernão Gomes for five years, with the obligation of 'discovering' five hundred leagues of coast during this period. And because he or his agents came upon the gold trade that they dubbed the 'Mina (Gold) Coast,' Gomes was given the surname of Mina, together with the correspondent coat of arms, and renamed Fernão Gomes da Mina.* [2]

At that time the Guinea trade was already a common practice amongst our people and the residents in those places; and they dealt with each other in matters related to commerce in peace and love, without those war raids and attacks which there had been at first. And this cannot be otherwise, above all because these are rude and barbarian people, both in law and in customs, as in the use of things from this Europe of ours – for they were always hostile before they started to take an interest in them. But after they had had some notion of the truth through the benefits they received both in their souls and in their reasoning, and in things for their use, they became so tame that, as soon as the ships from this kingdom arrived to their ports, many peoples would come from the backlands to trade our goods, which were given to them in exchange for souls, who came to receive salvation rather than captivity.

And with things thus running normally and regularly in those parts of the coast that had already been discovered,[3] and the King so occupied with the affairs of the realm that he did not think it was his service to cultivate this commerce, nor to leave it as it was, as regards what the parties paid, it having been thus suggested to him in

---

[1] João de Barros, *Da Asia de João de Barros e de Diogo do Couto*, Década I, liv. II, cap. II, pp. 141–51; cf. MMA, vol. 1, doc. 65, pp. 436–43. This and all documents that reference MMA uses Brásio's transcription as a starting point, but all such transcriptions were checked against the originals.'

[2] Unless otherwise stated, transcripts to most of the documents translated here have been published in Portuguese. Those that are not will be indicated in the abstract, though readers will also know from the initial footnote for each document's title, where published transcriptions, or sometimes translations, will be noted.

[3] João de Barros used the term *'descobrir,'* and its derivations, in the double sense of 'sighting' and 'exploring.'

November of the year one thousand and four hundred and sixty nine,[4] he leased it for a period of five years to Fernão Gomes, an honorable citizen of Lisbon, for two hundred thousand *reais* a year; with the condition that, in each of those five years, he would be obliged to discover one hundred leagues further along the coast, so that by the end of the leasing period five hundred leagues would have been discovered.

Which discovery should start in Sierra Leone, at the point reached by Pedro de Sintra and Soeiro da Costa, the last discoverers prior to this lease; for later this Soeiro da Costa discovered the river which we now call 'of Soeiro' and is located between Cape Palmas and [[Cape]] Three Points, near the House of Akyem, where the *feitoria* of the gold trade is done. And among other conditions included in this contract, there was one determining that all the ivory should go to the King, at the price of one thousand and five hundred *reais* per *quintal*;[5] and the King would give it at a higher price to a certain Martim Eanes Boaviagem, because he was obliged to do so by another, previous, contract[6] regarding all the ivory traded in Guinea. And because it was something much appreciated at that time, Fernão Gomes had permission to trade[7] one African civet in each of the said five years.

Which contract was celebrated in the year four hundred and sixty-nine: with the condition that he was not to trade on the mainland opposite the islands of Cape Verde, since, as they belonged to Dom Fernando, the trade pertained to their residents; nor was he given the trade of the castle of Arguin, because the King had given it to Prince Dom João, his son, as part of the *assentamento*[8] which the Prince received from him. But afterwards the said Fernão Gomes obtained this trade of Arguin from the Prince for a certain number of years, at the price of one hundred thousand *reais* per year. And Fernão Gomes was so diligent and fortunate in this discovery and its trade that, as early as January four hundred and seventy-one, through João de Santarém and Pedro Escobar, both knights of the King's Household, he discovered

---

[4] Unknown document. Before this date, we know Fernão Gomes was appointed *recebedor* (collector) of all Muslim men and women, as well as of any other articles from the Guinea trade. The document is dated 12-4-1455, ANTT, *Chancelaria de D. Afonso V*, liv. 15, fol. 47. (Note: I use the date format, *dd/mm/yyyy*, for archival references.) For one year, from September 4, 1469, Fernão Gomes, resident in Lisbon and *escudeiro* (squire) of the Royal Household, could send a 30-ton caravel to Africa, that is, to Safi and to the towns and villages of that *comarca* and coast, with as many and whatever goods he might want, except for arms, gold, silver, and prohibited items, and to bring whatever he might wish, in the same circumstances (*Ibid*, liv. 31, fol. 116, 4-9-1469). Fernão Gomes remonstrates with the king against the royal orders, which decreed everything from Guinea ('Moors,' malagueta, etc.) be taken to the customs house before being received, because this went against their contract. Document written in Carnide on 30-5-1472, *Ibid*, liv. 33, fol. 150.

[5] *Quintal*: see Glossary.

[6] A certain Martim Anes Boaviagem, merchant and resident in Lisbon, obtains a royal license to carry arms, dated 2-7-1431, ANTT, *Chancelaria de D. Afonso V*, liv. 16, fol. 125. An *escudeiro* (squire) with the same name, resident in Lisbon, obtains a similar license, dated 10-5-1468, *Ibid*, liv. 28, fol. 29. Addressed to the same person, for two of his retainers who were in Brittany, letters of marine insurance for their ships or even for those of the Bretons of the Dominion of the Duke of Brittany. Issued in Óbidos on 2-7-1472, *Ibid*, liv. 29, fol. 116.

[7] Depending on the context, and whenever the verbal form is used, the Portuguese term *resgatar* is translated herein as 'to exchange or trade.' See P. E. H. Hair, 'Portuguese Documents on Africa and Some Problems of Translation,' *History in Africa* 27 (2000): 96–7.

[8] *Assentamento*: see Glossary.

the gold trade in the place which today we call Mina; and the pilots were Martim Fernandes, resident in Lisbon, and Álvaro Esteves, resident in Lagos, who at that time excelled in his office over everyone else in the whole of Spain.

The first gold trade done in this land took place in a village called Esma[9] which at that time had five hundred residents:[10] and afterwards it was done further down, in the direction where today lies the fortress which king Dom João had built (as we shall see[11] in due course), which place was called by our people Aldeia das Duas Partes. And not only did Fernão Gomes discover this gold trade, but his discoverers, as stipulated by contract, reached as far as Cape Santa Catarina, which is thirty-seven leagues beyond Cape Lopez and two and a half degrees latitude south. And at that time Fernão Gomes made a very large fortune, with which he later served the King, both in Ceuta and in the conquest of Alcazar, Asilah and Tangier, where the King knighted him.

And in the year four hundred and seventy-four, the last of his lease, he [[the King]] granted him a new title and coat-of-arms, a crested shield with a field in silver and three black men's heads, each of them with three gold rings on their ears and noses, and a necklace on their necks, and 'Mina' as a surname, in remembrance of its discovery; and for this he issued him a writ, on the twenty-ninth of August of the said year.[12] Four years later, he [[the King]] appointed him to his Council, for at that time, due to the good industry of Fernão Gomes, the trade of Guinea and the trade of Mina was so fruitful, and contributed so much to the welfare of the Kingdom, that for this service and for other personal reasons he deserved all the honor and grace that was bestowed on him.

Furthermore, at that time the island of Formosa was discovered by a certain Fernão do Pó, and it now bears the name of its discoverer, having lost the one which had then been given to it. And the last discoverer during the lifetime of this King Dom Afonso was a certain de Sequeira,[13] a knight of his Household, who discovered the cape we called Catarina, which name he then gave to it because he had discovered it on that saint's day.[14] And not only at that time, by the King's command after he began to reign, but also through the said *Infante* Dom Henrique who, as we have seen earlier, lived until the year four hundred and sixty-three,[15] conquests and discoveries were continually taking place: as that of the coast whence the first *malagueta* came, which was carried out by the *Infante* Dom Henrique. And the little *malagueta* that could be had from Italy before this discovery was obtained from the Moors of these parts of Guinea, who crossed the vast region of Mandinga and the deserts of Libya, which they call the Sahara, until they reached the Mediterranean

---

[9] In Brásio's transcription, '*Sãmá.*' Esma was known as a produce export market.
[10] In Brásio's transcription, '*vezinhos*' ('*vizinhos*'): see Glossary.
[11] Cf. Liv. III, ch. I and II.
[12] Unknown document.
[13] Fernão de Sequeira.
[14] November 25.
[15] In fact, until 1460.

Sea at a port which they call Mundi Barca, and corruptly Monte da Barca. And because the Italians did not know where it came from, and it was so precious a spice, they called it Grana Paradisi, which is the name it bears among them.

The islands of São Tomé, Annobon and Principe, as well as other trades and islands, were also discovered by command of King Dom Afonso; and we shall not deal with them in particular, because we do not have the information of when and by which captains they were discovered. We do know, however, that more things are commonly said to have happened and more lands to have been discovered in the time of this King than what we have written; and, likewise, with an island which is still unknown and that was found in the year four hundred and thirty-eight years. And in order that what I say should not appear strange, I will bring forward a testimony, which includes many witnesses to its truth.

In the year five hundred and twenty-five, a fleet from Castile, whose chief captain was Friar García de Loays, Commander of the Order of St. John, sailed from the coast of Guinea to the coast of Brazil, heading towards our islands of Moluccas; of which voyage we have obtained a chart. Its author recounts an argument which occurred in that latitude[16] between a certain Rodrigo da Cunha, Andalusian *fidalgo* who was captain in that fleet of the *nau* Santiago, and Santiago Guevara, Biscayan and captain of a patache likewise called Santiago. And the argument was about who was entitled to take to the chief Captain a Portuguese ship which both had boarded[17] and which was coming from the island of São Tomé carrying black people and sugar. And from words alone the captains went as far as mortar fire, and in the end the caravel was taken to the chief Captain. Which chief Captain spoke to the pilot about taking him with him but decided not to do so because the ship was in such a latitude as would bring death to as many souls as sailed in her, since there would be no one left on the ship capable of bringing them back to this kingdom. Thus determined, he held him for a day to question him about matters related to the sea, until finally he let him go without any harm. From which pilot (according to the author of the chart) they learned that the Portuguese were in the Moluccas, where they had built a fortress; and that continuing their voyage, two degrees south, they had found an uninhabited island, called St. Mathew,[18] where there were two watering places, one of which was very good and the other not so much. And on two trees it was written that eighty-seven years earlier[19] the Portuguese had been there; and there were signs that they had already made use of it, since there was plenty of fruit, especially sweet oranges, palm trees and fowl, of the same kind that exist in these parts of Spain and of which many, which were in the trees, were killed with crossbows.

---

[16] In Brásio's transcription, '*parágem*' ('*paragem*'): see Glossary.

[17] In Brásio's transcription, '*arribaram*,' i.e. 'diverted the ship from its course,' though it is not possible to fully assert it was done by boarding it.

[18] In Portuguese, '*São Mateus*.'

[19] 1438.

He gives an account of many other things which were found there, of which I noted only these few as evidence for what we have said above: that our people had discovered more lands at that time than what we find in the writings of Gomes Eanes de Zurara. And to find this memorial inscribed on trees is not new, for it was a common practice among our people at that time; and some, in praise of the *Infante* Dom Henrique, wrote his motto, which was, as we have seen: *Talant de bien faire*;[20] because this memorial written on the bark of dragon trees and some wooden crosses was considered sufficient to mark their discovery. Afterwards (as we shall see below)[21] King João II in his time ordered that stone marks[22] be placed, with an inscription stating when and by whom that land had been discovered. And this was sufficient as a sign of royal possession, whereas today not even the fortresses built on the discovered land are enough, for the greed of men has invented laws in accordance with its purposes.

And as every prince spends the most part of his life on works for which he has a preference, King Dom Afonso came to neglect matters related to this discovery and to commemorate greatly the conquest of the towns of Alcazar and Asilah and of the city of Tangier (as we recount in our *Africa*) on the occasions when he was there in person. And he rejoiced so much with this war of Africa, for the good fortune he had in it, that he decided – insofar as the affairs of the government permitted – to go himself and conquer in person the city of Fez and all its kingdom, for which he had instituted a [[military]] order called Order of the [[Tower and]] Sword. And therefore he sent Gomes Eanes de Zurara, his royal chronicler, to the town of Ksar es-Seghir, in order that, based on what he saw with his own eyes, he might write down the deeds of that war; to whom he wrote a letter in his own hand, praising him for the trouble he had taken there for the work he was composing; and this not with sparing and meagre words, as is the use of princes, but in an eloquent manner, as befits the fluent orator he prided himself on being.

And Gomes Eanes, seeing the delight felt by the king in all things related to this military affair, wrote the chronicle of the conquest of Ceuta, and another chronicle of the deeds of Count Dom Pedro de Meneses, and yet another of his son the Count Dom Duarte, relating in great detail the deeds of that war, with such a clear style as to deserve the title of the office he discharged. And to give credit where credit is due, he also wrote the chronicle of this King Dom Afonso up to the death of the *Infante* Dom Pedro, and the chronicle of his father the King Dom Duarte; which chronicles Rui de Pina, who succeeded him in the office, made his own, for all that he corrected and added to them, above all to that of King Dom Afonso, concerning what happened after the death of the *Infante* Dom Pedro.

Gomes Eanes undertook yet another task in the royal archive[23] which shed much light on its affairs, and this was the making of the books of registers, through

---

[20] *Talant de bien faire*: i.e. 'the will to do well' (French).
[21] Cf. liv. III, cap. III.
[22] In Portuguese, '*padrões de pedra*.'
[23] In Brásio's transcription, '*tombo deste reyno*' ('*tombo deste reino*'), that is, the '*Torre do Tombo*.'

condensing in a certain number of volumes the substance of a large number of loose documents, from the time of King Dom Pedro up to that of King Dom João *of glorious memory*;[24] [[he did]] this for he was head of the same archives, an office which was much suited to chroniclers, since it constituted a kind of guardianship of all the official documents of the Kingdom. Which documents should be seen by the chronicler with his own eyes, in order that he may write, more truthfully and in more detail, the complete account of the deeds of the king of whom he is an official. Because here one may find decrees, [[assemblies of the]] *cortes*,[25] marriages, contracts, fleets, celebrations, works, donations, grants, both through the register in the Chancery and Exchequer and through accounts from all parts of the Kingdom, should one want and know how to use the copies of so much writing. And truly (going back to Gomes Eanes, who was both chronicler and head of the royal archives) I do not know how long he lived, or how long he held these offices; but I do know, from what he left done by his own hand, that he did not serve without profit, but was worthy of the offices he discharged, both as regards the style and the thoroughness of the matters he dealt with.

2 *Duarte Pacheco Pereira's View of Mina*[26] *(1490)*

ABSTRACT – *Duarte Pacheco Pereira (1460–1533) was a late fifteenth-century Portuguese navigator and then governor of the São Jorge da Mina fortress. Though Pereira wrote his account between 1505 and 1508, he was on the coast in the late 1480s or early 1490s. Although he knew Diogo de Azambuja's lieutenant, he was not present during the construction of the São Jorge da Mina fortress, yet he frequented the fortress, as evident by references to him in the 1495-99 inquiry featured in* **Document 7***.*

From Cabo das Tres Pontas [Cape Three Points] to the islets of Hanta is four leagues.... The region of Hanta extends for seven or eight leagues; it contains a gold mine, which although not very large yields 20,000 doubloons or more; the gold is taken to be traded at the Castle of São Jorge da Mina and at the fortress of Akyem.... The blacks of this country live on millet, fish, and yams, together with a little meat; they are naked from the waist up, are uncircumcised and heathen, but, God willing, they will soon become Christians.

The islet of Hanta lies northeast and southwest from St. John River [Pra River], eight leagues [farther] along the route, a very small and narrow river, at high tide only a fathom and a half at its mouth, and this mouth can only be seen when very close to it. Here is a place called Sama [Esma], with

---

[24] In Portuguese, '*de gloriosa memória.*'
[25] *Cortes*: see Glossary.
[26] Duarte Pacheco Pereira, *Esmeraldo de Situ Orbis* (Lisbon: Imprensa Nacional, 1892), 68–70.

500 households, the first place in this land where trading in gold was done, and at that time it was called the Mine. This trading place and its commerce were discovered, on the orders of King Afonso V, by João de Santarem and Pedro d'Escobar, his knights and servants, on a certain day in January 1471. These two captains carried as pilots Alvaro Esteves, citizen of Lagos, and Martin Esteves, citizen of Lisbon, the former being the most competent man of his profession in Spain [i.e. Iberia] at that time.... From the Bay of Sama to the village of the Crooked Man is three leagues.... From there to the Castle of São Jorge da Mina is three leagues....

Since in the paragraph before the last... we have previously spoken of how the excellent prince, King Afonso V of Portugal, had the Mine [Mina] discovered, and of the captains and pilots who for this purpose were sent, it is now fitting that we should tell how his son, the most serene prince, King João of Portugal, after the death of his father, ordered the first work in founding the castle of São Jorge da Mina to be done. On the command of this magnanimous prince it was built by Diogo de Azambuja, knight of his household and high commander of the Order of St. Benedict. On the first day of January 1482, having taken out and being accompanied on nine caravels by as many other captains, most honorable men, Diogo de Azambuja being commander, he took out two urcas, ships of 400 tons each, with lime, worked stone, and enough other material to construct this fort. And although there was much disagreement between the blacks of this land and our people about the building of this fort, for they did not wish to agree to it, finally it was done despite them, so that, with great service and diligence, there was completed what was then necessary for the lodging and defense of all our men. Afterward, as time moved on, the same King João II accepted as necessary that it was appropriate to construct much more. We know that in all Ethiopian Guinea, this was the first solid (stone) building to be constructed in this region since the creation of the world. Through this fortress trade so greatly increased [in] good fine gold.... It is traded from the black merchants who bring gold from distant lands. These merchants belong to various nations: the Bremus, Atis, Hacanys, Boroes, Mandinguas, Cacres, Andeses or Souzos, and many others....[27] These people have hitherto been heathen, but some of them have now become Christians. I speak of those who live near the fortress, for the merchants come from far and have not the same interaction with us as these neighbors and accordingly continue in their false idolatry....

Three leagues beyond the castle of São Jorge da Mina... there is a cape which we call Cabo do Corço [Oguaa ('Cape Coast')].... Twenty leagues beyond Cabo

---

[27] 'Cac(e)res' was the Portuguese term *cafres* (from Arabic *kāfir*, 'unbeliever, pagan'), signaling, since the days of imperial Mali, gold producers who did not follow the Abrahamic religions. The 'Andeses' were also recorded as 'Anteses,' which referred to Ahanta. The 'Bremus' can be identified confidently with Abrem, the Etsi with 'Atis,' the 'Boroes' with Bono peoples living in the northern forest-savanna transition zone and 'Mandinguas' with Manding peoples inhabiting savanna-Sahelian West Africa, around the Niger valley. The 'Souzos' were the Susu peoples.

do Corco is another cape which we call Cabo das Redes [Fetu], because of the many nets that were found here when this land was discovered.... All the country between these two capes is fairly high and mountainous, halfway along there are three fishing villages, Great Fante, Little Fante, and Little Sabuu [Asebu].... The blacks of this country speak the same language as those of Mina, and their word for gold is vyqua [*sika*, 'gold'].... Twenty leagues beyond this mountainous area is the Rio da Volta [Volta River], which is fairly large.

3 War Between Two Mina Communities[28] (1490)

ABSTRACT – *An excerpt from Rui de Pina's Chronica del Rey Dom João II, written around 1500, about a conflict between two communities, represented by rulers from or outside the village of Adena, who attempted to use knowledge of the Portuguese religion and their possession of firearms to settle the conflict. One group, however, provides us with an early glimpse into Akan local warfare, especially the ritual and military use of hyire ('white clay'), an Akan symbol of victory, purity, and innocence.*

[...] In this year one thousand four hundred and ninety, two black men from the district of the town of São Jorge, who were enemies, determined upon battle; and one of them, to whom it seemed best,[29] pretended to the other to be favored with the assistance, which he claimed to be certain, of the Christians who were in the said town, as he knew that the Christians were more feared among them than any others, especially in deeds of arms. And this [[black man]] did it with such cunning that he ordered many of his men, who were black, to cover their faces, legs and arms with white clay, and commanded them to go in front, disguising them in all other respects so that they might all the more readily be taken for Christians.[30] And the other king, at the moment when the fight was about to begin, believing that the Christians were coming to the assistance of his enemy, did not wait for the rout, and was defeated without a struggle; and he fled, amid the great destruction of his men, and to the accompaniment of a great victory and much joy which this gave to his opponent.

---

[28] Rui de Pina, *Chronica del Rey Dom João II*, ch. 40, in José Correia da Serra, ed., *Collecção de livros ineditos de historia portugueza* (Lisbon: Academia das Ciências de Lisboa, 1792), 2: 102–3. See also John W. Blake, ed., *Europeans in West Africa, 1450-1560* (London: The Hakluyt Society, 1942), 86.

[29] This phrase is missing in Blake's translation.

[30] The call 'to cover their faces, legs and arms with white clay' has little to do with the men being 'taken for Christians.' The writer misunderstands Akan color symbolism, especially in martial matters. The ritual and warfare use of white clay (*hyire*) has a long and enduring presence in Akan societies. On Akan color symbolism, see T. C. McCaskie, *State and Society in Pre-colonial Asante* (New York: Cambridge University Press, 1995), 287–88; George P. Hagan, 'A Note on Akan Colour Symbolism,' *Research Review* VII, no. 1 (1970): 8–13.

4 Instructions from King João II to Rui Gil[31]
(10/08/1493)

ABSTRACT – *Instructions ordering João da Mina, an enslaved person belonging to the King of Portugal, be given a new set of clothing. The moniker, 'da Mina,' suggests a region of origin and certainly by 1493 the Portuguese had been profiting from the export trade in gold and a regional commerce in captives for some two decades. Several captives found their way to Portugal.[32] The document is published for the first time.*

Rui Gil, we order you to give to João da Mina, our slave, a cloak,[33] and a tunic,[34] and hose of black *antona*,[35] and a doublet of black fustian, all newly made and sewn. And you shall take note of it in your notebook. And furthermore you shall give him two shirts made of local fabric. Written in Torres Vedras, on the 10th day of August – João Pais wrote it – year one thousand 493. And furthermore you shall give him a *carapuça*,[36] and shoes, and a belt.

[sign.] *The King*

[Bottom of page]:

De Castellaco

Clothing of *antona* and fustian to João da Mina

5 License for the Residents of São Tomé[37] (11/12/1493)

ABSTRACT – *License granted to the residents/settlers of the island of São Tomé, for as long as it be the king's will, to trade enslaved peoples, pepper, and any*

---

[31] ANTT, CC 1-2-47. In a similar document, on January 30, 1493, an enslaved man named João Primeiro ('João the first') was given similar yet not the same new clothing as João da Mina half a year later. Though it is tempting to think they are the same person, they probably are not because two new sets of clothes in just six months was significant and because João da Mina carries, like Lisbon merchant Fernão Gomes, the moniker 'da Mina,' pointing to a specific region of origin.

[32] Eustache de la Fosse, a teenage Flemish trader captured by the Portuguese on the Mina (Gold) Coast in 1479-80, observed two Portuguese caravels arriving 'which had gone 200 leagues further [east] on to the River of Slaves [Niger Delta], bringing back a large number of slaves, a good 200 each, and they sold most of them at Mina for gold.' See Eustache de la Fosse, *Voyage a la Côte occidentale d'Afrique, en Portugal et en Espagne (1479-1480)*, ed. R. Foulche-Delbosc (Paris: Alfonse Picard et Fils, 1897), 12–15; Peter E. Russell, 'Novos apontamentos sobre os problemas textuais do *Voiaige à la Guinée* de Eustáquio de la Fosse (1479–1480),' *Revista Portuguesa de História* 16 (1976): 209–21. Foulche-Delboc's version of de la Fosse's account can be checked against the manuscript, MS 493 of the Bibliotheque Municipale de Valenciennes, ff.134v-137r. For a modern French translation of de la Fosse's voyage, see Denis Escudier, *Voyage d'Eustache Delafosse sur la côte de Guinée, au Portugal et en Espagne, 1479-1481* (Paris: Chandeigne, 1992).

[33] In Portuguese, *'loba'* is a long cloak, with no hood, sometimes used like a cape.

[34] In Portuguese, *'pelote'*: see Glossary.

[35] *Antona*: an old type of cloth.

[36] *Carapuça*: see Glossary.

[37] ANTT, Livro das Ilhas, fol. 105v; MMA vol. 15, doc. 4, pp. 15–16.

other goods from Rio Real to the island of Fernando Po, and in the Kingdom of
Kongo. They could sell these goods, as well as sugar, to the factor of São Jorge da
Mina, who paid them according to the prices this writ established.

License granted to the residents of the said island, so that they may trade pepper
in that land, which is given to them, and the price that will be paid for it in the
town of São Jorge.

We, Dom João etc., make known to all those who may see this letter of ours
that, it being our wish to bestow grace and favor on the residents who have settled
in our island of São Tomé, it is our will and pleasure that henceforward they
may and do trade pepper in that land, which we have given to them by our writ,
namely, from Rio Real[38] and the island of Fernando Po and throughout all the land
of Manikongo, should there be [[pepper]] in the said delimited land. And when
they depart from the said island, they shall take regulations from our *Almoxarife*[39]
or Receiver of the said island to go to the said parts to make the said trades, as
stated in his [[the *Almoxarife's* or the Receiver's]] regulations. And it is our will
and pleasure that, for each *moio*[40] of pepper which they take and is delivered clean
and dry to our Factor in the town of São Jorge, they be given by the said Factor
sixty manillas and eight *cruzados* per *moio*;[41] and they shall pay all the costs of
[[taking]] the said pepper to the said town, where they shall thus deliver it. And
this shall be so for as long as it be our will. And it is our wish that, should there
be copper and other goods which could be exchanged for pepper in the said land
which we thus give them, it is our pleasure[42] that they may trade it and obtain it
for the said copper and goods, and that for each *moio* of pepper they be paid by
our said Factor of São Jorge the equivalent in money to the said sixty manillas,
which we thus order that they receive per *moio*, plus the said eight *cruzados*.
And furthermore it is our wish and pleasure that, in exchange for the said goods
which there might be in the said island and delimited land, they may there obtain
and trade for themselves slaves and any other goods which may exist there, so
that goods may pass from one land to the other within the said marks of the said
delimited land, and that, at the same time, by way of trade the said residents may
obtain a larger profit from them.

---

[38] Today known as 'Bonny River'; see Joseph B. Ballong-Wen-Mewuda, "Africains et Portugais: tous
des négriers: Aux XVᵉ et XVIᵉ siècles dans le Golfe de Guinée," *Cahiers des Anneaux de la Mémoire: La
Traite et l'esclavage dans le monde lusophone*, Nantes, 3 (2001): 28.
[39] *Almoxarife*: see Glossary, under '*Almoxarifado*.'
[40] *Moio*: see Glossary.
[41] The repetition is in the document.
[42] The repetition is in the document. On copper as a key metal and currency (copper alloy or brass
manillas) in African history, see Eugenia W. Herbert, *Red Gold of Africa: Copper in Precolonial
History and Culture* (Madison: University of Wisconsin Press, 2003). See also J. S. Hogendorn and
H. A. Gemery, 'Continuity in West African Monetary History? An Outline of Monetary Development,'
African Economic History no. 17 (1988): 127–46.

Furthermore it is our wish and pleasure to give to the residents of the said island half a *cruzado*, or its equivalent, for each *arroba*[43] of sugar which they deliver to our Factor in the said town of São Jorge; and for each slave which they deliver to him, the said Factor shall give them four thousand *reais*, or its equivalent in gold. And therefore we thus notify our Factor and officials of the House of Guinea in this Kingdom, and the Captain, Factor and officials of the town of São Jorge, to whom we order that, for as long as it be our wish, as has been said, they obey and keep this letter of ours as is stipulated therein. And in confirmation of this we had this letter issued, signed by us and sealed with our pendant seal.

Issued in our city of Lisbon, on the 11th day of December – Pantaleão Dias wrote this – year of one thousand 493 years.

The said goods and articles thus traded should not be among those prohibited by the Holy Father, and by our ordinances and civil and canon laws.

6 *Manumission of Beatriz Gomes[44] (20/04/1499)*

ABSTRACT – *Manumission letter for Beatriz Gomes, an enslaved African woman, perhaps born in Portugal, but sent to serve in the fortress of São Jorge da Mina. Hers is one of the earliest known manumission letters granted for an enslaved person on Africa soil in the early modern period. The document is published for the first time.*

[We], Dom Manuel, etc., make known to all those who read this letter that, for the service done to us by Beatriz Gomes, our slave, in our town of São Jorge da Mina, and to bestow grace on her, it has been, and indeed is, our wish, to liberate, manumit and set her free from any subjection. And furthermore we notify all our *Corregedores,*[45] Judges and Justices to whom this letter may be shown, and we order them, that they shall henceforward acknowledge as her manumitted, liberated and free from subjection, and that they shall honor her and treat her as such, not allowing any injustice to be done to her, rather bestowing on her every favor and fair treatment in those things which are just and honest, because this will be our pleasure. Written in our city of Lisbon, on the 20th day of April – Álvaro Fernandes wrote it – year one thousand 499.

Beatriz Gomes
Manumission

---

[43] *Arroba*: see Glossary.
[44] ANTT, *Chancelaria de D. Manuel I*, liv. 16, fl. 45v.
[45] *Corregedor*: see Glossary.

7 Residents of the Town
of São Jorge Da Mina[46] (23/08/1499)

ABSTRACT – *Transcript of an inquiry concerning the quantity of gold and enslaved peoples traded by both officials and residents in São Jorge da Mina, during the mandate of captain Lopo Soares (15 September 1495 – 30 June 1499), before they boarded a ship for Portugal. This transcript is valuable because it provides one of the earliest and most detailed accounts of Portuguese trading and slaving operations through São Jorge da Mina, fortress personnel, and their activities over a four-year period, as well as Portuguese relations with local rulers and merchants, including a female merchant recorded as Briolanja.*

On the twelfth day of the month of July of the year '99, in the town of São Jorge in Mina, Fernão Lopes Correia,[47] *Guarda-Roupa*[48] of Our Lord the King and his Captain in the said town, and João Fernandes, Factor of the said Lord, and the scribes of the said Factory – in the presence of Lopo Soares, *fidalgo* of the said Lord's Household and former Captain – made all the residents of the said town who had been there since the time of the said Lopo Soares come before them, and told them that they should declare, under oath on the Holy Gospels, upon which all of them laid their hand, all the gold and slaves and supplies which they had received during the period they had been in the said town, advising them first not to perjure themselves, for they themselves and all their things would be searched before boarding, according to what is contained in the newly-written regulations of the said Lord. And they declared under oath what is contained in their statements below.

   Item. Firstly, through a letter from His Highness which was given to him by the said Fernão Lopes, captain, the aforementioned Lopo Soares said he wished to be the first to give oath and declare all the gold and slaves and food allowances which he had received during the entire period in which he had been a captain here; and he presented to the said Captain and Factor and scribes two receipts which he had of what he had received during the said period, one issued by Diogo de Alvarenga[49] and the other by Brás Teixeira, former scribes of the said Factory, signed by Gil Matoso, former Factor, and Rui Gago,[50] also scribe of the said Factory; and he swore on the Holy Gospels, upon which he laid his hand, that he had not received more than what was mentioned in the said receipts, which is the following:

   •   two hundred and forty-four marks of gold two ounces seven drams[51] and twelve grains and three quarters of gold, as follows:

---

[46] ANTT, *Contos do Reino e Casa, Núcleo Antigo* 867. Transcribed in J. Bato'ora Ballong-Wen-Mewuda, *São Jorge da Mina, 1482–1637: A vie d'un Comptoir Portugais en Afrique Occidentale* (Lisbon: Fondation Calouste Gulbenkian, 1993), 2: 493–519. The transcription was checked against the original, and this will be the case for all transcriptions from this text.

[47] See MMA vol. 1, docs. 123–24; vol. 4, doc. 32; vol. 15, doc. 18 and doc. 20.

[48] *Guarda-Roupa*: see Glossary.

[49] See MMA vol. 1, doc. 52; vol. 4, doc. 22.

[50] See MMA vol. 4, doc. 22.

[51] In Portuguese, '*oitava*' (sing.), that is, an 'eighth' of an ounce.

- 1 ounce 1 dram and 46 grains, which he received as food allowance[52] for himself and ten of his men, from the twelfth day of the month of September of the year '95 to the fifteenth day of the said month, which amount to three days;
- 30 marks 7 ounces 4 drams and 24 grains in respect of his payment,[53] from the last 15 days of the said month of September to the end of the month of June of this present year '99, which amount to forty-five and a half months, making five ounces and three drams and three grains monthly; and this was checked with the regulations of the late King, may God keep Him, by the said João Fernandes, Factor;
- and 13 marks 1 ounce 1 dram and 29 and a half grains in respect of his food allowance for the entire period, at a monthly rate of two ounces and two drams and fifty-one grains, and this for himself; and this was checked by the said Factor with the said regulations;
- 18 marks 1 ounce 4 drams and 43 grains in respect of his *feitoria*[54] from the income of the said House during the entire period; and this was checked by the said Factor with the lists of the said payment of the said *feitoria*, in which the income of the said House during the entire period is declared;
- 20 marks 3 ounces 6 drams and 44 grains in respect of his *feitoria* of cloth and other items for which he obtained double the estimate, i.e. eight marks three ounces seven drams and seventeen and a half grains from what was bought by Gil Matoso, and twelve marks and twenty-eight and a half grains from what was bought by Jorge de Pina, Treasurer, according to what is recorded in the register and estimate books of the said cloth; and these were verified and checked by the aforesaid Factor;
- 10 marks 7 ounces 4 drams and 60 grains, which he received as food allowance for two female slaves of his, who were registered for allowance during the entire period, except for this month of June '99 when one of them was taken away, at a monthly rate of seven drams and 59 grains for each of them;
- 120 marks 4 ounces 6 drams and 69 grains which he received as food allowance for the people whom he fed in his house during the entire period, as follows:
  - for eighteen people during the last 15 days of the month of September '95;
  - 18 [[people]] during the month of October, with one slave;
  - 19 people during the month of November, plus one person for fifteen days of the said month;

---

[52] In the transcription, '*mantimento de conduto.*' This specific term, instead of the more generic '*mantimento*,' appears to be used specifically for the 'food allowance' of some officials (such as the captain, the physician, the factor, and the scribe of the expenditure).

[53] As in the transcription ('*taxa*,' i.e. a fixed value), the word used here has a generic meaning of fixed 'payment.'

[54] *Feitoria*: in this, as in similar cases in the document, '*feitoria*' probably refers to office-holding in the factory ('factorship'), which entitled its possessor to a portion of the profits or goods traded there.

- 20 people during the month of December;
- 21 people during the month of January '96;
- 20 people during the month of February, with three slaves;
- 20 people during the month of March;
- 24 people during the month of April, with four slaves, plus one person for fifteen days of the said month;
- 27 people during the month of May, with four slaves;
- 27 people, with the said four slaves, during the month of June;
- 28 people during the month of July, with the said four slaves, plus one person for 15 days of the said month;
- 29 people during the month of August, with the four slaves;
- 29 people during the month of September;
- 28 people during the month of October, with the said slaves;
- 28 people during the month of November;
- 38 people during the month of December;
- 29 people during the month of January '97, with two slaves;
- 29 people, with the said two slaves, during the month of February;
- 31 people during the month of March, with the two slaves;
- 24 people during the month of April;
- 24 people during the month of May;
- 23 people during the month of June;
- 22 people during the month of July;
- 21 people during the month of August;
- 21 people during the month of September;
- 20 people during the month of October;
- 20 people during the month of November;
- 20 people during the month of December;
- 20 people during the month of January '98;
- 21 people during the month of February;
- 21 people during the month of March;
- 63 people during the months of April, May and June, making twenty-one per month;
- 20 people during the month of July, with one slave;
- 80 people during the months of August, September, October and November, making twenty people per month, with one slave;
- 19 people during the month of December, the slave included;
- 15 people during the month of January '99;
- 15 people during the month of February;
- 14 people during the month of March;
- 42 people during the months of April, May and June, making 14 people per month.

Which food allowance for the said people who were fed by the aforesaid Lopo Soares, and which amount to the said one hundred and twenty marks four ounces six drams and sixty-nine grains, should be checked by comparing the register of residents with the lists according to which the said Lopo Soares was given the said gold, so as to see the names of the people in the said lists and in the register, and to check whether they served during the said period for which they have here received payment.

And this was not done by the Factor because there was no register book, apart from one which was shown by the said Lopo Soares and which was stained and written between the lines, so that the said checking could not be done. And the same happened with the amount he received as food allowance for the said slaves.

- three marks four ounces one dram and sixty-one grains, which he received as due payment for the slaves during the period in which they were assigned food allowance, as declared in the above register, and they were assigned payment and food allowance. And he received all of it because they were his [[slaves]];
- ten marks one ounce six drams and sixty-seven grains which were paid to him by the black people for sheep, pigs and goats from Portugal and the Rivers, and a cow and a calf which he sold to them, in addition to wax candles;
- 2 ounces 1 dram and 45 grains which were paid to him by Diogo Gue, his slave, for a blue tunic[55] which he bought from him;[56]
- 3 marks and 5 ounces which were paid to him by certain residents for pigs he had reared, which he sold to them, and for some beasts[57] which they bought from him;
- 12 marks 1 ounce 6 drams and 42 grains which he obtained through the sale to the black people, at the rate of one slave for each man, of thirty-two slaves whom he had bought in the Factory on behalf of himself and thirty-one of his men.

According to the regulations, he could have slaves to serve him, and he could also sell them, including here some male and female slaves whom he had on behalf of some of his [[men]] and who were assigned payment and food allowance.[58] Which sales of cattle and slaves and other things were checked by comparing the receipt by the said Factor and scribes with the register of the said sales. In the said

---

[55] In Portuguese, '*pelote*,' a popular kind of garment with wide armholes, which might also be translated as 'cloak' or 'robe.'

[56] It was not far-fetched for captive or enslaved persons to work or trade goods on behalf of their holder, in this case the captain of the Mina fortress, and then 'earn' part of exchanged value for gold. The Flemish trader Eustache de la Fosse, once captured by the Portuguese, was forced to trade his goods, and turn the earnings in gold over to his captors.

[57] In Portuguese, '*besta*' usually refers to beasts of burden, such as mules.

[58] In the transcription, this passage is unclear: '*Segundo o regimento podia haver para os servirem e bem assim os podiam vender contando aqui alguns destes que houve em nome de alguns seus escravos e escravas que haviam mantimentos deles taxas*' (modernized ortography), which could be translated literally as 'According to the regulations there could be to serve them, and they could also sell them, including here some of these whom he had in the name of some of his male and female slaves who [or 'because they'] received food allowance from them payment.'

receipt, it is stated that he gave to each person from whom he had received the slaves one ounce of gold, which, being deducted from the sale of the said slaves, gave the said profit of twelve marks one ounce six drams and forty-two grains.

Of which two hundred and forty-four marks two ounces seven drams and twelve grains and three quarters of gold that the said Lopo Soares declared and are included in the above totals, in accordance with the regulations of the late King, may God keep him – one hundred and thirty-five marks five drams and forty grains the said Lopo Soares received as food allowance for the slaves and men whom he fed, and slaves of his who were also assigned payment and food allowance, since according to the regulations the said Lord allotted the captains of this town six men on payment and food allowance, plus three should there be no workmen[59] here to do the work, which thus amounts to nine men; this adds up, during the said forty-five and a half months of payment and food allowance, to seventy-four marks five ounces seven drams and fifty-one grains, from which must be deducted the one hundred and thirty-five marks five drams and forty grains which the said Lopo Soares received as payment and food allowance for the men whom he fed, as well as male and female slaves; he therefore received, over and above what the said regulations stipulate for his nine men, sixty marks two ounces five drams and sixty-four grains. And the said slaves were also assigned payment and food allowance.

The lists of payment which Lopo Soares received during the period of his stay mentioned the following workmen[60] who were employed in work in this town, namely:

- 4 masons during the month of November '95 and 1 during the month of December of the said year, and
- 4 during the month of January '96;
- 3 during the month of February;
- 3 during the month of March;
- 3 during the months of May, June, July, and August, and September, and October and November;
- 1 during the month of December of the said year '96;
- during January, February, March, April, May, June, July of the year '97, one mason per month;
- and during August, September, October, November and December of the said year, two per month;
- and from January of the year '98 until the end of February '99, which amounts to 14 months, one mason;
- and from the last 15 [[days]] of March '98 until the end of April '99, which amounts to 13 and a half months, another mason;
- and for ten months and a half, until the end of January of the said year '90 [*sic*], another mason;

[59] In Portuguese, '*oficiais*': skilled workers rather than laborers.
[60] See previous note.

- and for 13 months, until the end of January of the said year '99, another [[mason]];
- and during 6 and a half months of the said year, two [[masons]]; These workmen[61] all received payment and food allowance.

And another received food allowance only for the said 6 and a half months.

And of the two hundred and forty-four marks two ounces seven drams and twelve grains and three quarters which the said Lopo Soares received during the period of forty-five and a half months in which he served as captain, he justified the expenditure as follows:

- 86 marks 4 ounces 5 drams and 73 grains which he sent to the Kingdom:

  nine marks and four ounces through Afonso de Banardilha in the caravel Salvador;
  and three marks in the caravel Sardinha, through Fernão de Pina;
  and twelve marks through Pedro Lopes, captain of the caravel Nazaré;
  and thirteen marks through Estêvão Fernandes of the caravel Santa Cruz;
  and one mark in the caravel Santo Espírito;
  and eleven and a half marks in the caravel Nazaré, through António de Sá, Captain;
  and one and a half marks in the caravel Santa Catarina;
  and eleven marks in the caravel Sardinha, [[through]] Captain Rui Quatrim;
  and twenty-one marks four ounces one dram and seventy-three and a half grains in the caravel São Pantaleão, [[through]] Lopo Cabral, Captain;
  and three marks in the caravel Nazaré;
  and 4 marks two ounces and eleven grains which he paid for fourteen slaves from the island of São Tomé, and which included a bill[62] and a slave from the Ambassadors of the King of Benin yonder.[63]

Which slaves are declared below as having been bought in the said island with his merchandise of cloth and supplies;

and 3 marks 6 ounces 1 dram and 40 and a half grains which he paid for cloth and tin for his office in the factory;
and likewise a cup and a glass of silver;

---

[61] See previous note.

[62] In the transcription, '*recadaçam.*' In this precise case, the Portuguese term '*arrecadação,*' which is the modern form, has perhaps as its closest equivalent in English 'bill (of exchange).' According to context, it has been translated throughout the text as 'bill' or, more frequently, 'receipt.'

[63] Ambassadors from Benin visited the Portuguese at São Jorge da Mina and the village of Adena – and perhaps other settlements on the Mina (Gold) Coast. The 'gift' of a captive person became a custom in the evolving transactions between African communities and Portuguese merchants and officials. In this instance, (former) captain Lopo Soares is justifying his expenses, that is, how much he paid for 14 captives from São Tomé, and a captive delivered or gifted to him by the ruler of Benin. These transactions took place at the São Jorge da Mina fortress, though they ultimately involved African mainland and island territories and Portugal.

2 marks which he gave in this town to ship captains for one hundred *cruzados* of
gold which they sold to him;

2 marks 6 ounces 2 drams and 43 grains which he paid and ordered to be paid
here to some people to whom he was indebted and who are mentioned in the
said receipt;

2 marks which he spent in the Factory on garments;

6 marks which he spent on certain jewels which he gave here to captains and
scribes and pilot[[s]] of ships, as well as to other people, who are mentioned
in the said receipt; and nine marks five ounces seven drams and nine grains
he spent on his own maintenance and for those he fed.

And the [[remaining]] one hundred and twenty-seven marks three ounces
one dram and four grains will be taken by the said Lopo Soares himself to the
Kingdom, according to what is declared in the said receipt; and it was weighed in
the presence of the said Captain and Factor and scribes.

And the said Lopo Soares added that he had had thirty-four slaves during the
entire period he had been in this town as captain, as follows:

–5 pieces[64] who were sent to him by the King of Benin and which were granted to
him by Our Lord the King through a decree that he showed; and 14 from the island
of São Tomé whom he obtained in exchange for his merchandise; and 15 who came
from said island and whom he bought here through someone else.

Of which he declared the following expenditure – fourteen [[pieces]] given to
the following persons:

– 2 to Gomes Soares, two to Dom Diogo Lobo, Overseer of the Exchequer,[65] two
to Antão Gonçalves, *Alcaide*[66] of Sesimbra, one to Gomes Xira, one to Sancho de
Pedrosa, one to Duarte Roiz, one to Antão Gonçalves, retainer of Dom Gonçalo,
one to A'Lebre [[*sic*]], one to Diogo Gil, another to Gonçalo de Oliveira, and one
to Rui Quatrim.

And one whom he sold to the black men in order to give alms to Santa Maria
da Graça, and this was one of those who had come from Benin; and two of them
ran away here, as attested by the scribes; and one died on him; and three were
sent by him to Portugal in the caravel Sardinha; and one whom he had left to
the Factor was sold on behalf of the King because the black men wanted him;
and the Factor will send another to Lopo Soares. And he is now taking the other
twelve with him.

---

[64] By the start of the 16th century, enslaved Africans of the Portuguese were counted as *peças* ('pieces'),
or *peças dos escravos* ('units of slaves'). The term *peça* (in Spanish, *pieza*) became a shorthand for
a captive African, though usually with the meaning of one adult captive and, in some instances, a
captive woman with a small child. The trademark *peças* was widely used in the 16th century and across
the Atlantic region as an explicit idiom of commodification and dehumanization.

[65] In Portuguese, '*Vedor da Fazenda*': see Glossary.

[66] *Alcaide*: see Glossary.

Chief Alcaide

And Gonçalo Roiz de Sequeira, former chief *Alcaide* of this town, declared on oath, which was administered to him, the following:

namely, that he had earned and received in this town eighty-four marks one ounce one dram and seventy-two grains of gold, as follows:

- 18 marks 3 ounces 1 dram and 26 grains in respect of his payment for forty-six months, starting from the last 15 days of the month of September of the year '95 and ending with the first 15 [[days]] of July of the year '99; and this was checked with the regulations of the late King, may God keep him, by the said Factor;
- 5 marks 4 ounces 6 drams and 14 grains in respect of his food allowance during the entire said period; and this was checked with the said regulations;
- 11 marks and 50 and a half grains in respect of his *feitoria* of cloth and other items for which he obtained double the estimate, namely,
- 1 mark 3 ounces 7 drams and 32 and a half grains which were paid to him by Gil Matoso;
- 9 marks 4 ounces 1 dram and 18 grains which were paid to him by Jorge de Pina; and this gold which he had from the Factory was checked with the register by the said Factor;
- 5 marks 4 ounces 6 drams and 30 grains which he received during the entire period as payment for two white slaves[67] of his who were registered as his men; and this was checked with the regulations of the late King, may God keep him, concerning what the residents should receive in payment and food allowance;
- 11 marks 1 ounce 4 drams and 18 grains which he received as food allowance for the said two slaves during the aforesaid forty-six months; and this was checked with the said regulations, which stipulate that the chief *Alcaide* shall have one man on payment and food allowance, and another, also on payment and food allowance, should there be no workmen[68] in the fortress;
- 4 marks 4 drams and 64 grains in respect of food allowance for a female slave of his, out of the total of seven women he had registered during thirty-three and a half months;

[67] It remains unclear who or what were 'white slaves.' They could have been Iberians or prisoners of European ancestry sentenced to labor in far reaches of the empire, enslaved Muslims born in northern Africa or the eastern Mediterranean or Iberia, or mixed-race individuals described in the records imprecisely as 'white slaves.' See Jerome S. Handler and Matthew C. Reilly, 'Contesting 'White Slavery' in the Caribbean,' *New West Indian Guide / Nieuwe West-Indische Gids* 91, 1–2 (2017): 30–55; James H. Sweet, 'The Iberian Roots of American Racist Thought,' *The William and Mary Quarterly* 54, no. 1 (1997): 143–66; A. J. R. Russell-Wood, 'Iberian Expansion and the Issue of Black Slavery: Changing Portuguese Attitudes, 1440-1770,' *The American Historical Review* 83, no. 1 (1978): 16–42.

[68] In the transcription, '*oficiãães dobres*' ('*oficiais dobres*'), though it should probably read '*oficiais de obras*,' that is, 'workmen.'

- 2 marks 6 ounces and 6 grains which he received for two black men of his who were given to him by the Captain and who, registered as ship's boys, served in the *caravelões*[69] for two years;
- 2 marks 7 ounces 2 drams and 18 grains which he obtained through the sale to the black people of eight slaves who had been allotted[70] to him and his men;
- 7 marks 2 ounces 3 drams and 15 grains which he received as a half food allowance for the supernumerary men[71] who were given to him by the Captain, and he receives a half food allowance to feed them from him, namely,
- four people during the last 15 days of the month of September '95;
- twenty people during the months of October, November and December of the said year;
- January, February '96, four per month;
- twenty-five people during the months of March, April, May, June and July, at the rate of five per month;
- four during the month of August;
- thirty-five during the months of September, October, November and December of the said year, and January, February and March of the year '97, five per month;
- 6 people during the months of April and May, three per month;
- four during the months of June and July, two per month;
- fifteen people during the months of August, September, October, November and December of the said year, three per month;
- six people during the first three months of the following year '98, two per month;
- three people during April, May and June of the said year, one per month; and as for these supernumerary men, during the entire said period, this was checked with the aforesaid regulations by the said Factor;
- 6 marks 2 ounces 7 drams and 35 grains which he obtained through the sale to the black people of pigs, goats and wax candles, by license of the Captain;
- 4 drams and 18 and a half grains which he obtained through the sale to residents of two female slaves, who were sent to him from the island;
- 5 marks 7 ounces 3 drams and 41 grains which the said chief *Alcaide* obtained through the sale to residents of chickens, pigs, sheep, rose sugar and tavern wine, during the entire period of his stay;

[69] *Caravelão* (sing.): see Glossary.
[70] In this translation, the term 'allot(ed)' stands for the cases in which one or more slaves were given to an individual, whether an official or a resident, who was officially entitled to receive them.
[71] In the transcription, here as elsewhere, '*sobre salentes*' ('*sobressalentes*'), which might also be translated as 'extra' or 'spare men.'

- 4 marks 5 drams and 28 grains which he brought from the island of São Tomé, from cloth, garments, women's headdresses, and wine and other articles which he sold there; Of which 84 marks 1 ounce 1 dram and 72 grains of gold, obtained in this way, he declared the following expenditure, namely,
- forty marks six ounces and thirty grains which he sent to the Kingdom;
- three marks through Afonso de Banidilha;[72]
- four marks through João de Coimbra, pilot;
- four marks through Afonso Gonçalves, pilot of the caravel Santa (Cruz);
- five marks through António de Sá;
- five marks through the pilot of the caravel São Vicente;
- four ounces in the caravel Santa Clara;
- one mark and four ounces through Gonçalo Afonso, pilot of the caravel São Vicente;
- five marks in the caravel Sardinha;
- twelve marks in the caravel São Pantaleão;
- 1 mark and 1 ounce which he paid here for part of his *feitoria* of cloth;
- 4 marks 4 ounces 5 drams and 71 grains which he paid for thirteen slave pieces, together with a boy, from the island of São Tomé, whom he bought in this town; and in addition to these, he bought others in exchange for the cloth he took there;
- 11 marks 5 ounces and 7 drams which he spent on his personal needs during the entire period of his stay;
- 26 marks 7 ounces 4 drams and 46 and a half grains which he is taking with him and which were weighed in the presence of the said Captain, Factor and officials.

And the aforesaid chief *Alcaide* added that, during the time of his stay, he had had twenty-one slave pieces from the island of São Tomé whom he had bought, from which the following must be subtracted: firstly, he sold one female slave to Diogo de Alcáçova[73] and another to Luís Zeimoto, and two of them died, and he sent two through António de Sá, and one through Heitor Lopes, and two through Gonçalo Leão, and ten through Rui das Armas, and he has two here whom he is taking with him.

And the said chief *Alcaide* added that he was taking with him one mark five ounces and fifty-two grains of gold which belonged to the late Afonso de Campo Frio, who had resided here and of whom he was the executor, the net weight of which gold is one mark five ounces five drams and seventy-three grains which he received during the period of his stay here; 1 mark 2 drams and 14 grains which he received as food allowance for supernumerary men during thirteen and a half

---

[72] It should probably read 'Banadilha,' as elsewhere in this transcription, or 'Bovadilha'/'Bobadilha' as in MMA vol. 1, doc. 61.
[73] See ANTT, *Fragmentos, Cartas para El-Rei*, cx.1, mç. 1, n. 9.

months; and this was checked with the sum in the regulations of what is due for each of the supernumerary men per year.

- 3 ounces which he obtained through the sale of a female slave who had been allotted to him;
- 2 ounces 3 drams and 59 grains in respect of his *feitoria* of cloth for which he obtained double the estimate.

And the remaining 5 drams and 73 and a half grains were spent by the said Afonso de Campo on items which he needed; which gold was weighed in the presence of the Captain and officials.

And the said chief *Alcaide* added under oath that he was taking two marks six ounces one dram and thirty-seven grains of gold [[…]][74] which belonged to Gonçalo Afonso, pilot of the *barinel*[75] São Pantaleão, and which were paid to him in this town by Martim Vaz, shell cleaner,[76] before he left; which gold was the payment received by Martim Vaz during his stay here, and he was owing it to the said pilot for the latter had lent it, or its equivalent, to him in Portugal. And the said Gonçalo Afonso had it delivered to the aforesaid chief *Alcaide* to do as he had instructed, and this is attested by a receipt he kept of it. And the said gold was weighed.

And he added under oath that he was taking with him one mark four ounces and six and a half drams of gold belonging to Pedro Coelho, his retainer, who is in Portugal, which is the net weight of two marks two ounces two drams and eighteen grains which he received in this town, namely:

- 1 mark 2 ounces 3 drams and 53 grains in respect of a half food allowance for twenty-one and a half months, because the other half was received by the chief *Alcaide* for feeding him; and this was checked with the regulations regarding the food allowance which was due to each resident per year; and
- 1 ounce which was given to him by the chief *Alcaide* from the proceeds of a female slave who was allotted to the said Pedro Coelho; and
- 6 ounces 6 drams and 35 grains which he received as fourteen months of payment, in addition to the twenty-one and a half months during which he served as man of Diogo Pereira, Scribe of the Revenue; and this was checked with the regulations. And the remainder of what he earned he spent on his personal needs. And the said gold was weighed in the presence of the said officials.

---

[74] The author repeats the quantities, though this time in the abbreviated form.
[75] *Barinel*: see Glossary.
[76] In the transcription, '*limpador das conchas*'; it is unclear whether '*conchas*' refers to seashells, such as those used in the Portuguese trade, or to the part of the cannon which contains the explosive (also called '*caçoleta*,' the equivalent of the breech).

Master Jerónimo, physician

And Master Jerónimo, physician, who declared under oath that he had received and been paid in this town twenty marks two ounces and fourteen grains of gold during the entire period of his stay, as follows:

namely – 9 marks 1 ounce 5 drams and 44 grains and a quarter in respect of his payment as physician during forty-five and a half months; and this was checked with the regulations regarding what is due each year to the said physician;

- 5 marks 4 ounces 2 drams and 22 grains in respect of his food allowance for the said 45 months; and this was checked with the said regulations;
- 5 ounces 5 drams and 21 grains which were paid to him for his *feitoria*, for which he obtained double the estimate, before the King's prohibition which was carried out by the Captain, and this when a message from the King arrived regarding [[what should be done]] if one was a Jew [[?]],[77] at the time when the said Lord was expelling the Jews from his Kingdom;
- 1 mark 6 ounces 6 drams and 57 grains which he received as payment for one of his men and the apothecary, whom he kept for thirty and a half months; and this was checked with the regulations;
- 5 ounces 3 drams and 41 grains which he obtained through the sale of certain items, cloth, flour, which he sold to residents, and a little bit of *malagueta*, which he sold to Serrão;[78] and
- 2 ounces 1 dram and 42 grains which were paid to him here by the Rabbi Juda, to whom he had lent them in Portugal;
- 5 ounces 1 dram and 47 grains which he obtained through the sale to the black people of two female slaves, one who had been allotted to him and another from the island; and this was done by license of the Captain; and he gave half the profit to the King as attested by the receipt he is taking with him of the said gold;
- 2 ounces 2 drams and 41 grains which he obtained through the sale here to residents of six slaves from the island;
- 2 ounces and 7 drams which were given to him by Serrão and Anxi in jewels, for having treated them in their illnesses;
- 3 ounces and 4 drams which he obtained through the sale to the black people of one male slave from the island, by license of the Captain, in place of another whom he would have through one of his men;
- 2 ounces which the Captain gave to him in jewels. And all the above mentioned sales were checked with their register.

[77] In the transcription, the sequence between the two pages is not clear; there are probably some words or lines missing in the modern edition.
[78] See CC 1-9-61, CC 1-13-48, and MMA vol. 4, doc. 22.

And the aforesaid Master Jerónimo presented the expenditure of the gold as follows:

namely – 3 ounces which he paid for part of his *feitoria*;

- 2 marks which he paid in this town for five slave pieces, one male and four females, of which three were sent by him to Portugal and two he is now taking with him. And 11 marks and 2 ounces which he is taking with him to the Kingdom and which was weighed in the presence of the said officials.
- 1 mark 4 ounces 2 drams and 52 grains which he spent on his own expenses;
- 5 marks and 5 drams which he has sent to the Kingdom, namely, 1 mark 5 drams and 37 grains through Afonso de Banadilha, 2 marks twice in the caravel Santa Cruz, and 1 mark in the caravel Cirne, and another mark in the caravel Sardinha; and this was checked with the register of the receipts.

Diogo Pereira, Scribe of the Revenue

And Diogo Pereira, Scribe of the Revenue, declared under oath that he had received, during the twenty-seven and a half months of his stay here, thirteen marks five ounces three drams and forty-three grains, as follows:

namely – 2 marks 1 ounce and 71 grains in respect of his payment during the said period; and this was checked with the said regulations;

- 3 marks 2 ounces 6 drams and ten grains which he received as food allowance during the said period; and this was checked with the said regulations;
- 3 marks 3 ounces 7 drams and 65 grains in respect of the food allowance for one of his men for two years and one month, and for a male Christian slave for two and a half months, for whom he also received payment because he was his [[slave]]; and this was checked with the said regulations;
- 3 ounces and 48 grains which he obtained through the sale of a female slave who had been allotted to him;
- 3 ounces 5 drams and 6 grains which he obtained through issuing receipts and writing proxies;
- 3 marks 6 ounces 6 drams and 68 grains which he received from his *feitoria* at the rate of one percent; and this was checked with the lists of the said payment, in which the proceeds of the House, whence came his *feitoria*, are declared.

Of which gold he gave the following account of expenditure:

namely – 1 mark which he sent to the Kingdom, 4 ounces in the caravel Salvador and 4 ounces in the caravel Santa Clara;

- 1 mark which he gave here to a certain João Álvares, his man, who had lent it to him;

- 4 ounces 6 drams and 48 grains which he paid for two slave pieces, namely, one young female, whom he has already sent to the Kingdom, and one young male, whom he is now taking with him;
- 2 drams and 70 grains which he spent on items which he needed.

And he is taking with him the [[remaining]] 11 marks and 2 ounces, which were weighed in the presence of the said officials.

Lopo Vaz

And Lopo Vaz, retainer of Gonçalo Roiz de Sequeira, said under oath that he had received during the entire period he had been here one mark seven ounces six drams and forty-six grains of gold as follows, namely:

- 1 ounce which he received for a female slave who had been allotted to him and whom the chief *Alcaide* took on his behalf, plus his due payment for the period of thirty-six and a half months.

Of which gold the said Lopo Vaz spent three ounces six drams and nine grains on the purchase of a female slave from the island and on his personal needs; and he is taking with him one mark four ounces and thirty-seven and a half grains, which were weighed in the presence of the said officials.

João Dias

And João Dias, who was resident in this town, declared under oath that he had received during the entire period of his stay here six marks one ounce six drams and seventy grains of gold as follows, namely:

- 2 marks 6 ounces 1 dram and 11 grains in respect of his payment for forty-five and a half months;
- 2 marks 1 ounce 3 drams and forty-three grains which he obtained through the sale to residents of supplies, linen and garments, and
- 1 ounce and 6 drams through the sale of things and garments in the island;
- 1 ounce and 2 drams of tableware which he sold to the black people by license of the Captain;
- 3 ounces and 3 drams which he received from the residents for being the supervisor of the oven-house;
- 3 ounces 5 drams and 50 grains which he obtained through the sale to black people of two slave pieces who had been allotted to him, and through the sale to residents of another from the island.

Of which six marks one ounce six drams and seventy grains he sent four ounces to the Kingdom for two bills and paid four ounces for two slaves from the island, one of whom he sent in the caravel Sardinha and the other he is taking with him; and he spent two ounces and fifty-nine grains on his own needs.

And he is taking with him 4 marks 7 ounces 6 drams and 11 grains, which were weighed in the presence of the said officials.

Cristóvão Lopes

And Cristóvão Lopes, who was resident here, declared under oath that he had received during the entire period of his stay here four ounces seven drams and eleven grains of gold, namely:

- 3 ounces 7 drams and 11 grains in respect of his payment for eight months, and one ounce which he obtained for a female slave who had been allotted to him.

Of which gold he is taking with him four ounces and five drams, for he spent the rest, which were weighed in the presence of the said officials.

Diogo Fernandes

And Diogo Fernandes declared under oath that he had received during the entire period of his stay here one mark three ounces and two drams of gold, namely:

- 1 mark 2 drams and 54 grains in respect of his payment for eighteen months, since his food allowance was given to Lopo Soares, who fed him.
- 3 ounces and 3 grains which he obtained through the sale of a female slave who had been allotted to him.

Of which gold he spent one ounce two drams and sixty-two grains on his own needs; and he is taking with him one mark and two ounces, which were weighed in the presence of the said officials.

Brás Teixeira

And Brás Teixeira, scribe of the Factory, declared under oath that during the period of forty-seven months in which he was here he had received forty-seven marks five ounces and two drams of gold, namely:

- 3 marks 7 ounces and 20 grains in respect of his payment as Scribe of the Expenditure during the period of forty months in which he served in that office; and
- 4 ounces and 37 grains in respect of his payment as Scribe of the Revenue for six and a half months;
- 5 marks 5 ounces 5 drams and 73 grains in respect of his allowance for forty seven months;
- 7 marks 7 ounces 3 drams and 79 grains in respect of his *feitoria* from the income of the House, expenditure deducted. And the said allowance

and payment was checked with the regulations, and the *feitoria* with the lists of payment where the income of the said House is declared;

- 6 ounces 7 drams and 57 grains that he further received as Scribe of the Revenue for six months, making in all 47 months;
- 2 marks 6 ounces 5 drams and 2 grains which he received during forty-six and a half months as payment for a white slave whom he had as his man;
- 5 marks 5 ounces 5 drams and 73 grains in addition to what he received as food allowance for the said slave during forty-seven months, because for fifteen days he received no payment but only the food allowance;
- 2 ounces 4 drams and 15 grains which he obtained for Afonso Pires, who was registered for allowance during ten additional months, for he gave him the rest;
- 2 ounces 3 drams and 35 grains in respect of the payment for Pedro Murzelo, a Christian slave of his, whom he had registered as Master Jerónimo's man for five months;
- 6 ounces and 3 drams which he obtained for three slave pieces who had been allotted to him, whom he had in his own name and in that of the two men he had;
- 8 marks 1 ounce 1 dram and 28 grains which he obtained through the sale to residents of supplies, garments and cloth;
- 3 ounces and 6 drams which came from the island for items and garments which he had sent there;
- 1 mark 7 ounces and 1 dram which he obtained through the sale here to residents of slaves from the island;
- 3 ounces and 60 grains which he obtained through the sale of some goats and *malagueta*, and these sales were checked with the register;
- 7 marks 2 ounces and 7 drams in respect of his *feitoria* for which he obtained double the estimate, namely 5 ounces and 4 drams from Gil Matoso and 6 marks 5 ounces 2 drams and 62 grains from Jorge de Pina, Treasurer.

Of which forty-seven marks five ounces and two drams the said Brás Teixeira gave the following account, namely:

- that he paid three marks 1 ounce 5 drams and 48 grains in the Factory for some cloth and things, which he bought here and sent to the island for slaves;[79] and
- 4 ounces and 4 drams which he says he paid for two slave pieces, one of whom he is taking with him and the other he sent to the Kingdom;
- 1 mark 7 ounces 5 drams and 43 grains which he paid for eight pieces of slave children[80] from the island, whom he bought from residents;

---

[79] Contrary to what appears in the published transcription, it seems this is only one item, with no change of line.

[80] In the transcription, '*escravinhos*,' literally 'little slaves.'

- 4 marks 6 ounces 5 drams and 16 grains which he spent on his own needs;
- 13 marks 3 ounces 3 drams and 16 grains which he is taking with him and which were weighed in the presence of the said Captain and officials;
- 23 marks 5 ounces and 3 drams which he sent to the Kingdom, namely:
  - 2 marks through Afonso de Banadilha;
  - 1 ounce and 7 drams through Rui Martins;
  - 1 mark through Fernão Vaz, pilot;
  - 6 marks in the caravel Nazaré;
  - 2 marks 3 ounces and 4 drams through Rui de Castanheda;
  - 6 marks which he sent in the said caravel Nazaré on another voyage;
  - 2 marks in the caravel Cirne;
  - 4 marks in the aforesaid [[caravel]] Nazaré. And this was checked with the register of the receipts.

And the said Brás Teixeira added that, further to the aforesaid ten slaves, he had had twelve slaves whom he bought here from residents, and from the island, and one who was sent to him by Álvaro de Caminha.

Of which one he sent to the Kingdom, 11 he is taking with him, and of the remaining 11 he exchanged one for another slave of his, Francisco, whom he sold to the black people by order of the Captain, another one escaped, another died, and he sold the other eight here to residents.

Diogo Rebelo

And Diogo Rebelo declared under oath that he had received during the time he resided here seven ounces and five drams of gold, namely:

- 6 ounces and 5 drams in respect of his payment for twelve and a half months, since his food allowance was given to the Captain, who fed him;
- one ounce which was given to him by the said Captain for the slave who was allotted to him.

Of which gold he spent one dram and thirty grains, and he is taking with him six ounces seven drams and twenty grains, which were weighed in the presence of the said officials.

Luís Vaz

And Luís Vaz declared under oath that he had received one mark one ounce four drams and twenty grains of gold in respect of his payment for fourteen months, since his food allowance was given to the Captain, together with what he obtained through the sale to the black people of a slave who had been allotted to him.

Of which gold he is taking with him six ounces six drams and twenty grains, for he spent the remainder on the purchase of a slave from the island and on his own needs, which were weighed in the presence of the said officials.

João Álvares Machado

And João Álvares Machado declared under oath that he had received one mark six ounces and two drams of gold in respect of his payment for two years [[*sic*]] and fifteen days, [[since]] his food allowance was given to the Captain, together with what he obtained through the sale to the black people of a female slave who had been allotted to him.

Of which gold he is taking with him six ounces and two drams, for he spent the remainder, which were weighed in the presence of the said officials.

Lopo Dias

And Lopo Dias declared under oath that he had received one mark five ounces three drams and eleven grains of gold in respect of his payment for twenty three months, [[since]] his food allowance was given to the Captain, together with what he obtained through the sale to the black people of a slave who had been allotted to him.

Of which gold he is taking with him one mark three ounces and one dram, which were weighed in the presence of the said officials, and he spent the remainder.

Fernão Besteiro

And Fernão Besteiro Coronheiro[81] declared under oath that he had received two marks seven ounces five drams and three grains in respect of his payment and food allowance for fifteen months, which was checked with the regulations, together with what he obtained through the sale of a female slave who had been allotted to him.

Of which gold he is taking with him one mark five ounces and five drams, which were weighed in the presence of the said officials, and of the remainder he only spent two ounces of gold which he sent to the Kingdom for a bill.

Mem Gonçalves

And Mem Gonçalves declared under oath that he had received two marks four ounces six drams and four grains of gold in respect of his food allowance for eighteen months, since during some months his payment was given to the Captain, together with what he obtained from the sale to the black people of a female slave who had been allotted to him.

Of which gold he is taking with him to the Kingdom one mark and two ounces, because he spent the remainder on food and on the purchase of a female slave

---

[81] It is unclear whether this is a surname or a reference to Fernão Besteiro's actual trade, that of '*coronheiro*,' i.e. 'stocker' or 'finisher,' someone who made and finished the stocks and other wooden parts of the gun.

from the island whom he is taking with him; and it was weighed in the presence of the said officials.

Diogo Trigueiro

And Diogo Trigueiro, retainer of Lopo Soares, declared under oath that he had received two marks seven ounces and six drams of gold in respect of his payment for forty-five and a half months, and also for the sale of a slave who had been allotted to him, the said sum comprising four drams and sixty-four grains which he obtained through the sale to the black people of a little soap, by license of the Captain.

Which gold he is taking with him to the Kingdom, for he did not spend any of it and the said Lopo Soares fed him as he received his food allowance.

Gonçalo de Sequeira

And Gonçalo de Sequeira, former chief *Alcaide*, further stated that he had, in addition to the gold he had already declared, two ounces and three drams of gold which the residents of this town gave as alms to Santa Maria de Estrela, as mentioned in the bill of the said gold, which he is taking with him and which were weighed in the presence of the said officials.

Fernão da Rocha

And Fernão da Rocha, retainer of Lopo Soares, declared that he had received two marks four ounces two drams and two grains of gold, namely:

- 1 mark 3 ounces 7 drams and 29 grains in respect of his payment for twenty-four and a half months, since the food allowance was given to Lopo Soares; and
- one ounce which was given to him by Lopo Soares in lieu of the slave who was allotted to him, and which he received the first time he was placed here;
- 3 ounces and 5 drams for another slave who was given to him, in addition to the one who had been allotted to him, the second time he returned from the Kingdom;
- 3 ounces 2 drams and 48 grains which he also obtained through the sale to the black people of a refuse slave, in addition to the aforesaid two, by license of the Captain;
- three drams which were given to him as a gift.

Of which gold he spent two ounces on the purchase of a slave from the island whom he is taking with him; and he is taking with him to the Kingdom two marks two ounces and two drams, which were weighed in the presence of the said officials.

Fernão Correia

And Fernão Correia, retainer of the said Lopo Soares, declared under oath that he had received three marks two ounces three drams and forty grains of gold, namely:

- 1 mark 2 ounces 1 dram and 57 grains in respect of his food allowance as supernumerary for ten and a half months;
- 1 mark 5 ounces 1 dram and ten grains in respect of his payment for twenty-seven months, since his food allowance was given to the Captain;
- 3 ounces and 48 grains which he obtained for a slave who had been allotted to him.

Of which gold he is taking with him one mark five ounces and three drams, which were weighed in the presence of the officials; and he has sent to the Kingdom seven ounces one dram and forty-five grains for two bills, and the rest he spent on his own needs and on the purchase of a female slave from the island whom he has sent to the Kingdom.

Pedro Luís Calafate

And Pedro Luís Calafate declared under oath that he had received three marks four ounces one dram and fifty-five grains of gold in respect of his food allowance for twenty-six and a half months, together with 2 ounces 1 dram and 45 grains which he obtained through the sale of a female slave who had been allotted to him.

Of which gold he is taking with him two marks, which were weighed in the presence of the said officials. And he has sent to the Kingdom one ounce, and the rest he spent on his own needs and on the purchase of a slave from the island whom he is taking with him.

João Nunes

And João Nunes, who was resident in this town, declared under oath that he had received thirteen marks five ounces five drams and fifty-two grains of gold, namely:

- 7 marks 6 ounces 5 drams and 18 grains in respect of his payment and food allowance for forty-three months;
- 5 ounces and 45 grains which he obtained through the sale to the black people of two slaves, a male one who had been allotted to him and a female one from the island, by license of the Captain;
- 2 ounces which he received from the residents for being the supervisor of the oven-house;
- 2 ounces 3 drams and 60 grains which were paid to him by certain people to whom he had lent money in Portugal;

- 4 marks 5 ounces 2 drams and 69 and a half grains which he obtained through the sale to residents of cloth, garments and supplies; and this was checked with the register.

Of which gold he spent seven ounces one dram and eighteen grains on the purchase of four slaves from the island, two of whom he has sent to the Kingdom and the other two he is taking with him; and 5 ounces and 54 grains which he spent on his personal needs; and he is taking with him 1 mark 4 ounces and 6[[?]][82] drams, which were weighed in the presence of the said officials; and he has sent ten marks four ounces five drams and forty-five grains to the Kingdom, namely:

- 6 ounces through Afonso de Banadilha;
- 4 and a half marks which he himself took with him on two occasions;
- 1 mark through Afonso Álvares, apothecary;
- 1 mark in the caravel Santa Cruz;
- 3 marks through António de Sá, in the caravel Nazaré;
- 2 ounces and 5 drams in another caravel, all of it for bills.

Luís Lopes

And Luís Lopes declared under oath that he had received two marks five ounces three drams and sixty-seven grains of gold, namely:

- 1 mark 6 ounces 4 drams and 60 grains in respect of his payment for thirty-one and a half months, since his food allowance was given to the Captain;
- 3 ounces 7 drams and 51 grains which he obtained through the sale to the black people of a slave which had been allotted to him;
- 2 ounces 7 drams and 27 grains which were given to him by the said Lopo Soares.

Of which gold he has sent to the Kingdom three ounces and four drams for bills, and another 4 ounces to the island for the purchase of a slave; and he is taking with him one mark one ounce and three drams, which were weighed in the presence of the said officials.

Nuno Leitão

And Nuno Leitão, who was resident in this town, declared under oath that he had received six marks two ounces six drams and forty-seven grains of gold, namely:

- 3 ounces 3 drams and 19 grains in respect of his food allowance as supernumerary for three and a half months;

---

[82] In the transcription, '*zj.*'

- 5 ounces 6 drams and 54 grains which were given to him by the Captain as additional[[?]][83] food allowance for six months;
- 2 ounces 1 dram and 39 grains in respect of four and a half months' payment;
- 4 ounces 3 drams and 3 grains in respect of his food allowance for the same period;
- 2 ounces 3 drams and 26 grains which he obtained through the sale of a female slave who had been allotted to him;
- 3 marks 2 ounces 4 drams and 51 grains which he obtained through the sale to residents of supplies, garments and cloth, this sum comprising a slave from the island whom he sold to Brás Teixeira;
- 2 ounces 3 drams and 65 grains which he obtained through the sale to residents of two slaves from the island;
- 3 ounces 4 drams and 12 grains which were paid to him by Serrão for a cow, which he sold to him by license of the Captain.

Of which gold the said Nuno Leitão declared he had spent one ounce six drams and twelve grains on the purchase here of a slave from the island, whom he has sent to the Kingdom; and he spent 4 ounces 7 drams and 33 grains on his own needs; and he is taking with him 5 marks 4 ounces and 63 grains, which were weighed. And the said Nuno Leitão further declared that he was taking with him five ounces and six drams of gold which Lopo Soares, to whom he had lent them while in the Kingdom, gave him.

Afonso Arães

And Afonso Arães, who was resident in this town, declared under oath that he had well and truly received during the entire period he had been here eight marks five ounces six drams and eleven grains of gold, namely:

- 2 ounces 5 drams and 2 grains in respect of his payment for five and a half months;
- 1 mark 4 ounces 3 drams and 30 grains in respect of his payment as *Meirinho*;[84] which office he served for thirteen months; and
- 1 mark 4 ounces 5 drams and 18 grains in respect of his food allowance for the same period;
- 1 mark 1 ounce 5 drams and 60 grains in respect of his *feitoria* as *Meirinho* at the rate of one percent from the income of the House; and this was checked with the lists;
- 5 ounces 6 drams and 54 grains in respect of his food allowance as supernumerary, which he became again, for six and a half months;

---

[83] Tentative translation of '*de fora*,' which might also be translated as 'extra.'
[84] *Meirinho*: see Glossary.

- 1 mark 3 ounces 5 drams and 33 grains in respect of his food allowance for a further twelvemonth;
- 1 ounce 6 drams and 30 grains which were sent to him from the island on account of shirts and wine that he had sent there;
- 2 ounces 1 dram and 45 grains which he obtained through the sale to the black people of a female slave who had been allotted to him;
- 1 mark 2 ounces 6 drams and 21 and a half grains which he obtained through the sale to residents of supplies, garments and cloth; and this was checked with the register of the sales proceeds.

Of which gold he declared that he had spent three ounces and three drams, namely:

- 2 ounces and 3 drams which he spent on the purchase of a female slave from the island, whom he is taking with him; and
- 1 ounce and 11 grains on his own needs;
- 7 marks 2 ounces 3 drams and 21 grains, which he is taking with him to the Kingdom and which were weighed in the presence of the officials; and he has sent one mark to the Kingdom, namely:
- 4 ounces through Estêvão Fernandes, who came here as captain, and 4 ounces through Pedro de Sintra, pilot.

Tomé Lopes

And Tomé Lopes, who was resident in this town, declared under oath that he had received during the period of his stay here one mark four ounces six drams and fifty-two grains, namely:

- 1 mark 1 ounce 7 drams and 66 grains in respect of his payment for twenty months and a half;
- 2 ounces 6 drams and 66 grains which he obtained through the sale to the black people of a slave who had been allotted to him. And during the period in which he received the said payment, his food allowance was given to Lopo Soares for feeding him.

Of which gold he declared he is taking with him five ounces six drams and sixteen grains, and the rest he spent on the purchase of a female slave from the island whom he has sent to the Kingdom and on his own expenses; and it was weighed in the presence of the officials.

Diogo Álvares

And Diogo Álvares, retainer of Gonçalo de Sequeira, declared under oath that he had received during the period of his stay in this town one mark five ounces seven drams and thirteen grains, namely:

- 1 mark 4 ounces 7 drams and 13 grains which were given to him by the said Gonçalo de Sequeira and which correspond to half the food allowance due to supernumerary men, since he fed him for twenty-six and a half months;

- 1 ounce which was given to him from the proceeds of the slave who had been allotted to him.

Of which gold he has sent to the Kingdom one ounce one dram and forty-five grains; and three and a half drams [[he spent]] on his personal needs; and he is taking with him the said one mark four ounces seven drams and thirteen grains, which were weighed in the presence of the said officials.

João Frazão

And João Frazão, who was resident in this town, declared under oath that he had received during the period of his stay here four marks four ounces seven drams and thirty-one grains of gold, namely:

- 1 ounce 2 drams and 28 grains in respect of his wage as ship's boy for two months, during which he served in the *caravelões*;
- 2 marks 4 ounces 1 dram and 43 grains in respect of his payment for forty-two months, [[since]] his food allowance was given to the Captain, who fed him; and this payment was checked with the regulations;
- 1 ounce which was given to him by the Captain from the proceeds of the slave who had been allotted to him;
- 2 ounces 6 drams and 6 grains which he obtained through the sale to residents of six slave pieces from the island, whom he had bought;
- 3 ounces 5 drams and 29 grains through the sale of supplies and wine to residents.

Of which gold he has sent to Portugal one ounce, and he is taking with him three marks two ounces five drams and thirty-two grains. And he spent the remainder on his personal needs. Which gold was weighed in the presence of the said officials.

João Leal

And João Leal declared under oath that he had received during the entire period of his stay here nine marks six ounces five drams and seventy-two grains of gold, namely:

- 1 mark 2 ounces 3 drams and 58 grains in respect of his payment for twenty-one and a half months;
- 2 marks 5 ounces 7 drams and 15 grains in respect of his food allowance for twenty-two and a half months, since for one month he did not receive payment because he was registered as supernumerary;
- 7 ounces 6 drams and 22 grains which were given to him in addition for the time he was not registered;

- 5 ounces 2 drams and 18 grains which he obtained through the sale to the black people of two female slaves, one who had been allotted to him and another a refuse slave;[85]
- 5 ounces which were paid to him here by Álvaro Domingues, retainer of the Captain, for certain things and money he [[João Leal]] had lent him in Portugal;
- 1 ounce 6 drams and 13 grains which he obtained through the sale to residents of two slaves from the island;
- 1 mark 4 ounces 4 drams and 39 and a half grains which he obtained through the sale of cloth, garments and supplies in the island of São Tomé;
- 1 mark and ten grains which he obtained through the sale here to residents and people from the caravels of fourteen slave pieces whom he had brought from the island; and these sales were checked with their register;
- 6 ounces and 47 grains which he obtained through the sale to residents in this town of some cloth and garments; and this was checked.

Of which gold he declared that he had sent to the Kingdom one mark and seven ounces, namely:

- 4 ounces through Luís Perdigão;
- one mark [[through]] Pedro Lopes, in the caravel Nazaré;
- 3 ounces through Álvaro Dias in the caravel Santa Catarina;
- 3 drams and 50 grains, which he spent on his own needs;
- 1 mark and ten grains which he spent on the purchase of four slaves from the island, whom he has sent to the Kingdom;
- 6 marks 7 ounces 2 drams and 12 grains which he is taking with him to the Kingdom and which were weighed in the presence of the said officials.

Fernão Gil

And Fernão Gil, who was resident in this town, declared he had received seven ounces two drams and twenty-five grains of gold in respect of his payment and food allowance for five months.

Of which gold he spent three drams and five grains, and he is taking with him 6 ounces 7 drams and 20 grains, which were weighed in the presence of the said officials.

---

[85] Captive Africans rejected at purchase, unsold at market, or left behind from a lot were called 'refuse slaves.' They were consequently sold cheaply to anyone who would buy them. Some were 'refused' on account of illness.

Jorge Álvares

And Jorge Álvares, resident in this town, declared under oath that he had received one mark six ounces three drams and sixty grains of gold in respect of his payment for nineteen and a half months, [[since]] his food allowance was given to Lopo Soares, including here what he obtained through the sale of a female slave who had been allotted to him and 2 ounces which he received from the residents for being the supervisor of the oven-house. And he is taking with him one mark three ounces and one dram and spent the remainder on the purchase of a female slave from the island and on his own expenses.

Gil Matoso, who was Factor here

And Gil Matoso, who was Factor in this town, declared and said under oath, which was administered to him, that he had received eighty marks two ounces six drams and thirty-two and a half grains of gold, as is shown by two receipts, one issued by Diogo de Alvarenga, Scribe of the Expenditure of this Factory, and another by Diogo Pereira, Scribe of the Revenue, in the following manner:

namely – 3 drams and 67 and a half grains in respect of his and four of his men's food allowance from the twelfth of the month of September one thousand 495 until the fifteenth of the said month, which amount to three days;

- 12 marks 5 ounces 1 dram and 63 grains in respect of his payment as Factor from the last fifteen days of the said month of September of the said year '95 until the first fifteen days of the month of July of the present year '499, which amount to forty-six months, at the monthly rate of two ounces one dram and forty-five grains;
- 5 marks 4 ounces 6 drams and 14 grains in respect of his food allowance for the entire said period, at the monthly rate of seven drams and fifty-nine grains;
- 18 marks 2 ounces 6 drams and 70 and a half grains in respect of his *feitoria* from the income of the said House during the entire period, the expenditure on salaries and food allowances having been deducted as shown in the lists;
- 3 marks 1 ounce and 61 and a half grains in respect of his *feitoria* for which at times he obtained double the estimate, since they were items of a kind which the black people wanted to buy;
- 22 marks 3 ounces and 56 grains of gold which he received as food allowance for four of his Factory men during the entire period, at the monthly rate of seven drams and fifty-nine grains each;
- 3 marks 2 ounces 6 drams and ten grains which he received as food allowance for Isabel Matosa, his female white slave, whom he had registered for allowance from the said last fifteen days of September '95 until the end of December '497, which amount to twenty-seven and a half months;

- 5 ounces and 66 grains which he further received as food allowance for Afonso Gonçalves, whom he has registered as supernumerary from the said 15 days of September until the end of July of the year '496, which amount to ten and a half months;
- 4 ounces 1 dram and 59 grains which he further received as payment for Fernão de Faria, his white slave, whom he had registered as man of the Factory by a writ of the King from the first day of April of the year '497 until the first fifteen days of July of the year '99, which amount to twenty-seven and a half months, at the monthly rate of one dram and seventeen and a half grains per man of the Factory;
- one mark two ounces two drams and fifty-one grains in respect of his *feitoria* from the income of the House during all the said twenty-seven and a half months of the said slave,[86] as shown in the lists; and
- one mark 6 drams and 72 grains which he also received as pay for João Martins, his Christian black [[slave]], whom he had registered as ship's boy in the *caravelões* from the first day of January of the year '497 until the end of the month of June of the year '98, which amount to eighteen months.

Gold from his sales, namely:

- 4 ounces 4 drams and 72 grains which he obtained through the sale to Afonso de Banadilha of a gold chain and a *bidem* [[*sic*]];[87]
- 2 ounces 3 drams and 45 grains which were paid to him by Luís Pestana, who was resident here, for two women's shirts and a black dress,[88] as well as for other items such as garments, headdresses and supplies; and
- 4 marks 3 ounces 4 drams and five and a half grains through the sale to residents, for the entire period of his stay, of women's and men's garments, wine and other supplies; and
- 1 ounce 4 drams and 41 grains which were brought to him from there [[as proceeds]] of the sale in the island of São Tomé of women's clothing, boots,[89] shoes and hatches; and
- 5 ounces 5 drams and 60 grains from the sale of flour and biscuit,[90] oil and fish and rose sugar, which were bought from him for the King;
- 4 drams from the sale to Briolanja, black woman, of a barrel of flour; and
- 5 ounces and 37 and a half grains from the sale to Serrão, Anxi and Gomarrão, black men, of a sow and some sheep, goats and quince preserve, by license of Lopo Soares, Captain;

---

[86] This passage is unclear, but it seems the reference to the 'said slave' is only made to identify the period at stake.
[87] Meaning unknown.
[88] In the transcription, '*sainho*': see Glossary.
[89] In the transcription, '*borzeguins*': see Glossary.
[90] In the transcription, '*biscoito*': see Glossary.

- 3 marks 3 ounces 6 drams and 15 grains which he obtained from the sale to the black people of ten slaves who were his or had been allotted to him, one in his own name, and another in the name of Isabel Matosa, his white female slave, and the other eight in the name of some of his men, to whom he gave one ounce each;
- 6 ounces 5 drams and 66 grains which were repaid to him here by Lopo Soares for Guiomar de Ataíde, female slave of the said Captain, whom he had bought for him in Portugal.

Which gold was checked with the regulations and the lists of payment, as well as with [[the lists of]] the payment of the *feitoria* of the one percent from the income of the House, and the gold from the sales was checked with their register.

Of which gold the said Gil Matoso gave the following account of expenditure: namely – 26 marks 7 ounces 7 drams and 67 and a half grains which he has sent to the Kingdom for certain bills issued by Diogo de Alvarenga, Scribe of the Expenditure of this Factory;

- and six marks of those for a bill of the Revenue by Diogo Pereira; and
- one mark two ounces and seven drams which he lent here to Duarte Pacheco;[91]
- 3 marks 7 ounces 2 drams and 53 and a half grains which he spent on the purchase of twelve slave pieces from the island whom he bought here as well as in the island, and also a young slave girl for whom he paid the King through Afonso Álvares, apothecary, and whom he is taking with him;
- 2 marks 6 ounces and 61 and a half grains which he spent on his personal needs;
- forty-five marks two ounces and four drams of gold which he is taking with him to the Kingdom and which were weighed in the presence of the said officials. And of the above mentioned twelve slave pieces he declared the following expenditure:

namely – ten of them were sent by him to the Kingdom for a bill, and one of them died in this town, and he is taking a female slave with him. And the said Gil Matoso further declared that he has sent to the Kingdom another two slave pieces for a bill, namely, one[92] whom he obtained in the island for a pipe of wine and some cloth, and the other[93] whom he exchanged here for another who will be paid for in the Kingdom by the wife of Fernão Martins, goldsmith, presently residing in the island. He is also taking a [[slave]] boy whom he has just bought on the caravel that came from the island in exchange for oil and cloth.

---

[91] Duarte Pacheco Pereira was the author of the well-known *Esmeraldo de situ orbis*, and later captain-governor of the São Jorge da Mina fortress.
[92] It remains unclear, since *'peça'* ('piece') is a feminine noun, whether the feminine pronoun refers to 'piece' or to a 'female slave.'
[93] See previous note.

And in addition to all these pieces he is taking with him another three who were sent to him by the King of Benin[94] by a writ which was given to him by the said Lord; and one of these three, who fell sick at the time of his departure and will be sent later, he is leaving behind. And he is taking these three slave pieces by writ of the said Lord, to be charged to his account and, when settling his account, their payment will be outstanding, and he will ask the King for them or hand them over to whomever His Highness should instruct.

[sign.] *Gil Matoso*

João Drago, Factory man

And João Drago, retainer of Gil Matoso and Factory man, declared and said under oath, which was administered to him, that he had received during the entire period of his stay in this town four marks four ounces three drams and forty-seven grains of gold, as attested by two receipts, one issued by Diogo de Alvarenga, Scribe of the Expenditure, and another by Diogo Pereira, Scribe of the Revenue, as follows:

namely – 7 ounces and 40 grains in respect of his payment as Factory man from the last 15 days of the month of September of the year '95 until the first 15 days of the month of July of the present year '99, which amount to forty-six months, at the monthly rate of one dram and seventeen and a half grains;

- 2 marks 2 ounces 2 drams and 62 and a half grains in respect of his *feitoria* from the income of the House, deducting the expenditure on salaries and supplies for all the said 46 months;
- 7 drams and 50 grains which he received for a cloak[95] and two scarlet caps for which in the Factory he obtained double the estimate, since the black people wanted to buy them;
- 3 ounces which he obtained through the sale here to the black people of a slave who had been allotted to him. Gold from his sales, namely: 6 ounces 5 drams and 44 and a half grains which he obtained through the sale at retail to residents of some supplies and Brittany cloth, as well as shirts and some linen and garments;
- 3 drams from the sale to Serrão, the black man, of a sheep, by license of Lopo Soares, Captain. Which gold was checked with the payment lists of the salaries and the *feitoria* of the one percent from the income of the House, as well as with the registers of the sales.

Of which gold he declared the following expenditure:

namely – 4 ounces which he has sent to the Kingdom for bills;

- 5 ounces which he paid here for two slaves from the island of São Tomé, one whom he has sent to the Kingdom and the other whom he is now taking with him;

---

[94] Words crossed out in the manuscript: 'who were granted by Our Lord the King as attested.'
[95] In the transcription, '*marlota*,' a short cloak of North African origin.

- 2 ounces 3 drams and 47 grains which he spent on his personal needs. And he is taking with him to the Kingdom three marks and one ounce of gold, which were weighed in the presence of the said officials.

[sign.] *João Drago*

Pedro Fernandes

And Pedro Fernandes, who was a man of the Factory in this town, declared and said under oath that he had received during the period of his stay here one ounce and seventy grains of gold in respect of his payment and *feitoria* of a quarter of the one percent, from the month of May '99 until the first 15 days of July of the present era, which amount to two and a half months, during which he served as Factory man.

Which gold he is now taking with him to the Kingdom, and it was weighed in the presence of the said officials.

Diogo de Alvarenga

And Diogo de Alvarenga, Scribe of the Expenditure of this Factory declared and said under oath, which was administered to him, that he had received during the entire period of his stay here thirty-seven marks five ounces two drams and one grain of gold, as attested by two receipts issued one by Rui Gago, Scribe of the Expenditure, and the other by Diogo Pereira, Scribe of the Revenue, as follows:

namely – 4 marks 4 ounces 4 drams and 56 and a half grains in respect of his payment as Scribe of the Revenue, from the first day of the month of September of the year '95 until the first 15 days of the month of July of this year '99, which amount to forty-six and a half months, at the monthly rate of six drams and fifteen and a half grains;

- 5 marks 7 ounces 1 dram and 73 grains in respect of his food allowance from the last 15 days of the month of August of the year '95 until the first 15 days of July '99, which amount to forty-seven months;
- 9 marks 1 ounce 3 drams and 35 grains which he obtained through his *feitoria* from the income of the House, expenditure with salaries and supplies having been deducted from the last 15 days of the month of September of the year '95 until the first 15 days of July of this year '99, which amount to forty-six months, as attested by the lists of payment;
- 2 marks 6 ounces 4 drams and 72 grains which he received as payment for Simão Pires, his white slave, during the said 46 months, at the monthly rate of three drams and sixty-seven grains;
- 5 marks 7 ounces 1 dram and 73 grains which he received as food allowance for the said Simão Peres, his slave, from the last 15 days of the month of August '95 until the first 15 days of July of the year '99, which amount to forty-seven months, during which he was registered as his man;

- 5 ounces 6 drams and 66 grains which he received from certain items for which in the Factory, from Gil Matoso, Factor, he obtained double the estimate, since the black people wanted to buy them. And this gold which he thus received as salary and food allowance for himself and his slave, as well as from the *feitoria* of the one percent, was checked with the regulations of the late King regarding what was annually due to them in gold from sales:

namely – 1 mark 6 drams and 30 grains which he obtained through the sale to the black people of four slaves whom he had in the Factory, one who had been allotted to him, another of Simão Pires, his white slave whom he had registered as his man, another in place of Gastão de Alvarenga, his brother, to whom he had been allotted, and a boy whom he received as a refuse slave;

- 4 ounces 1 dram and 63 and a half grains which were sent from the island of São Tomé for wine and supplies which were sold for him there;
- 3 ounces 1 dram and 36 and a half grains which he obtained through the sale to Mor Lopes, resident here, of a female slave from the island of São Tomé;
- 3 drams and 15 grains which were paid to him by Diogo Gue, a black man of Lopo Soares, for two sheets;
- 7 ounces 7 drams and 25 grains which he obtained through the sale to Serrão, Gomarrão[96] and Anxi, black men, of goats, sheep, dogs, chickens and wax candles, by license of the Captain;
- 1 mark 1 ounce 3 drams and 44 grains from biscuit, oil, flour and other supplies and things, which he sold for the King;
- 4 marks 2 ounces 4 drams and 23 grains from the sale to residents of supplies, garments and cloth;

Of which gold he declared the following expenditure:

namely – 20 marks which he sent to the Kingdom for some bills of expenditure and revenue;[97] and

- 2 marks and 3 ounces which he spent on the purchase of eight slave pieces from the island of São Tomé, five of whom he has sent to the Kingdom, another two whom he is now sending through Marcos Fernandes, and another who is staying here;
- 1 mark which he paid for some cloth which he bought here;
- 8 marks 4 ounces 4 drams and 12 grains which were found during the inspection of the gold of all the residents who were here. Which gold was weighed in the presence of the said officials and will be kept by him to take it when he goes to the Kingdom.

---

[96] In the transcription, '*Gomaram.*'
[97] In the transcription, '*recadações de despesa e receipta.*'

And he added that the gold spent on the purchase of the above mentioned eight slaves includes the purchase of a little girl whom he bought here from Pedro Fernandes, man of the Factory, to whom she had been allotted, and who will stay here for him to take as a payment when he goes.

And the five marks five ounces five drams and sixty-four grains which are left to make up the total he spent on his personal needs during all the time he has been here until the writing of this [[inquiry]].

And he further declared under oath that he had received another six slave pieces from the island of São Tomé in exchange for cloth and supplies, of whom he has sent two to the Kingdom for a bill, and the other four he still keeps with him here.

This record was copied by myself and will be kept by the scribes of this Factory. And the gold received by Jorge de Pina, *Meirinho*, and Bartolomeu de Agrala, *Almoxarife*, was not registered here because of the imminent departure of Fernão de Melo, and we will send it [[the register]] in the next [[caravel(?)]]; but their gold was weighed and registered according to what is ordered by the King in the regulations. And the Captain, Factor and officials signed here.

Written by me, Jorge de Pina, Scribe of the Revenue, on the 23rd day of August 1499.

> *João Fernandes*
> *Jorge de Pina*
> [sign.] *Fernão Lopes Correia*   *Diogo de Alvarenga*
> *Rui Gago*   *Pedro Barroso*

8 Gold from São Jorge Da Mina[98] (1500)

ABSTRACT – *A table accounting for gold brought from São Jorge da Mina to Portugal in 1500 and their valuation and equivalences in the Portuguese monetary system.*

[Table of the gold which arrives from the town of São Jorge da Mina]

Book of the account [...]
House of [...][99]

The [goldsmith] declares [...]
for each [[gold]] mark [...]
seven drams[100] [...]

---

[98] ANTT, *Contos do Reino e Casa, Núcleo Antigo* 928. Transcribed in PMA, 3: 92–99.
[99] In the transcription, '*Casa dos...*'; probably, '*Casa dos Contos*' (see Glossary).
[100] In Portuguese, '*oitava*' (sing.), an 'eighth' of an ounce.

56 *cruzados* [...] 19 [...]
in which [...] money [...]
whence comes [...] *dobra* 4

1 *dobra*	241 *reais* 2 ¼ *pretos*[101]
2 *dobras*	882 *reais* 4 and one half *pretos*
3 *dobras*	1,324 *reais* 6 ¾ *pretos*
4 *dobras*	1,765 *reais* 9 *pretos*
5 *dobras*	2,206 *reais* 11 ¼ *pretos*
6 *dobras*	2,648 *reais* 1 and one half *pretos*
7 *dobras*	3,089 *reais* 3 ¾ *pretos*
8 *dobras*	3,530 *reais* 6 *pretos*
9 *dobras*	3,971 *reais* 8 ¼ *pretos*
10 *dobras*	4,411 *reais* 10 and one half *pretos*
20 *dobras*	8,823 *reais* 10 *pretos*
30 *dobras*[102]	35 *reais* 8 and one half *pretos*[[sic]][103]
40 *dobras*[4]	147 *reais* 7 *pretos* [[sic]]
50 *dobras*[4]	59 *reais* 4 and one half *pretos* [[sic]]
60 *dobras*[4]	580[104] *reais* 3 *pretos*
70 *dobras*[4]	10,850 [...] *reais* 1 one half *pretos*
80 *dobras*[4]	30,790 [...]
90 *dobras*[4]	39,700 [...] [[one and a]] half *pretos*
100 *dobras*[4]	44,115 [...] *pretos*
200 *dobras*[4]	88,200 [...] *reais* 6 *pretos*
300[4] *dobras*	132,300 [...] *reais* 3 *pretos*
400[4] *dobras*	176,475 *reais*
500[4] *dobras*	220,593 *reais* 9 *pretos*
600[4] *dobras*	264,712 *reais* 6 *pretos*
700[4] *dobras*	308,831 *reais* 3 *pretos*
800[4] *dobras*	352,950 *reais*
900[4] *dobras*	397,068 *reais* 9 *pretos*
1,000[4] *dobras*	441,187 *reais* 6 *pretos*
2,000[4] *dobras*	882,375 *reais*

[101] *Pretos*: literally, 'black [*reais*],' a Portuguese copper coin. Most authorities consider one *real branco* ('white *real*,' which was made of tin) equivalent to 10 *reais pretos*. According to the dictionary of Antonio de Morais Silva (*Diccionario da Lingua Portugueza*, 1789), during the 15th century, the *real branco* was worth 12 *reais pretos*. Given the value is more than 10 *reais pretos* included in this list, at the time the table was first drawn up, the *real branco* was worth 12 *reais pretos*.

[102] Words and/or numbers are missing. Reconstruction based on folios 5 and 5v.

[103] When values are obviously wrong, this is indicated by [[*sic*]].

[104] It is possible there is a score over the first '*j*' missing in the transcription; this being the case, it should read '1,480.'

Table of the gold	
one mark has	8 ounces
one ounce has	8 drams

Ounces of marks	
one ounce is worth	6 ¼ *dobras*
2 ounces	12 and one half *dobras*
3 ounces	18 ¾ *dobras*
4 ounces	25 *dobras*
5 ounces	31 ¼ *dobras*
6 ounces	37 and one half *dobras*
7 ounces	43 ¾ *dobras*
8 ounces which make up one mark	50 *dobras*

Dram of dobra	
one dram of gold *dobra* in jewels is worth	57 *reais* 10 *pretos*
2 drams	115 *reais* 8 8/12 *pretos*
3 drams	173 *reais* 7 *pretos*
4 drams	231 *reais* 5 *pretos*
5 drams	289 *reais* 3 *pretos* 8 [...]
6 drams	347 *reais* 2 *pretos* [...]
7 drams	405 *reais* 4 *pretos* [...]
8 drams which is worth 1 *dobra*	462 *reais* 10 *pretos* 9 [...]

Drams of ounces of gold in jewels	
1 dram	361 *reais* 6 *pretos*
2 drams	1 *dobra* 723 *reais*
From one ounce of gold dust are lost[105]	27 [...]
2 ounces	54 [...]
From one dram of gold dust are lost	3 1/8 grains

[105] In the transcription, '*quebram*' (literally, 'break') from '*quebra*' ('melt loss'), i.e. 'are lost' (as impurities) during the process of smelting.

[For] one mark of gold in jewels the gold-finer declares [[59]][106] *cruzados* and 135 *reais*, making up 23,145 *reais*, which, divided into 50 *dobras*, amount per *dobra* of gold in jewels to 462 *reais* 10 *pretos* 9 twelfths[107] of *preto* and 3 fifths of one twelfth of one *preto*.

[For] one mark of gold ore the gold-finer declares 57 *cruzados* 360 *reais*, making up 22,590 *reais*, which, divided into 50 *dobras*, amount per *dobra* of gold ore to 451 *reais* 9 *pretos* and 3 fifths of one *preto*.

For one mark of gold dust the gold-finer declares 56 *cruzados* 219 *reais* 4 and one half *pretos*, making up 22,059 *reais* 4 and one half *pretos*, which, divided into 50 *dobras*, amount per *dobra* to 441 *reais* 2 *pretos* ¼.

Dobras of gold in jewels[108]	
1 *dobra*	462 *reais* 10 *pretos* 9 twelfths[109] of *preto* 3/5 of twelfth of *preto*
2 *dobras*	925 *reais* 9 *pretos* 7 1/5 twelfths
3 *dobras*	1,388 *reais* 8 *pretos* 4 4/5 twelfths
4 *dobras*	1,851 *reais* 7 *pretos* 2 2/5 twelfths
5 *dobras*	2,314 and one half *reais*
6 *dobras*	2,777 *reais* 4 *pretos* 9 3/5 twelfths
7 *dobras*	3,240 *reais* 3 *pretos* 7 1/5 twelfths
8 *dobras*	3,703 *reais* 2 *pretos* 4 4/5 twelfths
[9] *dobras*	4,166 *reais* 1 *preto* 2 2/5 twelfths
[10] *dobras*	4,629 *reais*
[20] *dobras*	9,258
30 *dobras*	13,887
40 *dobras*	18,516 *reais*
50 *dobras*	23,145
60 *dobras*	27,774 *reais*
70 *dobras*	32,403 *reais*
80 *dobras*	37,032 *reais*
90 *dobras*	41,661 *reais*
100 *dobras*	46,290 *reais*
200 *dobras*	92,580
300 *dobras*	138,870 *reais*
400 *dobras*	185,160 *reais*
500 *dobras*	231,450 *reais*
600 *dobras*	277,740 *reais*

[106] Blank in the transcription. The actual value is referred to again in fol. 8, line 1 of the table.
[107] In the transcription, '*dozeno*' (the same as '*dozão*').
[108] Fol. 4 is blank.
[109] In the transcription, '*dozãos*' (the same as '*dozenos*').

Dobras of gold in jewels[108]	
700 *dobras*	324,030 *reais*
800 *dobras*	370,320
900 *dobras*	416,610 *reais*
1,000 *dobras*	462,900 *reais*
2,000 *dobras*	925,800 *reais*
3,000 *dobras*	1,388,700
4,000 *dobras*	1,851,600 *reais*
5,000 *dobras*	2,314,500 *reais*
6,000 *dobras*	2,777,400
7,000 dobras	3,240,300 *reais*
8,000[110] *dobras*	3,703,200 *reais*
9,000 *dobras*	4,166,100 *reais*
10,000 *dobras*	4,629,000 *reais*

Dobras of gold ore	
1 *dobra*	451 *reais* 9 3/5 *pretos*
2 *dobras*	903 *reais* 7 1/5 *pretos*
3 *dobras*	1,355 *reais* 4 4/5 *pretos*
4 *dobras*	1,807 *reais* 2 2/5 *pretos*
5 *dobras*	2,259 *reais*
6 *dobras*	2,710 *reais* 9 3/5 *pretos*
7 *dobras*	3,162 *reais* 7 1/5 *pretos*
8 *dobras*	3,614 *reais* 4 4/5 *pretos*
9 *dobras*	4,066 *reais* 2 2/5 *pretos*
10 *dobras*	4,518 *reais*
20 *dobras*	9,036 *reais*
30 *dobras*	13,554 *reais*
40 *dobras*	18,072 *reais*
50 *dobras*	22,590 *reais*
60 *dobras*	27,108 *reais*
70 *dobras*	31,626 *reais*
80 *dobras*	36,144 *reais*
90 *dobras*	40,662 *reais*
100 *dobras*	45,180 *reais*

[110] In the manuscript, '*biij*,' without the score above the numbers, signifying 'thousand.'

110 *dobras*	49,698 *reais*
120 *dobras*	54,216 *reais*
130 *dobras*	58,734 *reais*
140 *dobras*	63,252 *reais*
150 *dobras*	67,770 *reais*
160 *dobras*	72,288 *reais*
170 *dobras*	76,806 *reais*
180 *dobras*	81,324 *reais*
190 *dobras*	85,842 *reais*
200 *dobras*	90,360 *reais*
300 *dobras*	135,540 *reais*
400 *dobras*	180,720 *reais*
500 *dobras*	225,900 *reais*
600 *dobras*	271,080 *reais*
700 *dobras*	316,260 *reais*
800 *dobras*	361,440 *reais*
900 *dobras*	451,620[[*sic*]]
1,000 *dobras*	451,800[[*sic*]]

Table of the gold from Mina[111]		
1 mark	59 *cruzados* 135	23,145 *reais*
2 marks	118 *cruzados* 270 *reais*	46,290 *reais*
4 marks	237 *cruzados* 150	92,580 *reais*
6 marks	356 *cruzados* 30 *reais*	138,870
8 marks	474 *cruzados* 300	185,160
10 marks	593 *cruzados* 180	231,450
20 marks	1,186 *cruzados* 360	462,900 *reais*
30 marks	1,780 *cruzados* 150	694,350
40 marks	2,373 *cruzados* 330	925,800 *reais*
50 marks	2,967 *cruzados* 120	1,157,250
60 marks	3,560 *cruzados* 300 *reais*	1,388,700 *reais*
70 marks	4,154 *cruzados* 90	1,620,150
80 marks	4,747 *cruzados* 270	1,851,600 *reais*
90 marks	5,341 *cruzados* 60 *reais*	2,083,050
100 marks	5,934 *cruzados* 240	2,314,500 *reais*

[111] Fols. 7 and 7v. are blank.

Ounces	
1 ounce 7 *cruzados* 163 *reais* 1 and one half *preto*	2,893 *reais* 1 and one half *preto*
2 ounces 14 *cruzados* 326 *reais* 3 *pretos*	5,786 [[*reais*]] 3 *pretos*
4 ounces 29 *cruzados* 262 [[*reais*]] and one half	11,572 *reais* and one half
5 ounces 37 *cruzados* 35 *reais* 7 and one half *pretos*	14,465 *reais* 7 and one [half] *pretos*
6 ounces 44 *cruzados* 98 *reais* 9 *pretos*	17,358 [[*reais*]] 9 *pretos*
7 ounces 51 *cruzados* 361 [[*reais*]] 10 and one half *pretos*	20,251 *reais* 10 and a half *pretos*
8 ounces 59 *cruzados* 135 [[*reais*]]	23,145 *reais*

Drams	
1 dram	361 *reais* 6 *pretos*
2 drams 1 *cruzado* 333	723 *reais*
3 drams 2 *cruzados* 304 *reais* and one half	1,084 *reais* and one half
4 drams 3 *cruzados* 276 *reais*	1,446 *reais*
5 drams 4 *cruzados* 247 *reais* and one half 1,807 *reais* and one half	
6 drams 5 *cruzados* 219 *reais*	2,169 *reais*
7 drams 6 *cruzados* 190 *reais* 2,530 *reais* and one half	
8 drams 7 *cruzados* 173 *reais* 1 and one half *preto*	2,893 *reais* 1 and one half *preto*

Grains	
1 grain	4 *reais* 9 *pretos* 9 twelfths and ten twelfths of twelfth
2 grains	9 *reais* 7 *pretos* 7 twelfths and 8 twelfths of twelfth
3 grains	14 *reais* 5 *pretos* 5 and one half twelfths
4 grains	19 *reais* 3 *pretos* 3 twelfths and one third
5 grains	24 *reais* 1 and one half *preto*
6 grains	28 *reais* 11 *pretos* 2 twelfths
12 grains	57 *reais* 10 *pretos* and one third
24 grains	115 *reais* 8 *pretos* 8 twelfths
36 grains	173 *reais* 7 *pretos*
48 grains	231 *reais* 5 *pretos* and one third

Gold ore	
1 mark	57 *cruzados* 360 *reais*
2 marks	115 *cruzados* 430 *reais*
3 marks	173 *cruzados* 300 *reais*
4 marks	231 *cruzados* 270
5 marks	289 *cruzados* 240
10 marks	579 *cruzados* 90
20 marks	1,158 *cruzados* 180
40 marks	2,316 *cruzados* 360
50 marks	2,896 *cruzados* 60 *reais*

Ounces
1 ounce 7 *cruzados* 93 *reais* 10 *pretos*
2 ounces 14 *cruzados* 187 *reais* 8 *pretos*
4 ounces 28 *cruzados* 375 *reais*

Drams of gold ore	
4 drams	3 *cruzados* 241 *reais* 11 *pretos*
2 drams	1 *cruzado* 320 *reais* 11 and one half *pretos*
1 dram	355 *reais* 5 *pretos* 3 quarters of one *preto*

And of gold dust, from each mark a loss of three drams should be deducted.[112]

Table of the value of the gold which arrives from Mina from the town of São Jorge of Our Lord the King.

9 Letter from Dom Manuel
to the Factor of Mina[113] (28/09/1501)

ABSTRACT – *The King of Portugal determines the chaplain at São Jorge da Mina shall celebrate a Mass of St Mary every Saturday and say prayers for the souls of the knights of the Order of Christ and for others, according to their obligation. This determination applies to all Portuguese bases in western Africa.*

---

[112] In the transcription, '*bater de quebra*' (translated here as 'deduct a loss'), which should read '*abater de quebra*' ('*abater*' meaning 'to deduct'). '*Bater*' means 'to beat' or 'to strike,' but in some cases, when used together with '*moeda*,' 'to coin money.'

[113] ANTT, *Livraria, Cód. pergamináceo* [parchment Codex] 516, pp. 53–55; MMA vol.1, doc. 49, 184–5.

[[We]], Dom Manuel, by the grace of God King of Portugal and the Algarves, on either side of the sea in Africa, Lord of Guinea and of the Conquest, Navigation and Commerce of Ethiopia, Arabia, Persia and India, as Regent and Governor and Perpetual Administrator of the Order and Knighthood of Our Lord Jesus Christ, make known to you, Factor and scribes of our town of São Jorge da Mina, that the *Infante* Dom Henrique, my [[*sic*]] uncle, may God keep him, has ordained in his testament that every Saturday, and in every place in Guinea where there be a vicar or chaplain, a Mass of Our Lady be said for him, with the Celebration of the Holy Ghost and the Prayer *Fidelium Deus*; and that, before beginning the mass, he [[the vicar or chaplain]] should face the people and ask them for the sake of God to say a *Pater Noster* for his [[the *Infante's*]] soul, and for those of the said Order and those for whom it was due and obligatory to pray to God. And that the said chaplain or vicar should receive one silver mark in silver [[*sic*]] per year for his work, paid out of the rent of the *vintena*[114] which he gave to the said Order.

And because it is our wish that all clauses of his testament be observed, we order you, from the day this letter is there presented to you onwards, to ensure that the aforementioned mass is said every Saturday, according to the order and in the manner stated above, and to pay the vicar or chaplain who shall say it the mentioned silver mark or its equivalent from our gold which you will be receiving there, of which you shall inform our House of Mina, so as to deduct that amount from that which is given to the Collector of the said *vintena*, which bears this expense.

And by the copy of this letter, which shall be registered in the books of that Factory, together with its receipt, it will be accounted for on your behalf. And we enjoin you and future Factors to always ensure that the mentioned mass is said and remind and tell the said chaplain and vicar on our behalf to say it. And if by chance you come to know that he has not observed it thus, you shall deduct the equivalent to this from his payment, and you shall have the masses which he has left unsaid said by someone else, so that the obligation is observed. And if on one or more Saturdays, due to some obstacle, it is not said, it shall be said on some other day of the week, so that nevertheless all the mentioned masses be said.

Written in Lisbon, on the 28th day of September – Gaspar Roiz wrote this – year of Our Lord Jesus Christ one thousand five hundred and one years.

10 Gold from Mina[115] (1502)

ABSTRACT – *In what would be an otherwise passing note about the gold from Mina to Portugal, court chronicler João de Barros draws an important connection between Mina gold and the prestige and wealth of the King of Portugal, and relates that Vasco da Gama's intention was to impress this idea upon the ambassadors*

---

[114] *Vintena*: see Glossary.
[115] João de Barros, *Ásia: Década primeira*, book 6, ch. 2.

representing sovereigns in the Indian Ocean. Indeed, Mina gold played no small part in Portugal's ascendency to empire from a tiny, backward economic country with a small population and without a base for a global maritime empire.

[Vasco da Gama],[116] departing from Restelo [port in Lisbon], set his course via Cape Vert [Senegal], and on the last day of February he anchored before it at a place called by ours Saly Portudal,[117] where he remained for six days, taking in water and a supply of fish. And there a caravel arrived, which had come from Mina, whose captain was Fernando de Montarroio, who was carrying two hundred and fifty marks of gold, all in manillas and jewels, which the black men are accustomed to wear. The Admiral, who was taking with him Gaspar da Índia,[118] whom he had taken on board at Anjediva[119] [island], together with the ambassadors of the King of Kannur[120] and the King of Cochin,[121] wished them to be shown this gold, not so much because of its quantity, but rather so that they might see it still unwrought as it was, and that they might know that King Dom Manuel was lord of the mine [[of gold]], and that normally twelve or fifteen ships arrived each year bringing him a similar quantity.

11 Letter from Diogo De Alvarenga to King Manuel[122] (18/08/1503)

ABSTRACT – *Diogo de Alvarenga shares with the King of Portugal that the King of Akatakyi ('Komenda') hopes to become a Christian, and refers to the baptism of the King of Fetu, made possible by the deception of the São Jorge da*

---

[116] Vasco da Gama, on this trip, would arrive in Calicut on 30 October 1502 and return in 1503. In 1499, he had returned from his first voyage to India, at a time when the Ottoman empire was at war with Venice, and disrupting the European spice trade. The Ottomans held sway in the eastern Mediterranean, but conflicted with Venice, who controlled the sea routes to Egypt and the Levant. Da Gama brought spices back from India and these made a good profit for the Portuguese crown. The king monopolized the pepper trade as he had done with the Mina gold trade, and sought to cut out Arab-Muslim traders who conveyed pepper from Calicut through the Red Sea to Egypt. They worked in partnership with the Zamorin, Hindu sovereigns of Calicut and surrounding areas, who refused to drive away the Arabs as da Gama had urged. So, da Gama found an ally in the Raja of Calicut, who controlled the port a hundred miles south of Calicut, and who was a rival of the Zamorin.

[117] In Barros's text, '*porto Dále.*'

[118] Gaspar da Índia was a Jew born in Poland around 1444. He traveled to Jerusalem and Alexandria and was then taken prisoner and sold as a slave in India, where he obtained his freedom and served the ruler of Goa under the name Yusuf Adil. He had greeted Vasco da Gama in 1498 and was seized and baptized a Christian by da Gama under the name Gaspar da Índia. Da Índia became a pilot in da Gama's fleet and the Portuguese king granted him a petition and used him as an interpreter in other expeditions, including the 1500 voyage with Pedro Álvares and Nicolau Coelho to Brazil, meeting Amerigo Vespucci at Cape Verde. He returned to India in 1502 and in 1505 with Portuguese fleets, and to Calicut in 1510, when he presumably died.

[119] In Barros's text, '*Anchediua.*'

[120] In Barros's text, '*Cananor.*'

[121] In 1505, Cochin became capital of the Portuguese Estado da India, yet with the conquest of Goa in 1520, Goa became the capital in 1535.

[122] ANTT, CC 1-4-32. Cf. MMA vol. 1, doc. 52, pp. 190–93; Blake, *Europeans in West Africa*, pp. 94–96.

Mina captain. He also relays the construction of a church and the first mass in the capital of the Fetu. Alvarenga requests a missionary for the permanent service of the church in Fetu and for the fortress of Akyem ('Axim').

My Lord,

Diogo de Alvarenga.[123] I kiss the royal hands of Your Highness, whom I inform that, on the old cloth,[124] from the first day of the month of November of the past year one thousand and five hundred and two years up to the fifteenth day of this month of August 1503, which add up to nine months and a half, I have raised five thousand and three hundred *dobras*, namely, five thousand from the merchandise and three hundred in addition. I did not raise more because, I assure Your Highness, the cloths were in such a condition and so spoiled that they were of no use. And now, My Lord, I will hand over this House to Paio Roiz, as Your Highness commands, and I will go to Akyem, where I hope in Our Lord, should it please Him to grant me health, to serve Your Highness, as I desire. I should count it as a favor if Your Lordship would remember to write to the Captain to finish this House of Akyem, in the manner ordered by Your Highness, because, as it is now, your merchandise, together with the people, is at great risk, for, in addition to the great diseases with no cure, everything is in the hands of the black people. Thus, for many reasons, it will be very much to your service that it be finished, because Your Highness should not forget a farm which bears such good fruits and should send lime and tiles and bricks and timber to finish it, because there are none here.

Item. My Lord, Your Highness will be pleased to know that on the 21st[125] day of the month of July, the distance of three bombard shots from this fortress, the Sharif, who now is the King of Akatakyi ('Komenda'),[126] with all his people, came here to clear the roads to the fortress and allow the merchants to come. And the Captain sent me there, with eight crossbowmen, to call on him and reaffirm our friendship with him, which, Our Lord be praised, is very firm and [he] very friendly with the fortress. May it please Our Lord that it will always be so and that his wish shall be fulfilled, since he says that he wants to be a Christian.

Item. My Lord, Your Highness will be pleased to know that Sasaxi [[Sakyi]], King of Fetu, thanks to the cunning of the Captain, who above all other wishes to be of service to you, and with great commitment, was made a Christian. And on the eve of Santiago, which was the 25th day of July, he sent the Vicar and myself there, where it pleased Our Lord that, when we arrived in Fetu, with our cross raised on high and all in procession, and went to where he was, immediately after he had received the embassy which the Captain sent him, he received the

---

[123] See ANTT, *Contos do Reino e Casa, Núcleo Antigo* 867; cf. MMA vol. 4, doc. 22.

[124] In Portuguese, '*roupa velha*': see Glossary.

[125] Due to an inkblot in the manuscript, it is unclear if this should read '21st'; another possibility might be '22nd' or even '20th.'

[126] In the manuscript, '*d'acomane*' ('of Acomane'). More than likely, references to the 'King of Acomane' signaled the ruler of the Eguafoɔ ('Aguafo'; 'Guaffo,' etc.), rather than the head or leading figure—called 'sharif' by the Portuguese—of Akatakyi, a coastal settlement under said overlordship.

Baptismal Water and was converted to the Faith of Our Lord, together with six knights, the most important of the place.

Item. My Lord, on the morning of the feast of Santiago, he [the King of Fetu] ordered that a house of prayer, where mass could be said, be made in the square as quickly as possible. And when it was over, the Vicar put on his vestments and there it pleased Our Lord to look upon them, and all the most important people of the place were made Christians, as well as two of the King's wives and a son, who is now with the Captain in this fortress. And these most important people number at least three hundred. And as soon as these were made Christians, all the other people who gathered there received the Baptismal Water with much devotion, and I assure Your Highness it was a wondrous thing to see the parents take the children on their shoulders and in their arms, striving to arrive first;[127] and there were at least one thousand people or more. And after we had made them Christians, the Vicar and I made the arrangements for their chapel, with its altar and cross, which is revered beyond words. And thus, My Lord, I believe that soon the King of Ampia [?],[128] according to what he says, will be made a Christian, and likewise the one of Akatakyi ('Komenda'), as I have said. May it please Our Lord that this Christianity is in His service, and for the salvation of His souls, and peace for Your Highness, to whom I report all this because I believe Your Lordship will be pleased with it and will consider it your service, and because all was done through me and the Vicar, whom I assure Your Highness to be a very good man and deserving of your grace. And the King is called Dom João and his son Dom Manuel because this was his[129] will.

Item. I believe that it is the service of God and Your Highness that a mass be sung and said in that chapel of Santiago of Fetu once every fifteen days, so there will be more devotion and the people better Christians. If you consider it to be in your service, Your Highness should write to the Captain so that he provides for it, in addition to sending another cleric who will not be able to excuse himself; where there are two spare clerics, to have three is much service of God and Your Highness, and rest for the Vicar, who will receive grace with this. May Your Lordship not forget to provide Akyem with a cleric, for men are dying there with no confession. May the Mighty God always be pleased ever to increase your royal estate with a long life. Written in this town of yours of São Jorge da Mina, on the 18th day of August 1503.

12 Letter from the Captain of Mina to King Manuel[130] (22/12/1503)

ABSTRACT – *Letter on the state of São Jorge da Mina and work needed on it, including suggested repairs. The captain disagrees with certain letters patent*

---

[127] Tentative translation of '*a quem primeiro chegarya*' ('*a quem primeiro chegaria*'); the verb seems to be missing.
[128] In the manuscript, '*Ampya*' (extended abbreviation).
[129] 'Their'; in the manuscript, '*sua.*'
[130] ANTT, CC 1-4-42; PMA, vol. 3, pp. 343–45; cf. MMA vol. 4, doc. 8, pp. 24–27.

sent to São Jorge da Mina concerning vacancies the king was to fill. He believes clergymen from Portugal were unnecessary in Akyem ('Axim').

+

My Lord,

In a letter which the Factor and officials and I have written to Your Lordship, we have informed you about the present state of this House,[131] regarding the cloth as well as other things. And as concerns some repair work in the Factory, My Lord, about whose necessity we have written to Your Lordship, so that the cloth which is getting spoiled be well kept, I think, My Lord, that this is of much service to you, as we have written, for it seems a great deficiency in a trade as important as this not to possess a proper building so as to prevent this cloth from constantly being spoiled, as it is now, without one being able to avoid it. For every time they are put on sale, the merchants are placed in such a way that, for ten *lambéis*, they may well bring down the House;[132] and because it is small, they tread upon [the cloth], nor can they be prevented from seeing all the cloth that there is in the House, because there is no building where it can be kept out of sight; and the cloth that does not fit into the Factory, since this is too small, is now in my house. Fernão Lopes[133] can tell Your Lordship how small this House is, so much so that it is not possible to fold or to shake the *lambéis*, which is most necessary. Therefore it seems to me that much is lost in this House by not taking care of the cloth, as would be necessary, nor having a place or another building in which to store it, and that what Your Lordship loses in one or two years because of this would be enough to have this work done, which would take only a short time to be done properly, were Your Lordship to provide the means.

Because, as regards lime and freestone for stonework, they can be brought from the island of São Tomé, provided a ship comes to carry it, and the position of this [[the building]] would be along the town's ditch, in such a way that all the cloth which there is here could fit in it, and also a house could be built to keep some cloth out of sight, so that the black people do not see it and do not tread upon it, as they do now with all the cloth that there is there.

May Your Lordship consider this and speak to Fernão Lopes, who knows everything about this House and the place where it can be built, as I say, because it seems to me, My Lord, that this is of much service to you, and I would be glad if this work should be started in my time, since it befits your service more than any other.

---

[131] In Portuguese, '*Casa*,' which, in this context, could also be translated to 'warehouse.' For a discussion on the meaning and translation of '*Casa*,' see P. E. H. Hair, 'Portuguese Documents on Africa and Some Problems of Translation,' *History in Africa* 27 (2000): 91–97.

[132] Tentative translation of '[...] *estão postos os mercadores em foro que por dez lambéis derrubam toda a Casa.*'

[133] See ANTT, *Contos do Reino e Casa, Núcleo Antigo* 867, CC 1-13-48, and MMA vol. 1, doc. 123.

I have asked there, My Lord, for some roof tiles and lime to cover these warehouses and to repair some things, which could well be done now, and [[later]] they could only be repaired with twice the expense of doing them now.

And as concerns, My Lord, some letters patent Your Lordship has issued regarding vacancies, God be praised, there have been only six this year, one of them filled by a new-Christian, a retainer of João de Mendonça, hardly fit to serve Your Lordship, either here or anywhere else. In the one [[vacancy(?)]] of Lopo de Soajo, may he be with God, Diogo Martins, a *moço do monte*[134] of yours; and [[in(?)]] another, of a man who died here, a retainer of Fernão de Loronha,[135] who is here with the trade of slaves and wine. And now, My Lord, there arrived further letters patent for Diogo Fernandes, tinsmith,[136] who is also coming and whom I registered, in spite of my instructions. These have occupied vacancies which I had already filled; thus, My Lord, it is unfortunate to have to put every day before Your Lordship my services and merits, so that you do not take away a grace you have bestowed on me, because Your Lordship must take into consideration that what I had I have spent in your service, and that what I will earn I only desire for your service.

And those who ask you, My Lord, for these letters patent for those who come here, may not have left captivity as recently as myself. I would be obliged to you, My Lord, if you would recall that you have granted me these vacancies, to carry out what until now, God be praised, I had to do. And from now on I start being Captain of Mina.

And if these men who ask you, My Lord, for these letters patent, do so in order to enrich the retainers who serve them, I, My Lord, have asked for them from you so as to free another two men who were in captivity with me, something which, God be praised, until now I have not been able to achieve. And for Your Lordship to bestow this grace on me, it would be enough for me to be with those who every day vacate.

And regarding, My Lord, a letter which Your Lordship has written about sending a clergyman to Akyem, I say, My Lord, that this is not necessary, nor is it your service. Because no sooner does any one of those who are there have a headache than, by boat,[137] in one night and one day, he is here, where the equipment which is possible to have here is, since we have no neighbors,[138] nor do they want to send them to us from Portugal.

Written in your town of São Jorge, on the 22nd day of the month of December 1503.

[sign.] Diogo Lopes de Sequeira[139]

---

[134] *Moço do monte*: see Glossary.
[135] On Fernão de Loronha, see, for instance, John L. Vogt, 'Fernão De Loronha and the Rental of Brazil in 1502: A New Chronology,' *The Americas* 24, no. 2 (1967): 153–59; William B. Greenlee, 'The Captaincy of the Second Portuguese Voyage to Brazil, 1501-1502,' *The Americas* 2, no. 1 (1945): 8–11.
[136] In Portuguese, '*batefolha*,' which could also mean 'gold beater.'
[137] In Brásio's transcription, '*almadja*' ('*almadia*'): see Glossary.
[138] In Portuguese, as in Brásio's transcription, '*vizinhos*'; see Glossary.
[139] See ANTT, Tribunal do Santo Ofício, Inquisição de Lisboa, Processo 11041.

13 Mina Captain António De Miranda De Azevedo to Mina Clerk[140] (05/07/1504)

ABSTRACT – *Order of Mina captain to the clerk of São Jorge da Mina, concerning gifts to be dispatched to specific local rulers on the Mina coast. This document is published for the first time.*

I, António de Miranda de Azevado, of the Council of the King our Lord, Captain and Governor of this city and fortress of São Jorge da Mina, order you Francisco Vaz, second clerk of this factory, to deliver to the account of factor Barnabé Henriques one *pintado*, two *aljaravias*, and five and a half rods[141] of lenço de Reão and one basin which I order to be given to the Kings of Esma and of Jamou; and also one basin, one *aljaravia* and two and a half rods of lenço de Reão, which I order to be given to the king of Aldea do Torto [[Akatakyi]].[142] Done by me João Leitão first clerk of this factory on the fifth day of the month of July 1504.

[signed] António Miranda de Azevado

14 Accounts of Paio Rodrigues, Factor in Old Cloth in São Jorge Da Mina[143] (07/05/1507)

ABSTRACT – *The factor's account of old cloth at São Jorge da Mina for the period of 28 August 1503 to 20 July 1505, tabulating the amount of gold received in exchange for cloth sold at the fortress. Officials, specifically the treasurer, of the Casa da Mina examined this and other accounts.*

We have commanded an account to be taken from Paio Rodrigues, knight of our Household, of all that he received while in the office of our Factor of the Old Cloth in our town of São Jorge da Mina, from the 28th day of the month of August 1503 to the 20th of July '505, wherein it is shown that he received in all 293 marks, 2 ounces, 3 drams, 37 grains of gold of the said mine; 924 *lambéis*[144] of different kinds, used, old, and some of them torn; and 1600 *aljaravias*,[145] great and small,[146] likewise used; and also other linen for beds and tables, and clothes, and old articles which could not be sold in our great factory of the said town where he received them. He spent and delivered up this gold, these *lambéis*, aljaravias and aforesaid things, so that he had nothing left; and of all he rendered a good

---

[140] ANTT, CC 1-8-98. Transcribed in University of Ghana, Legon, Furley Collection at the Balme Library, P1 1469–1522, L2. Cf. translation, *ibid*, P1 1469–1522, L3.

[141] In Portuguese, '*vara*' (sing.): see Glossary.

[142] Akatakyi, also known as 'Komenda.'

[143] ANTT, *Místicos*, liv. 5, fol. 28. Transcribed in Anselmo Braamcamp Freire, 'Cartas de quitação,' *Arquivo Histórico Português*, IV, n. 501, p. 479.

[144] *Lambel* (sing.): see Glossary.

[145] *Aljaravia*: see Glossary.

[146] In the transcription, '*grandes e pequenos*,' which might also mean 'long and short.'

account. [...][147] Wherefore we acquit and free him from obligation. [...] Issued in Punhete,[148] on the 7th of May – João de Barros wrote this – year 1507.

15 Accounts of Aires Botelho, Factor at Akyem ('Axim')[149] (16/02/1508)

ABSTRACT – *The factor of Akyem's ('Axim') account for the period of 1 May 1505 to 31 September 1506, tabulating the amount of gold received in exchange for cloth, metals, beads, and enslaved persons sold at fort St. António, near Akyem.*

We have now commanded an account to be taken from Aires Botelho, knight of our Household, of everything which he received and spent in the seventeen months during which he acted as our Factor in the trade of Akyem, which lies in the parts of Guinea, a period which began on the first of May 1505 and ended at the end of September '506, wherein it is shown that he received in gold 727 marks, 2 ounces, 3 drams, 15 grains, namely: 38 marks, 4 ounces, 2 drams from Diogo de Alvarenga, who was Factor there before him; and 688 marks, 6 ounces, 1 dram, 15 grains from the sale of goods which were delivered to him for the said trade; and he received in addition 67.094[150] common brass manillas, and 408 shaving bowls, and 714 chamber pots, and 501 *lambéis* of *mazona,*[151] and 10 kapok [[cloths]],[152] and 6 urinal pots,[153] and 69 pots with handle(?),[154] and 164 Anhara [[*sic*] *aljaravias* and another 78 Tenes *aljaravias,* and 93 small blankets from Flanders and another 10 from the Kingdom, and 32 *alquices*[155] of coarse weave, and 102 crimson caps, and 813 rods of French fabric,[156] and 181 shells; and in addition woolen and cotton cloth, slaves, corals, beads of many sorts, Akori (glass) beads[157] from the rivers, and other articles which are used in the chapel of the said Factory, and provisions for the upkeep of the said House; and also many other things of different descriptions and kinds, as are described and declared in detail in the receipt of his said account. Which gold and other things

---

[147] This and the next ellipses are in the transcription.
[148] Today called 'Constância.'
[149] ANTT, *Chancelaria de D. Manuel,* liv. 5, fol. 20; liv. das Ilhas, fol. 175. Transcribed in Anselmo Braamcamp Freire, 'Cartas de quitação,' *Arquivo Histórico Português,* I, n. 28, p. 205. Cf. Blake, *Europeans in West Africa,* pp. 97–98.
[150] In Blake's translation, but not in Braamcamp Freire's transcription, '67,095.'
[151] In Blake's translation, between square brackets, 'hambels of Messina.' For '*lambel*' (sing.), see Glossary.
[152] In the transcription, '*painas*,' cloths made of a very fine type of cotton.
[153] In the transcription, '*bacios machos*' ('male pots'), possibly urinal pots, as Blake has it, specifically designed for men.
[154] Tentative translation of '*caldeiras de aro*' ('*aro*' meaning 'ring').
[155] *Alquice*: a kind of cape, usually white (see *Dicionário de Morais,* under '*alquicé,*' and Blake's footnote on page 98).
[156] In the transcription, '*lenço,*' any type of cotton or linen fabric.
[157] On *Akori* (glass) beads from Benin, see Milan Kalous, 'A Contribution to the Problem of Akori Beads,' *The Journal of African History* 7, no. 1 (1966): 61–66.

are shown to have been spent by him correctly, according to our Regulations, which were issued to him, in such a way that nothing was left to be spent, as was also confirmed by the receipt of the said account,[158] which was examined and completed in our Exchequer, wherefore we acquit and free from obligation [...][159] the said Aires Botelho [...]. Issued in Almeirim, on the 16th of February – João de Barros wrote it – year 1508.

16 List of Residents at São Jorge Da Mina[160] (01/02/1509)

ABSTRACT – *List of Portuguese officials and residents, as well as enslaved and local African 'hostages' from ruling families, often a son, residing in São Jorge da Mina and Akyem ('Axim'), courtesy of a monthly list for those who will receive rations of bread. The details for each person listed surpasses the allotment of bread and provide insights into the inner workings of the fortress-city and its internal relations between officials, residents, captives, servants, and women and men.*

List of the residents in the town of São Jorge da Mina, among whom João Mealhas, Overseer of the Oven-house of the said town, will distribute the rations of bread during the month of February 1509.

Further: Instructions from Aires de Sequeira, Factor, Francisco Fróis, Scribe of the Expenditure and Factor of the Old Cloth, and Simão Fernandes, Scribe of the Expenditure, all of them of São Jorge da Mina, to the contadores[161] of the Royal Household to account on behalf of João Mealhas the flour spent in that distribution. 6 March 1509.

List of the persons who shall receive a ration of bread in this month of February '509, namely one ration per person:

Item: Cristóvão Lopes, Vicar	1 person
Item: Duarte Rodrigues, Chaplin	1 person
Item: Captain Afonso de Bobadilha, together with twenty-eight persons, namely, six men of his who are allotted to him, and two porters, and a caulker, and a stonemason, and eight vacant men from among those registered,[162] and nine supernumerary men,[163] and one woman, all of whom are allotted to him by letter-patent of Our Lord the King	28[*sic*] persons

---

[158] The passage from 'Which gold [...]' to '[...] the receipt of the said account [...]' is missing in Blake's translation.
[159] This and the next ellipsis are in the transcription.
[160] ANTT, CC-2-16-123; PMA, vol. 3, pp. 490–3.
[161] *Contador*: see Glossary.
[162] Tentative translation of '*avagamtes do numarro*' ('*vagantes do número*').
[163] In the transcription, '*sobressalemtes*' ('*sobressalentes*'), which might also be translated as 'extra' or 'spare men.'

Item: Diogo Botelho, chief *Alcaide*,[164] with one man of his, who is allotted to him	2 persons
Item: Aires de Sequeira, Factor, with four men of his	5 persons
Item: Simão Fernandes, Scribe of the Expenditure	1 person
Item: Francisco Fróis, Scribe of the Expenditure and Factor of the Old Cloth, with a man of his whom he is entitled to with the old cloth	2 persons
Item: Martim Mendes, Scribe of the Revenue	1 person
Item: Simão Nunes, Scribe of the Revenue	1 person
Item: Diogo Carreiro, *Meirinho*[165]	1 person
Item: Manuel Mendes, *Almoxarife*[166]	1 person
Item: João Mealhas, Overseer of the Oven-house	1 person
Item: Luís Álvares, Scribe of the *Almoxarifado*	1 person
Item: Gaspar de Sequeira	1 person
Item: Master Fernando, physician	1 person
Item: Pedro Gomes	1 person
Item: Diogo Fernandes, Factor of the Shells	1 person
Item: Miguel Enantolaço	1 person
Item: Manuel Dias	1 person
Item: the apothecary	1 person
Item: Sebastião Dias	1 person
Item: Luís Afonso	1 person
Item: Lourenço Lopes, Scribe of Akyem[167]	1 person
Item: João Álvares, bombarder	1 person
Item: Diogo Martins, cooper	1 person
Item: Lopo da Nova, blacksmith	1 person
Supernumerary man	
Item: Pedro Álvares Colaço	1 person
Extra men	
Item: Friar Diogo Zagalo	1 person
Item: Álvaro Fernandes	1 person
Item: João Álvares	1 person
Item: Francisco Enes,[168] clergyman of Akyem	1 person

[164] *Alcaide*: see Glossary.
[165] *Meirinho*: see Glossary.
[166] *Almoxarife/Almoxarifado*: see Glossary.
[167] In the margin: '*começou aver a b dias*' [['*começou a haver há 5 dias*']], 'he started receiving five days ago.'
[168] 'Eanes.'

Journeymen[169]	
Item: João, *Meirinho*[170]	1 person
Item: Rodrigo, stonemason	1 person
Women	
Item: Inês Rodrigues	1 person
Item: Catarina Vasques	1 person
Item: Catarina Pires de Barros	1 person
Item: Genebra Ripanço	1 person
Item: you shall give to the Captain's house for children of kings who eat at his table	half a ration
Item: Dom João Serrão[171]	1 person
Item: Fernão[172] Pepim	1 person
Slaves of Our Lord the King	
Item: Fernão de Ávila	1 person
Item: Catarina, his wife	1 person
Seamen of the *caravelão*[173]	
Item: Nicolau Lopes, pilot	1 person
Item: João Enes	1 person
Item: Álvaro Dias	1 person
Item: Pedro Lopes	1 person
Item: Pedro Martins	1 person
Item: João, cabin boy	1 person
Item: Lourenço, cabin boy	1 person
Item: Cristóvão	1 person
Item: Roque Malagueta	1 person

To each of these persons, contained in this list, you shall give his ration of bread, as instructed therein. Written on the first day of February '509 years.

Francisco Fróis

Aires de Sequeira

Simão Fernandes

In this list I have not given any ration beyond the fifteenth day of the present month.

---

[169] In Portuguese, '*oficiais jornaleiros*': skilled workers paid by the day.
[170] Probably, the office and not a surname; for '*Meirinho*,' see Glossary.
[171] In the transcription, 'Saram.'
[172] 'Fernando,' since these two names are interchangeable.
[173] *Caravelão*: see Glossary.

17 List of Residents and their Ration at São Jorge Da Mina[174] (01/03/1509)

ABSTRACT – *A list of Portuguese officials and residents at São Jorge da Mina and Akyem as in the previous month, but with some new and revealing details. This and the prior list provides rare monthly sets of activities which could have been—when extrapolated forward—representative of 'normal' activities during a given year.*

List of the residents in the town of São Jorge da Mina, among whom João Mealhas, Overseer of the Oven-house of the said town, will distribute the rations of bread during the month of March 1509.

Further: Instructions from Aires de Sequeira, Factor, Francisco Fróis, Factor of the Old Cloth, and Simão Fernandes, Scribe, all of them of São Jorge da Mina, to the contadores[175] of the Royal Household to account on behalf of João Mealhas the flour spent in that distribution. 31 March 1509.

List of the persons who shall receive a ration of bread in this month of March of the era of '509 years

Item: Estêvão Lopes, Vicar	1 person
Item: Duarte Rodrigues, Chaplain	1 person
Item: Captain Afonso de Bobadilha, together with twenty-eight persons, namely, six men of his who are allotted to him, and two porters, and a caulker, and a stonemason, and eight vacant men om among those registered,[176] and nine supernumerary men,[177] and one woman, all of whom are allotted to him and who, together with his person, make 28 persons in all	28[*sic*] persons
Item: the chief *Alcaide*[178] Diogo Botelho, with one man who is allotted to him	2 persons
Item: Aires de Sequeira, Factor, together with five persons who are allotted to him	5[*sic*] persons
Item: Simão Fernandes, First Scribe	1 person
Item: Francisco Fróis, Factor of the Old Cloth, with one man	2 persons
Item: Martim Mendes, Scribe of the Revenue	1 person
Item: Lourenço Lopes, Scribe of Akyem	1 person

---

[174] ANTT, CC-2-16-161; PMA, vol. 3, pp. 504–9.
[175] *Contador*: see Glossary.
[176] Tentative translation of '*avagamtes do numoro*' ('*vagantes do número*').
[177] In the transcription, '*ssobressalemtes*' ('*sobressalentes*'), which might also be translated as 'extra' or 'spare men.'
[178] *Alcaide*: see Glossary.

Item: Simão Nunes, Scribe of the Revenue	1 person
Item: Diogo Carreiro, *Meirinho*[179]	1 person
Item: Manuel Mendes, *Almoxarife*[180]	1 person
Item: Luís Álvares, Scribe of the *Amoxarifado*	1 person
Item: João Mealhas, Overseer of the Oven-house	1 person
Item: Master Fernando, physician	1 person
Item: Pedro Gomes, wine seller	1 person
Item: Miguel Colaço	1 person
Item: Gaspar de Sequeira	1 person
Item: Engriote[*sic*] Lopes	1 person
Item: the apothecary	1 person
Item: Sebastião Dias, barber	1 person
Item: Luís Afonso, resident	1 person
Item: João Álvares, bombarder	1 person
Item: Diogo Martins, cooper	1 person
Item: Lopo da Nova, blacksmith	1 person
Item: Diogo Fernandes, sheller, Factor of the Shells	1 person
Supernumerary men	
Item: Pedro Álvares Colaço	1 person
The ordinary	
Item: Friar Diogo Zagala	1 person
Item: Álvaro Fernandes, clergyman	1 person
Item: João Álvares, clergyman	1 person
Journeymen[181]	
Item: João, *Meirinho*[182]	1 person
Item: Rodrigo Eanes, stonemason	1 person
Women	
Item: Inês Rodrigues	1 person
Item: Catarina Vasques	1 person
Item: Catarina Pires	1 person
Item: Genebra	1 person
Black hostages	

---

[179] *Meirinho*: see Glossary.
[180] *Almoxarife/Almoxarifado*: see Glossary.
[181] In Portuguese, '*oficiais jornaleiros*': skilled workers paid by the day.
[182] Probably, the office and not a surname; for '*Meirinho*,' see Glossary.

Item: Dom João Serrão[183]	1 person
Item: Fernando Papim[184]	1 person
King's slaves	
Item: Fernão de Avela	1 person
Item: Catarina, his wife	1 person
Item: Francisco, blacksmith	1 person
Item: Jaca	1 person
Item: Francisco, of the oven-house	1 person
Item: Aneda[185]	1 person
Item: Papagaio[186]	1 person
Item: Manicongo	1 person
Item: João	1 person
Item: Tomé	1 person
Item: Alicaga,[187] who makes baskets	1 person
Item: Anicuiu[188]	1 person
Item: the Calle,[189] half a ration	half a ration
You shall give to nine slaves of Our Lord the King who serve in the kneading-house	9 persons
Item: you shall give half a ration to the Captain's house, for the children of the merchants	half a ration
Item: you shall give Gafa	half a ration
Item: you shall give Maria Afonso	half a ration
Seamen of the *caravelão*[190]	
Item: Nicolau Lopes	1 person
Item: João Enes[191]	1 person
Item: Álvaro Dias	1 person
Item: Pedro Lopes	1 person
Item: Pedro Martins	1 person
Item: João	1 person

---

[183] In the transcription, 'Saram.'
[184] 'Pepim,' which is a placename, as appears in Document 16.
[185] In the transcription, 'Amda,' though it seems the scribe added an 'e' to the word which the transcriber did not identify.
[186] In English, 'Parrot,' probably a nickname.
[187] In the transcription, 'Allyquaga.'
[188] 'Aniquiu'; in the transcription, 'Aniquyhu.'
[189] Meaning obscure; probably a name.
[190] *Caravelão*: see Glossary.
[191] 'Eanes,' which is interchangeable.

Item: Lourenço	1 person
Item: Cristóvão	1 person
Item: Malagueta	1 person
You shall give to Francisco de Brito, Factor of Akyem, together with a man who is allotted to him, two rations	2 persons
Item: João Henriques, Scribe	1 person
Item: Catarina Fernandes, a woman from Akyem	1 person
Item: you shall give a ration to two slaves from Akyem	2 persons

To each of these persons, contained in this list, you shall give his ration of bread, as instructed therein. Written on the first day of the said month.

Aires de Sequeira

Simão Fernandes

Francisco Fróis

Item:[192] to Rui Lobo, Factor of Akyem, with a man of his	2 persons
Item: to Francisco Enes, clergyman	1 person
Item: Francisco, formerly a man of the scribes of Akyem	1 person

Simão Fernandes

Contadores[193] of the Household of Our Lord the King, you shall account on behalf of João Mealhas, overseer of the oven-house of this town of São Jorge, three hundred and forty-seven *alqueires*[194] and four rations which he spent with the residents in this town, from the month [*sic*] of March '509 until the end of the said month, as shown in this list. Written on the last day of the said month of March '509 years.

Aires de Sequeira

Francisco Fróis

Simão Fernandes

---

[192] In the margin: 'These started receiving on the 21st day.'
[193] *Contador(es)*: see Glossary.
[194] *Alqueire(s)*: see Glossary.

18 Letter from Pedro Ferreira
to King Manuel[195] (05/10/1509)

ABSTRACT – *A letter to King Manuel about safeguarding the important caravels that procure gold from Mina. The letter also concerns the bundling of merchandise, the wine supply to Mina, and personnel salaries.*

We have received four letters from Your Highness, in which you order us to reply to them and give a reasoned opinion regarding some of the matters mentioned there concerning the government of the town of São Jorge da Mina, which have been discussed between us all, as Your Highness ordered.

As regards what Your Highness says, namely, that, in your opinion, the main thing that gives rise to these disservices is the lack of care as regards the guard of the caravels, and that you would be pleased that we should discuss the best manner of guarding the said caravels; and whether it would be a good thing to replace the present guards with other persons of a different quality; and whether they should be more or less [numerous], or what should be the ordinance issued as regards this matter for the better performance of your service; and furthermore that we should immediately write to Your Highness [informing you] how many guards there are at present, by name, and for how long each of them has been serving; and whether any of them has bought the office which he now holds by your license –

– My Lord, the guard which is now kept in the caravels of Mina is the same as has always been ordered by Your Highness's regulations, namely, before anything is loaded, most of the times, as often as we can, we go to the caravel and, in our presence, the hold is so thoroughly searched by the guards who will be guarding her, that nothing remains unsearched. And once this has been done, the Factor consigns to them the keys of the hatches, thereupon leaving the said guards inside the caravel, which nobody can leave, by day or night, without at least one of them staying in the caravel. And every day, at nightfall, the keys of the hatches are brought back to the said Factor, who returns them again on the following morning. And before the caravel sets sail, we always go on board and, in our presence, she is searched once more for chests, bundles and other articles we find on deck, because what is below deck cannot be searched and depends entirely on what the guards have already done. And a muster is taken, as ordered in the aforesaid regulations, and then we return and the caravel sets sail, taking the guards as far as Restelo.[196] And this, My Lord, is thus ordained and governed, and it seems to us in accordance with what is fitting for your service. And in this

---

[195] ANTT, CC 1-8-45; PMA, vol. 5, pp. 589–93; cf. MMA vol. 4, doc. 14.
[196] MMA (vol. 4, doc. 14) adds the following footnote to his transcription: 'The same as '*restolho*' ['stubble']. A place in Lisbon, currently occupied by the Praça do Império [Empire Square] and the [Monastery of the] Jerónimos, and whence ships used to depart to [the] open sea.'

case of the gold which is thought to come from Mina otherwise than as it should, we can only presume and believe that it is brought in return for what is taken from here against your regulations and through these guards and pilots of the caravels, who are often and sufficiently admonished and warned by Estêvão Vaz, as much as is proper and fitting to your service, though whether they err in this and do not observe it, until now we have not been able to ascertain or know for sure, notwithstanding our belief that thus Your Highness receives much disservice in this matter.

Also, My Lord, it is our opinion that, in the caravels that go to the island of São Tomé, many things are taken from here, which are then transferred from the said island to Mina with the collusion of those who are there and deal with them, this being another loophole through which the order of your regulations and guard may be seriously broken, and for which until now there has been no satisfactory remedy. And as regards the replacement of the said guards by persons of a different quality, it is our opinion that what these now do could be done by others, provided that[?][197] they are more or less robust and, possibly, with less fear and more audacity. And for these good men would be needed, known to be such, and not just anybody. And this is so well ordered and as befits your service, that we could not find a better solution for this, because its defects[198] lie only in the wrongdoing of the guards, which cannot in any way be prevented as long as they desire to do what they should not. The guards who are now serving here are ten in all. Namely, João Duarte and Francisco Ferreira and Tristão Roiz, a retainer of Dom Gonçalo Coutinho, to whom you granted their offices five years ago; and André Cubelos, who was *Moço do Monte*[199] of the late King – may God keep him – who sent him here to serve in this office more than 20 years ago, and he is still serving in it; and João Rebelo, who was formerly a member of the Guard of the Palace of Your Highness, who granted him the said office, and he [still] serves here; and Rui de Alagoa,[200] who used to be *Reposteiro*[201] of the late King – may God keep him – who granted him this office, [and] it is now 15 years that he has been serving in it; and Estêvão Martins, who was formerly a retainer of Fernão Serrão and obtained the office in the time of Fernão Lourenço by purchase from a certain Pedro Barroso, who was a porter and guard here by license of Your Highness, it is now seven years; and Pedro Lopes, who was a *peloteiro*,[202] to whom Your Highness granted this office two years ago; and João de Freitas, who was formerly *Fiel*[203] of the House of Ceuta, and Pedro Gomes, who was Scribe of

[197] In the manuscript, '*ajmda que*' ('*ainda que*'), literally 'even if,' which does not make sense here.
[198] In Portuguese, '*desconcerto,*' which literally means 'disconcertment.'
[199] *Moço do Monte*: see Glossary.
[200] '*Rui da Lagoa.*'
[201] *Reposteiro*: see Glossary.
[202] *Peloteiro*: a maker of pellets. In Brásio's edition (MMA vol. 4, doc. 14), the transcription (expanding an abbreviation) reads '*pelo tesoureiro,*' i.e. 'by the treasurer,' which does not make much sense in this context.
[203] *Fiel*: see Glossary.

the Unloading[204] of the Ships and Solicitor of the Customs House,[205] whom Your Highness favored with these offices a year ago. And as regards Your Highness's question, whether they be too many or too few, for the caravels of Mina alone they would be more than enough, but for the business and ships of India they could not be any less.

And as regards Your Highness's opinion that it is most inconvenient that the pilots and seamen of this House's caravels should themselves make up the dunnage and package the merchandise which is to go in each caravel inside the said House, as has been done until now, and that for this purpose the men appointed[206] by the Treasurer would suffice, for the business is scant and fitful – this manner of bundling by the seamen is still observed, and was always observed previously, because, though it may not seem to Your Highness very demanding, it is always necessary to employ in it at least eight or ten people for five or six days, which are occupied with shaking the *lambéis*, and folding and packaging them, and with counting and weighing the manillas and brass, which are always in great quantity and require much handling; and with fewer people it would not be possible to get the caravels ready to sail without several days' delay, which would interfere very much with other affairs of the House, and thus in this it is not possible to find a better solution. And because over the last few days Estêvão Vaz has suspected that the seamen put, or could put, some shells and Akori beads and other small items in these packs, since then, when the cloth is given out, we are present and the said packs are not to be made up except in our presence, so that we supervise it carefully, in order that, from now on, nothing to your disservice may take place.

And as regards the red wines that go for the supply of Mina, Your Highness has been informed that they are such as go bad, and they are no good either as wine or as vinegar, and in this you receive much disservice. And you order us to find out at once where these wines come from and the reason why they go bad, and where can one find better wines, so they do not go bad[207] and there be no disservice to you. In this, My Lord, we cannot give a reasoned opinion to Your Highness, because the said wines are bought and sent to Mina by Jorge de Vasconcelos[208] and officials of the storehouse who, by order and command of Your Highness, are in charge of supplying all provisions to Mina, as well as to other places. And we do not buy wines other than those from Caparica for sale at Mina, as they are sent as merchandise. Your Highness may have the said Jorge de Vasconcelos asked about this. And as to where can one find better wines, it is known that the best is those from Ribatejo and this city's environs,[209] whence Estêvão Vaz says that Mina always got its supplies, and likewise for the use of the

---

[204] In Portuguese, '*Escrivão da Descarrega.*'

[205] In Portuguese, '*Requeredor da Alfândega.*'

[206] In the manuscript, '*ordenados,*' literally 'ordained.'

[207] The passage '[...] and also where / can one find better wines, so they do not go bad [...]' is missing in Brásio's transcription (MMA vol. 4, doc. 14).

[208] See MMA vol. 4, doc. 32.

[209] In Portuguese, '*termo,*' the countryside around a village or city.

captains and scribes and seamen of the caravels, and he has already said this and written about it to Your Highness several times.

And as regards the salary which was paid to Francisco de Góis before he presented his accounts of the Factory of the Old Cloth,[210] he received the said salary at the same time as the other scribes and residents who came with Bobadilha,[211] after they had presented a certificate by Rui Gomes, Judge of Guinea, to João Martins of the Mint – who is in charge of making the payments on these bills together with João de Ferreira, who takes note of them – which states that there is no impediment on the part of Your Highness, and he was paid like all the others. And because he was not appointed here as the Factor of the Old Cloth but took office there through vacancy of André da Gama, it did not occur that anyone other than the Factor of Mina should present accounts, and this is why his salary has been held back. And now, as soon as we read this message from Your Highness, he was summoned to this House and pressed either to return his salary or to give some security for it until he presented his accounts. And he replied that he was a prisoner and that by order of Your Highness he had offered security for both accounts and salary, [and] that he would do whatever else Your Highness ordered. May Your Highness order what we should do for your service.

The regulations of the Captain, Factor and officers of São Jorge that were in this House and which Your Highness orders that we send to you, are carried by João Rebelo and are a copy of those which are kept there, together with the register of certain letters and other documents[212] which Your Highness sent there after the regulations had been concluded. There is no other [copy] here and it is advisable that Your Highness should return it because there is no time to copy it before it goes.

Written from Lisbon, on the 5th day of October 1509.

       [sign.] *Estêvão Vaz*   *Rui Gomes*   *Álvaro Barroso*

                                            João de Ferreira[213]

When Francisco de Góis was paid, I, Estêvão Vaz, was in Sintra by Your Highness's command.

[left corner]:
Letter from the House of Mina Already replied to
To Our Lord the King
From the House of Guinea

---

[210] In Portuguese, '*Feitoria da Roupa Velha*': see Glossary.
[211] MMA vol. 4, doc. 14, adds the following footnote: 'Cf. [MMA], [vol.] I, p. 212, where *Bouadilha* [or *Bobadilha*] is wrongly transcribed as Bonadilha.' See ANTT, *Contos do Reino e Casa, Núcleo Antigo* 867, and MMA vol. 1, doc. 61.
[212] In the manuscript, '*aluaraães*' ('*alvarás*'), a broad term used for different kinds of official documents.
[213] Signatures appear in Brásio's transcription (MMA vol. 4, doc. 14), though not in the manuscript.

19 Letter from Manuel De Góis
to King Manuel[214] (1510)

ABSTRACT – *Letter from Manuel de Góis to King Manuel, in which the signatory denounces certain irregularities officials of the factories committed against the Royal Exchequer, and puts forward measures to remedy the commerce of Mina.*

My Lord,

It is many days now that, based on experience, I have wished to show Your Highness [...] the fruit of my knowledge about the matters of your Exchequer and kingdoms [...] against, of which Your Highness presently has, for the little time that [...] wished to make use, because of the complaints against me presented to Your Highness by certain persons, whose faults and names I will not reveal, since I am a party concerned in this case and also because I am certain that, from long ago, Your Highness has known them as friends not of your property but rather of theirs, the evidence of which Your Highness may perceive by the growth of their wealth since they were appointed to your offices, and which may show you who serves you faithfully, among whom myself – not that this has brought me any rest, but rather much labor and the loss of my property and honor, from which I have suffered damage, and will continue to suffer until Your Highness is assured of who I am and how much I wish to serve you. Of this I am very doubtful, because I am certain that Your Highness does not know me, nor is there anyone who could speak to you about me – not ill, because I do not follow, or serve, or will serve anyone, but Your Highness, for no one can serve two people at the same time without vexing one or both of them. And I, My Lord, not to put myself in a position to disserve[215] Your Highness, if I were to serve another person I would necessarily have to steal from you and give to someone who would speak to Your Highness about me, with which offers I would make him praise me before Your Highness and say that I was what I was not, thus placing myself in your good graces at the expense of your Exchequer. Of these deceptions I have never wanted to make use and therefore, My Lord, I do not have anyone to favor me, except God; because this is true, and He shall favor it, and help whoever makes use of it, and open for me the path through which Your Highness may know who I am and how much I wish to serve you. This Your Highness may know from the time when, last year, in Almeirim, you began to hear it from me. As the time was short and the case I put forward obscure, because I wanted to put it in few words, though it would have been necessary to put it in many to make it clear,

---

[214] ANTT, *Fragmentos, Cartas para el-Rei*, Cx.1, Mç.1, n. 19; PMA, vol. 5, pp. 620–27.

[215] In the transcription, '*de sservir*' ('*de servir*' – 'to serve'), with a footnote added noting the repetition of the preposition '*de*.' In fact, in the manuscript it reads '*de desserujr*' ('*de desservir*' – 'to disserve').

and because of the shortness of time, Your Highness was not pleased to hear me about the case which I then put forward, as well as about another four cases, each of which might be worth above six thousand *cruzados* for your Exchequer. And I will make any person recognize this who may want to deny it. And so that Your Highness may see how certain I am of what I know, let Your Highness summon those who are best informed about your Exchequer, who are the Count of Vila Nova, and the Baron, and thirdly António Salvago, who are persons who must know it well, since these are matters which harm them. [And] I, My Lord, after expounding the cases, will make them acknowledge that what I say is true, because what I will tell Your Highness will be well told, for I know it very well, and not by speculation but rather by experience, because, My Lord, I went twice to Flanders, on one occasion during the time of Tomé Lopes and on another of João Brandão; and I went to Venice in the time of Vicente Roiz; and I have been in the factories of Castile in the time of João Carreiro, and afterwards of Nuno Ribeiro; and I have been in Mina in the time of Dom Martinho da Silveira; and I have stayed in the overseas territories for four and a half years; and I come from Beja, where Your Highness has wheat and other supplies bought; and in all these places, My Lord, in which I have been, as I say, I have seen your officials and factors, and the way they deal with your property, and how each of them serves you, which have never, and still do not, please me, since I saw how absolutely everyone steals from you. And may Your Highness be sure that, among those who deal with it, your property is contraband, as he who steals less is known as a fool. The description of which is unnecessary for someone who can learn it as easily as Your Highness, should you desire to watch for your property. And being able, as Your Highness is, to prevent them from serving you ill, you will not only benefit your Exchequer but also its profits, as they turn away from serving God and Your Highness, taking from your Exchequer more than what is allotted to them by Your Highness. Of which matters as I claim to know there is one Your Highness may now see, by starting with the matters of Mina. And this can be the way Your Highness may adopt to preserve its affairs and to be able, should you be willing, to dispense with guards to inspect the caravels, provided it be done according to the manner I will describe, which is the following and which will seem impossible to Your Highness before you see it.

Item: And so that Your Highness may better understand what I will say, it seems to me that it will be necessary to describe to Your Highness the ways, which are many, in which everyone tries to steal, and by no other means can you protect yourself except by this.[216] The manner of stealing is as follows: as soon as the caravels reach the port of Mina, without further delay and before any person goes ashore, an *almadia*[217] comes from the castle bearing two scribes and the

---

[216] In the transcription, '*e per nhũa outra vya sse defender podesse per esta nom,*' should read, in modern spelling, '*e por nenhuma outra via se defender pode, se por esta não.*' The translated phrase is then, 'and by no other means can you protect yourself, except by this.'

[217] *Almadia*: see Glossary.

meirinho,[218] according to Your Highness's regulations, who are believed to come to inspect the caravels in the manner stipulated by Your Highness, though [[in reality]] they come to trade, making their profit and your loss, through speaking with the captains, scribes and pilots of the caravels and, while pretending that they are asking them for news from Portugal, they ask them about the goods they are bringing, and they buy them, and they immediately take all they can with them […] these are cowries, and grey beads, and shells, and coral, and every other merchandise of the same type which can be taken in secret, since they are of small size and great worth. And the other large items, such as linen and colored cloths, and every sort of goods, are negotiated with their proprietors, saying to them that they will be ready at a given hour of the night; and at the hour agreed between them, they send an *almadia* to the caravel, at midnight or at eleven, and the one who is expecting it is ready and, bringing the *almadia* alongside [[the caravel]], throws the merchandise which he has into the boat, and he returns to shore and gives the merchandise to the one who had sent him to get it. And if the scribes and *meirinhos* who go to the caravels should be unable to trade with any people, such as seamen, because they do not trust them or because they do not show them their merchandise at that time, when they go ashore on certain days when they are allowed to, they get together in twos under an arbor which there is, and there, in secrecy, negotiate with one another and, while appearing to discuss and talk about matters related to Portugal, make their arrangements and sell their goods as well as they can. And as for those goods which they cannot take [[from the caravel]] since they might be caught, an agreement is reached between the parties and an *almadia* is sent during the night, as I have already said; and the one who delivers the goods keeps watch until the *almadia* arrives, and as soon as it arrives he hands over the goods which he has with him, and if those in the caravel sense that he [[in the *almadia*]] is there, he escapes, and goes away, and he returns as many times as needed until he is able to finish what had brought him there. And this is the manner, My Lord, in which those who are in Mina supply themselves with the merchandise which goes from here, and they cover up for each other so that they may succeed. And for Your Highness to be able to prohibit and forbid that goods be taken from here there is only one way, which is the following: that Your Highness may find a way to prevent these men from speaking in confidence with one another. And once confidences are forbidden and they not allowed to tell secrets, they will have no way of selling their goods; and once they know for sure that they will not be able to sell them there, they will not bother with taking them from here; and if they do not take them, there will be no need for guards, and we are certain that those who do not take goods will not bring more gold than that which they will be able to earn from [[the sale of]] those items which Your Highness allows them to take. Because, My Lord, [[gold]] is not given there for free but is rather more valued

---

[218] *Meirinho*: see Glossary.

by the black people of that land than by any others. And the reason why I say that those who take prohibited goods will not be able to sell them, or make any arrangements, if they cannot speak in confidence, is obvious: and no one can in effect deny that someone who has no way of speaking in confidence with those to whom he would sell his merchandise will be obliged to throw it into the sea or bring it back to Portugal; because if I would now take prohibited goods to Mina, while not being allowed to speak in confidence with anyone from there, there would be no way of saying out loud to the one who would buy them from me 'I, so & so, am bringing such & such goods, would you like to buy them from me?', because I cannot say this without being heard by all. Now, if someone would want to speak by gestures, they would not be understood, nor would it be possible for him to say what goods he had brought with him; and if it would be possible to understand by gestures, which it is not, it would not be possible to know what those goods were or what should be offered for them, nor would there be a way to send someone by night to the caravel to fetch them, because he could not be sure of anything, since neither the buyer would be able to know the hour or the day, nor the seller could know on what day and at what time the buyer should send someone to the caravel to fetch the said goods; and, not knowing the exact time, he would not wait. And even if the one making the purchase,[219] My Lord, had any means, during the night, of sending any goods he might have in an *almadia* which might have been sent to him for that purpose, it is not to be believed that there would be any man willing to put his property at risk by sending it to someone before speaking with the one making the purchase, and saying what goods he had brought and the price he [[the buyer]] should pay for them. And after he [[the buyer]] is informed about the goods [[the seller]] has brought and how much he should pay for them, he says to the one selling the goods 'Be ready on such night, at such time, and an *almadia* will be sent to you and will make a signal; and when the *almadia* makes the said signal, you will give him the goods, and not otherwise'. And when the seller is certain of this, he will be on the alert for the hour when the *almadia* will arrive, and when he sees it, together with the signal, he will gather that it is the one he was waiting for and give him the merchandise which he has brought, and not otherwise. Now, if they are forbidden to speak in confidence, they will have no way of selling their merchandise. Your Highness would agree that, if these men are certain that they will not be able to trade the goods which they may take from here to Mina, they will prefer not to take them rather than, having taken them, be forced to bring them back or throw them into the sea, since they would necessarily have to choose between one of these two. And the manner, My Lord, in which this should be dealt with, in order not to create a hindrance to either party, namely the residents and the caravels, is the following.

---

[219] This must be a mistake and should read 'seller' instead.

74 *Documents*

Your Highness will know that the castle of São Jorge da Mina is as far from
the sea as Your Highness's balconies from the stone pier.[220] So, My Lord, as I was
saying, if Your Highness approves of what I have written above, for this to be well
carried out and have the effect which Your Highness desires, which is to have a
way of keeping what is yours:

- Your Highness should have an enclosure built in the port, where the
  boats land, which is next to the sea, on an elevation which there is in the
  said port, very convenient for such a purpose and a good place to have an
  enclosure built, large enough for the people who should be there, made
  of stone and lime, or clay, or as Your Highness may order, circular or
  square, or as Your Highness may find best, of the height of a man's waist
  or slightly higher, built in a way that a man may lean on it and speak
  with those outside as from a stair or balcony parapet. Which enclosure,
  My Lord, should have two doors, one towards the sea and the other
  towards the land, with its doors and an arbor of the size of the enclosure,
  like the one which there is above, in the castle. And the making of all
  this, My Lord, will cost above sixty thousand *reis*;
- and Your Highness should order, under heavy penalty, the residents[221]
  as well as the captains of the caravels not to allow any resident[222] to
  enter the caravels, namely scribes, *meirinhos*, or any other persons. And
  Your Highness should order that, as soon as the caravel arrives, the boat
  be hoisted out, and the captain, and the scribe, and the pilot, and all
  of them, if they all want to, go on shore, and they shall be obliged,[223]
  under heavy penalty, to enter together the enclosure and arbor which
  was made for them immediately after landing. And the captain of the
  caravel, as soon as they are in the said enclosure and arbor, will have it
  shut. And those from the castle shall go there to fetch their letters and
  news from the Kingdom, though without getting close to the enclosure,
  from which they shall stand three or four steps apart, according to some
  marks which shall be made beyond the enclosure, so that they may not
  go beyond them or get close to the said enclosure. From that place they
  shall ask whatever they may wish, and they shall receive their letters,
  which shall be read publicly before being handed over to the parties.
  And on the day set for the delivery of the goods brought from here,
  the captain of the caravel shall order their men to put them on shore,
  outside the enclosure, towards the castle. And as soon as all the goods

[220] 'Your Highness's balconies from the stone pier': reference to the Paço da Ribeira ('Riverside Palace') and the stone pier just close by, in the Terreiro do Paço ('Palace Yard'), both built during Dom Manuel's reign.
[221] In the manuscript, '(a)os da terra,' literally '(to) those of the land.'
[222] See previous note.
[223] In the transcription, 'defesso' ('defeso'), which means 'prohibited,' though here clearly in the sense of 'obligatory.'

are put on shore, the captain of the caravel, together with all his men, shall return to the enclosure and, when they are there, he shall call the Factor and scribes to come and receive the goods, and from the inside of the enclosure he shall deliver them to the Factor and scribes, which, My Lord, may be easily done. And when they come to the delivery of the gold, they should deliver it from the same place where they receive the merchandise, which is outside the enclosure, since it seems to me, My Lord, that it is not necessary to weigh the gold before the scribe and captain of the caravel, given that the coffer is fastened and sealed, and the key is thrown into the sea; it would be sufficient to weigh it in the castle, in the presence of the scribes and the Factor, and this seems to me to be sufficient to dispense with weighing it before the captain and scribe of the caravel, since the coffer is fastened and sealed with a recognizable seal, and it is not possible to unseal or open it without it being detected. And should Your Highness nevertheless wish to have it weighed, the gold should be received in the same way as the merchandise. And on the day appointed for both parties to hold a fair, the manner shall be the same as in the delivery of the merchandise, those selling standing inside [[the enclosure]] and those buying outside everything they may have brought being sold at their will. And if this is carried out in this manner, Your Highness will be well served and those of the caravels will be glad, since they will remain the whole day on shore and they will return to their ships in the evening, which presently they cannot do, since they are always on board the caravel, except for those days on which they are allowed to go to the castle, and also to get water and firewood for the voyage; which water and firewood Your Highness should order the Factor of the castle to have brought by Your Highness's black people, who are there for the trade. And this should be done, My Lord, because if these people leave the ship, they may speak in confidence with the residents and, thus speaking, do what they want. And this manner, My Lord, should also be followed with the passengers, both those who go from here and those who come from there, so that those who will leave from here will only go to the fortress when the caravel is about to leave; and should a passenger come in the caravel, he should not mix with the caravel crew, except at the appointed hour and day for the departure of the caravel, so that they may not give warning beforehand. And if there should be two caravels or more in the port, then the procedure will consist in each of the caravels delivering her merchandise, one at a time; and on the day of the delivery by one of them, the men from the other caravel, or caravels, should not go on shore. And if there be two of them being made ready for departure on a certain day, provided they observe the conditions abovementioned, they [[the men]] may be on shore at the same time, in the said arbor and enclosure, and pass from one caravel to the other. This must be so when the two of them [[caravels]] are to leave together, and not otherwise. And if they cannot leave together, after delivering their merchandise, as I have already said, they [[the men]] cannot in any way, under heavy penalty, get together on land or on the caravels; and on the day when the men from one of the caravels are on shore, those from the other caravel, or caravels, should not go on shore on that day, but rather each of them [[the crews]] should do so on the day that should be appointed for them. And this can easily be done, My Lord, with no hurrying on the part of those which will be all day on shore, contrary to what happens today. If Your Highness orders that this [[manner]] be observed, you will confirm through experience that what I say is true. The more so, My Lord, since, by looking carefully though without experiencing it, it is well proven and cannot be denied what so clearly shows by itself to be very profitable and good for your Exchequer, and that is that Your Highness should order to have it seen[224] how few entreat you to bestow offices in those parts, and those who may require them will be those who expect to satisfy themselves with the salary. And if Your Highness should watch closely, you will find that the guards of the caravels may be dispensed with, since it will not be necessary to inspect the ships if things are done in this manner [[described above]], because one will not take goods to throw into the sea if one is certain that he will not be able to sell them; and if one does not take goods, one cannot bring gold, since this is not given there for free, but is rather highly valued. And also, My Lord, each caravel should take a chain to keep the boat fastened during the night, and it should be secured with a padlock. And should Your Highness have any doubts regarding any part of these notes, and wish to know about it from me, I will better present it to you by word of mouth rather than here, with a quill. Because, My Lord, these matters cannot be written as clearly as when they are spoken by word of mouth. And about these matters, My Lord, as well as about many others which are of great service to you, I will speak to you, should you care to listen to me, without asking for any other favor than that which Your Highness may find I am worthy of, starting with that which I have already twice asked Your Highness, which is issuing me a license to become a clergyman, something that has been my wish for many days now; and I would have already become one if I had this license, because I lack nothing to become one, except Your Highness's orders and license. All the rest I have, because, My Lord, I am […] all that a clergyman has to know. And Your Highness shall bestow a great favor upon me, and Our Lady shall be pleased, since Your Highness will find yourself better served by me in an ecclesiastical

---

[224] In the transcription, '*sse faça vera*' ('*se faça vera*'), does not seem to make sense; it should probably read '*se faça ver*' ('to have it seen').

habit than until now, in a secular one. And what makes me most wish for this, My Lord, is not witnessing the errors and disservices against Your Highness committed by many in their offices, and also because, My Lord, I cannot help exposing what seems wrong to me. Which disposition of mine, My Lord, since I chose to put it to use, has brought me to my present state – may God improve it, as well as Your Highness, for it is in your power – which is the lowest possible, for it was my fate to incur the displeasure of Your Highness, whose hands I kiss.

20 Letter from Manuel De Góis to King Manuel[225] (02/01/1510)

ABSTRACT – *The letter details an enslaved person named Fernão da Vela who acted as interpreter in the Portuguese trade with Benin, as well as the sad situation at São Jorge da Mina, due to scarcity of inland, local merchants.*

[…] one thousand *dobras* was cleared in seven days, and today, the 12th day of January, which is when she will leave, the caravel Santo Ildefonso(?),[226] which was the first to depart from the Kingdom, appeared at dawn in front of this House.[227]

There is a slave in this House who is called Fernão da Vela and who was sent from the Kingdom to act as interpreter in the trade which used to be done in Benin and the Rivers. And after he had served during some journeys, instructions arrived from Your Highness ordering that the said slave should go to stay in Benin with the Factor for three years, and that it was your wish that the said slave should be freed, of which the only certainty here is that he, and some people who saw the said instructions in the Factor's dispatches, say that it was so. And when the said slave came to this House, he brought 12 slave pieces of his, of which six were sold to the traders[228] in the trade, and four after that; and two little girls are still with him and his wife, and a small daughter, and this wife he brought from Benin. […]

This House, Our Lord be thanked, is in good health, but the local merchants come so rarely that there is very little trade. May it please Our Lord to fulfill my wishes in this respect. And as concerns the necessary measures regarding this and all other matters in your service, Your Highness may be certain that they will be

---

[225] ANTT, *Fragmentos, Cartas para El-Rei*, cx. 1, mç. 1, n. 37; PMA, vol. 5, pp. 629–30; cf. MMA vol. 4, doc. 17.

[226] In the manuscript, '*sant'ylafomsso.*'

[227] This first excerpt was not included in MMA's transcription (vol. 4, doc. 17). Rather than place it in the appendix, the transcribed excerpt appears as follows: 'mjll dobras foy despachada em sete dias / e oje xii dias de Janeiro, que sera sua partida, / amanheçeo d'avante desta casa a caravela / sant'ylafomsso que primeiro partio do Reyno.'

[228] In the manuscript, '*mercadores*' ('traders'), instead of '*moradores*' ('residents') as in Brásio's transcription.

carried out, and where there is so much obligation to do so, it would be unnecessary to give another reason.

From this town of yours of São Jorge da Mina, on the 12th day of January '510. [*Autograph*]: I kiss Your Highness's hands

Manuel de Góis[229]

21 Letter from Manuel De Góis to King Manuel[230] (22/01/1510)

ABSTRACT – *A letter from the Mina captain Manuel de Góis detailing the affairs at São Jorge da Mina, as well as matters about wine sales and the government of the fortress.*

+

My Lord,

The caravel Santo Ildefonso,[231] may God guide her safely, whose captain is Diogo Pereira, carries six thousand and five hundred *dobras* for one hundred and thirty marks. She arrived in this city on the day before the departure of the [[caravel]] Santa Cruz; she was cleared in eleven days because she is a large ship and because the Santa Cruz delayed her clearance by one day.

Your Highness has written me a letter ordering that the fairs for the goods brought by ships as provision for the residents should observe the chapter of the regulations, according to which they should be held on the shore and by two people. And I have written to Your Highness that it cannot be done on the shore because there is so much heat that it is inconceivable to keep the captain and officials and residents in the sun, which would cause an even greater need than we already have of the things for our provision, and no one would be willing to stay in the sun unless it were for something of much service to you. And if it were only one fair it should not be held, all the more so because many of them cannot be avoided, which is a cumbersome and troublesome process for the clearance of the caravels and the safekeeping of this House, because the communication of the residents with the seamen, as well as with the black people, has been cut, as I have written to Your Highness, and can only be done with a gate on the draw-bridge of the ditch, so that the black people cannot approach the Ramada[232] or places where there are residents without having been sent for.[233] Therefore, from

---

[229] See CC 1-9-61, MMA vol. 1, doc. 61; vol. 4, doc. 18.
[230] ANTT, CC 1-8-72; PMA, vol. 5, pp. 634–6; cf. MMA vol. 4, doc. 18, pp. 64–67. This letter is full of ellipses, and its meaning, out of context, is partly obscure.
[231] In Brásio's transcription, '*Santy lafonsso.*'
[232] The Ramada was a pavilion or free-standing structure near the São Jorge da Mina fortress, providing shade and protection from the rain.
[233] In the document, '*sem recado,*' which might also mean 'without caution.'

this ship onwards, I shall not allow any ship to put anything on land, so that no person from the ships may speak with anyone from the fortress. And I have taken this decision as a result of another letter from Your Highness, which was brought by this ship, whereby you once more order that in no circumstance should fairs be held anywhere other than the shore, which is a place that will not do, nor in Ramada, for Your Highness agrees that it should not be done. And you can be sure that it would be a greater service to you and advantage for the residents to find a way for them to get their provisions.

And [[I]] had also wanted to prevent any wine from being taken from the ships to be sold to the residents, to which he [[the Captain(?)]] replied that they were bringing it under Your Highness's regulations, issued by Estêvão Vaz,[234] and that they had always taken from here the money raised from it as bills of exchange, and that it had been paid to them, without any impediment having been raised. And although in this he did as much harm to the residents as to themselves[[?]], he was thinking only of the benefit that would accrue from the trade of the wine of this House, for each caravel carries at least three or four pipes, and though I order it all to be kept in the storehouse and given, as a rule, to its owners, it is reasonable to assume that anyone who buys it at nine and ten thousand *reais* a pipe will not sell it all to the residents, for it would bring little profit. May Your Highness provide in this matter, without forgetting the people who will be in this House, because, if they do not obtain from the Captain the wine which they have been accustomed to drink and are forbidden to buy it from any of the ships, it will be necessary that all the wine coming should, as a rule, be from Caparica, since all the other wine goes bad, and this is the reason they have always been allowed to buy it.

In the regulations of this House there is a letter whereby Your Highness orders the captains to hold at certain times of the year a general inquiry regarding certain items contained therein, about which I have spoken to Bobadilha,[235] and he said that it did not seem to him to be in the service of God or yours, and that therefore he would not make any [[inquiry]]. Then, in a memorandum, I suggested to him, among other things, that he should speak to Your Highness in order to decide about the procedure which would best befit your service, and in relation to this I have not seen any reply, and it is necessary to know what Your Highness thinks would be best.

The chief *Alcaide*[236] presented to me a warrant issued by Your Highness to Bobadilha, whereby a supernumerary[237] should be dispensed to him, without prejudice to the favor you had granted him, and after that it said that, when another Captain should come, it was your wish that he be one of those registered.[238] To

---

[234] See ANTT, CC 1-8-54, MMA vol. 4, doc. 14.

[235] See ANTT, *Contos do Reino e Casa, Núcleo Antigo* 867, MMA vol. 4, doc. 14, and MMA vol. 1, doc. 61.

[236] *Alcaide*: see Glossary.

[237] In Brásio's transcription, '*sobresalemte*' ('*sobressalente*'), which might also be translated as 'extra' or 'spare man.'

[238] In Brásio's transcription, '*hordenados*' (i.e. '*ordenados*'): literally, 'ordered' or 'ordained.' Possibly those entitled to receive an allowance.

which letter I presented in reply the instructions which I had brought from Your Highness, where the people were named[239] who would make up the stock of fifteen residents which completes the number of fifty registered persons.[240] And if Your Highness does not recall it, you may seek information from João da Fonseca, who wrote the said instructions. Therefore, I could not have registered his man, unless I dispensed him against Your Highness's orders and as he had been registered until then, given that he had filled the vacancy, which was in the gift of Your Highness, of a bombardier, since he was not one of the fifteen residents whose vacancies Your Highness has granted to the captains, and he will thus be the object of gratitude on your account.

And so that Your Highness should see how pleased I would be to observe your warrant above any other, if Your Highness had not determined the warrants which alone should be observed, and there being no mention of his [[warrant]] in the said instructions, I have granted him one of my allowances[241] and thirty thousand *reais* per year, and told him to write to Your Highness, for I could not register his man for the aforesaid reason. And he has now shown me a warrant [...][242] one of my men from among those registered, and that I register another [[man]] of his, which I think Your Highness would consider as false information. I do not know to whom Your Highness would do such great injustice without having been heard; and finding me[243] guilty, Your Highness would find the punishment to be of even greater quality than the fault; and if he had looked at it carelessly, as he informed Your Highness, Your Highness should bear in mind who was informing you and who was the object of the information.

This House is presently in good health; by the grace of Our Lord we have only three patients in the infirmary.

From this town of yours of São Jorge, on the 22nd of January 1510.

[*Autograph*]: I kiss Your Highness's hands.

Manuel de Góis[244]

ADDRESS: To Our Lord the King.

---

[239] In the manuscript, '*nomeadas*' ('named'), instead of '*nomeradas*' (i.e. '*numeradas*,' which means 'enumerated') as in Brásio's transcription.
[240] In Brásio's transcription, the preposition linking the two last sentences—which appears in the manuscript—is missing: '[...] *ho tromquo dos qujmze moradores com que se çessa ho numero* [...].'
[241] Probably, a food allowance.
[242] Half the line in the manuscript is unreadable.
[243] In the manuscript, '*achamdo-me*' ('*achando-me*') instead of '*achamdo-se*' ('*achando-se*'), as in Brásio's transcription.
[244] See CC 1-9-61, MMA vol. 1, doc. 61; vol. 4, doc. 17.

22 Accounts of Estêvão Barradas, Factor of São Jorge Da Mina[245] (22/03/1510)

ABSTRACT – *An account from the São Jorge da Mina factor for the period of 20 August 1504 to 10 January 1507, detailing the amount of gold received for merchandise, including enslaved peoples.*

We make known that João Vaz de Lemos, accountant of our Household, has now come to our Exchequer to explain the account which, by our command, he took from Estêvão Barradas, knight of our Household, of everything which he received and spent during the period when he was our Factor in our town of São Jorge da Mina; and the receipt of his account showed that he began to receive for the said Factorship on the 20th of August of the year '504 and finished on the 10th day of the month of January '507, and thus he served for two years, four months and twenty days. The said receipt showed that during the said period he received 4,563 marks, 4 ounces, 1 dram, 12 grains of gold from the said mine; and also he received 6,976 *lambéis* of Mezona[[*sic*]][246] of all kinds, and 2,507 Tenes *aljaravias*, and 69 *alquices*[[?]],[247] and 2,905 *aljaravias* of Aguara [[*sic*]],[248] and 1,582 shaving bowls, and 520 urinal pots,[249] and 3,192 chamber pots, and 1,133 shells, and 1,894 rods and one third of fabric of all kinds, and 287,813 manillas of brass and copper, and 440 slave pieces, both male and female, and also many other goods and other articles, which he is shown to have received, […] which we have not named here, because they are many and of many qualities. And forasmuch as the said Estêvão Barradas has rendered us […] a very good account with delivery […] we acquit him […]. Issued in Almeirim, on the 22nd of March – João Vaz de Lemos, accountant of our Household, wrote this – year 1510.

---

[245] ANTT, *Chancelaria de D. Manuel*, liv. 3, fol. 9v.; liv. das Ilhas, fol. 180v. Transcribed in Anselmo Braamcamp Freire, 'Cartas de quitação,' *Arquivo Histórico Português*, II, n. 181, p. 75. Cf. Blake, *Europeans in West Africa*, 107–8.

[246] In Blake's translation, between square brackets, 'hambels of Messina'; for '*lambel*' (sing.), see Glossary.

[247] In the transcription, '*alqueires*,' which was a measure of capacity; see Glossary. In Blake's translation, the word is '*algueires*,' which he describes as 'a kind of mantle,' though we were unable to confirm this.

[248] Possibly '*Anhara*,' as in the document with the accounts of Aires Botelho (16 February 1508), n. 18 of Blake's translations. According to Braamcamp Freire, the manuscript in the *Livro das Ilhas* reads '*Huara*.'

[249] In the transcription, '*bacios machos*' ('male pots'), possibly urinal pots—as Blake has it—specifically designed for men.

23 Letter from Manuel De Góis
to King Manuel[250] (18/04/1510)

ABSTRACT – *A letter from the Mina caption detailing the state of commerce, the donation of enslaved women to the settlers or residents of the fortress, sanitary conditions, and trade goods which can be exchanged with Africans and the quality they should have to be sold. Of crucial importance is the gold trade, which has slowed or dried up, in part because of apparently low supplies and in part because of the poor quality of Portuguese-supplied cloth and metal goods for trade.*

+

My Lord,

The caravel Santo Espírito, may God guide her safely, whose captain and scribe is André do Basto, retainer of the Queen your sister, is carrying seven thousand *dobras*, since the caravel Taforea is staying in the port and a similar amount cannot be taken, as now it is the trade of this House which is being carried, [[though]] not as I would wish, for there are no articles made of brass or copper except small basins, and not many of them, and the cloth from Oran arrives in such a spoiled condition that it is unlikely to be sold [[?]].[251] And among the black people there is so much Mandinga cloth, made of cotton, that it interferes greatly with the House's trade. And the main reason why there are no merchants coming, according to what they say, is because this year there has been no gold, for when God gives, He gives to everyone. Your Highness can be certain that there are so few merchants coming that the little gold, which is being carried would not be taken, were it not for the great diligence put in persuading them to come and trade. May God grant me so much grace that this year will be better than it has begun and [[better]] than the last, and that He will not punish my sins in this way, since one cannot doubt either His Justice or His Mercy.

I have received through the said Captain a letter from Your Highness in reply to another which I had written to you about the female slaves, wherein Your Highness expresses the wish that I be given four pieces and the *Alcaide*, Overseer,[252] Factor and scribes of the Factory one each, and the residents one for every three. Which I have executed as follows; and the remaining pieces will go in the first ships, and this one is taking seventeen pieces. And the remaining ones will go in the next, for they cannot go in this one, since she carries no provisions.

---

[250] ANTT, CC 1-8-116; cf. MMA vol. 1, doc. 61, pp. 210–14.
[251] Tentative translation of '[...] *que se leua muy mall*' ('[...] *que se leva muito mal*'), literally '[...] difficult to take.'
[252] In Brásio's transcription, '*uedor*' ('*vedor*').

item for me, four pieces	4 p.
item for the chief *Alcaide*, one piece	1 p.
item for the Factor, one piece	1 p.
item for Duarte Roiz, scribe, one piece	1 p.
item for João Henriques, scribe, one piece	1 p.
item for Rui Pinto, scribe, one piece	1 p.
item for Sebastião Colaço, scribe, one piece	1 p.
item for the vicar, Luís Henriques [[and]] Rui Carvalho, one piece	1 p.
item Rui Pires, André Gonçalves [[and]] Fernão da Gansa	1 p.
item Master Pedro,[253] physician, Manuel Fernandes [[and]] Estêvão Gomes	1 p.
item for Gonçalo Valada,[254] Pedro de Goios [[and]] the *meirinho*	1 p.
item Rui Gamito,[255] Afonso Gonçalves [[and]] Fernão Tarrim	1 p.
item Fernão Delgado, Vicente Medeiro [[and]] Sebastião Fernandes	1 p.
item Manuel Dias, Fernão Branco [[and]] Bartolomeu Dias	1 p.
item João Mealhas,[256] André Afonso [[and]] Cosme Eanes	1 p.
item Gaspar Roiz,[257] and the male nurse and Afonso Fernandes	1 p.
item João Ribeiro, Diogo Dias [[and]] Afonso Picado	1 p.
item the apothecary, Gomes Fernandes [[and]] the caulker	1 p.
item Bartolomeu Mendes, and the blacksmith and the barber	1 p.
item Álvaro Lobo, the factor of the seashells and Estêvão Lourenço	1 p.
item João Lourenço, Pedro Vicente [[and]] Cristóvão Fernandes	1 p.
item the pilot, together with the seamen of the *caravelão*,[258] and the women	1 p.
item João Fernandes, and Figueiredo and the cooper	1 p.
item Fernão Martins, Jorge Nunes [[and]] Rui Gonçalves	1 p.
item Pedro Gonçalves, bombardear, Salazar [[and]] João Pires	1 p.

And because Your Highness says in your letter that these pieces, which will thus remain here, should not have been in the fortress for more than two years, I have to inform you that, in the said House, there is not one who has been here for the time which Your Highness has defined, since as recently as in the time of

---

[253] See ANTT, *Fragmentos, Cartas para El-Rei*, cx. 1, mç. 1, n. 9.
[254] See ANTT, *Fragmentos, Cartas para El-Rei*, cx. 1, mç. 1, n. 9, CC 1-9-61, and CC 1-13-48.
[255] See CC 1-9-61.
[256] *Ibid.*
[257] The scribe in MMA vol. 1, doc. 49.
[258] *Caravelão*: see Glossary.

Bonadilha[259] Your Highness had already sent here instructions determining that no slaves should come from the islands; and the few pieces the residents bought from the refuse of the House's trade were taken with them, and those they had obtained from the islands were sold by them to the residents who came with me; as a result, all of them [[the slave pieces]] have been here for more than two years, since Your Highness's instructions have been in this House for approximately the same period of time. And as regards this, I took the step of sending all of the older ones, and if any of them should stay I will, until I take them with me to the House of Mina, take such good care of them and the others that Your Highness will not be ill served; therefore I beg Your Highness not to let more time pass than is ordered in your regulations. The chief *Alcaide* and the Factor each keep his slave piece, in addition to those Your Highness allots them, for they had brought them from the Kingdom by warrant of Your Highness: namely, that the chief *Alcaide* could have [[the slave]] in place of the man who was allotted to him, and the Factor in place of one of the four men of the Factory who were allotted to him; and because there were no other people to put in their places, I have let them have [[the slaves]] until Your Highness should decide.

These last months of February and March were rather difficult, for in addition to the lack of merchants coming here, Sebastião Ferreira, Second Scribe of the Expenditure, and Simão Nunes, First Scribe of the Revenue, and another two residents died; and the office of Second Scribe of the Expenditure was taken up by João Henriques, who came from the Revenue, and that of First Scribe of the Revenue was taken up by Rui Pinto, who was *Almoxarife,*[260] in accordance to what Your Highness orders in your regulations; and the office of Second Scribe of the Revenue was taken up by Sebastião Colaço, and that of *Almoxarife* by Rui Gamito, so that everything was distributed among Your Highness's retainers. And because afterwards a letter patent of Your Highness for Sebastião Colaço arrived, in which you express the wish that he serve in the first office which becomes free, and he is such a good scribe as Your Highness can see by this handwriting and as/ so fit to perform any duty better than anyone else; I will kiss the hands of Your Highness for bestowing him the grace of serving the office he now has, and your other retainers the offices they now have, until a captain is sent, for in each of these offices they have served and will serve you well.

The officials from the House of Mina have sent in these two caravels a kind of short *aljaravias,*[261] which I think were sold [[?]].[262] And similarly they have sent in the caravel Taforea a sample of painted *lambéis,*[263] which are quite eye-catching and of good quality, and which will be sold[[?]][264] if the dyes stick,

---

[259] It should probably read 'Bobadilha'; see ANTT, *Contos do Reino e Casa, Núcleo Antigo* 867, MMA vol. 4, doc. 14; vol. 4, doc. 18.
[260] *Almoxarife*: see Glossary.
[261] *Aljaravia*: see Glossary.
[262] In Brásio's transcription, '*despenderom,*' literally 'spent.'
[263] *Lambéis*: striped cloth for covering tables, etc.
[264] In the transcription, '*se leuará*' ('*se levará*').

because if they fade they will not be sold[[?]];[265] and thus, until one sees whether a year from now the black people will consider them as good as they now praise them for being, such a large amount of money should not be brought, because they can tire of them, like they do with other goods which they are continually asking for and then reject. And may Your Highness instruct them to make this cloth as light and with as fast dyes as possible, for without these two additions the incomplete ones are not worth as much as those from Oran, in which the wool is much finer. And it should also be instructed that the warp should be well covered by the weft.

The state of health in this House is now improving, although among the black people, in the surroundings, there are still sick people and some of them die, so much so that during these last three months, both among them and among the white people, many have been unwell.

From this town of yours of São Jorge da Mina, on the 18th of April '510.

[Autograph] Your Highness's servant and factor,

Manuel de Góis[266]

24 Letter from Rui Leite, Rui Pinto and Sebastião Colaço to King Manuel[267] (02/09/1510)

ABSTRACT – *Letter from Rui Leite, Rui Pinto, and Sebastião Colaço (officials at São Jorge da Mina), to Dom Manuel. In it they detail events which led Captain Manuel de Góis to arrest, and send an African merchant named Dom João Serrão to the island of São Tomé, together with the steps he took in order to restore the security of local Portuguese trade, which Dom João and the King of Fetu, his ally, had jeopardized.*

My Lord,

We did not write to Your Highness on previous occasions because there was no reason for doing so, since on matters pertaining to your service and the trade of this Factory, we were to inform the Factor and officials of the House of Mina. It is only that, as regards this affair of Dom João Serrão, and even though Captain Manuel Gomes has written in detail about it to Your Highness, we, for our part, would also like to make it known. This black man was so abhorred in this village[268] that people, both those who came from abroad and those who resided

---

[265] In the transcription, '*os leuarõ*' ('*os levarão*').
[266] See CC 1-9-61, MMA vol. 4, doc. 18; vol. 4, doc. 17.
[267] ANTT, CC 1-9-60; PMA, vol. 5, pp. 706–8.
[268] In the transcription, '*aldea*' ('*aldeia*'); see Glossary.

there, were continually complaining about him to the Captain – though, despite having been rebuked by the Captain several times, he was never punished – because he always took one and a half *pesos*[269] instead of one *peso* as he should[270] and, in addition, because of certain imbroglios which he had got into with the Sharif, to the detriment of this trade, as the Captain will have informed Your Highness in more detail. And he took the side of the King of Fetu, which is opposed to that of the Sharif, through whose land all merchants come, for which reason it is necessary to keep him satisfied the whole time. And he caused as much damage as he could, because the most important people of this village did not want to align with him, and he did them as much harm as he could, for which reasons the Sharif was displeased with this House and did not want to let pass a white man who was going to repair a road which was in bad condition. And then the Captain endeavored to send him to Fetu, and had a road opened through the brush for his man to go to the backlands, as indeed he went. And Serrão, together with the King of Fetu, told the Captain that the merchants could travel along that road and that it was safe. And the Captain told them that he would be very pleased if they would have them come; that if they made the road safe, it would be freed from duties; and he satisfied them both by removing the duties which used to be charged.[271]

And then both the King of Fetu and Serrão had someone sent to the backlands to inform that the road was safe and free from duties. And soon after, four or five merchants came along the said road, and went back; and after these came another one with six slaves, and, while he was buying, he ordered them to go back by(?) a salt road;[272] and on the said road three of them were killed, and the others escaped. And the merchant came to the Captain to make a complaint, and he was informed that the King of Asebu,[273] a neighbor of Fetu, had killed them; and he immediately sent a white man, with a black man from Fetu and another of Serrão, to the King of Asebu, to ask him why he had done it or whether someone had instructed him to do so. He replied that no one had instructed him, that he had done it because Fetu was his enemy, and owed him a large sum of money, and furthermore had opened a road across his land without discussing it with him or giving him any part of what the Captain had given him, and that he had deceived the said Captain and the merchants saying that the road was safe.

---

[269] *Peso(s)*: see Glossary.

[270] '…he always took one and a half *pesos* instead of one *peso* as he should': literal translation of '*no pesso que levava omde avya de ser hum peso levava peso e meo*' ('*no peso que levava, onde havia de ser um peso levava peso e meio*').

[271] '…and he satisfied them both by removing the duties which used to be charged': tentative translation of '*e comtemtou-os ambos por tyrarem os direytos que damtes levavam*' ('*e contentou-os ambos por tirarem os direitos que dantes levavam*').

[272] 'by(?) a salt road': tentative translation of '*com hum caminho de sall*' ('*com um caminho de sal*'), literally 'with a salt road.'

[273] The Portuguese identification of *Sabu* is Asebu.

And in view of this reply the Captain satisfied the merchant by [[giving him]] a Mazouna [[*lambel*]],[274] and told him to go to speak with the King of the Akan, that if they wished to come and destroy Asebu he would help him,[275] and if he wished to be paid in money he would see to it and compensate him. And with this the merchant went away feeling satisfied. And then Serrão, together with the King of Fetu, in order to have the residents of the village on their side by force, since they would not go to them willingly, had the Captain told that Alvarenga, and Dom Jorge, and Diogo Lopes had forced the King of Asebu to kill the merchant's slaves and throw them [[the merchants]] out of this village, otherwise he[276] would wage war against him. And the Captain replied to him that they would not have given money to harm the merchants, but rather had given money for opening that road, and that it was also true that they had offered some *aljaravias*;[277] but, if he wanted, he could send people from the village, and white men with them, to destroy Asebu. And he only wanted to wage great war, because the said Dom Jorge, and Alvarenga, and Diogo Lopes did not swear with him, or that they were thrown out.[278]

And he did not let any water, firewood and maize (?)[279] be taken out of this village, except those of Dom João, nor did anyone leave this village without him admonishing them straightaway. And he took an *almadia*[280] of Alvarenga, with three of his slaves and two of another merchant, and the *almadia* was loaded, and he destroyed the greater part of the maize [[fields]], and killed three slaves of Dom Jorge, and another of an Akan merchant. And then six or seven merchants got together here and came to make a complaint against Dom João to the Captain, telling him that he was doing everything [[that he wanted(?)]], and that he was playing the atabals and horns;[281] and they said[282] that he was the only one to have water, firewood and millet(?), [[and]] that they wanted to go away, and that the Akan would not come to this House anymore, and that [[on]] the road which he had made safe three slaves were killed, and that he had also ordered his [[slave]][283] to be killed on the road to Akatakyi ('Komenda'),[284] which had always been safe.

---

[274] For the identification of this type of *lambel*, which is mentioned in other documents of the same period, see John Vogt, 'Notes on the Portuguese cloth trade [...],' *The International Journal of African Historical Studies* 8, no. 4 (1975): 635.

[275] Literal translation of '*ho*' ('*o*'), *sing.*, though it probably should read '*os*,' *pl.* ('them').

[276] In the transcription, '*faria gera*' ('*faria guerra*'), *sing.* It is not clear whether this is a reference to the captain or, despite the singular form used by the scribe, to Alvarenga, Dom Jorge, and Diogo Lopes (which makes more sense).

[277] *Aljaravia(s)*: see Glossary.

[278] 'did not swear with him, or that they were thrown out': literal translation of '*porque nam juravam [...] co'elle ou os botassem fora*' ('*porque não juravam com ele [...] ou os botassem fora*'). The meaning of this passage is obscure.

[279] In the transcription, '*milhos.*' Though other documents point to maize/corn, millet cannot be completely ruled out.

[280] *Almadia*: see Glossary.

[281] In the transcription, '*corvos*' ('crows'), but in the manuscript '*cornos*' ('horns').

[282] In the transcription, '*dezia*' ('*dizia*'), *sing.*

[283] It is not clear to whom this enslaved person belonged.

[284] In the transcription, '*Comane.*'

And on hearing this, so as to pacify them, he had Serrão called to the Ramada, and he did not want to come and covered himself with flour,[285] which, among the black men, means they are resolved to wage great war.

All his men came armed with shields and assegais to fight us. And then we armed ourselves to bring him to the Captain by force, and the merchants threw themselves at the Captain's feet begging him not to do so immediately. Then the men went back, as it seemed to him that many of them did not want do to it, and it was, and still is, considered to be a good thing to have left the matter for the time being and to do as was done afterwards, namely, after the merchants were gone, the Captain contrived to seize him in his house and arrested him; and he ordered that all his people be thrown out of the village; and he took the slaves so as to collect the debts from the time of Bovadilha; and he sent him [[Serrão]] to the island of São Tomé, as he will inform Your Highness in more detail. And in addition he [[Serrão(?)]] ordered that fire be set to the houses of Rui Gago, the main merchant in this village, and they would have robbed, had the men not left the fortress. And then he retired to his house, as well as the others since he would do as much to each of them.

For which reason the Captain took counsel with us, the other officials and competent persons, and we agreed that it would be very much in Your Highness's service to send him to the island immediately, and this had been the opinion of us all for many days, but, as it seemed to us that this should not be done without orders from Your Highness, it was not done, and the Captain did not send him [[to the island]] until he met the Sharif. And they became close allies.[286] And he made his road safe and free from duties, so the Akan do not have to pay anything. And for this he offered him a son as hostage; and he knows how little they pay for children and so he asked him to give him his gold jewels; and then he gave him some gold jewels which weigh two hundred *pesos*: And he immediately sent one of his knights to the backlands to inform that the road was free from duties, and a white man is accompanying him also to assure them that this village is also safe and free from duties, so they do not have to pay anything. It seems to us, My Lord, that this has been done as befits your service. May God Our Lord increase your royal estate in His holy service. From this town of São Jorge da Mina, on the 2nd day of the month of September '510.

Rui Leite   Sebastião [Co]laço (?)

Rui Pinto

---

[285] In the transcription, '*emfarinho-sse*' ('*enfarinhou-se*'), from '*farinha*' ('flour'); the substance is powdered white clay or *hyire*, which the Portuguese misunderstood as flour.

[286] 'and they became great allies': in the transcription, '*e semtou com elle grandes amizades*' ('*e assentou com ele grandes amizades*'), literally 'and he established great friendship(s) with him.'

25 Letter from Manuel De Góis
to King Manuel[287] (02/09/1510)

ABSTRACT – *This letter from the Mina captain to the king chronicles the conflicts between the Portuguese at São Jorge da Mina, a notable African merchant named Dom João Serrão, the ruler of Fetu baptized by the Portuguese Dom Jorge, and a high-ranking official of Akatakyi ('Komenda') obliquely called the Sharif. The document is published for the first time.*

My Lord

The caravel Santa Cruz, may God guide her safely, whose captain is Álvaro Barreto, carries over five thousand *dobras* and arrived in this town on the 24th of August, and she does not carry more gold because, on the 15th of the said month, Santo Ildefonso[288] sailed from here taking what was in the House.

On the said caravel Santo Ildefonso, I wrote to Your Highness that it was being decided, in consultation with the chief *Alcaide,*[289] the Factor, the officials and the persons of this House, to arrest Serrão[290] should there be no other remedy, and [explained] why it was nevertheless necessary to do so. I shall inform Your Highness of what has happened from the day the said caravel Santo Ildefonso sailed until today, because about what happened earlier, I have already written.

The day after the said caravel sailed, I ordered that Dom João be summoned and, in front of the officials, I told him how he had every good reason to serve Your Highness well and how ill-advised he was to expect otherwise, and that the things he did I would nevertheless remedy, should he want to mend his ways; that he should go to the King of Fetu and ask him for an *almadia*[291] which he had taken, with a number of slaves as well as other things of the people of this village, and that he should not entertain thoughts of waging war, for I had learned that he himself, Dom João, had done so and that he would pay for all the damage caused and to be caused.

Because the same King of Fetu, when I requested the said *almadia* and slaves and things carried in it, sent me word that I should request it from Dom João, for he had him told to take it; and that he had him informed of the time of his arrival, and that he had himself boasted of it to the same parties, as well as of all the other things that had been done, the witnesses to which I promptly took to his presence. And then he went to Fetu, and he returned to this village before dawn, and he brought with him three hundred black people, who he sent to the maize [field] of Dom Jorge, which is on the road to Akatakyi ('Komenda'),[292]

---

[287] ANTT, CC 1-9-61.
[288] In the manuscript, '*Santyllafomsso.*'
[289] *Alcaide*: see Glossary.
[290] See ANTT, *Contos do Reino e Casa, Núcleo Antigo* 867, MMA vol. 4, doc. 22, and CC 1-13-48.
[291] *Almadia*: see Glossary.
[292] In the manuscript, '*Comanea.*'

and they killed two of his slaves and took one prisoner; and they also killed a slave of an important merchant, out of six or 7 who were being bought there. And when news arrived to the village, I ordered the readiest[?][293] people of the village to leave, and behind them the other important people, with some white people with crossbows, and they were already safe; nevertheless, Dom Jorge's bowmen contrived to shoot at them, and with their arrows they killed seven of them, and among these there was a *meirinho*;[294] and when the people returned with the news and they found the three dead black people, namely, Dom Jorge's two slaves and the one of the merchant, all the merchants came to me to complain that Serrão had killed his slave and that he had also killed the other three of the other merchant, who were killed on the new road, for he had gone to their houses to call them, so they came by that road which was safe and even so he had killed them; and that now they were playing their *atabaques*[295] and they were wee-ping for their slaves.

And then I had Serrão called there to Ramada, so that I could pacify them and remove from his mind whatever was upsetting him in this village, and he would not come. I sent another messenger and again he would not come. And he was with his armed people and said that the white people had gone there after him; and it would have been so if the merchants, when they saw the people getting out, had not knelt before me with such pleas that it was necessary to make them turn back, because otherwise many people could have died, and women and children, and some people could have died, which would have compromised the tranquility of the land. Then the merchants, with the chief *Alcaide*, went there and brought him to Ramada, all covered with flour [i.e. *hyire*]. I shouted at him a little and made him go back home to wash himself. And after the merchants had completed their buying and left, I disguised him and contrived to take him to my place, and had his son and his nephew called, and after that all his wives. And then I told him that he could not leave this fortress until everything had quietened down, for he caused trouble. And I told him to go to the top of the wall and speak to his people, telling them to leave their weapons and quieten down because he was with me, and that, if they were afraid of anything, I would send some white men to sleep with them. And he told them to be ready with their weapons and that, at midnight, the people from Fetu would come and, as soon as they heard the alarm, they should set the houses on fire and get out and attack the people of the village, on the inner part. I was immediately told of it, in his presence, by other black people who were there, as well as all the most important people of the village who were listening to him. And I had him put in shackles and ordered the people to leave the fortress with the Factor, and that he should put them all out and let no one hurt them, and that he should take the slaves, so as to raise by them what the said Serrão owed in

---

[293] In the manuscript, '*mais solta*,' literally 'freest.'
[294] *Meirinho*: see Glossary.
[295] *Atabaque*: see Glossary.

the Factory. And thus it was done, for everybody left and they were taken across the river, and only two black men died because they wanted to be killed.[296]

And the people from Fetu, when they saw what had been done by those whom they met on the way, went quickly back to their homes to guard them and have not left them until this day, nor do I believe they ever will. And another five black people remained hidden in the houses, and at night they set fire to the houses, and they threw water over themselves [?],[297] and two of them were taken by the guards and the others escaped. The people ran to the fire and it was put out, so that only Dom João's houses were burnt. And the following day, the Sharif, and the merchants who were still in Akatakyi ('Komenda'), and those of the *comarca*,[298] required that I have Dom João killed. I replied that Christians only kill those who wage war on them; that Serrão was Your Highness's slave and that I would send him to your Stable or to cultivate yam on the island, provided they made the roads safe and free. Then the Sharif sent word that he wanted to meet me and do as I ordered, as indeed he came, and we entered into a firm friendship and he freed the road through which nothing goes to the Akan, where I used to take two *pesos*[?][299] to each merchant, and he would give me a son[?][300] as pawn,[301] and I desired rather a vessel of water in my hands and asked for his jewels as security, which he gave me readily, and they are worth more than two hundred *pesos*[?]. He says their value is incalculable because they belonged to his father. And the said Sharif straight away sent one of his knights inland with Gonçalo Valada,[302] who is a very respected man among the black people and has served Your Highness very well, to give notice of the freedom and safety of the road, as well as of this village. To all of us, My Lord, it seems that things are now such as to remedy the decline which had affected this trade.

And after everything was settled, I sent Serrão to the island of São Tomé, together with one of his wives, and his son and his nephew, because they were only a little less troublesome than he was, and they would be more if they remained here; and I gave him eight slave pieces to cultivate his yam, and I wrote to Fernão de Melo's

---

[296] In the manuscript, '*que qujseram que os matasem*' ('*que quiseram que os matassem*'), which might also mean 'whom they wanted to be killed.'

[297] In the manuscript, '*poseram-/-lhe ho foguo e lançaram-se auga*' ('puseram-lhe o fogo e lançaram-se água'); another, less probable, translation might be '[...] and water was thrown over them [the houses or the slaves].'

[298] In the manuscript, '*comarcãos*,' i.e. the inhabitants of a '*comarca*'; see Glossary. It is not clear whether the term refers to the Eguafoɔ or, more specifically, to Akatakyi.

[299] In the manuscript, the abbreviation '*pºs.*'

[300] In the manuscript, abbreviated as '*fº*,' which could stand for '*filho*' (son).

[301] On pawning in Africa, especially during the transatlantic slaving period, there is a lot of literature. See, for instance, Paul E. Lovejoy, 'Pawnship, Debt, and 'Freedom' In Atlantic Africa During the Era Of The Slave Trade: A Reassessment,' *The Journal of African History* 55, no. 1 (2014): 55–78; Judith Spicksley, 'Pawns on The Gold Coast: The Rise of Asante and Shifts in Security for Debt, 1680–1750,' *The Journal of African History* 54, no. 2 (2013): 147–175; Paul E. Lovejoy and David Richardson, 'The Business of Slaving: Pawnship in Western Africa, C. 1600–1810,' *The Journal of African History* 42, no. 1 (2001): 67–89.

[302] See ANTT, *Fragmentos, Cartas para El-Rei*, cx. 1, mç. 1, n. 9, CC 1-13-48, MMA vol. 1, doc. 61.

wife asking her to give him a bit of land for him to work. And I sent it through Rui Gamito, Your Highness's *Reposteiro,*[303] in the *Caravelão,*[304] so as not to disturb the voyage of the merchant caravels and because at that time there was no ship here.

An inventory of the property found with him was publicly made by one of the scribes, before me and all the officials, which inventory I am sending to Your Highness. Not one of some manillas of gold, or of any other gold, if he had it, was taken from him. Only the slaves could be taken to raise what he owes in the Factory; and because so many [[slave]] pieces were taken that they exceed the amount of the debt, I did not care to take his gold, except for a few jewels that had been pawned in the Factory. They were executed for the value for which they had been pawned, and they were sent to the Kingdom, because I, without security in gold, will not have Your Highness's estate pawned.

I have ordered the other wives of Dom João, who did not go with him, to be delivered to their parents and to the persons to whom they belonged, and I will keep one of them, who is from Fetu, because they give her to me in recognition for what has been done for this village. The other wives are already in their houses, for they are on friendly terms with the fortress. They were six in all. Adding to this, another sign that he was so good a Christian was found with him, and they were eight idols which he had kept and hidden so well that no one knew he had them.

I had wanted to send the remainder of Dom João's property to the island, after Your Highness had been paid, and I again settled with these men, with whose advice and opinion I do everything of this nature, that it would be better to keep everything on deposit until Your Highness decides what should be done. If, by chance, Your Highness should wish to receive more detailed information about this business and the matters regarding Serrão, you may call a retainer of the Baron, known as João Mealhas, who used to be the supervisor of the oven-house here, for he may know it, as he departed from here carrying some messages to the Sharif about this case. May Our Lord increase Your Highness's royal estate. From your town of São Jorge da Mina, on the 2nd of September '510.

[sign.] *Manuel de Góis*[305]

26 Officials of the Casa De Guiné to King Manuel Concerning São Jorge Da Mina[306] (27/09/1510)

ABSTRACT – *Officials from the Casa de Guiné e Mina indicate they do not have the specific cloth in demand at Mina, without which it will be difficult to procure gold from there.*

---

[303] *Reposteiro*: see Glossary.
[304] *Caravelão*: see Glossary.
[305] See MMA vol. 1, doc. 61, MMA vol. 4, docs. 17 and 18.
[306] ANTT, *Gavetas*, 15, mç. 1, n. 14.

We have received a letter from Your Highness in reply to another, which we wrote you touching the affairs of Mina, by which Your Highness commands us to send to the Factor and officials the painted *lambéis*[307] and urinal pots,[308] for which they sent. We have already written to Your Highness many times to say that the said painted [[*lambéis*]] have been lacking in the House for some days, on account of which you commanded us to look for them in Oran[309] and other parts; and when we replied to this, you wrote to say that João de la Serra had shown how these might be obtained. We would again remind Your Highness that in this House there are no painted [[*lambéis*]] which we can send to Mina, and according to what your officials write from there without them gold cannot be obtained from the merchants, who do not ask for other cloth.

We pray Your Highness to order what may seem best for your service so as to obtain them, since they are so necessary. And we are sending the urinal pots and chamber pots by the caravels in the quantities required and of the kinds requested.

Written from Lisbon, on the 27th of September 1510.

Estêvão Vaz   Rui Gomes

Álvaro Barroso   João de Ferreira

[On the reverse]: To Our Lord the King.
From the House of Guinea.
From the House of Mina.

27 Instructions from Dom Martinho De Castelo Branco to Álvaro Raposo[310] (26/06/1512)

ABSTRACT – *Dom Martinho de Castelo Branco orders the Receiver of the Ovens of Vale do Zebro to deliver to Pedro Rosado, Almoxarife of the Supplies of Mina, two hundred quintais of biscuit for maintenance of the enslaved people from the Kingdom of Kongo. Mina, Benin, São Tomé, and Kongo formed a 'triangular' regional trade circuit involving gold, captives, shells, and other goods.*

+

Dom Martinho de Castelo Branco, Lord of Vila Nova de Portimão, of Our Lord the King's Council, and Overseer of his Exchequer,[311] orders you, Receiver of the

---

[307] In the transcription, '*lambees pimtados*' ('*lambéis pintados*'), i.e. 'printed *lambéis*'; for '*lambel*' (sing.), see Glossary. In his translation, Blake presumes *lambéis* and '*pintados*' are different articles. See, *MMA* vol. 1, doc. 61.

[308] In the transcription, '*bacios machos*' ('male pots'), possibly urinal pots, as Blake has it, designed for men.

[309] In the transcription, 'Ouram' (probably for 'Orão'/'Orã').

[310] ANTT, CC 2-33-76; cf. MMA vol. 15, doc. 8.

[311] In Brásio's transcription, '*veador de sua fazenda*' ('*Vedor de sua Fazenda*'): see Glossary, under '*Vedor da Fazenda.*'

Ovens of Vale de Zebro,[312] and the scribe of his office, to deliver to Pedro Rosado, *Almoxarife*[313] of the Supplies of Mina, two hundred *quintais*[314] of biscuit[315] of the inferior sort, which I order be delivered to him for maintenance of the slaves which may come from Manikongo and Arguin. And by this [[instruction]], with the bill of lading issued by the scribe and signed by both, in which he shall declare that he receives [[the biscuit]] from you and that it will be so posted, it will be accounted for on your behalf.

Written in Lisbon, on the 26th of June – Jorge Dias wrote it – 1512.

Deliver to him another two hundred *quintais*, so as to make four hundred in all.

a) Dom Martinho

28 Letter from Nuno Vaz De Castelo Branco to King Manuel[316] (07/10/1512?)

ABSTRACT – *Nuno Vaz de Castelo Branco informed the king that a son of the Akan ruler and the merchants who accompanied him had left São Jorge da Mina with Gonçalo Valada, a Portuguese whom Branco sent with them across a river. Branco learned the Akan ruler would wage war against the Etsi/Atis again because they had killed his son, though peace attempts would be made. The document is published for the first time.*

Letter from Nuno Vaz de Castelo Branco to the King, in which he informs him that a son of the King of the Acanes [[Akan]], together with certain merchants, went there and told Gonçalo Valada[317] that the King of the Acanes would once more wage war against the Etsi/Atis,[318] for they had killed a son of his, and that they would involve(?) the Sharif.[319] Written in Mina, on the 7th of October of Without era

After I had written to Your Highness, the son of the King of the Acanes, together with other merchants who had come with him, left, and I sent Gonçalo

---

[312] Vale do Zebro (Barreiro), south of Lisbon, was the place where, from the 15th century, the king's biscuit ovens were located.

[313] *Almoxarife*: see Glossary, under '*Almoxarifado.*'

[314] *Quintal* (sing.): see Glossary.

[315] In Portuguese, '*biscoito*': see Glossary.

[316] ANTT, *Colecção de cartas, Núcleo Antigo* 879, n. 180. John Vogt, in *Portuguese Rule on the Gold Coast* (p. 214), believes Nuno Vaz de Castelo Branco might have been the Mina captain in 1502, yet he provides no evidence to support his speculation. Branco left for India just before or after 1506, joining Afonso de Albuquerque's fleet. Gonçalo Valada served in the fortress between 1510 and 1514, when Branco was in the Indian Ocean, suggesting Branco, if he was captain, had been so around 1502 or thereabouts. This would make sense because his successor as Mina captain was Diogo Lopes de Sequeira, who served in that capacity between 1503 and 1504/6, but, like Branco, left to serve in India by 1509. There was a Nuno Vaz who served as the Mina captain in 1514. The matter remains inconclusive.

[317] See CC 1-9-61 (Letter from Manuel de Góis to the King) and CC 1-13-48.

[318] 'Antis,' in the original (both foliae).

[319] Of Arabic origins, the Portuguese *xarife/xerife*, or *sharīf*, usually referred to the chief advisor or representative of local polities in contact with São Jorge da Mina.

Valada with them to cross the river; and they said to him and declared that the King of the Acanes would once more wage war against the Antis, who had killed his son, and that it would take place before the end of the month, and they declare that the Sharif would be involved(?). I inform Your Highness of this, so that you should know that this land is not yet pacified. But it will please Our Lord that everything be done well and as pertains to Your Highness's service. And I, My Lord, will attempt all ways and means for making peace among them. And I am now sending Gonçalo Valada to visit the King of the Acanes, and from the news that comes back I will have a better knowledge of this and other matters of the land where they occur. And in the first vessel I will inform Your Highness about them. From Mina, on the 7th of October.

I kiss the royal hands of Your Highness,

[sign.] Nuno Vaz de Castelo Branco

29 Letter to King Manuel[320] (1512-13)

ABSTRACT – *Letter to the king underscoring two trends for the Portuguese at Mina—and any overseas Portuguese—in the sixteenth and seventeenth century: the infrequency of ships laden with necessary supplies and much needed merchandise for trade, and the changing roles of imperial agents, such as Manuel de Sande, who is ship captain but will become factor or chief merchant at São Jorge da Mina several years later. The document is published for the first time.*

My Lord,

Your Highness wrote to me some days ago saying that it was your wish that the supplies and merchandise carried by the ship of Mina on which Azambujo[321] is sailing should not be transferred to that of Álvaro Luís, as you had written to him, since for a long time no ship had gone [[there]], so that her [[Azambujo's ship's(?)]] departure would not be delayed, but rather that her clearance should be hastened, in order that she should depart as soon as Sebastião Vargues carried out an order which you gave him. And that the other [[ship]] which should go after this, whose captain should be Manuel de Sande, who would soon arrive here, should immediately be made ready; and that, as regards the pilots, one should follow the procedure you had indicated to me or what I thought best, so that Azambujo's ship should not be delayed. The weather here [now(?)] seems fine and this [ship] of Álvaro Luís is ready, and it would be [...] service if she should

---

[320] ANTT, *Fragmentos, Cartas para El-Rei*, cx.1, mç.1, n.7. The precise date of this document is unknown, but circumstantial evidence suggests 1512-13. Azambujo refers to Afonso Vaz Azambujo, a Mina pilot and ship captain (see CC-2-34-124, 3-10-1512), who was lost near the island named João da Nova on the India route in 1528. Manuel de Sande was Mina factor, c. 1517–19, but apparently ship captain before his stint as factor.

[321] Azambuja is also a town in Ribatejo, in the Tagus valley, suggesting a place of origin.

depart immediately, for it has been a [long] time since the last ship went, except for the Azambujo's, which left some days ago, as if he already knew whether he should go on her as captain,[322] [[and]] it would be good if she would come as soon as possible; and also the manner of proceeding with her [[Álvaro Luís's ship(?)]], because here it is said that Your Highness has already gathered the guards in order [...]

30 Afonso Caldeira to King Manuel about São Jorge Da Mina[323] (02/01/1513)

ABSTRACT – *A letter from the late Afonso Caldeira to the king informing him of the affairs at São Jorge da Mina, including the status of efforts to convert local African rulers to Christianity.*

Sir. After kissing the royal hands of Your Highness with due reverence, I report, Sir, that since writing that first letter to Your Highness, wherein I gave you an account of affairs here on the last day of January, the King of Fetu and the King of Ampya[[*sic*]][324] came here, who had given their hostages to Pedro Nunes and [João?] Serrão[325] and whom I welcomed with full honors, as Your Highness may learn from all who go to the Kingdom from here; and they brought with them some of their brothers and relations, their knights, above all Hemo[[*sic*]][326] who is the most important. I offered them of mine[327] in such a way that they were well satisfied, and Your Highness may rest assured that, as long as I remain here, they will always be peaceful and at Your Highness's service. This King of Fetu is a very honorable person, a very truthful man and well inclined towards the service of Your Highness. He is sending his son there and he says that, if needs be, he would take his place[328] to serve Your Highness.[329] He says that he wishes to be a

---

[322] The meaning of this sentence is not clear: '[...] *como ja sabera se ha d'jr capitam nelle* [...].' Another possible translation would be '[...] as if he already knew whether there should be a captain sailing in her [...].'

[323] ANTT, CC 1-12-72. Cf. Blake, *Europeans in West Africa*, pp. 112–14.

[324] In Blake's translation, between square brackets, 'Yabi?'

[325] In Portuguese, as in other Latin languages, the article is not infrequently used when referring to a person by his or her name or surname; '*ao será*' ('*ao Serrão*') could thus be translated simply as 'to Serrão.' The article is, in fact, used in other documents when referring to this same Serrão. Note that Blake's translation reads 'Afonso' as an expansion of '*ao*,' which he presumes to be an abbreviation, though this is usually written either '*aº*' or with a mark of abbreviation over the two letters.

[326] In the text, '*a hemo*,' where '*a*' is probably a preposition; the name could also be '*Ahemo*.' This mention is missing in Blake's translation.

[327] Literal translation of '*Eu lhe dey do meu*' ('*Eu lhe(s) dei do meu*'), i.e. 'I offered them my hospitality.'

[328] Tentative translation of '*ele em pessoa livrara.*'

[329] The passage from 'He is sending [...] to '[...] serve Your Highness' is missing in Blake's translation.

Christian and that all his land should become Christian. On the day of Our Lady, he attended vespers and mass, and he did everything which he saw me do, and he says that he thinks the ways of the Christians very good, and he asked me earnestly to write this letter to Your Highness in his presence, wherein he prays Your Highness to command a chapel to be built for him so that he may hear mass, and that I should see that he be made a Christian, and also his wives – for there are more than one – and his children, and likewise his knights and people, and this very earnestly. And he awaits a reply to this, and I shall not do anything until the command of Your Highness arrives. Also, he told me that he prayed Your Highness to make him a present of a mule, or an ass, or a horse, on which he might ride. And further he desired me to write to Your Highness that you might order a house to be built for him wherein he might live.

Item. Furthermore, he says that he prays Your Highness to send back after one year his son and Dom Simão, so that here they may teach his people to be Christians; and that he prays Your Highness to make him a present of two chests, covered with leather, to keep his belongings,[330] because he is afraid of fire; and moreover he says that he prays Your Highness to allow Pedro Nunes to take charge of his son and to accompany him when he is to return. This [[........]][331] a son, whom they call Afonso, who is a grave and truthful man, but I think him a great fool and a rogue, and as such I present him[332] to Your Highness. The other King of Ampya[[*sic*]], who had his son here, did not want him to go there, and I considered it in our interest not to press[333] him in this matter, because it is not necessary. This King of Fetu and that of Ampya[[*sic*]], and also all their knights, kiss the hands of Your Highness, and I have nothing more to report about this, except that I pray God to prolong the life and royal estate of Your Highness, as Your Highness desires. From Mina, on the 2nd day of January 1513.

From the servant of Your Highness, who kisses your royal hands.

Afonso Caldeira

[Center]:
To Our Lord, the King.
From the late Afonso Caldeira – may God keep him – which Pedro Nunes delivered. 1513.

---

[330] In Blake's translation, 'to hold gold,' though there is no reference to gold in the manuscript ('*pera ter ho seu*,' i.e. '*para ter o seu*').

[331] Gap in the manuscript.

[332] In the manuscript, '*ho uêdo*' ('*o vendo*'), literally 'I sell him,' which Blake translates as 'I hand him on.' The use is obviously metaphorical.

[333] In Blake's translation, 'to use force,' which in this context does not correspond to the meaning of '*forçar*.'

31 Letter from the Factor of Mina, Francisco De Góis, to King Manuel[334] (19/08/1513)

ABSTRACT – *A letter from the Mina factor to the king about the affairs of Mina, specifically its fiscal affairs, the fortress's need of captives from Benin, and conflict between two Akan societies in the interior. Document published for the first time.*

My Lord

Having kissed the hands of Your Highness for having been mindful of me and wished to use me in a matter such as this, in which so much is lost to your service, I have to say that I have written certain letters to Your Highness, in which, My Lord, I gave you a large account of affairs here both past and present, and to many, or to most, of them Your Highness did not provide an answer in this last [letter] you sent me. However, because in this cruel world men such as myself value their honor above everything else, I shall receive much grace from you, My Lord, if you hold it in such consideration as is due to someone who has damaged it in your service.

And as regards what will be done here for your service, Your Highness may rest easy, for it will be done with as much love and willingness as my desire is solely the desire to let Your Highness learn through a truthful report how I serve you with much honesty. And Your Highness must believe that, if I were provided with the merchandise which is necessary for this trade, I would not be satisfied only with doing as the treasurer of Fernão Lopes, because there is money in the treasury as it used to be. The truth is that in some years there is more than in others because the waters are more abundant some years than in others.

And even though this money is now [being drained by] this Mandinga competition, which has never been as open as it is now,[335] I have at present, God be praised, so many clients in this House that, if I had the slaves which are needed for the trade, together with the other goods which would come from there, I would send as much money as Your Highness might request, for, since I have been here, I have always known this House to be in great need of slaves, especially now that, for the past five months, the *caravelão*[336] which passes here has been in Benin, and has still not come back. We do not know what to say to this, except that, if this King of Benin wanted to fit out your ships, as he rightly should, this *caravelão* by itself would almost be sufficient; and doing things as they are now done, and I believe that they will be done every time, My Lord, four will not be sufficient, for with the delay in the journey to and from the Rivers, if they operate with due dispatch, it takes two to two and a half months.

---

[334] ANTT, CC-1-13-48. This document is quoted in Maria Emília Madeira Santos, 'Rotas Atlânticas: O caso da carreira de S. Tomé,' in *Actas do II Colóquio Internacional de História da Madeira* (Lisboa: Instituto de Investigação Científica e Tropical, 1989), 649–55.

[335] Tentative translation of '*E posto que este dinheiro tenha*[?] *agora este furo / de mandinga que nunca foi tão aberto / como agora* [...]' (modernized ortography).

[336] *Caravelão*: see Glossary.

And up to this day, Gonçalo Valada[337] has not yet come from the Akan, and every day [I wait][338] for his arrival and hope he brings all things of your service corrected and concerted as I ordered him, for I have this information. But the black people, My Lord, put so much delay in all their things that this is the reason why they never grow old.

And I sent to the island of São Tomé, My Lord, the *caravelão* which goes from here to Akyem to bring the wife and daughter of [João] Serrão,[339] according to what Your Highness commanded in your letters, the one you sent to Lopo Mexia and the other to Fernão de Melo. However, one of the main reasons for having sent it there, besides fulfilling your order, was because I was being so pressed on the part of Serrão, the Sharif, and Acuo,[340] and Atinco, his brother-in-law, to send [the *caravelão*] to bring her, that their annoyance with me for not doing it was indescribable. And because, My Lord, the man who will serve you in this *alcaidaria*[341] should be old in his knowledge, so as to understand the affairs of the black people, and young, so as to be able to endure his labor, and not as they may tell Your Highness there; because, My Lord, he who would serve you here as is due to your service, will not take a nap at regular hours[342] and will get up three times every night to go through the House. And he who does not do so, will then make friendships at the expense of your property; this would not be the case if he lost his sleep, which a man of fifty or over cannot endure.

And if this caravel does not carry the ten thousand *dobras* which are stipulated by your regulations, it is not my fault nor that of the officials here, but rather because when this caravel arrived we had not had, for a whole month and a half, any merchandise in this House from which we could obtain a single grain of gold. And this was because Afonso Mexia had written to the House two months before he left, saying that no merchandise should be sent to him, for he had plenty here; and because of the delay in the voyage of the galleon which carried our message, during the said period we remained without the said merchandise, for, as soon as the aforesaid Afonso Mexia left, I inspected the House and we auctioned off, in some cases cheaply,[343] in the Old Cloth, seven hundred *lambéis* of all sorts which were there, badly spoiled, and were damaging the unspoiled cloth. And these cloth have now all been sold, so that there are no more than six *lambéis*, which were sold for between five and thirteen *pesos*[?],[344] according to what was offered, and we are now in need of old cloth. We hope that they come in this galleon. And thus

---

[337] See ANTT, *Fragmentos, Cartas para El-Rei*, cx. 1, mç. 1, n. 9, CC 1-9-61, and MMA vol. 1, doc. 61.
[338] Inkblot in the manuscript.
[339] See ANTT, *Contos do Reino e Casa, Núcleo Antigo* 867, CC 1-9-61, MMA vol. 4, doc. 22.
[340] See ANTT, *Fragmentos, Cartas para El-Rei*, cx. 1, mç. 1, n. 9.
[341] *Alcaidaria*: see Glossary.
[342] In the manuscript, '*empresado,*' i.e. '*emprazado,*' which literally means 'previously scheduled.'
[343] In the manuscript, this passage (lines 8–10) is not totally clear. It reads: '[...] eu dey loguo varejo a casa / e lançamos por vezes em baixo na Roupa / Velha setecentos alanbes de toda sorte [...].' One meaning of the verb '*lançar*' is 'to auction.'
[344] The abbreviation in the manuscript is '*p°s.*'

there is nothing more to write about to Your Highness, except that all the black and white people are living in great peace and health, may Our Lord be praised.

And today, the 19th of August, an important knight[?][345] of the King of the Portuguese Akan, arrived here. His name is Aquempo, whom Afonso Mexia ordered to be expelled from here for having told him about his friendship with the Sharif, and he brought many people with him. I think that he always used to leave us a thousand *dobras*, and I treat him with the honor and courtesy which befits your service. However, he was unable to give me any news of Gonçalo Valada because it had been a month since he had departed from there and he stopped on the way. From this town, on the 19th day of August 1513.

My Lord, after I had written this [letter] to Your Highness, the merchant of the Castilian Akan arrived, who had been with Gonçalo Valada for two days among the Portuguese Akan, and he gave the news of their being already friends with one another. I thank the Lord, because in this there is much to your service. And [he said] that Gonçalo Valada had not yet come because he had been detained by the King of the Portuguese [Akan], saying that they wished him first to see a house they were building there as lodging for the white men who should go there, and that he comes with [......][346] his son, who will become king, is very quarrelsome and has all his sons and daughters married back there among the Castilian Akan.

From the servant and factor of Your Highness, who kisses your royal hands.

[sign.] *Francisco de Góis*

32 Letter to King Manuel[347] *(18/01?/1514)*

ABSTRACT – *A fragmented letter about the affairs of Mina, especially the internal politics of presumably Akan societies and of Portuguese trade on the coast. The document is published for the first time.*

My Lord,

As regards the death of Tinquouam,[348] [son of the King of the(?)] Akan, of which I have written to Your Highness [................] they killed while going from this fortress [................] children and wives, or rather, that [................] to depart totally lost[349] [................] 16th of January 1514, and I did so [................] [...] in which he/

---

[345] It is unclear, though probable, whether the abbreviation in the manuscript stands for '*cavaleiro.*'
[346] Faded in the manuscript.
[347] Fragmentary document, damaged by fire; about one third of each page is missing, along with the outer margin. Simple square brackets indicate reconstitution; double square brackets do the same for additions; lacunae and fragments of words which cannot be reconstructed are indicated by [.....]; cases in which reconstitution is uncertain are indicated by [xxx(?)]; and those where meaning and/or reading is unsure by (?).
[348] Tentative modernized spelling: '*Tincovão.*' Tinquouam, in this context, would likely be the name Ata Kwame. Ata means the Saturday-born Kwame was a male twin.
[349] *Dessachado*: possibly a negative form of '*achado*' ('found').

it(?)[350] is now going, through [Gonçalo] [Va]lada[351] was in Fetu, which [................]
had sent him, and with him [................] and a nephew of his, and a [.........] of
his [...] given his importance, and a nephew [of] [................] thus, My Lord, the
war(?)[352] cannot be [................] the King of the Akan, with all the [................]
Kingdom, in which there were 7 [.........] and [........] jurisdiction(?) only one and
before [................] I ordered that a request be made that [................] also of his/its/
their(?) that [................] because they wanted to come to [war(?)] [............]

[................] two [[female]] hostages, namely, one to be in the [................]
which is between the Akan and Fetu [................] divides a road, so that they may
go [................] Akatakyi ('Komenda'),[353] and another to Fetu, because Acuo[354]
[................] very safe, since he/it(?) was put in [................] the King of the Akan
that Acuo had given place [................] to kill the said Tinquouam and [................]
the truth was known, the said [[female]] hostage was delivered [................]
babble, one [...] of the sherif that the *tersos*[355] [................] some days ago of a
little [disagreement] [..............] between them. They have, however, [................]
that/than(?) ourselves, talk to each other and going to the house [................]
others, and have ill will against each other, and [...] [................] My Lord, I had
these [[female]] hostages delivered because/so that(?) [................] security for the
merchants [................] also not to do any [................] to no people of these, and
the [............] [hostages] are here now, who came [................] of the King. And as
soon as this was thus done [................] and they reached the Etsi/Atis, which are
two [places(?)][............] where they no longer found anyone, since all of them
were [................] a *meirinho* of the said Etsi/Atis [................] bush with many
people, saying that [................] and fought, and died, and [...] [................] they
ran away and set fire to the [................] that this they had thus done [................]
know that it is by the sea because he gave shelter to the Etsi/Atis when [................]
hunger did not let them/want to leave them(?) [................] to eat, and they
turned away/came back(?), and they say [................] is not finished, that how
much it amounts to [................] who has already finished and did what he should
[................] the war remains(?) to a son of the [................] and to 3 or 4 nephews
of his [................] to come against them, because the Etsi/Atis [................] place
as from another, gather [................] now again to do/make(?) a [................] a
stream here more [................] and thus that from then until now [................] no
Akan merchant or [................] this fortress, only these who [................] come
to buy go to [................] of the said King, and to ask for and [................] which
was taken from Tinquouam [................] [...] and some things can [................] it

---

[350] In cases where meaning is unclear, the options are indicated as alternatives.

[351] See CC 1-9-61, CC 1-13-48, and MMA vol. 1, doc. 61.

[352] It is not clear whether what is written in the manuscript is '*a gerra*' ('*a guerra*') or '*agua*' ('*água*'),
i.e. 'water'; in view of the context, the former seems more likely.

[353] In the manuscript, '*[Acu]mane.*'

[354] See CC 1-13-48. Acuo was probably the Akan name Akwao, a Thursday born male.

[355] Given the state of the manuscript, the meaning of '*tersos*' in this context is not clear: either
'lustrous'/'clean,' or (with the modernized form '*terços*') 'rosaries,' 'thirds,' or a type of military
administrative unit.

is not to be believed that [................] fill up 4 sheets of paper [................] even an elephant's beard[356] [................] sent to bring [................] that these should come, had [................] and they say that all that [................] Akan have told me [................] even though some may be missing [................]

[................] and the conclusion is that they do not have it unless [................] of saying that they give him back everything and [................] since now, My Lord, this is thus done [................] of Our Lord, which was just [settled(?)][............] otherwise I fear it might be late [................] and I wish that(?) the life [................] early(?) because this house [..........][................] that illuminate(?) only the Akan, and the [sharif] [..........Ac]uo(?) do not fear anyone, except(?) [...] [................] sherif(?)[357] says that he has no friends [................] Your Highness and the King of the Akan [................] a bad or a good road is not [................] all open, but the Akan [................] still for now coming from their [................] each of them fears, and as to/how much(?) [...]

[................] this part, this way I remain [................] [hope] in Our Lord that soon this [................]. [................] I am sending Your Highness eight thousand [*dobras*] [............] [S]ão Tomé much from where I/he(?) had[358] [...], and [................] [Your] Highness may believe that, were it not for the slaves, [................] we would not have a single *real* [................] of this last month of December [................] up in the cloth more than [................] *dobras*, being continued(?) [................] between 7 thousand and 9 thousand more or less [................] Your Highness how the Aka[ne] [................] this House and of the slaves of António Carneiro[359] are going in these [................] ninety-four marks and 2 ounces 2 [drams(?)] [................] which make *dobras* 4714 of [................] which [...][360] were obtained from one hundred and [................] which were sold in the said month of [December] [................] [...] prices, yet all of them were [................] 24 *pesos* each [[slave]] piece and the others that [............] [are lacking] to match the 199 c[................] Diogo de Alcáçova[361] sent here/was sent here(?) [................] in this other month of January and not [................] because we do not do the [................] at the end of the month, only the [................] as refuse. It seems to me, however, [................] which we have of them, since all of them were [taken(?)] [............] only one, 2 who ran away, and [................] that, if I/he(?) had

---

[356] Literal translation of '*barba de elefante*,' but most likely the elephant tail, a key symbol of wealth and power in Akan societies, especially among the Asante. See T. C. McCaskie, *State and Society in Pre-colonial Asante* (New York: Cambridge University Press, 2003).

[357] Since the beginning of the line is missing, it is also possible that, instead of '*xarife*' ('sherif'), this should read '*almoxarife*' (see Glossary).

[358] Due to the state of the manuscript, it is not possible to provide an exact transcription, and thus a translation, of this sentence. Another possible reading might be '[...] take much from which I/he(?) had [...].'

[359] See CC 1-8-54.

[360] Crossed out in the manuscript: '*venderam*' ('[were] sold'). On António Carneiro and the importance of his family in the 16th century Portuguese court, see Pedro Pinto and Robin Law, 'New Evidence on Relations between Portugal and the Kingdom of Allada in the Sixteenth Century,' *History in Africa* 47 (2020): 37–49; Pedro de Brito, 'The Stillbirth of a Portuguese Bourgeoisie: Leading Families of Porto (1500–1580),' *Mediterranean Studies* 5 (1995): 14.

[361] See ANTT, *Contos do Reino e Casa, Núcleo Antigo* 867.

here or [................] would have sold them, because [................] last month all of them(?) were [................]

And as regards, My Lord, your [................] I cannot [.....] them [.....] account [.....] until now, which is the 18ᵗʰ of J[anuary(?)] [...........] waited for one of the [................] who/which is there now and is not coming [................] as if today(?) still [.........] him [.........] to reach seven [................] yet I wait/hope(?) every [................] also because the Akan [................]

[................] of Our Lord, I hope that it be [................] may cost me two dozen *febres*³⁶² with [................] and also some jewels of my [................] I spend nothing of Your Highness, and [................] would go should it be fitting and necessary [................] I not one or two painted but ten(?) [................] of which I until now, God be [praised,] [...........] needed, nor do I believe that I have taken [................] wanted to correct by giving [................] they need another factory only [................]. [................] of the Roxo³⁶³ who justifiably may be there [................] this arrived/arrives(?), I forgot with other [................] of writing to Your Highness as(?) I gave [................] João Vaz, *moço de estrebaria,*³⁶⁴ who here [................] *almoxarife*³⁶⁵ of the supplies which were [agreed with(?) Francisco] Roiz, who used to be a scribe in the time [...] [................] *almoxarifado*, your *moço do monte,*³⁶⁶ with [................] given that the said João Vaz told me [................] should be in this land, and about this [................] me so(?) pensive, that I/he(?) feared that before(?) [................] might fall sick, and this Francisco Roiz with whom [................] knows very well how to do and [...] [................] *almoxarifado*, and yet, however, My Lord, [................] condition of writing it/so(?) to Your [Highness] [...] might wish so, that he would be and [................] ordered about it what [...] [................] your service.

Yet, My Lord, this Francisco Roiz is very poor and married and [...] [...] when he came, he has been serving [Your Highness] well [...] to come to have for being well/wellbeing(?). And Master Pedro,³⁶⁷ who has asked me [license/permission(?)], is going in this caravel and I gave it to him because here is staying/remains(?) [................] and he is called João Álvares, whom I [.........] you [.........] as much in this land, which I [.........] myself [.........] him, and with the best physician of [................] [...] that he has of the said land, that in [................] was/has been(?) here for three years and now [................] three that he is here, and is a man very [................] and I am always treated by him [................] and as regards Master Pedro, My Lord, he is going very [................] complaint, and ask for justice from [Your Highness] [...........] Cabedo³⁶⁸ who says that he raised

---

³⁶² *Febres*: coins below the stipulated weight (from the French '*faibles*').
³⁶³ Probably a nickname or a surname ('*roxo*' meaning 'red(haired),' but also 'purple' or 'scarlet').
³⁶⁴ *Moço de estrebaria*: see Glossary.
³⁶⁵ *Almoxarife/almoxarifado*: see Glossary.
³⁶⁶ *Moço do monte*: see Glossary.
³⁶⁷ See MMA vol. 1, doc. 61.
³⁶⁸ It is not possible to determine whether, in the manuscript, this word begins here or in the previous line (the end of which is missing). It is likely this is the complete form, probably a surname.

[........] him [........] to a merchant, of which case [................] [...] and I ordered/ sent to(?) Rui Gomes [................] of/from(?) the things of the said Álvaro de Ca[bedo(?)] [...........] pay to the said Master Pedro no [..............] [wages(?)] until Your Highness [........] him [........] however, now his [................] [pay] everything which was owed to him [................] and it is going through the said receipt[369] [...............] should not pay/does not depart(?)[370] until he shows [................] his/ its(?) release. From this town [................] 1514.

From Your Highness's creature and servant, who kisses your royal hands.

[Reverse of the letter]
From the chief
Alcaide of Mina

33 Letter from Gonçalo Mealheiro to King Manuel[371] (07/10/1514)

ABSTRACT – *A letter from a Portuguese official at São Jorge da Mina describing a conspiracy that implicates African merchant Dom João Serrão in connection with the King of Fetu, as they reportedly sought to kill the chief Alcaide and his people, and wage war against the Adena villagers and the Portuguese in São Jorge da Mina. Document published for the first time.*

[address] Our Lord the King

[left top corner]: Of the Sharif of Mina

My Lord,

Sharif Dom Manuel, and Buamam King of the Assas [Wasa], and Diogo Lopes, and Diogo de Alvarenga,[372] and Rui Gago, all servants of Your Highness, make known to you that Dom João Serrão[373] concerted with the King of Fetu to come, as they did, to this town and kill the chief *Alcaide*[374] with all the people, and thus wage war against all the people of this village of Your Highness as well as against us. The King of Fetu did all this on advice of the said João Serrão, who in everything disserves Your Highness. Therefore, My Lord, we beg you to do us the favor, in order to do Your Highness's service, and for our tranquility and for the peace of this land and the merchants, of ordering Nuno Vaz, Your Highness's

---

[369] In the manuscript, '*arrecadaço(m)*' ('*arrecadação*'): see Glossary.
[370] It is not clear whether this should read '*pague*' (present subjunctive of '*pagar*') or '*parte*' (present mode of '*partir*').
[371] ANTT, CC 1-16-30; cf. MMA vol. 4, doc. 22.
[372] See ANTT, *Contos do Reino e Casa, Núcleo Antigo* 867, MMA vol. 1, doc. 52.
[373] See ANTT, *Contos do Reino e Casa, Núcleo Antigo* 867, CC 1-9-61, and CC 1-13-48.
[374] *Alcaide*: see Glossary.

Captain in this town, not to allow the said Dom João to enter this village ever again, because he is continually involved in these tumults, and he is their leader, among other disservices done to Your Highness. Which matters could be remedied if Your Highness were to order that he no longer be admitted here, thus bestowing a grace on us, as well as order that a son of his, called Dom Simão,[375] should also not be admitted here, for he is someone who is cunning like his father. Your Highness should not trust Pero Nunes in this matter, because he is the main person doing these disservices to Your Highness. We all of us ask Your Highness not to send him here again, for each time he hinders the service of Your Highness. [May God] increase your estate at your service.[376]

From this town of Mina, on the 7th day of October one thousand five hundred and fourteen years.

34 Accounts of Gonçalo Lopes[377] (17/12/1514)

ABSTRACT – *Gonçalo Lopes, Almoxarife, provides an account of the gold and enslaved peoples procured during the period 1 January 1511 to 31 December 1513 for the House of Mina and Guinea.*

We have commanded an account to be taken from Gonçalo Lopes, knight of our Household, and *Almoxarife* of our slaves and the twentieth from Guinea, and Factor of our islands, of everything which he received and spent in the said *almoxarifado* and factories during the period of three years, which began on the 1st day of January '511 and ended at the end of December '513. And the receipt of his said account, which was taken and examined in our [[*Casa dos*]] *Contos*[378] by the overseers of our Exchequer, shows that he received during the whole of the said period 27,428,975 *reais*, which he received from the persons named below, namely: 4,236,927 *reais* from Rui Gomes, Treasurer of the House of Mina, for equally as much from the twentieth of gold which came from Mina during the whole of the said three years, in which were included 40,000 *reais* which he received from him for the expenses of his office; and 162,350 *reais* which he received from certain persons for the twentieth of slaves and other articles, which they brought to these Kingdom; and 31,300 *reais* from certain passengers who lived in Sierra Leone among the negroes; and 28,615 *reais* which he received from certain parties for the fourths of some slaves of theirs,

---

[375] See MMA vol. 15, doc. 55.
[376] In the manuscript, this passage reads, '[...] *acreçente sseu estado a seu serujço* [...]' ('[...] *acrescente seu estado a seu serviço* [...]'). This appears to be a case of ellipsis or unintended omission of keywords, probably for lack of space.
[377] *Chancelaria de D. Manuel*, liv. 11, fol. 69v.; *Místicos*, liv. 6, fol. 130. Transcribed in Anselmo Braamcamp Freire, 'Cartas de quitação,' *Arquivo Histórico Português*, II, n. 297, p. 440. Cf. Blake, *Europeans in West Africa*, pp. 117–18.
[378] *Casa dos Contos*: an integrant part of the Exchequer, which regulated and audited public accounts.

which they brought to these kingdoms; and 535,500 *reais* which he received from João da Fonseca, since he farmed the fourths, twentieths and tenths of the land of the island of São Tomé for two years, which began on the day of St John '511 and ended on the same day in '513, and this sum included the one percent which he paid; and 70,130 *reais* from Duarte Afonso and Duarte Belo, since they farmed the twentieth of the island of Annobon, which ended on the day of St John '513, and this sum included the one percent; and 55,550 *reais* from the Count of Portalegre, since he leased the orchil of the islands of São Nicolau, Santa Luzia and islets for one year, which ended on the day of St John '513, with the one percent; and 3,130,999 *reais* from António Rodrigues Mascarenhas and Nicolau Rodrigues, since they leased the islands of Santiago, Fogo and Maio for three years, which began on the day of St John '510 and ended on the same day in '513, with the one percent; and 1,125,162 *reais* which the said Gonçalo Lopes received from himself for the sale of 1,352 dozen and 4 goat skins, which he received from the islands during the said three years of his receipt,[379] at various prices per dozen; and 64,558 *reais* which he also received from himself for the sale of 57 *moios,*[380] 18 *alqueires*[381] of wheat at various prices; and 8,086,975 *reais*, being the value of 1,265 slave pieces, both male and female, which he received from the said Rui Gomes, Treasurer of the House of Mina, during the said three years of his receipt; and 32,200 *reais* which the said Gonçalo Lopes also received from himself for the sale of 10 slave pieces, both male and female, at various prices;[382] and 1,616,000 *reais* from João de Lila and João de Castro, since the trade of Sierra Leone was leased to them for three years, which began on the day of St John '510 and ended on the day of St John '513, and this sum included the one percent; and 393,900 *reais* from Francisco Martins, since he leased the Senegal River[383] for two years, which began on the first of January '511 and ended at the end of December '512, with the one percent; and 1,376,620 *reais* from the said Francisco Martins for an equal sum amounted during the last year and a half (which began on the first of January '511 and ended on the day of St John '512) of the three years during which he leased the Rivers of Guinea, and this sum includes the one percent, since João de Figueiredo, who was Receiver of the said slaves, had received as much before; and 1,363,500 *reais* from Master Filipe, since he leased the Rivers of Cantor and Gambia for three years, which began the day of St John '510 and ended on the same day in '513, with the one percent; and 1,212,000 *reais* from the said João de Lila and his partners, since they leased the Rivers of Guinea for one year, which began on the day of St John '512 and

---

[379] Literal translation of '*de seu recebimento,*' i.e. the period during which he was receiving.
[380] *Moio*: see Glossary.
[381] *Alqueire*: see Glossary.
[382] The passage from 'and 32,200 *reais* [...]' to '[...] at various prices' was omitted in Blake's translation.
[383] In the transcription, '*rio de Çenagues.*'

ended on the same day in '513, and this sum includes the one percent; and 1,050,400 *reais* from Calliro Redolho, since he leased the trade of malagueta for two years, which began on the first of January '512 and ended at the end of December '513, with the one percent; and 606,000 *reais* from the Secretary António Carneiro, since he farmed the fourths and twentieths of his said Island of Príncipe for four years, which began on the day of St John '510 and ended on the same day in '514, with the one percent; and 112,000 *reais* from André Rodrigues, the Receiver of the money from the sale of spices, for the expenses of his office, in two instalments;[384] and 1,504,800 *reais* from Heitor Nunes, in eleven instalments;[385] and 2,300 *reais* from Rui de Castanheda; and 82,788 *reais* from Bartolomeu Marchione[386] in two instalments; and 44,000 *reais* from Baltasar Fernandes, Receiver of the Paço of Madeira;[387] and 26,000 *reais* from João de Borba, Receiver of the ports of Entre-Tejo-e-Odiana; and 20,000 *reais* from Álvaro Dias, *Almoxarife*[388] of the island of Santiago; and 140,000 *reais* from Álvaro Pimentel; and 80,000 *reais* from Sebastião de Vargas, the Receiver of the money of the Treasurer of the House of Mina; and 197,000 *reais* from António do Porto, the Receiver of the House of the said slaves; and the remaining 39,600 *reais* from João Godinho, the Receiver of extraordinary money from all these eleven persons, for the expenses of his office. And 311 *moios*, 4 *alqueires* of wheat, whereof 55 *moios*, 3 *alqueires* he received from António Godinho, *Almoxarife* of the island of São Miguel, and 68 *moios*, 15 *alqueires* from Luís Gonçalves, *Almoxarife* of [[Vila da]] Praia on the island of Terceira, and 43 *moios*, 46 *alqueires* from Francisco Martins, *Almoxarife* of the island of Graciosa, and 60 *moios* from António da Veiga, *Almoxarife* of Faial, and the remaining 84 *moios* from Diogo Girão, *Almoxarife* of the island of São Jorge. And 25 *quintais*,[389] 2 *arrobas*,[390] 19 *arratéis*[391] and a quarter of redwood,[392] which he received from the traders of Sierra Leone, as the twentieth of 513 *quintais*. And also many other things of various kinds, as is contained in the said receipt, which are not enumerated by reason of their length. And by the closure of his account, he is shown to have spent the whole of the said money and the aforesaid articles well and as he ought. [...][393] And therefore [...] we acquit and free him from obligation. [...] Issued in Almeirim, on the 17th of December 1514.

---

[384] In Braamcamp Freire's transcription, '*per duas adições*,' literally 'by two sums.'
[385] See previous note.
[386] The Florentine merchant Bartolomeo Marchionni.
[387] The Paço da Madeira was a Portuguese administration office, linked to the system of customs and excise and charged with overseeing the trade in wood and other merchandise.
[388] *Almoxarife*: see Glossary.
[389] *Quintal* (sing.): see Glossary.
[390] *Arroba*: see Glossary.
[391] *Arrátel*: see Glossary.
[392] In the transcription, '*páo vermelho*' ('*pau vermelho*'), known as 'Brazilwood,' and not '*pão vermelho*' ('red corn') as Blake has it.
[393] This and the following ellipses are in the transcription.

35 Report by Alessandro Zorzi from
the City of Venice[394] (1517)

ABSTRACT – *Report on the Kongo, Mina, and Benin, but excerpts have only been taken from the brief passages relevant to the Mina (Gold) Coast.*

They say that the King of Portugal has on the coast of Ethiopia, towards the South,[395] beyond the Old Mina[396] de São Jorge, a lieutenant[397] where every year he sends ships. And between land and the Padrão River,[398] behind that southern coast, they say that there is an Ethiopian king as powerful as can be, who is called the King of Manikongo, which is a name taken from that country where he reigns, which is a very great kingdom, and is continuously at war with its neighbors and especially with those who are to be found towards the Cape of Good Hope, all of them savage and very cruel men, and especially those of the said Cape of Good Hope, who in previous years killed 60 Portuguese[399] who, in all safety, had disembarked on land thinking that they were civilized and tame men.

[...] They also say that on the borders of the King of Benin there is another king further inland, who borders on the Old Mina, like the King of Benin, and they say that his Kingdom is called Labidi.[400] He has horses, though they are small, but he is not as powerful as the King of Benin. But the King of Manikongo is the most powerful of them all. They say that they take horses to the said two kings, namely those of Benin and Manikongo, who do not have horses but only small cattle and goats. They have coarse millet and beans. The said Portuguese bring from that country ivory tusks, *malagueta*, and slaves who are well proportioned. Every year they send 12 *barze*, that is, one a month, and they go to Old Mina where the castle of São Jorge is. And that those black people who give obedience to the King of Portugal give him every month Tiber gold to the value of 10,000 to

---

[394] MMA, vol. 15, doc. 17, pp. 35–41. References to the foliation have been removed in Brásio's transcription, since the original source is not cited. The document is written in Italian, with one short passage in Latin. This text was the object of a study by Francisco Leite de Faria and Avelino Teixeira da Mota, 'Novidades Náuticas e Ultramarinas numa Informação dada em Veneza em 1517,' *Memórias da Academia das Ciências de Lisboa: Classe de Ciências* 20 (1977): 7–75.

[395] In Brásio's transcription, '*megio di*,' that is, '*mezzogiorno.*'

[396] Mina Velha (Old Mine) refers to São Jorge da Mina, to distinguish it from Mina Nova (New Mine) or Sofala.

[397] In Brásio's transcription, '*locotenente*' ('*luogotenente*'), in this context possibly a representative of the King; by extension, it may stand here for the territory under his authority.

[398] In Portuguese, 'Rio de Padrão,' literally 'Pillar River'; nowadays the 'Congo/Kongo River.' Diogo Cão served King João II in a war against Castile, and his voyage(s) of 1482–84 reached the mouth of the Kongo River, where he planted a pillar (*padrão*) in the name of São Jorge—patron saint of Portugal and the Portuguese cavalry—hence, Padrão River.

[399] The fame of 'very cruel savages' undoubtedly derives from when they murdered Dom Francisco de Almeida on March 2, 1510, while he was returning from India, together with approximately 60 of his men.

[400] It seems the Portuguese had only recently learned about the existence of the ruler of Labadi ('Labidan'), who was on the eastern extreme of the Mina (Gold) Coast proper, not Benin. The so-called 'porto da Gata' ('port of Gwato') is nowadays Ughoton. Labadi, near Nkrãn, was known for leathermaking and had a foul market.

15,000 *ducati* per month, and they go inland to the mountain caves[401] to fetch it. And thus, there are three powerful kings on the coast and inland in Guinea, one the King of Labidi, and the other, more powerful, the King of Benin; the third, who is more powerful than the other [[two]], is the King of Manikongo, who is beyond the island of São Tomé, at the Padrão River. [...]

36 Letter from Fernão Lopes Correia to the Factor of Mina[402] (20/10/1517)

ABSTRACT – *Mina captain Fernão Lopes Correia orders factor Manuel de Sande to supply emissary Nicolau Garcia with a variety of 'gifts' to indigenous rulers and leading figures of key polities, to persuade them to 'open the roads' and allow gold and traders safe passage to and from the interior to the Portuguese fortress. Document published for the first time.*

[[I]], Fernão Lopes Correia, Captain and Governor of this town of São Jorge da Mina, order you, Manuel de Sande, currently its Factor, to deliver to Nicolau Garcia the following items: *scilicet*, for the King of the Akan,[403] a painted [[*lambel*]][404] and a Tenes *aljaravia*, and two and a half rods of cloth, and a red cap;[405] and for the King of the Abrem,[406] some [[*lambéis of*]] mazona [[*sic*]][407] and a red cap, and two and a half rods of cloth; and for four knights of the King of the Akan, four short[408] *aljaravias*; and for the King of Bua [[*sic*]],[409] a short *aljaravia*; and for the passage by boat,[410] a chamber pot and four short aljaravias for expenses of the said Nicolau Garcia, since I am sending him to these parts(?)[411] to open the roads, through which[412] I will send him the said items, as this is in the service of Our Lord the King.

---

[401] In Brásio's transcription, *'fornace'* (followed by a question mark), which could be literally translated as 'ovens'; it probably should read *'fornacchie,'* i.e. the name given in the Apuan Alps to caves cut into rocky walls.

[402] ANTT, CC 2-72-26.

[403] In the manuscript, *'acanes.'*

[404] In the manuscript, *'hũ pintado'* (*'um pintado'*); see *MMA*, vol. 1, docs. 61 and 125 for the complete term *'lambéis pintados.'*

[405] In the manuscript, *'barete'* (*'barrete'*): see Glossary.

[406] In the manuscript, *'beremus.'*

[407] For the complete term *'lambel/lambéis* of *mazona,'* see, for example, Blake's translations, doc. no. 18.

[408] In the manuscript, *'pequenas,'* which might also be translated as 'small.'

[409] In the manuscript, *'Rej de bua'* (*'Rei de Bua'*), which might read *'Rei d'Ebua'* ('King of Abura'(?)). And Bua might be related to 'Buaman.'

[410] In the manuscript, *'barca,'* a term which may refer to different kinds of vessels of small or medium size.

[411] In the manuscript, the abbreviation *'pᵃˢ,'* which might stand for *'pessoas.'* In this context, it is likely this should read *'pᵉˢ'/'partes'* ('parts').

[412] It is not clear whether *'polo quall'* (*'pelo qual'*) refers to the roads being opened (though it should strictly read *'pelos quais,'* pl.) or the reason for sending the items (in which case it should be translated as 'for which reason').

And by these [[instructions]], which will be registered by the Scribes of the Expenditure, who will post it as expenditure, it will be accounted for on your behalf. Written by me, Gaspar de Vila Lobos, scribe of the Factory, on the 20th day of October 1517.

Gaspar de Vila Lobos

[sign.] *Fernão Lopes Correia*

37 Writ for the Brotherhood of the Black Men of Lisbon[413] (18/04/1518)

ABSTRACT – *King Manuel determines every caravel coming from Mina should donate 500 reais as alms to the Brotherhood of the Rosary of the Black Men, of the monastery of St Dominic of Lisbon. This documents links the Mina (Gold) Coast to an early modern African diaspora in Portugal.*

[[I]], Dom João, etc., make known to all those who may see this letter of mine that the majordomo and confreres of the Brotherhood of Our Lady of the Rosary of this city presented to me a writ by my lord and father, may he be in glory, which reads as follows:

We, the King, make known to you, João Gago, Treasurer of our House of Guinea, and to the scribes of that office, that it is our wish and pleasure to henceforth donate to the Brotherhood of the Black Men, sited in the Monastery of St Dominic of this city, five hundred *reais* as alms for every caravel coming from Mina, as we donate to the other houses[414] of brotherhoods in this city, and hence we order you to deliver as alms to the majordomos of the said brotherhood five hundred *reais* for each caravel that comes from Mina. And by the copy of this letter, which will be registered in the books of that House, they will be made known and accounted for on your behalf.

Written in Lisbon, on the 18th day of April – António de Neiva wrote this – one thousand 518.

As the aforementioned have asked me as a grace to confirm the said writ in writing, and their request having been seen by me, it is my wish that it be confirmed together with its contents in their entirety.

Gaspar de Figueiredo wrote this, in Lisbon, on the 8th day of August, year one thousand 529. And I, Damião Dias,[415] had this written.

---

[413] ANTT, *Chancelaria de D. João III*, liv. 22, fol. 100; cf. MMA vol. 2, doc. 49.
[414] In Brásio's transcription, '*Casas,*' here in the sense of organized bodies.
[415] See MMA vol. 4, doc. 40.

38 Instructions from Fernão Lopes Correia to Factor Manuel De Sande[416] (23/04/1518)

ABSTRACT – *Fernão Lopes Correia gives a brass cauldron to the 'Sharif,' a key local ally, and four hundred reais for making curtains for the altars of the Mina cathedral.*

+

[[I]], Fernão Lopes Correia,[417] Captain and Governor of this town of São Jorge da Mina, order you, Manuel de Sande,[418] who are Factor there, to deliver a brass cauldron to be sent to the Sharif, whom I have ordered to be visited, and furthermore that you deliver four hundred *reais* for the making of some curtains which I ordered to be made for two altars of this cathedral. And by these [[instructions]], which will be registered by the Scribes of the Expenditure, whom I order to post it for you as expenditure, it will be accounted for on your behalf.

Written by me, Gaspar de Vila Lobos,[419] scribe of this Factory, on the 23rd day of the month of April 1518.

a) Fernão Lopes Correia   a) Gaspar de Vila Lobos

39 Instructions from Fernão Lopes Correia to Factor Manuel De Sande[420] (13/08/1518)

ABSTRACT – *Fernão Lopes Correia gives the Vicar Rui Pires various vestments, which he enumerates, since the old ones were worn out serving the Mina cathedral. Captains had to pay equal attention to matters related to commerce and missionary work, whether baptism, conversion or rituals for sick and dying Portuguese residents.*

[[I]], Fernão Lopes Correia,[421] Captain and Governor of this town of São Jorge da Mina, order you, Manuel de Sande,[422] who are Factor there, to account on behalf of Rui Pires, who served here as Vicar, two bands, with an amice, of

---

[416] ANTT, CC 2-107-113; cf. MMA vol. 15, doc. 18.

[417] See ANTT, *Contos do Reino e Casa, Núcleo Antigo* 867, MMA vol. 1, docs. 123 and 124, MMA vol. 4, doc. 32, and MMA vol. 15, doc. 20.

[418] See ANTT, *Fragmentos, Cartas para El-Rei*, cx. 1, mç. 1, n. 7, CC 2-86-30, MMA vol. 1, docs. 123 and 124, MMA vol. 4, doc. 32, MMA vol. 15, docs. 18 and 20.

[419] See MMA vol. 15, doc. 20.

[420] ANTT, CC 2-109-129; cf. MMA vol. 15, doc. 20.

[421] See ANTT, *Contos do Reino e Casa, Núcleo Antigo* 867, MMA vol. 1, docs. 123–24; vol. 4, doc. 32; vol. 15, doc. 18.

[422] See ANTT, *Fragmentos, Cartas para El-Rei*, cx. 1, mç. 1, n. 7, CC 2-86-30, MMA vol. 1, docs. 123–24; vol. 4, doc. 32; vol. 15, doc. 18.

bead-embroidered damask, and two bands of black moire, and two gremials[423] and some cuffs,[424] and an amice with its band of purple velvet, and two amice bands of *brocadilho,*[425] and an amice band of the carmine-satin vestment, since they have been worn out in the service of this cathedral. And by these [[instructions]], which will be registered by the Scribes of the Expenditure, whom I order to post it for you as expenditure, it will be accounted for on your behalf.

Written by me, Gaspar de Vila Lobos,[426] scribe of this Factory, on the 13th day of August 1518.

a) Fernão Lopes Correia a) Gaspar de Vila Lobos

40 Letter from Fernão Lopes Correia to King Manuel[427] (08/10/1518)

ABSTRACT – *Fernão Lopes Correia provides reasons for the lack of commerce in Mina, the shortfalls in flour, and details the various events related to the administration of the fortress. Finally, he asks for royal permission to leave for Portugal.*

+

My Lord,

João Coelho, Captain of this ship, gave me a letter from Your Highness, and I am sending a reply to the officials of the House, whereby the estimate of the merchandise which they can send in each ship, based on ten per year, is declared, according to what Your Highness says in the letter.

Your Highness should not be surprised at the small quantity of cloth[428] mentioned in [[the estimate]], which is due to the great quantity that there is here,

---

[423] In Brásio's transcription, *'regaços,'* literally 'laps,' hence the cloth a bishop wore on the lap when sitting during some religious ceremonies (the precise term in Portuguese is *'gremial'*).

[424] In Brásio's transcription, *'manguitos,'* literally small sleeves used to protect or adorn the wrists, and thus a probable corruption of *'maniquetes,'* the name given to the ornamental fabric or lace used as trimming in the alb's sleeves. For the English equivalent, 'cuffs,' see *Thesaurus: Vocabulário de Objectos do Culto Católico* (Lisboa: Universidade Católica Portuguesa / Fundação da Casa de Bragança, 2004), 178, under *'Maniquete.'*

[425] *Brocatilho*: see Glossary.

[426] See MMA vol. 15, doc. 18.

[427] ANTT, *Chancelaria de D. Manuel I*, III, doc. 179; cf. MMA, vol. 4, doc. 32, pp. 117–23. On October 8, Fernão Lopes Correia asked the king to send a new captain from January until May, so he could return before winter. On September 26, 1519, the signatory of this letter was still captain of Mina (Cf. MMA vol. 1, p. 427), though on October 3 the same year, Duarte Pacheco Pereira had already been appointed to the captaincy (Cf. MMA vol. 1, p. 428). We surmise the present document is dated October 8, 1518. We have not found in the *Chancery* the royal writs appointing as captains either Fernão Lopes Correia or Duarte Pacheco Pereira. See CC 2-86-30, MMA vol. 1, docs. 125, 127, 129, 130, 131, 132; vol. 15, doc. 31; see also ANTT, *Contos do Reino e Casa, Núcleo Antigo* 867.

[428] In Brásio's transcription, *'roupa.'* Here, as elsewhere, MMA adds a note explaining *'roupa'* means 'light goods.' Every time the term is used in these documents, it designates different kinds of fabric or cloth (such as *lambéis*).

since one needs to find a way of selling it. And I do not know of another way apart from not receiving much; and let that which is coming be all, because otherwise it will never be possible to make an end of the remainder, since the greater part of these cloths which are here now do not make more than fifty; and when they [[the black people(?)]] find that they do not reach sixty, they do not want to take them, except when they have no alternative, since they are already here and they cannot find any other cloth. And therefore it is necessary to send always one hundred in each of the ships of Gonçalo Vaz,[429] or in any others which come here, so that, knowing that these have arrived, they [[the black people(?)]] may come and, when these cloths have all been sold, also take the others. And thus it will be sold, giving a lesser loss to Your Highness.

And I am also sending an opinion on the two *lambéis* of a sample[430] from Gonçalo Vaz which we have received here, and which are sold at twenty *pesos,*[431] as Your Highness ordered. And all things considered it is my opinion, and that of the Factor, that because of the price only a few will be sold.

And furthermore I am sending an opinion on the two Tenes *aljaravias*[432] which came as a sample[433] from Gonçalo Vaz, and which the black people do not want to buy because of their price, since they can see that they are not [[true Tenes *aljaravias*]], as the Tenes ones are woven with a different warp, and are thicker, and the inner side is like tapestry, though not with long hair, for they wear this reverse side directly on the skin, and they find it soft and warm, which pleases them much, as they use them both day and night, since the only mattress they have is a skin under [[the body]] and one *aljaravia* over it. And all things considered it is our opinion that, as long as there are no Tenes *aljaravias*, they will take these for five *pesos*, for they have already offered as much for these, and I have ordered that they should not be given to them before I have informed Your Highness.

And furthermore I am sending an opinion on the *aljaravias* from Fez, which we have now received here, and which could well be done without, for they are such that they are worthless, and because they [[the black people]] are already used to those of Gonçalo Vaz, which are so good that they could not be better; and Your Highness should not have others brought, since you have them in the Kingdom; and you should have it agreed that he give you three thousand per year, as well as the necessary *lambéis*, because once they arrive there will be no need for thinner ones. And the profit will stay in the Kingdom and Your Highness may be better served. And thus, you shall not need to send money to Fez.

---

[429] This seaman is unidentifiable. See MMA vol. 1, docs. 125 and 132.
[430] Literal translation of '*da amostra*,' which here might mean the articles were 'of the best quality.'
[431] Spanish coin, the same as *duro*, equivalent (at the time of the publication of the MMA) to five *pesetas*.
[432] *Aljaravia* (sing.): see Glossary.
[433] Literal translation of '*per amostra.*'

And though Your Highness, My Lord, is of the opinion that the great quantity of *aljaravias* might hinder the selling of the *lambéis*, Your Highness should not fear, since they are different both as to cost and as to use, for the *aljaravias* are worn by all men exclusively as a cloak, while the *lambéis* are cut for breeches[434] and for their wives' *fufus,*[435] with which they cover themselves. And thus, the one does not hinder the other, though one can sell as many *aljaravias* as one wants. I make this known to Your Highness because Gonçalo Vaz wrote to me, saying that Your Highness would be pleased to know it.

My Lord, this flour which comes for our sustenance has always been received according to the letters from Jorge de Vasconcelos,[436] where he says that he is sending ten *moios*[437] of flour in twelve pipes, at fifty *alqueires*[438] per pipe. And because, My Lord, the *Almoxarife*[439] feels he has suffered a great loss, for he received and gave a receipt for them on this basis – it being impossible to measure such a large amount – and now, when he gets through it he finds they [[the pipes]] do not contain the full fifty *alqueires*, he has asked me to have measured the capacity of one pipe from each ship; and, according to what was found in each case, he would accept the others on the same basis. And because this seemed to me to be fair and just, I ordered the Factor and officials to go to the underwater hull and, in the presence of the captains, to have [[the flour of]] one whole pipe sieved and measured, so as to estimate what the *Almoxarife* was receiving. And so, it was done, My Lord, in the presence of Duarte Borges and his scribe, together with the officials, and there was a shortfall of three and a quarter *alqueires*.

And now the same was done, in the presence of João Coelho and his scribe, and there were eight *alqueires* missing, the pipe being one of the largest. And because it seems to me, My Lord, that no person can give good account of what he does not receive, and because the captains are aggrieved by this, since they issue a receipt for them there, I have them issue their receipts for the full amount as stated in the letter, in order to avoid disputes between them and the Factor and *Almoxarife*, together with a declaration of how much was found to be missing. I make this known to Your Highness in order that you may provide in this matter as you consider best to your service, so that the pipes arrive as full as they should be, and because the officials [[responsible]] are not persons of whom it should be feared or presumed that they might appropriate anything at all, let alone this, which is worth so little. And because it is necessary to settle how it should be done in future, it is necessary that Your Highness should provide in this matter as you consider to be your service, and in such a way that the *almoxarifes* suffer no loss and your service may be kept.

---

[434] In Brásio's transcription, '*bragaas*,' i.e. '*bragas*': short and loose shorts, made of *bragal*, a type of coarse fabric.
[435] Skirts, dresses.
[436] See MMA vol. 4, doc. 14.
[437] *Moio* (sing.): see Glossary.
[438] *Alqueire* (sing): see Glossary.
[439] *Almoxarife*: see Glossary.

My Lord, Your Highness granted me this captaincy for the period stipulated in your regulations, on condition that I married Francisca de Miranda, for which I gave many thanks to God, as I know that my services can never be an excuse for not granting a favor to someone else with them. And I, My Lord, have done so rather as a service to you than for the pleasure I might receive from both one thing and the other. And I have discharged them as God may wish that Your Highness should know, and the fear I had of this land was rather of the opinions of the officials than of its infirmity. And thus, I told Your Highness that I would be obliged if you should send some officials with me, with whom I could serve you. And Your Highness told me that you would do so. And after this you rightly made me break with [[?]][440] Vasco de Pina. And then it was your wish to send[441] Manuel de Sande, who discharges it [[the office]] very well and as befits your service. And after him came Aires Botelho, whom I believe Your Highness does not know, and who, together with Baltasar de Barros, has now greatly offended the *Almoxarife* with words, [[though]] I had ordered him not to do so, for which reason I have imprisoned both of them in the lodge, and they may only go out to serve their offices. And I have given orders to have a hold put on their wages until I have made this known to Your Highness, so that you give them the punishment they deserve, for its having taken place where it did and with an official of yours. And furthermore, I am also sending under arrest a certain Francisco Eanes, who was a resident here, and who was also implicated in the matter [[?]],[442] as stated in the judicial action and examination which is being sent in the strongbox. And Your Highness may be sure that, if he were not a retainer of Our Lady the Queen, may God keep her,[443] he would receive his corrective here. And thus, I am sending him under arrest, so that Your Highness may have him punished as you consider best to your service. And regarding those who stay here, I would be obliged if you should send me instructions with the first ship, specifying what you wish to be done with these officials, because if it were not for the necessity I had of them in performing your service, in view of their offices, they would have been sent under arrest in this ship, so that Your Highness might have had them receive the corrective found to be just, according to the examination which was made.

My Lord, I feel that I am in no condition to remain here any further than Easter, and therefore I will kiss Your Highness's hands should you soon have a captain appointed from January onwards, in order that he may arrive here before May and that I may leave in the summer, and not in the winter, as was the case when I came here. And I would be obliged to Your Highness, and so would be whoever should come, should this take place earlier and with good weather. And thus it would be settled that the appointed captains should come and go with good weather. And let not Your Highness think that I say so with passion, let alone

---

[440] Literal translation of '*partyr com*' ('*partir com*').
[441] In Brásio's transcription, '*mudar*,' literally 'to change,' which does not make much sense in this sentence. It should probably read '*mandar*,' i.e. in this context, 'to send.'
[442] Tentative translation of '[...] *que tambem foy nyso*' ('[...] *que também foi nisso.*'
[443] Reference to Dona Maria of Castile, second wife of Dom Manuel, who died in Lisbon on March 7, 1517.

with the hope that Your Highness may give me more time, because I do not wish nor ask for[444] it, for I already know that I shall never be richer than I have always been. And in this I shall be very much obliged to Your Highness, since I would rather give up some of my time [[of service]] than ask for it, as I know that my condition makes it necessary to cut it short, lest I put myself at great risk.

My Lord, as I conclude writing this [[letter]], this entire land remains peaceful and quiet, and with all the roads unimpeded, and the House in better health than it has been for many days. May Our Lord be praised.

May Our Lord increase your Royal Estate with a long life, as we all wish and need.

From Mina, on the 8th day of October [1518].

[sign.] Fernão Lopes Correia

ADDRESS: To the King
SENDER: From Fernão Lopes Correia,
     Captain of Mina

41 King Manuel to António Porto Carreiro, Captain of Arguin[445] (02/12/1518)

ABSTRACT – *Letter from the king to the Captain of Arguin about the kinds and numbers of enslaved Africans to be shipped to Mina and orders it be ongoing.*

António Porto Carreiro, we, the King, send you greetings. We have now commanded Duarte Borges, who is going at present as captain in this ship which we are sending to Mina, to make for that Factory so that you may deliver to him forty or fifty slave pieces, in order that he may transport and deliver them to our Factor of the said Mina. Wherefore we enjoin and command you to deliver to the said Duarte Borges, or to any other person who may go as captain of the said ship, the said slave pieces. And you shall ask him for a receipt until you are given another formally from the said Factor of Mina. And moreover, we command you henceforward to send to the said Factor in all ships the slaves for which our officials of the House of Mina write to you. And whatever they ask of you by their letters you shall do, as if the letters were ours, because this is our wish, and for this we shall thank you. And you are to provide every favor, aid and quick dispatch which may be necessary, as we are confident you will. Written in Almeirim, on the 2nd day of December – Manuel de Moura wrote this – 1518.

And the said slaves, which you are thus to deliver to him, are to be all males, or as many of them as possible. If there can be seventy pieces, you shall

---

[444] In Brásio's transcription, '*preço*,' which could read '*prezo*' (from the verb '*prezar*,' 'to cherish'). Given the context and the following sentence, however, this should probably read '*peço*' ('I ask for').
[445] ANTT, CC 2-79-25. Cf. Blake, *Europeans in West Africa*, p. 126.

deliver this number to him. And they are to be the best to be had there, and they are to be neither boys nor old men but the most youthful adults which may be found there.

The King

To the Captain of Arguin about these slaves for Mina.

42 Receipt from Duarte Borges for Slaves Delivered to Him at Arguim[446] (04/01/1519)

ABSTRACT – *Ship captain Duarte Borges acknowledges receipt of enslaved Africans, which he will transport to Mina.*

Duarte Borges, Captain of the ship Santo Ildefonso, which is now going to Mina, acknowledged and admitted that he received from António Porto Carreiro, Captain of this castle of Arguin, thirty-five slave pieces, both male and female, which he is carrying to deliver to the Factor of the said Mina. And as a true record he gave him this receipt, signed by him and written by me, Nicolau Antunes, on the fourth of January 15[1]9.

[sign.] Duarte Borges

Nicolau Antunes

35 pieces which were posted as receipt in the ledger of João Gago[447] for the year '519 at folio 216, in an entry which states that he received them from António Porto Carreiro through the said Duarte Borges, to deliver them to Manuel de Sande, Factor of Mina. This is true.[448]

[On the reverse of one page]:
Receipt for 35 slave pieces, both male and female, which were taken to Mina Of Duarte Borges
These 35 slave pieces are posted as receipt for João Gago in the ledger for '519, at folio 216 of his book.

[On the reverse of another page]:
Letter from Our Lord the King about Duarte Borges, when I delivered him some slaves for him to take to Mina
By the King
To António Porto Carreiro, knight of his Household and his Captain in the castle of Arguin

---

[446] ANTT, CC 2-79-25. Cf. Blake, *Europeans in West Africa*, p. 127.
[447] Treasurer of the House of Mina (?).
[448] Blake's translation ends here.

43 Dispatch from São Tomé Officials to the Agents of São Jorge Da Mina[449] (17/01/1519)

ABSTRACT – *The cargo transported on the ship Santa Maria-a-Nova is as follows: 70 male and female enslaved persons, 2132 akori beads, 11 grey beads, and 14 coribombo cloths.*

Most Honorable Factors,

[[We]], *Licenciado* Bernardo de Sequeira, main *Corregedor*[450] and Provider of the Orphans in this Island of São Tomé by special warrant of Our Lord the King, and João de Lagos *Almoxarife,*[451] and Álvaro Frade,[452] and Jorge Vaz, make known to Your Graces that the ship Santa Maria-a-Nova, of which João do Porto is pilot and Pedro Velho scribe, sailed from this island. And the ship carries a cargo of seventy slave pieces, both male and female, plus two thousand and seventy-two Akori beads, and eleven grey beads and fourteen *coribombos,*[453] to be delivered there to Your Graces according to the terms of the contract; and there will also be delivered to Your Graces sixty Akori beads, which altogether amount to two thousand one hundred and thirty-two Akori beads to be delivered to Your Graces, and thus we inform you. Issued in this island of São Tomé, on the 17th day of the month of January one thousand five hundred and nineteen years, [[by]] Nuno Vaz, Registrar of the *Correição*[454] of the said island. I, João de Lisboa,[455] Registrar of the *Almoxarifado*[456] of the said island for Our Lord the King, wrote it.

[sign.]   *Jorge Vaz*   *B. de Sequeira*   *João de Lagos*

Álvaro Frade   *João de Lisboa*

44 Accounts of Gaspar De Villalobos, Factor of Old Cloth in São Jorge Da Mina[457] (06/02/1519)

ABSTRACT – *Account of Mina factor Gaspar de Villalobos for the period from 13 December 1516 to 21 March 1519.*

---

[449] ANTT, CC 2-79-67. Transcribed in Ballong-Wen-Mewuda, *São Jorge da Mina*, 2: 530.
[450] *Corregedor*: see Glossary.
[451] *Almoxarife*: see Glossary.
[452] See MMA vol. 4, doc. 33.
[453] *Coribombos*: meaning obscure.
[454] *Correição*: see Glossary.
[455] See MMA vol. 4, doc. 33.
[456] *Almoxarifado*: see Glossary.
[457] ANTT, *Chancelaria de D. Manuel*, liv. 44, fol. 46; liv. das Ilhas, fol. 215v. Transcribed in A. Braamcamp Freire, 'Cartas de quitação,' *Arquivo Histórico Português*, II, n. 273, p. 430. Cf. Blake, *Europeans in West Africa*, pp. 127–28.

We have commanded an account to be taken from Gaspar de Villalobos, knight of our Household and former Factor of the Old Cloth in our town of São Jorge da Mina, for the two years and two months and twenty days, which began on the 13th of December 1516 and ended on the 2nd of March '519, during which he was entrusted with the receipt of the said Factory. And it has been found that, during the said period, he received the following gold and articles, namely: 267 marks, 6 ounces, 2 drams, 66 grains of gold, by the sale of the goods here declared, namely: 114 *aljaravias*[458] of every kind, and 1,001 *lambéis*[459] of every kind, and 4 striped[460] blankets, 1 *alquice*,[461] and other things, which he received upon delivery from Baltasar de Barros, who was Factor of the said Old Cloth, and which are declared in his receipt. The said receipt, which was examined in our Exchequer by our overseers thereof, showed that the said Gaspar de Vilalobos, Factor, has rendered us a very good account of the said gold and other articles. [...] in view of which [...] we acquit and free him from obligation. [...] Issued in Evora, on the 6th of February – João do Porto wrote this – 1519.

Although it states above that the period of his receipt[462] ends on the 2nd of March, it is for two years and three months and eighteen days, which begins on the 13th of December, as has been said, and ends at the end of March '519.

45 Regulations of the Commerce of São Tomé[463] (08/02/1519)

ABSTRACT – *These regulations cover wages of crews and payment in enslaved persons; precepts to be observed in commerce; the branding of the king's slaves and their sustenance; the salary of the factor, the auditor, and other officials; the prohibition of embarking sick enslaved persons; the treatment of the enslaved on board and that accounts be rendered for those who die; the maximum price of the enslaved; sending the enslaved and merchandise to Mina; and the journeys from Mina to the Rivers of Benin for trade.*

We, the King, make known to you Álvaro Frade,[464] knight of our Household, whom we now appoint as Factor of our slave trade of the island of São Tomé, which used to belong to the traders, and Pedro Dinis, whom we appoint as Receiver, and João[465] de Ferreira and João de Lisboa,[466] scribes, that these are the

---

[458] *Aljaravia(s)*: see Glossary.
[459] *Lambel* (sing.): see Glossary.
[460] In the transcription, '*alambeladas*,' from '*lambel*,' which characteristically had stripes.
[461] *Alquice*: see Glossary.
[462] Literal translation of '*de seu recebimento*,' i.e. the period during which he was receiving.
[463] ANTT, *Leis e Regimentos de D. Manuel*, fols. 83-88v; cf. MMA, vol. 4, doc. 33, pp. 124–33.
[464] See CC 2-79-67.
[465] In fact, 'Lopo.' At fol. 89 of this codex, one can find the regulations Dom Manuel gave him. Cf. MMA vol. 1, p. 423.
[466] João de Lisboa was appointed scribe of the *Almoxarifado* of São Tomé by letter of 10-4-1514. Cf. ANTT, *Chancelaria de D. Manuel*, liv. 15, fol. 24. See CC 2-79-67.

regulations and manner which, in this commerce and trade, it is our will that you should observe.

Item: You shall choose as pilots and masters, and also as seamen and ship's boys, for those ships of ours which will serve in the said trades, the best and most trustful you can find there. And because we are informed that the traders used to pay, as annual wages, approximately, six slave pieces to each pilot, and four to the master, and five to every three seamen [[?]],[467] and two to each ship's boy, and this approximately, and that they could take them to the Kingdom, you shall try to have them serve for lower wages and settle it with them as best you can and as might serve me well, given that whatever the amount they shall be well paid. And this shall be settled with them in your presence, and whatever you settle, up to the said amount that was given to them by the traders, will be good, and from that [[amount]] down as far as you can, as has been said. And in the aforesaid manner you shall pay the officials, and workers, and provisions, as they [[the traders]] used to pay, and if it can be for less, so shall it be done.

Item: You shall be minded to inform our Factor and officials of the House of Mina, through the *carreira* ships[468] in which our slaves shall come or through any others which shall come from there, of the merchandise, stays and pitch of which the trade may be in need; and you shall likewise inform us, so that you may be provided with everything in time.

Item: You shall send persons to act as scribes of the ships that you shall send to the Rivers who are fit for it and trustworthy; and they shall be appointed by you and the Auditor,[469] since you will know which persons may be suitable, and they will have with them the regulations which they are accustomed to take, and these shall be signed by both of you. And in addition to what is stated in them, you shall on our behalf order them, under [[penalty]] for the scribes and pilots of forfeiture of their property and wages, not to give for each piece more than forty manillas, and from that [[amount]] down as far as possible. And at the other Rivers, and wherever the linen fabric of coral and crystalline color is of value, you shall immediately settle what they shall give for a slave piece, and ivory, and red fabric, as well as for other goods, and they shall not exceed it, for it is our wish and purpose to provide the said trades henceforward with good and appropriate regulations, and that they be ruled by them and not by the disorder into which they had lapsed.

Item: In addition to its being prohibited and declared in the regulations of the scribes of the said ships that, on the way back from the trades, no [[ship's]] boat be pulled out on that island without our officials being there first,

---

[467] Tentative translation of '*a cada mari-/nheiro com cimquo tres*' ('*a cada mari-/nheiro com cinco três*'), literally 'to each seaman with five three.'

[468] In Brásio's transcription, '*nauios da quarreira*' ('*navios de carreira*'): see Glossary.

[469] In Brásio's transcription, '*Contador*': see Glossary.

except in case of great necessity, you shall declare and order them on our behalf, under penalty of forfeiture of the property of the said pilot and scribe, not to pull out any [[ship's]] boat, nor to collect any person on the ships or on board. And you shall execute the said penalties on those who do otherwise, one half for whoever should denounce them and the other for the captives. And you shall immediately order that this prohibition be proclaimed, so that they cannot plead ignorance.

Item: You shall have a mark put on those slaves of ours who shall come from the Rivers, and it shall be a cross with a surround[[?]][470] on the right arm, as the Auditor said that they used to put there on our pieces [[of slaves]]; and you shall forbid anyone to brand with the said mark or on the said arm, under penalty of forfeiting the said piece.

Item: For each of the said farms, declared in the letter of the Factor, which he shall buy for the sustenance of our slaves, you shall find an overseer, a trustworthy white man, who shall look after and take very good care of them. And to each of them [[the factors]] you shall pay wages up to the amount, which was given by the traders, and from that down if possible, obliging them to take good care and be especially mindful of the said slaves. And furthermore, you, Factor and Auditor, shall often visit the said farms, and plantations, and slaves, to see and provide for the care of the said slaves, and the food which should be planted(?)[471] there, and what the said overseers shall do with the slaves and how these could be put to use; and they [[the enslaved]] shall be serviceable, because they know how to do it [[the farm work]] and have been accustomed to it in their lands, however unskilled they may be. And should there be some who might better perform the service and work of the said farms, they shall always remain there as foremen[472] and never be sent to the Kingdom like the others.

Item: Since you will need money for the purchase of the said farms and plantations, and the repair of the ships, it is our wish that any money which there may be from the crusade[473] and the deceased and the captives should be delivered to you there and charged as revenue against the Receiver; and receipts in due form shall be issued of whatever may be the amount, so that through them we may have the said money paid here to whom it may concern. And in addition to the said receipts being signed by the Factor and scribes, according to custom, they shall also be accompanied by a declaration signed by you, Factor and Auditor, stating that an amount was posted there, so that they shall be paid here by us. Which amount shall

---

[470] In Brásio's transcription, '*e[n]sserre*' ('*encerre*'), from the verb '*encerrar*,' i.e. 'to close' or 'to enclose.'

[471] In Brásio's transcription, '*seanear*,' which is meaningless; possibly should read '*semear*' ('to sow').

[472] In Brásio's transcription, '*mestres*' ('masters').

[473] It is unclear which 'crusade' the writers had in mind.

be posted as revenue of the said money, and you shall not sign them [[the receipts]] without first having seen it posted. And hereby we order those who shall keep the said money to deliver it to you in the manner declared above, and the Justices to oblige and constrain them to do so.

Item: The wages that you, the said officials, shall receive for the said offices are as follows.

Item: To you, said Álvaro Frade, Factor, thirty thousand *reais* in the Kingdom's currency per year, which you shall receive after you have finished repairing the buildings of the Factory and the ships, and from then onwards. And the other officials shall receive their wages from then onwards, according to what we pay to each of them, as declared below. And in addition to this, you, Álvaro Frade, shall receive the one percent of all the money which is raised from the sale of the slaves who are sent to the Kingdom and from all the merchandise which shall come from the said trades; which slaves and merchandise shall be sold here by our officials, all the sales being registered in a separate book, so that each year the one percent may truly and faithfully be taken from it and paid to you or to someone appointed by you.

And you shall receive the one percent for the slaves you shall send from there to Mina, and for the Akori beads, grey beads and other goods which come from the Rivers [of Benin] and you send there, namely, for the gold, should the said slaves and goods be traded in Mina. Which payment shall be made to you in this Kingdom by a certificate of our Factor and officials of the said town, whom we order to institute a book, or separate titles, of the sale of the slaves and goods which you shall send them, so that through them the one percent may be rightly paid to you.

Item: It is our wish that the said Auditor, Lopo Fernandes, shall receive, in addition to the twelve thousand *reais* he has as allowance of his office, a sixth of the said one percent from the slaves and merchandise which shall come from the said trade and be sold here by our officials, as well as in our town of Mina, in the manner declared above.

Item: The said Receiver, Pedro Dinis, shall receive twelve thousand *reais* in the Kingdom's currency per year, plus one third[474] of the said one percent.

....

Item: We hereby order the judges of the said island to have all and each of you swear on the Holy Gospels that you shall serve the said offices well and truly; and a record shall be made of this, and you shall be notified to take the oath before you start serving in the said offices.

Item: We remind you that you should not embark on the *carreira* ships slaves who are so sick or unwell that it seems that they might die if they travelled by sea.

---

[474] In Brásio's transcription, '*o terço*,' literally 'the third'; it is probable this was an unintended repetition.

And you shall leave these at the plantations to recover and come in the other ships, when they are well, advising the overseers to take good care of them and treat them well, so that they are cured. And yet you visiting and going to them is what will bring them the greatest benefit.

Item: We furthermore remind you that the *carreira* ships should have their decks floored with boards of white wood,[475] which exists there in great quantity, so that the slaves may travel well protected against the cold and the rain; and their beds should be made with the same wood, under the deck; and they should also be well provided with yam, and palm oil, and nuts[[?]],[476] and bananas, and some *malagueta*, and their sticks[[?]][477] to chew; and you should remind the pilots to take or have good care taken of them, and to put good order in the supplies, forbidding the seamen to exhaust them.

Item: You shall notify the pilots and scribes of the *carreira* ships that, should a slave die, they shall check his mark before he is thrown into the sea, so as to know if he is one of our slaves and if he bears our mark. And when a slave of ours dies, a record shall be made in the presence of witnesses, and they shall sign it. And you shall not acknowledge the death of the said slave to the pilot and scribes before the said certificate and register have been shown to you. And you shall remind our officials of the House of Mina to withhold their wages until the circumstances of the death of the said slave have been ascertained, so that his [[the slave's]] value can be deducted from his [[the pilot's(?)]] wages, unless a legitimate justification has been presented.

Item: When you send the ships to the [[places of]] trade, their pilots shall receive the necessary merchandise from the said Factor, and they shall issue a receipt for them in a separate book which shall be in the House for that purpose. And the scribe of the ship shall charge it as revenue against them [[the pilots]], so that he may account for it afterwards and so that, when they have gone and arrived at the [[places of]] trade, the said scribe may know which merchandise is being taken, since he must be present when they are traded, and he shall record in his book, as they buy them, the pieces and goods which are bought, and for what price, and what kind of goods, and everything in detail. And he shall be reminded not to allow more than forty manillas to be given for a slave piece, as has been said above, subject to the said penalty.

And if, during the return journey or while in the trade, a slave of ours should die, he shall not be thrown into the sea without it first having been checked whether

---

[475] White wood: literal translation of '*pau branco*'; whether some type of less valuable timber, as in English, or a specific type of wood coming from trees native to Brazil, the Azores, Madeira, or the Canary Islands.

[476] In Brásio's transcription, '*quaroço*' ('*caroço*'), which usually has a narrower meaning of the stone of a fruit.

[477] Meaning obscure; in Brásio's transcription, '*paaos*' ('*paus*').

he belongs to us. And if so, a record shall be made in the said book and under a separate title of how, on such a day of such a month of such a year, in such a port or journey, a slave was found dead and thrown into the sea in the presence of the pilot and master and other witnesses from the ship; and all of them shall sign the said record. And when they arrive at the island, they shall unload the slaves and merchandise into our Factory, before you, the above-mentioned officials of ours, as has already been said. And the very next day, or earlier, if possible, in the presence of all, the pilot and scribe shall account for the trade of the said cargo, [[checking it against]] the receipt which shall have been left of the merchandise which was delivered to him [[the pilot]] by the Factor. And all being present there, if you can be present, the scribes of the Factory shall post as revenue in the books of receipt of the Factor all the slaves which were bought, together with their price, as well as the ivory, redwood, and other goods; and as regards the said ivory and redwood, a declaration shall be written stating how many tusks, and pieces of wood, there are, and how much they weigh.

....

Item: You shall advise the pilots and scribes, should they be unable to buy the slaves for forty manillas apiece, to return and not offer more than that for them. However, the other goods shall be traded as may seem best to our service.

Item: You shall advise them not to take slaves who are ill or crippled, and rather try to ensure that they are young and healthy. And if they are not able to find such, they shall take others for the price which may seem best to our service and advantageous to the ship.

Item: Since the traders who contracted with us to send to Mina the slaves necessary for its trade did not and do not comply with the agreement, as they should and are obliged to, it is our wish that those who are needed be sent there from our trade, in addition to those that they may send, and this notwithstanding their contract. And we therefore order you to send them, as soon as the slaves from the [[places of]] trade arrive there, a ship loaded with them [[the enslaved]], the best possible; and also all the Akori beads, grey beads, *ortigas*[478] and cloth from Benin that you can get which could serve for the trade of Mina, which shall be delivered to the pilot who shall go on the ship, without a scribe going on board, since this is not necessary. And he shall leave a receipt with the Factor of that Factory regarding the slaves and the said goods which he delivers to him, so that he may bring a receipt in due form of all the cargo from the Factor of Mina, written by one of the scribes of the Revenue, in which they confirm that they have received the aforesaid [[merchandise]] and that this has been posted as revenue against them. And the slaves whom

---

[478] *Ortigas* (or '*urtigas*'): literally, 'nettles'; the meaning in this context is unclear.

you shall send them should be healthy, and well fed and nourished with the necessary sustenance, because the crossing and journey is not so long as to prevent all of them, if they travel like this, from arriving in good health. And should it occur that one of them should die, on the arrival [[of the ship]] you shall receive an oath from the crew, confirming that this is so. And if the death be confirmed, it shall be posted as expenditure against the Factor. And after the said pilot delivers a receipt in due form of the remaining slaves and goods issued by the Factor of Mina, the pilot shall be relieved [[of the charge]], and the receipt which he had delivered shall be returned to him, so that he may tear it up. And since we have written a letter to the Captain and Factor of the said town of Mina, which we are sending open to you, so that you may read it, together with these regulations, in which we order them to inform you about the number of slaves they need and to state when you should send them, you shall be minded to take special care to send them, and to send the full number that you were asked by them to send – and rather too many than too few – as well as all other goods of the said trade which should come from the Rivers.

And we remind you that, in addition to your obligation, as befits our service, to provide in this matter most diligently, because of what you receive from your share of the one percent mentioned above you should do so, in order that we may be fully served, and you rightly benefited.

Item: And if it seems to you to be a good thing and in our service that the ships you should send to Mina with the slaves shall sail directly from Mina to the [[places of]] trade, so as best to expedite the trade, when you do send them there with the said slaves you shall have a scribe and the necessary goods embarked in the said ships. And you shall order the pilot and seamen to do so, in order to avoid the possible delay caused by returning to the island, and from the island to the [[places of]] trade. And all of this we leave for you to decide there upon consultation[479] and do as you think best for our service and the trade.

Written in Almeirim, on the 8th day of February – Afonso Mexia[480] wrote it – year 1519.

Item: It is our wish that Álvaro Frade and Pedro Dinis, Receiver, have four men to serve in the administration and management of the trade, namely, two each; and each man shall receive every year two slaves from the trading of our cloth, and one of these men shall also serve as porter of the Exchequer,[481] for this shall be in the said Factory, and thus he may cater for any need.

---

[479] In Brásio's transcription, the verb form is '*comsulteis*' ('*consulteis*'), from '*consulta*': see Glossary
[480] See CC 1-13-48 and MMA vol. 2, doc. 43.
[481] In Brásio's transcription, '*comtos*' (from '*Casa dos Contos*'), a board of the Royal Exchequer.

46 Command by Fernão Lopes Correia, Governor of São Jorge Da Mina[482] (21/03/1519)

ABSTRACT – *Letter accounting for the sale of defective chamber pots. The sale or exchange of old, defective, or otherwise spoiled cloths and metals were a mainstay of Portuguese trade on the Mina (Gold) Coast, as it was elsewhere.*[483]

[[I]], Fernão Lopes Correia, Captain and Governor of this town of São Jorge da Mina, command you, Manuel de Sande, at present the Factor in it, to post as account and expenses to João Franco, Factor of Akyem, one hundred and forty-nine defective small chamber pots, which he sold at various prices, in addition to the fifty which you sent him from here for sale. And by this, which will be registered by the Scribes of the Expenditure, whom I order to post it as expenses, it will be accounted for you on your behalf. Written by me, João de Seixas, clerk of this Factory, on the 21st of March 1519.

[sign.]   João de Seixas

Fernão Lopes Correia

[On the left side of the page]:
Certificate for the lord Captain from the Factor of Akyem ('Axim') of one hundred and forty-nine defective [[pots]], and the instructions of the Captain.[484]

[Different page]:
We have examined the books of this Factory and we have found that, of the small pots, at various prices, one hundred and ninety-nine were sold, and thus there are still there for sale seventy-eight which are defective and broken, so much so that it seems to us that they will be poorly sold. And we certify it to be so to Your Graces. From this Factory, on the 21st of October '518[[?]].

[sign.]   Francisco de Mesquita
Pedro Lameira

47 Writ to the Captain and officials of Mina[485] (30/07/1519)

ABSTRACT – *Ban on entering the São Jorge da Mina fortress for any pilot coming from Portugal, except on the day of the appointed fair.*

---

[482] ANTT, CC 1-9-85. Cf. Blake, *Europeans in West Africa*, p. 128.
[483] On cheap European trade goods, see Walter Rodney, *How Europe Underdeveloped Africa* (London: Bogle-L'Ouverture Publications, 1972), 102; Stanley B. Alpern, 'What Africans Got for Their Slaves: A Master List of European Trade Goods,' *History in Africa* 22 (1995): 5–43.
[484] Blake's translation ends here.
[485] ANTT, *Livro de Registo de Leis e Regimentos de D. Manuel*, fol. 104. There is an identical writ for the factor and officials of the House of Mina, dated July 21, 1519: *Ibid*, fol. 104; cf. MMA vol. 1, doc. 122.

We, the King, make known to you all, the present and future Captain and Factor and officials of ours in our town of São Jorge da Mina, that, because we consider it our service, we henceforth order and forbid any pilot of any caravel going from here to the said town to go inside the said fortress, under penalty of losing all the payment due to him for the voyage, in addition to such physical punishment as we see fit. Only on the day of the ordained fair will he be allowed to come with his company to the Ramada, according to custom and our regulations; and when the fair is over, they shall all return to their ships. We thus inform and order you henceforth to obey it and to have it fully obeyed and observed, and not to allow the said pilots to go inside the said fortress as mentioned, because this is our wish. And if you do otherwise, we shall turn on you and reproach you greatly, as are to be expected in such case. And to the pilots who go there you shall give a certificate signed by yourself and the said officials, because without this certificate they shall in no circumstance be paid here in our House of Mina. And you shall do thus without any doubt or impediment whatsoever on your part, for we consider it to be our service.

Written in Evora, on the 30th day of July – Garcia de Resende made this – year 1519.

48 Instructions from Fernão Correia to the Factor of Mina[486] (26/09/1519)

ABSTRACT – *Instructions for giving a painted cloth, an aljaravia, and a cauldron to the newly installed local ruler in Akatakyi ('Komenda').*

[[I]], Fernão Lopes Correia,[487] Captain and Governor of this town of São Jorge da Mina, order you, Manuel de Sande,[488] who are Factor there, to deliver a painted [[*lambel*]],[489] a Tenes[490] *aljaravia* of the best quality,[491] and a large brass[492] cauldron, which I order be given to the newly-acclaimed King in Akatakyi ('Komenda').[493] And by these [[instructions]], which will be registered by the Scribes of the Expenditure, whom I order to post it for you as expenditure, it will be accounted for on your behalf.

---

[486] ANTT, CC 2-85-8; cf. MMA vol. 1, doc. 123.

[487] See ANTT, Contos do Reino e Casa, Núcleo Antigo 867, MMA vol. 1, doc. 124, MMA vol. 4, doc. 32, MMA vol. 15, docs. 18 and 20.

[488] See ANTT, *Fragmentos, Cartas para El-Rei*, cx. 1, mç. 1, n. 7, CC 2-86-30, MMA vol. 1, doc. 124, MMA vol. 4, doc. 32, MMA vol. 15, doc. 18 and 20.

[489] In Brásio's transcription, '*hũ pimtado*' ('*um pintado*'); see MMA vol. 1, docs. 61 and 125 for the complete term '*lambéis pintados.*'

[490] Tenes: reference to the provenance (Tenes in the Kingdom of Tlemcen) of the type or pattern of the fabric used.

[491] In Brásio's transcription, '*da mostra*,' though in this context it should probably read '*de amostra*' (literally, 'of sample'), that is, 'of the best quality.' The meaning of '*mostra*' presented in a footnote by MMA—'equipment, wardrobe, store'—is, as far as it has been possible to ascertain, incorrect.

[492] In Brásio's transcription, '*darã de arame*: a type of red-colored copper, from which, when mixed with calamine, brass is made.

[493] In Brásio's transcription, '*Acomane.*'

Written by me, Pedro de Seixas, scribe of this Factory, on the 26th day of the month of September 1519.

[sign.] F. Lopes Correia   Pedro de Seixas

49 Instructions from Fernão Correia to the Factor of Mina[494] (26/09/1519)

ABSTRACT – *Instructions for buying a blanket featuring the Pope in the middle as an offering or gift to the ruler of Fetu, whom the captain Correia now orders to be visited, so peace and trade can flourish.*

[[I]], Fernão Lopes Correia,[495] Captain and Governor of this town of São Jorge da Mina, order you, Manuel de Sande,[496] who are Factor there, to buy a blanket of *papa*[497] for nine *pesos*,[498] which I order be given to the King of Fetu, whom I now order to be visited, in order to make peace between them and those of Akatakyi ('Komenda'). And by these [[instructions]], which will be registered by the Scribes of the Expenditure, whom I order to post them [[the *pesos*]] as expenditure, they will be accounted for on your behalf.

Written by me, Pedro de Seixas, scribe of this Factory, on the 26th of the month of September 1519.

[sign.] F. Lopes Correia   Pedro de Seixas

50 Letter from Duarte Pacheco Pereira to the Factor of Mina[499] (03/10/1519)

ABSTRACT – *Duarte Pacheco Pereira orders certain items be offered to the rulers of Akatakyi ('Komenda'), Fetu, and Ampia to further lubricate relations between them and the Portuguese, and amongst each other for Portugal's interests.*

[[I]], Duarte Pacheco,[500] *fidalgo* of the Household of Our Lord the King, Captain and Governor of this town of São Jorge da Mina, order you, João de Figueiredo,

---

[494] ANTT, CC 2-85-9; cf. MMA vol. 1, doc. 124.

[495] See ANTT, *Contos do Reino e Casa, Núcleo Antigo* 867, MMA vol. 1, doc. 123, MMA vol. 4, doc. 32, MMA vol. 15, doc. 18 and 20.

[496] See ANTT, *Fragmentos, Cartas para El-Rei*, cx. 1, mç. 1, n. 7, CC 2-86-30, MMA vol. 1, doc. 123; vol. 4, doc. 32; vol. 15, docs. 18 and 20.

[497] Of wool: called as such for bearing the image of a Pope in its middle. In Brásio's transcription, '*cobertor de papa*' (the Portuguese term '*papa*' meaning 'Pope'). Note, however, Brásio's etymology is uncertain, as it is possible '*de papa*' derives from '*empapado*,' i.e. 'mashed' or 'thick pressed,' from the type of wool used. The term '*cobertor de papa*' is still in use.

[498] Name given in numismatics to a certain kind of metallic piece used in the past to ascertain the legal value of the coin.

[499] ANTT, CC 2-85-44; cf. MMA vol. 1, doc. 125.

[500] See ANTT, *Contos do Reino e Casa, Núcleo Antigo* 867, CC 2-86-30, MMA vol. 1, doc. 127, 129, 130, 131, 132; vol. 4, doc. 32; vol. 15, doc. 31.

Factor of Our Lord the King, to deliver three painted *lambéis*,[501] namely, two of Gonçalo Vaz[502] and one of Our Lord the King, and two Tenes *aljaravias* of the best quality,[503] newly painted, and one short *aljaravia*, and two large bowls, and five pieces of linen clothing, which I order be given to the King of Komenda and the King of Fetu and the King of Ampiar [[*sic*]], since as I am now ordering that they be visited anew.[504] And by this [instruction], which will be registered by the Scribes of the Expenditure, whom I order to post it as expenditure, it will be accounted for on your behalf.

Written by me, Pedro de Seixas, scribe of this Factory, on the 3rd day of the month of October 1519.

[sign.] Duarte Pacheco Pereira   Pedro de Seixas

51 Receipt from Manuel De Sande to Factor João De Figueiredo[505] (15/10/1519)

ABSTRACT – *Receipt attesting factor João de Figueiredo received the merchandise, enslaved peoples, and other items from Manuel de Sande, his predecessor. The document is published for the first time.*

+

The Factor João de Figueiredo acknowledged and confessed to having received from Manuel de Sande, formerly a Factor here, this merchandise and items further declared, *scilicet*:

Item: Of Fes painted [*lambéis*][506] of Our Lord the King, two thousand one hundred and forty-eight pieces .... 2[1]48

Item: Of painted [*lambéis*] from Safi, four pieces [[...]] .... 4 pieces

Item: Through the House of Akyem, [[...]] ten Fes painted [*lambéis*] from Fes.

Item: [[.....]] He also received fifty-two painted [*lambéis*] from Gonçalo Vaz's contract. [[....]] He also received five hundred and seventy-one Mazouna[507] *lambéis* from Oran and of all sorts.

Item: He also received two hundred and ninety-eight Tenes *aljaravias*.

---

[501] *Lambéis* are already striped by definition.
[502] See MMA vol. 1, doc. 32; vol. 4, doc. 32.
[503] In Brásio's transcription, '*da mostra*,' though in this context it should probably read '*de amostra*' (literally, 'of sample'), that is, 'of the best quality.'
[504] In Brásio's transcription, '*noua mente*' ('*novamente*'): it is unclear whether in this context this means 'again' or 'newly,' though the latter sense was more common at the time.
[505] ANTT, CC 2-85-75.
[506] In the manuscript, '*pintados*'; see MMA, vol. 1, docs. 61 and 125, for the complete term '*lambéis pintados*.'
[507] For the identification of these '*lambéis de mazona*,' which are mentioned in other documents of the same period, see John Vogt, 'Notes on the Portuguese cloth trade [...],' *The International Journal of African Historical Studies*, VIII (4), 1975: 635.

Item: He also received nineteen Tenes *aljaravias* from a sample[508] from Gonçalo Vaz's contract.

Item: He also received one thousand one hundred and thirty-one short[509] *aljaravias*.

Item: He also received eight hundred and ninety-seven short *aljaravias* from Benzemero's contract and from Safi.

Item: He also received, through the House of Akyem, one hundred and eighty short *aljaravias* from Gonçalo Vaz's contract.

Item: He also received four hundred and sixty-one rods[510] of white cloth, measured along the selvage.

Item: He also received, through the House of Akyem, thirty-one rods of white cloth, measured along the selvage.

Item: He also received eighty-seven *côvados* and three quarters of black cloth, measured in *côvados*.

Item: He also received, through the House of Akyem, fifty-two *côvados* and three quarters of black cloth.

Item: He also received ninety-four *côvados* of green cloth.

Item: He also received one *côvado* of the same type of cloth.

Item: He also received fifteen *côvados* of *grã*,[511] measured in *côvados* of the Realm, with some holes.

Item: He also received twenty-six and two thirds *côvados* of *grã*, with some holes and moth-eaten.

Item: He also received forty-seven *côvados* and three quarters of half-*grã*,[512] in seven large and small pieces.

Item: He also received one hundred and forty *côvados*, in the measure of the Realm, of blue *condado*, in four bolts, moth-eaten and with some holes.

Item: He also received forty and a sixth *côvados* of blue *condado*, torn and moth-eaten, in nineteen pieces.

Item: He also received twenty-eight and a half *côvados* of blue *condado*.

Item: He also received twenty-four *côvados* of red *condado*, in thirty small pieces, moth-eaten.

Item: He also received, through the House of Akyem, ninety-one *côvados* of red *condado*.

Item: He also received, through the said House of Akyem, seventy-nine *côvados* of blue *condado*, \in *côvados*/.[513]

---

[508] Literal translation of '*da amostra*,' which might mean the articles were 'of the best quality.'

[509] In the manuscript, '*pequenas*,' which might also be translated as 'small.'

[510] In Portuguese, '*varas*.'

[511] *Grã*: fabric dyed in '*grã*,' a scarlet or crimson dye; see Glossary.

[512] Half-*grã*: also listed as a type of cloth in John Vogt, *op. cit.*: 645.

[513] Added between lines.

Item: He also received sixty-one and an eighth *côvados* of yellow cloth, moth-eaten.

Item: He also received ten and an eighth *côvados* of red *condado*.

Item: He also received four tablecloths, very old and torn, of green cloth, which is twenty-seven and an eighth *côvados*.

Item: He also received a blue tablecloth, of the officials' table [?],[514] which is four *côvados* of the Realm.

Item: He also received seven *alquicés*, four with red bands and three white.

Item: He also received, through the House of Akyem, three *alquicés*, one white and two with red bands.

Item: He also received a *bedém*, with torn hood.

Item: He also received one hundred and ninety-four ox's horns and three stag horns.

Item: He also received fifty-six slave pieces, both male and female, from the contract of Duarte Belo, ship-owner.

Item: He also received a refuse slave of Our Lord the King, from those who came from Arguin.

Item: He also received two thousand five hundred and forty-two rods and two thirds.

Item: He also received, through the House of Akyem, one hundred and forty-nine rods of *naval* cloth.[515] And the two thousand five hundred and forty-two rods and two thirds above mentioned are of *naval* cloth.

Item: He also received two hundred and twenty and a half rods of painted Cambay cloth in forty-eight bolts.

Item: He also received twenty-three bolts of *bretangil*, head and tail.[516]

Item: He also received a piece of *bretangil* which is four and a half rods.

Item: He also received a bolt of fine *bretangil*, with borders of red and blue silk.

Item: He also received twelve whole bolts of tapseel.[517]

Item: He also received three bolts of *bretangil*, with silk borders.

Item: He also received one hundred and fifteen *côvados*, in the measure of the Realm, of red satin from Bruges.

Item: He also received one hundred and eleven and a half *côvados* of satin from Bruges in two bolts.

Item: He also received forty-two and a sixth *côvados*, in the measure of the Realm, of green satin from Bruges.

Item: He also received ten *côvados* and five sixths of purple velvet, in the measure of the Realm.

---

[514] Tentative translation of '*da mesa em que fazem os ofiçiaes*' ('*da mesa em que fazem os oficiais*'). On the possible meaning of '*mesa*' in this context, see Glossary.

[515] In the manuscript, '*lemço naball*' ('*lenço naval*'): see Glossary, under '*Naval.*'

[516] Literal translation of '*cabo e coa,*' possibly meaning 'entire' or 'intact.'

[517] In Portuguese, *tafecira.*

Item: He also received a *pelote* of panels of red damask.

Item: He also received a large Oran [*pelote*] from Oran of red taffeta.

Item: He also received a white *bedém*, trimmed with white silk thread,[518] with its fringes.[519]

Item: He also received a tablecloth[520] of Indian *beirame*, which is two and a half rods.

Item: He also received two hundred and forty-four rods of thin Indian cloth, resembling *baetilha*.

Item: He also received eighty-six and a half rods of Indian head wrap[521] [cloth(?)], still unbleached.

Item: He also received, of the said narrow head wrap cloth, four hundred rods.

Item: He also received sixteen and a half rods of Indian cloth, narrow and bleached, in three pieces.

Item: He also received two pieces of Indian cloth, torn and with holes, which are six and a half rods.

Item: He also received four large bolts of *beirame*.

Item: He also received a bolt of *beirame* which is seven and a half rods, with some holes.

Item: He also received a bolt of *beirame* and one piece of another [*beirame* cloth], which are ten rods minus one sixth.

Item: He also received [[.....]] seven Tenes[?][522] head wrap [cloths(?)], with silk borders, which are fifty rods minus one sixth.

Item: He also received a [cloth(?) of] head wrap linen, with its red and black welts, which is three and a third rods.

Item: He also received [one cloth(?) of] Indian head wrap cotton, which is seven rods, torn and with blue bands on the edges.

Item: He also received an *almalafa* of three panels, with large and colored silk outer bands, with their welts.

Item: He also received an *almalafa* of unbleached cloth of two panels, with a large and colored outer band.

Item: He also received an *almalafa* of white silk, with a band of spun gold, which is two rods long and one and a third rod wide, with some holes.

Item: He also received an *almalafa* with a blue border on one side [?],[523] of linen, which is two and a half rods long and two thirds [of a rod] wide.

Item: He also received another *almalafa* of painted silk *zarzagania*, with some bands with spun gold and others in red, which is two rods long and one rod and one third wide.

---

[518] Or 'sowing silk' (in Portuguese, '*retrós*').

[519] In the manuscript, '*cadilhos*,' which could also be translated as 'strings.'

[520] In the manuscript, '*toalha*,' which could also, but less probable in this case, be translated as 'towel.'

[521] In the manuscript, '*touquas*' ('*toucas*'), which could be translated as 'coifs' or 'turbans.'

[522] In the manuscript, '*tenoçes*,' probably for '*teneses*' (adj.).

[523] Tentative translation of '*por hũa parte*' ('*por uma parte*'), which might also be translated by 'partly [of linen].'

Item: He also received five white *doraos*[*sic*],[524] with silk bands.

Item: He also received an old large *dorao*, with red silk bands.

Item: He also received an old quilted *saio*, with no sleeves.

Item: He also received an old *marlota* of yellow fustian.

Item: He also received a greyish white cloth,[525] with black bands and red stripe.

Item: He also received a *caçote* of white fustian, in tatters.

Item: He also received an *almalafa* of yellow silk, with bands of spun gold, which is one and a third rod long and one rod wide.

Item: He also received a white *dorao* from India, with silk bands.

Item: He also received four small-sized cotton smocks, two of them embroidered in red, another in black, and another in white.

Item: He also received two small head wrap [cloths(?)] with their strings,[526] which are three rods.

Item: He also received four smocks of *cotonia*, with white embroidering.

Item: He also received five Indian head wrap [cloths(?)], *scilicet*, four of them with silk bands and one with its welts, and one of them with holes, which are fifty-three rods and three quarters.

Item: He also received three pieces of Indian bleached cloth, which were twenty-seven and a quarter rods.

Item: He also received a white Indian tablecloth[?], with red borders, which is two rods.

Item: He also received a blue head wrap [cloth(?)], with some holes, with red welts and bands, which is two rods and two thirds.

Item: He also received thirty-six rods of Indian and Cambay cloths in eight pieces, and some of them with holes.

Item: He also received four pieces of taffeta, *scilicet*, one red and one yellow, and two cross-color,[527] which are eight *côvados* and seven eighths.

Item: He also received thirty-nine and a sixth rods of colored Indian cloth, painted, in seventeen bolts, with some holes.

Item: He also received four pieces of colored Indian cloth, *scilicet*, three with black borders and one striped, which are nine and a half rods.

Item: He also received two blue Indian cloths, with silk borders, which are four rods and three quarters.

Item: He also received a painted tablecloth[?] from India, torn, with welts and bands, striped, which is two rods.

Item: He also received a torn old *baetilha* [cloth(?)], which is two and a half rods.

---

[524] *Dorao*: meaning obscure; possibly a specific piece of clothing from Oran (i.e. '*d'Orão*' or '*de Orão*' / 'from Oran').

[525] In the manuscript, '*hum pano branquo / de cor cinzento*' ('*um pano branco / de cor cinzenta*'), literally 'one white cloth / grey-colored.'

[526] In the manuscript, '*cadilhos*,' which could also be translated as 'fringes.'

[527] In the manuscript, '*catasoll*' ('*catassol*'); also called 'shot silk,' 'changeable taffeta' or 'changeant' in English.

Item: He also received a white Indian cloth, with blue stripes, which is two and a half rods.

Item: He also received one tablecloth[?] from India, with bands and welts, which is two rods.

Item: He also received an Indian cloth, with a silk border, which is four rods.

Item: He also received a piece of Indian cloth which is seven and a third rods, with some holes.

Item: He also received thirty-seven rods of tablecloths in four bolts.

Item: He also received a piece of the said tablecloths, which is seven rods.

Item: He also received one hundred and forty-one and a half rods of holland, with some holes, in six bolts and pieces.

Item: He also received, through the House of Akyem, five bolts of Cambay cloth which are fourteen rods.

Item: He also received, through the said House of Akyem, three bolts of Indian cloth, which are fourteen rods.

Item: He also received, through the said House of Akyem, two pieces of checkered Indian cloth which are three rods.

Item: He also received one thousand five hundred and nine shells of Our Lord the King, both small and large.

Item: He also received, through the House of Akyem, fifty-five shells.

Item: He also received sixty-two new chased cauldrons.

Item: He also received thirty-six chased cauldrons, very small, old and without handles.

Item: He also received, through the House of Akyem, nine large chased cauldrons.

Item: He also received, through the said House of Akyem, twenty-five chased cauldrons, old and very small.

Item: He also received six hundred and seventy-seven *bacios machos*,[528] both large and small.

Item: He also received, through the House of Akyem, sixty-seven *bacios machos*, large and small.

Item: He also received eighteen *painas*,[529] large and small.

Item: He also received eleven copper pitchers,[530] old and dented.

Item: He also received six hundred and forty-one barber's basins.

Item: He also received, through the House of Akyem, one hundred and eighty barber's basins.

Item: He also received one thousand and six urinal pots.

---

[528] *Bacios machos*: meaning obscure. John Vogt, *op. cit.*: 643, describes them as 'large, shallow pans,' though he provides no other information or source on the matter. Since '*macho*' ('hook knife') is a tool which was used to carve the hollow cavity, for example, of wooden bowls, possibly these vessels had a characteristic concave shape, being necessarily shallow in order to guarantee their stability. This, of course, remains a mere hypothesis.

[529] John Vogt (*ibid*: 645) lists '*paina*' as a type of cloth. In this manuscript, references to '*painas*' appear to be associated with utensils of various sorts, but mainly made of metal. One (remote) hypothesis is that this was a primitive form of '*panela*' ('pan'), from the Latin '*panna*.'

[530] In the manuscript, '*camtaros*' ('*cântaros*'), which are large vessels with a wide neck, to carry water.

Item: He also received, through the House <of Akyem>. three hundred and forty-four urinal pots.

Item: He also received one hundred and twenty-one brass cauldrons, including seven with metal bands.

Item: He also received fifty cauldrons, old and dented, and six of them with no handles.

Item: He also received eighteen brass cauldrons with no handles, very old and in pieces, which are used for manillas.

Item: He also received, through the House of Akyem, ten brass cauldrons, large and small.

Item: He also received [[one hundred and five]] large copper cauldrons[531] with covers, ninety-nine of them new and the other six old.

Item: He also received, through the House of Akyem, seventy-six large copper cauldrons, with their covers.

Item: He also received four thousand one hundred and five brass manillas.

Item: He also received through the House of Akyem nine thousand and forty-five brass manillas.

Item: He also received, of large copper manillas in two pipes,[532] six thousand eight hundred and thirty manillas.

Item: He also received one hundred and seventy-nine brass hand bells.

Item: He also received one thousand eight hundred and thirty-eight *castanes*[533] in [[…]] a large box,[534] many of them broken.

Item: He also received eighteen very small brass cauldrons, with their handles.

Item: He also received, through the House of Akyem, fifty-five *castanes*.

Item: He also received eight elephant tusks.

Item: He also received one thick rope of coral from João Fogaça, which has seventy-four corals.

Item: He also received a rope of coral, which has seventy [[.....]] corals and four ambers.

Item: He also received another rope of coral, barrel-shaped, with glass beads, which has forty-five corals.

Item: He also received another rope of coral, [...........?],[535] which has two hundred and nine small corals.

Item: He also received two thousand three hundred and seventy-two corals, barrel-shaped, very small, in broken ropes.

Item: He also received one hundred and seventy marks six ounces four drams of coral, large and small, of all sorts.

---

[531] In Portuguese, '*caldeirões*,' which are larger than '*caldeiras*'; large pots, here also translated as 'cauldrons.'

[532] In Portuguese, '*pipas*'; see Glossary.

[533] *Castanes*: meaning obscure; possibly a plural form for '*castão*,' the head of a cane or stick.

[534] In Portuguese, '*caixão*'; primarily a large box used for storage and transport.

[535] In the manuscript, '*feiçam de boa*' ('*feição de boa*'), which might be translated as 'of good quality.' The meaning, however, remains obscure.

Item: He also received, through the House of Akyem, forty-five ounces of coral, small and of all sorts.

Item: He also received, through the said House of Akyem, a rope which has three hundred corals.

Item: He also received one thousand five hundred and eight cowries of Our Lord the King.

Item: He also received, through the House of Akyem, four hundred and forty-three cowries.

Item: He also received thirty-three thousand eight hundred and seventy-five crystalline beads.

Item: He also received, through the House of Akyem, of margarites and small crystalline [beads], all mixed, seventeen thousand one hundred and eighty beads.

Item: He also received, through the said House of Akyem, sixty-five beads from Gonçalo Eanes.

Item: He also received nine hundred and seventy-two *laquecas*.

Item: He also received thirty-two thousand and eight margarite beads, large and small, and many-colored.

Item: He also received sixty-three *côvados* of red *solia*, with some holes, in four pieces.

Item: He also received seventy-three and a third *côvados* of black *solia*, with some holes and in two pieces, in *côvados*.

Item: He also received fifty-five *côvados* of yellow fustian, in three pieces, in *côvados*.

Item: He also received a cloth of *tresmesa*[?][536] of white and yellow fustian, which is thirty-six *côvados*, in six cloths [[.....]], old and worn.

Item: He also received, through the House of Akyem, seventy *côvados* of black *solia*.

Item: He also received eight old palm cloths.

Item: He also received seven painted palm cloths from Benin.

Item: He also received sixteen *conimbombos*[537] from Benin of Our Lord the King.

Item: He also received ten *conimbombos* from Benin from the contract of Duarte Belo, ship-owner.

Item: He also received twenty-two horse tails.[538]

---

[536] *Tresmesa* or *tres mesa*: meaning obscure. Since there is a type of cloth named '*trespano*' (a fabric woven with three warp threads), it is just possible this passage should read '*hum pano de tres [de] mesa*' ('a tablecloth of three threads'), or the scribe used '*tresmesa*' as a synonym of '*trespano*.'

[537] *Conimbombos*: meaning obscure.

[538] For the use in a royal apparatus of palm cloth and horse tails, see Garcia de Resende's *Crónica de D. João II*, when describing the King of Kôngo, quoted, for instance, in Mariza de Carvalho Soares, "Por conto e peso': O comércio de marfim no Congo e Loango, séculos XV-XVII,' *Anais do Museu Paulista: História e Cultura Material*, 25, no. (2017): 59–86: '[...] *posto em um estrado rico, e nu da cintura para cima, com uma carapuça de pano de palma, e ao ombro um rabo de cavalo guarnecido de prata, e da cinta para baixo coberto com panos de damasco, que el rei [de Portugal] lhe mandara, e do braço esquerdo um bracelete de marfim.'*

Item: He also received six thousand seven[?] hundred and twenty-two cowries from the contract of Duarte Belo, ship-owner.

Item: He also received ten grey beads from the said contract of Duarte Belo.

Item: He also received seven hundred and two cowries from the Secretary's[539] contract.

Item: He also received one thousand four hundred and sixty-four imitation grey beads from the Secretary's contract.

Item: He also received, through the House of Akyem, ten thousand four hundred and twenty-six cowries from the Secretary's contract.

Item: He also received a level half *alqueire*[540] of Indian small beads and cowries, all mixed and of very poor quality.

Item: He also received two thousand eight hundred and ninety-five bundles of yellow *matamungo*,[541] of ten strings per bundle.

Item: He also received three hundred and seventy-seven bundles of blue *matamungo*, six of them of yellow [*matamungo*].

Item: He also received seven hundred and fifty-five yellow beads.

Item: He also received a rope of yellow pierced beads, which has three hundred and ninety-one very small beads.

Item: He also received two hundred and seventy beads from Gonçalo Eanes.

Item: He also received thirty-two long *carampa*[542] beads.

Item: He also received one hundred and twenty-five painted beads.

Item: He also received, through the House of Akyem, two hundred and forty imitation grey beads.

Item: He also received, through the said House of Akyem, five thousand and nine hundred beads from Benin.

Item: He also received, through the said House, a small case full of Indian beads.

Item: He also received thirty-seven cases, both large and small, old, with no keys.

Item: He also received[543] sixty-nine coffers, both large and small, new, with their keys.

Item: He also received three hundred and sixty-two small cases, new, with their keys.

Item: He also received, through the House of Akyem, thirty large cases.

Item: He also received, through the said House of Akyem, twenty-four small cases.

Item: He also received thirty-two hooded cloaks[544] of red *condado*.

Item: He also received, through the House of Akyem, five hooded cloaks of red *condado*.

---

[539] Probably Dom António Carneiro, secretary of Dom Manuel, member of the Royal Council, and also Donatory (*Donatário*) of the island of Príncipe.

[540] *Alqueire*: see Glossary.

[541] *Matamungo* or *matamingo*: see Glossary. For the same term, see MMA vol. 2, doc. 26.

[542] *Carampa*: meaning obscure.

[543] At this point, there is an involuntary repetition of letters in the manuscript.

[544] In Portuguese, '*capuz(es)*,' which today means only the 'hood.'

Item: He also received seven hundred and twenty-one red *barretes* of *grã*.

Item: He also received, through the House of Akyem, one hundred and eighteen red *barretes*.

Item: He also received twenty-one Alentejo blankets,[545] one of them old.

Item: He also received two Alentejo blankets, through the House of Akyem.

Item: He also received half a blanket of *papa*,[546] very old and torn, which is of no use at all.

Item: The said Factor João de Figueiredo also received from the said Manuel de Sande, formerly a Factor here, sixty-seven marks seven ounces seven drams and thirty grains of gold of Our Lord the King.

Item: He also received seven marks five drams and fifty-three grains of gold from the third, as calculated,[547] of Duarte Belo, ship-owner, of thirty-seven slave pieces, both male and female, which were sold under his contract, during the entire months of July, August and September 1519, for seven hundred and sixty-nine gold *pesos*.

Item: He also received two ounces three drams and sixty-nine grains of gold from the Secretary's third of a female refuse slave and four hundred cowries, which were sold here, under his contract, for thirty-four gold *pesos*.

Item: He also received two marks five ounces six drams and fourteen grains of gold from the wines of Our Lord the King, which were sold in the time of the said Manuel [de Sande], formerly a Factor here.

Item: He also received six wine pipes from the vintry of Our Lord the King, which were short by eighteen *almudes* and six *canadas*, including one for filling up.[548]

Item: He also received six empty pipes.

Item: He also received[549]

Item: The said Factor João de Figueiredo also received from Manuel de Sande, formerly a Factor here, seven old and worn mattresses of lodging.[550]

Item: He also received an old blanket of half-*grã*.

Item: He also received five sheets, very old and in tatters.

Item: He also received of mixed items of this House.[551]

---

[545] 'Alentejo blankets' were made of wool. In John Vogt, *op. cit.*: 639, it is translated as 'Alentejo mantles,' which is incorrect.

[546] Blanket of *papa* ('*cobertor de papa*,' in Portuguese): a type of woolen blanket. It is possible '*de papa*' derives from '*empapado*,' i.e. 'mashed' or 'thick pressed,' from the type of wool used. The term '*cobertor de papa*' is still in use.

[547] Tentative translation of '*da terça parte que se montou / a terça parte de*,' perhaps an involuntary repetition the scribe made.

[548] In the manuscript, '*d'atestaçam*' ('*de atestação*'), i.e. a measure of wine used to fill up the pipe or cask to the top, whether to keep the wine from spoiling through oxidation or to prevent the natural loss of wine with time due to evaporation.

[549] At this point, the scribe interrupts the text.

[550] In Portuguese, '*aposentadoria*' or, in full, '*direito de aposentadoria*,' that is, the 'right of lodging,' which was a prerogative of the higher social strata.

[551] Literal translation of 'Item: *Recebeo mais das cousas / mistigas desta casa*' ('Item: *Recebeu mais das coisas / místicas desta Casa*').

Item: He also received two sacks of old and torn colored wool.

Item: He also received two old and torn flags.

Item: He also received two old inkpots, one of wood, the other one of leather.

Item: one old pickaxe. And one sieve[?].[552] And one medium-sized bell,[553] with no clapper. And a pair of large iron scissors for cutting gold. And ten metal plates. And also half a *Canada* of copper. And a large box with twenty-six reels of twine. And two bundles of thick twine. And three bundles of hanks of white threads. And eleven small collars.[554]

And four rings[555] of brass wire. And four reels of brass wire. And another large reel. And a lock with its bolt. And six staples. And another chest lock. And two latches.[556] And a small bolt. And a large key.[557]

And a wooden sphere[?],[558] which is used to hold the thread for tying quarters[?].[559] And a sea chart, torn into pieces, with two compasses. And five hundred and twenty-six tin crosses. And an iron bar. And a screw. And a small latch. And an old cooking pot, very small and with no handles. And a wooden sundial. And a large book, bound in red, with the [Portuguese] shields.[560] And a large wooden box where the weights are stored. And a linen sack. And six chests which are in the Factory, two of them new and the others already used. And three large boxes,[561] formerly used for storing sugar. And also seven large barrels, with small cases and red *barretes*. And a brush for silk. And six hourglasses, dismounted. And six sheets of paper[?][562] of grains for weighing gold. And two touchstones, with seven silver wands with gilded tips, in a pouch. And four hundred and thirty and[*sic*] bad[563] grains[?].[564] And five new flags,

---

[552] In the manuscript, '*pnera*,' possibly for '*peneira*' ('sieve').

[553] In Portuguese, '*campã*.'

[554] Literal translation of '*colarinhos*'; the meaning in this context is not clear.

[555] In the manuscript, '*manjlhas*' ('*manilhas*'), though probably not in the usual sense of 'bracelets.'

[556] In Portuguese, '*aldrabas*,' which may also mean 'knockers.'

[557] In Portuguese, '*chave mourisca*': see Glossary.

[558] In the manuscript, '*pomᵃ*,' which does not seem to be an abbreviation (as it would not stand for anything that makes sense in this context), but rather the result of a scribe's correction. This being the case, it should read '*poma*' ('sphere' or 'ball'), even though the meaning here remains obscure.

[559] In the manuscript, '*quartas*,' possibly the 'quarters' of units of measure such as the *alqueire*, the *arrátel* or the *vara* (rod). It might also mean an 'earthenware water pitcher' ('*vaso de água*'), according to Moraes da Silva's *Diccionario da Lingua Portugueza*. The meaning might also be the fourth part of a large water vessel (a '*pote*').

[560] In the manuscript, '*quinas*,' the blue shields, with their five white bezants, characteristic of the Portuguese flags almost since the foundation of the realm.

[561] Note that '*caixão*,' as in the manuscript, was the term commonly used for the boxes where sugar was stored and transported.

[562] In the manuscript, '*papes*,' possibly for '*papéis*' ('papers' or 'sheets of paper'); the meaning in this context remains obscure.

[563] In Portuguese, '*ruins*,' which could also mean 'defective,' 'deficient,' 'inferior,' or 'low-quality.'

[564] In the manuscript, because of a scribe's mistake, (probably) '*grs*,' which could stand for both '*grãos*' ('grains') or '*grãs*' (a type of cloth).

with crosses of Christ, and spheres[?],[565] and [Portuguese] shields. And two sheepskin buskins. And a large chest, which is in the Treasury, with four locks.

Item: five tables, *scilicet*, one of the store,[566] and another in the treasury, and another in the factory, and two old ones which are of no use. And an old sieve, which is used in the store. And five padlocks, one of them without key. And an anvil with a hammer. And a cutter which is used for cutting gold. And a book of the taxes on merchandise, and another of the fortress's regulations. And an old multiplication table.

And a balance [[...]] in a box lined with red cloth, with a gilded beam.[567] And [[.....]] three pairs of unornamented balances. And three *alqueires*. And one half *alqueire*. And a wooden quarter. And another half *alqueire* of wood. And also seven hundred and seventy metal weights for weighing gold. And an old balance with its small trebuchet.[568] And three pairs of old balances. And also three wooden *côvados* of the Realm, one of them iron-shod. And also two wooden [North African] *côvados*. And an iron rod. And a balance with gilded plates[?],[569] with its small iron trebuchet, in an old and broken wooden box, which is in the Treasury. And another balance with its small trebuchet, which is used for weighing the gold in the store. And two balances, one large and the other small. And three weight piles, *scilicet*, one of eight marks, which is lacking one dram; and another of four marks, which is lacking half a dram; and another of one mark, which is lacking four drams.

Item: He also received sixteen breastplates,[570] *scilicet*, two of them without backplates, old and rusty. And seventeen mail coifs, old and rusty. And also ten old crossbows, with their racks[571] and claws, with no strings or nuts. And also twenty-five halberds.

Item: The said Factor João de Figueiredo also received from Manuel de Sande, formerly a Factor here, the following items from the Cathedral: *scilicet*, a garment of crimson[572] velvet, [with][573] clavi of plain brocade.

---

[565] In the manuscript, '*esperas*,' which was formerly a synonym of '*esferas*' ('spheres'); possibly a reference to the characteristic armillary sphere present in the royal banner and other regalia from the time of Dom Manuel I. The term '*espera*' might also mean an antique small piece of artillery or small cannon.

[566] In Portuguese, '*venda*,' usually a 'grocery,' but also any 'store' or 'shop'; the word is still in use, especially in Brazil.

[567] In the manuscript, '*asteas*' ('*hastes*'), literally 'beams.' As a balance only has one beam, it is likely the scribe was referring to other parts of the balance, such as the lever.

[568] In the manuscript, '*trabuquete*' (diminutive form of '*trabuco*'), literally a 'small trebuchet,' this being a weapon for throwing stones. Maybe the scribe gave to the balance's 'lever.'

[569] In the manuscript, '*balanças*,' most probably the name the scribe gave to the 'plates' or 'bowls.'

[570] In the manuscript, '*corpos de piastroes*' ('*corpos de piastrões*')—'*piastrões*' literally meaning 'breastplates'—which, given that it is said they had no 'backplates,' should read '*couraças*' ('cuirasses').

[571] Also known by the French word '*cranequin(s)*'; in Portuguese, '*armatoste(s)*,' a device for spanning the crossbow.

[572] In the manuscript, '*cremjzam*,' most probably for '*carmesim*' ('crimson').

[573] In the manuscript, '*do*' ('of the'), though it should read '*com o*' ('with the').

Item: He received another garment of crimson velvet [[..]], with clavi of plain brocade.

Item: He also received another garment of crimson satin, with clavi of black velvet; there is no band in the amice.

Item: He also received some curtains of tapseel, with clavi of crimson satin.

Item: He also received a frontal of the said tapseel and of the same type.

Item: He also received four frontals of camlet, one black and blue and tawny.

Item: He also received a frontal of the main altar, with clavi of pearl-embroidered white damask, of velvety satin.

Item: He also received two frontals of velvety satin.

Item: He also received a cloth of the Rivers.[574] And some curtains of black camlet, very torn and old.

Item: He also received a cloth of the Rivers of Benin. And four cloths for the altars, which are twelve rods.

Item: He also received another old cloths for covering [[......]]. And four altar cloths. And two surplices. And two [...?][575] of Our Lady, one of Mercy.

Item: An image of Our Lady. And two old frontals of linen.

Item: He also received six altar stones. And seven candlesticks, *scilicet*, three large and three small. And eight cruets of pewter. And a pair of host presses.[576] And three call bells.[577] And two communion bells.[578]

And a brass cauldron. And two corporal boxes, one woven with purple velvet and another of wood, painted with a *divisa de espera*.[579] And five corporals, three of holland and two of linen cloth. And two old wimples[580] of silk.

Item: A black cloth which is used in Lent. And a towel[581] of sleaved silk. And a small towel with stripes. And a houseling cloth with red bands. And a very old book cover[?],[582] lined with green damask. And three small [[..]] missals, with their baptismal books.[583] And a paper book in which there is to be found the office for Maundy Thursday. And four small paper books

---

[574] In the manuscript, '*Ryoes*,' probably for '*Rios [de Benin]*' ('Rivers [of Benin]'). See two lines ahead.

[575] Unintelligible word, possibly '*sartais*' ('necklaces') or '*tarjas*' ('ornamented borders' or 'escutcheons').

[576] In the manuscript, '*obradejras*' ('*obradeiras*'), today known as '*ferros de hóstias*.'

[577] In the manuscript, '*synos de tamjer*' ('*sinos de tanger*'); probably 'sacristy bells,' or 'chancel bells.'

[578] Literal translation of '*campajnhas de comungar*' ('*campainhas de comungar*'), probably the 'sacring bells' rung at the elevation of the host and chalice.

[579] In the manuscript, '*deviza despera*': meaning obscure. This could be translated as 'device of waiting' or 'device of sphere' ('device' in the sense of a compound of a picture and a motto, or else only of an emblem). There is an obsolete meaning of '*espera*' as 'sphere.'

[580] In the manuscript, '*beatilhas*,' but here, unlike elsewhere in the document, in the sense of 'coifs' or 'wimples.'

[581] In Portuguese, '*toalha*,' whether a baptismal towel, a bishop's towel, a cere cloth, or a credence cloth.

[582] In the manuscript, '*funda de lyuro*' ('*funda de livro*'), whether a 'book cover,' from '*funda*' as a 'shield cover/sheath,' or a 'small case.'

[583] In the manuscript, '*bauticejros*,' most probably for '*baptistérios*,' and in this context, books containing the baptismal rite.

in which the processional offices are noted down. And a sacramental book.[584] And a [.........?].[585] And another old one, unbound, of the [Synodal] Constitutions. And a Librixa[586] vocabulary book. And a [[........]] silver lamp. And five chests. And a *lambel* blanket.[587]

And a monstrance of gilded silver, with a box with a rod of cloth. And two urinal pots. And two large plainchant books. And another two books, a missal and a [[..]] book of vespers. And a chrismatory. And a large missal. And a large gilded silver cross, with its crucifixion. And a silver thurible,[588] with its white chains and gilded *roseta*[589], which weighs three marks two ounces and three and a half drams. And a chalice in gilded silver, with its paten, which weighs three marks and four ounces, with gilded foliage, and with its leather box. And another chalice in gilded silver, with its paten, which has enamel thistle foliage on the pommel,[590] and which weighs two marks and an ounce of silver. And

item: Another gilded chalice, with its partly gilded paten, and with a Saint Anthony's cross[591] and a white sphere;[592] and the said paten [has] a similar gilded cross; and they weigh [[..]] one mark four ounces and two drams of silver. And three silver chalices, with their patens, gilded and plain in parts, and with gilded stems; they weigh together five marks and three and a half drams.

Item: A cope of pearl-embroidered purple brocade, with clavi and galero of crimson velvety[*sic*] velvet, and with fringes of crimson silk and gold thread.

Item: Another cope of crimson velvet, with clavi and galero of blue velvet, and with fringes of red and yellow floss silk.[593] Two copes of tawny damask, with clavi and galero of crimson velvet, with fringes of colored silk thread.

---

[584] Literal translation of '*lyuro sacramentall*' ('*livro sacramental*'). It is not clear whether the scribe is referring here to a generic type of doctrinal book, or the work of Clemente Sánchez de Vercial— *Sacramental*—which was written in the first half of the 15th century and published in Portugal in 1488, thus constituting the first known incunabulum in Portuguese.

[585] Unintelligible word(s), though clearly related to the Gospel. One hypothesis is that it reads '*um Evangelho ruim*' ('a Gospel in bad condition') or '*um Evangeliário*' ('an Evangeliary' or 'Book of the Gospels'). In either case, not all letters would have been drawn by the scribe.

[586] *Librixa* (or *Librija*): a name formerly given to Antonio de Nebrija. On Nebrija's works, especially the dictionaries, see for example Fermín de los Reyes Gómez, 'El privilegio de los *Diccionarios* de Antonio de Nebrija (siglos XV-XVIII): Otro enredijo de mil diablos,' *Corpus Eve* [online]: *La défense de la langue vernaculaire en Espagne (XVe-XVIIe siècles): Paratextes et textes*.

[587] In the manuscript, '*mamta alambelada*' ('*manta alambelada*'), a blanket in the style of a *lambel*.

[588] Or 'censer.'

[589] In the manuscript, '*Rozeta*,' meaning obscure, though it seems possible this be the name given by the scribe (i) to the spherical metal body for holding charcoal and incense, (ii) to the bells sometimes attached to the chains of the censer (both hypothesis by analogy with the small balls attached to the end of the thongs in penitents' scourges, which are called '*rosetas*'), or (iii) to the 'incense boat'— called '*naveta*' in Portuguese—given their phonetical similarity.

[590] That is, the 'bowl' of the chalice, by analogy with a sword's 'pommel' ('*maçã*,' in the manuscript).

[591] Saint Anthony's cross: the 'tau-cross' (also known as '*crux commissa*'), associated with St. Anthony of Egypt.

[592] In the manuscript, '*espera*,' for the obsolete meaning of '*espera*' as 'sphere.'

[593] In Portuguese, '*cadarço*'; also known, in English, as 'floss' of 'ferret silk.'

Item: Another cope of green satin, with clavi and galero of crimson velvet, and with fringes of red and yellow floss silk.

Item: Another cope of blue damask, *viz.* with clavi and galero of crimson velvet, and with fringes of many-colored floss silk. And a vestment of pearl-embroidered black brocade, with clavi of gold embossed brocade, and with fringes of crimson silk and gold thread, new and complete.

Item: Another vestment of crimson brocade, with its dalmatics of crimson brocade embroidered with gold, and with clavi of purple brocade; which dalmatics and vestment are lacking the bands of the amices, all three of them, and have crimson and green and gold-thread fringes. And three vestments of crimson velvet, with clavi of blue velvet, and with fringes of colored floss silk, with its offices,[594] except one which is lacking the gremials[?],[595] and the cuffs of the sleeves, and all amice.

Item: Another vestment, with two dalmatics of crimson *brocadilho* with clavi of embossed brocade, with fringes of blue silk and gold thread; which vestments are lacking two bands of the amices of the dalmatics.

Item: Another vestment of black camlet, with its dalmatics in the same fashion, with clavi of blue velvet and fringes of black and white floss silk, new, with all its offices, except for the bands of the amices of the dalmatics.

Item: Another vestment of plain brocade, lined with blue cloth, with fringes of green silk thread, with all its offices.

Item: He also received six vestments of white boccasine[596] linen, lined in black, with white crosses.

Item: Also four curtains and four frontals of the same kind, for Lent.

Item: Two curtains hanging in the small altars, of Cambay cloth, which are nineteen and a half rods, lined all over with *naval* cloth.

Item: Three altarpieces in the altars.

Item: Also four rods of *naval* cloth, which were used for making hand towels for the altars, and little angels[*sic*] on the chalices, and chalice bags.

Item: Also two altar linens of the main altar, which are seven rods.

Item: The Factor João de Figueiredo also received from Manuel de Sande, formerly a Factor here, through the House of Akyem, a silver chalice with its paten, gilded in places.

Item: A pair of host presses. And a vestment of purple velvet, with blue clavi, and with its alb in perfect condition.

Item: Another vestment of linen cloth,[597] white, in perfect condition.

Item: A box with some corporals.

Item: Two old cruets of pewter.

---

[594] Literal translation of '*oficios.*'
[595] In the manuscripts, '*Regaços*'; see Glossary.
[596] Boccasine, fine buckram; see Nathan Bailey, *An Universal Etymological English Dictionary* [...]. (London: Printed for R. Ware et al., 1770).
[597] In the manuscript, '*lemço*' ('*lenço*'), any kind of linen or cotton cloth.

Item: He also received an old frontal of colored camlet.

Item: A brass cross.

Item: Two altarpieces and a Saint Anthony.

Item: A broken mirror. And an altar stone. And two missal books, old and torn. And a hand bell. And two brass candlesticks. And four rods[?] of torn towels. And some blue torn curtains. And a sack-cloth with figures, in tatters. And a Tenes *aljaravia*, used as frontal.

Item: Some towels of *naval* cloth, amounting to three rods.

Item: A chest with the church's accoutrements. And an old curtain of black sack-cloth.

Item: A frontal of sack-cloth, old and torn.

Item: A veil of a rod and a half, which is used in the altar.

Item: A piece of what used to be the altar linen, torn. And another torn piece.

The said Factor João de Figueiredo also received from Manuel de Sande, formerly a Factor here, through the House of Akyem, the following mixed items.

Item: Two bombards. And five bombard [powder] chambers. And a brush. And eighteen spears.

Item: A call bell.

Item: An axe. And two sickles. And a hatchet. And an anvil, with two cutters and a hammer for cutting gold.

Item: Three iron stone hammers. And four iron picks. And three hammer eye punches of iron. And a hoe. And three pieces of a millstone, with its iron spindle.

Item: Three iron bars. And four halberds, two of them intact and the other two broken. And a bolt, with its lock without key. And a copper funnel. And half an *almude* of copper. And a pair of pincers. And a gimlet. And a table with its wooden feet. And two locks, one a nose lock[598] and the other with bolt, attached to the door of the Factory. And another lock with its bolt on the said door. And five torn sieves. And a barrel with gunpowder. And twenty-one bombard [stone] balls. And two bombard wedges. And an old chest, with no lock. And two bread kneading bowls. And two broken [dough] trays. And a wooden breadboard for rolling out bread. And half an *alqueire*, and two quarters, and an eighth, for measuring flour.

And an old chest, with no lock. And a linen kneading cloth of two rods, which is used for bread. And a broken crystal[?].[599] Three copper pitchers. Three *painas*. A copper cooking pot.

---

[598] Literal translation of '[*fechadura*] *de naris*' ('[*fechadura*] *de nariz*'), which might correspond to a 'buckle bolt.'

[599] In the manuscript, '*crjstell*' ('*cristel*'), literally 'clyster' or 'enema.' Probably for '*cristal*' (in English, 'crystal'), an object made of crystal glass.

Item: He also received three slaves of Our Lord the King, who serve in the House of Akyem, painted [*sic*] Duarte Estêvão. And two female slaves, Isabel [and] Inês, her daughter, a two-month-old baby girl.

Item: A wooden barrel with gunpowder. And four pavises, old and broken. And an *almadia*. Three pairs of balances, *scilicet*, a gilded one, a large black one, and another one small and broken.

Item: Another [pair of] balances, with its small trebuchet.

Item: A broken pile of eight marks, which lacks one dram. And seventy-one weights, which are used in the Factory's store. And two measuring *côvados*, one of them Moorish. And two measuring rods, one of them iron-shod. And two chests, *scilicet*, one which is in the Treasury and another one which is used for merchandise. And two hundred and thirty-four arrows, of them[*sic*][600] without head.

Item: The said Factor João de Figueiredo also received the following items from the infirmary.

Item: Twenty sheets and fifteen mattresses, one of them of gunny. And twelve old Tenes *aljaravias*. And five little bolsters And a *paina*. And two *bacios machos*. And five barber's basins. And a copper pitcher, with its cover. And a stone mortar. And a copper chamber pot.

Item: The said Factor João de Figueiredo also received from the vintry a wooden tub. And a pewter pitcher for measuring wine. And a wooden funnel. And another one of copper. And a chest. And a balance, with its small trebuchet.

Item: Also five metal weights for weighing gold. And a large wine tap.[601] And a one-piece hammer and gimlet.

Item: The said Factor João de Figueiredo also received from the kneading-house a large *paina*. And two large copper cauldrons. And two old small *aljaravias* for covering the bread. And an old large bowl. And an old chest. And one and a half *alqueires* made of wood. And a quarter and an eighth made of wood.

Item: The said Factor also received from the smithery, *item*: Two tongs. And two files. And some bellows, with their pipes. And a single-horn anvil.[602] And a hammer. And two iron lathes. And a caliper. And a mandrel. And two anvils. And two large hammers. And a tuyère. And a *paina*. And a large file. And a pair of pliers. And a pair of wedge tongs. And a pickaxe. And an axe. And a vise.[603] And a cutter. And a pair of hand tongs. And two chisels. And two punches.[604] And a hammer. And a large anvil. And an axe

---

[600] The scribe possibly forgot to note down the number of arrows without heads.

[601] In the manuscript, '*chaue grande de vinho*' ('*chave grande de vinho*'), as in the French term '*clef du tonneau*,' a large 'tap' or 'spigot,' which was placed in the bunghole of casks and pipes. Its mechanism was similar to a linchpin which crosses the basis of the threaded shaft in a wine (and olive oil) press, which is also called '*chave*' ('key').

[602] In the manuscript, '*cafra*,' probably for '*safra*' ('single-horn anvil').

[603] In the manuscript, '*perafuso*' ('*parafuso*'), which might also be translated as 'screw.'

[604] In the manuscript, '*ponteiros*,' which might also be translated as 'burins.'

mandrel. And a *tazinha*[*sic*].[605] And a pair of pincers. And a hand hammer. And a caliper. And a hammer eye punch.

And the said Factor João de Figueiredo also received [[..]] from the apothecary: Thirty-four small sugar bowls. And eleven pots. And a pair of balances. And one mark. And two mortars, a large one, and a small one with a pestle. And a small bottle. And ten wooden cases, large and small, both broken and intact. And a small box. And a spatula. And [[.]] a copper barrel, broken in two.

Item: The said Factor João de Figueiredo also received from the said Manuel de Sande, formerly a Factor here, the following slaves of Our Lord the King, who serve in this fortress,

item: Inês Fernandes, in the infirmary.

Item: Beatriz, in the infirmary, with two children.

Item: Catarina, in the infirmary, sweeper.

Item: Madalena, who serves in the oven-house.

Item: Isabel, wife of Jaca ['Jaqua' in ms], who serves in the oven-house.

Item: Margarida, with a son, who serves in the oven-house.

Item: Antónia, with two children, who serves in the oven-house.

Item: Catarina, and Margarida, and Cristóvão, who serve in the Captain's house.

Item: Catarina, and Francisco, and a girl who is the daughter of Catarina, who serve in the Factor's house.

Item: Inês, who serves in the house of Pedro de Seixas, with a breastfeeding daughter.

Item: Mécia, with a daughter, who serves the residents.

Item: Brígida, who serves the *Alcaide-mor*, with two daughters.

Item: Maria *a Velha* ['Maria the Old'], who serves the residents.

Item: Another Maria, who serves the residents.

Item: Another Maria, who serves the residents.

Item: Another Maria, who serves the residents.

Item: Graça, with four children, who serves in the kneading-house.

Item: Francisca, who serves Francisco de Seixas, with a little girl.

Item: Guiomar, with a son, who serves the residents.

Item: Also Maria, a little girl and daughter of Catarina, who died here.

Item: He also received António, a slave who serves in the fortress.

Item: Also João, blacksmith.

Item: Also Francisco, of the oven-house.

Item: Also Tomé.

Item: Papagaio.

Item: Pedro.

Item: João Jaca.

---

[605] *Tazinha*: meaning obscure. It is possible it should read '*tenazinha*' ('small pincers').

Item: João Redondo.

Item: Biuba.

Item: Pedro, Manikongo.

Item: Colhão, who came from Arguin – all men who serve in this fortress.

Item: He also received two brass cauldrons, which should have been added above under 'infirmary'.

Item: He also received a register book of this fortress, which comes from the time of Álvaro Salgado. And let there be no doubt concerning what is written between the lines regarding the blue cloth from Axim. And because it is true that the said Factor João de Figueiredo received from the said Manuel de Sande, formerly a Factor here, this merchandise and items above mentioned, and since they will be posted for him as receipt by Francisco de Seixas and João Afonso, scribes of this Factory, he gave him this receipt, issued by me, Pedro de Seixas, first [[.]] scribe of this Factory, and signed by the said João de Figueiredo and us, officials, on the 15th day of the month of October 1519.

     [sign.]   *João de*   *[Pedro] de Seixas*   *João Afonso*

                 Francisco de Seixas   *Figueiredo*

52 Instructions from Duarte Pacheco Pereira to the Factor of Mina[606] (20/11/1519)

ABSTRACT – *Duarte Pacheco Pereira orders two goats to be offered to the herald of the ruler of Wasa and other 'noblemen merchants.'*

[[I]], Duarte Pacheco Pereira, *fidalgo* of the Household of Our Lord the King, Captain and Governor of this town of São Jorge da Mina, order you, João de Figueiredo, Factor of Our Lord the King, to deliver three and a half *pesos* for two goats which I order be given to the herald of the King of the Assans [[Wasa]] and to other *cavaleiros mercadores*[607] who came with him. And by these [[instructions]], which will be registered by the Scribes of the Expenditure, whom I order to post it as expenditure, it will be accounted for on your behalf.

    Written by me, Pedro de Seixas, scribe of this Factory, on the 20th day of the month of November 1519.

          [sign.] Duarte Pacheco Pereira   P. de Seixas

---

[606] ANTT, CC 2-85-200; cf. MMA vol. 1, doc. 127.
[607] *Cavaleiros mercadores*: see Glossary.

53 Acceptance of Slaves by the Pilot
of the Santa Maria-a-Nova[608] (01/12/1519)

ABSTRACT – *Pilot Jorge Gonçalves took ten enslaved male and female captives, called 'pieces,' back to the agents of the contractors because they were ill and improper for trading. This document also serves as a certificate of unloading for the Factor of São Jorge da Mina, João de Figueiredo, who re-dispatched the human cargo to São Tomé.*

Jorge Gonçalves, pilot of the ship Santa Maria-a-Nova, acknowledged and declared that he received ten slave pieces, both male and female, from João de Figueiredo, Factor.

Namely, three out of the sixty he now brought, who he had to take back because they were ill with ringworm, and five who were here before the time of Manuel de Sande, and other two from Malagueta from the said time of Manuel de Sande.

Which ten pieces he received for delivery to Baltasar Roiz and Diogo Fernandes, Factor of Duarte Belo.

And because this is true, he gave him this receipt, which was written by me, Francisco de Seixas, Scribe of this Factory, and signed by both, on the first of December 1519.

[sign.]   *Pedro Afonso*   *Francisco de Seixas*

Jorge Gonçalves   *Duarte Pacheco Pereira*

54 Letter from King Manuel to the Officials
of Mina[609] (20/03/1520)

ABSTRACT – *Prohibition for white men of any quality, except for royal factors on behalf of the king, to buy enslaved Africans through the Portuguese fortresses at São Jorge da Mina and at Akyem ('Axim').*

We, the King, make known to you our Captain, Factor and officials of our town of São Jorge da Mina that, as we regard it to be our service and in the interest of our trade of the Factory of Akyem, from the notification of this [[letter]] onwards we forbid the Factor and scribes who are in the said Factory, or any other white men, of whatever quality, to buy there, themselves or through any other person, any slaves, or negotiate in this matter whether publicly or secretly, subject to the penalties which are incurred by any persons found guilty of and proven to have been involved in the trade of prohibited goods from Mina, and which it is our wish and

---

[608] ANTT, CC 2-86-30. Transcribed in Ballong-Wen-Mewuda, *São Jorge da Mina*, 2: 531.
[609] ANTT, *Leis e Regimentos de D. Manuel*, Fundo Antigo, n. 16A, fol. 162v; cf. MMA vol. 4, doc. 35.

order be executed on them should they fail to obey, except that it is our wish that the said factors of ours of the said Factory should buy them on our behalf and then sell them again when they consider it to be our service, doing everything in the presence of the scribes ascribed to their office, who shall post as expenditure the manillas and goods which they give for the said slaves, and as revenue the said slaves, so that they may render an account of them or of the gold in exchange for which they sell them again.

We notify you thus and we order you to have the Factor who is serving at present, and all others hereafter, immediately notified of this [[letter]], as it is our wish that they should keep and observe it, as stipulated herein. And you shall have this [[letter]] copied to the book of the regulations of that Factory and in that of the House of Akyem, so that it is made public to all and none may plead ignorance. And we order the Judge of the Cases of Mina[610] to have a copy of this [[letter]] made, so that he may know what we thus forbid; and [[we order]] our officials of the House of Guinea to record the copy of this [[letter]] in the books of the regulations of the said House; and they shall state on the reverse of this [[letter]] that they have made a copy of it in the manner stated; and they shall send it to you by the first ship, so that, in those matters which concern and pertain to you, you may have it observed and obeyed as has been said.

Written in Evora, on the 20th of March – António Afonso wrote this – year 1520.

55 *Instructions to the Factor of Mina*[611] *(07/05/1520)*

ABSTRACT – *Duarte Pacheco Pereira orders delivery of various items to the ambassador João Vieira as offerings or gifts to the King of Wasa.*

[[I]], Duarte Pacheco Pereira, *fidalgo* of the Household of Our Lord the King, Captain and Governor of this town of São Jorge da Mina, order you, João de Figueiredo, Factor of Our Lord the King, to give and deliver to João Vieira, whom I am now sending to visit the King of the *Asas* [[Wasa]], anew,[612] a painted [[*lambel*]],[613] and a Tenes *aljaravia*, of the best quality[614] and newly-painted, and a red cap,[615] and a pair of breeches[616] of *naval*[617] cloth, which makes up two and

---

[610] In Portuguese, '*Juiz dos Feitos da Mina.*'
[611] ANTT, CC 2-89-80; cf. MMA vol. 1, doc. 129.
[612] In Brásio's transcription, '*novamente*': it is unclear whether in this context this means 'again' or 'newly,' though the latter sense was more common at the time.
[613] In Brásio's transcription, '*hũ pimtado*' ('*um pintado*'); see MMA vol. 1, docs. 61 and 125 for the complete term '*lambéis pintados.*'
[614] In Brásio's transcription, '*da mostra,*' though in this context it should probably read '*de amostra*' (literally, 'of sample'), that is, 'of the best quality.'
[615] In Brásio's transcription, '*barrete*': see Glossary.
[616] In Brásio's transcription, '*braga*': short and loose shorts.
[617] *Naval*: see Glossary.

a half rods,[618] and a chamber pot. And by these [[instructions]], which will be registered by the Scribes of the Expenditure, whom I order to post it as expenditure, it will be accounted for on your behalf. Written by me, Vasco da Mota,[619] scribe of this Factory, on the 7th day of May 1520.

[sign.] Duarte Pacheco Pereira   Vasco da Mota

56 Instructions to the Factor of Mina[620] (08/05/1520)

ABSTRACT – *Duarte Pacheco Pereira orders the delivery of two and a half pesos to buy a goat for the brother of the King of the Akan.*

+

[[I]], Duarte Pacheco Pereira, *fidalgo* of the Household of Our Lord the King, Captain and Governor of this town of São Jorge da Mina, order you, João de Figueiredo, Factor of Our Lord the King, to deliver and pay two and a half *pesos* for a goat which I order be given to Nipa,[621] brother of the King of the Akan, and to other merchants who came with him. And by these [[instructions]], which will be registered by the Scribes of the Expenditure, whom I order to post it as expenditure, [[it will be accounted for]] on your behalf.

Written by me, Vasco da Mota, scribe of this Factory, on the 8th day of May 1520.

[sign.] Vasco da Mota   Duarte Pacheco Pereira

57 Letter from Duarte Pacheco Pereira to the Factor of Mina[622] (08/08/1520)

ABSTRACT – *Duarte Pacheco Pereira orders a quantity of cloth for a pair of breeches be offered to an official from Fetu.*

+

[[I]], Duarte Pacheco Pereira, *fidalgo* of the Household of Our Lord the King, Captain and Governor of this town of São Jorge da Mina, order you, João de Figueiredo, Factor of Our Lord the King, to deliver two and a half rods of *naval*

---

[618] In Portuguese, '*vara*' (sing.): see Glossary.
[619] See MMA vol. 1, docs. 130, 131, 132; vol. 15, doc. 31.
[620] ANTT, CC 2-89-82; cf. MMA vol. 1, doc. 130.
[621] *Nipa* means 'a person/human being' in Akan/Twi.
[622] ANTT, CC 1-91-28; cf. MMA vol. 1, doc. 131. Cf. Blake, *Europeans in West Africa*, pp. 130–31. Blake mistakenly gives the archival reference for the letter number 27, when it is, in fact, number 28, that is, CC-1-91-28.

cloth for a pair of breeches, which I order be given to a knight from Fetu, so as to observe the service of Our Lord the King. And by these [[instructions]], which will be registered by the Scribes of the Expenditure, whom I order to post it as expenditure, it will be accounted for on your behalf.

Written by me, Vasco da Mota, scribe of this Factory, on the 8th day of August 1520.

[sign.] Duarte Pacheco Pereira   Vasco da Mota

On the reverse: Instructions from the Captain, wherein he orders that two and a half rods of cloth be given to a black man. Posted as expenditure.

58 Letter from Duarte Pacheco Pereira to the Factor of Mina[623] (08/08/1520)

ABSTRACT – *Duarte Pacheco Pereira orders certain items to be offered to the kings of the Akan and the Abrem, to be delivered by João Vieira.*

+

[[I]], Duarte Pacheco Pereira, *fidalgo* of the Household of Our Lord the King, Captain and Governor of this town of São Jorge da Mina, order you, João de Figueiredo, Factor of Our Lord the King, to deliver a painted [[*lambel*]][624] of Gonçalo Vaz, and a Tenes *aljaravia*, three rods of *naval* cloth, and a red cap,[625] and a chamber pot, which I order be given to the King of the Akan,[626] and two short[627] *aljaravias* for two of his knights, for this is the custom and done as ordained by Our Lord the King upon the arrival of his captains in this town. And furthermore, I order you to provide a [[*lambel* of]] *mazona* [[*sic*]],[628] and a short[629] *aljaravia*, and two and a half rods of *naval* cloth, and a red cap, which I order be given to the King of the Abrem,[630] for it is ordained by the said Lord that they be given to him, as he is situated on the merchants' route. Which things I order you to give and deliver to João Vieira, whom I am now sending there to visit them anew. And I order you to give him six short *aljaravias* for his expenses, for himself and for

---

[623] ANTT, CC 2-91-28; cf. MMA vol. 1, doc. 132. Cf. Blake, *Europeans in West Africa*, p. 130. In Blake, the archival reference for the letter erroneously indicates number 27 instead of number 28, and the date is August 8, not 18, as Blake has it.

[624] In Brásio's transcription, '*hũ pimtado*' ('*um pintado*'); see MMA vol. 1, docs. 61 and 125 for the complete term '*lambéis pintados.*'

[625] In Brásio's transcription, '*barrete*': see Glossary.

[626] In Brásio's transcription, '*Acames.*'

[627] In Brásio's transcription, '*pequenas,*' which might also be translated as 'small.'

[628] *Amazona*: long skirt women use for riding. Brásio's definition of '*mazona*' does not appear to be accurate. In other documents, the complete term is '*lambel/lambéis of mazona*'; see, for example, Blake's translations, doc. n. 18.

[629] In Brásio's transcription, '*pequena.*'

[630] In Brásio's transcription, '*Abermus.*' Duarte Pacheco Pereira calls them *Bremus.* Cf. MMA vol. 1, p. 3.

two slaves who carry this load with him, and for an interpreter who is going with him. And by these [[instructions]], which will be registered by the Scribes of the Expenditure, whom I order to post it as expenditure, it will be accounted for on your behalf.

Written by me, Vasco da Mota, scribe of this Factory, on the 8th day of August 1520.

[sign.] Duarte Pacheco Pereira   Vasco da [Mota]

59 Instructions from Duarte Pacheco Pereira to Factor João De Figueiredo[631] (07/01/1521)

ABSTRACT – *Duarte Pacheco Pereira orders an aljaravia, a red cap, and two and a half rods of naval cloth be given to the chief Meirinho of the King of the Abrem, which has been the custom of all the Portuguese captains of São Jorge da Mina.*

+

[[I]], Duarte Pacheco Pereira, *fidalgo* of the Household of Our Lord the King, Captain and Governor of this town of São Jorge da Mina, order you, João de Figueiredo, Factor of Our Lord the King, to deliver a small[632] *aljaravia,*[633] and a red cap, and two and a half rods of *naval* cloth, which I order to be given to the chief *meirinho*[634] of the King of the Abrem,[635] as has been the custom of all the captains of this town to have them given, since the road through which all the merchants come to this fortress crosses it [[Abrem territory]]. And by these [[instructions]] I order the Scribes of the Expenditure to post it for you as expenditure, so that it will be accounted for on your behalf. Written by me, Vasco da Mota,[636] scribe of this Factory, on the 7th day of the month of January 1521.

a) Duarte Pacheco Pereira   *a)* Vasco da Mota

60 João De Barros, Chronica Do Emperador Clarimundo[637] (1522)

ABSTRACT – *In João de Barros's account of the adventures of the fictitious progenitor of the king of Portugal, titled 'Chronicle of the Emperor Clarimundo' and*

---

[631] ANTT, CC 2-93-87; cf. MMA vol. 15, doc. 31.
[632] In Brásio's transcription, *'pequena,'* which, in this context, could also mean 'short.'
[633] *Aljaravia*: see Glossary.
[634] *Meirinho*: see Glossary.
[635] In Brásio's transcription, *'Abermus.'*
[636] See MMA vol. 1, docs. 129, 130, 131, and 132.
[637] João de Barros, *Chronica de Emperador Clarimundo, donde os Reys de Portugal descendem ...* (Lisboa: na Officina de Francisco da Sylva, Livreiro da Academia Real, 1742), 389.

published in 1522, the author has a section that talks about the societies of Mina as the Portuguese perceived them in the first two decades of the sixteenth century.

And the rim of the land where thunderstorms are cause of torment and labors for seamen, with its most humble Lion mountains[638] will come and bow before his feet, barefoot, unclothed, and charred by the burning Sun, asking in a new language for doctrine to learn of Him who created them and all else in the world.

> Fetu,[639] Wasa,[640] with those of Akatakyi ('Komenda'),[641]
> And their great and powerful Sharif,
> Descrying a small vessel of his
> Joined those from Akan.[642]
> And coming all with great joy
> With full saddlebags they entered
> The golden town called São Jorge
> Because it was discovered on that day.
> The cruel[643] *Andiotes* [[Ahanta?]] from the great land of *Danda*,
> With the *Aciús* [[Etsi/Atis?]], *Lanús*, Abrem,[644]
> Hearing the news, will say 'Let us rise up
> And serve Him who commands.'
> By Land and Sea, His name
> Is everywhere so feared
> That it gives strength to the weak
> And it deposes and brings down the powerful.

61 Royal Letter to the Captain of Mina[645] (13/10/1523)

ABSTRACT – *Letter from King João III to Afonso de Albuquerque, Captain of São Jorge da Mina, about the importance of the village of Adena—called here 'our village of Mina'—and how they should be treated to ensure commerce continues to favor the Portuguese.*

Dom Afonso, we the King send you greetings. We have been informed that you are treating the knights of our village of Mina there harshly, in such a manner that the

---

[638] Lion mountains: i.e. Sierra Leone.

[639] In the original, '*Afutus.*'

[640] In the original, '*Asas.*' All words in italics have been transcribed exactly as they appear in the 1742 edition.

[641] In the original, '*Cumania.*'

[642] In the original, '*Akania.*'

[643] It is not clear whether '*Crús,*' in the original, is part of the name of an African group or is used as an adjective (meaning 'cruel').

[644] In the original, '*Beramús.*'

[645] MMA vol. 1, doc. 136, pp. 451–52; Jeremiah D. M. Ford, ed., *Letters of John III, King of Portugal 1521-1557* (Cambridge, MA: Harvard University Press, 1931), 3–4. Cf. Malyn Newitt, ed., *The Portuguese in West Africa, 1415-1670: A Documentary History* (New York: Cambridge University Press, 2010), 96–97.

village is depopulated and men are going away from there to other parts; and for these reasons, which have been pointed out to us, besides others which are said to exist, we regard it as a matter very prejudicial to our interest and to the welfare, and primarily the trade, of that town. Since they are Christians and have received the water of baptism, they must be defended, instructed and protected, and not banished; and this also, since they are our vassals, and live there in obedience to us and to you and to our captains of that town, serving in our name in everything ordered them for our service, and with their people and their *almadias* carrying on their heads the wood for all our ships and, furthermore, since many of them buy on a large scale in that Factory, and all, generally, in the [factory of] the Old Cloth, which is bought by them and sold in their *almadias*. Moreover, we are told that there were rich men among them, and that they have slaves, who are all of them at our command, or may be, if they be treated well and protected with that moderation in punishment, and also in instruction, which is meet and proper for our service and their well-being. These men tell us that for all their services they neither have, nor expect, from us any other reward than that we should protect them and have them provided with justice. For this reason, it seems to us that you will not be doing what is in our interest by expelling them; and if it is done to punish them, it seems harsh, because by being expelled they incur two dangers: being killed or robbed. And in other cases, should they deserve punishment, to pay a fine to that church, or something similar, would be enough. We thus enjoin and command you to treat them better and to dispense with banishments to the best of your ability; you shall rather protect them, and direct them to take the way most fitting for our service, taking care that they do not depart from it, because this is in the interest of that Factory, and that they do not go about, commenting what they ought not about you and the Factory; otherwise, besides losing them and the service which we receive from them, with such novelties[646] the merchants will not come, as they come when the land is free from them. Written in Tomar, on the 13th day of October 1523. António Afonso made this.

The King
To Dom Afonso, Captain of Mina
To Dom Afonso de Albuquerque, *fidalgo* of his Household and Captain of his town of Mina.

62 Writ of Confirmation for the Convent of Tomar[647] (03/12/1523)

ABSTRACT – *King João III confirms the writ of Dom Manuel I, exempting the preachers of São Jorge da Mina from contribution. The king removes the Vicariate of Mina from the jurisdiction of Tomar.*

---

[646] In the original, '*inovações*' (or '*novidades*'), i.e. things that disturb the normal course of events.
[647] ANTT, *Ordem de Cristo*, Sala 25 – 51-13, fols. 54v.-55; cf. MMA vol. 4, doc. 36.

[[We]], Dom João, by the grace of God King of Portugal and the Algarves, on either side of the sea in Africa, Lord of Guinea and of the Conquest, Navigation and Commerce of Ethiopia, Arabia, Persia and India, etc., make known to all those who may see this letter that the Prior and friars of the Convent of our town of Tomar have presented to us a letter from my lord and father the King, may he be in glory, that reads as follows.

[[We]], Dom Manuel, by the grace of God King of Portugal and the Algarves, on either side of the sea in Africa, Lord of Guinea and of the Conquest, Navigation and Commerce of Ethiopia, Arabia, Persia and India, make known to all those who may see this letter that, since the presentation of the Vicar of our town of São Jorge da Mina belonged to the Prior and friars of the Convent of Tomar of the Order of our Mastership of Christ, they have been used to present him until now. And because in the said town we have assigned him through our regulations a good payment, they have been used to impose on him a contribution of thirty thousand *reais* per year, to help with the cost of the wax of the said Convent and other commendable expenses in the service of God and ours, and for the good of the Convent. Due to this contribution paid by the said vicars, as we have been informed, learned clergymen, of exemplary lives and good customs, fit for preaching and who give good teachings, cannot be found, as they would be if they received their salary free from the payment of any contribution whatsoever. And since it is our wish that in the said town there always should be learned vicars, who may bear fruit within the Church, and convert the natives, and preach, etc., we have considered it beneficial, and in the service of God and ours, to order that the Convent be paid twenty thousand *reais* per year for the said wax, provided the said Prior and friars relinquish the presentation of the said Vicariate, and that it revert to us, to be given, free from any contribution whatsoever, to learned clergymen who preach, as has been said, so that they may serve the said Vicariate in the above manner.

And since they have been pleased with this, it is our wish and we order our Receiver of the one percent who serves now and those who shall serve in the future, from the first day of the coming January of the era one thousand five hundred and twenty-one onwards, to deliver each year at the request of [[?]][648] the said Prior and friars of the said Convent the said twenty thousand *reais* for the said wax, and to be given a receipt for it, and we order our auditors,[649] by this [[receipt]] and the copy of this letter, to account for it on their behalf.

Issued in our city of Evora, on the 6ᵗʰ of July – António Afonso wrote this – year of Our Lord Jesus Christ one thousand five hundred and twenty.

And this shall be so while this be our [[wish]], etc.

[[We, the King,]] having been entreated by the said Prior and friars to grant them the favor of confirming the said letter, and having seen their request, and wishing to bestow a grace and favor upon them, grant it to them, and confirm and

---

[648] In Brásio's transcription, '*a certo recado*'; the meaning is not entirely clear.
[649] In Brásio's transcription, '*contadores*': see Glossary.

acknowledge the letter as confirmed, thus and in accordance with what is stated therein, and we order that it be thus kept and obeyed, for this is our wish.

Issued in Montemor-o-Novo, on the 3rd of December – Gaspar Mendes wrote this – one thousand five hundred and twenty-three.

63 Nomination of Luís Álvares as Vicar of São Jorge Da Mina[650] (20/02/1524)

ABSTRACT – *Letter of confirmation by the Bishop of Funchal. The Bishop confirms the king's nomination of Luís Álvares as Vicar of São Jorge da Mina. The document is published for the first time.*

[We], Dom Diogo Pinheiro, by the grace of God and of the Holy Mother Church of Rome Bishop of Funchal, Primate of the Indies, of Our Lord the King's Council and his *Desembargador*[651] of the Palace and Petitions, Prior of [the Collegiate of] Guimarães, make known to all who see this letter of confirmation and possession, health in Jesus Christ, that *Bacharel*[652] Luís Álvares, priest,[653] came before us and presented to us a letter of presentation of the said Lord, which appeared to have been signed by His Highness and whose content is as follows: [We], Dom Manuel, by the grace of God King of Portugal and the Algarves, on either side of the sea in Africa, Lord of Guinea and of the Conquest, Navigation, Commerce of Ethiopia, Arabia, Persia and India, as Head[654] and Governor that we are of the Order and Knighthood of the Mastership of Our Lord Jesus Christ, make known to you, Dom Diogo Pinheiro, Bishop of Funchal and of our Council, that, trusting that Luís Álvares, priest, *bacharel* and solicitor, will perform well [in that office] and as is due to the service of God, and that he is able and suited for it, and wishing to bestow a grace and favor on him, it is our will to present him now as Vicar of the Church of São Jorge of our town of Mina, notwithstanding the letters patent we have given to Friar Amaro, who is now a vicar there, and whom we order to return; and we desire that with the Vicariate the said Luís Álvares should receive as allowance sixty thousand *reais* per year, and this for a period of three years. And the said Luís Álvares will have the duty of serving the said Vicariate, like the aforesaid Friar Amaro.

And therefore, we ask you to confirm him in the said Vicariate and give him your diploma of confirmation in form, according to the regulations. Issued in Lisbon, on the 17th day of July –Vicente Saraiva wrote this – one thousand five hundred and twenty-one. And having read the said letter of presentation of the

---

[650] ANTT, CC 2-113-99
[651] *Desembargador*: see Glossary.
[652] *Bacharel*: see Glossary.
[653] In the original, '*clérigo de missa*,' i.e. an ordained cleric, who is able to celebrate mass (as opposed to '*clérigo de evangelho*' (deacon) and '*clérigo de epístola*' (subdeacon).
[654] In Portuguese, '*Regedor*.'

aforesaid Lord, to whom the said presentation rightly pertains, and trusting the benevolence and prudence of the said Luís Álvares, through the imposition of our biretta on his head we have confirmed him in the said Vicariate of São Jorge of the town of Mina, which is now held by Friar Amaro, notwithstanding the letters patent which were given to the said Friar Amaro – presentation and report[?][655] of the said Lord, to whom the said presentation rightly pertains as Head and Governor, as the perpetual administrator of the said Order of Christ; and we recognize him as its [of São Jorge da Mina] Vicar for the said period of three years.

And the said Luís Álvares swore on the Holy Gospels, on which he laid his hands,[656] that during the said period he would always observe that reverence and obedience which is due to us and our canonically immediate successors, and that he would obey our orders and those of our deputy *ouvidores*,[657] and finally he promised to observe everything that is written in Pope Gregory's constitution and in the Bishop's addendum, or which is specified in more detail about similar oaths. And through this [writ], we order the residents of the said town to acknowledge the said Luís Álvares as their true Vicar and Rector during the said period, and to carry out and ensure the contribution of the dues owed to the said Vicariate. Issued in Lisbon, under our mark and seal, on the 19th day of the month of August – António do Couto, on behalf of Pero Eanes do Couto, wrote this – the year one thousand and five hundred and twenty-one. Written by me, Duarte de Paiva, first scribe of this fortress, on the 20th day of February '524.

[sign.] *António Couto*   *Duarte de Paiva*

64 Regulations Regarding the Portuguese Trade of São Jorge Da Mina and São Tomé[658] (07/02/1529)

ABSTRACT – *Introductory page of regulations of the town of São Jorge da Mina, with an explicit focus on pious works and guidance for the captain, factor, and other officials. The 94 folios that make up these regulations have not been translated because of the document's length, overall value, and formulaic nature. Scholars can consult the originals or transcriptions elsewhere.[659]*

---

[655] Tentative translation of '*rolaçam*' ('*relação*').
[656] In the manuscript, '*por ele corporalmente tangidos*,' which literally means 'which he touched with his body.'
[657] *Ouvidor*: in this case, an ecclesiastical magistrate.
[658] BSGL, *Regimentos da Cidade de São Jorge da Mina, São Tomé, e Obras Pias*, Reservado A-55, fols. 1-1v.
[659] Transcriptions of the complete regulations can be found in Ballong-Wen-Mewuda, *São Jorge da Mina*, 2: 542–620, and University of Ghana, Legon, Furley Collection at the Balme Library, P3 1529, 'Regimento da Mina,' pp. 1–89. A partial analysis of this *regimento* (regulation) appears in David Birmingham, 'The Regimento da Mina,' *Transactions of the Historical Society of Ghana* 11 (1970): 1–7. For a broader look at such regulations from King Manuel onward, see Damião Peres, *Regimento Das Cazas Das Indias E Mina* (Coimbra: Faculdade de Letras da Universidade de Coimbra, Instituto de Estudos Historicos Dr. Antonio de Vasconcelos, 1947).

A

Regulations of the Factory of São Jorge da Mina: Regulations of the Captain

[[I]], Dom João, by the grace of God King of Portugal and the Algarves, on either side of the sea in Africa, Lord of Guinea and of the Conquest, Navigation and Commerce of Ethiopia, Arabia, Persia and India, etc. – – make known to all those who may see these regulations of mine that, considering that the regulations and laws which have until now been applied in the town of São Jorge da Mina did not sufficiently provide for many matters pertaining to the governance and regulation of the said town, and thus that it has become necessary to remove some things and establish others, I have determined to proceed in this matter as seemed fit to my service and judgement, and had these regulations drawn up, as specified below. And it is my wish and command that, from the day of the arrival in the said town of São Jorge da Mina of Estêvão da Gama,[660] *fidalgo* of my Household, whom I now send as Captain, onwards, the regulations shall be fully observed and obeyed, notwithstanding any other regulations and letters, and that those of the King, my lord and father, may he be in holy glory, which have until now been applied in the said town, be sent to me, because I desire that only these now be observed, in accordance with what is stated therein.

The first are the Regulations of the Captain of the said town.

Chapter One

Of the number of officials and residents in the said town.

It is my wish that the permanent [[number]] of officials and residents in the said town be sixty-six persons, including in the said regulations the four women who will be in service in the said town, distributed as follows:

The Captain and ten men;
One Vicar;
Three Chaplains;
One Factor with four men;
Two Scribes of the Factory, both of the Revenue and of the Expenditure [...].

65 Regulations of the Captain of Mina[661] (08/02/1529)

ABSTRACT – King João III recommends special care in attracting African peoples to the Catholic religion by teaching them to read, write, and count. Zeal and care should be 'to persuade the black people to become Christians.'

---

[660] See MMA vol. 1, doc. 152. Estêvão da Gama was appointed captain of Mina by letter of Dom João III, dated February 4, 1529, See ANTT, *Chancelaria de D. João III*, liv. 45, fol. 158v.
[661] BSGL, *Regimentos da Cidade de São Jorge da Mina, São Tomé, e Obras Pias*, Reservado A-55, fols. 7-7v; cf. MMA vol. 1, doc. 150, pp. 502–4.

Chapter Ten

Of how the Captain shall take care to persuade the black people to become Christians, and of what the Vicar shall teach, and of the salary they shall both receive for it.

I enjoin and order the said Captain, for the service of God and mine, through whatever honest ways and means, and to the best of his ability, to be particularly mindful and careful in encouraging the black people of the *comarca*,[662] and any others who might come to the town, who may wish to convert to the faith of Our Lord Jesus Christ, so that they, and others who will come after them, may achieve salvation. And as regards the black people who reside in the village, he shall take special care to order them to have their children taught how to read and write, and to serve in the church by praying and singing and in all other offices of the Divine Office, which matter I entrust to the Vicar and chaplains who are in the said church and who may wish to take charge of it, or any other person who may better know how to do it, should they [[the Vicar and chaplains]] not be able to do it, and any of the aforementioned to whom the Captain entrusts it.

It is my wish, in order that it be done with good will and diligence, that each year two gold *justos*[663] or their equivalent be given to each boy, up to a total of fifteen, who teaches [[religious]] matters, and who writes and serves in the said church, and that another two *justos* be given each year to the Captain for each of the said boys, up to the said total of fifteen, for taking good care of this. And in addition the said Captain shall receive one *justo* for each black person from the said village who becomes a Christian through his diligence. And I order the Factor to pay each year to the Vicar, or to any other person who may be entrusted with it by the Captain, by order of the said Captain, the said two *justos* for the boys he thus teaches, up to the said total of fifteen. And the scribes of the Factory will register in their books at the beginning of each year the number of boys, as well as that of those of the said village whom the said Captain persuades to become Christians, and they will post the amount paid for them [[the boys and the converted black people]] by the Factor to the said Captain as expenditure, so that by the said register and orders it is accounted for in his behalf. And should some of the said boys begin to learn and then give up or die, the said salary will be paid proportionally up to that date, taking into account the said two *soldos*, that is, *justos* per year, and how long he [[the Vicar]] had taught them.

---

[662] *Comarca*: see Glossary.

[663] Gold coin of the reign of Dom João II, of 22 karats, weighing 121 grains or 38 marks. In Brásio's footnote, '*peças em marco*,' literally 'pieces in marks.' It was worth 380 white *reais*. Its name derived from the first word of the motto written on the reverse: *Justus ut palma florebit*, which encircled the image of the king seated on the throne. On the obverse, it bore the coat of arms of Portugal (already reformed) and around it the name of the monarch and his titles (cf. *Grande Enciclopédia Portuguesa e Brasileira*, vol. 14, p. 421).

Chapter 11

That the Vicar and chaplains ensure that the church be adorned with the necessary ornaments

I enjoin and order the said Vicar and chaplains to maintain the church always very clean and in good order, with its vestments, and chalices, and books, surplices, thuribles [[?]],[664] wax, and all other ornaments and necessary things for the service of Our Lord, and that the Divine Office be performed with perfection. And should the said church be in need of the said articles, or of some of them, the said Captain will have them requested to my Factor and scribes of the House of Guinea, who, according to my regulations, will send them when they see his message.

....

Manuel de Moura wrote this in Lisbon, on the 8th day of February of the year 1529.

66 Letter from Duarte Roiz to King João III[665] (10/05/1529)

ABSTRACT – *After going to the Kingdom of Kongo, Duarte Roiz was detained for six[666] months, his journey having thus failed. From this vantage point, he informs the king of irregularities observed in the commerce of São Tomé, Akyem ('Axim'), and São Jorge da Mina.*

+

My Lord,

[[I,]] Duarte Roiz, knight of your Household, make known to Your Highness that I went to Kongo as captain in a fleet of Damião Dias,[667] scribe of your Exchequer, very highly recommended as I was to the King of Kongo by Your Highness, and [[that]] he detained me for 7 months, for which reason the ship on which I went was eaten by shipworms, and all my cargo,[668] and pilot, and master, and several seamen, and factor died. I wrote from the island of Príncipe to João Lobato, your Factor, asking him to provide me with a ship to take the slave pieces of the cargo together with the crew to the island of São Tomé, so that Your Highness

---

[664] In Brásio's transcription, '*tribos*' ('tribes'), which does not make any sense in this context. It seems likely, however, that '*tribos*' might stand in the document as an abbreviation for '*turíbulos*' ('thuribles').
[665] ANTT, CC 1-42-116; cf. MMA vol. 4, doc. 40, pp. 144–46.
[666] In Brásio's transcription, '*bij meses*' ('seven months').
[667] See MMA vol. 2, doc. 49.
[668] That is, the enslaved.

might receive your duties, and he sent me a *caravelão*[669] of Your Highness, whose pilot was a certain Duarte Luís,[670] who has been doing a great disservice to Your Highness in Akyem and Mina. And this Duarte Luís lives in Vila Nova,[671] in the Algarve, and has been for his part doing a great disservice to Your Highness.

Your Highness is certainly aware that I have been writing to you from the island of São Tomé about the great amounts which, from the island of São Tomé, are being stolen from you in Mina and Akyem; and I will not mention the people who thus ordered things until I go and kiss Your Highness's hands, since I expect to receive distinguished favors from Your Highness for having made it possible for Your Highness to order punishment for those who have been stealing from you, Your Highness having bestowed many favors upon them.

I have written to Your Highness recommending that you should close the doors of the island of São Tomé, so that no ships should go from the island to Mina, for you must believe that it is through them that Mina and Akyem are being robbed, and not the contrary. Because I have truly come to know the truth by serving you, being in addition a man who knows Mina very well, as well as all Guinea and Brazil, and there is no shipworm that I do not know. And as my desire to be of service to Your Highness is very true, I venture to write to you, informing you about what is going on and what should be done for your service, and do so because my desire to serve you is great.

Your Highness has a territory in the Ambos,[672] which is located between the island of Fernando Po and the mainland, in which there is much *malagueta*, and it seems to me that one can take 30 or 40 *moios*[673] per year, and much more if the soil becomes accustomed to it. This *malagueta* is concealed from you since no factor of yours who has been in the island of São Tomé has ever declared it to you. I have informed you of this, and because I have a great desire to serve you, I was pleased to look out for everything so that I could make it known to Your Highness, as it seems to me that, by doing so, I am rendering a great service to you.

I have made known to Your Highness many things concerning your service in a letter of mine which I sent you from the island of São Tomé, and by all that I have written I inform you that in no matter regarding the island of São Tomé are they acting honestly towards you: namely, the Akori beads which come from the Rivers [i.e. Benin], and which are so valuable in Mina, are placed in the hands of a factor of Jorge Arbote, who does what he wants with them, and he may well keep them for himself, as Your Highness does not have a scribe [[there]], and they may well do what is said throughout the island of São Tomé to be a disservice to you.

---

[669] *Caravelão*: see Glossary.
[670] See MMA vol. 15, doc. 53.
[671] That is, 'Vila Nova de Portimão' (today 'Portimão').
[672] Possibly, the island of Annobon, also known as Ambo. Edwin Ardener identifies 'Ambos' with the Ambas Bay in Cameroon. See Edwin Ardener, *Kingdom on Mount Cameroon: Studies in the History of the Cameroon Coast, 1500-1970* (London: Berghahn Books, 1996), 7–18, 24–25, 28, 35, 352, and 362.
[673] *Moio*: see Glossary.

Your Highness should not send slaves from the island or Akori beads to Mina, for you may be sure that it is not your service, if not of all Portugal;[674] and if it is more costly it will be more in your interest and service, for otherwise Mina will never have goods which are severely prohibited, which are taken via the island of São Tomé. And you may be sure of this being so, because, believe me, for the past two and a half years so much stealing and disservice has been done to you in Mina that I do not know how you can receive your dues [[?]],[675] and believe me that in everything you are robbed in the island of São Tomé, even, as we say, with the sugar. All this I write to Your Highness for I write to you very truly, as a man who desires only to be of service to you.[676]

I have arrived in Caliz[[?]][677] on a ship from the island of São Tomé, and because I am ill I have not still gone to your court to kiss your hands and give you a fuller account of many matters of your service, which I do not dare to declare in this [[letter]], because I do not know how you will be when you read it, and because I have a great number of highly secret things to tell Your Highness, which I am not telling now for the reasons I have already mentioned, from which I expect many favors from Your Highness. May God increase your royal estate and the days of your life.

Today, on the 10th day of May 1529 years.

Duarte Roiz

ADDRESS: To Our Lord the King
This letter is highly secret; it should be opened in Your Highness's presence. Sent from Caliz [[?]]

67 Letter to Estêvão Da Gama, Captain of Mina[678] (25/06/1529)

ABSTRACT – *Letter from King João III ordering the captain of São Jorge da Mina give a food allowance[679] only to those chaplains of Mina and Akyem ('Axim') provided with letters of authorization from the Bishop of Funchal.*

[674] In Brásio's transcription, '*senã só de Portugall*' ('*senão só de Portugal*'), which literally means 'rather only of Portugal.' But what seems to be written in the manuscript is '*senã tode Portugall*' (probably, '*senão todo Portugal*'), i.e. 'if not all Portugal.'

[675] In Brásio's transcription, as in the manuscript, '*onra*' ('*honra*'), which may refer to kinds of payments.

[676] Although the transcription has only '[...] *todo jsto scprevo a V.A. por que só desejo o seu servyço*' ('all this I write to Your Highness for I desire only to be of service to you'), in the manuscript this passage reads '*todo jsto esprevo a v.a. porque lhe esprevo muita verdade como omem que [so] deseja o seu servyço.*'

[677] In Brásio's transcription, '*Coly(m)*' (or '*Cali(m)*,' as noted by the editor). In the manuscript, what seems to be written is '*Caliz*' or '*Calez*'; although the author of the letter was referring to a Portuguese port, he may be referring to 'Cadiz.'

[678] BSGL, Reservado A-55, fl. 68v-69; cf. MMA vol. 1, doc. 152, pp. 519–20. Estêvão da Gama was appointed captain of Mina by letter of Dom João III, dated February 4, 1529, ANTT, *Chancelaria de D. João III*, liv. 45, fol. 158v.

[679] It is not entirely clear what '*mantimento(s)*' stands for in this case, but it probably means 'food allowance' and not 'supplies/food,' as Brásio has it.

Estêvão da Gama, I, the King, send you my greetings.

I am informed that some clergymen go to that town of São Jorge and to Akyem to administer the Holy Sacraments without taking with them the letters patent and licenses to administer the said Sacraments, whereby I command you and the captains who shall occupy the office, even though the said chaplains bring an authorization for receiving their food allowance and what is due to them, not to give anything to them, or to allow them to administer any Sacrament, unless they first show the letters patent and licenses issued by whomsoever has the power and competence to do it. And this shall be recorded in the book of the regulations of that town, to be obeyed at all times.

Álvaro Neto wrote it in Lisbon, on the 25th day of June one thousand 5 hundred and 29.

This license shall be issued by the Bishop of Funchal or by someone on his behalf, and it shall be recorded in the House of India and Mina; and the officials of the said House should be reminded to notify all clergymen who are going to Mina to carry with them letters of curateship(?),[680] for whatever is necessary, without which they will not be allowed on board.

68 Letter from Fernão De Carvalho to Dom João III[681] (03/06/1530)

ABSTRACT – *Fernão Carvalho gives news of the Gaia (Mahin) and Volta rivers, and of the service the king would receive if there are precautions against the trade of some individuals in those places, since much gold is found in those parts.*

+

My Lord,

Since I arrived in this island of São Tomé with the charge granted to me by Your Highness, which is that of Captain of the *caravelão*[682] that takes the slaves from this island to Mina, I have always tried to serve you in all things, both in those pertaining to my charge and in those in which Your Highness might be disserved by someone else in these parts. And I have learned from several people who know it for certain, that one of the main rivers in these parts, whence comes the greatest part of the Akori beads brought to this island, is the Gaia River,[683] which is fifty

---

[680] In the transcription, '*curaida*,' a word which does not exist; it should probably read '*curato*,' i.e. 'curateship,' the office of a curate.

[681] ANTT, CC 1-45-31; cf. MMA vol. 1, doc. 156, pp. 154–55.

[682] *Caravelão*: see Glossary.

[683] The Gaia River is the Mahin River in the (former) kingdom of Benin; the Portugues also named it Rio Primeiro ('First River'). See Robin Law, 'Early European Sources Relating to the Kingdom of

leagues behind Mina, and where many people, both white men and manumitted black men, choose to remain. And between the Gaia River and Mina there is another river which is called the Volta River, of which it is said that there is much gold and that a great amount of it goes from there to Mina; and because it is so close to the Gaia River, where the white men reside, it is possible that some of them, since it is so near, may have the audacity to go overland to the Volta River and beyond, to trade with the black men, from which will follow great disservice and loss to Your Highness. [[Therefore,]] I have decided to give you this information, so that Your Highness may provide as seems fit to your service. And should you desire that, on my return journey from Mina to this island of São Tomé, I should go to Volta River to sound the bar, and to sound out the black people as to whether they want peace or agree to trade, and to find out what they want and what has value among them, I will do what Your Highness orders me, for I desire that Your Highness should entrust me with matters of your service and I know how easy it will be for Your Highness to provide in this matter, as you will know by a letter from the Captain of Mina and by another from the *Corregedor*[684] of this island, both of which I enclose.

From this island of São Tomé, on the third of June 1530 years.

Fernão Carvalho[685]

+

ADDRESS: To Our Lord the King.

69 Merchandise Delivered by Gonçalo De Campos to the House of Mina Treasurer[686] (30/08/1530)

ABSTRACT – *List of trade goods factor Gonçalo de Campos delivered to the pilot of the São Miguel, and ultimately to the House of Mina in Lisbon. These metals, cloths, and trinkets were the staples of the commerce between Portugal and Mina—and, for that matter, western Africa. The document is published for the first time.*

[On] the thirtieth day of the month of August one thousand 530, the Factor Gonçalo de Campos delivered to Afonso Martins, pilot of the ship São Miguel,

---

Ijebu (1500–1700): A Critical Survey,' *History in Africa* 13 (1986): 247; idem, 'Trade and Politics behind the Slave Coast: The Lagoon Traffic and the Rise of Lagos, 1500–1800,' *The Journal of African History* 24, no. 3 (1983): 322–4; A. F. C. Ryder, 'An Early Portuguese Trading Voyage to the Forcados River,' *Journal of the Historical Society of Nigeria* 1, no. 4 (1959): 294–5.

[684] *Corregedor*: see Glossary.

[685] See MMA vol. 15, doc. 38.

[686] ANTT, CC 2-164-118. Fragmentary document with stains and torn paper. Dots between simple square brackets, except where a footnote has been added, indicate words which are illegible; simple square brackets are also used to indicate reconstitution.

whose captain was Francisco Monteiro, eight old [....] with seven *gafas*,[687] and eighteen [.........] with their *nivilheiras* [*sic*],[688] and [........] and four old cubic rulers,[689] [......] eight cauldrons with lid with [.....] and four lids and an old pan [....] a big old copper cauldron and nine[teen] old jackets,[690] and sixty-eight [...........], and seventy-three pots [....] among which six pots [....] iron handles[?][691] and eight copper jars [....] seven shovels[692] and eighty-five hoods [...........] and fourteen *aljaravias*[693] from [Fernão] de Álvares's trading, in which were packaged [....] hoods.[694] Which items the said Factor deli[vered to] Afonso Martins to take for shipping to the Kingdom, [to be delivered] to the Treasurer of the House of Mina, [according to] what [the afore]said Lord orders [.....][695] in his re[gulations]. Written by me, Nuno Antunes, scribe of this [Factory], on the aforesaid day, month and era.

[sign.] *Nuno Antunes de Barros*

[...] day of the month of September [...][696] [one thousand] [five hun]dred and thirty, the said [Factor Gonçalo] [de Ca]mpos delivered to Pedro Fernandes, pilot of the ship [......] [...] which merchandise was delivered by the said Factor to the said Pedro Fernandes for him to take to the Rossio[?] and give it to the Treasurer of the House of Mina, according to what the aforesaid Lord orders in his regulations. Written by me, Nuno Antunes, scribe of this Factory, on the aforesaid day, month and [era].

[sign.] *Nuno Antunes*

On the ninth day of September 1530 years, the Factor Gonçalo de Campos [deli]vered to Afonso Martins of the caravel São Miguel, whose captain is Francisco Monteiro, four *aljaravias* from Fernão de Álvares's trading, to be delivered to the T[reasurer of the] House of Mina.

[sign.] *Nuno Antunes de Barros*

[sign.] By *Fernão de Gama*

---

[687] In the manuscript, '*gafos,*' i.e. 'lepers,' which would make no sense in this context. '*Gafa*' may have here three different meanings: it either means a boathook, a hook used in spanning the crossbow, or a vessel for transporting salt in a salt mine.

[688] Obscure meaning.

[689] In the manuscript, '*páreas*': see Glossary.

[690] In the manuscript, '*alabardas,*' which literally means 'halberds.' However, given the items listed in the document, it is probable the correct spelling would have been '*albardas,*' which could stand for 'jackets,' and also for 'pack saddles.'

[691] In the manuscript, '*bordas*,' literally 'rims.'

[692] In Portuguese, '*sapas.*' A more accurate translation, but probably betraying the broader sense of the term in the original, would be 'trenching shovels.'

[693] *Aljaravia*: see Glossary.

[694] Word between lines.

[695] Crossed out in the manuscript: '*fejto por*' ('*feito por*'), that is, 'done/written by.'

[696] Crossed out in the manuscript: '*entre*[*gou*]' ('delivered').

On the fourth day of the month of March 1531 years, the Factor G[onçalo de Campos] delivered to Vasco Fernandes, pilot of the caravel São Cristóvão, whose captain [...], [...] thirty *aljaravias* from Fernão de Álvares's trading, to be [delivered] to the Treasurer of the House of India and Mina, according to what the aforesaid Lord [orders] in his regulations.

On the aforesaid day, month and era, the said Factor Gonçalo de Campos delivered to Pedro Eanes of the caravel Espera, whose Captain was António Lobo, thirty *al[jaravias]* from Fernão de Álvares's trading, to be delivered in the Kingdom to the Tr[easu]rer of the House of India and Mina, according to what the aforesaid Lord orders in [his] regulations.

[sign.] By *Fernão da Gama*

70 Bill of Lading of Lopo De Pina[697] (17/06/1532)

ABSTRACT – *Bill of lading for the cargo of the caravelão Santo António, of Sesimbra, comprising enslaved peoples, yam, and Akori beads, to be taken from São Tomé to São Jorge da Mina.*

+

I attest, and Lopo de Pina,[698] Factor of Our Lord the King in this fortress of São Jorge da Mina,[699] acknowledges that he received from Gabriel Fernandes,[700] Receiver in the island of São Tomé, through Fernão Carvalho,[701] Captain of the *caravelão*[702] Santo António, of Sesimbra, the articles mentioned below: namely, sixty-five slave pieces, both adult and young, male and female. And of cowry three thousand seven hundred and forty-three Akori beads,[703] which weighed, including the tare weight of the small bag of palm [[leaf]] and paper, five marks one ounce and five drams.[704] And of yam forty *quintais*,[705] which came as provisions for the said vessel. And of palm oil, a small quantity in a barrel of six *almudes*.[706] And of rice, fifty-four *alqueires*[707] in two pipes; and he is taking the pipes back.

---

[697] ANTT, CC 1-176-56; cf. MMA vol. 15, doc. 38. In the title MMA gave to the document, '16-6-1532'; but according to the transcription, this should read '17-6-1532.'
[698] See MMA vol. 15, doc. 46.
[699] Lopo de Pina was appointed factor of Mina on September 27, 1539, ANTT, *Chancelaria de D. João III,* liv. 26, fol. 262v.
[700] Tentative translation of an otherwise obscure phrase; instead of '*recebedor de Gabriel Fernandes*' ('receiver of Gabriel Fernandes'), as in Brásio's transcription, this should probably read '*receber de Gabriel Fernandes*' ('receive/received from Gabriel Fernandes'). See MMA vol. 15, doc. 46.
[701] See MMA vol. 1, doc. 156.
[702] *Caravelão*: see Glossary.
[703] The repetition is in the document.
[704] In Portuguese, '*oitava*' (sing.), that is, an 'eighth' of an ounce.
[705] *Quintal* (sing.): see Glossary.
[706] *Almude* (sing.): see Glossary.
[707] *Alqueire* (sing.): see Glossary.

And because it is true that the said Factor received the aforesaid articles, and they have been posted for him as revenue by me, Lopo Sardinha, [[with]] Jorge Cotrim,[708] scribes of this Factory, I give him this bill of lading, written by me and signed by all, on the 17th of June 1532 years.

a) Lopo de Pina / *a)* Jorge Cotrim / *a)* Lopo Sardinha

Posted as expenditure.

71 King João III to the Count of Castanheira[709]   (03/02/1533)

ABSTRACT – *Letter from the king to Dom António de Ataíde, overseer of his exchequer, about the gold-bearing caravels from Mina and hopes that the flow of gold, measured in dobras, continues as in the time when Estêvão da Gama was captain of São Jorge da Mina.*

[…] I thank you greatly for the news which you have sent me about the caravels from Mina. It is very likely that the reasons why they did not bring more than ten thousand *dobras* are the ones you wrote. From now on, I hope they may bring what the ones from the time of Estêvão da Gama[710] used to bring. And furthermore, I strongly enjoin you to ensure supplies to Mina, and that now, since the contract of the pepper, in which Francisco Lobo has one thousand *quintais*,[711] has terminated, you complete the contract of the merchandise for Mina, as was ordained and seems to you to best befit my service.

The King
Reply to the Count of Castanheira.
[On reverse side]
By the King.

To Dom António de Ataíde, Count of Castanheira, Overseer of his Exchequer.[712]
    [Évora, 3rd February 1533]

---

[708] See MMA vol. 15, doc. 46.
[709] MS Port 4491, letter 47, Houghton Library, Harvard University. Transcribed in Ford, *Letters of John III*, p. 85. See also ANTT, *Colecção de São Lourenço*, liv. 1; Elaine Sanceau, *Colecção de São Lourenço*, vol. 3 (Lisboa: Centro de Estudos Históricos Ultramarinos da Junta de Investigação do Ultramar, 1973–83). Many of Dom António de Ataíde's letters to João III can be found in ANTT, MM, vol. 4, though there are several in MS Port 19, Houghton Library, Harvard University.
[710] See MMA vol. 1, doc. 152.
[711] *'Quintais'* (sing. *'quintal'*): see Glossary.
[712] In Portuguese, *'Vedor da Fazenda'*: see Glossary.

72 King João III to the Count of Castanheira[713]
(08/02/1533)

ABSTRACT – *Letter from the king to Dom António de Ataíde, overseer of his exchequer, about a letter he (the king) received from the Mina factor, indicating the Mina captain is ill, though the fortress has plenty of goods and supplies.*

[...] The Factor of Mina has written me this letter, which I enclose, since the Captain is ill and because in it he gives an account of the situation in Mina, the plenty of goods and supplies that there exist, as well as when the caravels should sail. I send it to you, so that you may maintain and arrange matters in the House as best befits my service and according to what is written in it.

[...]

Fernão de Álvares wrote this, in Évora, on the 8th day of February 1533.

73 Bill of Lading of Lopo De Pina, Factor of São Jorge
Da Mina[714] (05/08/1533)

ABSTRACT – *Lopo de Pina acknowledges having received the goods mentioned from Gabriel Fernandes, for which he issues the due bill of lading.*

I attest, and the Factor Lopo de Pina,[715] of this fortress of São Jorge da Mina, acknowledges that he received from[716] Gabriel Fernandes,[717] Receiver of the island of São Tomé, through João Gomes, Captain of the *caravelão*[718] Santo António, of which Pedro Gomes is the pilot, ninety-five slave pieces, both male and female, adult and young. And furthermore, he received from the said Receiver one thousand seven hundred and seventy-four Akori beads, which weighed, including the tare weight of a small bag of palm [[leaf]], two marks and five ounces. And furthermore he received an amount of yam, which was left over from the voyage, as maintenance for the said slaves. And furthermore he received a small quantity of palm oil in[719] a wooden barrel of six *almudes*,[720] which was also left over from [[the maintenance of(?)]] the said slaves.

---

[713] MS Port 4491, letter 54, Houghton Library, Harvard University. Transcribed in Ford, *Letters of John III*, p. 92.

[714] ANTT, CC 2-184-71; cf. MMA vol. 15, doc. 46.

[715] See MMA vol. 15, doc. 38.

[716] In Brásio's transcription, '*e*' ('and'), though it should read '*de*' ('from').

[717] See MMA vol. 15, doc. 38.

[718] *Caravelão*: see Glossary.

[719] In Brásio's transcription, '*e*' ('and'), though it should read '*em*' ('in').

[720] *Almude*, sing.: see Glossary.

And because it is true that the said Factor received the abovementioned items, and they have been posted for him as revenue by me and by Jorge Rodrigues, scribes of this Factory, this bill of lading was issued for him and signed by all. Written by me, Jorge Cotrim,[721] on the fifth day of August 1533 years.

a) Lopo de Pina *a)* Jorge Rodrigues *a)* Jorge Cotrim

74   King João III to the Count of Castanheira[722] (1533/04?)

ABSTRACT – *Letter from the king to Dom António de Ataíde about the need to prepare a fleet for Mina to meet the needs of São Jorge da Mina.*

Count, my friend, I, the King, send you greetings as to one whom I dearly love. I have seen the letter you sent to me through Fernão Álvares, and he gave me an account of everything that was going on there, and of the situation in which you found everything in that town, and of the scarcity there of *naus* and ships,[723] as well as of all other things which he was minded to tell me. And I thank you greatly for the detailed account you had given me. And through this [[letter]] I reply to you concerning immediate needs and what it is my wish that should be done.

Item: as regards the fleet of Mina, and considering the reasons given by Fernão Álvares, it is my wish that the galleon São João should sail with it, should no other *nau* arrive to that town which you think may serve this purpose; because if there is, I will be pleased that she be bought[724] and that she sails with the fleet in place of the said galleon. And given the need that is felt in Mina, as it has been so long since any ship was sent there, I strongly enjoin you to make haste in making the fleet ready as quickly as possible. And you will have it given regulations, regarding what the chief Captain and the Captains are to do during the voyage, signed by you, and I will send it instructions ordering that they be observed as if they had been signed by me. And there you shall have discussions concerning the people who should be left in the castle of Mina, as well as whether any caravels should remain there for some time. And as soon as you decide on these matters, you will provide for them and order that it be declared in the regulations, because what you do I will consider to have been done well, for I know that you will regard it as befits my service.

Item: Fernão Álvares also gave me an account of the course of action you had taken regarding the *nau* São Roque, and how you had her inspected so she could be repaired and equipped to stay in the harbor, which seemed to me very

---

[721] See MMA vol. 15, doc. 38.

[722] MS Port 4491, letter 109, Houghton Library, Harvard University. Transcribed in Ford, *Letters of John III*, pp. 153–54.

[723] In the transcription, '*navios*,' which is the common term to designate any large vessel.

[724] Literal translation of '*se compre*,' though in this context it might also read '*se cumpra*' ('it be done/ observed').

well done and most necessary. I strongly enjoin you to have her, as soon as possible, repaired and equipped, and very well armed with artillery and equipped
with everything needed, so that she may lie in that harbor ready for whatever
befits my service. And should any *nau* arrive which may serve in the fleet of
Mina, I will be pleased that the *nau* São Roque and the galleon São João be both
equipped, armed and made ready in that harbor to assist in whatever occurs and
is necessary.

75 Embassy from Mina to Rome[725] (15/02/1535)

ABSTRACT – *Letter from D. Martinho de Portugal, Archbishop of Funchal,
to the Count of Vimios, about an emissary named Dom Filipe from Mina to the
Vatican. Dom Filipe had a meeting with the Pope. Filipe is the rare case of an
embassy from Mina to the Vatican, and thus significant when compared to the
various and well-known delegations from the Kingdom of Kongo. Unfortunately,
this excerpt from a longer yet irrelevant letter does not permit any meaningful
comparison with the Kongo or another African polity.[726]*

Dom Filipe has arrived here; this Pope was very pleased with him. He found this
embassy so miserable that he had garments made, and he recovered his spirits a
little. He seems[727] to be a good young man; he says he is poor and that he wants to
go to Mina. Help him, for the love of God, if it seems right to you. I took care of
him, but not as well as I wished. My companion is a very suspicious man; I never
speak to the Pope nor to any other person without him, and thus I did with Dom
Filipe. [...][728]
     From Rome, on the 15th of February 1535.

[sign.] Dom Martinho de Portugal,

Archbishop of Funchal

---

[725] ANTT, CC 1-54-77; cf. MMA vol. 2, doc. 13.
[726] On Kongolese emissaries to Europe, including the Pope and Portugal, see Cecile Fromont, *The
Art of Conversion: Christian Visual Culture in the Kingdom of Kongo* (Chapel Hill: University of
North Carolina Press, 2014); John K. Thornton, 'The Origins and Early History of the Kingdom
of Kongo,' *International Journal of African Historical Studies* 34, no. 1 (2001): 89–120; Richard
Gray, 'A Kongo Princess, the Kongo Ambassadors and the Papacy,' *Journal of Religion in Africa*
29, no. 2 (1999): 140–54; John K. Thornton, *The Kongolese Saint Anthony: Dona Beatriz Kimpa
Vita and the Antonian Movement, 1683-1706* (New York: Cambridge University Press, 1998); Ann
Hilton, *The Kingdom of Kongo* (New York: Oxford University Press, 1982); Graziano Saccardo,
Congo e Angola con la storia dell'antica missione dei Cappuccini 3 vols. (Venice: Curia provinciale
dei Cappuccini, 1982–83); David Birmingham, *Trade and Conquest in Angola* (New York: Oxford
University Press, 1966).
[727] In the manuscript in Torre do Tombo, '*parece,*' which MMA incorrectly transcribed as '*para o*'
('to the').
[728] According to the original manuscript, the letter does not end at this point; the remaining lines,
however, bear no relation to Mina.

76 Book of Cargo*[729]* and Regulations of the Ship Santa Maria Do Cabo*[730]* (24/04/1535)

ABSTRACT – *Instructions from the regulations which should be observed, detailing also what the pilot received from the factor of São Tomé to be delivered in Mina, the expenditure with the ship's cargo, the receipt for what the pilot received from the factor of Mina, and the expenditure with the ship's costs.*

Σ

COPY OF THE REGULATIONS

The regulations and manner which [[you]], the most honorable Duarte Luís,[731] Captain and Pilot of the ship Santa Maria do Cabo, and Jerónimo de Orta,[732] scribe, shall observe during this journey which you will make to Mina, are as follows:

Σ   As soon as you have been searched by the *Corregedor*[733] or judges who should be with you, and thus with the scribes of this Factory or each of them, as is stipulated by Our Lord the King in his regulations, you shall in our presence release the moorings immediately, and make sail, and while you sail in sight of this island you shall be mindful[734] not to let any *batel*, *almadia*,[735] or any other [[boat]] approach you, but rather you shall ensure that you immediately follow your route directly towards the said Mina, because the said Lord commands that, should you in any way do otherwise as regards this matter after releasing the moorings from this port, you shall be arrested, and lose your wages, and receive the other penalties mentioned in his ordinances.

Σ   After you have departed from the said island and port, as soon as you are on the coast of Mina, you shall be mindful[736] to endeavor, and to be very careful and vigilant, not to sail leeward of Mina, but rather you shall endeavor to sail as far windward as you can, since it often happens that,

---

[729] In Portuguese, '*Livro da/de armação*,' the book where all transactions, together with the ship's costs, were noted down by the scribe who travelled on board (thus distinct from the logbook); see José Virgílio Amaro Pissarra, 'Livros de armação,' in *Navegações Portuguesas* (Lisboa: Instituto Camões, 2002–2006). For an alternative and approximate English translation of '*livro de armação*' ('book of cargo'), see Joshua Montefiore, *Commercial Dictionary: Containing the Present State of Mercantile Law, Practice, and Custom* (London: The Author, 1803), under 'Book of Cargo or Loading'; another, less precise, alternative might be 'ship's book.'

[730] ANTT, CC 2-200-127; cf. MMA vol. 15, doc. 53, pp. 110–14.

[731] See MMA vol. 4, doc. 40.

[732] See MMA vol. 15, doc. 40.

[733] *Corregedor*: see Glossary.

[734] In Brásio's transcription, '*farês hauizados*' ('*fareis avisados*'), which is meaningless; it should read '*sereis avisados*' ('you shall be mindful).'

[735] *Batel* and *almadia*: see Glossary.

[736] In Brásio's transcription, '*farês hamizades*' ('*fareis amizades*'), literally 'you shall make friends with'; to make any sense, this should read, as above and below (see following paragraph), '*sereis avisados*.'

for want of care and vigilance, ships are unable to make port in Mina, from which great loss derives for the said Lord; which same care and diligence you shall also have in being vigilant that the slaves do not rebel or create any disorder.

Σ   As soon as you have made yourself known[737] to the land where you will make port, you shall be mindful to sail, from there to Mina, in such a way and with such caution as not to go past it either by night or by day, since it has often occurred that a ship has passed by without being recognized,[738] in doing which you shall be very vigilant; and you shall also be very vigilant lest any *almadia* come alongside your [[ship]] either by day or by night, nor shall you speak with any of their [[men]] either during the outward or the return journey. And should you do otherwise, you shall lose your wages and salaries, and receive the other penalties mentioned in the ordinances.

Σ   As soon as you arrive in front of Mina, should you have anchored by night, you shall signal with a bombard, or with a flag should it be day, and you shall not pull out any *batel* by night, but only by day, after they signal to you from land, at which [[signal]] you shall pull out the *batel* and leave [[the ship]] together with the scribe. And you shall take with you the letter from the House to the Factor and officials, which you shall deliver in the presence of the Captain; [[and]] you shall go on the *batel* directly to the exact place where the flag is put for you, which will be in Ramada. And once the letters[[*sic*]] have been read, you shall establish as briefly as possible that they should immediately receive your delivery of slaves, and Akori beads, [[and]] supplies, so that you make sail again before night. And should you be unable to finish it on time, you shall retire to your ship, to which you shall tie the *batel* in such a way that it be secure. And on the next day, as soon as they set the signal for you, you shall go ashore and finish your delivery, of Akori beads as well as of any other goods [[and]] supplies, for all of which you shall obtain a receipt in due form, so that you may bring it for the account of the Factor and Receiver.

Σ   As soon as you have delivered the slaves and any other goods which you may take from this Factory, and obtain a receipt in due form, you shall immediately retire, and make sail, and move away from land so that no *almadias* come alongside [[the ship]], which you shall not allow subject to the penalties mentioned in these regulations of yours, which you shall most fully observe. And you shall come to this island without touching any other land but this port and bar, where as soon as you arrive you shall signal with two bombards, in order that we may immediately go to you to bring the said ship, thus and in the same manner as when you departed from

---

[737] Tentative translation of '*houverdes conhecimêto*' ('*houverdes conhecimento*'), from the infinitive '*haver conhecimento*,' literally 'to have knowledge.'

[738] In Brásio's transcription, '*hauer conhecimêto*' ('*haver conhecimento*'): see previous note.

here, with the *Corregedor* or judges,[739] so as to check whether any of you, or any other person, has done anything contrary to these regulations. And before we go to you, you shall not pull out any *batel*, nor shall any other [[*batel*]] be brought alongside [[the ship]], subject to the said penalties.

Σ You shall not take, or allow any person to take, or to bring in the ship, any letters, because His Highness so orders and considers it to be his service, subject to the same penalties as those who take the prohibited articles. And so that they do not plead ignorance should they commit this or any other act contrary to these regulations, the scribe shall make them public before the crew and copy them at the beginning of the book he shall make during the said journey, in order that it may always be known that regulations were issued regarding what should be done. And in his book he shall register the slaves and any other goods which may be delivered to the Pilot, and the supplies, thus and in the same manner in which they are given; and thus, when the delivery is carried out in Mina [[the charge]] shall be cleared to the said Pilot, even though he shall bring a receipt in due form of what he delivers. Of which regulations a copy of the original, which is kept in this Factory, was given to him, signed by the said Pilot. One thousand five hundred and thirty-five years.

Σ

On the 24th day of the month of April one thousand 535 years, the ship Santa Maria do Cabo, may God guide her safely, whose Pilot is Duarte Luís, departed to Mina from the bay of the island of São Tomé, in front of the Factory. And as soon as she departed, I, the scribe, read and published these regulations, both to the Master and to the whole crew. And, on the part of the said Lord, I demanded that they should keep and obey them as stipulated therein. And I, Jerónimo de Orta, scribe of the said ship, wrote this.

Revenue [[posted]] for the said Pilot of what he received from the Factor of the island of São Tomé to deliver in Mina.

Σ I post as revenue for the said Pilot one hundred slave pieces, both male and female.

Σ I post as revenue for the said Pilot four hundred and fifty *pesos*[740] of yam, which he received to be spent with the [[slave]] pieces and crew of the said ship.

Σ I post as revenue for the said Pilot six *quintais*[741] of iron, [[divided]] into eight *bares*.[742]

Σ I post as revenue for the said Pilot one *quintal* of lead paste.

---

[739] A similar passage of the regulations inserted in a book of cargo of another ship (the São Cristóvão – MMA vol. 15, doc. 55) reads 'without the *Corregedor* or judges.'

[740] *Peso* (sing.): see Glossary.

[741] *Quintal* (sing.): see Glossary.

[742] *Bar* (sing.): see Glossary.

Expenditure of the cargo which Duarte Luís, Pilot, delivered to the Factor and officials of Mina.

Σ   I post here as expenditure for the Pilot one piece, who died on the 7th day of the month of March.

Σ   I post as expenditure for the said Pilot one piece, who died on the 9th day of the month of March.

Σ   On the **11**[th] day of the month of March I post here as expenditure for the said Pilot one piece, who died.

Σ   I post here as expenditure for the said Pilot ninety-seven slave pieces, both male and female, which he delivered to the Factor and officials of Mina, on the 17th day of the month of March.

Σ   On the said day I post here as expenditure for the said Pilot a chest with three thousand Akori beads, which he delivered to the Factor and officials of Mina.

Σ   On the said day I post as expenditure for the said Pilot one *quintal* of lead paste, which he delivered to the Factor and officials of Mina.

Σ   On the said day I post as expenditure for the said Pilot four hundred and fifty *pesos* of yam: namely, [[divided]] into two and a half *bateladas*,[743] which he delivered to the Factor and officials of Mina. And the remainder was spent with the cargo and crew of the said ship.

Revenue of what the said Pilot of Sebastião Pestana,[744] Factor of Mina, received to be delivered to Manuel Vaz,[745] Factor of the island of São Tomé.

Σ   I post as revenue for the said Pilot twenty thousand brass manillas, which he received from the Factor of Mina to deliver to the Factor of the island of São Tomé, which [[manillas]] he received on the 17th day of May one thousand 535.

Σ   I post as revenue for the said Pilot one barrel which he says contains two *quintais* of gunpowder, which he received from the Factor of Mina to deliver to Manuel Vaz, Factor of the island of São Tomé.

Expenditure with the ship's costs.

Σ   I post as expenditure for the said Pilot an old cable,[746] which is broken.

Σ   I post as expenditure for the said Pilot the main halyard [[?]],[747] because it is old and broken.

Σ   I post as expenditure for the said Pilot the stay of the main mast because it is not for use.

---

[743] *Batelada* (sing.): see Glossary.
[744] See MMA vol. 15, doc. 55.
[745] See MMA vol. 15, doc. 55; CC 2-205-21.
[746] In Brásio's transcription, '*callabrete*' ('*calabrete*'), a thinner type of cable; see Glossary.
[747] In Portuguese, '*ostaga*.'

Σ   I post as expenditure the sheets[748] of the main sail because they are both broken.

Σ   I post as expenditure for the said Pilot the braces, with their topgallant stays,[749] of the main sail.

Σ   I post as expenditure for the said Pilot the halyard [[?]] of the foresail because it is broken.

Σ   I post as expenditure two studdingsails [[?]][750] of the foresail.

Σ   I post as expenditure for the said Pilot a topping lift[751] of the foresail.

Σ   I post as expenditure for the said Pilot four shrouds of the mizzenmast [[?]].[752]

Σ   I post as expenditure for the said [[Pilot]] the halyard [[?]] of the mizzen mast, because it is old and broken.

Σ   I post as expenditure for the said Pilot the yard lift [[?]][753] of the mizzen.

Σ   On the 17th day of May of the era one thousand 535 years, in Mina, after Duarte Luís, Pilot of the ship Santa Maria do Cabo, had received the abovementioned manillas, three buckets [[with manillas]] fell into the sea; and since he does not know how many [[manillas]] were lost, because some of them, which fell in the presence of the Captain and officials, were caught, I will not post them as expenditure for him until they are counted in the island.

Σ   On the 11th day of June of the aforesaid era I post here as expenditure for the said Pilot [20,000] manillas, which he delivered to the said Factor before me, the scribe, out of which 20 thousand manillas eighty-one were missing, which are those that fell into the sea, [[and]] which I post as expenditure for him to make up the abovementioned 20,000, since the sea was very wild, as I, the scribe, may attest, and the slaves who were putting them on the *batel* fell with them into a breaking wave.

77 Logbook[754] of the São Cristóvão[755] (05/12/1535)

ABSTRACT – *Logbook of a ship carrying merchandise from São Tomé to São Jorge da Mina. The cargo loaded at the port of departure was as follows: 80 male and female enslaved adolescents (described as handsome and healthy), 17,000 cowrie*

---

[748] In Brásio's transcription, '*estotas*,' though it should read '*escotas*.'

[749] In Brásio's transcription, '*reigadas*,' that is, '*arreigadas*.'

[750] In Brásio's transcription, '*coetos*,' which should perhaps read '*cutelos*.'

[751] In Brásio's transcription, '*hamãtelho*,' that is, '*amantilho*.'

[752] In Brásio's transcription, '*meza*,' probably an abbreviated form of '*mezena*' ('mizzen' or 'mizzen mast').

[753] In Brásio's transcription, '*troca*' ('*troça*').

[754] This seems to be part of a '*livro de armação*' rather than of a 'logbook'; the '*livro da armação*' being the book where all the transactions, together with the ship's costs and relevant events, were noted by the scribe who went aboard.

[755] ANTT, CC 2-205-21. Transcribed in Ballong-Wen-Mewuda, *São Jorge da Mina*, 2: 539–40.

pearls, 400 pesos of yam, one barrel of palm oil. The text of the voyage regulations,
which is always the same and made public for the members of the crew at the begin-
ning of each voyage, is missing from this logbook.

Item.   On the fifth day of the month of December one thousand five hundred and
thirty-five years, Sebastião Álvares, pilot, received from Manuel Vaz,[756]
Factor of the King, eighty slave pieces, to be delivered to the Captain of
Mina. Which slaves were boys and girls of a good age, with no warts or
injuries of any kind.

Item.   On the same day, in the Factory of the said Lord, before me, the scribe,
together with the judge who was there at the time, Manuel Vaz and the
officials of the said Factory counted seventeen thousand Akori beads,
which Akori beads were delivered to Sebastião Álvares, pilot, to be
delivered to the Captain of Mina.

Item.   The master of the said[[*sic*]] ship received four hundred *pesos*[757] of yam,
in exchange for the said pieces, before me, the scribe.

Item.   On the same day, the master of the said ship received a barrel of oil in
exchange for the said pieces, before me, the Scribe.

Item.   On the sixth day of the month of December one thousand five hundred and
thirty-five years, the ship São Cristóvão, whose pilot is Sebastião Álvares,
the master João Luís and the scribe Fernão Roiz, sailed from the island of
São Tomé to Mina.

Item.   On the twenty-first day of the said month, we arrived at Mina, and on the
next day Sebastião Álvares, pilot, delivered to the Captain of Mina eighty
slave pieces, both male and female, before me, the scribe; of which pieces
two were refused. In addition, the Captain of Mina delivered to the pilot
seventeen pieces out of those he had in Mina, which were deducted from
those we carried for them. And they did not want to acknowledge more
than sixty-one.

Item.   Furthermore, on the same day, Sebastião Álvares, pilot, delivered to the
Captain of Mina seventeen thousand Akori beads, before me, the scribe.

Item.   On the twenty-fourth day, we sailed from Mina to the island of São Tomé.

Item.   On the twenty-sixth day of the said month, two pieces of the said Lord
died and they were thrown into the sea in front of the company; which
pieces were aged between ten and fifteen and were branded on the right
upper arm; and the brand is this: 66. Fernão Roiz.

[sign.] [[five-pointed star]] *Vaz*

Item.   On the first day of the month of January one thousand five hundred and
thirty-six years, we arrived at the island of São Tomé.

---

[756] See MMA vol. 15, docs. 53 and 55.
[757] *Peso*: see Glossary.

78 Logbook Fragment of the São Cristóvão[758] (19/03/1536)

ABSTRACT – *a Logbook[759] or fragment of a logbook (the text of the voyage regulations is missing) of a slave ship, São Cristóvão, between the island of São Tomé and the Portuguese Factory of São Jorge da Mina. The island's authorities delivered a cargo to the pilot composed of 100 'slave pieces, both male and female' and 400 pesos of yam. The outward journey between the two ports lasted from 19 March to 8 April 1536, and the return from 10 to 28 of April the same year).*

Book of lading of the pieces which Manuel Vaz, Factor of Our Lord the King, delivered to Pedro da Costa,[760] Captain of the ship São Cristóvão, which travels between the island of São Tomé and Mina. Fernando Roiz.

Item.   Firstly, I post as expense on behalf of Pedro da Costa, Captain of the said ship, four hundred *pesos* of yam which he received from Manuel Vaz, Factor of Our Lord the King, for the said load. Fernando Roiz.

Item.   On the eighteenth day of the month of March one thousand five hundred and thirty-six years, Captain Pedro da Costa received from Manuel Vaz, Factor of the said Lord in the island of São Tomé, one hundred slave pieces, both male and female, for delivery to the Factor in Mina. Fernando Roiz.

Item.   On the nineteenth of the said month, we sailed on the said ship from the island of São Tomé to Mina, with the aforesaid cargo. Fernando Roiz.

Item.   On the fourth day of the month of April one thousand five hundred and thirty-six years, a piece of the said Lord, aged twenty to twenty-five years, died and was thrown into the sea, in front of the company and myself, the scribe. Fernando Roiz.

Item.   On the sixth day of the said year [*sic*], a piece who was aged fifteen to twenty years died and was thrown into the sea, in front of me, that is, in front of the company and myself, the scribe. Fernando Roiz.

Item.   On the seventh day of the month of April, a piece fell into the sea in front of the company and myself, the scribe, and we could do nothing about it.

Item.   On the eighth of April of the said era, we arrived at Mina; and on the same day, Pedro da Costa, Captain of the said ship, delivered to Fernando Cardoso, Factor for the said Lord in Mina, ninety-seven slave pieces, both male and female, of which thirty-one pieces of the said load were refused; in addition, the said Fernando Cardoso gave the said Pedro da Costa three

---

[758] ANTT, CC 2-206-75. Transcribed in Ballong-Wen-Mewuda, *São Jorge da Mina*, 2: 540–41.

[759] Like Document 77 in this volume (ANTT, CC 2-205-21), this seems to be part of a '*livro de armação*' (which may be translated as 'book of cargo' or simply 'ship's book') rather than of a 'logbook.'

[760] See MMA vol. 15, doc. 55.

refuse pieces of our load; therefore the said Fernando Cardoso was left with sixty-six pieces of the said load. Fernando Roiz.

Item. On the tenth day of the said month, we sailed from Mina to the island of São Tomé. Fernando Roiz.

Item. A halyard wore out which was fixed to the foremast, and the mast broke. And more in repairing the said ship. Fernando Roiz.

Item. Further I post as expense two large oars which wore out on the mizzen yard which broke in two. Fernando Roiz.

Item. We arrived at the island of São Tomé on the twenty-eighth day of the month of April one thousand five hundred and thirty-six years. Fernando Roiz.

79 Letter Bestowing the Office of Mina Captain on Manuel De Albuquerque[761] (20/08/1536)

ABSTRACT – *Letter bestowing the captaincy of São Jorge da Mina to Manuel de Albuquerque for two years, with an income of 800,000 reis, with no other emoluments. The document is published for the first time.*[762]

Registered [.......][763]
Registered in the Chancery
Registered in the House of Mina
[sign.] *Francisco Dias*

[right side]:

Registered in the book of registers of this Factory of Mina by me, Cristóvão Roiz, scribe.

[sign.] *Cristóvão Roiz*

[He] paid nine thousand and three hundred and sixty *reais*, and gave his oath in the Chancery, in Évora, on the fifth day of September one thousand 536.

[cross]
[sign.] *Martim Ferreira*

[writ]

[I], Dom João, by the grace of God King of Portugal and the Algarves, on either side of the sea in Africa, Lord of Guinea and of the Conquest, Navigation and Commerce of Ethiopia, Arabia, Persia and India, etc., make known to all those who may see this letter that, considering that the office of Captain of this

---

[761] ANTT, CC 1-57-87. See also ANTT, Tribunal do Santo Ofício, Inquisição de Lisboa, Processo 11041.

[762] To the best of my knowledge, this document has not been published before, but I reserve the right to be corrected.

[763] Illegible because of faded and blotted ink.

town of mine of São Jorge da Mina is of a quality which requires the appointment of a person of great confidence, and one who is able to and knows how to perform well [in that office], and because I trust Manuel de Albuquerque, *fidalgo* of my Household, will serve me well there, and with all the prudence and fidelity which is due to my service, as he has done until now in all matters in which he has served me; and bearing in mind his services, and because it pleases me to bestow a favor on him, it is my wish and my pleasure to grant him the Captainship of the said town of São Jorge da Mina for the period of two years and with a remuneration of eight thousand *reais* each year, with no other remuneration or emoluments.

And I order the Captain who is now in the said town, and the Factor and the town's officials, to hand over the said Captainship to the said Manuel de Albuquerque as soon as he arrives there, and to let him possess and serve in it during the said period, and receive the said remuneration, without any doubt or impediment whatsoever, for this I grant him. And thus I order the Factor and officials of the Houses of India and Mina to give him shipping according to the regulations. And he shall swear in the Chancery, on the Holy Gospels, that he will serve the said Captainship truthfully, in everything observing my service and the rights of the parties. And before he leaves this Kingdom, he shall do me homage according to custom, and he shall take with him a certificate and patent from me to prove it. And to confirm it, I have him given this letter which has been signed by me and sealed with my pendant seal. Manuel da Costa wrote this in Évora, on the twentieth of August, the year of the birth of Our Lord Jesus Christ one thousand five hundred thirty-six. And each of the ten men who are assigned to him shall receive twenty thousand *reais* each year, which shall be paid to the said Manuel de Albuquerque for him personally to pay the said men the value that will be agreed with them. Fernão de Álvares had it written down.

[sign.] *The King*

Letter concerning the Captainship of the town of São Jorge da Mina, which Your Highness grants to Manuel de Albuquerque for a period of two years and with eight thousand *reais* of remuneration, with no other remuneration or emoluments. And he shall do his homage according to the regulations and give his oath in the Chancery.

80 King João III to the Count of Castanheira[764] (29/08/1536)

ABSTRACT – *Letter from the king to Dom António de Ataíde about the commerce in enslaved persons between São Tomé and São Jorge da Mina and whether to buy 600 captives at auction.*

---

[764] MS Port 4491, letter 232, Houghton Library, Harvard University. Transcribed in Ford, *Letters of John III*, pp. 266–7.

Count, my friend, I, the King, send you greetings as to one whom I dearly love. Because certain doubts have been raised in my Exchequer, on behalf of the traders of the island of São Tomé, as to whether or not to buy at auction the six hundred slave pieces which the said traders were to give for the commerce of Mina, it is my wish that you order it to be suspended until the fifteenth day of the coming month of September, even though it was supposed to be held at the end of this month of August, in order that during this period the said doubts may be settled. Manuel da Costa wrote this, in Évora, on the 29th of August 1536.

The King.

To the Count of Castanheira, on the purchase at auction of the slaves that the traders of the island of São Tomé were to give for the commerce of Mina; that he orders its suspension until the fifteenth day of September, even though it should be held at the end of this month.

[On reverse side]

By the King.

To Dom António de Ataíde, Count of Castanheira, Overseer of his Exchequer.

[Different handwriting:]

For this auction is to be held tomorrow, the last day of August.

81 King João III to the Count of Castanheira[765] (26/09/1536)

ABSTRACT – *Letter from the king to Dom António de Ataíde, concerning a large amount of gold buried somewhere close to São Jorge da Mina. The king claims the gold as his but will give those who know of its whereabouts no more than half, if found.*

Count, my friend, I, the King, send you greetings as to one whom I dearly love. I have read the letter you sent me, in which you say that Afonso de Albuquerque told you that two or three men, who are in that town, knew that in a certain place there were buried eighteen to twenty thousand cruzados or gold *pesos*, and that, provided some agreement be reached with them that would satisfy them, they would immediately disclose the place where the gold is, and that they proposed to give you one fifth. I thank you for your diligence in warning me about it, for what you have done in this affair, and for what you relate about it in your letter. I strongly enjoin you to enter into an agreement with those who are talking about it, or with whom you will discuss it, as you think best, provided you do not give them more than one half of what is found. And should they not be the

---

[765] MS Port 4491, letter 242, Houghton Library, Harvard University. Transcribed in Ford, *Letters of John III*, pp. 275–76.

same persons as traded and buried it, you will do as seems best to you and to my service; and I will order that everything you decide shall be fully obeyed. And you shall tell Afonso de Albuquerque on my behalf that I thank him greatly for the warning he gave you, as someone who desires much to serve me; and that I enjoin him, in the agreement he shall make, to explain to those people that they should feel satisfied with what is fair, for the gold is mine and they cannot take it or possess it by any good title. And once you conclude the agreement you will inform Master de Albuquerque of what he shall do there, as you are aware should be done in such matters. Fernão de Álvares wrote this, in Évora, on the 26th day of September 1536.

The King.

Reply to the Count of Castanheira.

[On reverse side]
By the King.

To Dom António de Ataíde, Count of Castanheira, Overseer of his Exchequer.

82 King João III to the Count of Castanheira[766] (05/02/1537)

ABSTRACT – *Letter from the king to Dom António de Ataíde concerning a fleet to be sent to Mina with necessary supplies and trade goods for the gold trade, but armed to ward off pirates.*

Count, my friend, I, the King, send you greetings as to one whom I dearly love. I have read the letter you wrote me, in which you tell me about what is being done regarding those fleets, and how people are beginning to be enrolled to go to India, without any money having been received until now as interest for the loans you made there; and I had already been informed of it through Fernão Álvares, and it pleased me very much. As regards the contracts of slaves which you ordered be done there, it seemed very well to me and I thank you greatly for what you have done, since I have been well served in that matter.

As regards what you say about your discussion with the officials of the depot[767] concerning the fleet of Mina, since the time has come for its departure, and that it seems to you that only the galleon Trindade should sail, with no other ship[768] or caravel, and for the reasons you give in your letter, it is my wish and my service that you have it done as soon as possible, and that she take all the necessary supplies and merchandise and bring all the gold that there may be in Mina.

---

[766] MS Port 4491, letter 276, Houghton Library, Harvard University. Transcribed in Ford, *Letters of John III*, pp. 305–7.
[767] In the transcription, '*allmazem*' ('*armazém*'): see Glossary.
[768] In the transcription, '*navio.*'

I strongly enjoin you to have her armed and equipped, in such a way as to go and return safe from pirates, and that you write to me concerning the person whom you think should go as captain in the said galleon, and when you think everything can be ready, so that I may send you the necessary letters patent and write to Mina ordering that all the gold which is there at the time of the departure be delivered [[to the Captain of the ship]].

[...]

Manuel da Ponte wrote this, in Évora, on the 5th of February '537.

The King.

83 King João III to the Count of Castanheira[769] (09/02/1537)

ABSTRACT – *Letter from the king to Dom António de Ataíde concerning the year's expenditure and debts to Flanders to be paid with money borrowed against gold from Mina. The letter also tells us something about European credit systems in the sixteenth century as it relates to Mina's gold.*

I thank you greatly for the accounts you sent me regarding ways of meeting this year's expenditure, without drawing on the money for Flanders; and I was very much pleased with this. I hope in Our Lord that with your help and prudence the debts will be paid, and the expenses met; and even if to achieve it some interest has to be sold, I will very much consider it my service, as I wish to see the debts of Flanders paid. And in order to pay them more efficiently, expenses here are being and shall be cut as much as possible. There is no reply to be given to the remaining of your letter, only that it seemed to me that the effort to have money borrowed against the gold that shall come from Mina was your doing, for the later the interest rate was sold, the greater the service done to me. And for these expenses I strongly enjoin you to make the most, as I am sure you will, of whatever sales can be affected of pepper and spices to Castile and other places, without prejudice to the remittance to Flanders. Fernão de Álvares wrote this, in Évora, on the 9th day of February 1537.

The King

Reply to the Count of Castanheira.

[On reverse side]

By the King.

To Dom António de Ataíde, Count of Castanheira and Overseer of his Exchequer.

---

[769] MS Port 4491, letter 277, Houghton Library, Harvard University. Transcribed in Ford, *Letters of John III*, p. 308.

84 *King João III to the Count of Castanheira*[770] *(05/05/1537)*

ABSTRACT − *Letter from the king to Dom António de Ataíde concerning the payment of loans and debts with money derived from Mina gold transported one or more caravels to Portugal.*

Count, my friend, I, the King, send you greetings as to one whom I dearly love. Fernão de Álvares informed me of the letter you sent him about the payment of the five thousand *cruzados* that the Bishop of Viseu will receive this year for the first half of the 10 which he lent me; and because he felt content in doing it, with all the good will that you know, and for all the other reasons which you mention in your letter, I will receive much pleasure from their prompt payment. And because presently there is no money from contracts, nor any other more certain than that of the caravels of Mina, and all the money which will come in the first [[caravels]] of this year is already spent, I cannot devise a better way of paying it than with the gold from the other caravels of Mina, which, with the help of Our Lord, shall come after those we are presently awaiting. Thus I strongly enjoin you to have the said five thousand *cruzados* paid to him from the gold of the said second caravels which are due to come from Mina; and that you immediately ordain that they be paid to him at the Mint or at the House of Mina, where it suits him best, so he is assured of being paid, as has been said, for that is my wish. Pedro Henriques wrote this, in Évora, on the 5th of May '537.

The King

To the Count of Castanheira, about the payment of the 5 thousand *cruzados* for the first half of the 10 which were lent by the Bishop of Viseu.

[On reverse side]
By the King.
To Dom António de Ataíde, Count of Castanheira, Overseer of his Exchequer.

85 *Letter to King João III*[771] *(28/08/1537)*

ABSTRACT − *Letter to King João III about captives for gold and a prisoner's plea for freedom. The document is published for the first time.*

---

[770] MS Port 4491, letter 310, Houghton Library, Harvard University. Transcribed in Ford, *Letters of John III*, p. 341.
[771] ANTT, *Fragmentos, Cartas para El-Rei*, cx.1, mç. 1, n. 20.

My Lord,

Since my wish is always to search for and obtain those things which are in your service, and because the following matters are so much so, I have determined to make known to Your Highness through this [[letter]] what is happening, of which I have been informed by a man who wishes to oblige by giving you one hundred and fifty slave pieces which have been misappropriated by all [[your]] officials, the least valuable of them being worth fifty thousand *reais*, and 30-odd marks of gold from Mina, and 30 *cruzados* and more, which belong to Your Highness since they were obtained with Akori beads and grey beads in the gold trade of Mina, in addition to many other slaves which belong to him[?][772] and six or seven articles [[of merchandise(?)]], through means of which this man and I myself, given what I have learned from him, will inform you; and thus other most substantive matters much for your service of which it is advisable only to speak personally to Your Highness, to be attended to and provided for very secretly so that the sky be not covered with dust[?],[773] and to endeavor to hide and conceal in order that what is so clear may not be known or found out.[774]

And in these kingdoms too, if Your Highness so wishes, you may obtain a great amount of money each year for aid to the places of Africa, which, should I explain it to you, would seem good to you and the right thing to do. And should you consider it to be in your service that I should go to you to account for this man and for everything else I have told you, you may grant me a writ ordering that I should be set free [[from prison]]; and that four months after the day I am set free, I may show myself guiltless of [[the crimes]] for which I am imprisoned [......] the town for prison or the lodge, and from it [...........] of this man and of what I say in this [letter], and my imprisonment [................] Antão Gonçalves, [that] Jorge Dias, who serves as [your] [.........................] sent you[?][775] a letter saying that you should arrest me [...............................] accounts I had come back without authorization, they should [.............................] never was *almoxarife*[776]-collector [..........................] nor should he[777] need the [.............................] accountant rather than the account. And [.............................] torment me with cunning and [.............................] my adversaries that I ordered what I could not order, you may tell me so, because my adversaries wish to see me destroyed, since they fear that I may show Your Highness that they have been maliciously taking two *contos*[778] of *reis* and more from your Exchequer. My Lord, if you consider it your service to

---

[772] 'you'; it is not clear whether the pronoun ('*lhe*') refers to the king or to the man the author mentions in the letter.
[773] In the manuscript, '*jueyra*' ('*joeira*'), which means 'winnow,' though it should probably read '*poeira*' ('dust').
[774] The meaning of the last part of this passage is not clear in the manuscript: '[...] *e se trabalhe por se encobrir e esconder por que se não saiba nem ache o que tão claro está*' (modernized ortography).
[775] Or 'him'; unclear from the manuscript.
[776] *Almoxarife*: see Glossary.
[777] Or 'I'; unclear from the manuscript.
[778] *Conto*: one million.

wish to know what I say, you should order that the said writ be issued and I be set free in the manner I have mentioned above, which, in addition to be much in your service, is a greater advantage than my imprisonment, [[and]] it is much more in the service of God and Your Highness to order that I be set free in the manner I have asked than for me to be imprisoned here without cause, badly, without cause,[779] suffering hunger and abandonment, eaten alive by vermin, which is not God's service nor yours. I kiss the hands of Your Highness, whose life and royal estate may God greatly increase and make prosper, as well as [[that]] of the Queen and Prince [[and]] children. At your service, from this [[prison of]] Limoeiro, on the 28th of August 1537.

[Reverse]: To Our Lord the King.

Of his service.

86 *Writ for the Captains of Mina*[780] *(22/11/1537)*

ABSTRACT – *King João III orders the reward of a 'justo' ordained in the regulations not be paid to Mina captains, since they are not observing the conditions stipulated for the conversion of the indigenous peoples of Mina.*

I, the King, make known to all who may see this letter of mine that, through the Regulations of Mina, I had granted that its Captain should receive, at the expenses of my Exchequer, one *justo*[781] for each village black person who, through his industry, became a Christian. And because I am informed that some past captains have received the *justo* without having deserved it, for they behaved in such a way in this matter that they rather deserved punishment than the said reward.

And because the captains who shall not behave thus, that is to say, who shall not observe it – all of those who go to Mina, or the majority of them, may attempt more than simply to induce the said black people to become Christians using those ways and means which they ought to use to make them become so – more for the great harm they will do to Our Lord than for other benefit that they should receive from it,[782] – in order to avoid the evils that in this case may at any time occur, it is my wish and my pleasure that, henceforth, the Captain of Mina shall not and cannot receive the said *justo* which he used to receive for the black people who, through his industry, had become Christians, according to what is referred at greater length in the tenth chapter of the said regulations,[783] for in spite of it [[what is there stipulated]] this is my wish.

---

[779] The repetition is in the manuscript.
[780] BSGL, Reservado A-55, fol. 69-69v; cf. MMA vol. 2, doc. 24, pp. 64–65. Corrections and additions to the transcription in Ballong-Wen-Mewuda, *São Jorge da Mina*, 2: 609–10, using Brásio's transcription.
[781] *Justo*: Portuguese gold coin.
[782] As transcribed by MMA, the meaning of this paragraph is still relatively obscure.
[783] Cf. MMA vol. 1, doc. 150, pp. 502–3.

And I order Manuel de Albuquerque, who is now the Captain of Mina,[784] not to take the said reward for any black person who becomes a Christian, and to have this decree recorded in the books of the Factory, with a note signed by him in the margin of the said Chapter of the Regulations whereby I order that the said *justo* should not be given, so that at all time it should be known that this is what I have ordered.

I enjoin and order the captains of Mina who should occupy the office from now on to obey in this way and to stimulate the said black people to become Christians through every good means they can use, for, in addition to the great service that in so doing they will do to Our Lord, they should know that there is nothing else they can do in Mina that would be of greater service to me or make me more content. And another such note will be placed by the said Factor and officials of the House of India in the said Chapter of the Regulations of Mina, which is kept in the said[[*sic*]] *Mesa*,[785] and at the end of it this decree will be copied verbatim; and it is my wish and command that it be observed and obeyed in its entirety, notwithstanding what is ordained to the contrary.

Álvares do Avilar wrote it in Lisbon, on the 22nd day of November one thousand 5 hundred and thirty-seven.

87 Inquisition Trial Dossier for Graça[786] (17/09/1540)

ABSTRACT – *An enslaved and elderly African woman baptized Graça was accused of engaging in 'idol worship' and 'witchcraft' at São Jorge da Mina. Graça was dispatched to the Holy Office in Lisbon to stand trial in front of the judges of the Inquisition. She appears to be the first African and perhaps the first woman to come before the newly established Portuguese inquisition. The document is published for the first time.*

Criminal case against Graça, slave who came under arrest from Mina and is now in this city's prison.

The scribe ——————— [sign.] António de Paiva

Briolanja de Saneiro

1540

Sentenced to life imprisonment and sent to be indoctrinated.

N. 11041

Year of the birth of Our Lord Jesus Christ of MD forty years, on the XVIIth day of the month of September of the said year, in the very noble and ever loyal city of Lisbon, at Rua do Saco, at the abode of the Most Magnificent and Most

---

[784] This nobleman of the Royal Household was appointed captain of São Jorge da Mina, by writ dated August 20, 1535, ANTT, *Chancelaria de D. João III*, liv. 21, fol. 160.

[785] *Mesa*: see Glossary.

[786] ANTT, Tribunal do Santo Ofício, Inquisição de Lisboa, Processo 11041, fls. 1–30.

Reverend Lord Dom Diego Ortiz de Vilhegas, by the mercy of God and of the Holy Church of Rome Bishop of São Tomé and Mina, of Our Lord the King's Council, and his Dean, etc.

His Lordship being there present and before me, António de Paiva, his scribe, appeared Gaspar Tibão, Treasurer of the Casa da Mina, and presented and delivered to him, the aforesaid Lord Bishop, a slave named Graça, who belonged to the King, who came under arrest from Mina, [and] whom Doctor Álvaro Esteves, the Judge of the King's Cases,[787] had ordered him to consign, for it was said that the aforesaid Graça had been arrested because of matters regarding the Faith, which were said to have been committed by her in the said Mina, and for this reason, it was to him, the aforesaid Lord Bishop of Mina, that pertained the cognizance of her case. This having been examined by him, the aforesaid Lord Bishop, he ordered me, the aforesaid António de Paiva, to receive the said slave and take her, prisoner as she was, to the clerics' prison of this city, which was carried out by me, the scribe. And the [[...]][788] record of the consignment of the aforesaid slave is as[789] follows. And I, António de Paiva, who wrote this. Do not doubt the word *as* between the lines and the word *copy* that was crossed out, because it was truly thus amended.

[blank page]

On the 17th day of September of one thousand five hundred forty years, in the city of Lisbon, in the clerics' prison, before me, António de Paiva, scribe, being there present António Feio, gaoler of the aforesaid prison, I, the scribe, by order of the Lord Bishop, delivered to him Graça, a slave who came under arrest from Mina, whom he acknowledged to have received and committed himself to take charge of from then on and not to release her without a warrant from the aforesaid Lord Bishop. Written in Lisbon by me, António de Paiva, scribe, on the day, month, era *ut supra*,[790] and he signed here.

[sign.] António Feio de Castelhaco

And after this, on the nineteenth day of the aforesaid month of September of one thousand five hundred forty years, Gonçalo Pinto, scribe of the King's Cases, gave to me, António de Paiva, certain records concerning the case of Graça, imprisoned Defendant, which were remitted from Mina together with an order of Doctor Álvaro Esteves, Judge of the aforesaid Lord's Cases, and which were handed to him by me, the scribe, in order that it should be known to whom pertained the cognizance of the charge and case. [And] the said records and order are the following. I, António de Paiva, wrote it.

And after this, on the twenty second day of the said month of September of the said year of MDXL years, in the city of Lisbon, at the abode of the aforesaid Lord

---

[787] In Portuguese, *Juiz dos Feitos do Rei*: an office similar to that of a judge of the king's bench, but with somewhat narrower jurisdiction. He judged cases regarding the king as concerns rights pertaining to the Crown.

[788] Word crossed out: 'copy.'

[789] Word added.

[790] '[...] as above' (Latin).

Bishop Dean, by the said Lord Bishop it was at once ordered that I, the scribe, should bring the aforesaid Graça, imprisoned Defendant, who was in the prison, to ask her many questions that were due in the name of justice, which order I, the scribe, executed. And the record of the said questions is the following. I, António de Paiva, scribe, who wrote it.

Record of the questions asked by the Lord Bishop to Graça, slave, imprisoned Defendant: Year of the birth of Our Lord Jesus Christ of MDXL years, in the city of Lisbon, at Rua do Saco, at the abode of the Most Magnificent and Most Reverend Lord Dom Diogo Ortiz de Vilhegas, Bishop of São Tomé and Mina, of Our Lord the King's Council, and his Dean, etc. His Lordship being present and before me, the scribe, named below, by His Lordship it was at once ordered that I, the scribe, should bring Graça, imprisoned slave, who was in jail by his, the Lord Bishop's, warrant, which order I, the scribe, executed. And thereupon she was brought under arrest, and His Lordship asked her, Graça, the following questions: the said Lord Bishop asked her whether she was a Christian, [and] she said yes; asked her what her name was, [and] she said Graça; asked her whether she had been baptized, [and] she said yes, in the church of the castle of the aforesaid Mina; asked her who was the priest that had baptized her and what his name was, [and] she said that she did not know his name; asked her who her christening godparents had been, [and] she said João Machado and Graça[791] de Leão, who, after they had completed their time, had come back to Portugal; asked her if her said godparents had taught her the Pater Noster and the Ave Maria, [and] she said no; asked her whether she knew the Pater Noster and the Ave Maria, [and] she only said the first words of the aforesaid prayers; asked her if she knew the Creed, [and] she could not say any word of it and said that the priest was now beginning to teach it to her, and said she had been baptized in the time of King Dom Manuel, God rest his soul, and said that no one had ever taught her the Pater Noster nor the Ave Maria nor the Creed; asked her who was her God, [and] she said that He was the Lord of all and that He was in the church, and that she had no more than one God, who was the one that was in the church; asked her if the bowl that had been found in her possession was her god, [and] she said the bowl was for serving food and that it was not god; asked her if the sticks which were in the bowl were intended for casting spells, [and] she said no, that a grandson of hers, by the name of Martinho, had placed them in the bowl to play with them; asked her if she knew how to cast spells, [and] she said no, that she believed in God and in the Virgin Mary and that she renounced the devil; asked her whether Jesus Christ was the son of Our Lady the Virgin Mary, [and] she said she did not know, and that neither the priest nor her godparents had ever taught her such a thing. These questions were asked by His Lordship, before me, the scribe, and he ordered that a record of them be written, along with her responses, as has been written earlier and above. And I, António de Paiva, scribe of the Chamber of the aforesaid Lord Bishop, who wrote this, on the twenty second day of the month

---

[791] The scribe amended the name from 'Garça' to 'Graça.'

of September of the said year. Do not doubt where it reads *Garça*, for it should read *Graça*, because it was truly thus amended.

[sign.] Bishop Dean

And the said records having thus been presented, as has been said, together with the record of the questions asked by His Lordship to Graça, imprisoned Defendant, as written above, he, the aforesaid Lord Bishop, ordered me, the scribe, to prepare this case with them. And I, António de Paiva, who wrote it.

Ready [for decision].

These records and the quality of the faults of Graça, imprisoned Defendant, having been examined, I order the Prosecutor to proffer the charges against her *ad primam*.[792] And Our Lord the King's Attorney be notified to defend the aforesaid Defendant, belonging as she does to His Highness.

[sign.] Bishop Dean

The above written order was published by the Lord Bishop Dean at his abode, before me, the scribe, and without the knowledge of the party and of the Prosecutor, to whom, I, the scribe, pursuant to the warrant of the aforesaid Lord Bishop, took these case records, in order that he should come to the first hearing with charges against the aforesaid Graça, imprisoned Defendant. All this took place on the twenty fourth day of the month of September of one thousand five hundred forty years. And I, António de Paiva, scribe, who wrote this.
Submitted to the Prosecutor on the XXIVth of September.

And after this, on the twenty seventh day of the month of September of the said year of MDXL, the *Licenciado*[793] Manuel Manriques sent this case record to me, the scribe, together with the following charges. And I, António de Paiva, the aforesaid scribe, who wrote it.

My Lord

Says the Prosecutor of Justice against Graça, Our Lord the King's arrested slave, who is now held in this city's prison: And that it be done. [The Prosecutor of Justice] seeks to prove that being the aforesaid Graça a Christian and having received the water of the Holy Sacrament of Baptism in the city of São Jorge da Mina, the said Graça, oblivious of our Holy Catholic Faith, did not perform the acts of a true Christian or take care to know the Pater Noster, Ave Maria, Creed or Salve Regina as she was obliged. Rather, oblivious of everything and with little fear and reverence towards the Lord God, made idols and kept them and worshipped them, and cast spells and had them hidden in her house, and because of this she was publicly defamed [[...]], and there was much public voice and fame[794] against her, the Defendant Graça, in the said city of São Jorge, where she lived.

---

[792] '[...] at the first [hearing]' (Latin).
[793] *Licenciado*: holder of a university qualification higher than that of a *bacharel*, usually someone qualified to exercise a profession (law, medicine, etc.).
[794] Rumor.

[The Prosecutor of Justice] seeks to prove that, thus insisting the aforesaid Defendant Graça in her pertinacity and treachery, on the seventh day of the month of April of the present era of Our Lord of 1540 years, in the fortress of the said city of São Jorge, in the oven-house and lodgings of the aforesaid Defendant, there were found with her certain idols, namely, a small bowl the size of a small plate, and inside it four round sticks four fingers long, all of them covered with flour or whitewashed so as to become whitened. And the Defendant being asked what that was, she replied that it was her god, who she worshipped. And after a while, being asked by someone else about it, she again said with haughtiness and great obstinacy that it was her god, making it clear that she believed in it and held to it, and with a clouded face whenever people doubted it, and she held it without any doubt, that they were, and she considered them to be, idols. [The Prosecutor of Justice] will prove that, on the aforesaid day and place, there were found with her spells, contrivances, and materials to make them, namely, two clay mugs between two chests, namely, one mug and the bottom of another, both fixed to the floor with clay, and in them feathers mixed with something disgusting, like porridge. And being asked what that was, she, the Defendant, replied that it was for her father and mother to eat from, as they would eventually come there to eat, her father and mother having been deceased a great many years ago from this worldly life; the aforesaid Defendant firmly believed, as a bad Christian and infidel, that they would come, and as an idolator she believed in and worshiped the idols and believed in them, at night saying gentile and idolatrous prayers over the aforesaid mugs.

[The Prosecutor of Justice] seeks to prove that, thus obstinately persisting the Defendant in her evil customs, not seeking to learn about our Holy Faith, as she is obliged, when asked whether Jesus Christ, Our Savior, was the son of the Virgin Mary, she replied that she did not know, as someone who took little care of knowing the matters of Faith, necessary to the salvation of her soul, instead doing the opposite in everything. For this reason and for what was said above, she deserves to be severely punished. Of this there is public voice and fame. Considering what has been said, *peto*[795] that she be sentenced to the penalty she deserves by law and to pay the legal costs.

> *Peto admitti et cetera. Non se astringens et cetera. Super quibus omnibus et singulis petit justitiam ministrari.*[796]

These case records having thus been presented, together with the aforesaid charges, as has been said, His Lordship ordered me, the scribe, to prepare the case in order for him to pronounce on it according to justice. And I, António de Paiva, scribe, who wrote it.

---

[795] '[...] I ask [...]' (Latin).
[796] 'I ask that it be admitted, etc. Not being guilty etc. / In relation to each and every one of which he asks that justice be administered' (Latin).

I receive the Prosecutor's charges. Let them be submitted to the Attorney of Our Lord the King, to whom the Defendant belongs, so that he may present the contestation[797] *ad secundam.*[798]

[sign.] Bishop Dean

The above-written order was published by the Lord Bishop Dean at his abode, before me, the scribe, and without the knowledge of the party and of her Attorney, as well as of the Prosecutor, on the twenty seventh day of the month of September of one thousand five hundred forty years, and His Lordship ordered that it be done. And I, António de Paiva, who wrote it.

And thereupon on the aforesaid ‹day›, I, the scribe, pursuant to the warrant of the aforesaid Lord Bishop, took this case to the Attorney of the King's Cases of the Casa da Mina, whom I, the scribe, notified with the two orders of the aforesaid Lord Bishop, and I notified him to come with his contestation to the second hearing, as he had been ordered by His Lordship. And I, António de Paiva, who wrote this.

Submitted to the King's Attorney on the 27th of September.

And after this, on the 5th day of the month of October of the said year of one thousand five hundred forty years, at the abode of the aforesaid Lord Bishop, His Lordship being present and before me, the scribe, and with the knowledge of the Prosecutor, this case record was brought by a Solicitor of Our Lord the King with the following arguments.

Most Reverend Lord

Of this case I do not have any information, except what *constat*[799] in these records, that this slave only now came to the Kingdom, therefore *casus est talis*[800] that nothing more should be said, *nisi tantus que fiat Justitia.*[801]

And this case having been presented, with the arguments written above, by Our Lord the King's Solicitor it was said that he had no other contestation but what he said above. All this having been examined by the aforesaid Lord Bishop, he ordered me, the scribe, to prepare this case, which order I, the scribe, executed. And I, António de Paiva, scribe, who wrote this.

Ready [for decision] on the Vth of October.

Before any further order, may the Defendant be notified to give information to Our Lord the King's Attorney, given that, in his arguments above, he says that because he has no information he will not contest. And may it again be submitted to him, so he comes with his contestation to the 2nd [hearing].

---

[797] In Portuguese, '*contrariedade,*' that is, the contestation the defendant's attorney presents to the prosecutor's charges.
[798] '[...] at the second [hearing]' (Latin).
[799] '[...] is contained [...]' (Latin).
[800] '[...] the case is such [...]' (Latin).
[801] '[...] but only that justice be done' (Latin).

[sign.] Bishop Dean

The order above was written by the Lord Bishop Dean, at his abode, with the knowledge of the parties and their attorneys, before me, the scribe, on the sixth day of the month of October of one thousand five hundred forty years. His Lordship ordered that it be done. And I, António de Paiva, who wrote it.

And after this, thereupon on the said day written above, I, the scribe, pursuant to the warrant and order of the aforesaid Lord Bishop written immediately above, went to this city's prison, where the aforesaid Graça, Defendant, is held, and I, the scribe, notified her of the order above and read it to her and notified her to instruct someone to provide information to Our Lord the King's Attorney, who will be her attorney, and she replied that she had no one to do it on her behalf and asked the aforesaid Lord Bishop to decide her case according to justice. And I, António de Paiva, who wrote this.

And this having thus been done, as has been said, I, the scribe, after having thus notified the aforesaid Defendant with the above, took these case records to Our Lord the King's Attorney, whom I told he could go and receive the statement of the aforesaid Defendant at the clerics' prison, where she was held, for she told me she had no one to send it through, so he would be able to bring his contestation to the second [hearing] according to the order of the aforesaid Lord Bishop. And I, António de Paiva, scribe, who wrote this.

Submitted to the King's Attorney on the VIIth of October.

And after this, on the XIVth day of the aforesaid October of the said year of MDXL, at the abode of the aforesaid Lord Bishop, His Lordship being present and before me, the scribe, Our Lord the King's Solicitor gave to me, the scribe, these case records, and he stated that the said Lord's Attorney sent him with the following contestation. And I, António de Paiva, scribe, who wrote it.

Contesting, the King's Attorney says, and that it be done: The said Lord's Attorney seeks to prove that Graça, the aforesaid Lord's slave, is about sixty to seventy years old, a woman of little knowledge and newly-arrived, unable to speak [our tongue] except in the manner of a newly-arrived black woman, for the most that the aforesaid slave understands is by gestures and pointing to things, so that through them she can understand what is said to her; and the reason is that the aforesaid Graça lived in Mina, without ever coming to this Kingdom, and most of the time had to do with black people, who she talked to, and therefore it is only to be expected (?) that she should not have enough instruction to know and do what is required by justice.

The said Lord's Attorney seeks to prove that the accusation against her was made by a capital enemy of hers, one João da Mata, the supervisor of the oven-house of the castle of São Jorge da Mina, wherein the aforesaid Defendant Graça lived, and was a kneader in the said oven-house, and baked bread for the people. And thus the aforesaid João da Mata, being the oven-house's supervisor, entered into conversation[802] with a mulatto woman by the name of Margarida,

---

[802] Though Portuguese officials did their best to scrub details about intimacy from their records, the phrase 'entered into conversation' has unclouded sexual connotation, especially in gendered relations between superiors and subordinates, as João da Mata and Margarida Rodrigues were.

who lived in the aforesaid Mina, and having thus entered into the said conversation with the said mulatto woman, he contrived to set the said mulatto woman to work in the oven-house and to put out the Defendant Graça, saying against her, the Defendant, that she was a witch and that she had made the contrivances of the bowl and everything else she is now accused of, for it was all set up by the said mulatto woman together with Mata; and they took the sticks with which a grandson of Graça, the Defendant, played tipcat,[803] and put them in the bowl and right away went to the priest to make the said accusation, and all this for the purpose of putting out the Defendant and placing the aforesaid mulatto woman in the oven-house, as in fact she was, and today she is there. *I ask* that, this being so, no proceedings be taken against her in any respect.

[The said Lord's Attorney] seeks to prove that the said Graça, the aforesaid Lord's slave, is a good Christian, and because she knows the acts of a Christian, she did all she could but, being a newly arrived slave and not knowing how to speak [our tongue], she was unable to learn the prayers that every faithful Christian is obliged to know. However, in everything she could do, she has always attended the church which is in the aforesaid castle, both on Sundays and on the other days whose observance the Holy Church commands, and on the other days when the divine office was celebrated she was soon in the church, and with her heart and external acts she performed and showed that she was a Christian, and did whatever she could; because of her tongue, she was not and is not able to know and learn anything else. Therefore, in everything, she, the aforesaid Defendant Graça, has no guilt for which she should be punished in the face of (?) everything that [is alleged] against her. Absolution requested. Of this there is public voice and fame. *Petit admjti.*[804] And proved, may she be acquitted.

And these case records having thus been presented, together with the aforesaid contestation, as has been said, the aforesaid Lord Bishop ordered me, the scribe, to prepare the case, for him to pronounce on it according to justice. And I, António de Paiva, scribe, who obeyed it and wrote it.

Ready [for decision] on the XIVth of October.

I receive the contestation of Graça, the Defendant. If the Prosecutor has any reply, let him bring it *ad primam*.

[sign.] Bishop Dean

The order above was written by the Lord Bishop Dean, at his abode, before me, the scribe, and with the knowledge of the Prosecutor and Our Lord the King's Attorney. And His Lordship ordered that it be done. And all this took place on the sixteenth day of the month of October of one thousand five hundred forty years. And I, António de Paiva, scribe, who wrote it.

And thereupon I, the scribe, on the day written above, pursuant to the said Lord's warrant, took this case records to the Prosecutor of Justice, so he should

---

[803] In the original, '*bilharda,*' a children's game played with sticks with tapered ends, similar to tipcat.
[804] 'Requests that it be admitted' (Latin).

present his reply against the aforesaid Defendant at the first [hearing]. And I, António de Paiva, scribe, who wrote it.

Submitted to the Prosecutor on the XVIth of October.

And after this, on the 19th day of the month of October of the said year, at the abode of the Lord Bishop, His Lordship being present and before me, the scribe, named below, with the knowledge of Our Lord the King's Attorney, appeared the *Licenciado* Manuel Manriques, Prosecutor, and he said he had no reply and asked him, the Lord Bishop, to assign a term of proof for the charges received and to order that Our Lord the King's Attorney be notified on behalf of the Defendant whether the judicial examination conducted in Mina existed. This having been submitted to the said Lord Bishop, he exempted him, the Prosecutor, from the reply which he was due to give, and assigned fifteen days for the parties to present their proof of the items[805] received and ordered me, the scribe, to notify Our Lord the King's Attorney whether the judicial examination which had come from Mina existed. And I, António de Paiva, who wrote this. And, moreover, he ordered me, the scribe, to further notify the aforesaid Attorney of Our Lord the King of the deferment now assigned. And I, António de Paiva, who wrote it.

Awaiting proof ——— XV days

And after this, on the 20th day of the said October of the said year, I, the scribe, pursuant to the warrant of the aforesaid Lord Bishop, went to the house of Our Lord the King's Attorney and notified him, on behalf of the said Lord, whether the judicial examination which had come from Mina existed. And moreover I notified him that fifteen days had been given to them to present their proof of the items received, to which the aforesaid Attorney of Our Lord the King replied and said that the aforesaid judicial examination that had come from Mina existed, while declaring that he would bring forward the objections to its witnesses in due time. And as to the term of proof he said nothing, and he signed here. And I, António de Paiva, scribe, who wrote this.

[sign.] Fionirus

Records to be submitted to the Prosecutor

[sign.] Georgius *Licenciatus*

Rector(?)

The above-written order was requested in Lisbon by the *Licenciado* Jorge, [who] had been an Inquisitor at the Holy Inquisition's prison, the *Licenciado* João da Fonseca, Prosecutor, being present, on the XXIVth day of May of MDXLI years. I, António Roiz, wrote it.

The request having been made, as it is said, I, the scribe, read the case records aloud to the Prosecutor, so he would come forward with whatever he wanted. I, António Roiz, wrote it.

My lord.

---

[805] Charges and counter charges.

The deferment assigned to the Defendant has now been exceeded, and above all I ask Your Grace to prevent her from presenting any more evidence and to assign her a time limit to come forward with any objection to the opening and publishing of the court examination. *cum expen.*

With these the case is ready [for decision].

I, António Roiz, wrote it.

Ready [for decision].

The quality of the imprisoned Defendant's evidence having been examined; I grant her ten days to provide evidence to her already delivered contestation.

[sign.] Giorgius *Licenciatus*

Rector(?)

The above-written order was requested in Lisbon by the *Licenciado* Jorge Roiz, Inquisitor in the hearing he conducted at the Holy Inquisition's prison, on the XXXIst day of May of MDXLI years. António Roiz wrote it.

And after this, on the XVth day of the month of November of one thousand DXLI years, in Lisbon, at the hearing there conducted by Doctor João de Melo, Inquisitor, which he conducted in the Holy Inquisition's prison, the Prosecutor, *Licenciado* João da Fonseca, being present, he reported(?) this case, stating that the case records had been given to establish terms, and that he had examined them, and that the terms of this case included summoning the Defendant and asking her whether she had any objection both to the examinations and to the witnesses(?).[806] And the aforesaid Lord Doctor Inquisitor thus ordered that, before the first hearing, the Defendant be notified. I, Jorge Coelho, wrote it.

After this, on the XIInd day of the month of November of one thousand DXLI years, in Lisbon, the Attorney of Our Lord the King remits this case record with the following arguments. I, Jorge Coelho, wrote it.

My Lord

The ten days which were assigned to this imprisoned Defendant for reformation were not notified to me, therefore I ask Your Grace that they may be granted to me again, for this case remained obscure (?), and news of her, slave, was sought at the Santa Misericordia[807] from the Bishop of São Tomé in Coimbra, without anything else being found until now. *Quod peto et res scriptibus* (?).[808]

And after this, on the XXIInd day of the month of November of one thousand DXLI years, in Lisbon, at the hearing conducted there by Doctor João de Melo, Inquisitor, which he conducted in the Holy Inquisition's prison, the Prosecutor and *Licenciado* João da Fonseca, who addressed this case, being present; and

---

[806] Uncertain transcription of 'witnesses' (in the original, '*testemunhas*').

[807] Literally, 'Holy House of Mercy,' a charitable organization of royal foundation caring for the sick and poor.

[808] 'Which I request, together with the matters in writing (?)' (Latin); uncertain transcription of '*scriptibus.*'

information having been given by me, notary, on the above terms of what Our Lord the King's Attorney had said, and everything having been examined by the aforesaid Doctor Inquisitor, he ordered, and he desired(?), and prevented the King's and the imprisoned Defendant's Attorney of their objections, and he declared the examinations open and published, and he ordered that they be added to this case with the knowledge of the parties, that they might pronounce on its justice. Pursuant to his warrant, I wrote down the said examinations here, and they are the following. I, Jorge Coelho, wrote it.

[blank page]

Act of presentation of some records, which were brought from Mina, about Graça, slave of Our Lord the King. Year of the birth of Our Lord Jesus Christ of one thousand and five hundred and forty years, on the XVIth day of the month of September, in this city of Lisbon, at the dwelling house of Doctor Álvaro Esteves, of Our Lord the King's *Desembargo*[809] and Judge and *Desembargador*[810] of the Cases and Charges of Guinea, Mina and Indies etc., before him, the judge, appeared António de Paiva, scribe of the Bishop Dean, and presented to the aforesaid Judge *Desembargador* certain records, which are the following. I, Gonçalo Pinto, who wrote this.

Record concerning Graça, who is imprisoned for being a witch, and criminal case.

Year of the birth of Our Lord Jesus Christ of MDXL years, on the 7th day of the month of April, in this fortress of São Jorge da Mina, being there present in the customs house Pero Lopes, the Vicar and Visitor of the aforesaid church of the fortress on behalf of the Reverend Lord Dom Diogo Ortiz de Valhegas, Bishop of São Tomé etc., before the said Vicar at once appeared João Vaz de Paiva, *Bacharel*[811] and Physician of the aforesaid fortress, and he told the Vicar that on the said day, as he was going to the oven-house of the said fortress for some noodles which they had there, he met some black women who worked in the oven-house who were shouting, these being Margarida Roiz and Bárbara Lopes, women who worked at the kneading-house, and he asked them why were they shouting, and they told him that Graça, slave of Our Lord the King, had some things related to sorcery and idolatry, of the gentile kind, and that she (*sic*) told him about it to unburden her conscience, [marginal note: vertical line on the left, from bottom to top: on the XVIth of Setember of 540, by António de Paiva, the Bishop Dean's scribe] for she was a Christian. And the Vicar, at the said customs house, being there present Captain Manuel de Albuquerque, Captain and Governor in the aforesaid city and fortress, at once said that, the aforesaid Bachelor having told him the above, he should send the aforesaid Graça to his presence, which he immediately did, and with her João da Mata, the oven-house's

---

[809] *Desembargo*: the equivalent of the Supreme Court of Justice.
[810] *Desembargador*: a judge of a higher court.
[811] *Bacharel*: holder of a first degree from the university.

supervisor, together with the spells and idols which had been found with her and which the said João da Mata found in a small little wooden bowl, the size of an eating vessel, and inside it four wooden sticks, each of them four fingers long, all of them looking alike and whitened with flour,[812] along with two clay mugs, which were also found with her and which were broken in the confusion. And the aforesaid Captain at once ordered that she be put in the pillory and prison of this fortress and told the aforesaid Vicar to make a judicial examination of the matter in order to apply the law.

And thereupon, on the aforesaid day, month and era above written, the said Vicar, accompanied by me, the scribe, went up to the pillory where the aforesaid Graça was held and asked her if she was a Christian, and she said yes; and what her name was, [and] she said Graça; and where had she been made a Christian, [and] she said that in the church of this fortress; and moreover he asked her who was the captain at the time when she was made a Christian, [and] she said that Diogo Lopes de Sequeira; and moreover he asked her what the name of the priest who had baptized her was, [and] she said she could not remember, only that he was a large man, who shortly after left for the Kingdom and who lodged with the overseer, who was called de Barros. And he said no more. And I, Ambrósio Cosairo, who wrote this.

Examination

Item. João da Mata, supervisor of the oven-house of this fortress of São Jorge da Mina, a witness sworn on the Holy Gospels, which were given to him by the aforesaid Vicar, and asked the customary [questions][813] whether he wished evil or good to the said Graça, he said that he did not wish her either evil or good, only that she served there in the kneading-house, just like all the others, who he has in his charge because he supervises the oven-house. And he said no more. And I, Ambrósio Cosairo, who wrote this.

Item. The said João da Mata being asked about the said oath that had been given, read and declared to him, the first information that had been given to the aforesaid Vicar against the said Graça about the spells and idols which had been found with her, and further what he knew about the said case, he, the witness, said that it is true that, almost as soon as he arrived, Captain Manuel de Albuquerque had told him one day to beware of a black woman who was called Graça [and] not to give her anything, for people said that she was a great witch.

And thereupon, on the said day written above, the aforesaid João da Mata being in the kneading-house, he heard a tumult and hastened to it, and arriving at the door he saw Margarida Roiz coming with a soiled clay mug in her hand, and she said that they were spells that Graça had

---

[812] Here the scribe crossed out the expression 'of clay.'
[813] In Portuguese, *'costume.'* In trial documents, a witness is asked 'the customary questions' regarding any enmity existing between himself and the accused.

there and that she had more of them, and having seen this he went out of the oven-house, where the aforesaid Graça had a chest, and he looked between this [chest] and another one, and he found a clay mug out of sight between the chests, which was fixed to the floor with clay, and so was the bottom of another mug that the aforesaid Margarida Roiz had taken and which showed that the other mug was fixed as well. And when he, the witness, saw this, he asked her what the purpose of those things was, and she remained silent, and he slapped her a number of times to make her tell the truth, and she said that one of them was for her father and the other for her mother, so they would come there and eat, which was a custom of her land, and that was how black people did [[things]]. Furthermore, he added that the aforesaid Margarida Roiz said that there were other spells which the other black women could tell him about. And then, he, the witness, told the cooper to move a box belonging to the said Graça, and under it they found a small bowl made of wood, with a base, the size of an eating vessel, with four round sticks in it which were about three or four fingers long, whitened with flour or lime. And he had asked her what the purpose of it was, and she had been silent for a little while, and he had pressed her to say what it was, and she had replied that it was her god, and he had asked her again what she was saying, and she had again said that it was her god; and then, he, the witness, ordered that the aforesaid bowl be taken and kept, so it could be shown if necessary when he was asked about it. And he said no more. And I, Ambrósio Cosairo, scribe, who wrote this.

Item. João Vaz de Paiva, *Bacharel* and Physician in this fortress of São Jorge da Mina, a witness sworn on the Holy Gospels, and asked the customary [questions], whether he wished evil or good to that slave named Graça, he, the witness, said that he did not wish her either good or evil and that he would tell the truth of what he knew. And he said no more.

Item. The witness being asked by the aforesaid Vicar what he knew about the said information which he had given to the said Vicar against the said Graça, and further what he knew about the aforesaid case, he, the witness, said that it was true that he had seen [it] while going to the oven-house in the morning for some noodles that they had there, and he had met Bárbara Lopes, a black woman, and Margarida Roiz, a mulatto woman, who serve in the kneading-house and who came from the Kingdom, and they were shouting and having words with the said Graça. And the said women of the kneading-house, as soon as they saw the aforesaid *Bacharel*, told him to come and look at the spells which that black woman had there. And then they showed him two mugs made of clay and fixed on clay like cloth rolls, and then they found one of the mugs under a bed of the said black woman, and they showed it to him, and inside it he saw a feather and other things which he did not care to look at because they were disgusting, and so they again took another mug and broke it along with the one he had already seen, and the clay on which it was fixed to the floor. And right after that, the said women of the kneading-house told him, *Bacharel*, and João da Mata, who was present, to look under a chest that was there, that they would find more spells, and that they only knew what the other black women had told [them]. And thereupon [the *Bacharel* and João da Mata] told <u>the cooper, who was present, to move a chest aside, and they found a small bowl, with a base, the size of an eating vessel, with four round sticks in it, around four fingers long each</u>, which bowl and sticks were floured with flour or lime, he did not know which. And when her mugs were found, the oven-house's supervisor, João da Mata, asked her what the purpose of that was, and she, the aforesaid Graça,[814] <u>said that it was for her father and mother, who were already dead, to come there and eat, and that this</u> was a custom of black people. And further by the said *Bacharel* and João da Mata she was asked what those sticks were or what it all was about, and she, leaning against the aforesaid chest where they had taken them from, said with <u>a serious face that it was her god. And then the aforesaid João da Mata said, 'Your god?,' and she, the aforesaid Graça, said 'Yes!' with great steadiness,</u> and he, the aforesaid *Bacharel*, had started shouting at her, rebuking her. And that at that point the black woman who served the *meirinho*[815] and others told him, in their tongue, he did not know what, and that she again had said that <u>her spells</u> could kill no one, and that she had taken the said sticks and rubbed her breasts with them, and that the aforesaid *Bacharel* had gone out, shouting at other women who were there and rebuking them. And that he knew no more. And I, Ambrósio Cosairo, who wrote this.

Item.   Bárbara Lopes, a black woman of the kneading-house, sent to this fortress, a witness sworn on the Holy Gospels, on which she placed her hand and which were given to her by Pero Lopes, the Vicar, and asked the customary [questions] and matters pertaining, she, the witness, said that she did not wish her either evil or good and that she would say the truth about what she knew. And I, Ambrósio Cosairo, who wrote this.

Item.   The witness being asked about the aforesaid information written above, which was given to the aforesaid Vicar, against the said Graça, which was all read and declared to her, and a question having been asked by the said Vicar about what she knew of it, as well as any other thing about the aforesaid Graça related to the aforesaid case, she, the witness, said that it was true that this morning, the seventh days of the aforesaid month of April, while she was in the oven-house of the said fortress with other black women, namely Margarida Roiz and Beatriz, a black woman who pertained to Our Lord the King, as she, Bárbara Lopes, was going to get

---

[814] 'Aforesaid Graça': words added.
[815] *Meirinho*: officer of justice, similar to a bailiff, who carries out arrests and other judicial warrants.

a small bowl which she had under the corner of her chest to take some embers in it, she saw some clay mugs under the said small bowl, and then she asked what it was and the aforesaid Beatriz told her that it was one of Graça's spells and that under the chest there were others, and she, the said witness, had told it to Margarida Roiz, and the said Margarida Roiz tried to take the mugs, and Graça went for her to take them back, and they broke them. And Margarida Roiz had first shown one to João da Mata and the *Bacharel*, and there were chicken feathers in it, and white powder, and at that point João da Mata had come and slapped her a number of times, while asking her what it was, and she had told him that she gave it to her father and mother to eat. And then they told the aforesaid João da Mata to have her chest removed, for the black women said that under it there were other spells; and thereupon he had commanded it to the cooper and under it he had found a small bowl, with a base, and four round sticks the size of about three or four fingers each, floured white with something which he did not know whether it was lime or flour. And that the aforesaid João da Mata had asked her some questions, and likewise the *Bacharel*, and that she had not heard them because she was taking bread out of the oven. And that she heard people say that she [Graça] spoke with those mugs at night and prayed over them, but if it is so or not she does not know. And she said no more. And I, Ambrósio Cosairo, who wrote this.

Item. Margarida Roiz, a mulatto woman who serves in the kneading-house, witness, being asked the customary [questions] and matters pertaining, i.e. what she knew and whether she wished evil or good to the aforesaid Graça, and sworn on the Holy Gospels, which were given to her by the aforesaid Vicar and on which she placed her hand, she, the witness, said that she did not wish her either evil or good and that she would say all that she knew. And I, Ambrósio Cosairo, who wrote this.

Item. The said witness being asked about the aforesaid information against the said Graça, written above, which was given to her by the said Vicar and which was told, read and declared to her, and asked the question of what she knew about it, she, the witness, said that it was true that this morning, seven days of the month of April, she, Margarida Roiz, being in the oven-house of this fortress, had been told by Bárbara Lopes that the said Graça had spells which were between two chests, and she, the witness, went there to look and had found two clay mugs with chicken feathers in them and fixed on clay, and she had picked up one of them and had shown it to João da Mata, and the said João da Mata had come there and had broken one of them and she had broken the other, and that the said João da Mata had asked her [Graça] what those mugs were and that she had remained silent. And then he had slapped her a number of times and she had said that those mugs were for her father and mother to come there and eat. And this having been done, that he had ordered her to move the chest aside and that he had found there a small bowl with a base, and that in it there were some small round sticks, which were whitewashed; <u>and that she heard that she had said that it was her god,</u> though she did not heard it herself because she went away immediately. And she said no more. And I, Ambrósio Cosairo, who wrote this.

And she begged me, Ambrósio Cosairo, to sign in her place, for she did not know how to sign. And the said examination having been copied, as has been said, the aforesaid Vicar ordered me, Ambrósio Cosairo, his scribe, to prepare it, so he could pronounce according to justice. And I, Ambrósio Cosairo, who wrote this.
Sentence of the Vicar

These records, and what is shown through them, having been examined, and as Graça confessed being a Christian, together with the idols which had been found with her, along with the rest that is shown by them, as it is a criminal case and I cannot determine it criminally, I remit these records, along with the aforesaid imprisoned Graça, to the Lord Bishop of São Tomé, to whom the case pertains for it is in his diocese, and I beg Captain Manuel de Albuquerque, on my part, if he pleases, and on the part of the Holy Mother Church I require him to send under arrest the aforesaid Graça, along with these records, to the said Lord Bishop, for him to determine according to justice. This sentence was published by the Vicar Pero Lopes, in this city of São Jorge da Mina, on the fourteenth day of the month of April of the year of MDXL years, in absence of the party. And the sentence having been published, as has been said, I, the scribe, on the said day, month, and year, at once delivered this case record to Captain Manuel de Albuquerque, so he could examine it and decide according to justice. And I, Ambrósio Cosairo, scribe, who wrote this.

In testimonium[816] of the Captain

Having examined this Vicar's sentence and the quality of the case, as well as what he requires from me on the part of the Holy Mother Church, it seems to me the service of God and of Our Lord the King to send this black woman to the Kingdom in order to avoid any further impropriety which will not be the service of Our Lord for it is between black people. And therefore, I order the *meirinho* of this fortress to deliver her under arrest to the Captain who comes in the first merchant ship, so that, arrived in the Kingdom, he should consign her, along with these records, to the Judge of the Casa da Índia and Mina[817] and then remit it whomsoever its cognizance pertains. This order, written above, was published by Lord Manuel de Albuquerque, Captain of this city of São Jorge da Mina, in its keep, where he resides, on the twentieth day of the month of April of one thousand and five hundred and forty years, before me, Ambrósio Cosairo, scribe, and he ordered that it be obeyed, according to what is said in it, [including] where it is crossed out and says *of clay*, and between the lines where it says *aforesaid Graça,*

---

[816] 'Testimony [...]' (Latin).
[817] House of India and Mina.

because it was truly thus amended. And I, Ambrósio Cosairo, who wrote this and signed it with my wonted mark. [sign.] Ambrósio Cosairo

Item. Which record was combined with the original which I keep with me, together with the aforesaid Pero Lopes, the Vicar and Visitor. And in truth we both signed it, for it is well and faithfully copied and concerted. [sign.] Ambrósio Cosairo

[sign.] Pero Lopes

Which examination, after being concerted, was counted by me, Ambrósio Cosairo, and it is written on seven half sheets, including this one, and signed by the said Pero Lopes, the Vicar, and by me, Ambrósio Cosairo, [........].[818]

[sign.] Ambrósio Cosairo

On the fifteenth day of the month of September of MDXL years, in the city of Lisbon and at the abode of the Most Magnificent and Most Reverend Lord Dom Diogo Ortiz de Vilhegas, Bishop of São Tomé and Mina, of Our Lord the King's Council and his Dean etc., His Lordship being present and before me, the scribe, named below, appeared Rui Dias Freitas, Captain of the Caravel Galga that has now arrived from Mina, and presented to His Lordship these records, which he said had been given to him by the Vicar of Mina, and which came secured and sealed, so that they arrived without any suspicion of having been opened, and His Lordship, before me, the scribe, ordered that they be opened and read in order to pronounce on them according to justice. And I, António de Paiva, scribe of the Chamber of the said Lord Bishop, who wrote this.

[blank page]
[blank page]
[annotation on reverse side of sheet]
Criminal case which was made against Graça, slave of Our Lord the King, which is sent to be consigned to the Lord Bishop of São Tomé, and is borne by Rui Dias de Freitas, Captain of the Caravel Galga.

And having been thus presented, as has been said above, the aforesaid António de Paiva, scribe, told the aforesaid Judge that these records had been given to him, which had come from Mina, and that he brought them to him, the Judge, so he would remit them to the said Bishop of São Tomé, Dean, to whom they pertained, as being concerned with matters of Faith and done by the Vicar of Mina, because they were directed to him, the Judge, to remit them; and by him, the Judge, it was said that he by himself could not remit them and that he would take them to the Court of Appeals to be examined for the Court to pronounce according to justice. And he ordered me, the scribe, to conclude the record. Gonçalo Pinto who wrote this.

Ready [for decision].

Ruling by the Court of Appeals. Those [members] of Our Lord the King's *Desembargo*, who remit these records to the Bishop of SãoTomé. Given their

---

[818] Illegible.

quality and how they are made concerning the arrest of Graça on matters of Faith, let the said Graça be imprisoned as she was consigned, [and] justice be required for it pertains to the Chapter(?)[819] [sign.] Bartolomeu Álvares

[T]he case examined in Mina.

[sign.] The *Doctor* Francisco Georgius

Pero Moniz Fernandus

The order of the Court of Appeals written above was published by Doctor Álvaro Esteves, *Desembargador* and Judge of Guinea, in Lisbon, at his dwelling house, on the XVIIth day of the month of September of one thousand and five hundred and forty years, with the knowledge of the party, and he published it in his home because the Court was in vacation and no hearings took place. Gonçalo Pinto, who wrote this.

Of Graça, arrested slave

On the IXth of November, in the prison, Cosme Dias, in prison.

Examiner of the Customs House's Judge.

Item.   António Feio, gaoler in the prison of this city, a sworn witness on the Holy Gospels, and asked the customary [questions] and matters pertaining, to all he said *nihil.*[820]

Item.   Asked about the first article of the contestation of the aforesaid Defendant Graça, which had been read in its entirety and declared to her in detail, he, the witness, said that it is true that the said Defendant is in prison and, judging by her looks, seems to be about sixty years old, and she understands and speaks our tongue very poorly; and that, when she came here under arrest, they had told him that she had come from Mina and that she had been a Christian there. And he said no more.

Item.   Asked about the second article of the aforesaid contestation, he, the witness, said *nihil.*[821]

Item.   Asked about the third article of the said contestation, he, the witness, said that the only thing he knew was that, since the aforesaid slave have been in prison in his custody, he saw her commend herself to God and comporting herself like a Christian. And concerning the other articles and article he said no more. And I, António de Paiva, scribe of the aforesaid Lord's Chamber, who wrote this. And the aforesaid witness and Examiner both signed here.

[sign.] Cosme Dias   António Feio de Castelhaco

Item.   Caterina da Fonseca, the wife of António Feio, gaoler of this city's prison, a sworn witness on the Holy Gospels, and asked the customary [questions] and matters pertaining, she, the witness, said *nihil.*[822]

---

[819] Uncertain transcription of 'chapter' (in Portuguese, '*cabido*').
[820] '[...] nothing' (Latin).
[821] *Idem.*
[822] *Idem.*

Item. Asked about the first article of the Defendant's aforesaid contestation, she, the witness, said that it was true that the said Defendant has been held in this prison for about two months now, or whatever is ascertained to be the case. The said slave, Graça, seems to her, the witness, to be a woman of about sixty years old, and that she is a black woman and newly-arrived, and who understands little and speaks our tongue even worse. And about the aforesaid article she said no more.

Item. Asked about the second article of the aforesaid contestation, she, the witness, said that she only knew that, when the imprisoned Defendant arrived here, people said that she came from Mina. And she said no more.

Item. Asked about the third article of the Defendant's aforesaid contestation, which had all been read in its entirety and declared to her in detail, she, the witness, said that it is true that, since this Defendant has been imprisoned in this jail, she saw her performing the acts of a Christian, and that one day, probably about a month ago, in the morning, when she, the witness, was in a place where the aforesaid black woman could not see her and there was no one present with her, the Defendant, she saw her kneeling down and lifting her hands while commending herself to God, raising her eyes to the sky, whence it seemed to her, the witness, that the Defendant is a good Christian. And this is all she, the witness, knows and nothing more. And about the article and articles she said no more. And because she did not know how to write, she begged the Examiner to sign in her place. And I, António de Paiva, scribe, who wrote it.

[sign.] Cosme Dias

Item. Álvaro Gonçalves, a retainer of Manuel de Albuquerque, a sworn witness on the Holy Gospels, and asked the customary [questions], he said *nihil*.[823]

Item. Asked about the first article of the Defendant's aforesaid contestation, which had been read in its entirety and declared to him in detail, he, the witness, said that it is true that he, the witness, had been in Mina acting as a supervisor for Manuel de Albuquerque and that at that time this slave, Graça, was in Mina and served in the kneading-house, and that of her age he, the witness, does not know it, only that she is very old and does not speak as well as the slaves of this place. And about the rest of the article, he said no more.

Item. Asked about the second article of the Defendant's aforesaid contestation, which had been read in its entirety and declared to him, he, the witness, said that it is true that João da Mata, cited in the article, was the supervisor of the oven-house of Mina, and that the aforesaid Defendant belonged to the King and also attended at the kneading-house and she kneaded, and that it is true that he, the witness, saw him, João da Mata, complaining about this slave for being a bad servant; and whether for this reason the said João da Mata bore ill will against the Defendant, he, the witness, does not know. And he said no more.

Item. Asked about the third article of the Defendant's aforesaid contestation, he, the witness, said that several times he saw the said Graça going to church and praying while kneeling and lifting her hands as if she was commending herself to God, and that this took place in the church at Mina. And about the other articles and article he said no more. And he, the witness, signed here. And I, António de Paiva, scribe, who wrote it.

[sign.] Cosme Dias   Álvaro Gonçalves

With the said witnesses and examinations thus opened and published, I submitted it to the Prosecutor of Justice to pronounce as he thinks right. I, Jorge Coelho, wrote it.

After this, on the first day of the month of December of one thousand DXLI years, in Lisbon, the Prosecutor sent this case record with the following arguments. I, Jorge Coelho, wrote it.

My Lord.

The charges were not contested by the Defendant, *Jndo ante nam oportet prolis contestetur ne fratur suciam lite nom contestat, et ad bonum causse loquendo.* Everything contained in the said charges is clearly proved, because, as confessed by the Defendant [.....],[824] in the questions which were asked to her it is stated that she did not know the Pater Noster nor the Ave Maria nor the Creed; and not knowing the Creed, she could not be a good Christian, for she ignored the articles of Faith. She also said that she did not know whether Our Redeemer, Jesus Christ, was the son of Our Lady, the Holy Virgin Mary, which the aforesaid Defendant and every Christian is obliged to know and is one of the main articles of our Holy Catholic Faith. *Ibi natus ex Maria Virgine,*[825] and if *dubius in fide infidelis est, a fortiori ille qui oio(?) ignorat.*[826] And further it is proved that with her were found some small, round sticks, covered with flour or whitewashed, that had been placed in a small bowl and that the aforesaid Defendant said were her god, which she worshiped, and she was an idolator despite being a Christian and having received the water of the Holy Baptism, as she confesses in the aforesaid questions. And she had two mugs which were behind some chests, with porridge or something of the kind, and said that her father and mother come there to eat, which was *gentilica superstitio propter*[827] which she *fide catholica apostatasse non est dubius et ideo graviter punienda quod peto cum sumtibus.*[828]

---

[824] Illegible word due to torn paper.
[825] 'There He was born of the Virgin Mary [...]' (Latin).
[826] '[...] someone uncertain in matters of faith is an infidel, all the more so is one who is ignorant of them' (Latin).
[827] '[...] a gentile superstition, on account of [...]' (Latin).
[828] '[...] there is no doubt but that [she] is an apostate from the Catholic faith and should therefore be severely punished, which I request, with costs' (Latin).

I have submitted the crimes to Our Lord the King's Attorney for his attention (?). I, Jorge Coelho, wrote it.

On the ninth day of December of 1541, in Lisbon, by Our Lord the King's Attorney this case record was given to me, with the following arguments.

My Lord.[829]

Constat[830] that this [..] [.......................................

.............]. And when she was made a Christian [...................], and given what in truth [...................] she was made a Christian [..................] because she had no master in Mina for she belonged to the King, given that she [......] deputy [........................] Mata [...........................] his office [.......................................] of the scribe [..........] [......] *laborat* [.....] Mina for her interest, and she a black woman and newly-arrived and does not speak [..............] very badly [...................] for her to be quick-witted enough to know what is really required to be a Christian, and therefore the questions which were asked in Mina, when she answered she said what she knew, being a person of little knowledge and newly-arrived. However, to exempt from proof [..............] *libat causa* [......] *cum ignorantia Juris et in dilictis excusar a dolo*[831] *ut in ligitur In prinad be quam flaujo de plagear unde litel in tall casu non ita excusant tanten atento,* being a black slave from Guinea who had never come to this Kingdom to be *ita instructa in fide*[832] *pro octa participationes fidelium [...]ysto est sufinone cum tanta jgnorantia lydat ut etiam atenditur indilistes excusat estas[[...]].*[833] *ubo absoluat [...] et cum sumptibus.*[834]

With these the case is ready [for decision]. I, António Roiz, wrote it.

Ready [for decision].

The Deputies of the Holy Inquisition and of the Ordinary rule that, these records having been examined, namely, the Prosecutor's charges and the evidence given, and as it is shown that the Defendant, Graça, being a Christian, said that certain sticks which were hers were her god, in addition to the other facts referred in the records; and yet, considering the quality of the evidence, as well as [the fact that] the aforesaid Defendant, after being made a Christian, was not instructed or indoctrinated in our Holy Faith, they sentence the said Defendant to life imprisonement, where she will be instructed in the Faith, and they assign her as her prison the Monastery of Santa Clara of this city of Lisbon, and they charge in conscience the Mother Abbess and nuns of the said monastery with taking very great care in her instruction and salvation.

[sign.] The Bishop of Angra Didacus Antonius João de Melo

Luís Pinto *Doctor* Fernandis D. Mendus

---

[829] Paragraph full of illegible words, hidden by inkblots, as indicated by square brackets.
[830] 'It appears [...]' (Latin).
[831] '[...] ignorance of the law and in transgressions exclude malice [...]' (Latin).
[832] '[...] thus instructed in the faith [...]' (Latin).
[833] Crossed out, illegible.
[834] '[...] be acquitted [...] and with costs' (Latin).

Criminal case of Graça
supra.
Published on the 22nd of December of 1541.

And after this, immediately on the aforesaid day, month and era written above, in the monastery named below, the aforesaid Defendant Graça was delivered inside the Monastery, and to the nuns, of Santa Clara of this city, and they received her there to carry out [the sentence] (?). By me, Diogo Tristão, secretary, who wrote it.

88 Black Man from the Malagueta Coast Appointed as Interpreter[835] (30/09/1540)

ABSTRACT – *André Dias, described as a black man and an interpreter for the Portuguese on the Malagueta Coast, will receive a salary usually paid in the Houses of India and Mina. Because of this region's proximity to the Mina (Gold) Coast, Dias would have also worked with the Portuguese forts at Akyem ('Axim') and São Jorge da Mina.[836]*

[[I]], Dom João etc., make known to you, Factor and officials of the Houses of India and Mina, that, trusting that André Dias, a black man [[and]] interpreter of the Malagueta Coast, will serve me well and faithfully in the said post of interpreter, as befits my service, and wishing to bestow a favor on him, it is my wish and my pleasure that he should serve as interpreter of the said Malagueta Coast, and receive for the said post the salary usually paid in the said Houses to those who serve as interpreters, together with all the fees and emoluments which are rightfully due to him.

I notify you thus and I order you to let him serve in the said post of interpreter and receive the said salary as has been said, and to observe and obey this letter of mine, as is stated therein. And he shall swear in my Chancery, on the Holy Gospels, that he will serve in the said post well and truthfully.

Diogo Neto wrote this in Lisbon, on the thirtieth of September, year of the birth of Our Lord Jesus Christ of one thousand 540. Do not have doubts concerning the crossing out of [[the word]] 'Mina,' because it was done truly.

---

[835] ANTT, *Chancelaria de D. João III*, liv. 40, fol. 215; cf. MMA vol. 15, doc. 58.

[836] The Portuguese recorded a group of people which they called 'Alandes,' who inhabited an area near Cape Palmas to Akyem ('Axim') and who exchanged goods, such as ivory, cotton cloth, and captive peoples—described as 'usually very good ones' by a 16th century observer—for bracelets, porcelain beads, and leather goods. Described as peaceful people, perhaps because they were friendly with the Portuguese. See A. Teixeira da Mota and P. E. H. Hair, *East of Mina: Afro-European relations on the Gold Coast in the 1550s and 1560s: An Essay with Supporting Documents* (Madison: University of Wisconsin, African Studies Program, 1988), 75.

89 Letter to the Factor and Officials of the Houses
of India and Mina[837] (23/12/1541)

ABSTRACT – *King João III orders that whoever has resided in Mina or Akyem ('Axim'), even though he be a vicar or a chaplain, shall not return there without a special warrant from the king. He orders a register of personnel be made.*

I, the King, make known to you, Factor and officials of the Houses of India and Mina, that it is my wish that henceforth, for a number of just reasons which lead me to so decide, no one shall go to the town of São Jorge da Mina and the Factory of Akyem who is an official of whatever office or position, or a resident, vicar or chaplain, who returns after having gone and resided[[?]][838] in the said town and Factory of Akyem, unless in the letters patent I issue him, or in some other, it be declared that he may return despite having gone and been there before – under penalty, for whomsoever goes against this order, of losing his entire wages. And you shall notify everyone in writing, and you will post [[the notification]] on the door of that House, so they cannot plead ignorance. Because when I make an exception[[?]][839] for some people and let them go there despite having already gone there once before, it will be after having received information that they had served well and faithfully their offices during the time they had been in the said town of Mina and Factory of Akyem, since, if they had not done so, it is to be presumed that they would not return there fully desirous of serving me well.

And since I am informed that some officials and residents, retainers of the captains, and other persons, return from Mina without completing the term of service determined in their letters patent, it is my wish that, so that they serve the time remaining to them within the determined period, they shall not serve the said [[remaining]] time without my special warrant. And after you have made known this writ of mine and given a copy of it to Doctor Álvaro Esteves, Judge of the Cases of Guinea and the Indies[[*sic*]],[840] for them to copy it into the regulations, it is my wish that you send it to the said town of São Jorge da Mina to be presented to the Captain, Factor and officials who are presently there, whom I order to record it immediately in the books of the regulations of the said town, so that they and those who shall be there in the future shall observe and obey it as stated therein.

And I order them to institute immediately a Book of Register, in which they shall make note of all those who are now and shall be in the future in the said town of Mina, as well as in the Factory of Akyem, specifying their names, and those of their fathers and mothers, and their place of birth, in order that through the said

---

[837] ANTT, CC 1-71-37; cf. MMA vol. 2, doc. 43, pp. 114–16.
[838] In Brásio's transcription, '[...] *tiuer* [...] *estado d'asemto* [...]' ('[...] *tiver* [...] *estado de assento* [...]'), that is, probably registered as a resident.
[839] In Brásio's transcription, '*descompensar,*' literally 'to unbalance.'
[840] See ANTT, Tribunal do Santo Ofício, Inquisição de Lisboa, Processo 11041.

Register it be known who violates this prohibition and, that being the case, that the abovementioned penalty be executed. And they shall send certificates attesting that the said book has been set up and [[the writ]] copied into the regulations, and [[you]] shall sign on the reverse of the copy you will make in the books of the regulations of that House, and you and they shall observe this fully, for I consider it to be in my service.

Diogo Neto wrote this, in Lisbon, on the 23rd day of December 1541. This is to be obeyed, even if it does not go through the Chancery, notwithstanding any disposition to the contrary. Written by Afonso Mexia.[841]

This copy was checked by me with the original; and because this is true, I have signed here. In Lisbon, on the 16th day of October five hundred and forty-two.

Gaspar Pires

90 Female Slave from São Jorge Da Mina Accused of Offenses Against the Faith[842] (16/10/1542)

ABSTRACT – *Orders that an enslaved female baptized Graça from Mina accused of offenses against the faith be posted as revenue for Pedro da Mota, and the Bishop of São Tomé would deal with her case. This is the case of Graça featured in the 1540-1 inquisitional trial in* **Document 87**.

My Lord, the Auditor[843] Diogo Rodrigues,

I order you to post as revenue in advance for Pedro da Mota, Receiver of the Extraordinary Duties, a female black slave of Our Lord the King, called Graça,[844] who came under arrest from Mina for a case pertaining to the Faith, was sent to this Kingdom by the Vicar of the said town of São Jorge da Mina, [[and]] was delivered by ruling of the *Relação*[845] to Dom Diogo Ortiz,[846] Bishop Dean of São Tomé, to be dealt with according to justice, as attested in a receipt of the said Bishop, [[written]] on the reverse side of the said ruling, stating that he had received the said slave from Barnabé Henriques, Factor of the said town, for whom she had been posted as receipt. Which slave you shall post as receipt for the said Pedro da Mota, so that he may establish whether she has been released and what has become of her. And should he find that she has been released, he shall seize her for His Highness, since she belongs to him, and a certificate in due form should be issued for the account of the said Barnabé Henriques, Factor.

---

[841] See CC 1-13-48 and MMA vol. 4, doc. 33.
[842] ANTT, CC 2-237-139; cf. MMA vol. 15, doc. 59.
[843] In Portuguese, '*Contador*': see Glossary.
[844] See ANTT, Tribunal do Santo Ofício, Inquisição de Lisboa, Processo 11041.
[845] *Relação*: see Glossary.
[846] See ANTT, Tribunal do Santo Ofício, Inquisição de Lisboa, Processo 11041, MMA vol. 2, docs. 2 and 21.

In Lisbon, on the 16ᵗʰ day of the month of October 1542. And the said ruling and receipt of the said Bishop shall be delivered to the said Pedro da Mota.

a) Jorge Dias

91 Letter by Jorge Vaz to King João III[847] (1542)

ABSTRACT – *Excerpt of letter from Jorge Vaz to King João III about Manding traders who did business at São Jorge da Mina for gold, but this trade is now threatened. Manding traders on the northwest edge of the Akan forest were well known, but their presence was rare on the sixteenth century coast, if they were there at all.[848] The document is published for the first time.*

[…] Furthermore, the said Afonso de Torres has flooded the River Cantor [[River Gambia]] with so many goods which are sold in Mina that the merchants who pass through the country of the Mandinga, who used to go to the trade of Mina, because they are able to find the same goods at a lesser price and in great abundance all the year round at the said river, started to go there, as they still do, with much gold; and the merchants stopped travelling to Mina, which caused, and has been causing, great losses to Your Highness, as long as you do not provide in this case and in those mentioned above. And this information came now to my notice and, since Your Highness might not yet be aware of it, it seemed to me that I should demonstrate it to you, as I have done with all other matters of your service. […]

92 Letter from João Gomes Souro to King João III[849] (08/01/1543)

ABSTRACT – *Three Castilian ships went to trade on the Mina coast, but lacking in means, the São Jorge da Mina garrison was unable to repel them. A ship sunk on the coast, and one survivor became a Muslim and another was sent by João Gomes Souro to Lisbon. A Muslim interpreter, whom João Gomes Souro had*

---

[847] ANTT, *Colecção de cartas, Núcleo Antigo* 877 (Cartas dos Governadores de África), n. 220. Transcribed in Avelino Teixeira da Mota, 'The Mande Trade in Costa da Mina According to Portuguese documents until the mid-16ᵗʰ century,' unpublished paper presented to the Conference on Manding Studies, SOAS, London, 1972, p. 23. The Arquivo Nacional dates this document to 1537, whereas Mota dates it to 1542 based on two letters by Jorge Vaz, that is, ANTT, CC 1-72-38 and CC 1-72-47.
[848] Ivor Wilks' belief Manding traders were at São Jorge da Mina and Adena when the Portuguese arrived and eager to trade firearms 'has no support in the early [Portuguese] sources,' as Paul Hair rightly noted. See P. E. H. Hair, *The Founding of the Castelo de São Jorge da Mina: An Analysis of Sources* (Madison: African Studies Program, University of Wisconsin, 1994), 53 n. 33; Ivor Wilks, 'A Medieval Trade-Route from the Niger to the Gulf of Guinea,' *The Journal of African History* 3, no. 2 (1962): 339.
[849] ANTT, CC 3-15-87; cf. MMA vol. 15, doc. 59, pp. 137–38.

*brought from Lisbon, stayed in Timbuktu for four months, where Souro reckoned
the journey from Mina to Timbuktu was at least 10 months.*

Σ

My Lord,

I have written a letter to Your Highness in which I made known to Your Highness
that the Castilians of the Canary [[Islands]] came to sack this coast with three
ships, and they took themselves to trade; and as I found this castle so lacking in
everything, I had no means to drive them off. And according to what I learned
from the Moors, they traded a good 30 slave pieces; and one night, sometime
later, a ship of theirs went to the coast and was lost, together with all the merchandise she was carrying, and everyone was saved. Two of the men reached
the shore, where they were captured by Moors, and one of them became a
Muslim, while the other was brought to me here by the Moors, [[and]] I am
sending him on this ship to the Court Corregedor,[850] so that he may deal with him
according to justice.

I have learned that they will keep coming back here until the end of March.
May Your Highness order me what to do regarding this case, since, if they are
allowed on this coast, this castle will have no trade, because they will take
everything, given that they pay the Moors 20 *dobras* for each slave piece, and in
addition they bring captives whom they trade in exchange for the pieces.

I brought a Moor from Portugal by instructions from Your Highness which
were given to me by Francisco de Lemos, interpreter, according to whom[851] Your
Highness was going to send him to Timbuktu. And he left here and may have
stayed there for four months, and when he came he said he had gone to Timbuktu,
though through the Moor who took him it is known that he did not go any further than near Guinea; and if he says a different thing there to Your Highness,
you should know that this is the truth, since I have learned from Moors from the
mainland who have already gone there that it takes ten months or a year, and he
was gone for four months, as António Lopes, scribe of this Factory, may better
inform Your Highness.

And at present there is plenty of trade arriving in this castle, and I have 1,150
slave pieces. May Your Highness order the officials of the House of India to provide this castle with the necessary goods, since it is ill-provided with everything,
as I have told Your Highness.

May Our Lord God increase Your Highness's royal estate with a long and
healthy life. I kiss Your Highness's hands.

---

[850] *Corregedor*: see Glossary.
[851] In Brásio's transcription, '*o quall*' ('*o qual*'), which may refer either to the 'Moor' or to Francisco
de Lemos; it seems equally likely it should read '*a qual*,' i.e. in this context, 'according to which
[instructions].'

Written today, on the 8th of January 1543 years, and by this ship I am sending 150 pieces, as much as she will take.

João Gomes Souro

[*On the reverse*]: To Our Lord the King,
   of his service.

93 Letter from Gonçalo Toscano De Almeida, Vicar of Mina, to the King[852] (14/04/1548)

ABSTRACT – *Letter of Gonçalo de Almeida Toscano to King João III telling him about the shameful and unchristian acts of the Portuguese residents in relation to the 'black women' in and around the fortress. Toscano also comments on the local politics and figures. The document is published for the first time.*

[cross]

My Lord,

The office of Vicar which I hold here in this town and fortress of yours of Mina gives me the audacity to write to Your Highness and make known to you the many evils and great public sins which exist there, and from which ensue great damage and loss both to the property and to the lives of those who live there. Therefore I make known to Your Highness that in this fortress there are fifteen manumitted black women, who used to be your slaves and now are free at the expense of the property and salaries of the poor residents, and with whom these and some of your officers live so dishonestly and publicly as if they were their lawful wives, they [the residents] being married there [[i.e. Portugal]], with wife and children, of whom they are very unmindful. Of these black women each of them takes one for himself into his house, and through them [the women] they take[853] [...] and they have children[?] with them,[854] which is a great disservice to God and Your Highness and from which many evils follow. And this from the death of António de Brito until now, and at present more than ever; to such an extent do the men live in sin and participate in this concubinage, that they strive to stay for a long time in the land and they would prefer living and working forever in Mina and not there. Who will gainsay this, apart from the poor sick Vicar, who meets with so much opposition and who so loathes rebuking that he is forced to keep silent. Because, as I say, the principal people of this land live in this vicious path which is followed by the small [folk], and here I do not have

---

[852] ANTT, CC 1-80-74.
[853] In the manuscript, '*tomam*,' which, depending on the context, might also be translated as 'get' or 'catch.'
[854] Tentative translation of '[...] *e tomam por elas* / [illegible] *e de que ha fil*[*h*]*os*[?] [...]' (modernized ortography).

anyone to help me. And if Your Highness does not provide in this matter, this town will be a second Sodom and Gomorrah, may God Our Lord forbid it, for the labors and evils which at present take place here are but a retribution and scourge that God Our Lord imposes on us for this sin. I remind Your Highness of the death of four captains and many other people, who have died during these last two years.

What is this if not a punishment from God, who takes them to Him, since when they come [here] they strive only to act in your service, disregarding that of God Our Lord, and when they wish to do it they have no time. And furthermore, each year, once or twice, the French and pirates come to this coast to trade, bringing great trouble to this land, with little benefit to you, as the examinations and letters from the Captain will show in more detail. And furthermore, the great wars between the black kings within this fortress's *comarca*,[855] above all those of the big Akan against the small Akan,[856] from which Your Highness receives great loss, because since the death of Dom Filipe they have always been at war and have not returned to this fortress. And this is proceeding in such a way that it will last for a long time if Your Highness does not provide. And there used to be no greater trade done in this Factory of yours than that of these Akan. And thus also in the *comarca* of Akyem, where everywhere the roads are obstructed, together with the great wars waged by a black man whose name is Captain Acaa,[857] who has raised himself from nothing and become a thief and a highwayman, so that everyone is afraid of him and pays him a tribute. This Acaa brings with him three hundred armed men, who are very brave; he does much harm throughout this land, and because of it no merchants come to this Factory from anywhere. And it is my opinion that all this trouble and evils which occur at present were given by God for the sins committed in this land: the public men live in sin and engage in much usury and much perjury, and they mistreat the divine person of God and the saints, and they greatly disobey the Church and its ministers, and so time is wasted in the things I have mentioned above and which are the cause of God Our Lord punishing us. I write these things to Your Highness so you may provide, according to the service of God and yours. And I wish to remind you of an authority of Saint Paul, of a great city of the Corinthians, of a man who lived there in sin and because of whom those of the said city received many evils from God, namely, sickness, and death, and drought in the storms,[858] and hunger, and other tribulations, not knowing where these came from. Saint Paul, who, at this time, shared our Holy Faith, wrote to them, saying: 'it is reported commonly, i.e. notoriously,[859] that there is fornication among you, and such fornication as is not so much as named among the

---

[855] *Comarca*: see Glossary.
[856] In Portuguese, '*Acanes grandes*' and '*Acanes pequenos*.'
[857] That is, 'Acá,' since the double 'a' usually means the vowel is accentuated.
[858] In the manuscript, '*temporaes*' ('*temporais*'): most probably meaning the 'the rainy season.'
[859] That is, 'notoriously': added to the quotation by the writer.

Gentiles, that one should have his father's wife'; and it continues: 'that he that hath done this deed might be taken away from among you'; 'know ye not that a little leaven leaveneth the whole lump?'; [and] 'therefore put away from among yourselves that wicked person' (*1 Corinthians, 5*).[860]

Therefore may Your Highness provide, and God Our Lord will be with us in all things, by sending these manumitted black women to the Kingdom or to São Tomé, because in addition to their being the cause of what I have said above, they are pernicious to the lives of men, of which I assure Your Highness; and since I came to this land, during the past two years, six or seven men have died solely as a result of going after these black women, having no other disease, amongst other things of which they [the women] are the main cause. Thus they are very pernicious, because, in addition to all that was said above, they, or part of them, and some of your slaves, have committed great errors and other yet greater evils in this fortress, which are wondrous and fearful, and of which I cannot tell Your Highness because I have learned it *like God, in confession.*[861] I beg Your Highness, for the love of Our Lord Jesus Christ, to provide in this matter and send them away, because it will be much service to God and yourself, and health and life to the men. And may Your Highness give permission for the residents to bring black female slaves with them, to use them here as their servants and to take them back when their time is over, because they will not be as pernicious as these. I write these things at such length because it is in reality part of the charge and office of Vicar which I hold, and also to unburden my conscience, which in this matter is discharged now that I have told you about it.

And if Your Highness wishes to know whether I tell you the truth and who I am, Doctor Diogo Gonçalves, your *Desembargador*[862] and Provisor of the Archbishopric of Lisbon, knows me, for he has already given me a similar charge and knows how much I strive to do the service of God and what pertains to my office, and he can give you information [about me]. I beg Your Highness to provide as soon as possible and may God Our Lord increase your life and royal estate for many years to come, with Our Lady the Queen and Our Lord the Prince, for His holy service, Amen. Written in this town and fortress of yours of Mina, on the 14th day of April 1548 years.

[sign.] *Gonçalo Toscano de Almeida*

---

[860] Quoted in Latin in the manuscript: '*Omnino scilicet notorio / auditur inter vos fornicatio et talis for- / nicatio qualis nec inter gentes ita ut uxorem / patris sui aliquis habeat; sequitur: tollatur de / medio vestrum qui hoc opus fecit; nescitis quia mo- / dicum fermentum totam massam corrumpit; auferte / malum ex vobis ipsis; Prima [epistula] ad Corinthios V.*' The translation of these passages was taken from the King James Version of the Bible.

[861] In Latin in the manuscript: '*sicut Deus / in confessione.*'

[862] *Desembargador*: see Glossary.

94 Letter from the King to Lopo De Sousa, Captain of Mina[863] (12/10/1548)

ABSTRACT – *A letter which King João III wrote to Lopo de Sousa,[864] Captain of Mina, informing him of Jorge da Costa's arrival as overseer of the works in the fortress.*

Lopo de Sousa,[865] I, the King, send you many greetings [[…]].[866] Jorge da Costa,[867] knight of my Household, is now going there to serve as Overseer[868] of the works of the said town. And since in order to take care of the said affair, as I command him to do and according to the regulations given to him, it is necessary that he be informed and discuss the said work, I order and enjoin you to inform him of what has been done prior to his arrival, and discuss and decide with him and the master of the said works what will be done from then on, which shall be in accordance with the notes you took with you, without making any change or innovation in the substance of the works. And in everything else you shall deal kindly with him, as is proper, and should be done thus so that I may be well served; and you shall deal kindly with Jorge da Costa as long as he serves me well.

The galleon São João, which it had been decided to leave in that town to be dismantled, turned out to be in a better and finer condition than it then appeared, and for this reason, and also because it seems that the galleon Esperança, which is there, will be sufficient to shelter the people who will stay on board, I considered it to be my service that it should not stay there but return, since it can still be of service. And, thus, as soon as the stone and ammunition carried in that vessel and in the other vessels of the said fleet is unloaded, [………………][869] you shall give clearance in order that you leave without doing there [...............] which cannot be done without for the said unloading [...............] in another letter I order you to do it [...................] and thus is my service.

Bartolomeu Fróis wrote this, in [Lisbon, on] the 12th of October '548.

---

[863] ANTT, CC 3-17-6; cf. MMA vol. 2, doc. 71, 189–90.

[864] See Ford, *Letters of John III*, p. 376.

[865] Lopo de Sousa Coutinho, *fidalgo* of the Royal Household, was appointed to the captaincy of São Jorge da Mina, first by writ dated September 29, 1541, and issued in Lisbon, and then by vacancy of Filipe Lobo, who had taken the office by royal letter dated April 17, 1548. See ANTT, *Chancelaria de D. João III*, liv. 70, fols. 42v.-43.

[866] Cancelled: *'eu tenho mandado'* (*'I have ordered'*).

[867] Jorge da Costa received a writ appointing him as factor of the town of São Jorge da Mina, for three years, after the renunciation of Ambrósio Roiz, issued in Lisbon on June 12, 1548. On the same date, he received a writ appointing him, for three years, to the office of overseer of the works which the king had then ordered to be done in that town. See ANTT, *Chancelaria de D. João III*, liv. 67, fols. 55v.-56. By royal writ dated December 7, 1554, he was appointed Provider of the Royal Exchequer in São Jorge da Mina. See ANTT, *Chancelaria de D. João III*, liv. 63, fol. 162.

[868] In Brásio's transcription, *'vedor.'*

[869] Damaged parts of the document, which cannot be reconstituted from the meaning of the sentence.

95 Letter from the Captain
of Mina to Dona Catarina[870] (03/04/1550)

ABSTRACT – *The Mina captain details Portuguese relations with neighboring local rulers, the condition of the land, and describes persecution of which the captain claims to be a victim. The captain wrote to Dona Catarina, regent and wife to João III, because the king was ill.*

+

Madam,

I sent Your Highness a letter by the ships that sailed from here in October, in which I informed you about this land and the long time that has passed since any merchant came, and also about the care I have taken regarding Dom João,[871] King of Fetu, a very pernicious neighbor to this fortress and Your Highnesses' service. Thus he rapidly sent his son Dom Luís, and I two white men who went with him, to the Akan, where they have remained until now; and they are already on their way, bringing with them the son of the King of the Akan, and they will stay in Branna (?), which is four days' journey from here. But they wrote to me from there saying that they had encountered secret obstacles on the part of this Dom João. I have already asked him for an explanation; he is so vicious that nothing can stop him. I do not know where this will end. Nevertheless, should anything happen before this ship sails, even if only an hour beforehand, Your Highness shall be informed of it.

I assure Your Highness that, when I arrived in this land, I found it ruined, and I have spent much energy so as to leave it as it is due to your service, as my many gray hairs can testify, adding to the […] the many evils that […] and not because I let […] of them, which, as I hindered it[[?]],[872] suffers harm. In order that Your Highness may check what is said there against what I do here, [[namely]] that I have now escaped the poison which many times has been prepared for me, for which I greatly praise Our Lord, I ask you to find out from the interpreters. One of those who wanted to give it to me was a certain Simão Veloso, retainer of Fernão de Álvares, chief Treasurer, and the other a certain Lopo Somido, who has been here for many years and of whom it is said that he did not come as a saint. I will not write about how I came to know this so not to vex Your Highness with so wretched an affair. To the King […] in detail and I send him the in[[formation(?)]] […] is well attested by this […] gave for goods which were [taken?] from them,

---

[870] ANTT, *Fragmentos*, mç. 17; cf. MMA vol. 2, doc. 85, pp. 246–47. Brásio claims the sender of this letter is Dom Martim de Castro, *fidalgo* of the *Infante* Dom Luís, the king's brother. A writ issued in Almeirim, on 20 January 1546, appointed him captain of Mina for three years. Cf. ANTT, *Chancelaria de D. João III*, liv. 33, fol. 82.
[871] See MMA vol. 4, doc. 69.
[872] Tentative translation of '*como eu atalhase*' ('*como eu atalhasse*'). The meaning is unclear.

and take from him [...] and proved, of which I send the records. If what they say there regarding my debaucheries is true, why do they give me poison; and if they want to give it to me, how am I debauched [?]. These, Madam, are clearly demonstrated things. It is a habit of old for people to speak ill to the princes of the vassals who serve them best, and for them [[the princes]] to know the truth and to bestow grace and honor on them, and for the people to be surprised with it, for they are not able to understand that the kings possess divine judgement and counsel whereby they cannot err, and the populace suppose that the hatred of any idler should call forth a punishment from the prince.

I remind Your Highness of these things and their basis, so that God may take me from [this?] unhealthy land in good health, for I have no other person who may say this to you [...] ignorant words, uttered from afar, and I hope in God that Your Highness still reads them.

I am sending you a sugar bowl *dalgua* [[*sic*]][873] through Belchior Ruiz, *moço da câmara*[874] of Our Lord the King, whom Your Highness gave me so that I might bring him with me [...]; I am keeping some cats[875] to give you when I go. May God increase Your Highnesses' life and royal estate for many years to come. Amen.

From Mina, on the third of April 1550 years.

ADDRESS: To Our Lady the Queen.

SENDER: From the Captain of Mina.

96 Letter to the King Regarding the Mina Trade[876] (1547–53?)

ABSTRACT – *The author of the letter informs an ailing King João III of the disservice being done to His Majesty in the Mina trade and provides several illustrative cases. He promises to make other disclosures of the same kind, provided the king grants him a certain favor he has asked for, or another.*

+

My Lord,

For further declaration of the disservice done to Your Highness in the trade of Mina and Guinea, since, as they are not made public, many of these traders remain unpunished and free from the chastisement of their faults, and your Exchequer is

---

[873] *Dalgua*: unknown meaning.

[874] *Moço da câmara*: see Glossary.

[875] In Portuguese, '*gatos*': since Dona Catarina was herself a renowned collector of exotica, these 'cats' are probably the much-appreciated African civets (in Portuguese, '*gatos-de-algália*'). See MMA vol. 1, doc. 65 (excerpt from João de Barros, *Década* I, liv. II, cap. II) and MMA vol. 2, doc. 135.

[876] ANTT, CM 4-151; cf. MMA vol. 4, doc. 142, pp. 633–37. This document is neither dated nor signed. But as it mentions events from the time of the captaincy of Francisco de Barros Paiva in São Tomé (1547–1553), it may be surmised it belongs approximately to the same period.

much diminished from its right and true value, as to a King and supreme lord rightly befits; and from this it follows that not even a half of what they should receive and collect according to the regulations arrives into the hands of your treasurers and officials in charge of it; and since he, the petitioner, is not able to prove entirely that which needs to be proved by legitimate evidence – he will declare those [[cases]] which, relying on the evidence presented, can be proved with the greatest likelihood.

He will prove that a certain Francisco de Andrade, your retainer, having been granted favors by Your Highness and appointed to an honorable office, and being an affluent and wealthy man, and free from obligations regarding children, driven by greed, colluded with a certain António Roiz, and João Roiz and Duarte Roiz, his wife's brothers, and with two sons-in-law of these two brothers-in-law of his, sons of Diogo Roiz, who was *adail*[877] of Goa, who [[the sons]] received as legitim from their father and mother over three thousand *cruzados* each, to disserve Your Highness, one of them in the trade of Mina and Guinea, in order that, going in with them for payment, he might divert a large amount of the gold from Mina, and for that purpose they formed a partnership and bought three vessels, which they manned and loaded with forbidden goods. And with the said António Roiz as captain and principal, the first two ships went to the Malagueta Coast, trading in those goods which were most valuable there, while the said Francisco de Andrade, and his brothers-in-law and their sons-in-law remained here, getting ready other goods and matters related to the said trade, and collecting information about the said journeys and the others which they expected to make to the town of São Jorge da Mina, for your much greater disservice and their own benefit.

He will further declare that, after the said António Roiz arrived from the said parts, carrying much *malagueta* and sharing it with the said partners and associates of his, and bringing information regarding the best way of getting closer to the town of São Jorge da Mina and making port where the merchants who bring the gold to the said town of São Jorge often come to rest from their long journeys, he, with the help and favor of the aforesaid, manned for the third time a sailing ship with the crew which he trusted. And departing from the port of Sesimbra with many forbidden goods, he got as far as nine leagues from the said town of São Jorge, where, while trading, he was discovered by its Captain. And he [[the Captain]] sent many *almadias*[878] and men against the said ship, and finding some people on shore they arrested them, together with much merchandise which they had there. And some of them were tried[[?]][879] and sentenced, and others, through appealing to the orders, were practically acquitted by the judges[880] of the Archbishop of this town, and it is believed that they received favorable

---

[877] *Adail*: see Glossary.
[878] *Almadias*: see Glossary.
[879] In Brásio's transcription, '*foraõ prouydos*' ('*foram providos*'), that is, 'proceeded with.'
[880] In Brásio's transcription, '*desembargadores*'; a more exact equivalent would be 'appellate judges,' though, in this particular case, the term '*desembargador*' seems to be used as a direct synonym of the broader term 'judge.'

sentences because of the gifts they made or because these same judges say that the Sacred Canons do not punish such offenders, and this should be provided for by requesting a bull from His Holiness preventing them from benefiting from clerical privilege.[881]

He further declares that the said António Roiz escaped on the said ship, taking much gold with him, and with two partners of his came to the island of São Tomé. And Francisco de Barros, Captain of the said island, whether through not being informed that this [[António Roiz]] was dealing in things contrary to your service, or through comradeship, since they were both factors of Bartolomeu de Paiva, your preceptor, may he be with God, so favored him that he was not arrested there, even though the said Captain had immediately been asked to have him arrested and to have the ship on which he came searched; all of which was not done as it should, but rather delaying the search of the ship and the arrest of the offender, so that he escaped on the same ship and came to the islands, where he was imprisoned and escaped from prison, setting himself and others free, and [[then]] came to this Kingdom bringing seven or eight thousand *cruzados* in gold bars, put into a doublet and hose as if they were padded, which he shared with his aforesaid brother-in-law, and brothers, and associates. And from here he went to Seville to be the guide[882] of two Castilian ships [[…]],[883] which, under great necessity, he later denounced to Your Highness, as a result of which he was relieved of the grave crimes he had committed, and nevertheless arrested and put on board the *nau* Burgalesa, where he ended his days, according to his desserts. And the said Francisco de Andrade, and his brothers-in-law, and their sons-in-law remained safe with their interests, of which cases and crimes Your Highness has not been informed until now. And even today, resorting to their usual mischief, they have placed in Guinea Baltasar de Carvalhal, one of the sons-in-law to whom they send forbidden goods and weapons and assegai[884] blades, all for your disservice and their own benefit.

He further declares that Cristóvão de Melo,[885] son-in-law of João de Barros,[886] Factor of your House of India, has done much disservice to you in this trade, because when Jorge Rui de Melo, your Master of Ceremonies,[887] was appointed Captain of the said town of São Jorge, the said Cristóvão de Melo found him houses to lodge his wife and daughter next to him, and colluding with him there, before his departure, he obtained through the good offices and favor of his said father-in-law three posts of residents of the said town, [[which

---

[881] Cf. MMA vol. 2, p. 513.

[882] In Brásio's transcription, '*g[u]yador*' ('*guiador*'), someone who guides; in this case, probably, the 'pilot' of the ship.

[883] In Brásio's transcription, the omitted phrase reads: '*que per sua hordenança*' ('*que por sua ordenança*')—literally 'which by his/your ordinance[?]' —the meaning of which, also for syntactical reasons, is unclear.

[884] In Brásio's transcription, '*dazagayas*' ('*d'azagaias*').

[885] See MMA vol. 5, docs. 78, 84, 96, 106 and 109.

[886] See MMA vol. 3, doc. 16.

[887] In Portuguese, '*Mestre-Sala.*'

were taken up by]] someone who was his preceptor, and a certain Correia, his servant, and a certain Loureiro, his servant, which [[posts]] they sold to other persons for forty and fifty thousand *reais*. And the said Loureiro went with the said Rui de Melo with goods of his said preceptor and brought him in return above one thousand and five hundred *cruzados*. And now, on these ships, he is expecting other one thousand and five hundred *cruzados*. And counting on this and on what else he expects, he has bought from a certain Filipe Lopes Correia twenty-odd *moios*[888] for sale,[889] and from him, petitioner, a farm[890] of the Order of Avis, which the said Cristóvão de Melo had rented from him for nine and a half *moios* of wheat and other payments, concerning which there is a lawsuit going on between them, the sale being disputed because he has not paid the price promised at the time, and because he does not have a license from Your Highness with which to validate the said sale, as he is obliged to by a public deed, given that a license was required since the said farm belonged to the said order. And because this man [[Cristóvão de Melo]] and his father-in-law, in their offices, have done much disservice in other ways which the Overseer of the Exchequer[891] of these parts of India and Mina is not able to identify, not having been informed about them and having innumerable tasks which do not allow him to attend to it, he, the petitioner, undertakes to reveal them, should Your Highness consider it your service.

Item: He declares that a certain Roque Lopes, Master of the galley on which Diogo Soares went to the said town of São Jorge, as well as a certain Pedro Gomes and Tristão Gomes, brothers, and Margarida Gomes, their mother, have done and still do much disservice to you in the said trade of Mina and Guinea, as he will prove to you. And other things which are very much in your service, should [[Your Highness]] grant him the favor requested in his petition, or any other, in accordance with his worthiness and the danger which he incurs by it, for which he will be obliged.

97 *King João III to the Count of Castanheira*[892] *(05/02/1551)*

ABSTRACT – *Letter from King João III to Dom António de Ataíde concerning the prospects of new gold mines not far from São Jorge da Mina. The king orders this matter to be investigated.*

---

[888] *Moio* (sing.): see Glossary.
[889] Literal translation of '*de vemda*' ('*de venda*').
[890] In Brásio's transcription, '*casall*' ('*casal*'), which usually denotes a farm smaller than a '*quinta*' or a '*fazenda.*'
[891] In Brásio's transcription, '*veeder da fazemda*' ('*Vedor da Fazenda*'): see Glossary.
[892] MS Port 4491, letter 345, Houghton Library, Harvard University. Transcribed in Ford, *Letters of John III*, p. 376.

Count of Castanheira, my friend, I, the King, send you greetings as to one whom I dearly love. Lopo de Sousa, who has now been as Captain in the town of São Jorge da Mina, has written me a letter, which I enclose, in reply to those I had sent him about the new gold mines, which he says are roughly fifty leagues[893] from Mina; and, according to what he writes, this seems to be an affair worth being looked into, for without much expenditure it is possible to ascertain the truth. You will see the letter of Lopo de Sousa and all he says in it. And if you think talking about this with my officials, or with whomever may give you more information, would be of service to me, you shall do so, with the discretion which seems to you to be required by this affair; and you shall write to me immediately saying what ought now to be done in relation to it, or whether it will be of [[more]] service to me to obtain more information from the Captain and from my officials who are at present in Mina, so as to send the letters in the ships which are now being prepared to go to Mina, if that be the case. André Soares wrote this, in Almeirim, on the 5th of February 1551.

The King

To the Count of Castanheira, about the new mines.
[On the reverse side]
By the King.
To Dom António de Ataíde, Count of Castanheira, Overseer of his Exchequer.

98 Letter from Simão Roiz to Dona Catarina[894] (12/04/1557)

ABSTRACT – *Mina factor Simão Roiz (Rodrigues) writes to Queen Catarina about the piracy from European competitors disrupting Portuguese trade. He argues that provided there was a fleet every year for defense against pirates, it would be possible to trade and make much money in the São Jorge da Mina fortress.*

+

Madam,

Last year, through the ships in which Gaspar Henriques[895] went as chief Captain, I sent Your Highness a letter, wherein I informed you that I had raised two African civets for you, which I wanted to send through him to Your Highness;

---

[893] The Portuguese, '*légua*': see Glossary.
[894] ANTT, CC 1-101-18; cf. MMA vol. 2, doc. 135, 399–400; Mota and Hair, *East of Mina*, 59 (see appendix for transcript, under Document A). See also the annotated notes in *East of Mina*, for documents A–D.
[895] Gaspar Henriques, squire-*fidalgo* of the Royal Household, was appointed captain of the ship '*Samtresprjto*' ('Santo Espírito'), which was being prepared to sail to the town of São Jorge da Mina for an 'outward and return' voyage issued in Lisbon on 23 October 1555. Cf. ANTT, *Chancelaria de D. João III*, liv. 63, fol. 316v.

and because Afonso Gonçalves de Botafogo, Provider, did not want to give me permission to do so, preferring those he himself was sending to Your Highness, I let him do it. And I am sending them now through Adão Ferreira, who goes as a scribe in the ship whose captain is Francisco de Sá;[896] and he is also taking a cage with some tailed birds. May Your Highness accept the service as from a poor man, who only wishes for more if it is in order to better serve Your Highness.

As regards the land, if Our Lord the King were to send a fleet every year to guard it well from the many pirates who come to it and hinder its trade, as they have done this year, much money would be raised in this Factory; and if this coast is not guarded against pirates, it will not be possible to raise any, due to the great bargains they offer the black people.[897]

May Our Lord increase [[Your Highness's]] life and royal estate for many years to come for His holy service.

From this fortress and town of São Jorge da Mina, on the twelfth day of April of the year 1557.

Simão Roiz

+

ADDRESS: To Our Lady the Queen.
SENDER: From Simão Roiz, Factor of Mina.

99 Letter from Francisco Pires to Dona Catarina[898] (17/04/1557)

ABSTRACT – *Mina Alcaide-mor Francisco Pires writes to Queen Catarina about the presence of pirate ships from European competitors, the effect it has had on Portuguese trade in gold, and the need to have the Mina (Gold) Coast guarded from them. Setting up a trading-post at Nkrãn ('Accra'), he notes, had not been undertaken.*

Madam,

I wrote to Your Highness about how this coast was full of pirates through Gaspar Henriques, and to say that you should persuade the King our Lord to be pleased

---

[896] Francisco de Sá, squire-*fidalgo* of the Royal Household, received writ of scrivenership ('*carta de escrivaninha*') on one ship of the Mina run, for an 'outward and return' voyage issued in Lisbon on November 3, 1552. Cf. ANTT, *Chancelaria de D. João III*, liv. 71, fol. 380.

[897] These pirates, both English and French, are included in volume six of Richard Hakluyt's *The Principal Navigations, Voyages, Traffiques and Discoveries of the English Nation*, 12 vols. (Glasgow: James MacLehose & Sons, 1903–05), in particular Willem Towrson's third voyage (1556–7), in which he refers to French ships on the coast.

[898] ANTT, CC-1-101-23. Cf. Mota and Hair, *East of Mina*, 59–60 (see appendix for transcript, under Document B).

to give orders to have it guarded. This year so many pirate ships sailed to it that they flooded the whole coast with many commodities of all kinds, as Cristóvão de Oliveira will tell Your Highness. He sent two pirate ships to the bottom [[of the sea]], which was an honorable deed and worthy of much reward. May Your Highness reward him. As for the establishment [[of a trading-post]] at Nkrãn,[899] it was not undertaken, because Baltasar Rebelo [only] arrived in March, when it is already winter on this coast, and the ships get into difficulties and the boats cannot make land. It will be done when the King our Lord commands, which can be from November to the end of March, which is summer on this coast. These ships carry to the King our Lord 53,500 or so *cruzados*, and Your Highness will realize that if the pirates did not come it would be double that. I write no more to Your Highness because you will see the letter I am writing to the King our Lord. Your Highness should nor consent to the loss of this orchard because there will always be much good fruit from it, provided that this coast is guarded, as I say.

 May the Lord God extend the life and royal estate of the King our Lord and of Your Highness, for His holy service, From this city and fortress of São Jorge da Mina, on the 17th day of April 1557.

Francisco Pires

For the Queen our Lady,
From Francisco Pires, *Alcaide-mor* of Mina.

100 Letter from Afonso Gonçalves De Botafogo to Dona Catarina[900] (18/04/1557)

ABSTRACT – *Afonso Gonçalves de Botafogo writes to Queen Catarina about the financial shortfall related to the gold trade at São Jorge da Mina, due to pirate ships. He requests a fleet to defend that trade against other European nations, while promising the queen the civet cats and musk she desires.*

+

Madam,

By way of the São Tomé caravel I wrote […] about the pirates who have come this year to this coast and the money which […] they would trade on it. And about what was done in this and other matters, I have already written to Your Highness at greater length in another letter.

---

[899] In the manuscript, 'Cara.'
[900] ANTT, CC-1-101-24. Cf. Mota and Hair, *East of Mina*, 60-61 (see appendix for transcript, under Document C).

In this fleet I am sending to the King our Lord 53,000 *cruzados* which I made in the six months until the pirates began to come, after which I never again opened this Factory to sell anything except some cooking pots. And may Your Highness truly believe that, in terms of the takings that used to be the case, I could have sent Your Highness close to 100,000 *cruzados* if these pirates had not come. By way of São Tomé I sent word that the King our Lord should send a fleet to defend the trade and I wrote that it should come as early as possible, so Your Highness should insist that the fleet be here on this coast during the whole of November.

The amount traded this year by these pirates, according to what I have discovered from blacks who are well-informed, could be 130,000 *cruzados*, because the galleass bv itself took all the *dinheiro* [[i.e. gold]] of Dom João and these kings, and it had dealings with them to the extent of some 30,000 *pesos* in all. The pirates trade freely this year and the last ships on the coast were trading near to Nkrãn[901] until they sailed off on March 15th, leaving the land stripped of goods for sale that there is absolutely no gold remaining. Nevertheless I will be striving, as pleases Our Lord, to do what I can despite these ships. In this matter, as in all accomplished in the service of the King our Lord and of Your Highness, I shall take such good care as Your Highness will see.

In the last fleet I sent Your Highness four civet cats and 40 ounces of musk. The death of one cat I much regret, but I shall make amends by continually sending Your Highness more live ones.

I now send Your Highness, on this fleet which is bringing *Freitas*, the servant of mine who last year brought the others, six very good cats and more than 42 ounces of musk, also very good [[... missing words...]], namely: two monkeys and a parrot. Freitas will endeavour to convey all of these safely and in good condition to Your Highness [...] for all he brings the things which are necessary [...] fleet. I shall strive to send more musk [...] although I have few cats left, but I shall still do the best I can.

May Our Lord increase the life and royal estate of the King our Lord and of Your Highness and the prince. From Mina, 18th of April 1557.

Afonso Gonçalves Botafogo

From Afonso Gonçalves Botafogo, April 18th.

The pirates traded 130,000 *cruzados* and [...] Mina 53,000 *cruzados* in six months.

To the Queen Our Lady [...] from Mina

---

[901] In the manuscript, 'Cara.'

101 Letter from Afonso Gonçalves De Botafogo to Dona Catarina[902] (18/04/1557)

ABSTRACT – *Afonso Gonçalves de Botafogo writes to Queen Catarina about the presence of pirate ships from European competitors, the effect it has had on Portuguese trade in gold, and the need to have the Mina (Gold) Coast guarded from them. Still, the establishment of a trading-post at Nkrãn ('Accra') had not been undertaken.*

+

Madam,

By way of the Cape Verde caravel which is now going there, and which arrived at this port on December 10th, I learned of the fleet that the King our Lord had sent under Cristóvão de Oliveira to guard this coast. Because of its delay at Cape Verde and the bad weather encountered, the fleet reached this port on the last day of the octave of Christmas, with its supplies used up and with men dead.

Eighteen days previously the great galleass, which had been on the coast of São Vicente, and which was very well supplied with merchandise, and with guns and men to defend it, passed within sight of this fortress. When the galleass was as far advanced as this fortress, it observed the caravel, which was anchored here in the port, and it began to survey the land with three pinnaces while staying out at sea itself, with the intention taking the caravel where it lay. I put forty men from this fortress inside the caravel immediately I saw the intention of the galleass and the caravel was placed inside the reef and there saved. The galleass resumed its passage along the coast and came to anchor in the port of the Fante,[903] eight leagues from this fortress. Six or seven days later another ship appeared and anchored opposite the fortress. It appeared to be the consort of the galleass, since the next day it came to anchor beside it. Both ships traded for almost a month. Dom João and his son-in-law and the whole coast traded with them to the extent of more than 30,000 *pesos*.

---

[902] ANTT, CC-1-101-25. Cf. Mota and Hair, *East of Mina*, 61–66 (see appendix for transcript, under Document D).

[903] In the manuscript, 'Afantes.' The reference is to a port, perhaps Akong, in coastal areas the Fante people inhabited. The Fante migrated from Takyiman, deep in the forest interior, and settled along the Atlantic seaboard and hinterlands by the 15th century. Though they belong to the 'Akan' cultural-linguistic grouping, their exchanges with various foreigners on the coast over the past five centuries have shaped cultural forms and norms, including their iteration of the Akan/Twi language. For more, see Kwasi Konadu, *Akan Pioneers: African Histories, Diasporic Experiences* (New York: Diasporic Africa Press, 2018); Rebecca Shumway, *The Fante and the Transatlantic Slave Trade* (Rochester: University of Rochester Press, 2014); Randy J. Sparks, *Where the Negroes Are Masters* (Cambridge, MA: Harvard University Press, 2014).

When Cristóvão de Oliveira was unloading in this port on January 4th, news was brought to me that in the *burel*[904] below Akyem ('Axim'), eight leagues from this fortress, there was already another ship trading. I immediately reported this to Cristóvão de Oliveira and he made ready to go there, as in fact he did, taking the caravel and pinnace. They reached the ship at dawn and the bombardment went on all day until towards evening, when the ship went to the bottom [[of the sea]] in sight of the blacks, which was the best reward there could be for us. Only one Frenchman was saved from the ship, in the boat which Cristóvão de Oliveira took there.

A few days later news was brought to me that at Esma,[905] eight leagues from this fortress, five pirate ships were trading, together with their pinnaces. I reported this to Cristóvão de Oliveira and he began preparations to attack them. He took along with him the large caravel, which I gave him rigged out and manned from this fortress. When he arrived at the [[pirate]] ships, he found there were two more of them, making seven in all, or eleven sail counting the pinnaces. He fought them and drove them away from the port, and it is said that the next night, opposite this fortress, one of them went to the bottom [[of the sea]] during the night.

This year these pirates started to arrive on December 11th past, from which it seems that they come earlier each time. For this reason it is essential for the service of His Highness that the fleet should come here in November. And may I again remind Your Highness to give orders that the ships come well rigged and with sufficient supplies but not to put the men/crew in irons, because in truth with so much water to traverse, out of so many persons/crew, there is none who cannot be of use in guarding the service of His Highness as thoroughly as needed. It does not seem right that ships which have to come as a fleet to fight and defend this coast should travel loaded [[*sic*]], and the time spent in unloading would be better spent on what they have come for. That is, [[to secure]] the whole coast from one end to the other, the fleet being divided into two, namely one part from Akyem to this port, and the other from here to Nkrãn. And since they will have come from Portugal, on the orders of the King our Lord and Your Highness, committed to this, they will straightway carry out what befits his and your service.

When Cristóvão de Oliveira reached this port I was beginning to recover from a serious illness which I had, and the labors I endeavored to undertake caused a relapse. Because the *aleaide-mor* was also very ill, I entrusted the unloading of the ships to Cristóvão de Oliveira and to the factor and officers, and they carried it out. Cristóvão de Oliveira will give Your Highness an account of what was done in this matter, and how things went.

Baltasar Rebelo arrived at this port on March 3rd. When he had travelled as far as Esma, eight leagues from the fortress, with Tomé Rodrigues, captain of the

---

[904] Perhaps a place. If so, it is unidentifiable, though 'Butri' cannot be ruled out.
[905] In the manuscript, 'Cama.'

leading ship, he came upon two vessels which were trading and this made them raise anchor, out of fear that unless they fled he would close on one of them. Through Baltasar Rebelo, His Highness wrote to me about the fortress which, for his benefit and service, Cristóvão de Oliveira was to have built at Nkrãn. Iimmediately offered him all help and support from this fortress to enable him to go and build it quickly, as the King our Lord wrote to me. But by the time Baltasar Rebelo arrived at this fortress it was already winter on the coast, and some of the ships had been unrigged and were leaking and without hawsers. For these reasons Cristóvão de Oliveira accepted the advice of his captains and master pilots, not to build the fortress this year, because of the great risk that the fleet and men would run, it being already winter. Hence, as it was now late, it seemed to be better for His Highness's service if the ships set off for Portugal. Since Cristóvão de Oliveira agreed, I ordered all necessary assistance to be given to the ships immediately, and he prepared for his voyage.

Concerning the priests and artisans whom His Highness wrote to me to lodge in this fortress, I have done this and have housed their effects, and I am ordering their stipends to be paid according to his regulations. I lodged the priests and put them in the church in the company of the others, and all serve and perform the holy offices as they are obliged, using such sacred vessels as His Highness has sent here, which this church was very much lacking. May it please our Lord to extend the life and royal estate of the King our Lord and Your Highness, and the Prince, so that you may send and provide other and better ones when these are worn out.

Up to the time of the departure of these ships the stone masons and other artisans have not been carrying out major work on this fortress, because at the moment there is no lime, there having been no stone to make it. However, when these ships leave, I shall order a batch to be fired, in order to repair the kiln which collapsed last winter, and then I shall have both kilns fired so that they can proceed with the works as His Highness shall order, and I shall also share some of the stone masons and artisans with Akyem. Until they can be so employed, I am ordering this trading post and fortress to be repaired and restored. Thus I am resolved to have the church repaired, for all of it is falling down, and it allows the rain in as much as if one were out in the street.

The planking and ironwork and all the other necessary things which came for Nkrãn, all of which arrived safely, I ordered to be received and stacked in the appropriate places so that they would be conveniently stored and kept together. I ordered a shelter to be built along the inner side of the wall to house all the timber, and I put the ironwork in one room, and the bricks and tiles inside a locked cellar, and thus I shall keep everything until the King our Lord and Your Highness command what more is to be done in his service. But as regards the ironwork I cannot guarantee that it will be able to be of any use here in a year's time, for being iron, if it is not worked within one month, it becomes of no use and is completely eaten away with rust.

From the quarrymen whom His Highness sent to quarry stone it is useless to extract any service because of the risk, to their lives, the great labor which the job requires being excessive in the sun. Previously, whatever number of quarrymen came here none escaped and all died, and up to now I have kept the stone-quarrying going by using three or four blacks whom I ordered to be taught this, so that if it were not for the quantity of stone which the ships take from here as ballast, the work here would be maintained by these men alone. From this it seems that were Your Highness to have ordered some blacks to come from Portugal, it would have been possible for these works and those at Nkrãn to have been undertaken. Had they been made to come, they would have been of great service, not only in stone-breaking but in all the other tasks, because they are lacking here, and [[Your]] Highness would be able to excuse white men who put their lives at such risk.

It seemed good to Cristóvão de Oliveira, before leaving for Portugal, to send Pero da Costa to Nkrãn with gifts for the king and his brothers, gifts which, at the his request, I gave the latter from this trading post. With him he sent his ship's master, and I sent the pilot of the caravel, and the master mason who was here, to investigate and observe where it will be best to build the fortress, and in what way the coast can be approached, and whatever else they can find out. I shall send a report to the King our Lord and Your Highness, and what they discover about all this Your Highness will see there.

The gifts which the King our Lord sent from Portugal for this King of Nkrãn it did not seem right to give at present, since the fortress is not built. I sent other gifts, as I now inform Your Highness, and the former ones will be kept until the King our Lord and Your Highness order what is to be done with them.

I wrote to Your Highness by the previous fleet about how I had sent a man to the kings of the Big Akan and the Small Akan[906] to get them to get them to mend relations and open up their roads to this fortress. This man spent more than eight months there and reconciled these kings and made them friends, and he opened roads that had been blocked for many years. As a sign of reconciliation and friendship he brought to this fortress a son of each of the kings. The son of the King of the Big Akan is his oldest son and heir, and is called António de Brito, the António de Brito who used to be captain here having once visited him. These hostages I received at this fortress very warmly, and I ordered them to be given their customary food.

After these roads had been opened up and all was completed, there happened to come here a brother of the King of the Small Akan, and over a black whom he killed in this town a great fight broke out. Some men and I hurried there, but the black came out of it dead, without my being able to intervene. To have this set right also cost me afterwards a great deal of trouble, and in bringing the matter

---

[906] In the manuscript, 'Acanes Grandes' and 'Acanes Pequenos,' respectively.

to a peaceful conclusion some expense. Dom João also helped in this, and now I have everything settled and all runs well.

After these ships came to port, the wife of António de Brito came here to be with him, I warmly welcomed her and soon made her a Christian, and she took the name Dona Caterina, in recollection of Your Highness, and I and Cristóvão de Oliveira were her godparents. Opening up these roads, like opening the others I have cleared from restrictions, has cost me a great deal of trouble and I have spent on this activity some of the property of this establishment and also some of my own salary. Since all is for the service of the King our Lord and of Your Highness, it must be counted well-spent.

I also wrote to Your Highness to say that this establishment could clear annually 100 R [[*sic*]] ells of Rouen cloth if the coast were rid of pirates. I ask forgiveness from Your Highness if I have not cleared this amount. But as many ships came this year as the year before, and with more and better merchandise, and they all traded as they willed, especially the galleass and ship which came first, for these took all the *dinheiro* of Dom João and his son-in-law, and all these ships traded up and down the coast. This year they came between 11 December 1556 and 15 March 1557, which was the latest they were here, and there were in all eleven large vessels, apart from the pinnaces, which makes a total of twenty. The information I gained from blacks who were well-informed was that these pirates were able to trade this year some 70,000 *pesos*, which is more than 100,000 *cruzados*. [[Only]] half this amount was taken at this establishment. And this is not ail, for most of it is in the form of gold ornaments, which the blacks break up when they see so much gain, twice as that offered at this establishment.

By this fleet I am sending Your Highness 53,522 *cruzados*, divided up in the way the King our Lord commands. In truth, I can hardly explain to Your Highness how I gained the amount I did in only six months, for when the time these blacks were waiting for came and these pirates arrived, which was in November and December, from then until now I opened up this establishment only for the sale of a few cooking pots. May Your Highness believe that, in terms of the takings that used to be the case, it could send close to 100,000 *cruzados*, this territory alone being capable of producing this much [[gold]], if there were no pirates and the trade was protected against them. While Your Highness is not expecting any [[more]] gold from here, because more ought to be sent I will work extremely hard to obtain it, as Your Highness will clearly see.

With this fleet lam sending Your Highness six civet cats and 42 ounces of musk in three sugar bowls, and a piece of very beautiful *anime* wood, and two booby monkeys, all of which are coming in the charge of Cristóvão de Oliveira, in order to be handed over to Manuel de Almeida. As for the cat which died, I shall make up its loss with another and yet another. As long as I live I shall serve Your Highness with whatever I have, since I owe all to the one for whose increase in life and royal estate I pray Our Lord, so that further favor may be extended to me.

Concerning the basins which the King our Lord writes may be or are made here into rejects, as well as others there may be in pieces. May it never be God's will, as long as I am in this land and this office, that the King our Lord should in this way or any other be badly served. But the truth is that, with such an abundance of trade goods as this establishment holds, and over such a long period of time, there cannot fail to be waste among them. All the goods which this time came in these ships were in excellent condition. May it please God that the sale of them does not fail.

So that the King our Lord and Your Highness may not blame me for not making approaches to the kings of the surrounding districts, to persuade them not to trade [[with European competitors]], as I did last year, [[let me explain]]. I was very ill when the pirates began to arrive, despite which I did not fail to approach the kings, through men I sent to the kings of Fetu and Aguafo]/Akatakyi,[907] for these are the leading kings in terms of wealth and power, and if they withdrew from trade what was left would be little. I ordered the men to offer them gifts and other things if the kings desired them, just as was done successfully by me the previous year. Notwithstanding all this, I was quite unable to bring the kings to agree to renounce trading. Dom João, in whom I most trusted, gave as an excuse that it was only because his people were compelling him against his own wishes. Last year they had not traded it was because they were bribed and given more than 500 *pesos*, but now he did not dare to quarrel with them. Nevertheless neither he nor his son-in-law was trading. But all this was mere words, an evasive reply from blacks who do not recognise or keep to the truth, especially when self-interest is involved. I have found out through spies that Dom João and his son-in-law, and the people of the king of Aguafo]/Akatakyi, traded more than 30,000 *pesos*. Whenever pirates come they will do this and will not forbid trading, because self-interest and the profit they gain count for more than whatever this fortress can give them in bribes.

As yet we have no definite news of the galleon *Comgo*. It is rumored that it reached the Malagueta coast, where it encountered the ships which Cristóvão de Oliveira met, and that when it attempted to fight them, it was set on fire and burned it out completely. What I actually learned from blacks was that the galleon made a fight of it, but in the end one ship cannot do much against seven, and so they captured it and burned it. Yet it still may be the case that it returned to port in the islands, and please Our Lord may this be so.

Concerning the money (*dinheiro*) which I informed Your Highness by the previous fleet that they would take when it arrived from Akyem, after the ships departed I did so much about this and put in such hard work that I collected it by counting it all by hand again, and I had it charged on receipt to the fator.

Although I said that Cristóvão de Oliveira is conveying the civet cats, musk, hides, and *anime* I am sending to Your Highness, in his charge he brings nothing

---

[907] In the manuscript, 'Afuto' and 'Acomane,' respectively.

other than Freitas, a servant of mine, who last year brought the other things to Your Highness. Freitas did not come here for any other reason, nor does he travel except to bring these things to Your Highness.

May Our Lord prolong for Your Highness the lives of the King our Lord, of Your Highness, and of the prince. 18th of April 1557.

Afonso Gonçalves de Botafogo

102 Letter from Francisco Da Costa Pontes[908] (05/08/1564)

ABSTRACT – *Francisco da Costa Pontes advises a fleet was being hastily prepared in England to be sent to the Mina coast, though under the pretense of heading towards Florida. There is bad business in Moscow and Flanders.*

+

My Lord Ambassador,

The information I present to Your Lordship is that, in the Kingdom of England, up to eight or ten sails are being prepared as quickly as possible to be sent to Mina and the Coast of Guinea, among them three large and powerful *naus,* namely, the flagship, of more than 400 tons, which is called Jesus of Lübeck[909] and belongs to the Queen; and another *nau,* of just a few [[tons]] less; and also the *nau* Minion;[910] and another two *naus* which belong to the London contractors, *naus* of between one hundred and one hundred and ten tons each; and in addition to these, three brigantines. These are the ones which are known, apart from others which are [[also]] reported to be going to Florida.

Item: I should state that the said [[*naus*]] are as well equipped with men and ammunition as can be. Others [[are]] as large as the ship owners who fit them out, who are important people, lords of the Kingdom as well as aldermen of London, all of whom intervene in this trade, since the business they had in Moscow, and Flanders, and other parts did not thrive as they had expected. And therefore everyone endeavors to venture into Guinea.

---

[908] ANTT, CC 1-107-4; cf. MMA vol. 4, doc. 69, pp. 246–48.

[909] In Brásio's transcription, '*Jesus de Libigue.*' The Jesus of Lübeck was one of John Hawkins' ships used in 1564 and 1567 for transatlantic slaving. The document refers to preparations for Hawkins' second voyage.

[910] In Brásio's transcription, '*Minhona.*' Like the Jesus of Lübeck, The Minion in 1564 was also involved in transatlantic slaving but was captained by David Carlet, who did travel to Mina. Both came in the decade of 1560 to be part of John Hawkins' fleet. See volume six of Hakluyt's *The Principal Navigations.*

Item: I was assured by many people that, together with these *naus*, there would
          sail a galley whose deck is lined with removable boards, so that they can
          be removed later in the Coast of Mina. I am not as sure of this galley as
          I am of the other sails mentioned above.

Item: I should state that the only talk along the west coast, as well as in the
          south coast, is concerning Mina, Guinea, Guinea.[911] And the majority of
          the seamen from the said parts, valiant men, have already been assigned to
          it [[the undertaking]]. And they say that this time they will destroy the said
          Mina, which may the Lord God not permit, but rather may they come in a
          worse state than last year and be definitively destroyed, as they deserve.

Item: This being a matter of so much importance to Our Lord the King, I have
          desired to inform the aforementioned to Your Lordship personally, or
          rather, to inform Your Lordship of the aforementioned case, which may
          the Lord God remedy as may be best for His service.

Item: The said sails will be ready to depart within approximately 8 days after St
          Bartholomew,[912] and it is determined that a certain number of them, after
          they have arrived at Mina, in the Coast of Guinea, shall capture black
          people and, from there, go to Hispaniola[913] to trade – so they say – the said
          black people, as one of these captains did last year. And Your Lordship
          may be sure that they are going as though to perform some great deed, as it
          seems by the way they are being, and have already been, fitted out, which
          may it please the Lord God shall be for our benefit and their loss.

Item: Some Englishmen have sometimes said that this last time that they came
          from Mina, or rather, that they were in the Coast of Mina, there were 2
          black men who spoke English on board the English *naus*; which black
          men told them that an important black man from that land, who calls him-
          self Dom João,[914] had told them to say, and he promised them so, that, if
          the English went with a fleet by sea, they would help them on land, I do
          not know with what purpose, only that the said English are relying on this
          promise. And this time they brought two black men with them, who were
          on board when our galleys chased them away. And they were unable to
          put them back on shore. And one of them died in Portsmouth,[915] on the
          arrival of the *naus*; and the other is returning on these *naus* which are now
          going to Guinea.

Item: these are the ports where [[vessels]] are fitted out, namely: in London,
          in Southampton(?),[916] in Portsmouth, in Gillingham water;[917] it is also
          said that from Bristol, presumably. And Your Lordship may inform Our

---

[911] The repetition is in the document.
[912] St Bartholomew's day is celebrated on August 24.
[913] In Brásio's transcription, '*Santo Domjnguos*' ('*Santo Domingo(s)*').
[914] See MMA vol. 2, doc. 85.
[915] In Brásio's transcription, '*Porsesmua.*'
[916] In Brásio's transcription, '*Antona.*'
[917] In Brásio's transcription, '*Ribeira de Gylyngamo.*'

Lord the King that all of this is certain. And I conclude by praying to Our Lord for the life and health of the Most Illustrious person of Your Lordship. Amen.

In Paris, on the 5ᵗʰ of August 1564 years.

Your Lordship's faithful servant,

Francisco da Costa Pontes

103 Royal Decree Ending the Offices of Almoxarife and Registrar of the Supplies[918] (16/05/1566)

ABSTRACT – *Copy of decree through which the king expressed his wish that henceforth in Mina there shall be no Almoxarife[919] or Registrar of the Supplies of São Jorge da Mina.*

I, the King, make known to those who may see this decree that I am informed that the offices of *Almoxarife* and Registrar of the Supplies of the town of São Jorge da Mina can be done without, and that, therefore, I have determined not to appoint another person to these offices. It is my wish and my pleasure that henceforth they shall cease to exist, and that the Factor of the said town shall receive and dispense the supplies, which until now were delivered to the said *Almoxarife*, in accordance with the regulations and instructions issued on the matter, according to which the scribes of the said Factory shall post the said revenue and expense in a separate volume, which shall be kept for that purpose alone, where nothing else shall be written. And therefore, I order the said Factor and scribes to serve in the said matter in the said manner, without receiving any more for it, as regards food allowance, than what they receive as Factor and scribes of the said Factory. And because certain persons have already been appointed to the offices of *Almoxarife* and Registrar of the Supplies, but have not yet served, when the time comes for them to take the office and to claim it, as well as to claim shipping so as to go and serve in it, the Factor and the officials of the House of India and Mina shall take care to ensure that the Overseers of my Exchequer[920] are informed about it, so that I may be informed and have the said persons given the equivalent of the said offices, or be satisfied in another way, as it may seem best and may be of greater service to me. Of this I notify the said Overseers of my Exchequer, and I order them to obey and to have fully obeyed and observed the contents of this decree, which shall be registered in the book of the regulations of the said Exchequer

---

[918] BSGL, Reservado A-55, fl. 69v-70v. Transcribed in Ballong-Wen-Mewuda, *São Jorge da Mina*, 2: 610–11.

[919] *Almoxarife*: see Glossary.

[920] In the transcription, '*vedores de minha fazenda*'; see Glossary, under '*vedor da Fazenda*.'

and in that of the House of Mina; and it shall be as valid as if it had been made in my name, signed by me and submitted to the Chancery, even if it does not pass through the Chancery, notwithstanding the contrary ordinance of the second book, title 20.

Ambrósio da Costa wrote it in Lisbon, on the 16th of May '5 hundred and 66.

I, Miguel de Moura, had it written down. And the copy of this decree, signed by the Factor and officials of the House of India and Mina, shall be sent to the said town in the first ship going there, to be recorded in the town's book of registers.

Checked with the original which was kept in the Exchequer, today the 26th of May one thousand 5 hundred and 66, and the copies will be sent to Mina in the ship São João, according to what is said in the above writ. Jorge Lobato.

104 Regulations for the Augustinians Who are Going to Mina[921] (23/02/1572)

ABSTRACT – *Regulations for how the Augustinian from Portugal should travel on the ship to São Jorge da Mina, what they should do, and how they should live when they arrive in Mina.*

[[From]] Friar Agostinho de Jesus, unworthy Provincial of the Order of the Hermits of St Augustine in this Province of Portugal, to the most beloved Fathers who, by holy obedience, are going from the said Province to Mina to preach the Holy Gospel. [[May they find]] good health and peace in the same Lord whom they are going to serve in spirit. [...]

Deinde proximus:[922] the love of men which God has brought to earth will take you to Mina, and all that you should do to win them [[the men]] and bring them to God will be nothing compared to what He did to save us. I remind you, my Fathers, that this is the gold which you are going to get, and that thus you should understand how much more one single soul is worth than all the riches and precious things in the entire world. It will be a great shame should there be a trader who may resort to more inventions and contrivances to set hands on a small bar of gold than Your Reverences to convert a little black boy or to deliver a bad

---

[921] MMA vol. 15, doc. 90, pp. 242–47. ADB, *Colecção Cronológica*, cx. 46. Friar Agostinho de Jesus, born in Lisbon of noble and affluent parents, was called Pedro de Castro before he joined the Hermits of St Augustine, in the Convent of Graça, where he changed his name after having become a friar. After serving as prior of the convent of Vila Viçosa and rector of the college of the Order in Coimbra, he was elected provincial. He wrote this document while serving his first term as provincial. He was Archbishop of Braga, having been consecrated by Dom Miguel de Castro, in the church of the Convent of Graça on January 3, 1589, while serving a second time as Provincial. He died on November 25, 1609, and was succeeded by another Hermit of St Augustine, Friar Aleixo de Jesus or de Meneses, who was Archbishop of Goa.

[922] 'Then your neighbor [...].' (Latin).

Christian from sin. To this you are called, to this you go, to this you should devote your entire life, leisure, and labor, as there is already nothing for which you live except for your neighbors, all of whom you should love in God, and through God, and for God. May you honor in all the image of the Creator, and do not allow in your hearts any neglect of any of them but assist them all with sweet charity and kind words. And you should go prepared to endure the labors and infirmities of everyone, and to assist their needs, and to forgive the offenses that may be committed against you, and in general have mercy with all, without preference for any person. [...]

And furthermore I enjoin them to set up in Mina a brotherhood of this saint [[St Nicholas]] and to bless their cakes[923] for remedy of the diseases[924] which are to be found there at all times; and after this they shall sprinkle holy water upon all of them. At daybreak, when they get up, they shall go and bid everyone good-morning, and first of all the Captain, with whom they shall exchange many greetings, and they shall sprinkle[[*sic*]] *asperges* upon everyone, and at the end the priest shall say *dignare Domine die isto & coet.*[925] and *Domine Deus omnipotens.*[926] [...]

Once they have arrived in Mina, they shall disembark with raised cross, and they shall walk towards the church [[intoning]] the *Te Deum laudamus* to offer themselves to the Most Holy Sacrament; and from there they shall go where the Captain who goes with them shall recommend. They shall immediately begin to organize their own affairs, and the first [[thing]] shall be to place themselves in seclusion;[927] and they shall do everything so quietly and with so little fuss that the people may understand that they are not going there to take care of themselves but rather of the souls of their neighbors. On the first possible day, they shall deliver a sermon in which they will declare to the people the reason they went to that land, to bring them light. Let them make a seclusion with a gate, inside which on no account shall any woman enter, or anywhere else where they may reside, so as not to give occasion to any public scandal.

Their life in that land as regards clothing, eating, drinking, and sleeping, and the rest, shall be in accordance with what the land will allow. The same shall apply to the other observances of the religion:[928] everything shall be ordered in accordance with the land.

---

[923] In Brásio's transcription, '*bolos*,' a mass of dough, usually round, which is cooked in an oven.

[924] In memory of Our Lady having blessed some pieces of bread which were eaten by St Nicholas of Tolentino and cured him, every year, on his feast day on September 10, in the churches of the Hermits of St Augustine—to whom he belonged—small loaves or cakes of St Nicholas are blessed (accompanied by prayers approved by Pope Eugene IV) and are said to cure all kinds of illnesses.

[925] '[...] vouchsafe, O Lord, this day etc. [...]' (Latin), the final lines of the hymn *Te Deum laudamus*, ascribed to St Augustine.

[926] 'Lord God Almighty' (Latin), a prayer included in the Roman Breviary and Liturgy of the Hours.

[927] In Brásio's transcription, '*recolhimento em que se matað*' ('*recolhimento em que se matam*'), literally 'seclusion in which they kill themselves'; it should read '*recolhimento em que se metam*,' that is, 'seclusion in which they may place themselves.'

[928] In the sense of 'religious order.'

Nocturnal and diurnal hours should be said by each of them alone, as the Fathers of the Company [[of Jesus]] do in their colleges, since our intention is not to submit the fathers who go there to the laws of the convent, but rather free them so that they may, at all hours, take care of what brought them there, which is to preach, to confess, and to convert the infidels. And as this cannot be done without much prayer, which achieves everything, I order that every day there should be two hours of prayer in common, one in the morning and the other in the afternoon or at night, in which the fathers will ask the Lord for a spirit of fervor for the work of conversion. [...] In the village[929] of the black people they shall take great care to teach the little ones, because in this way God will illuminate the earth; and see whether they can be brought up away from their parents, as in a college, at the King's expense. [...]

[A]nd we do not go there to become rich but to convert the infidels. [...]

Written in Penafirme, on the 23rd of February 1572.

Let each of Your Reverences copy this letter to keep it with you and know how to act with the help of the Lord.

Regulations for those who went to Mina.

105 Information Regarding Mina[930] (29/09/1572)

ABSTRACT – *One of the most extensive yet anonymous reports on the land, people, places, and imperial ambitions of Portugal, most evocatively a plan to colonize the Mina (Gold) Coast so the Portuguese crown and its merchants might reap all the benefits.*

As I was about to send Your Grace a more detailed account of what I consider to be beneficial to this land, in order to devote my life in some way to the service of him, who, after God, had granted it to me, God saw fit to send me so serious an illness that I was unable to obtain as full information as was required in this matter, and because of it I have lost a great part of the memory of my previous reflections. And, thus, Your Grace will please excuse the mistakes and the confusion of what I write, and not be annoyed should I repeat to Your Grace some of the things about which I wrote last year.

There are four manners to reap benefits from Mina: leaving matters as they are, provided some reforms take place; bringing about changes so that the same, or more, benefit can be obtained at lesser cost; leasing it out, which, as I shall explain later, should not be considered; or expanding it, so as to populate it, which is what I think most befits the service of God and of Our Lord the King.

---

[929] In Brásio's transcription, '*aldea*' ('*aldeia*'): see Glossary.
[930] MMA vol. 3, doc. 15, pp. 89–113; BNL, *Fundo Geral*, Ms 8457, fols. 100v.-110. Cf. Mota and Hair, *East of Mina*, 73–88 (for transcript, see appendix under Document E).

Regardless of the ways in which matters in Mina are disposed, everyone can see that galleys are needed, though not in such bad shape as those which are here now (scarcely any of which can be of any service, even though they be patched up before leaving the river) but, on the contrary, well repaired and kept ready for any eventuality; and great care must be taken over this.

And similar care should be taken that no white prisoners be put on the galleys – for several reasons: because they are not good for work in this land, and a black man rowing is worth two of them; and because most of the time they are sick, making the infirmary incur in expenses; and, what is incomparably worse, because many of them live unlawfully with native black women, who, as has been ascertained, waste[931] births, whether killing them [[the babies]] after they are born or provoking miscarriages, which is proved by the fact that, though they live maritally together and the women's bellies grow, there is not one mulatto in the whole village, whereas there are many in those places where black women give birth safely; and, in addition, these prisoners are in great part responsible for the goods of seamen, who come with the fleets, and of soldiers falling into the hands of the black people before time and contrary to the Law and customs, for the bargains they offer, so that they can give the money to their owner; and I have heard from some of them that they keep it [[the money]], or part of it, and they are in the habit of going and selling things to them [[the black people]], though they belong to residents. And I cannot but regard this as harmful to the Exchequer of Our Lord the King, since the black people will not come to the Factory to obtain goods as eagerly as they could. And even though Captain João Roiz[932] was able to partly remedy the situation by ordering them to sleep in the galley when the fleet arrives, given the little service they do to His Highness and the damage they cause to the land, it would be better to commute their punishment to other parts, rather than sending others to do the same as these.

Some may ask how could new galleys be brought here without white rowers? I say that they could be brought with men the punishment for whose crimes could be served during the voyage, before they arrive here. And then they could be sent back to Portugal or left on one of the islands. And those who are sentenced to death, or deserve it, could be sent here as rowers, as there is no lack of timber here for gallows. And this I would do above all to thieves, from what I know of their ways and that the Law treats them harshly, as it should.

In order that there be sufficient crew for the galleys when those who are here are sent back, it does not seem to me a bad idea to sentence the black criminals of São Tomé and of the island of Fogo to the galleys, whether for a certain period or for good, according to the quality of the crime. And those who commit a crime here could also be put on them [[the galleys]], as I believe is done. And between

---

[931] Literal translation of '*esperdição*' ('*desperdiçam*').
[932] João Roiz Coutinho was appointed captain of Mina by writ dated the 1-4-1586, ANTT, *Chancelaria de Filipe I*, liv. 15, fol. 287. See also MMA vol. 3, doc. 129.

them, and with fifty others that His Highness may have here now, they will make up a sufficient number. And above all the foreign pirates and the Lutherans who come to make raids, if they are not hanged straight away, should be put to the oars until they die, with no more courtesy than is used with black people.

For this purpose, it would be advisable to order that no black *cabeceira*,[933] as they are called, or principal lord, should have jurisdiction to punish whatever crime, or to order or sentence as a judge, but this should rather be reserved for those who are empowered to do so in Mina. Because they punish many of them with one *arroba*[934] of wine, with which they all get drunk; and if there is [[enough]] wine for that, then it would not be unreasonable to set them to the oars for one or two years.[935]

Therefore, should Mina stay as it is, in order to reform it, it seems to me advisable to order that the address and conversation with these black men be of such a kind as to make them understand that, as long as they remain good and faithful vassals of Our Lord the King, His Highness will take care of them and protect them as subjects, and not in such a way that they might imagine that they are friends with Our Lord the King in the same way as the King of Castile is friends with that of France. It would thus be advisable that not one of them be in any way given the title of King. Because, even if it seems that it means nothing, it matters much, for when one of these black men calls himself, or wants to be called, King, he fancies that being King of Akatakyi ('Komenda') or Fetu, which are peoples of up to one hundred grass shacks, or huts, at the most, is the same as being King of Portugal, which is a kingdom so worthy of this name.

And if it is to remain in its present state, I believe it will be most advantageous to have a fortress built, not where that of Nkrãn[936] used to be – which I have heard they want to rebuild – but next to some salt pans which are very close by, and to have the salt pans repaired by slave workers under the command of white men, which I think would be most advantageous; and if the land were populated, it could be made even more so by forbidding the black people to make salt through boiling sea water, which is how they presently do it.

If the rowers are black men, who will better endure continuous work, it would not be advisable for the galleys to be inactive, but they should keep sailing from here to Cape Palmas, and from here to Nkrãn, and further down, protecting the land and capturing any robbers who may go there; and if they take with them a caravel or a small vessel to carry goods according to their destiny, they can be loaded with ivory from Akyem upwards, and from there downwards they can exchange them for gold.

---

[933] *Cabeceira*: literally 'head,' as in 'head of the bed/table'; hence 'headman.' The title given to someone who governs over others.
[934] *Arroba*: see Glossary.
[935] In Brásio's transcription, the meaning of the last sentence is unclear.
[936] In Brásio's transcription, '*Cará*.'

The Alande, whose lands extend approximately from Cape Palmas to near Akyem, do not take cloth[937] and do not have gold, but they do have much ivory, which they exchange for manillas, porcelain beads, *laqueca*[938] and, I believe, cowries; and I have it on good authority that this will bring much profit, for there is so much ivory, and so cheap, especially if it is bought with the articles I have mentioned and with the cargo carried by the small vessel so as to go up the rivers in that *comarca*,[939] where the people are friendly to us and in themselves peaceable. And they use to come to Akyem (as I saw them) to sell their ivory and other small articles, such as lizard skins and *bandas*, which are two strips of cotton one or two palms wide that the native and white people buy from them, the natives for covering themselves and the white people to sell them when the occasion arises[[?]];[940] the natives put the skins on the handles of their daggers and on the assegais, on the part which they hold when they shoot; they also bring slaves to sell, and these are usually very good.

It seems to me that it would be advantageous to the land, without expenditure of labor, to have a certain number of goats, pigs and sheep brought in the *caravelão*[941] which is here now, or in other vessels, and give them to the black people in threes, which will not be expensive; and let them keep not less than the number given to them, but, on the contrary, more; and let them not kill the females to stop them from reproducing; and let them raise herds and have shepherds, to take them to the bush during the day and bring them back to the house of their owners at night; and assign wages to these shepherds; and teach them in every aspect how they should live, since these people do not have the least understanding or industry.

I have already written about the confusion there used to be in selling and buying goods, especially small goods, because no kind of currency is used, and therefore I thought fit to point out that it would be advisable for His Highness to create some currency, which would circulate only here, and order that it be used by both white and black men and be accepted without exception; and it could be introduced in the land by using it to pay some of the wages of the soldiers and officials.

It does not seem to me unreasonable, should there be mines – as there are – to build, as soon as a mine is found, a fortress, or an ample house for white people; and for the black people, because it is easier, to make a paling with large wooden beams, which they call *rochoada*,[942] next to which, and next to the house, huts could be made for the black people working [[there]].

---

[937] In the transcription, '*roupa*,' which in a footnote, MMA defines as 'light goods.' Considering the context, it seems probable in this case '*roupa*' means 'cloth,' which is one of its most common meanings.

[938] *Laqueca*: see Glossary.

[939] *Comarca*: see Glossary.

[940] In Brásio's transcription, '*a tempo que se aproueitão*' ('*a tempo que se aproveitão*'), literally, 'in time to be profited from.'

[941] *Caravelão*: see Glossary.

[942] In MMA, vol. 9, p. 336, Brasio adds the following note to the term '*rochoada*': 'an assemblage of rocks, a small fortress.'

I also think that it is not senseless for there to be others, besides the black people who will dig in the mines, to break the soil together with them and plant corn and yams, and for them to bring palm wine and nuts, and anything else which could provide for their subsistence and for that of those who dig; and also others to procure some livestock for use of the white people, and to go on breeding more every day, so that there is no need to send from Portugal anything beyond some flour and wine; and olive oil could be done without, since that of the palm is good enough to eat, as I know by experience. And if this were arranged in this manner, there would be no need in the Kingdom to be concerned about supplies, for even if there were no bread,[943] one can easily live on corn, as I myself also know, and the *bordão*[944] wine is also better than the Portuguese, though I believe it does not last more than two days; but it can be harvested all the year round, and is best in the Summer; but this only exists in that *comarca* of Akyem. Palm wine is more common and lasts longer, and I believe that all year round there is always some to be harvested.

I would also be of opinion, should Mina remain as it is, that no one should stay here for more than two years, three at the most, and that nobody, not even a factor, a scribe, a *meirinho*[945] or an oven-house overseer, should [[be allowed to]] return here in a higher position, or in any other way. Because the lower the position he held at the beginning, the worse he becomes when he returns in a better position, unless he is a man so well-known for being good and such a servant of God and the King that he might come a hundred times. And because it is not in my nature to speak of the disadvantages, they should be known through someone else, although they are not so concealed that they cannot be perceived by anyone who reflects about them.

I do not think that selling the offices of this land is sensible, because when the official has property in his hands, he has many means of satisfying himself if he thinks that the office was sold to him for more than it was worth.

As I have come to conclude since I have been here, His Highness loses much in not taking advantage of the *malagueta*, from Cape Palmas and beyond; and it seems that the two galleys would be sufficient to protect this coast, and that of Malagueta, and upwards, especially since, as I have been told, only very few robbers now go to those parts. Because King Felipe ordered in the Indies that no black people should be bought, which would take these people from where they gave great profit; but he also obtains it from the *malagueta*, which they take to Flanders. And the merchandise taken to be sold could be left in Cape Verde, and from there they could go and trade in ivory, *malagueta*, and slaves.

And I do not agree with those who object that this would lead to reducing the [[trade in]] spices from India, but rather know for certain that they are

---

[943] It should read 'wheat bread.'
[944] *Bordão*: see Glossary.
[945] *Meirinho*: see Glossary.

totally mistaken, for I believe that the amount of *malagueta* which is taken to those parts [[Portugal(?)]] by robbers is the same as, or even greater than, what can be sent there; and if the galleys are on the alert, with captains who desire to serve well, no raider will dare to come to this coast, of the many who, as I have been told, are coming now; and in relation to some of them there is some information, for a few days ago they badly ill-treated the man who has leased it [[the coast]].

And if they say that it is good for it [[the coast]] to be leased, I say that it would not be very bad if the galleys were there, as they ought to be; but I fear that, as long as there continue to be no ships of His Highness carrying out this service, there will be neglect, and lessees will profit little and foreign robbers much.

There is a law issued by His Highness many years ago, which is wonderful, and came to be ill-observed: which is that no new-Christians should come to this land;[946] and it should be observed. And those who are able to have it observed, and do not do so, know this better than I do. And thus it goes without saying that they are greedier, more cunning, more mischievous, more shameless in [[defending]] their own interest, and more interested in others' property,[947] than befits a reputable man.

Concerning religious matters, there has been improvement, for the Vicar Martim Gonçalves[948] has already put things in better order as regards the black people coming to mass and doctrine; and the same is being done out there in the village by the priests who came, where I am told that each of them in his own place teaches doctrine and reading, and I see many black people, boys and young men with sheets of paper and books in their hands. I hope in Our Lord that, with the diligence of all, the understanding of these people will be opened up, so that every day they may grow fonder of that which they need so much.

I am very pleased that they have started saying mass for them at a fixed hour and teaching them prayers by the cross,[949] and I believe they will be summoned by means of a roll, as is done in many parts, and [in] Spain, which seems to me to be most necessary as they are slack and negligent people and as a way of making them repeatedly hear their Christian names, since I believe that later, when they leave and go to their village, all of those who are Christians are called by their gentile names, and someone who is called 'João' is called there 'Tabo', and someone who is called 'Maria', 'Aduá'.

Among these Christian black people there is much filthiness – which could be called something much worse – because Christian men marry gentile women, and

---

[946] Cf. MMA vol. 2, p. 570.

[947] The Portuguese idiomatic expression, as in Brásio's transcription, is '*amigo do alheio*,' which literally means 'friends of what belongs to others.'

[948] Martim Gonçalves was appointed vicar of Nossa Senhora da Conceição and administrator of the ecclesiastical jurisdiction of Mina by royal writs dated December 12 and 15, 1571. See ANTT, *Chancelaria da Ordem de Cristo*, liv. 2, fol. 43v.

[949] In Brásio's transcription, '*cruzeiro*,' most probably an outdoor cross; depending on the context, it could also mean the crossing in a cruciform church.

Christian women gentile men, according to their gentile uses, and none of them is married as the Holy Mother Church commands, and it amazes me that, during the ninety-some years (so it is said) since Mina was discovered, no order has been given that they should marry *in facie Ecclesiæ*, so that more of them become Christians and so that those who say they are such understand what it means.

It seems reasonable to me that, in order that these black people become better Christians, they should live together in the area which is closer to the fortress, given that it is very prejudicial for a Christian to be among twenty gentiles, where I think they all live as gentiles, and cast their spells, and make use of superstitions and indecency, both those who are baptized and those who are not. And Father Friar Jerónimo[950] has written something about this, which he knows best from living with the black people.

A second manner (though I do not think that it should be adopted) would be to have the galleys watching the coast, as was said, and trading in it, and not to have so many people around here doing nothing, and to have an honorable captain with twenty-five soldiers, or more if necessary, and three or four bombardiers, as there are now, and the fortress well provided with ammunitions and supplies so that there be no lack of them, and few officials, and little communication with the black people, and only very few of those on duty should be inside the fortress, and only one servant for every three [[soldiers]] of the same company, and not two pairs for each [[soldier]], one for scratching the head, another for the feet, another to fan, and another to oversee these offices.

And if the galleys do this, as I say, they can be of avail, and the people from the fortress will profit from them, and they from the people, and it would be easier to sell the merchandise along the coast, as it is sold, and this would not make the people from inland[951] stop coming to the fortress, for necessity will bring them, as it does now, even if not as much as it used to.

I am quite aware that this will sound odd, because people will reply that no soldiers would be willing to come, but with good wages and some further profit they will do so; and even if there were none of these, among so many thousands of prisoners, as there are in that Kingdom, there will certainly be 25 honorable men who could serve their exile here, as they do in Brazil and other parts; and these would be enough, for although I know that there are only a few good men in prison, still there are some who are.

And in order to avoid the danger of their rebelling, they can be men who will leave women and children or property in the Kingdom, and who have the prospect of returning there, and thus none of them should be transported for life; and

---

[950] In the Chancery, we have only been able to find a certain Jerónimo Dias, '*clérigo de missa*' (an ordained cleric), who was examined in letters and virtue by the Fathers of the Company of Jesus, and who was granted the office of chaplain of the church of Nossa Senhora da Conceição of Mina, on 28-10-1571. See ANTT, *Chancelaria da Ordem de Cristo*, liv. 2, fol.44.

[951] In Brásio's transcription, '*mediterraneos*' (i.e. '*mediterrâneos*'), literally 'Mediterranean,' in the original Latin meaning of the word, 'in the middle of land.'

someone who was to be exiled for life somewhere else would rather be sent here for five or six years, in the hope of returning there [[to the Kingdom]].

I am not mentioning this as something which would be advantageous [[in itself]], but more could be achieved at a lesser cost than if Mina were to remain as it is now without being reformed.

The 3rd manner, that of leasing it out, would be so harmful to His Highness and his subjects that I do not want to speak about it. And at the end of the first lease the situation would be such that it would not be possible to find further lessees; and if there were any, it would be at a great loss, for the land would be so full of what is profitable for only a few years that nothing would be sold except at a very low price. But I move on to the fourth manner.

Last year I declared what I am now going to state clearly, that this land should be given to be populated, and could very easily become a new Portugal, or new Indies, richer than those of Castile, which will be a greater reason for the descendants to be proud and not to complain (when they find out what kind of obstacles were encountered) about their predecessors, who missed the opportunity which had been there for so long and would have been so easy to seize. For, if this state of affairs remains as it is now, I believe that these black people will endeavor to learn (if possible) how to defend themselves from us, and how to expel us from their lands, and not how to be Christians, and how to receive us there. And even though this might seem impossible now, with the passing of time, and with continuous communication, and the ill-disposition they display, they might reach a point where they wage war against the incautious, convinced that they are doing nothing here.

The advantage will be greater, though some may say that not so much: most advantageous to the royal majesty and estate, because it will add new kingdoms to those it already possesses – thus enlarging its name – as there are in this enormous Ethiopia, submitting them to its laws and having the divine laws preached. And, with the favor of Jesus Christ, they will thus acknowledge better the virtue of both, rather than through the spindles[[?]][952] and manillas which travel from kingdom to kingdom, and from hand to hand, and which they say come from a certain kingdom, called Portugal, that they estimate to be inferior to their own [[kingdoms]], because of the gold which exists there and that they must know to be a better metal than that of the manillas, just as we know that Portugal is better than Guinea.

If this meets with approval (as people tell me is beginning to be the case, and would to God that it were already so), it seems that the 1st thing that should be done is the same as was done in the government of India, [[namely]] that a grand nobleman come to this land as Viceroy of Ethiopia, as he goes to India and used to go to Brazil, with succession in the government should God dispose of him, as is done in India, so that such a nobleman, and with a name so close to the royal one, should endeavor to perform deeds worthy of his nobility and name.

---

[952] In Brásio's transcription, '*fusos.*'

And let not the Viceroy, Governor or anyone else, however delicate he may be, imagine that, just because he is sent to Guinea and Mina, he is coming to certain death, for, as far as I have been able to understand in relation to this land, it does not kill any more than that [[land]], and whatever kills here would also kill in the healthiest part of Spain, namely a scarcity of products from their own country, for there can be no abundance of them, and of those provided by the land, which frequently cannot be obtained; [[and]] going around naked and sleeping on the floor; walking barefoot exposed to the sun and the rain; and the lack of physicians and medicines when they are ill, because the greater part of the physicians take too long to understand the diseases of the land, and when the medicines do arrive they are so only in name; and in addition to these, bad diets which, by themselves, would be enough to kill people in healthy lands. This is what kills, because the land in itself seems to me to be one of the good things seen by the sun, since God has made it so abundant in things spontaneously generated, and of which not only may it be said that *Deus dat incrementum*[953] to what is sown and watered, as St Paul tells the Corinthians,[954] but that He Himself sows and waters it, and makes it grow; and for a hundred years He has been inviting the Portuguese people to give Him infinite thanks for having shown it to them, so that they could benefit from it. And this, and how good the land is, can be better understood if one considers the many things which it generates spontaneously; and from these it may well be deduced how much it will generate if helped by human industry, with which these things, which grow naturally, would also be much better.

There are oranges, lemons, and citrons, and sugarcane, meadows of green amaranth,[955] much purslane, and a kind of eggplant which is very good to eat; there are peppers[956] similar to those of the Indies, of the shorter type, and borage, though somewhat different from the kind that grows there [[in the Kingdom]]. There are white and red pumpkins, which are very good, and both of them look like melons. There are a thousand kinds of fruit good to eat, as one which is the size of small peaches[[?]],[957] without a pip but with seeds inside, like a very tasty pear, so marvelous that it whets the appetite; and another which looks like a very yellow plum; and another very similar to brownish figs, and many others about which I will not write, since I do not know what to compare them with, and the black people eat them all, and the white men the greater part, when they feel like it. And all of them grow naturally.

Of the seeds which have been brought from Portugal, I have not heard of any that has not grown here. There is radish, cabbage, coriander, and mint, and clove, [[and]] basil, which I believe grows wild. Every seed grows, and if it does not

---

[953] '[...] God gives increase' (Latin).

[954] *First Epistle to the Corinthians*, III, 6–8.

[955] In Portuguese, as in Brásio's transcription, '*bredo.*'

[956] In Brásio's transcription, '*pimentos,*' i.e. species of the genus *capsicum*, probably 'bell peppers,' whether hot or not.

[957] In Brásio's transcription, '*durázio*': here, probably a kind of peach ('*pêssego-durázio,*' or '*durazno*' in Castilian) and not a type of olive, which bears the feminine name form ('*durázia*').

bear any grain (as happened with a few wheat seeds, which grew as high as a man and with many ears) it seems to me that this is not due to the nature of the soil, but rather to its being very fertile; and I think that, if it were cultivated and became tired, it would also bear seeds, for the same happens in Spain, in very fertile soils, before they are cultivated and become exhausted.

In an orange and lemon orchard nearby there are fig-trees bearing figs, and pomegranate trees bearing pomegranates, and the vines from Portugal thrive and they bear grapes; and whatever is sown grows, and much would I have seen and tried if God had given me health.

The black people sow a large type of corn which they call *bruy*, and in Castile it is called Indian wheat and millet, which seems to me to be the same as grows there. They sow yams, which in this land provide good nourishment, and others, which they call *cocos*,[958] but in fact is food for pigs in Castile, but the black people, especially in Akyem, eat a lot of it. They also grow bananas, which in the Castilian Indies are called *plátanos*; it is a gentle kind of fruit, and on the road to Agri I have seen it in the bush, where it seemed improbable that it could have been planted. They grow very good cotton in this land, which could be of much profit.

The domestic animals, as far as I know, are only goats, sheep, and cows. The goats very small, the sheep of the same size of those there, their hair like that of the goats; and all those I have seen are spotted in white, orange, and black. The cows are very small, and their color is similar to that of the cows there. The pigs which are brought adapt well here, but not so in Akyem, where the Governor's horses and a donkey died. Dogs adapt to the land, and the Alande bring them here to sell them; and they make merry, and they eat them here, and it is a very special occasion, with many guests, whenever a dog is eaten in the houses of these black people.

There is an infinite number of wild animals here, as well as of birds.

From Cape Palmas to here, along the coast, at almost regular intervals – from what I have heard and seen – freshwater rivers enter the sea, where many sugar mills might be built, since there is an infinite quantity of timber along their banks.

The variety of trees which provide timber is endless; I have not seen any similar to those there. Among them there is redwood,[959] with which they dye; they tell me that this is a small tree. There is also wood from which they take a yellow dye and with which the black people dye a kind of conical caps[960] made from a certain type of grass.

In the mountains inland, there are swarms of bees in hollow trees, from which it is said that sometimes they bring pots with honeycombs to sell.

---

[958] *Cocos*: it is difficult to determine whether the author is using a local term or the Portuguese word for 'coconuts.' The latter seems likely.
[959] In Brásio's transcription, '*pao (pau) vermelho*': known as Brazilwood, a leguminous plant used in dyeing.
[960] In Brásio's transcription, '*carapuça*': see Glossary.

Truly, if one would want to write in detail about all the things this land gives, one would never end; but this is no reason to leave the palm trees out, which give so much wine and oil, even though I leave many other things out, all of them proof of the generosity of the land.

In reply to those who say that populating this land will be prejudicial to India, because there will not be enough people to go there, it might be proposed that no people come from Portugal, and that permission only be given to those from all these islands, from São Tomé to the Azores, which, I believe, are overflowing with people. And a friend of mine, who came in the *caravelão* from São Tomé, where he went for supplies, assured me that there were many people in that island eager to come to this land, provided it were increased and that [[lands were]] given in *sesmaria*;[961] and that he had been told that there were 20 men or more who would come, each of them bringing one hundred of his captive slaves, among whom many very worthy craftsmen of all the crafts necessary now at the beginning, as builders, masons, blacksmiths, and the like, and there is no doubt that, when they become undeceived and realize that this land is not a killer of men, many men, with all their property and household, will come from the other islands.

And even if people do come from the islands, Justice should not be entrusted to them, nor [[should they be made]] officials, but [[these positions should be reserved for]] native-born Portuguese, because even though there may be many men in the islands capable [[of occupying them]], the elders[[?]][962] do not generally acknowledge their worth and truthfulness.

And even if Mina does increase, it seems to me that what I have said about the galleys is necessary – those from Cape Palmas to these parts, as well as [[the two]] which will cruise along this coast; because the former can be and are most advantageous, carrying *malagueta* and ivory with a *caravelão* to the Factory of the island of Santiago, and are of great service to God, not giving way to the annexation, and robbery and frequent killing of Christians by the Lutherans; and the latter two will be a shield to whatever settlements be built in these parts, and they could not be better protected than by them [[the two galleys]].

And if, for the preservation of the Republic, those men harmful to it should be banished, it is advisable not to let come to this [[Republic]] those who will later need to be expelled; and it is wiser to remedy now with a simple concoction than to wait until later, when many and elaborate medicines are needed. It is not so much the case of robbers (though these are slow to mend their ways) and murderers, and trouble makers, and of others who may be transported here, since time and punishment gradually mend the ways of most of them, but that of new-Christians, who do not steal property, or kill men, or make trouble, but kill the whole Republic with their greed, [[and]] rob it with their deceptions. The trouble they make does not do much harm to it, but they do grievous harm

---

[961] *Sesmaria*: see Glossary.
[962] In Brásio's transcription, '*os antigos*,' literally 'the ancient' or 'old ones.'

to its entrails in pursuit of their own benefits; and in this land they would do much worse, because it would be easier for them and the gold would whet their appetite.

If people do come to populate this land, it would be wise not to let vessels be built here, and that no vessel should be allowed to navigate more than from coast to coast, and that nothing should be loaded from here except it be in King's ships or in those which come here with his warrant.

And in order to reap more benefits from this land, and to populate it more rapidly with white Christians, it does not seem unreasonable that the fleet coming here should belong, as it does, to the King – and not as in Castile, where I believe it does not – so that no one may take from here the articles which His Highness might reserve for himself, or bring from there, or from other parts, what according to those lords should only be brought on His Highness's behalf.

I say that, in my opinion, more benefits would be reaped from this land and it would become more populated by Christians if the ships came, as I have said, because they would not have the equipment to go trafficking along the seashore, and they would therefore concentrate on the mines, of which they would pay the fifth[963] to His Highness, and on their farming, and cattle breeding, and plowing the land, from which they would also reap much benefit.

Even though I do not know whether in Castile the King has reserved certain articles which should not be taken to the Indies, or brought from there (it seems to me that all people with license to go there are allowed to take everything except quicksilver, and bring everything that there is in the Indies, with a register, for duties to be paid, like gold and articles of most value, such as pearls), His Highness might forbid that there be brought here manillas, cauldrons, basins, cowries, beads, or be taken *malagueta* or ivory, as has been done until now, or wood for dyeing, or whatever might be harmful to what His Highness might want to reserve here, as he has reserved in other parts, or allow to be taken with a register, for duties to be paid.

Regarding currency, as I have mentioned in relation to the first manner, there can be some danger in it, as at the time when malicious coiners used to bring counterfeit *patacões*.[964] But if all vessels belong to His Highness, and the guards are very careful regarding whom they may trust, and new-Christians are not allowed to come to this land, it seems that what was proposed in relation to currency could be carried out. And, finally, for everyday trade [[?]],[965] order should be given that some currency should circulate.

If the land is populated and the black and the white people live side by side, I fear that the white people might be bad neighbors to the black people. And if some remedy could be found for this (which, I think, will be difficult) it would

---

[963] In Portuguese, as in Brásio's transcription, '*quinto*,' here a fixed amount of one fifth.
[964] The *patacão* (sing.) was a copper coin from the time of Dom João III.
[965] In Brásio's transcription, '*comércio da vida*,' or 'commerce of life.'

be a good thing if they lived together in the villages, for thus the black people would benefit from human civilization, and learn the methods of cultivating the land and raising stock used by the Portuguese; and they would also benefit from the Christian religion, the children of the black people being raised together with those of the white people and learning the language. And this would also be a way of preventing the houses of the white people from being set on fire, since the greater part of them (at least, now in the beginning) will be made of palm leaves and straw. And when the black people outnumber the white, they can be mixed with each other as seems best. And those who, in the same village, do not finish their conversion, can always be made useful until they finally convert.

Even though these black people are of less use in matters related to war, as in all other things, it is my belief that, dealing with the Portuguese, they will become more courageous; and this boldness might incite them to commit some betrayal in one of the villages which were to be built. And in order to prevent it, even if they want to do it, it would be wise to forbid them the use of any kind of Spanish arms, while ensuring that the white people do not let theirs get rusty; and in order that they [[the white people]] be more prepared, they should be ordered to take muster every so many days, and live in such a way among the black people that these, without being hurt, are afraid of them, because no matter how pampered they are by the white people, believe me, they will never be their friends.

It will be necessary to do with these black people the same that is done in Spain with the vagabonds who are made to look for a master and start working, punishing them monetarily and even physically if they do not do so, for they are the most idle and lazy people in the world. And to what extent idleness is an evil thing has been shown by experience and by human and divine laws: *otium reges prius, et beatas perdidit urbes.*[966] And since it is something that is so abhorrent to God, and from which stem all wickedness and roguery, he who renovates the new Republic should not allow it. And I consider this to be one of the best pieces of advice one can receive regarding this matter.

I have been told here that a certain number of boys used to be sent from this land to learn good customs and letters, so that afterwards they would teach their fellow natives. A wonderful thing, for sure, though it seems to me that it is equally good to have the priests, should they come, do the same here by teaching the doctrine in which they are so diligent, so anxious to serve God, and giving such an example, as I see them, that those who come after must, if they are to do it very well, endeavor to imitate them; but would that the doctrine of religion, which is now being taught to them, should find these black people living according to some principles of good human institution and the composure of reasonable people. Because even if it is indisputably true, as it in fact is, that we should first seek to bring to these people the Kingdom of God, there would be no inconvenience in starting with the Kingdom of men and teaching them the order and

---

[966] '[...] in times past, idleness has ruined kings and prosperous cities' (Latin) – Catullus, poem 51.

concert we have in human matters, so that through this demonstration, based on visible things, they can be more easily persuaded to believe in the matters of our Faith, which they can only see with the eyes of the soul. And Your Grace should not think that what I am saying is contradicted by the fact that in the Indies of Castile they have been discovering, populating, and converting at the same time, for there is so great a difference between the condition and the ways of these black people and those of those Indians, that we may call those from the Indies meek and simple lambs, while these are wild wicked wolves. And from what I have been able to gather of their cunning ways, they want to see in order to believe, while, on the other hand, they want others to give credit to their words and things without having seen them, since they are very deceptive towards the Christians, as they are among themselves.

And because the judgment and opinion of these people seem to me to be most incoherent and completely illogical, it will be wise not to leave it to their discretion what they will do, but rather, if they have slaves and are given land, to make them clear the land, sow bushels of corn and plenty of yams, plant trees, cultivate gardens and orchards, raise stock, etc.

Regarding the implements which they should use in cultivating the land, I believe I wrote to Your Grace last year that these should be mattocks, hoes, axes [[and]] sickles, and that it would be a good thing for them to report on this on certain days of the year. And these are things through which part of what is spent with the fleets can be saved, not allowing anybody to bring them privately.[967]

These black people wear their hair in many different ways, one of them with so many knots and tangles, in which they put gold beads, and others which they buy, and reels like those for linen, and loops and slipknots, that I think it is not convenient to permit it if one wants to eradicate idleness from among them: because it is a thing of sensuality and brazenness, and it must necessarily take much of their time.

I have not written about the gold, which I believe exists in this land, as I was waiting until I had more information about it and could do so, though my being unwell has also been an obstacle to it. But I am absolutely convinced that there is much gold. And one of the reasons that convinces me of this is seeing that, almost everywhere that the black people are said to have searched for it, they have found it. And if they do not know of more mines than those which exist, it is because they do not search for them, nor do they possess industry, diligence or will, for it is said that when they want to pay for something, the black people from the backlands buy it; then they go and take the gold from the mines.[968] And it is also said that the great majority of these black people do not hoard because of the lack of trust between them, since the most powerful, when he so desires, takes the

---

[967] In Brásio's transcription, the verb used is '*trazer*,' which can mean 'to bring' but also 'to have.' Therefore, an alternative translation of this last sentence would be '[...] not allowing anybody to possess them for their personal use.'

[968] In Brásio's transcription, the meaning of this sentence is unclear.

possessions of the less powerful, and also because of the many wars which are often waged between peoples.

I also think that, when the land is cleared and cultivated, what is already being raised will become immense, since [[now]] the land does not benefit from the sun because of the thickness of the trees, where animals do not reach let alone the black people, who do not open mines or search for gold in places which are not close to the water that is used to separate it from the soil. And even if they find it elsewhere, they do not dig there because of the labor of taking the soil to where there is water. And this will not hinder the white people from opening mines anywhere, even if they are far from water, because they will make wells, or aqueducts, wherever there are conditions for bringing water from the rivers, or else they will take the soil on beasts of burden, which they will raise, or on the black people themselves, who of all things are best at carrying.

And for taking care of the mines there should come not only a single miner – as I believe – and who is here in the infirmary almost as much as myself, but rather all those who can come with knowledge of this art, until they have found the mines and where they are located, etc.

A black man has now arrived here who is said to be son of the King of the Great Akan,[969] who was baptized during the time of António de Brito, who was Captain here,[970] and took the same name. He is a black man of distinguished appearance, and he brought with him a son of up to 20 years of age. And being asked about that land in the presence of the Vicar, and in his house, he said (for he speaks Portuguese reasonably well, since he has stayed here with his father) that that land was very rich, but that the gold which came from there was not extracted in the lands of his grandfather, who is still alive, but further away, in another kingdom, which he says it took him five days to reach. The name of that kingdom, or lands, where the mines are to be found is called Tafo. He says he saw the mines and pieces of gold, some of them the size of his head or fist, and larger and smaller according to what the earth gives, because even if they are no bigger than hazelnuts, it still is much gold. And what the black man said seemed true to me, from what I could judge from his bearing. And he also told me that, generally, whenever a black man or woman went to take gold, he [[or she]] would take twelve *pesos*[971] in one day. I asked him whether the soil where the gold was loose or stone? And he answered me that there were all kinds of soil, but in such a way that I could only surmise that it was like clay, and hard, from which some pieces emerge almost like stones, and he said that these were white.

Some days before this, the Vicar, urged by me, had asked another black man whether that land had much gold; and he answered, through the interpreter,

---

[969] In Brásio's transcription, '*Asaens.*'

[970] António de Brito was appointed captain of Mina by royal writ dated 10-1-1545. See ANTT, *Chancelaria de D. João III*, liv. 25, fol. 4.

[971] Subdivisions or multiples of the standard, i.e. of the type or model used for weighing metal.

through whom we put the question, that it was so. And when asked what size the pieces were he had seen taken from the soil, he looked all around the room, where there were bigger and smaller things which he could point out, and he said that he had seen pieces the size of some oranges which were there.

I cannot abide the indifference of almost all those who come to this land in trying to find out about these things, and it makes me very sad, and I do not know the reason, except that of having on my mind he who I wish be served by everyone, as pertains to a King and Lord. And this lack of care is made clear by the fact that one can hardly meet a man who, when asked where the richest gold mines are located, would not say those of the Big Elephant; and another one told us that it was a five-day journey from there, which means that from here (so I gathered) to there it is around one hundred or one hundred and ten leagues, which is not much, and they could be travelled without much difficulty and effort; though to say in what way would be never-ending.

As to the history of Caia, it has been extensively written there; it is a very large village, and a very good place with good soil, surrounded by and intertwined with palm groves, and more worthy to be inhabited by Christian people than by gentiles. And when I see myself limping, I would be glad if it had been from an arrow that had been shot at me there.

In the beginning of the month of August an ambassador from Caia came here to make peace, which they had broken with their betrayal; and at the end of four or five days, before the first one returned to his country, another black ambassador came and brought a gold necklace as a sign that he wanted to make peace. I do not know what was discussed with them; some say that a condition was imposed of compensating for a large part of the yield[972] of Caia which had been lost and which would amount to fourteen thousand *cruzados*; others say that the contract was suspended until the Governor expressed his opinion; and others still that no contract will be signed until a decision comes from the Kingdom regarding what should be done. And this would be the best thing to do, and that an agreement should not be reached except under the conditions I read about, many days ago, in regard to a similar case, which consisted in compensating for the losses and delivering the main rebels so to have justice done. And I think it would also be advisable that, throughout Caia and its villages,[973] no black man should be allowed to reside unless he paid a certain tribute for both land and dwelling, which could in all justice be taken from them completely because of the betrayal they committed. And in fact, if this land [[Mina]] is increased in order to be populated, it would in this case be better not to leave the land with them on any condition and to start by building there the main settlement, without accepting in those parts any black people apart from slaves, because the land is considered to be healthier and richer than this one, and more abundant in all things, and it will be a punishment feared by the other black people, just as they fear it now, ever since Caia was destroyed.

---

[972] In Brásio's transcription, '*fazenda*,' meaning 'wealth.'
[973] In Brásio's transcription, '*aldeas*' ('*aldeias*'): see Glossary.

And I am almost certain that these ambassadors are not such, but merely merchants, who, in exchange for the sign of peace-making they gave, will make a lot of money, taking property from both parties and non-parties independently of the agreement being in effect or not; and they will postpone the payment of what they stole, in the hope that thus this affair will be forgotten, and come here whenever it seems best to them, bringing a little in exchange for earning a lot.

Therefore, it seems to me that, after the sign is received, no one from Caia should be allowed to come here before peace has been confirmed, and that those caught should be put in the galleys or hanged, as this is how I think these people should be dealt with. And should there be some loss to His Highness's Exchequer, since it can be argued that no traders will come from there, it would be a small one. I believe that these black people are such rogues that they will not want to complete the payment, and if they do want to do so they will not be able to pay, especially now that they are at war against those of another black man who they call King of the Bush,[974] who is said to have died a few days ago at the hands of those from Caia, as did another five hundred and above on both parties. And those of the [[King]] of the Bush once again put fire to Caia after it had been burned down by the Christians, which means that they are on bad terms; and it would not be a bad idea to seize this land of Caia, as seems most reasonable and fair, and it would be a good thing to subdue them, for they are probably the worst enemies of their neighbors [[and]] because in this battle it is said that there were 20,000 black men; but for this number two hundred good Portuguese are enough.

There may be other people who understand better of all these things. And if I write about this, it is because Your Grace orders me so, and to show that I know the graces I have received and that I was willing to serve: my wish is good, and it grows each day; my strength little, and each day less; but God is great and merciful, and mighty, so as to restore my strength and let me fulfil the wish for His service. May He be with Your Grace and give you a long and healthy life.

From Mina, on the 29th of September 1572.

106 Memorandum from Jorge Da Silva to King Dom Sebastião[975] (22/08/1573)

ABSTRACT – *Jorge da Silva of the king's council makes the case that the Popes have given the land of the 'infidels' to the king and offers advice for effectively remedying Mina's spiritual and commercial neglect.*

[974] In Brásio's transcription, *'El-Rei do Mato.'*
[975] MMA vol. 3, doc. 16, pp. 114–19; BNL, *Fundo Geral*, Ms 8058, fols. 107–111; *Fundo Geral*, Ms 3776, fols. 79–83; *Fundo Geral*, Ms 8920, fols. 76–78. BNM, Ms 2422, fols. 145–148. Cf. Mota and Hair, *East of Mina*, 88-91 (for transcript, see appendix under Document F).

Popes have given the lands of the Infidels to the King of Portugal and to the King of Castile *ad propagandam fidem*,[976] and since the ministers of the Gospel are not free to teach the Catholic Faith because of the insolence of the barbarians, it is necessary that they take arms and troops for their defense. Because of these expenses, the Christian Kings may lawfully take advantage of the produce and proceeds of the lands of the Infidels.

St. Dionysus says that God is *sui ipsius defusivum*,[977] because, since He is the highest good, the nature of true good is that of being communicative.

As is well known, God has bestowed many graces upon the Christian Kings whose purpose, in their Territories[978] and Conquests, has been the conversion of souls and that their subjects should partake of the riches of the land.

Mina was discovered ninety years ago; not a soul has been converted, or any attempt been made in that direction, during all this time, even though the gentiles from Ethiopia are more willing to receive the Faith than any others in the world.

Never, during all this time, have the Christian Kings tried to have their subjects partake of this gold and of the riches of that land; on the contrary, all sorts of extortions and wrongs have been done to them by the officials, and a great many thefts committed against Your Highness's Exchequer.

Thus it is the will of God that, while making money in Brazil with sugar, cotton, wood,[979] and parrots, Your Highness should lose much revenue in pure gold and, although lord of the purest gold in the world, should not benefit from it, as do the French, English, Sharif and Moors of Africa.

I heard the Factor João de Barros[980] say that the King your grandfather[981] had been losing money in Mina for many years, and Your Highness's Exchequer has been losing and wasting over four hundred thousand *cruzados* during these three unnecessary years of Martim Afonso[982] and António de Sá,[983] for they took a fleet and soldiers sufficient to incur huge expenses, and hinder and damage the trade of Mina, but not sufficient to populate and conquer Mina.

It would be advisable that Your Highness should return to the first two principles: taking care of converting souls from the roots and of populating the

---

[976] '[...] for the propagation of faith' (Latin).

[977] '[...] emanation of himself' (Latin).

[978] In Brásio's transcription, '*Demarcações*,' literally 'Demarcated Territories.'

[979] Brazilwood (*Paubrasilia*): red leguminous plant, used in dyeing, from which, in view of its abundance, derived the name of Brazil, originally called Land of *Vera*, or *Santa*, *Cruz* (True, or Holy, Cross).

[980] João de Barros, the famous chronicler, was appointed as factor of the houses of Guinea and Indies by writ issued in Evora, on 23-12-1533. Cf. ANTT, *Chancelaria de D. João III*, liv. 19, fols. 243v.-244. On 25-5-1529, he was appointed to the office of scribe 'for the Judge of the Cases and Matters of Guinea and India,' which his father, Afonso de Barros, had also held and renounced in his son's favor. Cf. ANTT, *Chancelaria de D. João III*, liv. 48, fol.16. See also MMA vol. 4, doc. 142.

[981] Reference to D. João III, D. Sebastião's grandfather.

[982] See MMA vol. 12, doc. 61.

[983] António de Sá was appointed to the captaincy of S. Jorge da Mina and allowed to take one hundred men with him to serve the king, by writ issued in Sintra, on 20-9-1570. Cf. ANTT, *Chancelaria de D. Sebastião*, liv. 27, fol. 100v.

land, for when there is no gold, or when it has been exhausted, there will still be sugar, cotton, slaves, and possibly ginger and other valuable goods.

And Your Highness would do well to avoid having this business carried out at the expense of your Exchequer, for the profit will go to a few officials and other individuals, and the business will never be completed perfectly, because lacking in these two principles it is without foundations. Your Highness should already be weary of so many things being done at your expense.

The ancients say that experience *est mater rerum*;[984] to no avail have I racked my brain with Mutapa, Mina, lawful exchange, drawing up remedies and regulations for the *comendas*,[985] and other matters. I have always taken God and time for my witnesses. May God and the experience time has given us, in the name of His Five Wounds, help us now; and I know that what I say is of little worth. It is not in vain that the wise man says: *Dives loquutus est et dicunt quis est hic?*;[986] but I comply with my obligation and the love I have for the service of Your Highness. As I have mentioned the *comendas*, the zeal you have awakened in me has led me to this digression: Your Highness spends rivers of money on four *moços fidalgos*[987] in Tangiers; if you revised the regulations of the *comendas* and corrected some things which ought very much to be corrected, Your Highness would have a thousand spears in Tangiers at the expense of the Masterships' *comendas*: oh!, if men acknowledged they are men, whose office is to err from morning to night, and whose wisdom lies in acknowledging their errors! All the Psalms of David are full of acknowledgement of his guilt, and, in his *Confessions*, Saint Augustine speaks of nothing else. After Christ Our Lord had risen to Heaven, when Saint Peter took His place on earth and was confirmed in Grace by the Holy Ghost, even so he erred, and Saint Paul says that he rebuked him face to face *quia reprehensibilis erat*;[988] and we, miserable and most miserable sinners, want our opinions to be articles of faith, and our designs divine and infallible truths, when to err is human and not to confess one's error is devilish.

Returning to [[the subject of]] gold, if Mina is populated Your Highness will profit from the gold, and, added to the other goods which will then be traded, from the revenue of the custom houses; and from the Houses of Lisbon[989] you will have the profit of your subjects, which is a greater profit for Your Highness

---

[984] '[…] the mother of things' (Latin).

[985] *Comenda*: see Glossary.

[986] 'The rich man speaks, and they say: who is this?' (Latin). The full text is as follows: *Dives locutus, et omnes tacuerunt, et verbum illius usque ad nubes perducent. Pauper locutus est, et dicunt: Quis est hic?* (*The rich man spoke*, and all were silent, and what he said they extol even to the clouds. The poor man spoke, *and they say: who is this?*). Cf. *Ecclesiasticus*, XIII, 28–29. The author of the letter has collapsed the two verses into one, ascribing to the rich man (*dives*) what wisdom says of the poor man (*pauper*), thereby completely altering the meaning of the original text.

[987] *Moço fidalgo*: see Glossary.

[988] '[…] because he was to be blamed.' (Latin) – St. Paul, *Epistle to the Galatians*, II, 11.

[989] In Brásio's transcription, '*Casas de Lisboa*,' also known as '*Sete Casas*' ('Seven Houses'): these specialized in the collection of the *sisa*, a tax imposed on certain kinds of products. See António Manuel Hespanha, 'As Finanças Portuguesas nos Séculos XVII e XVIII,' *Cadernos do Programa de Pós-Graduação em Direito/UFRGS*, vol. VIII, n. 2 (2013), p. 109.

than it is for them: a King is never poor when his subjects are rich, nor rich when his subjects are poor.

And should Your Highness not have any of the benefits which I mention, at least you will not incur the large expenditure which you incur with the fleets of Mina and with maintaining them. And I believe that, if Your Highness had an account[990] made of the profit and losses of Mina during the past twenty-five years, you would find that the losses were of one hundred thousand *cruzados* per year, which, in twenty-five years, amount to two and a half *contos*[991] of gold; which is the best proof of the bad government that there has been until now and of the little service done to God, for so much gold was spent in searching for gold so certain and so close to home.

When the Cardinal[992] was governing, after gathering much information about Mina and after much discussion about it, he agreed with all those of the Council in giving up Mina, but the regulations drawn up – which I have always opposed – were so dangerous and filled with obstacles that there was no one willing to deal with Mina. And therefore I would say that, if Your Highness should give it up, you should rather take care of the conversion of the souls and populating the land, than of your private benefit, because, as I have said, the profit of your subjects is more Your Highness's profit, than your profit theirs.

As regards spiritual matters, I have nothing to say, for through the goodness of Our Lord, and the miracles and victories that we have each day, God shows Himself to be well served.

Concerning the Exchequer, Your Highness should be aware that the revenue is more certain than that from the silver and gold mines, for when the mines are exhausted there will be no more silver and gold, and this for many years after; but pepper is a fruit of the land, yielded every year, and it will last while the world lasts.

I will wager my property, which is worth much, and my head, which is worth nothing, that if Your Highness accepts this advice of mine, you will be the richest king in Europe.

Your Highness should keep all the pepper which comes to this kingdom and leave the spices and other goods to your subjects, as you do now. You will still receive the taxes from these spices and goods as you do now, and Your Highness, being lord of the pepper alone, will in a short time raise one hundred thousand *quintais*[993] of pepper, which are worth four *contos* of gold; and every time Your Highness wants one *conto* of gold in cash, you will find it by paying the merchants two hundred thousand *cruzados* in pepper. And this way you will always have a living treasure from which you may spend and pay as you wish. And as things stand now, Your Highness is like a day laborer who earns and

---

[990] In Brásio's transcription, '*maça*' (i.e. '*massa*'), probably in the sense of 'group,' 'collection' or 'totality.'

[991] *Conto*: see Glossary.

[992] Reference to the Regent Cardinal Dom Henrique, paternal great-uncle of Dom Sebastião.

[993] *Quintal* (sing.): see Glossary.

eats; and if you want to fit out part of a fleet, your officials will take money from the orphans, make bad payments to the parties, and other things which God knows and may His Mercy forgive them, and in my view very contrary to the Christian religion.

And what I say to Your Highness are not the opinions of alchemists or innovations contrary to the service of God and harmful to your subjects; nor do I say that Your Highness should take the salt or the products of the land. They are pure truths and mathematical demonstrations of great service to God, and for the increase of the royal estate and the benefit of your subjects. Your Highness should consider all other innovations which disregard these as highly suspect. Theologians say *quod bonum ex causa integra*:[994] the business which is partly defective cannot be a good business.

And if Your Highness is told that I have a private interest in this, God is witness that I have never sought it, as were Our Lord the King, may he be with God, and the *Infante* [[Dom Luis?], and as are Our Lady the Queen[995] and the Cardinal. And I swear on Your Highness's life, which is an inviolable oath, that [if] India and Mina were given to me I would have no business [in] either of them; my purpose is to perfect my life, give alms to the poor, trust myself to God, and wait for death.

I will kiss Your Highness's most royal hands for reading this paper before the Holy Sacrament, and devoting your attention to it for a while, because in fact the spirit can never be right if it does not listen to the voice of its Creator. Would that it had pleased God for Adam never to have spoken to anyone; he would not then have killed himself and us.

From Lisbon, the 22nd of August 1573.

107 Proposal for Making Effective His Majesty's Regulations Regarding Goods from Mina[996] (n.d.)

ABSTRACT – *The anonymous author proposes duties to the king on 'slaves leaving Mina for the Indies' and details how much profit the crown could make by instituting transatlantic slaving between Mina and the Spanish Caribbean and the mainland. The document is published for the first time.*

His Majesty being informed of the little profit coming from Mina for his Exchequer and the great expense incurred with the garrison which he has there, he was served

---

[994] '[...] for good comes from an entire cause' (Latin), in the sense that all the causes that concur must be good.
[995] Catherine of Austria, D. Sebastião's grandmother, and former regent of the kingdom in his minority.
[996] Biblioteca da Ajuda, 51-IX-25, fols. 1–2. I have placed this undated document here because it belongs to the latter part of the 16th century, and because the author's proposal matches other proposals made during the period.

to have permission given so that any person could send to the said district of Mina as many goods as he might wish, as long as he registered them first in the House of India and paid the duties of twenty per cent upon the said goods in Mina, whence they would be allowed to obtain, and trade, slaves, gold and all other things which might be found there; and that they should bring all of it directly to Lisbon, and pay the duties upon the slaves of a quarter and a twentieth which have always been paid, and upon all the other goods the usual duties. Though the said Regulations were issued seven years ago, until now not one person has sent anything to Mina, nor has there been any benefit for [His] Majesty's Exchequer, and the outlay and expense has always been continuous, amounting each year to twenty-five or thirty thousand *cruzados*. In addition to such an ordinary expense with no significant return, His Majesty's Exchequer incurs risk with the ships which carry the said goods, which are sometimes wrecked and seized by the enemy, as recently happened with Captain Miguel de Sequeira, who was heading towards the said fortress in one of His Majesty's ships, loaded with goods for the provision of that garrison.

I would here like to put forward to His Majesty that, in order for the Regulations of Mina to have effect and the duties of twenty per cent in kind be paid to his Royal Exchequer, he should be served to allow that the slaves thus traded may be taken to the Castilian Indies, as is done with those from all other trades of the Portuguese conquests, in which there is no inconvenience, since the said slaves thus traded will come from outside the ten leagues limit of the fortress of Mina, as is the case with all those which are taken from there to Portugal. And with this permission the duties of twenty per cent in kind upon those goods which may enter Mina for the said trades will be paid, together with four thousand *reais* for His Majesty's Exchequer for each piece of slave leaving Mina, the case being that nothing is paid for the slaves who are sent to Portugal when they leave Mina, but only – for those who are still alive when they arrive – little more than one thousand *reais* each upon entering the House of India, since those who are alive arrive ill, skinny and ill-treated, and are therefore worth almost nothing. And for this reason, it is to be found that the greater part of them is valued at around four to eight thousand *reais*. And, on the other hand, the slaves who are brought to Lisbon are so few that the duties of a caravel are not worth more than forty to fifty thousand *reais* at most.

And with the said duties of twenty per cent upon the goods entering Mina, and with the four thousand *reais* for each slave leaving Mina for the Indies, His Majesty will provide for that garrison most bountifully, without cost to his Royal Exchequer; on the contrary, by beginning to frequent the said commerce, His Majesty will profit, over and above what is spent with the garrison, from the income of the said duties. And in addition to so great a profit, the trade of gold will be reserved to His Majesty since the said shipowners[997] will only trade slaves. And His Majesty may send his

---

[997] In Portuguese, '*armadores.*'

Factor there, as in the past, for trading gold, sending him goods of his choice in the vessels of the ship-owners, with no cost to His Majesty's Exchequer. And the said ship-owners will commit themselves before the House of India to deliver to the said Factor everything which they might receive there. And when the payment in Mina of the duties of twenty per cent upon goods[998] entering Mina, as established in the Regulations, is put into effect, the same duties of twenty percent may be imposed upon entry into Angola and all other conquests where slaves are traded – duties which until today have not been paid. And since His Majesty, through the Regulations which he was served to have issued concerning Mina, orders that the twenty per cent be paid, there will be no inconvenience in having all the other conquests pay it, even more so as the four thousand *reais* of exit duties which are paid for slaves in the other conquests will be paid in Mina.

And if this duty is imposed, it will yield more than fifty thousand cruzados per year for His Majesty's Exchequer. And these twenty per cent upon entry can be more easily paid in the other conquests than in Mina, since in Angola the profit from the goods which are taken from Portugal reaches more than two hundred per cent, as is well known. And in addition to the advantage for His Majesty in having his Royal Treasure increased, there is also the advantage of this trade hindering the enemy, who is trading on that coast of Mina, because the black people, finding in abundance in His Majesty's fortresses all that they need, will not go to the Dutch to obtain it – because in addition to the men of commerce treating them well so that they bring them slaves promptly, which is the merchandise less valued by the black people, they will come to His Majesty's fortresses to trade rather than to those of the enemy, since they do not buy slaves from them. And in addition to the above reasons, it is necessary that slaves be taken from these parts of Mina, in order that there be no lack in the number of those His Majesty orders to enter each year the Castilian Indies, because in Angola, Guinea and Cape Verde there is lack of black people and their price is rising, so that, to load a ship in Angola or in Guinea, one has to trade for two years. And the slaves pay so many duties in the Indies to the Crown of Castile, that if the ship-owners do not have a place whence to obtain slaves without spending much time, which wastes and wears them out, there will be no people to do the said commerce.

And presently, in the Indies, there is the need for more slaves for the new Kingdom of Granada, for which purpose people are being sought who may want to commit themselves to take slaves to the said parts, which slaves cannot be sent, not even the quantity which is contracted, unless there are more places where they can be traded. And for this trade to get started and frequented, the petitioner commits himself, should His Majesty give permission to take slaves from Mina to the Indies, to point out a person who may send to the said fortress two ships with their Portuguese crew, loaded with goods, registering them first in the House

---

[998] In the manuscript, '*roupas e fazendas*,' which in this context are probably synonyms. '*Roupas*' could also be translated as 'cloth' 'r 'fabric.'

of India, and paying the exit duties of the *consulado*,[999] and the duties of twenty per cent in kind upon entering Mina, in accordance with the Regulations, and four thousand *reais* for each slave leaving Mina for the Indies, and this in addition to the duties which are paid in the Indies to the Crown of Castile for all the slaves of the other Portuguese conquests, which amounts to little less than twenty thousand *reais* each [ship(?)] – it being declared that the said two ships, which are thus obliged to begin this trade, should be given the number of slave pieces which is usually given per hundred in the other conquests [to compensate(?)] for those dead, which will not be subject to the payment of the four thousand *reais* in exit duties from Mina; and with a further declaration which His Majesty will send to the Governor of Mina, ordering him to give all help and assistance to the said ships and trade, not ill-treating them, or delaying their clearance, given that the said ships will be carrying slaves of the said Governor, or forcing the said ship-owners to sell or buy anything from him. And should he do otherwise, His Majesty's Royal Exchequer will compensate them for any damage caused to the said ship-owners because of the said Governor. [...]

108 Letter from Cardinal Alberto to King Filipe About the Mina Trade[1000] (25/10/1586)

ABSTRACT – *The Viceroy of Portugal, which was under the Spanish rule of King Filipe and his successors (c. 1580-1640), argues for leasing the trade of the fortress of Mina.*

+

My Lord,

I have ordered that the Board[1001] should deal with the matter about which Your Majesty wrote to me, as to whether the trade of the fortress of São Jorge da Mina should be put on lease or open to the natives of this Crown, and the manner in which this could be done so as to benefit Your Majesty's service and your Exchequer; and that, in order that this matter might be better addressed, an estimate should be made of the income from Mina for several years and of the expenditure with it, and that all other documents should be examined which might shed light on the best way of resolving this matter.

A report on the opinion of the Board has been drawn up by Diogo Velho,[1002] which is enclosed in this dispatch.[1003] And it seems to me that the best and most

---

[999] *Consulado*: see Glossary.
[1000] AGS, *Secretarias Provinciales* (Portugal), liv. 1550, fol. 567; cf. MMA vol. 15, doc. 113.
[1001] In Brásio's transcription, '*junta.*'
[1002] Diogo Velho was overseer of the exchequer (*Vedor da Fazenda*) and secretary of the Council of State.
[1003] In Portuguese, '*despacho*': see Glossary.

secure thing to do would be to lease the trade and that, Your Majesty being agreeable, it should be made public, and the people who negotiate this contract should be checked, together with what they offer, so that it may be concluded. And because I have learned that Vasco Fernandes Pimentel has delivered some notes regarding these matters of Mina, I have ordered that, if they have not yet been examined in the Board, they should be, because it may happen that, after they have been seen, something new may arise of which [[the Board]] should inform Your Majesty.

May Our Lord keep the most exalted and most mighty person of Your Majesty for many years, and increase your royal estate, as is my wish and I ask Him.

From Lisbon, on the 25th of October 1586.

Holy Catholic Royal Majesty[1004]
[*Autograph*]: Kisses Your Majesty's hands,
Your most humble nephew,
The Cardinal[1005]

109 Letter from Cardinal Alberto to the King About the Fortification of Mina[1006] (25/10/1586)

ABSTRACT – *Due to the significant threat posed by ever increasing European competitors on the Mina (Gold) Coast, the viceroy makes a case for fortifying the castle of São Jorge da Mina against those pirates.*

+

My Lord,

The Council having dealt with the great quantity of pirates who are abroad, and the state of the fortress of Mina, and the lack of people there, it seemed to me to be Your Majesty's service to send a *caravelão*[1007] there, with twenty to thirty Portuguese soldiers, and that Álvaro Roiz de Távora should go with them, with some harquebuses, gunpowder and ammunition, and that they should be left in that fortress to assist in whatever may be necessary, and that Your Majesty should have a letter sent to João Roiz Pessanha informing him that, since you have this news about pirates and it is possible that they may head towards that latitude,[1008]

[1004] In Brásio's transcription, '*S.C.R. Magestade*' ('*S.C.R. Majestade*'), the abbreviation for '*Sacra Católica Real Majestade*,' Portuguese version of a title the Spanish monarchs used from the 16th century onwards.
[1005] Albrecht VII. von Habsburg (known in English as Albert VII, Archduke of Austria), who was viceroy of Portugal between 1583 and 1593.
[1006] MMA vol. 15, doc. 114; AGS, *Secretarias Provinciales* (Portugal), liv. 1550, fol. 572.
[1007] *Caravelão*: see Glossary.
[1008] In Brásio's transcription, '*parajem*' ('*paragem*'): see Glossary.

you are sending him these men and ammunition, and that he should ensure the necessary vigilance and order, as Your Majesty believes he would (even if you had not now had him reminded), in accordance with what you have already ordered and is his obligation.

And because this message should be sent as quickly as possible, it seemed to me to be Your Majesty's service that this letter should be signed [[by me]].

May Our Lord keep the most exalted and most mighty person of Your Majesty, and increase your royal estate, as is my wish and I ask Him.

From Lisbon, on the 25th of October 1586.

Holy Catholic Royal Majesty

[*Autograph*]: Kisses Your Majesty's hands,
Your most humble nephew,
The Cardinal

110 Events Which Took Place in Mina[1009] (1592)

ABSTRACT – *Copy of various letters describing certain facts which took place in Mina, including complaints of the chaplain Friar Máximo against Captain João Roiz and Roiz's reply to the chaplain's letter, French pirates, and competition for the gold trade.*

João Álvares Sardinha, Captain of one of the galleys which there are in Mina, says in a letter of his that Captain João Roiz Coutinho[1010] sent the two galleys to a *nau*[1011] from Flanders which was trading in the Port of Cardes [[*sic*]], João Álvares sailing as chief Captain in the galley São Vicente, and Ambrósio de Barros, retainer of João Roiz, as Captain in the galley Santo António; and that, reaching the *nau* on the 17th of April, at one in the morning,[1012] they attacked her for three hours, and that she surrendered by hoisting the white flag of peace, some of the French party having been killed and many wounded; and that when he wanted to board the surrendered *nau*, they did not allow it and wanted to ward off the galley Santo António; [[and that]] João Álvares, without waiting for his order, with some men on a launch rowing in her direction, boarded the *nau* from the launch; and that, though he shouted at him not to do so, he did not obey him, and they wanted to pillage the *nau*.

[1009] ANTT, CC 1-112-3; cf. MMA vol. 3, doc. 129, pp. 454–59.
[1010] João Roiz Coutinho was appointed captain by writ dated April 1, 1586. See ANTT, *Chancelaria de Filipe I*, liv. 15, fol. 287. See also MMA vol. 3, doc. 15.
[1011] Given the specificity of the types of vessels mentioned in this text, the original Portuguese term '*nau*' (the name generally given to large vessels) will be used in the translation.
[1012] In Brásio's transcription, '*antemenhaã*' ('*antemanhã*'), literally 'before morning'; it is possible that '*uma hora antemanhã*' meant 'one hour before dawn,' but it is more likely the meaning was 'one o'clock in the morning.'

And that then he went in an *almadia*[1013] to show Ambrósio de Barros the regulations; and he did not look at them, saying that he knew them already. And that he asked him for help in taking the men off the *nau*, and they went to do so. And there he met a certain António Fernandes and a certain Estácio de Sousa, retainers of the Captain João Roiz; [[and]] he set them to guard the goods of the *nau* until they went to the fortress, as ordered by João Roiz. And they removed the men from the *nau* and began furling the sails and removing the stays(?), and he put a pilot on the *nau*, and provided for everything necessary. And that Ambrósio de Barros went to his galley and did not come back. And that, with everything in order on the *nau*, he went to his galley to take care of the wounded, for which he had someone ask Ambrósio de Barros for a French surgeon who was on his galley, and that he [[Ambrósio de Barros]] did not want to send him.[1014] And that a certain Diogo de Barros, a guard on the same *nau*, came to him saying that the retainers of the Captain, who were guards, had a cabin full of goods and some bundles in the hull of the *nau*. And that they said that it was all theirs and of Captain Ambrósio de Barros. And also that a Frenchman from the *nau* had told him that, in the stern cabin, there was a coffer with gold, which had been obtained through trading, containing 25 pounds and five ounces per mark of France. And that it contained other valuable goods. And that it immediately began to be said there that the two guards who were retainers of the Captain had been the first to enter the said *nau* and to take the said cabin, and that between them they had stolen the coffer with gold, and that they had let [[him(?)]] take part of the goods as they had told him what they had done. And that when he saw this, he wrote to Captain João Roiz asking him to have guards put on the galleys, in order to know what they had taken, and that he did not comply. And that he ordered the guards not to obey him, except in giving him a hawser to tie the *nau*. And that, until they arrived at the fortress, there were *almadias* coming and going, and retainers of the Captain back and forth between the *nau* and the galley, and that it is widely known that many goods were stolen. And that if the goods had been well kept, His Majesty's goods would have been worth thirty thousand *cruzados*, and that what went into the Factory could be worth a thousand *cruzados*. And that, after the *nau* was unloaded, a retainer of Captain João Roiz went to the fortress to sell as supplies part of these goods which had been taken from the *nau*.

He also says that, in March '89, a *nau*, and a small vessel, and a fusta which was said to bring Dom António de Mñs,[1015] went to that Coast; and that, when they passed in sight of the fortress, he sent a person of his household to João Roiz, who he says stayed there until they finished doing the trade, and that they took nearly three months, and they are said to have taken sixty thousand *cruzados*, and that the

---

[1013] *Almadia*: see Glossary.
[1014] In Brásio's transcription, '[...] *e que diz que lho não quer mandar*,' literally '[...] and that he says that he does not want to send him (to him).'
[1015] *Mñs*: possibly the abbreviated form of '*Martins*,' or '*Martínez*' if he was Spanish, as suggested by the preposition '*de*.'

galleys did not prevent it, the Captain having said that he did not have men and that he was afraid lest more sails should come. And he says that he could have had more men and supplies if he had sent a launch with two white men and some black men to São Tomé to ask the Captain for a ship with men in order to supply both the fortress and the galleys, which would have been sufficient to prevent the trade. And that he wanted to inform Your Majesty how the Captain has been humiliating him, and treating him very badly, and that he [[the Captain]] took from him some letters of warning, which he was going to send Your Majesty.

In another letter, the factor João Marques da Costa also reports on the lawlessness and excesses committed by the retainers of the Captain regarding these goods from the French *nau* which was seized, and on how Captain João Roiz did not act as he should in relation to these same goods, in which report he is in agreement with João Álvares. And he adds that the Captain has been having goods brought from São Tomé, which he keeps in his house without any authority and disregarding the regulations, and that he gives money from Your Majesty's coffer, without any authority, to whom he pleases.

And thus complains the Chaplain Friar Máximo[1016] by letter, and he says that Captain João Roiz ill-treats everyone, and in particular the Vicar and himself, and, according to what he says, he has been using words against men of religion for which, this being the case, and, in his opinion, he deserves to be rebuked.

In a letter dated the first of July '88, João Roiz says that, in April of that same year, there came to that coast a French ship of fifty tons, bringing thirty-six men, two Portuguese, and a Biscayan, and one of them, who was called António Beirão, was well-known among the people of Mina. And he sent the galleys to the ship, and they battled with her for three hours, and boarded her, and captured 27 of them alive together with the Captain, who was wounded and died within four days, and Beirão was burned and died within 21 days. And he says he promised the soldiers who seized this ship some part in it, which he mentions because he thinks that a letter from His Majesty is necessary, confirming what His Majesty has given him, in order to quash any scruples which may arise from the excommunications that the Vicar imposed, intending to receive a share of what was seized in the ship.

And in another letter, he also says that Dom António de Mñs went to that coast, and that going to the fortress he prepared himself should the Re[1017] wish to disembark, and that he hoisted flags on the bastions, and that he appeared off the coast with two *naus*, one the size of the galleon São Filipe and the other one

---

[1016] Friar Máximo das Chagas, professed Brother of the Convent of Christ in Tomar, was appointed chaplain of one of the chaplaincies of the *Infante* Dom Henrique, in the church of São Jorge da Mina, by writ dated 28-7-1584. See ANTT, *Chancelaria da Ordem de Cristo*, liv. 6, fol. 132. By a writ dated the 3rd of August, he was provided with the legal allowances. *Ibid*, fol. 132. Another writ dated 15-12-1584 granted him the faculty to take a man with him to help him, entitled to the same '*fato*' (goods) which was given to the men of the factor of Mina. – *Ibid*, fol. 132v. He received another writ granting him allowances dated 6-8-1594. *Ibid*, fol. 132.

[1017] The abbreviation was not expanded and the meaning of '*Re*' in this context remains obscure.

smaller, and a fusta of 16 benches on the sides and two launches. And that on the morning of the next day he had him visited by a certain Ambrósio de Barros, captain of one of the galleys, who knew him from India, together with a soldier with refreshments on another vessel, to see who was coming on it and figure out what their purpose might be, offering to trade a certain amount of money with him. And that Dom António recognized Ambrósio de Barros and ordered the soldier on his word to get on board; but he did not keep his word since, being asked for a reply, he did not want to let him disembark, and they did not release him until they had left the coast. And that [[he]] understood[1018] that his purpose was to sail along the coast selling goods. And that he sent João Álvares Sardinha to examine the vessels, to see whether with one galley they could prevent the trade. And that through him he sent a letter to him [[Dom António]] complaining that he had broken the word he had given to the soldier; and he replied to this by a letter, which he says he keeps with him. And that, when he saw that he could not prevent the trade, he sent some *almadias* to the ports, and that even this was not enough to prevent them from raising much gold. And that, through consorting with the black people, he could only find a Frenchman, of the Greek nation, who told him that there were three hundred and fifty soldiers and that they were coming to disembark on the castle; and that they had changed their mind because some of their principal soldiers had died from disease. And that through this [[Frenchman]] he came to know that Dom António had died seven days after arriving in sight of the fortress. And that they took in excess of three hundred pounds in gold; and that they brought so many goods that they were not able to get rid of them all during the nearly three months they were on the coast.

Then, in the letter of July '90, João Roiz Coutinho also speaks of the ships with which Dom António went there, and he says that he did not intervene[1019] because, in addition to having one galley on top of another with the keel and the stem destroyed, and the sides completely exposed,[1020] he considered that he would commit a serious mistake in doing it, for when he had been able to do so he had not asked for more than one galley, and this with few men, and he would have put the fortress at risk in the event of a disaster.

I do not give an account of some other matters which João Roiz mentions for the good of the fortress, because I thought it did not correspond to Your Highness's intentions in asking me to do so and having addressed the matters I have already dealt with.

There is no other evidence for the complaints made against João Roiz besides what is said by the parties, for until now there has been no examination of the witnesses regarding the substance of their complaints, and I consider that this

---

[1018] In Brásio's transcription, '*entendi*' ('I understood'), which makes no sense in this context.

[1019] In Brásio's transcription, '*naõ se meteo*' ('*não se meteu*'), which literally means 'he did not go inside.' Whether the expression had a more aggressive connotation is difficult to say.

[1020] Tentative translation of '[...] *além de ter uma galé sobre a outra com a quilha e rodas fora e o costado todo aberto* [...]' (modernized ortography). The meaning of this sentence remains relatively obscure.

matter should be clarified in relation to the business of the goods and gold which were taken from the *nau* and the ill-treatment of which the parties complain. And through the person who examines João Roiz, who should be examined[1021] there, it might be possible to know something about the goods which he allegedly ordered to be brought from São Tomé, and about other things he is charged with. This is my opinion. Your Highness should order what you think is of service to you.

111 Letter from the King to the Viceroy of Portugal[1022] (24/04/1606)

ABSTRACT – *King Filipe II appoints Dom Duarte de Lima as Captain of Mina to succeed Dom Cristóvão de Melo, and allows him to embark at the earliest opportunity.*

In a letter from His Majesty dated the 24th of April '606.
I have seen a consultation[1023] of the Council of India nominating persons for the Captaincy of the castle of São Jorge da Mina, and because I trust Dom Duarte de Lima[1024] to serve in it to my satisfaction, as I may expect from his person, and because it pleases me to bestow a favor on him, it is my wish to do so by appointing him to the said Captaincy. And I enjoin you to send for him immediately, and declare this to him, in addition to telling him to get ready to embark at the earliest opportunity, since it is very necessary (as you will have understood) that a successor to Dom Cristóvão de Melo[1025] be sent out.

112 Letter from the King to the Viceroy of Portugal[1026] (28/08/1606)

ABSTRACT – *The letter deals with the aid to be sent to the castle of Mina with the new captain Dom Duarte de Lima. The viceroy would nominate the captains of the caravels, informing the Council of India.*

In a letter from His Majesty dated the 28th of August '606.
On the first of this month of August, there arrived intelligence from Holland informing that a certain person had come from the castle of São Jorge da Mina to

---

[1021] The precise term for the act of examining an official regarding his conduct in office was *'tomar (a) residência'*—as in this case—or *'tirar (a) residência,'* literally 'to take (the) residence.'
[1022] BAL, Ms, 51-VIII-48, fol. 85; ANTT, CC 3-27-55; cf. MMA vol. 5, doc. 84.
[1023] In Portuguese, *'consulta'*: see Glossary.
[1024] See MMA vol. 5, doc. 85, doc. 105, docs. 116–17, doc. 119, doc. 123, doc. 186, docs. 225–7, and vol. 6, doc. 48.
[1025] See MMA vol. 4, doc. 142; vol. 5, doc. 84, doc. 96, doc. 106, and doc. 109.
[1026] BAL, Ms. 51-VIII-48, fols. 99–100; cf. MMA vol. 5, doc. 84, pp. 216–18.

that[[*sic*]] island, offering to deliver it to the rebels,[1027] provided they sent some ships with armed men,[1028] and that they were determined to send seven or eight ships. And it was furthermore reported that they intended to seize the said castle from an elevation[1029] which dominates it. And though there is no other assurance of this being so, apart from this report, or of this determination on the part of the rebels having been carried out, since it is most advisable to preserve that garrison due to its antiquity and for other reasons regarding my service and the benefit of this[1030] Crown for doing so, and being informed that there are few people in it [[the garrison]], and that it is much in need of things necessary to its protection – as a way of remedying all of this, I have determined to have sent there, as soon as possible, one hundred and fifty soldiers, men fit for service, and among them two or three who have served in Flanders and have much knowledge and experience of the way of making war. And that these people and those who are in the said castle should be sent muskets, pikes and other necessary weapons, and the amount of gunpowder and ammunition which seems fit; and similarly, wine, flour, oil, and the other supplies which are usually sent to that garrison, sufficient to maintain the people who are now going and those who are already there, as well as fabric for clothing. And that some artillery with carriages (if there are any) should be taken, and if it is not possible to take artillery, at least some carriages should go, so as to mount what there is in that fortress (since there is information that, for lack of them, it [[the artillery]] is all lying on the ground), and two or three experienced bombardiers; [[and]] that stone and lime should be taken, in order that, should it seem necessary to build a platform or a bulwark on the aforementioned elevation so as to place guards to protect it from the enemy, it can be done immediately.

And so that this aid may be sent, the necessary caravels should be taken and equipped, and the money which will be needed for all the expenses should be taken from that kept by the treasurers of the customs houses[1031] and from any other revenue.

And even though I have entrusted the fitting out [[of the ships]] to Dom Estêvão de Faro,[1032] I strongly enjoin you to assist him most particularly in everything that may be necessary, so that it can be done as well and quickly as possible.

And since Dom Duarte de Lima, whom I have appointed to the captaincy of that castle,[1033] is[1034] here at present, and given that, despite being in poor health, he is prepared to embark immediately and will depart as soon as possible when he

---

[1027] Reference to the Dutch.
[1028] In Brásio's transcription, '*gente de guerra*,' literally 'people of war.'
[1029] In Brásio's transcription, '*padrasto*': see Glossary.
[1030] In Brásio's transcription, '*dessa*' ('that'), which makes no sense in this context.
[1031] In Brásio's transcription, '*Alfândegas e Consulado*'; see Glossary, under '*consulado.*'
[1032] See MMA vol. 5, doc. 10, docs. 118–19; vol. 6, doc. 48.
[1033] Dom Duarte de Lima was appointed captain by royal writ dated Lisbon, 27-4-1607. See ANTT, *Chancelaria de D. Filipe II*, liv. 23, fols. 15–15v. However, he had been nominated successor to Dom Cristóvão de Melo on April 24 of the previous year.
[1034] In Brásio's transcription, '*se achou*' ('was'), which would make no sense here.

arrives there, I enjoin you to make sure, with this in mind, that in the meantime the equipment of the caravels is taken care of, without wasting any time.

And it is my wish that you should nominate their [[of the ships]] captains, presuming that I trust you to choose such persons that I will consider myself well served by the choice you should make. And you shall communicate this resolution to the Council of India and order it to issue the letters patent for the said Dom Duarte immediately, together with the other documents which those appointed to that captaincy are accustomed to take with them; and that they come with the first [[post(?)]] so that I sign them.

And if the caravels are ready, and with order to depart, before the said Dom Duarte arrives there (since, due to his not being well, this may happen to be the case), you shall have them depart with orders that this aid should be delivered to Dom Cristóvão de Melo, who is in that captaincy, and that they pledge allegiance [[to him]], as if it were owed to the said Dom Duarte.

And you shall have the necessary documents sent to Dom Cristóvão, so that he may understand the reason for ordering this aid, and what he should foresee and secure with it, and what else may seem necessary. And so as to avoid any delay, everything shall be signed by you.

a) Cristóvão Soares

+

[*On the reverse*]: From His Majesty

To the Council of India

113 Letter from the King to the Viceroy of Portugal[1035] (30/11/1606)

ABSTRACT – *King Filipe II orders aid should be sent to the fortress of Mina. That aid should support the building of galiots (single-masted Dutch cargo vessels) and the building of ships.*

In a letter from His Majesty dated the 30th of November 1606.

I have appointed captains for the fortress of Mina and the island of São Tomé, as you will have learned, and ordered that they embark as soon as possible. I enjoin you, should they have not yet [[embarked]], to make most haste, and to inform me of the progress with fitting out the caravels which I have ordered to be sent with aid to Mina. And as regards the galiots to cruise along the coast, it seems to me to be a most advantageous and necessary thing, to be effected with no further delay,

---

[1035] BAL, Ms. 51-VIII-48, fol. 112v; cf. MMA vol. 5, doc. 88.

for which reason I enjoin you to have it discussed in the Council of India, [[so as to determine]] what instructions should be given concerning the building of the said galiots, and whence the money necessary for it could be taken, or whether it would be advisable to have them built by contract. And you shall inform me of the opinion [[of the Council on this matter]] as soon as possible, so that no time should be wasted.

And as for the remainder of what is addressed in this consultation, I shall have a reply sent to you shortly.

a) Cristóvão Soares[1036]

114 Memorandum from Dom Estêvão De Faro to the Viceroy[1037] (1607)

ABSTRACT – *Council of the State member Dom Estêvão de Faro offers the viceroy measures to restore the commerce of Mina the Dutch have taken over. In turn, the viceroy replies.*

+

Since in the discussion held in the Counsel about the matters of Mina Your Lordship showed that you consider it a good service done to His Majesty to grant a license to the subjects and natives [[of the Kingdom?]] to barter and trade freely in the port of Mina and nearby places, under certain conditions and restrictions which were mentioned in the same discussion, I felt myself obliged to offer Your Lordship some further remarks, given that on another occasion I started to talk about this matter and pointed out, as being advantageous to His Majesty's Exchequer, many reasons to apply this license and franchise; and since I have been unable to find a paper which I then wrote, I will here detail those reasons which present circumstances have made more effective.

For some days now (as we know) His Majesty, and his Exchequer, has not been receiving any revenue from Mina, and has been spending and wasting [[money]] on that castle without receiving any benefice in return. And the persistence of the trade and commerce of the Dutch throughout that coast, starting from the sight of that same castle as far as Nkrãn,[1038] which is forty leagues, does not

---

[1036] See MMA vol. 4, doc. 25; vol. 5, doc. 61, doc. 84, doc. 186; vol. 6, doc. 14, doc 48, doc. 75, and doc. 81.

[1037] ANTT, Cx. 19, tomo II E, pp. 235-38; cf. MMA vol. 5, doc. 10, pp. 20–25. The document is undated; its contents and circumstantial evidence for Dom Estêvão de Faro suggest the year is 1607. De Faro was a member of the Council of State for kings Dom Filipe II and Dom Filipe III of Portugal, and it was in this capacity he issued the view recorded in the present document. The Marquis Viceroy is likely Dom Cristóvão de Moura, special favorite (*valido*) and intimate of Filipe I. Estranged from the court of Felipe III of Spain, he received a grant-letter dated 29-1-1600, appointing him as viceroy of Portugal for three years.

[1038] '*Acra*' ('Accra,' in English).

only do away with His Majesty's and his subjects' hopes of ever again obtaining any profit from the commerce of those coasts and seas, but is also, in front of our eyes, making them richer and wealthier with much gold, ivory, civet[1039] and other goods through which they become more powerful every day. And, in addition to this, as in those parts they have ports where they can take their goods and the products and goods of their land, they do not take them to the ports of Portugal and Castile, for which reason there is less movement in His Majesty's custom houses, since they have other places and fairs where, without having to pay duties, and with greater profit, they can sell and trade the said goods of theirs.

For which reason it seems not only useful and profitable, but also necessary, and almost obligatory, for His Majesty to issue the authorization and license which has been proposed, because in the first place it does not diminish or remove any profit from His Majesty's exchequer, since it has none, nor has it received any from Mina for many years, nor is it today in any condition to take part in or make use of that commerce, as it used to in other times.

This said, it seems a most useful remedy for removing the Dutch from the commerce of that coast, and for preventing the great profit and gain they obtain from it, to give free and general license to his subjects, so that they may barter and trade there. Because if there be many sailing there and trading in those ports, the abundance of goods will lower the price of those taken by the Dutch, and the profit being smaller they will not care as much to sail there; and furthermore it is only fair that the gain and profit which they obtain from this commerce in detriment to His Majesty's service should belong to your subjects, which would also be to the greater benefit of your Exchequer and, above all, the great amount of goods and the movement of a large number of merchants will make that coast expand, putting it into a more useful condition for the service of His Majesty, should he want to establish a monopoly and impose restrictions on others regarding this commerce.

And this license and authorization may be beneficial for His Majesty's Exchequer if it be given with the restrictions and conditions which I will detail.

That all those who take or send goods to Mina, and to that coast and its places, should first register them in Lisbon and at the House of Mina, whence the register shall be sent to the officials of His Majesty who reside in its castle; and all goods which arrive there without this having been done shall be lost, and he who takes it shall be punished.

And given the great profit from the trade and commerce in that coast and ports, that they should pay for all goods which are taken there for passing through the custom house or factory which His Majesty shall have established in the said castle of São Jorge, at a rate of forty per cent, by a fair assessment of the same place.

[1039] In the transcription, '*algalea*' ('*algália*'): here, probably, the glandular secretion produced by the civet, which is used in perfumery, and not the civet itself.

That an authorization and license should be given so that all subjects of His Majesty of this Crown may sail to Mina and take there all the goods which they wish, and they shall pay for them the duties mentioned above; and after the duties have been paid in the customs house or factory, they may take the goods with them to any other rivers and ports and sell them there.

As regards gold or civet, that they should not pay on return, whether there or here, any duties, considering the first duty of forty per cent.

That His Majesty may exclude the ivory trade, so that he may establish a monopoly as he finds best for his service.

That His Majesty may establish a monopoly of wine, both from this Kingdom and from abroad, as was done in past times with the contract of João Gomes or in any other way which seems best.

And His Majesty should settle this matter as soon as possible so that he may see its benefits in the damage inflicted on his enemies as well as in the profit of his subjects, and finally in the enlargement of his Exchequer, since it seems that the duties of the goods which are taken there, and the monopolies of ivory and wine, may be used to cover part of today's expenditure, and in future they may be even more relevant. Ours, etc.

Dom Estêvão de Faro[1040]

+

Reply to the above paper by Dom Estêvão de Faro, which I gave to the Marquis the Viceroy.

I have seen the paper concerning the Mina trade which Your Lordship has given me, and although I would agree with its main purpose, which is to open this trade to the subjects, seeing that the present state of this Kingdom and the many duties of His Majesty do not allow the business of commerce to be continued, as was done by the former Kings of this Kingdom, since this requires a great deal of oversight on the part of its owner, without which the ministers are generally careless (which is a general reason to reform other matters which I will not deal with now) – I do not agree, however, with the manner [[of doing it]] that is presented.

Firstly, because it is to be presumed that the coast of Mina, which is 200 leagues and many more long, is at both ends occupied by Dutch enemies with their factories, [[and that they are]] well settled on sea with their *naus* armed with cannon, as a result of which they all profit from that trade, without leaving any worthwhile river outside their control. And if His Majesty should open this trade today to his subjects, there would be not one who would be willing to go there, because he would go not to trade but to conquer. And this is well proven by the fact that, though the trade of the coast of Guinea, where there are very profitable goods, has been contracted, and though the contractor entreats and offers good deals to the merchants, there is no one willing to go there, merely because they know the danger which they incur with the pirates who control all that coast and its commerce.

[1040] See MMA vol. 5, doc. 84.

Therefore, before His Majesty takes any decision concerning the Mina trade, he shall have to clean that coast from pirates; and when that happens, and His Majesty controls the trade*s*, which he now does not, then may he decide about the trade in the manner which should seem best to him.

Nor do I agree with the conditions pointed out in this paper as regards establishing a monopoly of ivory, because this is the principal good on which the wealth [[of the subjects]] of this Kingdom will be spent, nor with a monopoly of wine, for no kind of trading is fitting for His Majesty.

As concerns duties I say nothing for now, as those which are proposed seem to me to be too high, and I am of opinion that duties should never be such that subjects may find that the advantages of avoiding them are greater than the danger which they incur by doing so, but rather that they should be such that they [[the subjects]] be glad to pay them instead of risking the loss of their property.

And the reason which is offered in this paper to argue that the Dutch will abandon this trade when they see that our people are going there and the land is being filled with goods, thus lowering the price of their own goods, is neither sufficient nor certain, but rather very doubtful, because the Dutch pay less in their own land for the goods which they take than we do, and they counterfeit them so that they pay less for them, and they also fit out the ships for less money than we do, and thus they can better maintain the trade even though it be with less profit, and therefore we will be the first to give up, and this is a matter which raises no doubts.

Therefore it is my opinion that, before making the coast its own, His Majesty should have it cleared of pirates, as I have said, and then he shall order as may seem more advantageous to trade, and this is necessary not only for Mina, but for all the coast of Guinea, from Arguin up to Angola, which is one thousand and seventy leagues of coast, since today all of it is in the hands of the enemy, and they have been profiting from it for many years, with considerable damage to the royal Exchequer and to the subjects' property.

+

Copy of a paper which Dom Estêvão de Faro gave to the Viceroy, and he gave it to me in the end of September.

115 Letter from Dom Cristóvão De Melo to the King[1041] (05/02/1607)

ABSTRACT – *Mina captain to King Filipe II on the state of the fortress of Mina, the struggle against the Dutch pirates, the state of the fortress of Akyem ('Axim'), and the urgent request for aid.*

[1041] AGS, Secretarias Provinciales (Portugal), liv. 1476, fols. 376-377v; cf. MMA vol. 5, doc. 96, pp. 249–51.

+

My Lord,

On the first days of September, I received intelligence that six ships had appeared seventeen leagues upwind from this fortress. I sent a man to reconnoiter them; they arrested him; from the information the black people gave me, I gathered that they were war ships. And though very ill and bedridden, as I still am, I made myself as ready as time, and the many and great needs of this fortress, allowed. I found myself with forty men able to use weapons and gathered some one hundred and thirty native black men. And on the sixth day of the said month they [[the Dutch]] reached shore when it was still night, and they began disembarking immediately, and in the morning, there were nearly six hundred men. And they set out on foot immediately, so that at nine they were a bombard shot [[from the fortress]].

I sent some eighty black men with their hurling weapons and ten shotguns[1042] to stall them [[the Dutch]] while I was gathering the women and the captains of the village[1043] as hostages, together with some livestock and supplies. God was served that these men should handle the Dutch with such good order that, watching it from the bulwarks and seeing that the Dutch were fighting in an elongated pike square,[1044] because the bush did not permit any other form, I sent forty men from among those who remained with me to break them up through the bush, where their flags were, which they did with great fury. And the Dutch were already so tired because of the heat that they [[the forty men]] broke them up in an instant, and those in the vanguard started to back away, and in two hours there was nobody left to pull a weapon. We killed one hundred and seventy of their men, and we sank a launch while embarking with forty-five men, and a *batel*[1045] with twenty-odd men, and a launch loaded with ammunition. And I came through it with thirteen men dead, and twenty-seven seriously wounded, [[and]] many others less seriously. Our Lord was served to give this victory miraculously to Your Highness, and St George to fight visibly.

I remain bedridden and the fortress in such need that cannot be described. I do not know what faults of mine make me deserve to be as neglected and forsaken as I have been for so many years. My Lord, I have been exhausting all my meagre means, and I am in debt and, above all, very ill. May Your Majesty grant me the favor of sending a captain and aid, since, if he does not come soon, he will neither find me nor, even less, the fortress. Because the enemy is numerous, and I am now left with fifteen ships – albeit merchant ships – in front of the fortress, although there is reliable information that at Cape Lopez[1046] there are eight Dutch ships

---

[1042] In Brásio's transcription, '*espjingardas*' ('*espingardas*'), which, unlike rifles, were smoothbore firearms.
[1043] In Brásio's transcription, '*aldea*' ('*aldeia*'): see Glossary.
[1044] In Brásio's transcription, '*esquadraõ perlongado*' ('*esquadrão prolongado*'), a military formation, usually of three aligned squares.
[1045] *Batel*: see Glossary.
[1046] In Portuguese, 'Cabo de Lopo Gonçalves.'

which were heading towards India and had turned back[1047] from the Cape of Good Hope. And it could well be that these will come here.

This man who is called Ambrósio Ferreira came forward and offered to go under water[1048] to São Tomé to ask for help, and from there to the Kingdom with this letter and report for Your Majesty, at his own expense. He is practically going amongst the enemy, since he is sailing on an English patache which made port here,[1049] and I paid him, and bought him gunpowder, and muskets, and harquebuses which he was lacking. He served as second scribe, is a prudent man and a most trustworthy one. And Your Majesty should show him great favor, as he trusts.

The Dutch also left one ship in Akyem, with one patache and two launches, and a hundred or so men to seize the castle. The Factor who is there now, Luís Soares,[1050] [[served]] most honorably, and defended it, and paid many black men at his own expense, and scattered them [[the Dutch]] when [[they]] landed on shore. He deserves to have Your Majesty write a letter to him and then grant him many favors, which will be as he deserves, for he did not have more than eight shotguns in his company, and he has been repairing the castle, which was in ruins, at his own expense.

I could write and tell Your Majesty many other things regarding this matter, but I will only add that for two years now not one thing has been received from Your Majesty in this fortress with which to buy a drop of water, nor has anyone been paid anything. And I have been providing for these wants with my lack of means. May Your Majesty be mindful of me, who have served you for thirty years under arms, with great trouble.

May God keep the Catholic person of Your Majesty.

From Mina, on the 5th of February '607.

Dom Cristóvão de Melo

116 Letter from the King to the Viceroy of Portugal[1051] (31/05/1607)

ABSTRACT – *Departure of the governors of Angola, Mina, and Brazil; aid to be sent to the Guinea Coast against the Dutch 'rebels'; source of the money for the expenses created by said aid discussed, as well as the dilapidated state of the Royal Exchequer.*

[1047] In Brásio's transcription, '*ar[r]ibaraõ*' ('*arribaram*'), past tense of the verb '*arribar*,' which in this case means to make an unscheduled call at a port (although, in other contexts, it may simply mean 'to make port').

[1048] Literal translation of '[...] *a jir por bajxo dagoa*' ('[...] *a ir por baixo de água*').

[1049] In Brásio's transcription, '*a[r]ribou.*' It is possible the meaning here be that the ship made port unexpectedly, turning back from some point; see previous note.

[1050] See MMA vol. 5, doc. 119.

[1051] BAL, Ms. 51-VIII-48, fols. 147–147v; cf. MMA vol. 5, doc. 108, pp. 305–6.

In a letter from His Majesty dated the 31st of May 1607.

I have seen the consultation[1052] of the Council of India about the common pact which the rebel[1053] provinces have now established, in order to pursue with greater strength, the damage they have been inflicting in India and in the conquered territories of Brazil and the Guinea Coast, and I approve of everything which is detailed in the said consultation. And although I understand that the Governors of Angola, Mina and Brazil have already departed, I strongly enjoin and entrust you, should they have not yet done so, to order that their departure should not be delayed, since in those garrisons, in the present state of affairs, their assistance and the aid they bring with them are clearly needed.

And because I greatly desire that all of them be provided for, not only with what is needed for their defense, but also in such a way that they may be able to harm and punish the enemies who attack them, and that, furthermore, all effort be made so that those who infest the Guinea Coast be chased away once and for all and be unable to further their design of perpetuating the commerce and trade which they have started there, and from which it is known that they take the bulk of the money with which they maintain their fleets – all the preventive measures which are mentioned in the said consultation seem to me most appropriate to obviate these assaults and damages. And if my Exchequer were in such a state that ready money could be provided to implement them, I would order so without delay; but because it is in the state you know, and I am forced to attend to other needs no less important, I enjoin you to order the Council of the Treasury[1054] to examine and consider most carefully whence the money necessary for these things might be taken, and whether there is any way of doing so which can be put into effect; and to inform me of its opinion as soon as possible.

And as regards the instruction which the mentioned consultation says should be given to private *navios*[1055] and caravels which sail to the said parts of Brazil and the Guinea Coast, to do so escorted [[by the King's fleet(?)]], on both the outward and return journeys, in order that I may take a decision I enjoin you to have a search made for the law or regulation on this matter that King Dom Sebastião, my cousin, who is with God, ordered to be drawn up, and to send it to me with the first post.

a) João Brandão Soares[1056]

+

[*On the reverse*]: From His Majesty

To the Council of India.

[1052] In Portuguese, '*consulta*': see Glossary.
[1053] Reference to the Dutch.
[1054] In Portuguese, '*Conselho da Fazenda.*'
[1055] *Navio*: a term generally used to signify any kind of large ship.
[1056] See MMA vol. 5, doc. 109.

117 Letter from the King to the Viceroy of Portugal[1057] (31/05/1607)

ABSTRACT – *Governors of São Tomé and Mina; revocation of powers of the Apostolic vice-collector; examination of the Governor João Barbosa; and departure of Dom Duarte de Lima.*

In a letter from His Majesty dated the 31st of May 1607.

I have seen two consultations of the Council of India, which you have sent in the dispatch of the 12th of this month, regarding the governance of both São Tomé and Mina; and, as you will have understood from another letter of mine, I have ordered that a letter should be sent from here to Dom Fernando de Noronha, appointed to the Governorship of São Tomé,[1058] instructing him to go immediately to that town and embark to serve his office. Should he do so, as I expect, one could avert the need – which I feel there is now – of coming to the aid of that island and the inconvenience of Constantino Lobo going first to São Tomé rather than to Mina. Nonetheless, should the departure of the said Dom Fernando be delayed, it will be necessary for the said Constantino Lobo to depart immediately with orders to remove João Barbosa from that governorship and embark him to the Kingdom, and to remain serving in his place until the arrival of the said Dom Fernando or whomever I wish, as is also explained in the said letter.

And as regards the Governor of Mina because the aid to that garrison depends so greatly on Dom Duarte de Lima taking it there, I enjoin you to send for him immediately and to tell him on my part that I will consider myself well served if he should embark as soon as possible to take up his office. And so that shipping may be arranged, I am writing a letter to the Count of Sabugosa which will go with these dispatches, in accordance with what you have told me about this matter, which you have discussed with him, and you shall have him receive the letter and proceed to execute it immediately, in order to save as much time as possible. And should Dom Fernando de Noronha depart to São Tomé immediately, Constantino Lobo shall embark with Dom Duarte de Lima to examine[1059] Dom Cristóvão de Melo, and from there, after this has been done, he shall go to São Tomé. And should Dom Fernando not depart immediately, then the said Constantino Lobo shall go first to São Tomé and, after having been given letters patent here charging him with that governorship, he will go on to Mina.

In view of the information about the conduct of João Barbosa, it is advisable not to delay assistance to that garrison any further, and it would be worse not to

---

[1057] BAL, Ms 51-VIII-48, fols. 149-149v; cf. MMA vol. 5, doc. 109, pp. 307–9.

[1058] Dom Fernando de Noronha was appointed by royal writ only on 8-1-1608. Cf. ANTT, *Chancelaria de D. Filipe II*, liv. 20, fol. 37v.

[1059] The precise term for the act of examining an official regarding his conduct in office was, as in this case, '*tirar (a) residência*,' literally 'to take (the) residence,' roughly equivalent to present-day 'debriefing.'

do so than for Constantino Lobo to go from São Tomé to Mina. And since in the actual state of both these fortresses any delay will cause great damage, as you will have understood, I hope that accordingly you will endeavor that there be none, despite any difficulties which might present themselves.

And as regards the powers of Vice-Collector which the Dean of the Cathedral of São Tomé possesses, you will have seen from the said letter what I order on this matter, and I once more enjoin you to use your best offices in making the Collector[1060] revoke the said powers. And you shall on my part enjoin the Bishop of that island to order the Dean, his brother,[1061] while João Barbosa is being examined, to remain five or six leagues outside the town, according to what was indicated by the Council of India, which is necessary for carrying out this measure properly. And you shall inform me of all that is done regarding this matter.

a) João Brandão Soares[1062]

[*On the reverse*]: From His Majesty

To the Council of India.

118 Ecclesiastical Administrator of Mina[1063] (09/07/1607)

ABSTRACT – *In view of the high cost of living and the commercial decay of Mina, the royal stipend paid to the vicar of Mina is raised by 40,000 reais. In the vicar's petition for a raise, he provides some details of the Dutch commercial presence and liaison with local communities.*

+

My Lord,

The Vicar and Administrator of São Jorge da Mina, Pedro Álvares de Fontes,[1064] has presented a petition to Your Majesty in this Council, saying that he has an income of only one hundred and ten thousand *reais* for the said administration. Given the letters patent he has been able to find, and given that there the cost of living is very high and the income low, and that for some years they have not been receiving goods from the Kingdom, as the Dutch have almost completely taken control of trade and commerce with the gentiles,[1065] and since in those parts one suffers many tribulations and the bulk of them falls on the petitioner,

---

[1060] Fabrizio Caracciolo, Neapolitan, referendary, acted as collector in Portugal from 22 December 1604 to 30 January 1609. Cf. Henry Biaudet, *Les nonciatures apostoliques permanentes jusqu'en 1648* (Helsinki: Suomalainen Tiedeakatemia, 1910), 259.
[1061] Reference to Pedro Fernandes Barbosa. See MMA vol. 5, doc. 127.
[1062] See MMA vol. 5, doc. 108.
[1063] AGS, Secretarias Provinciales (Portugal), liv. 1476, fol. 354; cf. MMA vol. 5, doc. 111, pp. 316–17.
[1064] See MMA vol. 5, doc. 72, doc. 118, doc. 120; vol 15, doc. 149.
[1065] By 'gentiles,' the vicar means the indigenes or local, non-Christian communities.

as Administrator, and thus it is right that he should have enough to provide himself with – he begs Your Majesty to have his share of the said Vicariate and Administration raised, as you did with all other overseas territories, considering what he has alleged, and that the Vicariate has not been raised for many years, and that the Administration of Rio de Janeiro will be raised once more, even though its income, and its profit and gains, are greater than those of Mina.

And [[he also says]] that Your Highness has granted the said Administrator, when he left from this Kingdom to Rio de Janeiro, a single payment of one hundred *cruzados* for his shipping, and that he should receive his salary starting on the day of his departure from this Kingdom, among other favors. And that he, the petitioner, is going to a very sickly country and offers himself to go there to serve Your Majesty, putting his life at risk, for which he deserves ample favors.

This [[petition]] having been seen in this Council, together with the certificates which he has presented of what was given to the Administrator of Rio de Janeiro, as well as to his predecessor, the former Vicar of Mina, it is [[our]] opinion that Your Majesty should grant him a raise of forty thousand *reais*, in addition to the one hundred and ten thousand *reais* which he receives as stipend, so that altogether he should receive one hundred and fifty thousand *reais* per year, considering what he has alleged and that that vicariate has not yet been raised.

In Lisbon, on the ninth of July 1607.

And that he should receive his stipend starting from the day he shall leave this city, provided Your Highness consider it to be in your service.

And the Count of Santa Cruz did not sign because he was not present at the vote.

[Four initialed signatures of the Councilors]

119 Regulations of the Vicar of Mina[1066] (04/08/1607)

ABSTRACT – *Detailed regulation of the communal and apostolic life of the clergymen at São Jorge da Mina. Only relevant excerpts, which cover Portuguese relations with local communities, especially the village of Adena, are included here.*

I, the King, as Governor, etc., make known to those who may see this writ of mine that it is my wish and pleasure that the Vicar who now serves, and those who will serve in future, the office of Vicar of the church of São Jorge da Mina should use and serve the said office according to the way and manner stipulated in these regulations of mine. […]

[1066] ANTT, Chancelaria da Ordem de Cristo, liv. 17, fols. 254–257v; cf. MMA vol. 5, doc. 114, pp. 321–27. In book nine of the same chancery, fols. 341–343, a similar document was registered, dated Lisbon, 25-1-1611, and written by Manuel do Rego, the secretary being António Viles de Cima.

The said Treasurer shall be obliged, every Sunday and holy days, at least an hour before vespers, to hold doctrine classes[1067] and teach it to the children who have been made Christians and to the children of the inhabitants of the village;[1068] and the Vicar shall teach doctrine to the catechumens and, should he see that the adults who have already been baptized need to attend and continue with the said doctrine classes, he shall admonish and compel them to be present at the said doctrine classes. And whenever he is not able to hold the classes himself, he shall entrust them to one of the chaplains who knows how to do it well, and he shall always take special care in this matter, since this is the most important part of his office and necessary for the good instruction both of the baptized and of the catechumens.

The said Vicar shall admonish and, if necessary, compel – as he can do by virtue of his office – those inhabitants of the village who are Christians to come to mass and be present at the divine offices at those times [[of the year]] when they are obliged to do so. And furthermore, he shall tell them of their obligation to confess and receive the Holy Sacrament at least on the four main feasts of the year, in addition to Easter, when it is obligatory, as has been ordained by the Church.

And he shall further enjoin them, should they or any other person in their house who may be in their care fall sick or be in such condition that they are unable to go to church in person, to inform him, the Vicar, diligently, so that the sacraments – *scilicet*, Confession, Communion and Extreme Unction – may be administered to them in time, taking great care to advise them that, should a Christian who may be in their care die without receiving any one of the said sacraments, as they are obliged to do, proceedings shall be taken against them, according to law and the obligation of his, the Vicar's, office. And he shall issue them the same reminder as regards sons or daughters who may be born to them, that they take care to bring them to church within eight days, so that they may be baptized as ordained by the Holy Mother Church.

If the said Vicar is asked by Christian inhabitants of the said village to go to administer any of the said sacraments to a sick person, because this person is unable to go to the said church to receive them, he shall go and do so in person. And if he cannot do so or is absent, the obligation shall be fulfilled by one of the chaplains, who shall be entrusted with it by him or whose office entails it, and who shall discharge it subject to the penalties which the said Vicar may decide. And so that they may perform the said office, no obstacle shall be put in their way by the captains of the fortress, but rather they shall favor and aid them with the necessary protection.

The said Vicar shall strongly endeavor that the residents[1069] from various parts who go to the said fortress to trade be informed of the matters of our Holy Faith and listen to them, [[the Vicar]] presenting them distinctly [[and]] with as much love and simplicity as can be; and so that it be known that he does not hold other

---

[1067] In the document, '*fazer doutrina*,' literally 'to make doctrine.'

[1068] In Brásio's transcription, '*aldea*' ('*aldeia*'): see Glossary.

[1069] As, further down, the reference is to '*mercador*'; it is possible this should read '*mercadores*' ('merchants') and not '*moradores*' ('residents').

conversations with them about temporal matters, he shall do so publicly. And should any of them, moved by the Holy Spirit, after being sufficiently instructed in the matters which all adults should know before being baptized, ask for the Holy Baptism, he shall administer it to him. And should he, after having been baptized, wish to return to his homeland, the Vicar shall take great care to warn him of the danger in which he places his salvation by living in a place where he cannot receive the sacraments or attend mass and the divine offices, and discharge all other obligations as a Christian; and he shall try hard to persuade him to move his house to the village, where he can be taught and comforted. And yet, in spite of these reasons, should the said merchant wish to return, he [[the Vicar]] shall entreat him to remain thus for a few more days so that he may depart better instructed in the matters of our Holy Faith, and he shall impart to him an instruction and way of life which he should keep while he is away from the said fortress. Furthermore, through the interpreters in the village, he shall tell him the Articles of Faith and common prayers of the Christians, and the precepts, and commandments, and other obligations of the Christians, strongly urging him, both during the journey and in his homeland, to endeavor to proclaim the name of Christ Our Redeemer and the matters of our Holy Catholic Faith in particular; and declaring to him, as regards his wife, if he has one, that he may not have her as his wife should she hinder our Holy Faith or do anything in contempt or scorn for it; and, if he is a bachelor, he shall declare to him that he may not marry a woman who is not a Christian. [...]

The said Vicar shall serve the office of Administrator of the Ecclesiastical Jurisdiction and visit the town of São Jorge da Mina and [the] village and settlement of Akyem at least once a year and whenever he thinks it necessary to do so, and he shall carry it out according to law. And should he discover offenses which pertain to the Holy Office of the Inquisition, he shall remit them to the inquisitors of the city of Lisbon, together with the accused, should he think it necessary to put them in prison; and if there appears to be no danger in waiting for the reply of the inquisitors, he shall send only the accusations, closed and sealed, and well-guarded. [...]

Jerónimo da Costa made this in Lisbon, the fourth of August one thousand six hundred and seven, and I, the secretary Pedro da Costa, had it written down.

Registered by me   Gomes de Azevedo[1070]

120 Letter from the Bishop Viceroy to King Filipe II[1071] (11/08/1607)

ABSTRACT – *The Bishop Viceroy acknowledges receipt of the letter from the Governor of Mina and its contents. He asks the king to send immediate aid, Dom Duarte de Lima, and ships.*

[1070] See MMA vol. 6, doc. 1.
[1071] AGS, Secretarias Provinciales (Portugal), liv. 1476, fol. 371; cf. MMA vol. 5, doc. 116, pp. 329–30.

+

My Lord,

Dom Cristóvão de Melo, Captain and Governor of Mina, wrote the enclosed letter,[1072] in which he gives information (of which Your Majesty will obtain confirmation according to the letter) about the state of that fortress, and of the rebels from Holland who went there and still remain on that coast. And since it is advisable to remedy these matters given their importance (as may be considered), Your Highness should be pleased to order that Dom Duarte de Lima[1073] (who was appointed Captain of this fortress by Your Majesty) be sent from that Court as soon as possible, so that he may embark immediately to it [[the fortress]], and that, in addition, some ships be equipped, so as to escort him to expel the rebels from those parts; and it is also most advisable to send the galiots, to cruise along that coast. And for all this Your Highness should be pleased to send a money order with which to pursue these matters with the required haste, as I have sometimes written to Your Majesty, who shall order as may seem best.

May God keep the Catholic person of Your Majesty.

In Lisbon, on the 11th of August 1607.

a) The Bishop Dom Pedro

121 Aid to São Jorge Da Mina[1074] (15/08/1607)

ABSTRACT – *Due to the critical situation of São Jorge da Mina, on account of Dutch attacks on the fortress, the king orders the departure of two caravels with supplies and the new governor. The king also appointed experienced persons to command them.*

In a letter from His Majesty dated the 15th of August 1607.

In the letter from Alexandre de Moura (which deals with the information he received of the arrival in Angola of the two ships which are expected from India and of the caravel which is coming from Malacca) it is said that, through the same means whereby he knew this, he was also informed [that] twenty-five rebel ships were besieging the castle of São Jorge da Mina, and that they were pressing it very closely. And although it is doubtful that at this time they should have gone in such numbers to those parts, since, however, at any time they cannot fail to

---

[1072] The Bishop Viceroy is referring to a document dated the 5-2-1607. Dom Cristóvão de Melo was appointed captain of Mina by royal writ dated the 14-1-1597. See ANTT, *Chancelaria de D. Filipe I,* liv. 31, fol. 158.
[1073] The royal writ appointing Dom Duarte de Lima is dated Lisbon, 27-4-1607. Cf. ANTT, *Chancelaria de D. Filipe II,* liv. 23, fols. 15–15v.
[1074] AHU, Cód. 283, fol. 55; BAL, Ms. 51-VIII-48, fol. 165; MMA vol. 5, doc. 117, pp. 331–22.

put that garrison under great pressure, considering the great lack of supplies that there must be, given the long time that has passed without their being sent to them, and since it is therefore advisable, as you will have understood, that the two caravels which I have ordered to be equipped should depart without delay, so that supplies be sent there, and that they take Dom Duarte de Lima,[1075] [[who has been]] appointed to that governorship – I strongly enjoin and entrust you to order it and have it effectively thus carried out.

And since the said Dom Duarte remains sick here and might not be able to arrive there as rapidly as required for the departure of the said caravels, in this case you shall, with an opinion issued by the Council of India, appoint experienced persons as their captains, who one may trust will make this journey as soon as possible and succeed in delivering to that castle the people and supplies which they take. And I trust that you will execute this diligently, so that there be no difficulties which may hinder or delay it, and you shall inform me that it has been done so.

a) João Brandão Soares

[*On the reverse*]: From His Majesty

to His Lordship the Count of Sabugal[1076]

122 Consultation of the Council of Portugal[1077] (18/08/1607)

ABSTRACT – *Examination of the problem of aid for the fortress of Mina, including Portuguese military success against the Dutch but not without local African support in arms. The king considered the councilors' proposal and opinion of the council, and he agreed with the latter.*

+

My Lord,

Thursday[1078] evening, the 16th of this month, the enclosed letter from the Viceroy[1079] was received, together with that from Dom Cristóvão de Melo, Governor of the fortress of São Jorge da Mina, which it acknowledges, in which he relates the success he obtained against nearly six hundred Dutchmen, who disembarked on land from six ships (in which they made port there) to seize the said fortress, and

---

[1075] See MMA vol. 5, doc. 78, doc. 84, doc. 109, doc. 116, doc. 119, doc. 123, doc. 186, doc. 226–27.
[1076] See MMA vol. 5, doc. 126.
[1077] AGS, Secretarias Provinciales (Portugal), liv. 1476, fols. 372–375v; cf. MMA vol. 5, doc. 119, pp. 335–40.
[1078] Written in Castilian (*'jueves'*).
[1079] Cf. document dated 11-8-1607.

how, finding himself with only forty Portuguese men who could bear arms and one hundred and thirty native black men, he crushed them and made them retreat, with the death of two hundred and forty-odd [[men]], one hundred and eighty of which died on land and the remainder while embarking, and with the loss of two launches, one of them loaded with ammunition, and one [[ship's]] boat which he sank; and he informs of the success that the Factor Luís Soares[1080] also obtained against other Dutchmen, in the castle of Akyem, where he was attacked by them – all of which is referred in more detail in the copy of the said letter, which is enclosed and translated into Castilian.

Together with this letter and that of the Viceroy, a consultation[1081] of the Council of India was examined, in which it is said that, through a letter from the master of a caravel which was heading towards São Tomé and was seized by two Dutch ships, it was learned that they were cruising the coast of Guinea split up into thirteen ships, and that they showed those of the said caravel a great quantity of gold and ivory which they had traded and writings of *ladino* black men[1082] from Mina about the friendship which they had established with them, and they told them that the fortress had no provisions, since these had not been sent there for two years, and that there were only thirty men and the injured Captain.

In view of the above, and of the great damage caused to Your Majesty's and your subject's property by these rebels remaining on that coast, it is this Council's opinion that Your Majesty should have them expelled from there, sending for that purpose three or four well-armed ships, which will be sufficient to do so since this enemy is divided; and that they should go escorted by the said four galiots that Your Majesty has ordered to guard the said coast; and that the departure of the new Governor, with the necessary provisions for the fortress, should be hastened.

The Viceroy is of the same opinion (in the enclosed letter, with which he sent that of the said Dom Cristóvão), recommending that for all this it is most convenient that Your Majesty should order that the necessary money be effectively provided and that Dom Duarte de Lima (who is now here), who has been appointed to that governorship, should embark immediately.

All which has been said having been seen and considered, the opinion [[of the Council]] was (as regards Dom Cristóvão de Melo) that, since he is in the state of necessity that is known, because much time had passed without provisions or men having been sent to him, and is in such need of everything, and of health, as he himself recalls, much to be esteemed and thanked is his willful resolve in resisting these enemies who had disembarked, surrounding them and, what is more, crushing them and making them retreat, with the death of so many [[of them]] and the loss of vessels. And thus it is the opinion of Francisco Nogueira,

---

[1080] See MMA vol. 5, doc. 96.

[1081] In Portuguese, '*consulta*': see Glossary.

[1082] Though in Brásio's transcription a footnote was added explaining '*ladino*' means 'astute, cunning, malicious,' it should be noted the term '*ladino*,' when opposed to '*boçal*,' refers to enslaved persons (or 'black men') who have assimilated elements of Portuguese culture and language.

Diogo da Fonseca, Afonso Furtado de Mendonça,[1083] Henrique de Sousa, Dom Estêvão de Faro[1084] and the Count of Ficalho[1085] that Your Majesty should order that this most particular service be kept in mind, so that, when Dom Cristóvão makes his request for favor, he may receive, in view of it, as much favor and advantage as possible; and that, for now, he should be thanked through a letter from Your Majesty for what he has done, and informed that his successor has already been appointed, as he has insistently requested.

The Count of Salinas[1086] is of the opinion that the conduct of the said Dom Cristóvão in this occasion, and the difficulties he overcame, and the resolve which he displayed, and his great merit in all this, make it necessary to grant him a favor immediately, and that therefore Your Majesty should grant him one of the vacant *comendas*,[1087] or something else, so that a message about it be sent in the caravels which are ready to depart, mindful as you will also be that this will be a matter of example and consequence for others, who serve in similar garrisons, to be encouraged in these times (when they are so infested by rebels) to do the same, and that the contrary could contribute to discouraging them; in addition to it being just that, the reward for present services, of a quality such as this one of the said Dom Cristóvão, should not be held over into the future.

And as regards what he writes about what the Factor Luís Soares did in defense of the castle of Akyem, it was the opinion of all that the acknowledgement of this should be written in a letter from Your Majesty to the said Luís Soares, so that on another occasion he may be pleased to do the same. And letters in accordance with what was said were immediately written to him and to the said Cristóvão de Melo, and they were sent to be signed by Your Majesty, so that they might go by the said caravels, since through them they will learn that Your Majesty has been informed of what they [[Luís Soares and Cristóvão de Melo]] have done.

And as regards the state of the fortress of Mina, and the persistence with which the rebels frequent that coast, the Council has in various consultations been representing to Your Majesty the importance for your royal service and the benefit of your Exchequer, and for the remedy of your subjects, to have this commerce return to its previous state, when great gains were made from it in the trade of gold, ivory, amber and other things which can be found on that coast, and to prevent the enemy from profiting from all this (as they do), taking from there a great part of the wealth with which they maintain themselves and carry out so many new exploits; and that, if this is not remedied once and for all, the damage will later become irreparable, especially since the rebels have now even attacked that fortress and that of Akyem (from which it may be deduced that they plan to settle and continue there), and because it is to be believed that, in spite of the success

[1083] See MMA vol. 5, doc. 61, and doc. 116 for an identical surname.
[1084] See MMA vol. 5, doc. 10, doc. 84, doc. 118; vol. 6, doc. 48.
[1085] See MMA vol. 5, doc. 118.
[1086] See MMA vol. 5, doc. 118.
[1087] *Comenda(s)*: see Glossary.

they have obtained (as they know about the scarcity of provisions and men in those fortresses, and they already have more information about the land and whence the damage was inflicted on them), they will return there with the same purpose.

And although Your Majesty has ordered that, so as to remedy this, all that is necessary be effectively provided, and although it has always been considered to be of great importance to send some well-armed ships to that coast to cleanse it of this enemy, nevertheless, for lack of money, none of this has been done until now, nor have the galiots been sent that Your Majesty has ordered to guard the said coast. Therefore, the Council having now been informed that, through the *Junta de Fazenda*,[1088] the necessary for the said galiots has been provided, it was considered that, in order to obtain with them what is intended, Your Majesty should be pleased to further order everything that is needed to also send some ships together [[with the galiots]] because, once the enemy have been definitively expelled with their help, and the ports of that coast which shelter them have been punished, the galiots will then be able to guard it better.

And [[the Council]] dealing with the number and the fitting out of the said ships, and considering the difficulties which may arise in this matter for lack of money, Dom Estêvão de Faro proposed that it would be a quicker and inexpensive remedy for Your Majesty to order Dom Luís Fajardo,[1089] while retiring[1090] during the entire month of October, to separate five or six ships of his fleet which may seem to him more suited and, providing them with the food supplies which may remain from the others, to send them from the latitude which should be more convenient for the navigation of that coast, with the purpose mentioned above, which will be achieved without these ships being missed in the fleet, since they will sail when it retires. And it is advisable that this be done at sea and that for these secret instructions be immediately sent to Dom Luís because, on reaching land, the soldiers and seamen will disembark and after that there will be no way of embarking them again on the ships. And because the [[ships]] which will go might need some repair (which will not be much, given that they took to sea so recently) and of more provisions, he recalls that, for all this, the necessary [[material and provisions]] can be sent by sea.

The opinion of the remaining [[Councilors]] is that if this could be carried out it would be the most convenient thing to do, but that they see difficulties, given that the ships of the fleet, whenever they retire, are damaged and in need of repair, and, if this is not done, the workmen[1091] and seamen will raise objections and refuse to start a new journey; and similarly the food supplies and other provisions which they take cannot fail to be needed by the fleet, just as there will be no lack of occasions to prevent their being sent from Lisbon on time. Therefore, they consider this remedy doubtful, and it appears to them that, if the difficulties in fitting

---

[1088] *Junta de Fazenda*: literally, 'Board of the Exchequer.'

[1089] Portuguese for 'Don Luis Fajardo.' See MMA vol. 5, doc. 123; vol. 6, doc. 41 and doc. 49.

[1090] In Brásio's transcription, '*recolhendosse*' ('*recolhendo-se*'): reference to the period during which ships stay anchored in the port.

[1091] In Brásio's transcription, '*offiçiais*' ('*oficiais*'): skilled workmen rather than laborers.

out these ships from any others which may be at the bar of Lisbon could be overcome, that would be most convenient for the service of Your Majesty in attending to such an important business.

And Henrique de Sousa adds that, should this not be judged appropriate, Dom Jorge de Mascarenhas,[1092] with the men from his *tercio*[1093] with whom he serves in the fleet, could be sent for this purpose, orders being given that, before entering Lisbon, he should make sure that the men do not disembark, and that the necessary provisions be ready for him so that they may be loaded immediately onto the ships and that these may return without delay.

And since Dom Estêvão de Faro mentioned that, before leaving Lisbon, he sent a caravel with provisions to Mina (which, considering the success which Dom Cristóvão obtained, and the state in which he was left, should reach him in good time), it seems that with these, and those which are now being sent to him in two caravels, he may repair the damage and hold out until additional aid is sent.

In Madrid, on the 18th of August 1607.

[Six initialed signatures]

[Decision[1094] *in the margin]*: I was pleased to hear of this, and thanks and whatever seems fit should immediately be sent by letter to Don Cristóbal de Melo,[1095] and the Council should consult me as regards the favor which ought to be granted to him. The two caravels should immediately be sent with food supplies and provisions, in addition to those which were sent to him before. And a letter should be written to the Viceroy telling him to have it checked, and to inform immediately about the ships which may be taken from those which there are in that river, to be sent to cleanse the coast of Mina, and how much the journey will cost, and whence the supplies can come, for then, considering this information and the state of the fleet, a decision may be taken.[1096]

[Initialed signature of the King]

123 Consultation to the Council of Portugal Concerning the Castle of Mina[1097] (08/10/1607)

ABSTRACT – *The captain informs the king about the deplorable state of the fortress, how he resisted the Dutch, and the urgent need for aid. The Council of State and the king provide their view of the situation.*

[1092] See MMA vo. 5, doc. 123.
[1093] From the Castilian; in Portuguese, '*terço*,' a type of military administrative unit.
[1094] In Portuguese, '*despacho*': see Glossary.
[1095] Castilian for 'Dom Cristóvão de Melo.'
[1096] This paragraph is written in Castilian.
[1097] AGS, Secretarias Provinciales (Portugal), liv. 1476, fols. 369–370v; cf. MMA vol. 5, doc. 123, pp. 346–49.

+

My Lord,

Through the enclosed consultation[1098] Your Majesty has been informed of the success which Dom Cristóvão de Melo, Governor of Mina, obtained against the Dutch who attacked that garrison. And together with this was represented [[to you]] what he has written[1099] about the danger in which he would find himself should they [[the Dutch]] try to attack it again, since they have seen how badly [[the garrison]] was in need of men, artillery, and ammunition; and that therefore he should be assisted as soon as possible with aid, and that it should be ordered that some galleons be sent there to expel this enemy definitively from that coast and to deprive them of the great gains they obtain there. And Your Majesty replied to what was proposed to you regarding this matter, writing in the margins of the said consultation with your royal hand.

The Viceroy[1100] was informed of this resolution by Your Majesty's letter, and this having been sent to him on the 4th of last month, today, the 5th of October, by the ordinary [[post]] of the 29th of the same month, a consultation arrived from the Council of India dated the 18th of August, sent by him, in which it is reported that the second scribe of the fortress of Mina, sent by the said Dom Cristóvão, had arrived in Lisbon to inform Your Majesty of the success he had obtained there against a Dutch fleet, and of the state of necessity and danger of defeat in which he had been left; and that, even though the said scribe had upon his arrival delivered to the Viceroy the letters which he had brought from the said Dom Cristóvão, and even though he will have informed Your Majesty of this success, nevertheless it was the opinion of the said Council to recall to Your Majesty that during the last four years the only aid sent to that fortress was that which went in a caravel that departed last April, which was not known to have arrived, and that, from what the said Dom Cristóvão informed concerning the ships which remained there, it could be conjectured that this aid might have reached them, and that if it did reach them it would have been so scant that it could have but little effect, and likewise with that which was said to have been sent from São Tomé, since it was of only forty men and because, [[the ship]] having turned back once (as it was learned), the enemy could have tried to seize the said fortress again. And since this is the most renowned of those [[fortresses]] Your Majesty possesses in the Guinea coast, given that it was the first to be founded by the former Kings of Portugal and the great profit which has always been, and still can be, made from it, it is the opinion of the said Council that Your Majesty should order that aid be sent there as soon as possible, and that Dom Duarte de Lima, who has been appointed to that governorship, should embark with enough forces, not only to defend it, but also, if

---

[1098] In Portuguese, '*consulta*': see Glossary.
[1099] Cf. document dated 5-2-1607.
[1100] The Viceroy of Portugal was then Bishop Dom Pedro de Castilho.

needs be, to punish the natives who shelter them [[the enemy]], and that he should take instructions with him regarding what he should do if he finds it occupied by the enemy. The Viceroy says he approves of this recommendation, and that, given that the needs of that fortress cannot withstand any delay in its receiving assistance, should Dom Duarte de Lima not be capable of embarking immediately because of his illness, Your Majesty should be pleased to appoint another person in his place. And he says that, meanwhile, the caravels were being equipped and would depart soon; and that, when Dom Duarte goes, or the person whom Your Majesty appoints, the ships will be armed to punish the rebels, as Your Majesty has ordered.

[[The Viceroy's letter]] having been seen by the Council, and [[it having been noted]] that the Viceroy does not reply to Your Majesty's orders to find out whether there were any ships in the river of Lisbon which might be sent to that coast, nor to the other things mentioned in the reply written by Your Majesty's royal hand, and that, while speaking of ships, he does not mention what Your Majesty has ordered him to do regarding them, nor is it known from any other letter of his that he has done so – it was considered that, this being a matter of such importance and in which any delay might cause great damage, the Viceroy has been very careless in this respect and therefore that Your Majesty should thus admonish him, so that his dissimulation regarding his lack of care in this particular matter does not lead him to do the same in others. And furthermore, the opinion was that the information about the affairs of Mina given through the said consultation having been checked against what the Governor Dom Cristóvão de Melo wrote to Your Majesty, they are one and the same matter, and that this should be stated to Your Majesty so that you know that there was not a second one.

And regarding what ought to be provided for the security of that garrison, given the dire straits in which it was left, and the doubts as to whether the caravel which departed in April had reached it, and, even if she did, whether it had been possible to unload the provisions she took, and given that all this makes it necessary not to waste any more time before sending aid to it [[the garrison]], both to secure it from these enemies and to expel them from that coast – the opinion was that, for now, the two caravels which were being equipped should depart immediately, if they had not already done so; and that, considering that fortress's evident need of aid, and the danger in delaying, and that the said caravels (should [[that fortress]] be besieged by enemy ships) will be unable to drive them out of there or even unload the provisions which they take (even though, with that purpose, the Viceroy was ordered to appoint persons of valor as their captains), and that presently there are no ships ready to depart except those from Dom Luís Fajardo's fleet,[1101] and that this is the most convenient monsoon[1102] to go to that coast – Your Majesty should have it ordered that the said Dom Luís should choose four or

---

[1101] Portuguese for 'Don Luis Fajardo.'
[1102] In Portuguese, '*monção*': see Glossary.

five of the said ships which may seem most fit and send them immediately, and, should he receive this order before entering Lisbon, he should do so before the men disembark, and that Dom Duarte de Lima should go as chief Captain[1103] of these ships, if the lack of health with which he left here so permits; and that Dom Cristóvão should return on [[the said ships]] holding the same post; and that, if Dom Duarte is not able to go, Dom Jorge Mascarenhas[1104] should do so.

And if Your Majesty is agreeable, the opinion [[of the Council]] is also that urgent orders should be sent to the Viceroy to foresee what provisions these ships may need, so that for lack of them they are not prevented from departing immediately and no other obstacles arise afterwards which may impede it [[their departure]]. May Your Majesty order as may seem best for your service.

In Madrid, on the 8th of October '607.

[Seven initialed signatures]

[*Decision*[1105] *in the margin*]: A new letter should be sent to Don Cristóbal de Melo[1106] to thank him, and the departure of his successor should be much hastened; and [[a letter should be sent]] to the Viceroy that he should, as he was ordered, inform about the ships in that river which are most fit for this purpose, except those from the Ocean fleet; and, if Dom Duarte de Lima is not in a condition to go, a letter should be sent to the Viceroy, ordering him to appoint persons.[1107]

[Initialed signature of the King]

124 Letter from Dom José De Melo to the King[1108] (16/10/1607)

ABSTRACT – *Dom José de Melo asks for the creation of the Ecclesiastical Administration of Mina, in the image of Rio de Janeiro, Brazil. In the 1570s, Brazil had also served as the model for the potential (yet aborted) Portuguese colonization of Mina. Strident missionary work amid a commercial fight with the Dutch would seem odd if Portugal was not also a missionary empire.*

By the ordinary [[post]] which left on the 16th of October 1607.

In another dispatch Your Majesty ordered me to ask His Holiness, on your behalf, that he may be pleased to erect and order that, in the district of Mina, an Ecclesiastical Administration be created, in the image of that of Rio de Janeiro and with all the other attributes which were mentioned in the information which I received together [[with the dispatch]]. I drew up a memorandum accordingly and

---

[1103] In Brásio's transcription, '*cabo*,' the person who is the head.
[1104] See MMA vol. 5, doc. 119.
[1105] In Portuguese, '*despacho*': see Glossary.
[1106] Castilian for 'Dom Cristóvão de Melo.'
[1107] This paragraph is written in Castilian.
[1108] Arquivo Cadaval (Muge), Cod. 937, fol. 115v; cf. MMA vol. 5, doc. 125, pp. 351–52.

spoke to His Holiness representing to him the zeal which moved Your Majesty to ask him for this grace, in addition to the reasons which there were to grant it; and although His Holiness replied to me that he would consider everything and would endeavor to satisfy Your Majesty, he referred the affair to the Congregation of the Council, since, as this district of Mina belongs to the Bishopric of São Tomé, and this implies dismembering it, the matter has to be discussed there. And since this is a vacation month, without any meetings of the congregation, as soon as the month is over, I will ensure that a good conclusion is reached. And should this be the case, if I have the money, I will have the petition signed and the bull dispatched.

125 Aid to São Jorge Da Mina[1109] (30/10/1607)

ABSTRACT – *In view of the precarious situation of the castle, the king orders it be provided with 80 soldiers, while the soldiers and residents who are not necessary for the service should return.*

In a letter from His Majesty dated the 30th of October 1607.

I have seen a consultation[1110] of the Council of India concerning certain notes which were written by Ambrósio Ferreira de Araújo,[1111] second scribe of the castle of São Jorge da Mina,[1112] and given that it is advisable that the said castle be better prepared to defend itself should the occasion arrive, it is my wish that it be provided with eighty soldiers on active service, including in this number the residents who have been assigned to it,[1113] who may take and keep only their wives with them in the said castle. And since the state of need in which it has been left makes it necessary to come to its aid, I once more strongly enjoin you to ensure that the aid of the two caravels is sent, as I have ordered, with all possible dispatch (if they have not already departed) and that the necessary soldiers and residents, up to that number, be sent on them, so that those who are not on active service there may return, advising the Captain to inform of what each of them has done during the previous events, in order that I may have them granted the favor which each deserves. And you shall inform me directly[1114] of all that is done regarding this matter.

João Brandão Soares

[*On the reverse*]: From His Majesty
   to His Lordship the Count of Sabugal

[1109] AHU, Cod. 283, fol. 95; cf. MMA vol. 5, doc. 126, pp. 353–54.
[1110] In Portuguese, '*consulta*': see Glossary.
[1111] See MMA vol. 5, doc. 127.
[1112] Dom Cristóvão de Melo described the deed of this man in his letter to the king dated 5-2-1607 (see MMA vol. 5, doc. 96). The 'notes' mentioned here are probably the 'letter and report' which is referred to by the captain of Mina in the aforementioned document.
[1113] In Brásio's transcription, '*ordenados*,' literally, 'ordered' or 'ordained.'
[1114] In Brásio's transcription, '*particularmente*,' which could also mean 'in particular.'

126 Letter from the King to the Council
of India[1115] (30/10/1607)

ABSTRACT – *The king orders repairs to the fortress of Mina as a top priority, in addition to delivering gifts to leaders of the 'black people' who helped the Portuguese against the Dutch. Provision of 80 soldiers on active service seems necessary to the king.*

In a letter from His Majesty dated the 30th of October 1607.

I have seen six consultations of the Council of India: one about a book with the title *Examination of Pilots*, and to this you shall have a reply as soon as the reading of the copy you have sent me has been concluded.

Another which deal with the notes written by Ambrósio Ferreira de Araújo,[1116] second scribe of the castle of São Jorge da Mina. And it is my wish, since that fortress is made of stone and clay and is gradually falling apart, that it be repaired with stone and lime; and that each of the captains of the black people who assisted in the defense be given four pipes of wine and a scarlet[1117] *cabaia*,[1118] as they will thus be encouraged to fight on a similar occasion, should it occur; and, since it is advisable that the said castle be better protected should the occasion arrive, that it be provided with eighty soldiers on active service, including in this number the residents who have been assigned to it,[1119] who may keep only their wives with them in the said castle. And since the state of necessity in which it has been left makes it necessary to come to its aid, I once more strongly enjoin you to ensure that the aid of the two caravels is sent, as I have ordered, with all possible dispatch (if they have not already departed) and that the necessary soldiers and residents, up to that number, be sent on them, so that those who are not on active service there may return, advising the Captain to inform of what each of them has done during the previous events, in order that I may have them granted the favor which each deserves. And you shall inform me directly[1120] of all that is done regarding this matter.

Another about Pedro Fernandes Barbosa,[1121] Dean of the Cathedral of the island of São Tomé.

[1115] BAL, Ms. 5-VIII-48, fol. 175; cf. MMA vol. 5, doc. 127.

[1116] See MMA vol. 5, doc. 126.

[1117] In Portuguese, *escarlata* (from the Persian *scarlat*: red fabric), fine crimson but not as fine as carmine (in Portuguese, '*grã*,' a crimson pigment derived from cochineal insects).

[1118] From the Arabic '*cabaia*.' A kind of tunic, low-cut, closed in front and open at the sides, of mid-leg length, which was originally made from a certain type of light silk called *cabaia*.

[1119] In Brásio's transcription, '*ordenados*,' literally, 'ordered' or 'ordained.'

[1120] In Brásio's transcription, '*particularmente*,' which could also mean 'in particular.'

[1121] See MMA vol. 5, doc. 109.

Another about the religious of the Order of St Dominic, whom the King of Kongo asks for. And to these a reply will be given soon.

+

[*On the reverse*]: From His Majesty
   to the Council of India.

127 The Exploration of the Manso ('Ankobra') River[1122] (1608)

ABSTRACT – *Details of Menda Mota and his son, among others, who ventured into the interior along the Manso River ('Ankobra,' or 'Snake river') in 1573, seeking gold mines of great significance. Mota died before he could submit a report of the journey and its findings.*

In the year of [15]73, together with Martim Afonso, may God forgive him, as I went by order of the Cardinal Henrique [Archbishop of Lisbon, ca. 1564-70; then regent, then king, ca. 1578-80] to the Coast of Mina as Captain-general to discover the Guire mines, going up the Manso River:

The Castle of Akyem is 30 leagues[1123] north of the fortress of Mina, before one reaches the fortress of the said Mina.

It is a castle with 4 metal falcons and a stone mortar also of metal, and 4 *berços*[1124] also of metal, which are supported by large wooden stakes that are fixed in the ground with their iron tritons.

It is a bastion on a knoll, which is beaten by the sea, and from that same bastion starts another one in the direction of the upper village, which is on the south side, and between one and the other there is a big building which serves as Factory.

On the north side, there is another village, the lower one, and both are very close to the said bastion, so that, when there is war, both of them are under artillery fire.

The mouth of the Mansu River, which is a good half a league from the castle of Akyem, is the width of a crossbow shot; only canoes enter through the said bar, because they are vessels made from a single log.

[1122] BA 51-IX-25 ff 69-69v. Cf. Luciano Cordeiro, *Viagens explorações e conquistas dos Portuguezes: Collecção de documentos, 1516-1619* (Lisbon: Imprensa Nacional, 1881), 18–20. In the modern manuscript index of Biblioteca da Ajuda, the document is dated 1608, confirming the date at the end of this document.

[1123] The Portuguese league (*légua*) at this time varied from about 5.5 to 6 meters.

[1124] *Berço*: a small breech-loading cannon, of the same category as the falcon, but of a smaller caliber, probably the equivalent of the falconet.

[The river] is 60 leagues in extent up to Guire Serafee; at several points it is much wider and at others much narrower.

And when the river carries less water, the black people who take the canoe carry it on their backs, in addition to the other load, until they have crossed the dry passage.

The river has plenty of trees which they call *mangues*,[1125] so much so that they hide the sun from those underneath. There are plenty of palm trees, which yield a wine as white as milk; it is very sweet. And there are plenty of mitzeeri (?) trees, citrons and some sugar cane, all of which the land yields without cultivation.

There are plenty of elephants, which come to the river and dive in it and only the tip of the trunk shows; they cover the rest with water because of the flies.

There are plenty of boars, and they kill many of them with rifles, because as soon as one of them falls, the others go to sniff at it with their snouts; the rifleman has only to shoot to bring them down.

There are plenty of monkeys and apes, and brown and blue parrots, plenty of gazelles which look like does, plenty of buffalos which are like wild bulls, and plenty of wild goats.

The sea-tide travels 5 to 6 leagues up the river.

There are many fish throughout the river.

There are plenty of guineafowl,[1126] which are like peacocks in size and taste. They have a blue color.

The Bugio mines are located 8 leagues from the river mouth. They have gold in the flaked stone, but not much.

The Guire Serafee mines, where the King is, are located by the river. They are washing mines and produce gold dust; the gold is fine. Of these, the ones which produce most are 30 leagues inland, in a place called the Big Elephant, where until now no man has been except Mendo Mota, accompanied (*sic*), by command of Martim Afonso, may God forgive him. These are very rich.

15 leagues inland from the castle of Akyem, in a place called Gri, there is gold; and after they had excavated it and discovered gold, a provision by the Cardinal Henrique was shown, whereby He ordered that the mine be closed and no further digging be done, and thus Martim Afonso was immediately ordered to come to the Kingdom.

From the fortress of Mina to Cará it is 4 leagues northwards; it is a city full of people, the greater part of whom make a living with trade. They are not brave people. They put poison in their arrows, which are made of strong cane.

24 leagues inland from there, in a place they call the Aborós, there are mines with much gold, because they were discovered by the dogs of the hunters who were after monkeys. Dom Cristóvão de Melo brought plenty of *caquereos*[1127] born in the land of gold, of very great weight. And he intended to ask His Majesty to

---

[1125] 'Mangroves' in English.
[1126] More precisely, the '*galinha do mato*' is the equivalent of the 'helmeted guineafowl.'
[1127] Obscure meaning.

allow him to produce them, but it all ended with his death at sea, after he had left from São Tomé, the year [1]608.[1128]

Bernardo da Mota, married in Setúbal, has the list of the Guire Serafee mines, with the lands painted and illuminated, which his father, whom they called Menda (*sic*) Mota, left him when he died.

128 Letter from King Filipe II to the Council of India[1129] (11/02/1609)

ABSTRACT – *Arrival of the captain (now governor) Dom Duarte de Lima in Mina. The king orders the money of the deceased be repaid and aid sent to São Jorge da Mina because de Lima 'found the factory lacking in everything.'*

In a letter from His Majesty dated the 11th of February 1609.

Through a consultation[1130] of the Council of India, I learned that Dom Duarte de Lima has arrived in the Castle of Mina, and the rest of what he informs concerning the state of that garrison, and [[what he]] asks for its fortification and maintenance and for restoring that commerce to its former state. And seeing his will to fulfill the duties of that governorship and to justify the confidence I placed in him when I entrusted him with it, I saw fit to thank him with a letter of mine which will be sent in different copies, which you shall order be sent by the first vessels. And since he says that, because he had found the factory lacking in everything, and it was necessary to come to the aid of both the soldiers to whom some payments and allowances were due and the people of the *nau*[1131] Nossa Senhora da Ajuda, he took some money from the deceased; and because for the just considerations for which I forbade that any captain or any other minister of mine should take this money, however much they may need it, this should be observed – the said Dom Duarte shall be advised to pay at once and effectively all the money that he may thus have taken, and a copy of the instruction which I have ordered to be issued (of which the *Mesa da Consciência*[1132] shall be informed) shall be sent to him, so that it be known what is determined by it, and, to the same effect, it shall also be sent to all other overseas governors and captains.

And since it is convenient to attend as soon as possible to everything that Dom Duarte asks for, even though, according to what you say, I am sure that the galiots which he is expecting will set sail together with the *naus* which are now due to depart for India, nevertheless I thought fit to strongly charge and enjoin you (as I do) to

---

[1128] A note added to this document in different handwriting says: 'These mines were discovered ten years ago.'

[1129] BAL, Ms. 51-VIII-48, fol. 239; cf. MMA vol. 5, doc. 186, pp. 500–01.

[1130] In Portuguese, '*consulta*': see Glossary.

[1131] Given the specificity of the references to vessels in this document, the original Portuguese term '*nau*' (the name generally given to a large vessel) will be used in the translation.

[1132] *Mesa da Consciência*: see Glossary.

ensure that it be so, and that they go with provisions according to what he indicates and is necessary for obtaining with them the intended results. And you shall ensure that one or two caravels will go with the said *naus*, with goods to be traded, and the materials and workmen[1133] which he requires for the work on that castle. And you shall inform me whether any of these things were sent in those [[caravels]] which went to get the money of the said *nau*.[1134] And you shall ensure that this will be carried out with the care that is required by the great convenience in keeping that garrison.

a) Cristóvão Soares

+

[*On the reverse*]: From His Majesty
to the Council of India.

129 Dom Duarte De Lima, Captain of Mina[1135] (19/07/1610)

ABSTRACT – *As supplies of lime, bricks, and tiles are slated to go to Mina, a disagreement about the conduct of the Captain de Lima emerges.*

Opinions in a consultation which was made on the 19th of July '610 about a letter written by Dom Duarte de Lima, Captain of Mina.

As regards the Factor, it was considered that the Captain exceeded himself in removing him from office, even if in the audit it was found that he had kept for himself three hundred and fifty thousand *reais*, since he returned them; and that it would have been sufficient to check the balance sheet and make him return the money, which would have been a good thing, for his death, as is reported, ensued from that [[measure]]; and that he [[the Captain]] should be ordered to send the chapter of the authentic regulations which he says gives him the power to remove the factors, as it seems convenient, if it does exist, to amend this passage and, if it does not, the said Dom Duarte should be considered guilty as a result of the examination;[1136] and that, if such chapter does exist, he should not make any use of it until Your Majesty has replied, as regards the passage which says that he may arrest and remove both the Factor and the scribes of the Factory.[1137]

[1133] In Brásio's transcription, '*officiaes*' ('*oficiais*'): skilled workmen rather than laborers.
[1134] Possibly the '*nau*' Nossa Senhora da Ajuda, which has been mentioned above.
[1135] BNM, Ms. 9419, fols. 68-68v; cf. MMA vol. 5, doc. 225, pp. 591–92.
[1136] In Brásio's transcription, '*rezidençia*' ('*residência*'): see Glossary.
[1137] In the margin: In the same letter dated 5-10-1610, His Majesty says the said Dom Duarte does not deserve what is said of him but is rather worthy of praise for his zealous behavior in this matter, and his jurisdiction should not be limited. And that since one of the captains of the galiots is dead, and the other has been sent to this kingdom, they should be appointed anew.

And as regards the captains of the galiots, since one of them is dead and the other has been sent to this Kingdom, it was considered that they should be appointed anew and that the said Dom Duarte should be admonished not to arrest or remove them from office, except in the case of divine or human lese-majesty. Should there be an accusation, however, he should send it authenticated to Your Majesty, so that you may order as you think best, and meanwhile he should not introduce any changes. And regarding the factorship, there should be due warning of when an appointment should be made, at the end of the term of service of the present incumbent, who is a soldier.

2nd: It was the opinion of three of the members,[1138] since experience has shown that it is not possible to find enough clergymen to go to Mina, though edicts have often been posted and other measures taken for that purpose, and since those who did go have disagreements with the governors which give rise to many drawbacks, that Your Majesty should order that four religious of the Order of Christ be sent, as is their obligation, one as Administrator and another two as his companions in Mina, and one other to reside in the Castle of Akyem. And it was the opinion of one member that, if enough clergymen are found, it is they who should be sent rather than friars.

3rd: By the letters from Dom Duarte it can be seen that nothing of this was sent in the caravels which went to get the money of the *nau*, or in the one which has now arrived. It was therefore considered that Your Majesty should be pleased to order that, in any case, all those ships which go to that fortress should take all the limestone, bricks and tiles which they can carry as ballast or wherever possible.

130 Dom Duarte De Lima, Captain of Mina[1139] (19/07/1610)

ABSTRACT – *A Portuguese official hopes the fleet will be equipped and depart for Mina to 'cleanse the seas of Guinea.' Considerations for building a fortress, after thorough examination of the problem, at Nkrãn ('Accra'), given the good relations the Portuguese claim to have with the 'King of Accra.'*

Opinion of a consultation which was made on the 19th of July '610 about a letter from Dom Duarte de Lima

It was the opinion of all, in view of what Dom Duarte writes and the other information which was gathered, that it is most convenient to the service of Your Majesty, and the good of this State and its subjects, that a fleet should be equipped as soon as possible, as Your Majesty has ordered, to go to cruise along the Guinea coast,

---

[1138] In Brásio's transcription, '*Vottos*' ('*votos*'), literally 'votes'; that is, the members (of a council) entitled to vote.

[1139] BNM, Mss. 9419, fols. 68v.-69; cf. MMA vol. 5, doc. 226, pp. 593–95.

starting with the rivers of Cape Verde, which are on the way, and from there to Mina, to cleanse that coast of the ships which may be there; and the galiots will join them there, as Dom Duarte writes, and therefore it is convenient that all the necessary equipment for the galiots be sent to him immediately, according to the lists which he has sent, and that a person of authority and with experience in warfare at sea should sail in the said fleet, who can be expected to perform Your Majesty's service well and to whom it shall be ordered to check or to have checked, after cleansing that coast and expelling the foreigners from there, the place where it is said that a fortress[1140] should be built, and to find out about everything which may be relevant for deciding whether it will be convenient that it be built, and how many people should remain there to defend it, and the cost[1141] of both building the said fortress and maintaining it, and whether it will be profitable or it will be sufficient to have plenty of goods for trading in that of Mina and the coast cleared, so that the gold from Nkrãn[1142] may be traded there, maintaining good relations with its King, captivating him by treating him well since, whether there is a fortress in Nkrãn or not, it seems that it will always be preferable and more convenient to deal with the trade than to possess the mines, given the necessary expense involved, as has been seen in other parts; and that, all the necessary having been done there, he should go with the fleet to the coast of Angola, to Port Pinda,[1143] to drive the foreigners from there and do everything else Your Majesty has ordered. And thus, with only one fleet, three objectives are attained, as through many consultations Your Majesty has had represented to you the convenience of coming to his [[Dom Duarte's]] aid, given the losses suffered by both the royal Exchequer and the subjects of this Crown. And since there are no galleons of this Crown in this river, which would by themselves be sufficient, for they are powerful and strong, it was considered that six ships and two caravels should go in this fleet, as well armed and equipped as possible and with as many men as can be taken in them, so as to provide them to Mina as well as to any other parts where they may be needed.

[*In the margin*]: In a letter dated the 5 October 1610, His [[*sic*]] Majesty says that it is most convenient that this work be carried out immediately, and that, to this effect, a fleet should be assembled which should take all the necessary materials for the building of the fortress and, in addition, for cleansing that port of the Dutch who trade there. While it is being built, because of the interest they will have in this, it is to be believed that they [[the Dutch]] will endeavor to hinder this work which, when finished, and with the aid of the galiots, may keep it [[that port]] free from this enemy without the need to send fleets from the Kingdom, which can never be of much assistance for this purpose, as the expense involved will necessarily be substantive, especially since they cannot go every year and because one can be sure

---

[1140] In Brásio's transcription, '*estaleza,*' which should be read '*fortaleza.*'
[1141] In this point, it seems a conjunction is missing, either in the manuscript or in the transcription: '[...] *e a despeza* [*que*] *se fará* [...].'
[1142] In Brásio's transcription, '*Cará.*'
[1143] Later, Port Alexander and, today, also known as Tombwa.

that, as soon as they return, they [[the Dutch]] will also return to occupy the places from which they had been driven, given the profit they obtain there. Therefore, Your Majesty should order the Viceroy to verify as soon as possible which ships may go in the fleet to the said port, and whether in the river of this city there are any which may be fit for this purpose and, if there be none, whence can one take them for this purpose; and that he should inform of the state of the galleons which were being equipped to go to Malacca, and whether they will be able to go in this journey, together with their names; and that the captains who shall sail in it [[the fleet]], and those he [[the Viceroy(?)]] will appoint, should be persons of valor, experienced in military affairs, and this shall be done in great secrecy, so that it be not known where the said ships which are being equipped are to be sent.

131 Dom Duarte De Lima, Captain of Mina[1144]
(23/07/1610)

ABSTRACT – *On the trial of the imprisoned Dutchmen, but their sentence will not be executed without the king's approval.*

On the Dutchmen which Dom Duarte sent under arrest and the terms of the truce as regards Mina and Guinea
On the 23rd of July '610.

It was the opinion of all, in view of what has been reported in this consultation,[1145] that the said Dutchmen incurred the penalties of Your Majesty's ordinance and instructions, and that, given the notoriety of the case and what has been learnt from the questions which were posed, proceedings should briefly and summarily be taken against them by judges of integrity who have given most satisfaction, who shall try them before the Marquis Viceroy as war general and in the presence of this Council, so that it may be notorious to the estates that Your Majesty has ordered this affair to be carried out with all due consideration, also because it will comprise the determination and establishment of the conditions to be maintained for the duration of the truce; and that the sentence should not be executed without previously informing Your Majesty, so that [[you decide]] what may seem best for your service. And the opinion of one of the members was that this Council may be excused from being present at this sentence and determination, and that, until Your Majesty takes a final decision regarding this matter, orders should be given to the overseas captains to arrest all the Dutchmen who are found in those parts and to seize their property, making an inventory and sending it, and to put the Dutchmen on the galiots, whatever their quality may be.

[1144] BNM, Ms. 9419, fol. 69; cf. MMA vol. 5, doc. 227, pp. 596–97.
[1145] In Portuguese, '*consulta*': see Glossary.

[*In a different hand*]: A copy of this consultation and of the others regarding Mina was sent again to the Marquis Viceroy, at his request, on the 8th of October '610.

132 Journey from Lisbon to Mina[1146] (21/11/1613)

ABSTRACT – *The author indicates the distance in leagues between different ports on the African coast, from Cape Verde to Mina.*

Information from Pilots who are used to go to Mina

Departing from here before the first of December. Cape Verde is at 14 degrees and two thirds, and from here to there is 500 leagues. And from there to the Cacheu River is 60 [[leagues]], and it usually takes from 18 to 20 days to go from this town to there. And anyone wanting to go from there to Mina should steer around the shallows and the Bissagos islands, for which he shall sail 50 leagues out from the coast, avoiding the shallows of Saint Anne; he shall head towards a place at a latitude of six degrees which is called Cape Mount,[1147] and from Cacheu to there is 220 leagues; and should he so desire he can sail along the Malagueta Coast; and, if he has nothing to do there, he should head towards Cape Palms.

From Cape Mount, which is at a latitude of 6 degrees, to Cape Baxas[1148] is 30 leagues. From Cape Baxas to Cape Palms is 54. At this latitude, the waters pull greatly to the shore, and it is necessary to bear this in mind. And at this latitude there are usually many French ships trading with the people who live there. This Cape Palms is at a latitude of 4 degrees north.

From Cape Palms to Akyem is 85 leagues.

From Akyem to Mina is 30 leagues, and if one makes little delay along the coast of Cacheu towards Mina, one can arrive there in 30 days; and this if the ships are few.

From Mina to [[Oguaa ('Cape Coast')]][1149] is three leagues.

From Mori[1150] to Kormantin three leagues.

From Kormantin to *Daio* is 8 leagues.

From *Daio* to Apam[1151] two leagues.

From *Apam* to Winneba[1152] six leagues.

[1146] ANTT, *Miscelânea Manuscrita*, cx. 19, t. 2 E, fols. 281–284; cf. MMA vol. 6, doc. 46, pp 162–3.

[1147] In Brásio's transcription, '*Cabo do Monte.*'

[1148] 'Cape Baixos'; also known as 'Noti Cornu,' 'Southern Horn' or 'Cape Shallows.'

[1149] In Portuguese, '*Cabo Corso.*'

[1150] In Brásio's transcription, 'Boure.'

[1151] In Brásio's transcription, 'Pam.'

[1152] In Brásio's transcription, 'Bianda.' Winneba featured leathermaking, livestock, and a 'slave' market.

From *Winneba* to Bereku[1153] 8 leagues.

From *Bereku* to Nkrãn[1154] eight leagues, which altogether make up 40 leagues from Mina to Nkrãn. And all of this are rivers and bays where one can anchor.

From the Castle of Mina to Port Pinda is 370 leagues, and the true monsoon[1155] is to depart from Mina at the beginning of February. They will see Cape Lopez[1156] and they will sail with land-winds and sea breezes, which arise every day, but if they set sail later the weather will not be so good, but instead very stormy. And on the way, should they wish to do so, they may return to the island of São Tomé.

If they pass Pinda, it will be necessary to take provisions of wine, oil, and vegetables for a year. And if they do not go beyond Mina, six months of provisions will be sufficient. And if they depart from here later than mid-December, it is evident that they will not be able to go beyond Mina.

+

[*On the reverse*]: Copy of a paper which I gave the Bishop Viceroy on the 21st of November '613, regarding the fleet which will go to the Guinea Coast, Mina and Pinda.

133 Aid to the Fortress of Mina[1157] (08/01/1614)

ABSTRACT – *Measures taken to provide military aid to Mina against attacks from Dutch fleets.*

In a letter from His Majesty dated the 8th of January 1614.

I have seen a consultation of the Council of India regarding the news which arrived from Mina about the death of Dom Duarte de Lima and the state in which the fortress was left, which caused me particular displeasure, because the things of the sea are so uncertain that it is possible (may God forbid it) that Pedro da Silva[1158] may have died or not have reached that fortress. And since it is so lacking in everything and the enemy is so close, [[and]] it is [[thus]] very advisable to come to its aid as rapidly as possible, I strongly charge and enjoin you to ensure, as soon as you receive this dispatch, that two ships be equipped with all haste, and that the largest possible quantity of gunpowder and ammunition be sent there, together with some muskets, and other guns, and enough provisions for some months,

---

[1153] In Brásio's transcription, 'Bereca.' Bereku was known for metalworking, livestock, and a fowl market.
[1154] In Brásio's transcription, '*Cará.*'
[1155] In Portuguese, '*monção*': see Glossary.
[1156] In Portuguese, '*Cabo de Lopo Gonçalves.*'
[1157] AHU, Cod. 284, fol. 22; cf. MMA vol. 6, doc. 48, pp 167–8.
[1158] See MMA vol. 6, doc. 40, doc. 75, and doc. 81.

to that effect sending Indian black cloth[1159] and the things which are known to be most used there, and carpenters, blacksmiths and masons for mending and repairing both the fortress and the guns, since it is possible that those which went with Pedro da Silva have not arrived.

And that a person of valor, and trustworthy, and experienced in the matters of those parts should go as commander[1160] of the said ships, so that, should Pedro da Silva have not arrived or have died, he may govern that Captaincy, for which purpose he shall secretly take a writ with his appointment.

A good conclusion of this purpose depends on the rapid execution of all this, [[and]] therefore I again charge you with taking care of [[this matter]], with great attention and diligence, ensuring that the ships depart as soon as they, and the things which are to be taken on them, be ready, without waiting for the Indiamen[1161] or any other company[1162] [[of ships]]; and with informing me of everything that is done, sending, as soon as they have departed,[1163] authentic and very thorough and detailed certificates of the provisions, arms and ammunition taken [[on them]].

[*On the reverse*]: From His Majesty

To His Lordship Dom Estêvão de Faro

a) Cristóvão Soares

134 Letter from the Governor of São Jorge Da Mina[1164] (13/10/1615)

ABSTRACT – *Mina Governor requests urgent and serious assistance be sent to the Mina fortress. Orders are made to send help immediately.*

A paper by the secretary Cristóvão Soares was seen in this Council, which he had sent there on behalf of the Archbishop Viceroy to be seen there together with a letter from Pedro da Silva, Governor of the fortress of São Jorge da Mina, so that it be provided with assistance as soon as possible and a report sent to Your Majesty.

[1159] In Brásio's transcription, '*roupas pretas*,' a specific category of eastern fabrics. See Nigel Tattersfield, *The Forgotten Trade: Comprising the Log of the* Daniel and Henry *of 1700 and Accounts of the Slave Trade from the Minor Ports of England, 1698-1725* (London, Pimlico, 1998), ch. 7.

[1160] In Brásio's transcription, '*cabo*,' the person who is the head.

[1161] In Brásio's transcription, '*naos da Jndia*' ('*naus da Índia*').

[1162] In the sense of 'fleet.' See John Mason Good, *Pantologia: A New Cabinet Cyclopaedia, Comprehending a Complete Series of Essays, Treatises, and Systems [...]*, vol. IV (London: Printed for J. Walker etc., 1819).

[1163] In Brásio's transcription, '*partidas*'; strictly speaking, the word should be '*partidos*,' as it refers to '*navios*' ('ships'). Alternatively, though less probably in this context, as the letter seems to have been originally written in Castilian, the word might refer to the 'certificates' ('*certidões*') and mean 'registered.'

[1164] AHU, Cod. 1192, fols. 139–139v; cf. MMA vol. 6, doc. 75, pp. 227–9.

In which letter the said Governor represents to Your Majesty the said fortress's present great need of both provisions and men, since most of those who were there have died; and that mass has not been said there for a long time, because there is no flour for making holy wafers; and that he sent for some help from the island of São Tomé, together with drugs and concoctions, for he saw the people dying of deprivation, and had a request made to the Governor of the said island for a mason, since those he had taken with him were dead; and [[that]], because of the great earthquakes that have taken place, the bulwark is almost completely in ruins; [[and]] that he has been left there with only twenty-five white men and many [[of them(?)]] sick, and unable to keep watch; [[and that]], the enemy seeing the state [[of the fortress]], they attacked it three times, and God was served that they should retreat with great loss on their side and none on ours; and after that they set fire to the village[1165] twice, with the intent, should the Governor come to its aid and the doors of the fortress be opened, of encountering him.[1166]

And then, with the native black men, he set fire to the enemy village, together with many goods and two large ships. That he has the galiots almost completely repaired, and that they were not finished because the blacksmith and caulker, whom he had also requested from the said island of São Tomé, had died.

That after this he informed Your Majesty, by last year's hulk, of the state of the enemy fortress, and that it used to be built of clay, and today most of it is made of stone and lime; and that presently there remained in the trade of that coast thirty-six enemy ships with goods which they sell, and they take counterfeit black cloth from Flanders, of a better quality than that from India, and thus ours loses all its value.

And the said paper and the abovementioned letter having been seen, the said Council immediately took care that a ship be sent to the said fortress, with goods and provisions, which will depart sometime during the next week; in which [[ship]] will be sent the blacksmith, mason and caulker, with their apprentices, together with a pharmacopoeia, which the Governor requests, and fabrics of the kinds which he indicates in the said letter, a report about which, as ordered by Your Majesty, is not being sent with this [[letter]] because they are now being loaded; once they have been loaded, it will be sent, and further information regarding whatever else may seem relevant [[to the Council]] will be given to Your Majesty.

And [[the Council]] recalls to Your Majesty that you should be pleased to order that an end be put to so considerable a damage as that which Your Majesty's Exchequer suffers from the trading of the Dutch on that coast, before they grow even stronger, because by delay greater damage will be caused, since this is a

---

[1165] In Brásio's transcription, '*aldea*' ('*aldeia*'): see Glossary.
[1166] Tentative translation of '[...] *para da uolta serem com elle*' ('[...] *para da volta serem com ele*').

matter more important than it seems; [[and that you should]] thank the Governor for his conduct during the [[events]] related in this consultation.

[*In the margin*]: In a letter from His Majesty dated the 13ᵗʰ of October '615.

I have seen a consultation of the Council of the Treasury which deals with what Pedro da Silva, Governor of Mina, wrote about the present state of that fortress for lack of men and provisions, and about those who are to be sent now from there [[to the fortress]] in a ship which is about to depart. And I strongly enjoin you to ensure that everything which is needed there be sent in the ship in large quantities, as I have ordered, and that great care be taken over this, without there being any delay. And should she have already departed at the time you receive this letter, you shall have aid sent through the first vessel, together with the other provisions which may seem to be lacking in the said fortress, in order that there should never be any shortage of them there, since it befits my service that it be provided with the necessary things. And that Pedro da Silva be thanked on my part for his good conduct during the events related in the said consultation, which is in accordance with what I always expect from him, with which I consider myself well served.

Cristóvão Soares

135 Aid for São Jorge Da Mina[1167] (October 1615)

ABSTRACT – *In view of the precarious state of the Mina fortress, King Filipe II and the viceroy agreed to send as much aid as possible. While gifts were offered to local rulers, to keep their support on the Portuguese side, soldiers from Portugal refused to enlist for Mina.*

In letters dated the 3ʳᵈ, 6ᵗʰ and 13ᵗʰ of October of the present year, Your Majesty says that the amount of aid and provisions sent to the fortress of São Jorge da Mina should be as large as possible. Your Majesty strongly charged the Viceroy to devote all his efforts to it, while ordering this Council to endeavor to guide him, as this is one of the things of most service for Your Majesty; and that, in addition to the cloth and supplies, to the material which is required to finish the galiots and to have them always equipped, and to the carpenter, caulker and blacksmith to work on them, some men should be sent to meet the need for them in that fortress; and [[that]] of all that is taken by the ship which will depart to [[the fortress]] a report should be sent to Your Majesty, which should be very particular and distinct so that he may be fully informed.

And that the regulations which were issued concerning the commerce of the said fortress should be observed; and that the Provider of the House of India

---

[1167] AHU, Cod. 1192, fols. 167–168; cf. MMA vol. 6, doc. 81, pp. 243–5.

should deal with the men of business [[who]][1168] may desire to come according to the manner stipulated in the said regulations; and that, for their [[the merchants']] protection, instructions should be issued for the Governor of Mina to give them all possible assistance and favor.

And that, should the ship which was to go to that fortress have already departed, aid should be sent to it by the first vessel, with the other provisions which would seem to be lacking in the said fortress, in order that it should never be any lack of them; and that Pedro da Silva should be thanked for his good conduct regarding the affairs of the said fortress.

And in compliance with the said letters, as Your Majesty orders, [[the Council]] replies that, in his letter, Pedro da Silva, Governor of Mina, does not ask for material, but rather for a metalworker,[1169] a blacksmith, and two masons, who will be sent to him on the said ship; and for the neighboring kings of that fortress and friends, four *farragoulos*[1170] of red carmine, six colored hats and another six fascine knifes,[1171] which are those which were being taken by João Roiz Roxo,[1172] who, having been seized in Cadiz,[1173] has returned to this city; and, of different parties[[?]],[1174] the cloths, wine, beads, *laqueca*,[1175] coral, oil, flour, as declared in the two certificates from the Provider and officials of the House of India, which are being sent to Your Majesty with this letter.

And the said Governor was ordered to take all the men he wished, from those who went on the said ship, to serve in the said fortress, leaving those necessary for the protection and navigation of the said ship, since there were no soldiers who wanted to enlist to go to Mina, as it seemed to them that they would remain in the said fortress; and likewise [[he should take]] one of the carpenters and caulkers taken on the said ship, since there were none willing to enlist to stay in that fortress, to serve in the galiots.

And in the March monsoon[1176] of next year, which is the first during which ships will be able to go to that fortress, all other assistance ordered by Your Majesty will be sent there. And as regards observing the regulations, this was put into effect and, accordingly, the merchants loaded [[the goods]] in the manner declared in the abovementioned certificate of the House of India. And thus, will it be done from now on. And the Provider of the said House will be thus charged,

---

[1168] At this point, it seems the relative conjunction '*que*' (translated by 'who') is missing, whether in the manuscript or in Brásio's transcription.

[1169] In Portuguese, '*serralheiro*,' someone who, in addition to being a locksmith, performs similar work with metal.

[1170] *Farragoulo*: a short-sleeved hooded cloak with a mantle appropriate for cold weather.

[1171] In Brásio's transcription, '*treçados*' ('*terçados*'), a short broad sword. See Antonio Luiz M.C. Costa, *Armas Brancas: Lanças, espadas, maças e flechas: Como lutar sem pólvora da pré-história ao século XXI* (São Paulo: Editora Draco, 2015).

[1172] See MMA vol. 6, doc. 49 and doc. 117.

[1173] See MMA vol. 6, doc. 49.

[1174] Tentative translation of '*de partes*,' literally 'of/from parts/parties.'

[1175] *Laqueca*: see Glossary.

[1176] In Portuguese, '*monção*': see Glossary.

as Your Majesty commands. And a letter was sent to the Governor [[instructing him]] to favor the merchants, by giving them all necessary favor and assistance.

In Lisbon, October '615.

Luís da Silva, Luís Pereira, Cosme Rangel,

Simão Soares

[*In the margin*]: In a letter from His Majesty dated the 18th of November '615.

I have seen a consultation[1177] of the Council of the Treasury, complying with everything which I had ordered through the letters of mine which are mentioned there regarding the things which ought to be sent to Mina and the observance of the regulations of its commerce, which is well done and of which I was pleased to learn. And since, because the ship which was sent to that fortress at the expense of my Exchequer was compelled by storms to make port in Vigo and jettisoned the goods that she was carrying, it is convenient to provide it [[the fortress]] with more, I strongly enjoin you to order the said Council to endeavor as much as possible to have this ship sent there again – as it is convenient, given the state in which it [[the fortress]] has been left, to provide for it as rapidly as possible – and to send on her everything needed for that purpose. And you should verify whether, under contract, any other ship might want to go there according to the manner of the regulations, on which whatever else that might be missing in the said fortress could go. And you should inform [[me]] about everything that is done regarding this matter.

Cristóvão Soares

136　Memorandum Concerning São Jorge Da Mina[1178] (1616?)

ABSTRACT – *The author argues for the value of Mina to Portugal, outlines the problems the Dutch presents, 'as though they were masters of that conquest' of Mina, and details a plan to recapture the Mina (Gold) Coast and its gold trade from the Dutch. The document is published for the first time.*

1. Portugal's Mina has always received greater attention from the kings of this Kingdom than any other of their overseas conquests, given that it yielded so much and in view of the income derived from it, without the expenses and the risk of other conquests. And before India was discovered, this was the only [conquest] to cater for the huge costs and expenses made by the previous kings in both war and peace, all ships being sent to fetch that much celebrated chest which was called 'the chest of Mina', with five hundred to six hundred

---

[1177] In Portuguese, '*consulta*': see Glossary.

[1178] Biblioteca da Ajuda, 51-IX-25, fols. 21–22v. The manuscript has an uncertain date ('16..'), but the specific context of the memorandum suggests the year 1616.

thousand *cruzados* in gold, which were carried in a ship by qualified and trustworthy persons.

2. Over the last twenty years – seemingly because, with some negligence, attention has not paid to the facility and liberality with which the Dutch have continued to trade along that whole coast – they have become its masters, so that the gold which formerly came to this Kingdom is now going entirely to Flanders. Your Majesty spends each year twenty to thirty thousand cruzados, as can be seen by the books of revenue and expenditure of the House of India and Mina, in which they are posted.

3. Not only does Your Majesty incur this expense through your Treasury, diminishing it, but you also increase that of the enemy, giving him strength to pursue a war as unjust as that which Your Majesty wages with the states of Flanders, all credit and reputation being lost which might otherwise be achieved by putting an end to it.

4. And seeing that their trade and commerce in Mina is not being hindered, every day the number of their vessels rises, and the *resgate* increases; and there are ships all along that coast, up to Cape Lopez, which is more than two hundred leagues, dispersing and occupying posts remote from one another, which is more to their advantage, where the black people go and give them gold for goods which are cheaper than ours, both because they cost them less and are of worse quality, and because, with that, they [the Dutch] attract them and get them on their side.

5. Greed has grown so much among these Flemish that, moved by it, they built a fortress three leagues away from that of São Jorge, where Your Majesty's Governors serve, in a place called Boure, which they use as both Factory and Customs House, as well as a garrison for those who remain there, protected and aided by the black people who maintain them, abusing the natives, neither letting the *resgate* come to Your Majesty's and your subjects' fortress, nor your Governors administer justice, as though they were masters of that conquest, those who discovered and won it.

6. And in the time of the Captain and Governor *Dom* Cristóvão de Melo, they attacked and tried to enter the fortress of São Jorge, which, being in great danger, he defended, aided by the effort and industry of those same black people. And with[1179] neighbors so close, made greedy by the great amount of gold they take from those parts, and the little remedy which is given to it, there is always the fear of their doing the same thing at all times if Your Majesty does not order [...][1180] and drive them off, which will be easy should Your Majesty desire it, according to the intelligence I have obtained from knowledgeable people who [...][1181] in the said conquest many years of experience.

[1179] In the manuscript, '*como*' ('as'), though it probably should read '*com*' ('with').
[1180] Illegible in the reproduction of the manuscript.
[1181] Illegible in the reproduction of the manuscript.

7. I have learned that Your Majesty has more gold now in that conquest than in any other time, and that in the Nkrãn(?)[1182] River, forty leagues from the fortress of São Jorge, there are large gold mines, which the King of those parts did not let the black people discover, in order that they would not take it to the Dutch. And this King is so loyal to Your Majesty that, though the Dutch had offered him much money so that he might let them built a fortress there, with the purpose of becoming masters of all that gold, he did not let them do so, saying that he was a vassal of the King of Portugal, and that he acknowledged him alone as his Lord and would allow no one else to have a fortress in that Kingdom of his, as he in fact has been asking Your Majesty for many years to have it built, which will be possible at minimal cost; and it will be of great importance for Your Majesty's Exchequer and the safety and freedom of your subjects.

8. And though some of these black people are very loyal, others are inconstant, and it may happen that, when this [King] dies, another will succeed him who will allow the Dutch to do what they have been desiring for so long.

9. A stop can be put to all this damage with as easy a remedy as a small fleet which Your Majesty could order to sweep that entire coast and seize the ships which they might find there, because although they may be many they are dispersed along the coast with little strength, with no artillery or soldiers, [and] in addition to being small ships, they are merchant vessels of traders, designed only for carrying goods. And since they have never found any impediment to their sailing and *resgate*, they feel as safe as if they were at home; and thus unwary are they all the year round; and if the fleet to be sent remains in secret, they will seize every one of them [the Dutch ships].

10. The ships having been seized, those who trade with them should be punished, for which Your Majesty will give powers; and that no black person, under severe penalties, should be allowed to live by the sea, and those who do so should have their houses burnt down. This having been done, those in the fortresses will surrender, given that the black men, who are naturally timorous, will not help them or go to their aid, but will rather kill them all, because even though they trade and barter with them, they do so for all the pampering they receive from them [the Dutch] and the goods they take to them. They bear great ill-will toward them and, if it were not for ours treating them badly, they [the black people] would have already subdued them; and they very much wish that Your Majesty would expel the Dutch with your power,[1183] and they have offered themselves to undertake this, to that purpose, and to seize the fortress, having frequently called upon the Governors *Dom* Duarte de Lima and Pedro da Silva.

[1182] Partly erased in the reproduction of the manuscript, most probably '*Carâ*' ('*Carâ*').

[1183] Probably in the archaic sense (in both Portuguese and English) of an 'armed force.'

11. Above all, since it [the fortress] can be seized without their aid, both because it is not strong and because they [the Dutch] cannot maintain it without the sea trade, which may be completely taken away from them by the punishment inflicted by the one and the other. And the black people seeing that Your Majesty is sending a fleet to that intent, will always be afraid that it may return whenever they intend to trade with the Dutch.

12. Should Your Majesty be served to apply the remedy as described above, may Your Majesty bestow on me the favor of charging me with this enterprise, given my wish and desire to commit myself to it, and to all other most hazardous enterprises in the service of Your Majesty, having given such a good account of myself in some enterprises in which I have participated and in others which Your Majesty has charged me with for the last seventeen years, during which I have served Your Majesty, that Your Majesty found me worthy of charging me with the government of Mina, for which letters patent have already been issued and which Your Majesty has already granted to me, making me feel even more obliged to take care of matters belonging to the service of Your Majesty and that state, wishing to restore in my time the former trade and commerce, which was so profitable to this Kingdom and Your Majesty's Exchequer, should Your Majesty do me the honor which I hope to win in this occasion, with no other interest in mind at present than serving Your Majesty well, trusting that, in your magnanimity, you will bestow on me all the honors and favors of which I may be deserving, withholding my request for them until that time.

13. And so that this might be done in secrecy and without much cost to Your Majesty's Exchequer, I will present to you what appears to me to be the easiest way.

14. When Your Majesty sends the Governors of Mina to their government, you have them given four or five ships to escort them, and this in times of peace with the Dutch. Today it seems that they should rightly sail better escorted, since that peace is over. And Your Majesty spends a great amount of money with them and in sending them.

15. This expense in ships and men may be avoided by using some ships from the Portuguese fleet, in which Your Majesty has presently put much money and expense. It seems reasonable that you should use them in this occasion, when they are not necessary for protecting the ships of India and the Portuguese coast, because when they retire[1184] to the port of Lisbon, towards the end of September and the beginning of October, it is the monsoon[1185] for the journey to Mina.

16. Six ships from the fleet, of the larger ones(?),[1186] together with two smaller and swifter pataches, will be sufficient. And there should be(?)[1187] ready supplies for five or six months: *scilicet*, as soon as the fleet arrives to retire, they

---

[1184] In the manuscript, '*recolhem*': reference to the period during which ships stay anchored in the port.
[1185] In Portuguese, '*monção*': see Glossary.
[1186] In the reproduction of the manuscript, the word—probably, '*maiores*'—is not completely visible.
[1187] In the reproduction, the word—probably, '*estejam*'—is not totally visible.

should be put on these six ships and two pataches, without letting anyone disembark, and they should immediately depart, and [...]¹¹⁸⁸ with them in a ship, for which I could be ready, taking care of what it is advisable to take to Mina, without saying a word about the fleet and that these six ships will again cruise along the coast. And we should all leave with escort, Your Majesty sending enclosed orders to be opened only twenty leagues out at sea, stipulating that they should obey me and follow those orders which regard(?)¹¹⁸⁹ both them and me in the Regulations which Your Majesty may issue.

17. This enterprise will take five to six months at most, and the desired success, with God's favor, being achieved, the ships may return to this port of Lisbon in March or April, if they depart at the time stated above. And there will be more than enough time for them to be renewed¹¹⁹⁰ and serve in the fleet, without losing time, which will be a great gain.

18. This was the manner adopted with *Dom* Luís Fajardo, when he went to the Castilian Indies, to the salt pans at the border,¹¹⁹¹ and seized the Dutch ships which were there with no risk, as I witnessed since I took part in that journey, which enabled me to realize how easy this journey is, in which I will also take advantage of the experience of some men who were in Mina. [...]¹¹⁹²

137 Memorandum By João Roiz Roxo¹¹⁹³ (1618?)

ABSTRACT – *Mina captain's memorandum about the situation at São Jorge da Mina, and the measures to be taken against the Dutch, including the 'counterfeit merchandise' of the Dutch traders.*

MEMORANDUM ON MATTERS RELATED TO THE CASTLE OF SÃO JORGE DA MINA

At present this castle does not yield anything at all to His Majesty; on the contrary, more than ten thousand *cruzados* are spent from his Exchequer every year, and

---

¹¹⁸⁸ Illegible due to the quality of the reproduction.
¹¹⁸⁹ In the reproduction, the word—probably, '*enderece*'(?)—is not totally visible.
¹¹⁹⁰ In the manuscript, '*refformarem*' ('*reformarem*'), which may also mean renewing crews and supplies, in addition to repairing the ship.
¹¹⁹¹ Reference obscure.
¹¹⁹² Fol. 23 is lacking in the manuscript.
¹¹⁹³ BAL, Mss. 51-VIII-25, fols. 46-46v; cf. MMA vol. 6, doc. 117. This document is undated. João Roiz Roxo received an appointment to go as captain of a ship of the India run in 1616, which did not become effective because around the same time he went to Faial island to get cargo from the flagship *Nossa Senhora da Luz*, which had been lost there while returning from India in 1615. For this he was praised and received an appointment for the ship of the 1617 India run (Cf. ANTT, *Chancelaria de D. Filipe II*, liv. 36, fol. 172). Roxo had previously been appointed as commander of two caravels with supplies for the Mina fortress, for the duration of a round trip only. See ANTT, Ibid, liv. 26, fol. 178v., writ dated 17-1-1610. He had already been appointed to the same post, for India, by writ dated 2-10-1609, ANTT, Ibid, liv. 21, fol. 86v. In 1614, João Roiz Roxo commanded an expedition to Mina which failed, since four of the six ships which he took were lost.

the Dutch help themselves to what is to be found in this coast of Mina, whether gold, *malagueta*, ivory, cotton or other things, to which they help themselves [[*sic*]], and each year they take from this coast one million in gold, which they use to wage war against His Majesty by both sea and land, and there are thirty to forty ships continuously to be found along the entire coast, not counting the pataches, which are everywhere.

And since His Majesty today makes no profit from this coast, it would be a good thing to populate it with convicts, as this land is very fertile, with tame people, and thus a state better than that of Brazil could be established there, as there could be many sugar plantations, since there is plenty of [[sugar]] cane, and fresh-water rivers, and a great quantity of wood and slaves.

Instructions could also be given in this castle to send slaves to the Indies and to Brazil, since the backlands of this coast are very vast, and His Majesty will greatly benefit from this because there are more black people to be found here than in Angola. And if there is trading in slaves, they will soon enter into war against one another and stop looking for gold since they will be at war, which is what they most seek. And as soon as the trade of the Dutch begins to fail, they will stop going to that coast, and they will all come to our castle. And our people should be allowed to cruise along the coast with their vessels, collecting everything there is, and bring it to the castle to pay the duties due to His Majesty.

I should likewise recall that at present that castle is poorly supplied with many things which are necessary and has very few people. And if one should break with the Dutch, it could happen that they try to seize it, and any carelessness should thus be avoided.

Everything that the Dutch take to that coast to be sold is fake and counterfeit, and the black people complain of this, saying that, if we had a trade and goods to sell, they would rather come to us than to the Dutch; thus, if plenty of wines, fabrics and other goods were sent to this castle, selling them for the time being at a reasonable price, the trade of the Dutch would be greatly hindered. These people have been progressively taking over this coast, since it is now over twenty years that they have been going there and there is already a great number of mulatto men and women, and this matter should thus be attended to with the best remedy possible.

Captain João Roiz Roxo wrote this.

138 Memorandum by Gaspar Da Rosa[1194] (1618?)

ABSTRACT – *Discussion about the causes of the decadence of Mina and remedies for its restoration. In this discussion, Gaspar da Rosa spoke on behalf of the subjects and residents of Mina and Akyem ('Axim').*

[1194] BAL, Ms. 51-VIII-25, fols. 115-116v; cf. MMA vol. 6, doc. 118, pp. 346–5.

MEMORANDUM ABOUT THE STATE AND REMEDY OF MINA

Gaspar da Rosa, knight of Your Majesty's House, who has been serving you in the fleets of this Kingdom since the year 1576, and in those of India for nine years, and in Mina as Factor, and before that as Captain and Factor of Akyem,[1195] who has performed many services, and in the year '617 went as Captain of the 2nd ship on the journey of the 3 [[ships]] which went with the Governor Manuel da Cunha de Teive[1196] to the said fortress – out of zeal in his duty of serving God and Your Majesty, calls to your attention the changed state in which the coast and trade of Mina is to be found today, and the causes which led to the said state, and the means through which it can be restored.

Because despite of a great amount of gold coming each year from the trade of the said coast of Mina to this Kingdom, and though presently three times more gold than before is arriving to the said coast, all of it goes to Holland. And those who are vassals of Your Majesty's fortress, both Christians and non-Christians, all of them so loyal, flee to the backlands and other parts, even though they had often fought in Your Majesty's service against the Dutch, and the cause and reason for this is the unreasonable treatment they receive from the governors.

So that Christianity, vassalage, trade and trade may be increased in the said coast, instructions were issued determining that for 10 leagues inland and along the coast of the fortress no black man should be made captive, pawned, or sold, and that they should be governed by leaders, whom they call *cabeceiras*,[1197] who made up for them[[?]][1198] with the deals they made with the white men. And these black men used to go throughout the backlands and the coast to trade gold, and they used to bring it with immunity from being sentenced to pawning, sale or captivity of their persons, wives, children and relatives, or from being pawned, sold, and made captive as payment for anything.

And because the black people are very fond of wine, and above all those who are vassals, and would even sell themselves, and their wives and children, for wine, it has also been formally determined that only the necessary number of barrels should be sent, to avoid there being any occasion for sentences of sale and captivity.

[1195] Gaspar da Rosa, or Gaspar da Rosa de Meira, *cavaleiro fidalgo* (knight *fidalgo*), was appointed to the office of factor and *Almoxarife* of São Jorge da Mina for three years, in the vacancy of those who had been appointed, as had been the case with Mateus Gonçalves, who was serving at that time. He was to embark on the ships, which were about to depart. Cf. writ dated 13-8-1593, ANTT, *Chancelaria de D. Filipe I*, liv. 32, fol. 34. I could not find the writ appointing him to the captaincy and factorship of Akyem ('Axim').

[1196] This is confirmed by a writ dated 26-11-1616, ANTT, *Chancelaria de D. Filipe II*, liv. 35, fol. 141. Manuel da Cunha Teive was appointed to the captaincy of Mina by writ dated 167-4-1616, ANTT, *Chancelaria de D. Filipe II*, liv. 31, fol. 231. By writ dated 6-12-1616, he could take an enslaved person or white woman with him as one of the four female kneaders who there should be in Mina, as established by the regulations. See ANTT, *Ibid*, liv. 36, fol. 121.

[1197] *Cabeceira*: see Glossary.

[1198] Tentative translation of '*os compunhaõ*' ('*os compunham*'), from '*compor*,' which—among other meanings—can signify 'to satisfy' or 'to repair.'

But since the governors' and captains' only intention is to bring much more gold, in the interest of their own transactions they have everything sent in wine beyond the [[limit stipulated in the]] regulations,[1199] and they have the wine and other goods sold at a higher price than they are worth, [[and]] they have ordered that there should be sentences of sale and captivity of persons, wives, children and relatives throughout the coast and the backlands, which was the reason for them [[the black people]] to leave for the backlands and throughout the coast to keep themselves free from vassalage, trade and commerce, and for this reason the trade has gradually come to be lost.

In addition to this, the Dutch have been going to the said coast with 20, 25, 30 ships to trade for so many years, and with so many goods and at such low prices, that they [[the black people]] would rather trade with them than for goods sent from this Kingdom.

And the situation has reached such a point that the Dutch even go with the said ships of theirs to the ports of trade of São Tomé, Benin, Jabù, Forcados River, [[and]] Cameroon River,[1200] where they trade plenty of fabrics, cotton, *polhos* [[*sic*]],[1201] cowries and other stones which have value on the coast of Mina, and ivory and pepper which can be found in Benin, and the only trade left for São Tomé is that of slaves, since all other goods are traded by the said Dutch.

In addition to this, since the captains and governors rely on the fact that they are *fidalgos* with blood ties [[to each other]], and are not asked to account for the excesses they commit when bringing gold and other goods, every year they exhaust in two months all the provisions which are sent, and the people are left with no provisions and without being able to provide for themselves, and without the fleet cruising along the coast, since, by not doing so, the governors make better trades, which is the only thing they are interested in, and not in preventing the trade which the Dutch have been making.

REMEDIES FOR RESTORING [[THE SITUATION]]

The main remedy is to send there a Captain who does not rely on his blood ties and who has shown that he places the service of God and Your Majesty above gold, and more gold, and that he will be satisfied with the favors Your Majesty may grant him in this Kingdom.

The 2nd [[is]] to have a visit made by the *Corregedor* and a commission sent[1202] to make an enquiry about those who have not obeyed the instructions

---

[1199] In Brásio's transcription, '*em uinhos e mais do regimento*' ('*em vinhos e mais do regimento*'), which could be literally translated as 'in wine and other [goods?] of the regulations.' It is, however, probable that it should read '*em vinhos a mais do regimento*' (the copulative conjunction '*e*' being substituted by the preposition '*a*'), i.e. wine in a quantity above that the regulations stipulated.

[1200] In Brásio's transcription, '*rio do Camarão*,' which could be translated literally as 'Shrimp River.'

[1201] Meaning obscure. Though not in use anymore, in Portuguese '*polho*' used to mean 'chicken' (as the Castilian '*pollo*'), which seems inappropriate in this context.

[1202] In Brásio's transcription, '*hũa correiçaõ & alçada*' ('*uma correição e alçada*'), '*correição*' being the name given to the visit of a *corregedor* (see Glossary) to administer justice in the places of his jurisdiction, and '*alçada*' a kind of itinerant tribunal.

and Regulations, and who have not kept the vassals but rather ill-treated them, and have not prevented the Dutch from trading, because, if this is punished, the vassals, together with their children and relatives, will feel reassured, and they will return and bring the trade to the fortress, and they will not weep or moan, saying that the Kings of Portugal are no more.

The 3ʳᵈ [[is]] to order that many favors be granted to vassals, both lesser and greater *cabeceiras*, and for that purpose to send goods in abundance, which should be sold at prices similar to those of the Dutch, until they stop going there, after which [[those goods]] may return to their previous price.

The 4ᵗʰ [[is]] that, since the great amount of goods which the Dutch have taken and still take has made everyone leave farm work and become merchants, as they still do, and those who cannot pay become thieves to those other merchants – as there are no plantations or farms – and all the neighboring kings of the said coast suffer and weep that they have been and are becoming ruined, and that they will eventually be totally ruined, as they see that they are starving to death – the remedy for this, as they know and are sure of, is for the Dutch to stop going there.

And though the King (by name of Satim) of Nkrãn, 40 leagues from Your Highness's fortress, where the Portuguese used to have a fortress, has offered it many times to the governors of the said Mina, and has enjoined and said that much is being done to have the Portuguese build a fortress there so that they may not be definitively defeated, which fortress will cost little, since there are instructions there to prepare lime and [[to cut]] stone, with which the fortress of São Jorge may also be repaired, before it definitively falls to the ground, as it is now – even so it is not advisable to build a fortress in Nkrãn because, in addition to its cost, it cannot receive aid from Mina if the Dutch go there; but if there is a fleet, the trade is secure, and to that effect they pledge their children and noblemen.

And even those from the borders of Boure, where the Dutch have their fortress, have at times come to offer themselves to the previous Governor, as they saw that they were being ruined for the said reasons, [[saying]] that they would kill the Dutch and deliver the fortress; and the reply was that it was not the right time to provide them with aid, both in people and in money.

The 5ᵗʰ [[is]] that, in order that the neighboring kings of the coast be more confident and willing not to trade with the Dutch, it is advisable to send a fleet with abundance of goods to the said coast of Mina, the round trip taking six months; and if it is not possible for all of them [[the goods]] to be sent at the expense of Your Majesty's Exchequer, they should go at the expense of merchants and be sold there at a price similar to that of the Dutch goods. And instructions should be issued to repair the galleys, and vessels, and *balões*,[1203] for which two carpenters

---

[1203] *Balões* (sing. *balão*): a fast vessel, similar to the brigantine (see António de Morais Silva, *Diccionario da Lingua Portugueza composto pelo Padre D. Rafael Bluteau, reformado, e accrescentado por [...]*, t.1. Lisbon: Na Oficina de Simão Tadeu Ferreira, 1789); 'a kind of an Indian long light ship, with oars' (António Vieira, *A Dictionary of the English and Portuguese Languages [...]*, pt.2. Lisbon, Printed for Rolland, 1861 [1ˢᵗ ed. 1773]).

and two caulkers will be necessary, so that during the summer, which there lasts from the month of October to March, they may prevent the Dutch from trading on the coast; and during the winter months it should be done as may be possible, with armed *balões*, since, with the favor of the neighboring kings, this will be sufficient to prevent the Dutch from trading. And if they cannot [[trade]], they will not go to the said coast. And to help in the said service, Your Majesty usually has 200 black slaves, and thus it can be performed more easily.

The 6th [[is]] that, as many black and white men have been serving Your Majesty well and ask for their reward in this Kingdom, and are very dispirited, so as to raise their spirits and give an example, it seems that it would be in Your Majesty's service to have them satisfied.

And because Gaspar da Rosa is experienced [[in these matters]] and well-liked by the black vassals of the fortress of São Jorge and the castle of Akyem, as well as by the residents,[1204] he was asked to submit all the aforementioned to Your Majesty and your Council, so that you may attend the matter with the remedy which this case has, and for this purpose he has come to this Court.

Gaspar da Rosa

139 Account by Garcia Mendes Castelo Branco[1205] (1620)

ABSTRACT – *Excerpted from this early, wide-ranging account of the Western African coast from Mina to Angola are relevant sections that deal with Castilian/ Spanish views of Mina and Portuguese-Dutch rivalry. Bear in mind, Portugal is under King Filipe II (or Felipe III in Spain).*

ACCOUNT OF THE AFRICAN COAST

from Mina, which is the castle of São Jorge, to Cape Negro, which is given to Your Most Illustrious Lordship by Captain García Mendez Casteloblanco,[1206] who is one of the first conquerors of the Kingdom of Angola and knows this coast very well, since he has frequently been there and to the other *rescates*[1207] which there are there, during the forty-six years he is been living there.

The castle of São Jorge da Mina is a good fortress of His Majesty, where there is a Governor. There were [[in the fortress]] about three hundred *vecinos*,[1208] and five hundred soldiers altogether. The trade of the said fortress consists of trading gold, namely buying it from the gentiles who come from inland and who give it in

---

[1204] In Brásio's transcription, '*uezinhos*' ('*vizinhos*'), a term which is normally used to designate resident members of a community, but that can also, when referring to outsiders, mean 'neighbors' (in this case, the neighboring 'black people').

[1205] BAL, Ms. 51-VIII-25, fols. 73-77v; cf. MMA vol. 6, doc. 138. Document written in Castilian.

[1206] Castilian for 'Garcia Mendes Castelo Branco.'

[1207] Castilian for '*resgates*' (trades or commerce).

[1208] *Vecinos*: the same as the Portuguese '*vizinhos*'; see Glossary.

exchange for cloth from Portuguese India, and necklaces of glass [[beads]] such as rosaries and others. And formerly every year a ship used to come for the kings of Portugal loaded with the finest gold, as the gold from those parts is the best which can be found. In the said Mina there is plenty of civet which comes from those parts, and [[civet]] cats which give very good civet, as those from there are excellent.

Below the said castle, just a few leagues away, the Dutch have a factory where the gentiles of that country bring the said gold and ivory to sell because [[there]] they are better paid for it than they are by our people, and similarly with the ivory,[1209] and civet, and hides, and whatever else is to be found there, since the said Dutch ordinarily have a very well-armed vessel, which is called the factor,[1210] at anchor in the said port, where other ships which they bring there take goods, and they cruise along the entire coast trading – and this in the ports where we used to trade – and when they finish their *rescate* they take it to the said factory of theirs, and they do the same with some goods which they seize from our ships which cruise along that coast.

They also bring other ships which take to Flanders this gold, and ivory, and hides, and the goods which they have stolen and which they can use there.

Hence it is necessary to remedy this [[situation]], with His Majesty sending to that coast a fleet of three or four galleys, well equipped and with good men, to seize and raze the fortification which they have on land, and to sink the said factor ship, and in this way, they may cleanse the Guinea coast of robbers, who throughout this coast are countless. And the onslaught against them will be terrific, so that they never return there, as these [[ships]] which have been trading throughout those parts and robbing us are not that strong, since they all belong to merchants; only the said factor ship which is in the port which is called Nkrãn is powerful, as we need to be if we want to seize it or sink it, and together with it raze the fortress which is on land. And this will be a great service done to His Majesty, given that, if our ships which go [[there]] to trade black slaves, ivory and gold, hides and civet, are not robbed, His Majesty will receive duties which will be more than sufficient to cover all the expenditure which would be made with this fleet, in addition to it being convenient to his [[His Majesty's]] estate to seize the fortification from the enemy, together with this enormous profit they make, and to restore a trade of such great importance to His Majesty's Exchequer and to his subjects. […]

140 Christendom of São Jorge Da Mina[1211] (23/02/1623)

ABSTRACT – *Various liturgical objects, a clergyman, and a pharmacopoeia for the infirmary of the Mina fortress.*

[1209] The repetition is in the document.
[1210] In Brásio's transcription, '*la factora*' (the feminine genre deriving from the genre of the subject '*nave*,' i.e. 'vessel').
[1211] AHU, Cod. 35, fol. 52v; cf. MMA vol. 7, doc. 28.

The Governors remitted to this Council a homage[1212] which was done by[1213] the Governor of Mina, together with orders to examine the matter as seemed fit; in which memorandum it is said that the main provisions being sent to that fortress are wine, flour for holy wafers, wax for the celebration of divine offices, oil for lamps, a clergyman, a pharmacopoeia for the infirmary, lentils, raisins, prunes, and sugar.

And because the ship which is now being sent to that fortress with provisions is not large enough to carry too much cargo, it seemed best for now to send in this [[ship]] a maximum of six pipes of wine, the abovementioned flour, wax, oil, pharmacopoeia, lentils, raisins, prunes, and sugar, and that for these things to be bought Your Majesty should send the necessary money.

And as regards the clergyman requested for the fortress of Mina, his appointment does not pertain to this Council, and Your Majesty should have the appointment of the clergyman remitted to the *Mesa da Consciência*,[1214] to which it does pertain. Your Majesty will order as seems best for your service.

In Lisbon, on the 23rd of February 1623.

141   News from West Africa[1215] (1624–1625)

ABSTRACT – *Arrival of the new governor in Mina.*

The new Governor Dom Francisco de Souto Maior[1216] has reached Mina safely, and Manuel da Cunha[1217] arrived victorious, since, before his departure, knowing that there were four Dutch pataches on Cacheu River, he attacked them one night with 15 canoes, and finding part of the people on land he stripped them of all the gold and ivory which they had [[with them]] and, after sinking them[1218] [[the pataches]], he returned victorious to the fortress with all [[their]] contents. [...]

142   The Dutch in São Jorge Da Mina[1219] (25/10/1625)

ABSTRACT – *Account of the battle waged against 2,000 Dutchmen at the castle of São Jorge da Mina. The Portuguese victory is attributed to the special protection rather than their local African allies.*

[1212] In Brásio's transcription, '*menagem*,' the same as '*homenagem*' ('homage'), that is, a ceremony where a vassal pledged submission to a lord. In this case, probably a formal account of a ceremony of this kind.

[1213] Given the lack of other contextual data, it is not possible to determine whether '*da parte do Governador da Mina*' means 'by' or 'on behalf of the Governor of Mina.'

[1214] *Mesa da Consciência*: see Glossary.

[1215] BNL, Fundo Geral, Ms. 241, fols. 198v.-199; cf. MMA vol. 7, doc. 96.

[1216] See MMA vol. 7, doc. 125.

[1217] See MMA vol. 6, doc. 94, doc. 118; vol. 8, doc. 116; and vol. 15, doc. 205.

[1218] In Brásio's transcription, '*dandolhes furo*' ('*dando-lhes furo*'), literally 'giving them a hole' or 'making a hole in them.'

[1219] AV, Nunziatura di Portogallo, vol. 16, fols. 238–241; cf. MMA vol. 7, doc. 125, pp. 389–93.

ACCOUNT OF THE MIRACULOUS VICTORY
OBTAINED BY DOM FRANCISCO SOUTO
Maior,[1220] governor of the fortress of São Jorge da Mina, against
the Dutch rebels and enemies, with nineteen ships,
the year one thousand six hundred and twenty-five, on the
twenty-fifth of October, Saturday, feast day of the
glorious martyrs St Crispin &
Crispinian: the contents of which
are as follows.
(.!+!.)

On the same day that the nineteen ships arrived, they directed their batteries against this town and fortress, which they thought they could raze by bombard fire, or reduce it to a state whereby it could be easily seized by the two thousand men who had been disembarked; and of these men one thousand and five hundred were musketeers, while I had only fifty-seven soldiers in this fortress, including myself – and many of them were not able to handle or manage their weapons well – together with nine hundred black men with three captains, to whom, once I had told them what was convenient for Your Majesty's service and the orders they should follow, I gave the gold which they requested, and even more than they had imagined; and thus [[feeling]] glad and satisfied, they promised me they would die in Your Majesty's service.

I gave the remaining gold to this fortress's neighboring kings of Akatakyi ('Komenda')[1221] and Fetu, with which I secured that that of Akatakyi ('Komenda') would not be our enemy on this occasion. And it was of great value to us that these kings remained neutral, that of Fetu having come with provisions to the aid of all these people much more attentively than he used to in times of peace.

On the same day, at two o'clock in the afternoon, or even before, every one of their ships began shooting against this fortress and town, while the two thousand Dutchmen, among whom (as I have said) the one thousand and five hundred musketeers, were already marching across the field of the Pilicada,[1222] [[which is]] a musket shot from this fortress. The three captains waited for them hidden in holes and behind bushes as they could. As the enemy was approaching, very much lords of the field, convinced that there would be no more opposition and marching with great security, I signaled with three pieces[1223] of this castle to the three captains, who emerged so close to the enemy that they [[the enemy]] could not do more than turn[1224] the muskets and fire off a charge against our men,

---

[1220] See MMA vo. 7, doc. 96.

[1221] Or Eguafoɔ. In Brásio's transcription, '*Acumane*.'

[1222] It is not clear whether '*Pilicada*' is a placename or rather the equivalent of '*paliçada*,' that is, a 'palisade.' See MMA vol. 8, doc. 38.

[1223] The exact term would be 'pieces of ordnance,' that is, mounted guns, or cannons.

[1224] In Brásio's transcription, '*não teue elle maes lugar pera voluer*' ('*não teve ele mais lugar para volver*'), literally 'they had no opportunity to turn,' which makes no sense in this context. The transcription published in 'Inéditos da Bibliotheca da Universidade de Coimbra,' *Archivo Bibliographico*, vol. VIII, n.8 (Agosto 1908), p. 124, however, offers a different version of this passage, which is the one adopted in this translation: '*não teue elle maes lugar que pera voluer*.'

which they awaited face down on the ground and [[with]] their shields raised, and after the tempest of the muskets the black men charged with courageous and Numantian[1225] spirit, and they attacked them with spears, halberds, partisans, pistols, and dispersed them and made them flee. Then followed soon after, until nightfall, the completion of the victory, without regard to quality, dignity, and age, with every one of them beheaded; and no more than forty-five [[Dutchmen]] managed to escape, saved by the darkness of the night and the aid from the said Aldeia[1226] do Torto ([[whose inhabitants]] are their friends). Fifteen flags were seized, and another fifteen drums, and over one thousand muskets, pistols, spears, [[and]] partisans, together with many other spoils, consisting of costly weapons, garments, [[and]] large hats which served as morions and protection from the sun.

This most miraculous victory was granted to us by the Virgin, Our Lady, on her [[feast]] day, which was Saturday, which thus coincided with the feast of the glorious martyrs St Crispin and Crispinian. And this fleet was one of the fleets which was going to the aid of Brazil, and it was divided at Sierra Leone, taking the route to Mina, where the finest and the best of them came to die at the hands of black men from Mina, Your Majesty's vassals. Thirteen on our side died in this battle, including three *cabeceiras*,[1227] and as regards the remaining soldiers thirty-four were wounded, fourteen of whom died, most of them from improper treatment or from having treated themselves.

On the next day, which was Sunday the 26th of the said month, in the early hours, during the watch[1228] before dawn, the flagship fired a piece to signal retreat, and set sail upwind from this coast, one league ahead of its pier, to a place which is also their [[the Dutch's]] confederate, called (Ampiari[1229])[[*sic*]], between the said Aldeia do Torto and this fortress; and there they remained anchored for eleven days, that is until the fifth of November, persuading the said neighboring kings of this fortress, especially the King of Fetu, by giving them offerings, to refuse us provisions, which he had never failed to give us; [[and]] those of Akatakyi ('Komenda') to give them black men to fight in revenge against the black men of this Mina. And as I had kept them neutral, as Your Majesty orders in your regulations, and also because they had seen the great victory which the black men from Mina (naked people) had achieved, they replied to them with vague words.

Undeceived at last, on the fifth of the following month of November, at ten o'clock in the morning and on Wednesday, they returned here to fire against this castle and town, and thus they continued Thursday and Friday, which was the

---

[1225] In the sense of 'heroic'; from Numantia, the last Celtiberian bastion against the Roman conquest of the Iberian Peninsula, which endured a siege of 13 months before surrendering, though not before the inhabitants had set fire to their own town.

[1226] That is, 'Village of Torto,' which can be identified with Akatakyi, itself rebranded 'Komenda' by the Portuguese; for '*aldeia*,' see Glossary.

[1227] *Cabeceira(s)*: see Glossary.

[1228] In Brásio's transcription, '*quarto*,' most probably the nautical term used to describe a period into which a day aboard a ship, together with the assignment of duties to the crew, is divided.

[1229] Possibly the same as 'Ampia.'

seventh of the said month, firing against this castle and town over two thousand [[cannon]] balls, among them balls of 25 *arráteis*.[1230] This castle received them as befitted such guests, and there they found the welcome they deserved, with many of them being killed on the ships, so much so that, on the said Friday, the seventh of the said month of November, at night, seeing that they had been so ill-treated by this castle, they retreated beyond the range of our cannon. And thus, they remained until the 14th of the said month, which was Friday, and [[after]] going back and forth by launch with messages for a fortress of theirs, which is situated in a place called Bonirem [[*sic*]], they eventually sailed there, and remained there until the 29th of the said month, Saturday, and [[then]] they went to Flanders, where they arrived – as became known in this fortress – with some of the ships badly damaged.

The dead in this battle were only two: *scilicet*, on the first day, the 25th of October, a black man who was taking and repairing cartridges in this castle's hall; and, on the final day of the battery fire, a soldier who was helping to pull a piece.

This fortress of Your Majesty has three bulwarks; only the two [[bulwarks]] on the shore were firing, for lack of men, so much so that I did not even have here Your Majesty's black men, since a month and a half earlier I had put them, with masons and workmen[1231] from this fortress, to repair the castle of Akyem, which was in ruins, together with black men of private individuals and of retainers of mine, and with some of the few white men there were, since the majority of them were with the corps of guards, working their guts out in Your Majesty's service. This victory was achieved with Heaven's favor and the ample good fortune of Your Majesty, and I also did my part with visit and assistance.

Dom Francisco Souto Maior

We hereby approve this Account for publication, and once it is printed it should be returned to be checked against the original, so that a license to circulate be granted, and otherwise it shall not circulate. Lisbon, on the 14th of January 1628.

João Álvares Brandão G. Pereira[1232] Francisco Barreto
Friar António de Sousa Pedro Novais
Let this Account be printed. Lisbon, the 19th of January '628.

Gaspar do Rego da Fonseca

Let this Account be printed, and once it is printed it should be returned to be taxed, and otherwise it shall not circulate. On the 19th of January '628.

Araújo Cabral Salazar

[1230] *Arrátel* (sing.): a unit of weight, equivalent at the time to approximately 0.460 kg.
[1231] In Brásio's transcription, '*officiaes*' ('*oficiais*'): skilled workmen rather than laborers.
[1232] 'G' most probably stands for 'Gaspar' (Pereira), inquisitor and member of the *Mesa da Consciência*.

This Account is taxed at five *reis*. On the 21st of January 1628.

Araújo Cabral Salazar

Printed in Lisbon. By Jorge Rodrigues. Year 1628.

143 Letter from the Apostolic Collector to the Secretary of State[1233] (05/02/1628)

ABSTRACT – *Ships arrive from Mina with news of Portuguese victory against the Dutch.*

Most Illustrious and Most Reverend Lord, my Most Honorable Father,

Through a ship which arrived this week from Mina we were informed of a notable victory achieved against the Dutch, thanks to the efforts of the Castellan of a small fortress, which is the last remaining one in Portuguese hands in those parts, as is described in detail in the enclosed printed account, whose information, however, is out of date.

[…]

From Lisbon, the 5th of February 1628.

Most Humble and Most Obliged Servant,

Lorenzo, Bishop of Gerace[1234]

144 Aid Sent to Mina[1235] (01/04/1630)

ABSTRACT – *Regulations given to Cosme do Couto, so he may take aid to Mina. Do Couto is asked to elude the Dutch 'enemy', which he may find at the castles of Akyem ('Axim') or Mina.*

We have examined the enclosed regulations which were given to Cosme do Couto in the year 1628, when he went as Captain of the ship which took aid to Mina, together with the paper newly given by him, as well as the information requested from Manuel da Cunha, former Governor of that fortress.

The said regulations and information having been seen, it is our opinion that there is nothing to correct or add anew, since they are as they should be, and we should only enjoin Captain Cosme do Couto, as regards the aid he is taking to

---

[1233] AV, Nunziatura di Portogallo, vol. 16, fol. 237; cf. MMA vol. 7, doc. 190. Document written in Italian.

[1234] See MMA vol. 8, doc. 8, doc. 15, doc. 31, and doc. 48.

[1235] AHU, Cod. 376, fol. 67v; cf. MMA vol. 15, doc. 205.

the said fortress, to endeavor to carry it out in every way possible, seeking every means to accomplish it, even if he finds the castle of Akyem and the fortress of Mina with enemy ships which may hinder aid from being delivered through the openings and slopes [[?]][1236] of the said fortresses, since it is most necessary for their preservation that they do not fail to receive this aid. Your Majesty shall order as best for your service.

In Lisbon, on the first of April '630.

Ls. / Rs.[1237] / SS. / – Roque de Silva. L.M.B.

[*In the margin*]: *Reply from the Government*

In conformity with the opinion expressed in this consultation, regulations have been issued for Cosmo do Couto, which will be given to him by the [[State(?)]] Department. As regards the provisions that he is taking, the necessary instructions will be given to him by the Council.

In Lisbon, on the first of April '630.

Dom Diogo

145 Letter from the Apostolic Collector to Cardinal Ludovisi[1238] (14/06/1631)

ABSTRACT – *Collector's opinion concerning the special powers requested from the Propaganda Fide by the vicars of Mina. Of note are the 'few Christians' around the fortress.*

Most Eminent and Most Reverend Lord, my Most Honorable Father,
     In order to give you as exact a report as I could on the vicars of Mina – which is situated on the African Coast – who request from this Sacred Congregation the same power of absolving occult cases which the Council of Trent in the chapter *Liceat* confers on bishops, and furthermore that of blessing the vestments, and consecrating chalices and altar stones, I first turned for information to a most honorable person, who was once Governor of that State, from whom I obtained the report which I enclose with this letter to Your Eminence, in the same manner as he gave it to a priest, minister of this Tribunal, whom I sent to him [[the Governor]] for this purpose. I should further say to Your Eminence (since you order me to include my opinion in this [[letter]]) that, as

---

[1236] In Brásio's transcription, '*nós* e barros' (probably, '*nós e esbarros*').
[1237] Possibly 'Rui da Silva'; see MMA vol. 15, doc. 209.
[1238] APF, SRCG, vol. 99, fols. 13-13v; Acta, vol. 7 (1631), fols. 12 v.-122, n. 13; cf. MMA vol. 8, doc. 8. Document written in Italian.

it is not possible to know how reliable these vicars are, I believe one should bear the following considerations in mind:

First, not to grant those powers to anyone except the Vicar of Mina, since it appears that he alone will be sufficient for the few Christians to be found in those parts. [...]

Lisbon, the 14th of June 1631.

Of Your Eminence
Most humble and obliged servant,
Lorenzo, Bishop of Gerace [...]

146 Report on the Coast of Mina[1239] (14/06/1631)

ABSTRACT – *The Apostolic Collector, based on information given by the previous governor, reports on the poor state of religion in the Ecclesiastical Jurisdiction of São Jorge da Mina, and proposes remedies.*

The town of Mina is situated on the Guinea Coast, at five degrees and minutes below the Equinox [[line]] to the north side and is more than 200 leagues from the island of São Tomé, which is below the said Equinox line.

In the said town, inside its fortress, there is a church called São Jorge; it has a Vicar and four Chaplains. The Vicar is suffragan to the Bishop of São Tomé, from whom he receives the Holy Oils, and has all the administration *in temporalibus.*[1240]

There is another priest in the town of Akyem, where another fortress is to be found; only one Vicar resides in that [[fortress]], subordinate to that of Mina.

And there are no other priests, apart from these two, in the entire Jurisdiction of Mina.

The aforementioned town of Mina has around 400 Christians, since, although there are 800 inhabitants to be found there, almost half of them are Christians; and the other half are no longer Christian for lack of clergymen, in view of the fact that, instead of zealous ministers, fruitful in propagating the Faith, as ought to be the case, persons who are far from exemplary are being sent to those parts. And this matter is even more serious as those Gentiles are pliable in following the Sacred Religion when encouraged and assisted by the aforementioned ecclesiastical ministers. And it seems that the fruit could be even greater given that the whole of that mainland of Africa has the same pliability and disposition to become Christian.

[1239] APF, SRCG, vol. 99, fols. 14-14v; Acta, vol. 7 (1631), fol. 106, n. 32; Lettere Volgari, vol. 11, fol. 86; cf. MMA vol. 8, doc. 9, 44–46. Document written in Italian.
[1240] *In temporalibus* (Latin): 'in temporal matters.'

In the aforementioned town of Akyem there are around 200 Christians and 300 Gentiles, who, at this hour, would be Christians if only the said clergymen did not fail in their obligations in the aforementioned manner.

There is another place called Esma, which belongs to His Majesty. It has some 200 *vicini*,[1241] [[and there]] lives a Portuguese soldier who is the sole Christian, and he lives there to collect the fish tithe for the said Majesty. This place lies between Mina and Akyem, and there could be another priest, as was put forward for consideration by that Governor to His Majesty at the *Mesa da Consciência*,[1242] which until now has not approved it, either as regards this [[matter]] or in replacing those ecclesiastical ministers, sending such [[priests]] as are able to fructify. And here ends what the Governor says.

Presently this conquest of Mina, from where a good quantity of the most excellent gold used to be extracted every year, is almost totally abandoned because of the Dutch, who have built a good fortress and every year send ships there to trade with the natives and to take everything which formerly belonged to the Portuguese, and so it is presently without a governor, because no successor has been sent for the one who died two years ago.

In the cardinals' congregation of the *Propaganda Fide* of the 29th of July 1631, the matter mentioned in this document was dealt with as follows:[1243]

The same Most Reverend Assessor of the Holy Office referred the report concerning the site and condition of the region of Africa called Mina, sent by the Spanish Nuncio, which states that Mina is a certain town on the Western part of Africa, between the Bishopric of Cape Verde in the island of Santiago and the Bishopric of São Tomé.

Some days later, the *Propaganda [[Fide]]* wrote to the Nuncio in Spain:

This Sacred Congregation was pleased to receive the report on the temporal state of the island of Mina which was sent by Your Lordship. But because it would be more pleased to receive one on the spiritual [[state]], it is its wish that you endeavor particularly to obtain it, so that one may take the resolution which was requested in the enclosed memorandum which has already been sent to you. That etc.

Rome, the 9th of August 1631.

147 Letter from the Apostolic Collector to Cardinal Borgia[1244] (01/11/1631)

ABSTRACT – *The letter deals with sending missionaries to Mina at a time when the Portuguese are losing Mina to the Dutch and Portuguese reliance on local African support is waning. The letter notes the dispatch of a new governor for São Jorge da Mina, who will depart in March.*

[1241] *Vicini*: the same as the Portuguese '*vizinhos*'; see Glossary.
[1242] *Mesa da Consciência*: see Glossary.
[1243] The record of the meeting is written in Latin.
[1244] APF, SRCG, vol. 74, fols. 316–316v; cf. MMA vol 8, doc 15, pp. 82–3. Document written in Italian.

Most Eminent and Most Reverend Lord, my Most Honorable Father,

With the last post from Madrid, I received a [[letter]] from Your Eminence dated the 20ᵗʰ of September last in reply to [[a letter]] of mine, which I had sent to that Sacred Congregation, about the report on the town of Mina, situated in Africa, on the Guinea Coast; [[and,]] seeing from this [[letter]] that it is the wish of the said Sacred Congregation that I endeavor to have as many ecclesiastical workers as possible sent to those parts, I will not fail to do all I can in order to achieve this holy end. And since what is now to be done is to send there as Governor a *fidalgo* who is my friend, I will make every effort to convince him to take as many [[ecclesiastical workers]] as he can.

Meanwhile I will be waiting for the brief on the spiritual powers, which the Sacred Congregation has decided to request in favor of the Episcopal Vicar of the said town of Mina, so that it may be sent with the Governor, who will sail in March, once his departure is decided. I have encouraged the Archbishop of Goa, a Dominican religious[1245] who is at the Court of Madrid, to spare no effort to obtain missionaries, and he has [[sent me a letter]] with this last post saying that His Majesty has granted him 18 for the parts of Mutapa, [[and]] that, once these have been found, they should go, [[as]] it will be a great help for the considerable need [[for missionaries]] in those parts.

Through the ship now arrived from India, I have received the two enclosed letters for the Sacred Congregation, which I am sending to Your Eminence together with this one, and I humbly bow before you.

From Lisbon, the first of November 1631.

Of Your Eminence

[*Autograph*]: Most humble and obliged servant

Lorenzo, Bishop of Gerace

Signor Cardinal Borgia

148 Letter from the Governor of Mina to the King[1246] (04/03/1632)

ABSTRACT – *Mina Governor Pedro Mascarenhas requests the power, in King Filipe III's name, to give soldiers' pay to the wives and children of the 'black men' of Mina who, when the Dutch 'rebels' attacked that garrison, distinguished themselves in the fight.*

By decree of the Government of the first of this [[month]] it was ordered that this Council should examine a petition from Pedro Mascarenhas,[1247] whom Your

---

1245 D. Manuel Teles de Brito.
1246 AHU, Cod. 39, fols. 105–105 v; cf. MMA vol. 15, doc. 209, pp 571–2.
1247 See MMA vol. 8, doc. 52, doc. 60, docs. 65–66, docs. 73–74, doc. 80, doc. 83, and doc. 85.

Majesty appointed as Governor of Mina, in which he argues that, in his opinion, for the increase of Christendom and Your Majesty's service, the black people of those parts should be granted some favors, which would place them under obligation to defend that fortress and make them fight with a grateful heart; and, to the said effect, that those who fought when the Dutch attacked the said fortress should be rewarded for their good conduct, their manifest valor and their wish to defend [[the fortress having led to]] the death of three or four [[of them]], according to the information which the Petitioner has.

He requests that Your Majesty, should you think it right, may grant him the power, in Your Majesty's name, to have them given soldiers' pay for their wives and children, or for whomever it may befit most, so that with it, seeing that Your Majesty grants favors to those who die in your service, they may take heart in situations of war that may occur; and, to this effect, that Your Majesty may have the necessary writs issued.

And the said petition having been seen in this Council, together with the matter discussed therein, the opinion was that, if Pedro Mascarenhas were to collect information about the black men who, on the past occasion (the clash which took place in the said fortress against the rebels from Holland), distinguished themselves, and fought with valor, and died in the fighting, [[and]] who, being married, left wife and children, Your Majesty should be pleased that he, the Governor, may grant to each of them [[the wives]] a soldiers' pay, so that they may benefit from it for life, and similarly with up to three children who may have been left by these black men.

And of what should be done as regards this matter, information should be sent to Your Majesty, so that you may have his procedure in this matter examined.

In Lisbon, the 4th of March '632.

Rui da Silva / Roque da Silva / João Sanches

[*In the margin*]: Reply from the Government
In agreement with the opinion, and this consultation to be returned

Lisbon, 15th of March 1632

The Count of Castro

149 Report from the Vicar of Mina to the Propaganda Fide[1248] (13/10/1632)

ABSTRACT – *A report on Christianity in the area surrounding São Jorge da Mina. It details the superficiality of the Christianity of the inhabitants subject to the fortress, the supposed rites and 'superstitions' of both non-Christians and Christians, and the unsuccessful measures Portuguese governors adopted against indigenous healers (called 'sorcerers').*

[1248] APF, SRCG, vol. 103, fols. 85–86; cf. MMA vol. 8, doc. 38, pp. 185–7. Document written in Italian.

REPORT ON THE CHRISTIANS OF MINA

Mina – thus called by the Portuguese, because the [[original]] name of that land is Adenà – was discovered in the time of King Dom João II, of glorious memory, in the year 1482,[1249] which is 150 years [[ago]], by a certain Diogo de Azambuja,[1250] *fidalgo* of the House of the said King Dom João, and was handed over to him, and he was given possession of it, by a black Lord of the land named Caramanza,[1251] whom Diogo himself insistently asked to become a Christian, but he never wanted to do so, a sure indication of the little Christianity which must have existed among the black people, before they had seen the example of their King and Lord accepting the Christian Faith.

After the fortress was built there, and the white people gathered in it, they proceeded to their *riscatto*[1252] and commerce, together with reducing the people of the village to receive the Holy Baptism, which they did not then want to accept, although afterwards, through conversation with white men, some of them did become Christians, and a church was built in Akatakyi ('Komenda'),[1253] a country which belongs to a King who is our neighbor and lies to the west of this fortress, and another one in Fetu, which lies to the north, countries which belong to neighboring kings, who killed and beat up the religious who were there, and took the sacraments and furnishings of the churches, and thus there were no more Christians left there.[1254]

As regards that [[church]] of Mina, everything is *pro forma*, given that they are Christians in name only, since, as for the rest – knowing what excommunication is or confessing directly – they only observe it out of obligation and fear of being condemned. If they go to the confessor,[1255] the only thing they do is to deny all that is asked of them, and so such as is their Christianity so is their absolution. But the most important result of all this is that the innocent small children die baptized.

They are great sorcerers, and greatly inclined to spells and superstitions. They mainly resort to pyromancy,[1256] and lighting a small fire, which they make for that purpose, they throw in a piece of green wood, and seeing from which part the fire comes, they interpret it as a signal of what they wish to know, etc.

They have also other forms of superstition, but what they resort to most is divination, pretending – according to how the lots are cast – to know whatever they desire; and this kind of divination, given that in reality there is implicit

[1249] The Portuguese came upon the region dubbed 'Mina' in January 1471, during the reign of King Afonso V.
[1250] Diogo de Azambuja was charged with erecting the fortress by King João II in 1482–3.
[1251] Italian for '*Caramansa*.' The Portuguese referred to the local ruler of Adena as 'Caramansa.'
[1252] Italian for '*resgate*' (trades or commerce).
[1253] In Brásio's transcription, '*Cumane*.'
[1254] On Christianity in Akatakyi and Fetu, cf. MMA, I, pp. 191–2.
[1255] In a slightly different copy of the document (MMA, vol.8, doc. 46), 'If they go to church to the confessor [...]' ('*Se vanno alla Chiesa à piè del confessore* [...]').
[1256] In a different copy of the document (MMA, vol. 8, doc. 46), '*chiromantia*' ('*chiromanzia*'), i.e. 'chiromancy.'

dealing with the devil, is nevertheless with them so implicit that they do not fore-tell anything, nor does the devil assist them in any matter, and thus they learn nothing of what they desire to know, or even whether ships or anything else from the Kingdom[1257] will arrive to this coast. But the same does not occur with the black people of Mozambique and Eastern India, and this way the devil keeps them deceived, considering that these do not deserve any better.

The Gentiles from this village have a black vicar, whom they call Sofo,[1258] to whom they give full credit, and they go to him to get water, which they call holy, and they sprinkle themselves with it; nor do many black Christians refrain from going to him in secret, as they give more credit to the said Sofo than to the Christian priests.

These people are so beastly that they say that stones soiled with mud and pigs' filth are saints, and they worship them and put out food for them to eat, saying that the Stone Saint eats.

On a field, which they call *paliçada* [[?]],[1259] which is one musket shot from this fortress, there is a stone that they call the Great Saint,[1260] which they go to visit and worship once a year. And since the sea often covers the said stone with sand, it frequently happens that people search for it for a whole day and do not find it; and when they do find it, they make a great feast, which consists in the gathering of Christians and Gentiles for eating and drinking.

Black women perform the same rite, apart from a few of them, brought up among white Christians, who do not take part in such things, and to these alone is Holy Communion given, if they are considered able to receive it.

All these black Christians and Gentiles have innumerable superstitions which cannot be taken from them, since, if one has eight children, four will be Christians and the other four Gentiles, and thus the former feed on the errors of the latter.

They are very fond of casting spells and calling sorcerers to their lands, who are most ignorant and have no dealing with the devil, and they are deceived every time by them [[the sorcerers]], who eat castrated ram or goat meat and other things which they demand for the said[1261] spells, which they only cast so as to make a living. And much as the Governors try to expel them from the land, there is no remedy. It could be said of these what Tacitus said in the first book of his *Histories* about the judicial [[astrologers]] of Rome: *genus hominum Principibus infidum, credentibus fallax, a Civitate nostra semper prohibentur, sed nunquam expulsum.*[1262]

[From Mina, the 13th of October 1632].

[1257] Reference to Portugal.

[1258] 'Sofo' is the Akan/Twi ɔsofoɔ, one of several indigenous terms for a spiritualist-healer.

[1259] In Brásio's transcription, '*pagliazza*,' though in a different copy of the same document (*MMA*, vol. 8, doc. 46) the transcription reads '*paglizzata*,' which is closer to the term '*pilicada*' used in vol. 7, doc. 125, possibly the equivalent of 'palisade.'

[1260] In Brásio's transcription, '*Santo Grande*.'

[1261] In this transcription, '*le tali*' ('the said'); but in the copy transcribed in MMA, vol. 8, doc. 46, this reads '*letali*,' i.e. 'lethal.'

[1262] '[...] a kind of men who are treacherous to Princes, deceitful to those who trust them, always prohibited but never expelled from our City' (Latin).

150 Letter from the Apostolic Collector to the Propaganda Fide[1263] (30/04/1633)

ABSTRACT – *Appraisal of the report by the vicar of Mina, in which Portuguese evangelization and commerce are symbiotically linked—the presence (or absence) of one affected the other.*

Most Eminent and Most Reverend, my Most Honorable Lord,

I have received a letter from the Vicar of Mina in Western Africa dated the 13th of October of last year, through which he confirmed the receipt of the brief of Our Lord, which I had sent him as ordered by the Sacred Congregation of the *Propaganda Fide*, with powers to bless corporals and sacerdotal vests. And as he enclosed a report on his church, I did not want to fail to send Your Eminence the enclosed copy, translated into Italian; because, even though I have on other occasions received very different reports about the character of the people from noblemen who have served there as governors, and even though I suspect this man speaks about them with little charity or too much zeal, as someone who wished that they would become Christians without effort on his part, nevertheless I thought that nothing should be hidden from Your Eminence, to whom pertains giving to each thing the remedy which is most appropriate; it being much to regret that in this, which was one of the first conquests of the Kingdom, and so close[1264] to it, the propagation of the faith has been almost forgotten, as this priest appears to believe. And for this reason it is not to be wondered (as I have said to several of these gentlemen) that temporal profits and trade have also been forgotten, nearly all having passed into the hands of the Dutch, who manage them as they will, and they take a great quantity of the finest gold, without the Portuguese having any more hope or will to recover them, as perhaps God will command that a day will come when human means will be less decisive.[1265]

With which I most humbly bow before Your Eminence, and I pray to the Lord God for your ever greater happiness.

From Lisbon, the 30th of April 1633.

Of Your Eminence

[*Autograph*]: Most humble and obliged servant,

Lorenzo, Bishop of Gerace

[1263] APF, SRCG, vol. 103, fols. 84–84v; cf. MMA doc. 8, doc. 48, pp. 223–4. Document written in Italian.

[1264] As is well known, São Jorge da Mina is not at all 'close' ('*vicina*' in Italian) to Portugal. The phrase may also mean 'close to the heart,' in which case there would be no incongruity.

[1265] The meaning of this last phrase is not entirely clear.

151 Letter from the King to Francisco De Lucena[1266] (24/06/1633)

ABSTRACT – *About the aid to be sent to São Jorge da Mina, at the request of the Governor Pedro Mascarenhas. Some priests would also be sent to convert the indigenes.*

I have seen the consultation of the Council of State of the 23rd of April last regarding the letter sent by Pedro de Mascarenhas, Governor of Mina, in which he informs of the success he obtained against the Dutch and of a letter written to him by an English general, who went to that state with four ships. And aid will be dispatched as rapidly as possible to that fortress, by sending there three caravels with all that may be necessary and required, [[and]] which is requested by the Governor, in order that he may resist the attacks from the enemy; and also some religious will be sailing in them for the conversion[1267] of the Gentiles, since, in addition to thus attaining the main purpose of reducing them to the Faith, this is also a means of strengthening their obedience to me, with which matters will be safer. And a letter shall be sent to the Governor thanking him for his good conduct in his clash with the Dutch, as well as in the reply he gave to the English, considering that he did not have information about the peace treaty signed with that nation, and ordering him also to thank on my behalf the persons who distinguished themselves on that occasion. And as regards removing the enemy from that coast, I have decided that this should be done with the utmost vigor. It is not convenient at this time, however, to delay the aid for Pernambuco, where it is so necessary and urgent, as will be understood from other letters taken by this courier, who should make all haste, as I have already ordered. As concerns this letter, and in particular the English, the articles of peace will continue to be examined so that this matter be provided with the appropriate remedy.

Written in Madrid, [the 24th of June 1633].

152 Letter from the King to the Count Viceroy[1268] (08/03/1634)

ABSTRACT – *About the aid needed at São Jorge da Mina at the governor's request, and further losses of a caravel, a French captain seized.*

[1266] BNM, Ms. 3014, fols. 274–274v; cf. MMA vol. 8, doc. 52, pp. 235–6.

[1267] In Brásio's transcription, '*conseruaçaõ*' ('*conservação*'), i.e. 'conservation.' A footnote to his transcription states the correct reading should be '*conversão*' (i.e. 'conversion'), as the continuation of the text makes clear.

[1268] BNM, Ms. 3014, fol. 277; cf. MMA vol. 8, doc. 60, pp 257–8. In a document dated 11-3-1634 (BNM, Ms. 3014, fols. 279–79v), King Filipe III insists on the momentous and never resolved problem: 'By ordinary [[post]] of the forth of the current month of March we have received a consultation of the Council of State regarding the information given by Pedro Mascarenhas, Governor of Mina, about the lack of provisions with which that fortress has been left, and the caravel which he sent to São Tomé for aid and was seized by a French captain while returning. And seeing what Pedro

I have seen your letter dated the 18ᵗʰ of February, and what is said in the one you sent me from Pedro Mascarenhas, Governor of Mina, about the straits in which they found themselves for lack of supplies for the people who serve there, and the caravel which was seized by a French captain while sailing from São Tomé to that garrison. And it seemed to me that I should strongly charge and enjoin you to see whether some aid could be sent to Mina, as you are aware of the importance of this garrison, and as its state of need should be clear from the long time that has passed since Pedro Mascarenhas informed about it and from its only having as a resource the caravel which was seized. And though the aid you refer to has been sent from that Kingdom, nevertheless, since the things of the sea are uncertain, it is to be feared that it may not have arrived. And as regards the loss caused by the seizure of the caravel, I have ordered by the appropriate means that this be satisfied.

Written in Madrid, [the 8ᵗʰ of March 1634].

153 Letter from the Captain of Mina to the King[1269] (15/05/1634)

ABSTRACT – *The Mina governor indicates the assistance received is insufficient for effective defense. The Dutch siege prompts his appeal for help once more.*

+

My Lord,

By the ship of Lübeck[1270] which you have sent with aid to this fortress, I am sending Your Majesty a detailed letter, with an account of how she arrived here fighting against two enemy ships during a whole afternoon and part of the night, and how I went to her aid with soldiers, which is the reason why she was not boarded and the enemy suffered great damage; and they were so outraged, that seven of them came into sight, and today, as I am writing this [[letter]], two of them remain almost within the range of our pieces.[1271]

And as I considered that it would be more convenient for the service and reputation of Your Majesty [[that the ship]] did not leave this port than for it to

---

Mascarenhas says about the state of necessity in which that fortress was left, and considering that this would eventually become worse, and that the people who serve there would become very dispirited with the seizure of the caravel, with whose arrival they hoped to remedy in part the straits [[in which they find themselves]], and all of this requires that all possible aid be sent to the said garrison without delay, in the manner which may seem best to the Council of State—I strongly charge and enjoin you to do so, and to deal with this with the diligence which you use in all matters of my service, for you must understand how advisable it is to send this aid. And the remainder of what is dealt with in the consultation will continue to be examined, and I will have a reply given to it shortly.'

[1269] AHU, S. Tomé, cx. 1, doc. 105; cf. MMA vol. 8, doc. 88, pp. 276–7.

[1270] In Portuguese, as in Brásio's transcription, 'Lubeque.' See MMA vol. 8, doc. 74.

[1271] The exact term would be 'pieces of ordnance,' that is, mounted guns, or cannons.

be seized in sight of the fortress without our being able to assist her, I ordered the Captain João Henriques not to set sail until we saw what time would bring.

In the first and second copies I represent to Your Majesty the sparing assistance which you sent me, and what was its import, and how much every three months' payment amounts to, with which I clearly demonstrate to Your Majesty that I am presently in the same straits as before the arrival of this aid, and even more so because I am now besieged by the enemy. It is not this which makes me feel dispirited and dejected; on the contrary, I must express my indebtedness to you for giving me the occasion for showing my desire to serve Your Majesty and to die in your service – but rather the lack of the necessary provisions, since without them the soldiers become dispirited and the black people lose their faith and loyalty.

This is the state in which I am left. If Your Majesty should consider that sending me aid would be convenient for your service, you should do it; otherwise, I submit to whatever God and Your Majesty should require of me and these poor soldiers. I have learned that there is an English ship ready to depart, [[which could]] leave this report in São Tomé, for the Governor to send it to Your Majesty, whose Catholic person may Our Lord keep for the protection of Christendom and your subjects.

Mina, the 15th of May '634.

Pedro Mascarenhas

154 Letter from the Governor of São Tomé to the King[1272] (24/09/1634)

ABSTRACT – *The letter details the continuing needs and state of the Mina fortress, the death of Pedro Mascarenhas, dealing with the Dutch as well as English ships, and news from Manuel de Barros about Mina.*

The Governor of Mina Pedro Mascarenhas, seeing that he was besieged and in dire straits in which he had been put by the Dutch, had sent[1273] by an English ship to this island the report which I have sent to Your Majesty in two copies, informing me that he could not do it by the [[ship]] in which Your Majesty had sent him aid, [[and]] of which Romão de Bocete was Master, because she had been surrounded by seven Dutch ships in sight of the said fortress and its port, with the purpose of seizing or sinking her. And finding himself in such straits and seeing the great need to inform Your Majesty about this, he offered the Master of this English ship, for bringing this

---

[1272] AHU, S. Tomé, cx. 1, doc. 112; cf. MMA vol. 8, doc. 73, pp. 303–5.
[1273] Brásio's transcription reads '*o obrigou a mandar*' ('made him send'), which makes no sense in this context. The correct reading is possibly, as translated, '*obrigou a mandar*' (or, alternatively, '*me obrigou a mandar*,' that is, 'made me send').

report to this island, one thousand and five hundred *cruzados*, which he did not want to accept, and so he brought it at his own expense to this island, as he explained before its Justice, in addition to the said Governor Pedro Mascarenhas informing me of it in his letters and through the letters patent which he says he issued to the Master of the said ship.

Pedro Mascarenhas is dead. He has been succeeded in the governorship of that fortress, as I have been informed, by a friar who served as vicar there, who is a cripple and is always bedridden.[1274] Besides, the Gentiles of the land are said to be restless because of the death of the said Governor, and this explains the changes observed in them as a result of the great insistence of the Dutch, through every means they can. It is advisable for Your Majesty's service to send with all haste the remedy which may seem best to you.

The Master of this English ship, who brought this report which is of such import for the good of that fortress and Your Majesty's service, presented a petition to the Provider of Your Majesty's Exchequer, Manuel Correia, since he was bringing it [[the report]] at his own expense. He gave him license to load the ship with twenty thousand *arrobas*[1275] of sugar, for which he immediately paid the duties due to Your Majesty's Exchequer, both those which were due in this island and in the Custom House of Lisbon and the *Consulado*,[1276] as is attested in the books of the Factory regarding the clearance of this sugar, with which money part of the overdue allowances was paid to the clergymen and officials of Justice and the Exchequer, [[since]] there was nowhere in this island from which to satisfy [[their payment]], given its miserable state and its being incapable of yielding the wherewithal with which to pay the obligations Your Majesty has here, as its trade is not leased.

To this island's port arrived an English patache from the trade of Benin, loaded with fabrics,[1277] which [[patache]] I ordered to be seized given that she came to the said trade without license or lease, as is obligatory, under penalty of forfeiture of goods, and because it goes against Your Majesty's regulations. The Provider of the Exchequer determined the forfeiture to Your Majesty's Exchequer of the said patache and of the goods which she was carrying, which amounted to nine hundred seventy-eight thousand five hundred and seventy *reais*, which are kept in the safe which is in the Factory, so that Your Majesty may order what to do with them, or the allowances to be paid.

[1274] Friar Duarte Borges, professed member of the Order of Christ, had been appointed chaplain of the fortress of São Jorge da Mina by royal writ dated 1-3-1619. Cf. ANTT, *Chancelaria da Ordem de Cristo*, liv. 22, fols. 166v. See also MMA vol. 8, doc. 74, and docs. 82–83.

[1275] *Arroba*: see Glossary.

[1276] *Consulado*: see Glossary.

[1277] In Brásio's transcription, '*panaria*,' whose dictionary meaning is, and was, 'granary,' which makes no sense in this context. It seems that in parts of the former Portuguese empire, '*panaria*' also carried the meaning of 'cloth' (as a collective noun); see, for example, António Carreira, *Panaria Cabo-Verdiana Guineense: Aspectos históricos e sócio-económicos* (Lisbon: Museu de Etnologia do Ultramar/Junta de Investigações do Ultramar, 1968).

The land is now peaceful and their inhabitants friendly; they only feel the lack of a Bishop, which is a great lack. Your Majesty should send him with all haste, as this is most advisable for Your Majesty's service.

I have represented to Your Majesty the present needs of the fortress, for lack of the necessary means for its defense, and since this is of such importance for Your Majesty's service, I entreat you as a favor to proceed as is most convenient for your service. May Our Lord keep your Catholic person.

São Tomé, the 24th of September '634.

The above [[letter]] is the one I have sent to Your Majesty in three copies. I must inform Your Majesty again that, on the fifth day of the month of November last, an English ship made port in this island, proceeding from the fortress of Mina, and had there disembarked a soldier of the said fortress, named Manuel de Barros,[1278] who, in order to serve Your Majesty, sailed in her so that he might give information in this island and the letters here enclosed might be sent to Your Majesty. And from him I learned about the state in which the said fortress was left, and that the Vicar Friar Duarte, who had succeeded to the Governor Pedro Mascarenhas, had died a sudden death, and that he had been succeeded by André da Rocha Magalhães, who had served there as chief *Alcaide*, with whose appointment I am informed that part of the disorders which were raging among the Gentiles are now improving. But, above all, we request from Your Majesty that you assist the said fortress with your aid. May Our Lord keep your Catholic person.

São Tomé, the fifth of January '635.

Lourenço Pires de Távora

155 Letter from the Chief Captain of Mina to the King[1279] (10/10/1634)

ABSTRACT – *Manuel de Barros departs carrying information about the state of the fortress, the wine used for trade is deteriorating (except that from Madeira), and the Dutch presence around the fortress is such that Indian cloth is requested from King Filipe III to pay the soldiers.*

Following the death of Pedro Mascarenhas and Friar Duarte Borges, who were governors of this fortress,[1280] I have succeeded them in the said post while serving Your Majesty as chief Captain, with applause from all its population, and, after having ordered Your Majesty's officials to take stock of the factories

---

1278 See MMA vol. 8, doc. 74.
1279 AHU, S. Tomé, cx. 1, doc. 111; cf. MMA vol. 8, doc. 74, pp. 306–8.
1280 Friar Duarte Borges served as governor for only three months, without being appointed by royal writ.

and warehouses, they checked what was kept in them against what was spent as payment every three months and found that the provisions for the existing garrisons were only sufficient for the present month, not including the quarters[1281] of each of them (which amount to much, as Your Majesty will already have been informed). And since this garrison has no other means of sustenance other than what Your Majesty sends from that Kingdom (as it has no commerce with other [[garrisons]]), I felt bound (and the residents so requested me) to send this report to Your Majesty through the island of Madeira, I mean of São Tomé, for which purpose there came forward the master of an English ship which was about to leave this coast for the city of London, and Manuel de Barros,[1282] who was serving Your Majesty in this fortress and has done so in other situations of danger, in which he displayed great courage, as he did on this occasion, driven only by his desire not to fail on any occasion to show his wish to commit himself to Your Majesty's service, for which Your Majesty should consider yourself well served.

As for the account I could give Your Majesty about this coast, I refer to him and to my predecessors' letters, since there is no news to give Your Majesty apart from their information. Of the misery in which this fortress is left I ought to inform you by various means, but I shall not describe them in detail in this [[letter]] so as not to tire Your Majesty with reading such an extensive letter. This soldier will inform Your Majesty of the [[miseries]] which are suffered, as he has also experienced them.

The wine which Your Majesty sent with the commander[1283] Tomé Matoso was altered[1284] when it arrived at this coast, and thus not even the black people bought it for more than half a *tostão*,[1285] and had it not been put up for sale so quickly Your Majesty's Exchequer would have lost it entirely. Therefore, Your Majesty should give orders for wine not to be sent to this garrison, except that from the island of Madeira, since the same will happen to wine from elsewhere.

The Dutch frequent this coast as before, and [[Dutch]] ships arrive here every month. Presently they have seven or eight [[ships]] in different ports, whence they make much profit; and I have been informed that they are waiting for some from Holland, the exact number of which is unknown. I remain as watchful as is advisable for the good protection of this fortress, to whose defense I will commit my life. There is no lack of gunpowder or balls, though some of those which came on the ship of Lübeck[1286] are of too large a bore,[1287] since the artillery which there is here will not take any [[balls]] over twelve pounds.[1288] There are plenty

---

[1281] In Brásio's transcription, '*quarteis*' ('*quartéis*'), probably the money falling due every three months.

[1282] See MMA vol. 8, doc. 73.

[1283] In Brásio's transcription, '*cabo*,' that is, the person who is the head.

[1284] Literal translation of '*se mudaraõ*' ('*se mudaram*'), in the sense that the wine had deteriorated.

[1285] *Tostão*: see Glossary.

[1286] In Portuguese, as in Brásio's transcription, '*Lubeque.*' See MMA vol. 8, doc. 66.

[1287] In the sense of 'caliber.'

[1288] In Portuguese, '*libras.*'

of soldiers, although of those who came with Pedro Mascarenhas, who added up to ninety-something, there are no more than nineteen left; but these, together with those who were here, have already overcome the first illness, which here is the most dangerous one, and are fit for every occasion which might offer itself, whether on sea or on land. The important thing is that Your Majesty should send cloth from India with which to pay them, since, if these are not lacking in the Factory, the soldiers will take heart and the neighboring black people will keep the faith and the loyalty due to Your Majesty, whose Catholic person may God keep for the increase of Christendom and the protection of your kingdoms and subjects.

In Mina, on the 10th of October 1634.

André da Rocha [Magalhães][1289]

156 Information from André Da Fonseca to the King[1290] (02/03/1635)

ABSTRACT – *A report on the military and commercial situation of Mina, and the need for reinforcements, a new governor, special consideration for the English and vice versa, and how to chase the Dutch away from their fortress of Moure/Mori.*

André da Fonseca, who recently arrived from Mina on the ship São João Baptista, proceeding from the island of São Tomé, declared:

- That he sailed to Mina on the ship of Dunkirk [[?]][1291] which, from here, went to the aid of that fortress, carrying the Governor of the island of Madeira.
- That on the coast of Mina, seventeen leagues from our fortress, the said ship had met another Dutch ship which seemed to be waiting for her there, and that, although they engaged with each other, our ship had continued her course and further ahead had met another [[Dutch ship]], thus finding herself caught in between, battling with them both, four leagues from the fortress.
- That, when the Governor Pedro Mascarenhas learned about it, he had aid sent to her by canoe, with 20 soldiers, who were taken on board, and with them she continued defending herself until she found shelter beneath the fortress's artillery, where afterwards they continued to pursue her.
- That, after the aid which was being carried had been disembarked, the two ships, which would have 30 pieces[1292] each, were joined by another five, thus making seven in all, [[and]] they surrounded her, both[[*sic*]]

[1289] See MMA vol. 8, doc. 73, docs. 82 and 83.
[1290] AHU, S. Tomé, cx. 1, doc. 115; cf. MMA vol. 8, doc. 80, pp. 316–8.
[1291] In Brásio's transcription, '*Vnquerque.*'
[1292] The exact term would be 'pieces of ordnance,' that is, mounted guns, or cannons.

within the range of artillery [[fire]], and thus they remained for a period of three months, until on a dark night the said Dunkirker[1293] ship set sail and came to São Tomé, where she remained to see whether she would have a cargo to bring to this port; and that, even though she was followed by the enemy, she managed to give them the slip which such adroitness that they were unable to find her.

- That the Governor Pedro Mascarenhas had died on the 27th of June from an abscess, having there given satisfactory and valuable service.
- That the fortress of São Jorge had been left with sixty or seventy Portuguese, including clergymen and some officials.
- That it will have fifteen or sixteen pieces of good brass-artillery, albeit in need of restoration and repair, but nevertheless still serviceable.
- That it still has gunpowder and ammunition, since there was no occasion for using up what there was, which had been brought by Pedro Mascarenhas and went on the ship [[of]] Dunkirk.
- That [[the fortress]] is in great need of two to four long-range pieces, as was seen on this occasion with the ship of Dunkirk.
- That the person who is now governing is satisfactory. That he left here with Pedro Mascarenhas, and that he had made him chief Captain, and that he was elected by the people of the fortress.
- That the Gentiles of that coast are restless and hand-in-glove with the Dutch, and this because in our fortresses there is nothing with which to barter and trade with them.
- That in the castle of Akyem the Captain is Gaspar de Almeida.
- That the enemy makes much profit on that coast from ivory, *malagueta*, gold and civet. And that to him, the declarer, it was said that last year one ship alone had taken from there thirty *quintais*,[1294] and that this is not much compared to what can be taken.
- That at every time of the year there remain many enemy ships, and also ships from England, though from the fortress of São Jorge we supply the English with water and provisions, and this under the peace [[treaty]]; and that, in the same manner, they help us without fail whenever they are asked.
- That the Dutch fortress is situated in Boure, three leagues leeward from ours, where their ships make port. And that at Aldeia do Torto, which is windward from our fortress, they permanently have a ship of state[1295] with 40 pieces; and that from there they sail along the coast to their [[places of]] trade, and all the hinterland goes to the enemy; and that this ship is the only obstacle to the aid which is sent from here.

[1293] In Brásio's transcription, '*Vnquerqueza.*'
[1294] *Quintal* (sing.): see Glossary.
[1295] Literal translation of '*nao destado*' ('*nau de estado*'), possibly a ship government representatives used, or a ceremonial one.

- That, if aid is sent to Mina without the enemy sensing it, with two galleons and two pataches, these four vessels will be sufficient to seize their fortress and any ships which may be there, without any more [[vessels]] being necessary, and that with this, together with the fortification of the post of the island of Torto and there being goods for trade, the enemy will be kept out, since the black people only go to them because they need their trade.

And he thus declared that the said André da Fonseca is a *cavaleiro fidalgo*[1296] of Your Majesty's Household, and 48 years of age, and to certify everything he signed. Lisbon, on the 2nd of March '635.

André da Fonseca

157 *Letter to the King About Mina*[1297] *(10/03/1635)*

ABSTRACT – *List of objects to be sent for aid to the Mina fortress for it to be effective, but there is a lack of money for putting this plan into effect.*

+

My Lord,

In view of what Your Majesty orders regarding the preparation of two caravels to be sent with aid to Mina, I must say that an inquiry having been made at this River [[in Lisbon]], only two fitted out caravels have been found which may be of service. Either of them will make this voyage against their will, but should Your Majesty be served, they must needs do it. The only doubt concerns what this aid should consist of, since it appears to me that it would be advisable to send now to Mina up to one hundred soldiers, three thousand *cruzados* in cloth[[?]],[1298] both for them and for those who are there, two thousand [[*cruzados*]] in provisions for [[Mina]], not counting those for the journey, fifty *quintais*[1299] of gunpowder, four sixteen- to twenty-four-pounder pieces[1300] of brass-artillery with field carriages for the fortress, four thousand balls to fit the bore of these pieces, six skilled artillerymen, twenty *quintais* of rope, another twenty of musket and harquebus bullets, one hundred fully-equipped muskets, one hundred harquebuses, also fully-equipped, one hundred pikes, fifty half-pikes,[1301] two hundred iron spades, two hundred mattocks, one hundred axes, one hundred cutting sickles, one

---

[1296] 'Knight *fidalgo*,' a rank of the nobility.
[1297] AHU, S. Tomé, cx. 1, doc. 116; cf. MMA vol. 8, doc. 81, pp. 319–20.
[1298] In Brásio's transcription, '*roupas*'; it is not totally clear whether the word refers to 'cloth' or 'clothing.'
[1399] *Quintal* (sing.): a unit of mass.
[1300] The exact term would be 'pieces of ordnance,' that is, mounted guns, or cannons.
[1301] Also known as 'spontoons.'

hundred pruning sickles, a man who knows how to refine gunpowder, twenty *quintais* of saltpeter for [[the gunpowder]] which may have become spoiled over time, two metalworkers,[1302] two blacksmiths, two masons to carry out and rectify repairs, all of them with their tools and smith's implements, sixty *quintais* of iron, ten *quintais* of steel, and an engineer of fortifications – this seems to me to be what should be sent as aid to Mina. To occupy vessels the weather has been fine [[?]][1303] since March; there is no ammunition or people on the land, nor do I know that there is any substance in Your Majesty's Exchequer, and therefore I do not see how this aid can be carried out. It is necessary that Your Majesty should give orders to determine how much [[aid]] it should be, where it can be found, and whence the money is to be taken for whatever is to be bought, and with this I will do whatever is in my power and Your Majesty should order.

In Lisbon, the 10th of March '635.

Rui Correia Lucas

158 Letter from Luís Galvão De Melo to the King[1304] (17/03/1635)

ABSTRACT – *Information obtained about the situation of the fortress of Mina and the island of São Tomé, according to the official inquiry.*

+

My Lord,

Your Majesty has ordered me to inform you about the state of the affairs of Mina and about the foreign ships which go to the island of São Tomé to trade, and to obtain this information from persons who have recently arrived from Mina, and what I have learned is as follows.

From Manuel de Basto,[1305] who was constable[1306] of Mina for more than four years, [[and]] who arrived in Setubal on a caravel of the same town, [[whose]] Master [[was]] Pedro Bravo,[1307] which departed from the island of Madeira, I have learned that the Governor of Mina, Pedro Mascarenhas,[1308] had died, and that of the one hundred and sixty men he had taken with him from this Kingdom only

---

[1302] In Portuguese, '*serralheiro(s)*,' someone who, in addition to being a locksmith, performs similar work with metal.

[1303] In Brásio's transcription, '*em*' (i.e. 'in'/'on'), which makes no sense in this context; it is thus possible this should read '*bem*' (i.e. 'fine').

[1304] AHU, S. Tomé, cx. 1, doc. 109; cf. MMA vol. 8, doc. 83, pp. 327–9.

[1305] See MMA vol. 8, doc. 82.

[1306] In Portuguese, as in Brásio's transcription, '*Condestável*,' in this case, either commander of the artillery or keeper of the fortress.

[1307] See MMA vol. 8, doc. 82.

[1308] See MMA vol. 8, doc. 52, doc. 60, docs. 65–66, docs. 73–74, doc. 80, doc. 82, doc. 85.

eight were alive, and that they died of illness; following whose [[the Governor's]] death the soldiers of that fortress elected as Captain and Governor Friar Duarte Borges, a friar of Tomar, of the Order of Christ, who was Vicar of the fortress, [[and]] who governed for three months and died.

And following his death the same soldiers elected as Governor André da Rocha, a former retainer of Pedro Mascarenhas, a person unfit for the office he holds; this information was [[also]] given to me by other men who came from the island of São Tomé.

The said Manuel de Basto further added that the fortress of Mina is in great danger, for lack of both Captain and artillery, but that it is not lacking in ammunition; and that in the fortress of Mina and its forts of Esma and Akyem, which are situated thirty leagues from the coast, there would be little more than eighty men. And that the black people of the land do not trade with the Portuguese because Your Majesty's Factory has no goods. And that the soldiers are not paid because there is not a thing to be found in the factories. And that the black people go to trade with the Dutch and the English who frequent that coast for the trade of gold. And that the fortress is in need of a constable.

And as regards the matters of São Tomé and the foreign ships which go there to trade, the persons from whom I have obtained the information say that, some two years ago, the Governor of the island of São Tomé, Lourenço Pires de Távora, allowed an English ship which had come from England, [[whose]] Master [[was]] João de Soto,[1309] an Englishman, to trade in the said island with its merchants and Your Majesty's factors, since all of them entreated the said Governor to let them trade with the English, which they did.

And as at that time Francisco Barreto arrived as Governor[1310] of the said island, the Englishman left the port; and complying with a message that he received from him [[the Governor(?)]], he put to sea. And that last September the same Englishman had been [[there]] with another, larger ship; and he sold to and bought from the merchants of the said island, since he was allowed to do it by the said Lourenço Pires de Távora, who on the death of the Governor Francisco Barreto was again elected Governor by the local people; and that he is now governing.

At the time of the departure of these men from São Tomé, two English ships anchored [[there]]; but because there was no sugar, they did not load. This is what I was able to gather as quickly as Your Majesty ordered, and for that purpose I labored to find these men, who were not present at the appointed hour and time for taking down this information, which I could not do immediately upon receiving the order for lack of a scribe. May God keep Your Majesty's Catholic person.

Lisbon, March the 17th '635.

a) Luís Galvão de Lemos[1311]

[1309] Portuguese form of an unidentified English name (possibly, 'John of Southampton [Soton]').
[1310] Francisco Barreto de Meneses was appointed governor of São Tomé by royal writ dated 8-6-1630. See ANTT, *Chancelaria de D. Filipe III*, fols. 145v.-146.
[1311] See MMA vol. 8, doc. 82.

159 Consultation of the Council of Portugal
About Aid to Mina[1312] (10/01/1636)

ABSTRACT – *The council examines the requests of the new governor of Mina, and the aid which he requests to take with him, including a physician, surgeon, and pharmacopoeia. Delays, however, stall the aid requested.*

My Lord,

In the instruction of the 7th of December last Your Majesty ordered this Council to examine two enclosed memoranda of Jorge de Mendoza Pazaña,[1313] one about his petition for an *encomienda*,[1314] and the other in which he requests armed ships to take with him to Mina; and on whatever opinions the Council should issue about each of the matters Your Majesty should be consulted.

In the memorandum which deals with the armed ships to be taken to Mina, it is said that Your Majesty has granted him the governorship of Mina, which he has accepted trusting that Your Majesty in your grandeur will grant him favors worthy of it, in consideration of the services which he has rendered to Your Majesty with notorious satisfaction, valor and disinterestedness; and that in the said governorship he expects to be worthy of Your Majesty, by defending that garrison from the enemy who now infest and threaten it, which he will not be able to do without Your Majesty granting that he be given armed ships which may take him and escort him so that he may protect himself from the dangers of the journey, and which may take the soldiers, and the persons with experience and information about that coast, whom Your Majesty should order to be given to him and to remain there, since at present that fortress is greatly lacking and in great need of people. And may Your Majesty be served to give him gunpowder, ammunition, supplies and all the other things required in sufficient quantity for him to defend himself, given that, should the occasion arrive, the Kingdom is too far away to be able to aid him. And Your Majesty should also have him given a smelter to fit bushings in many pieces of artillery which are out of service, and that he be given six pieces of artillery to take so as to replace another six which lie destroyed in the fortress, which he will send back to the Kingdom in the ships which may take him coal and charcoal,[1315] nails of every sort, iron, steel, and carpenters for repairing artillery, a physician, a surgeon, a barber and a pharmacopoeia. And in addition to the abovementioned, may Your Majesty grant that he be given two light caravels

---

[1312] AGS, Secretarias Provinciales, liv. 1649, fols. 12–12v; cf. MMA vol. 8, doc. 91, pp. 344–7. Document written in Castilian.

[1313] Castilian for 'Jorge de Mendonça Pessanha.'

[1314] *Encomienda*: in this context, probably the granting of the dignity of *comendador*, together with the lands and rents ascribed to it (rather than the right to explore indigenous labor, a system characteristic of the Spanish colonization of the Americas).

[1315] In Brásio's transcription, '*carbon* [...] *de bresso*' ('*carbón* [...] *de brezo*'), which is a type of charcoal made from briar.

to be at the said fortress permanently, so that with them he may inform Your Majesty of everything which he may find necessary, so that Your Majesty be better served and that he may better perform his duty.

The Council having examined everything, the opinion was that Your Majesty should be informed that, for the purpose of sending aid to Mina, the necessary orders have been given, a letter having been written on the 6th of September of last year to Her Ladyship the Princess, [[saying]] that, even though Your Majesty was certain that Her Ladyship the Princess was taking due care of having aid sent to that garrison in the manner considered suitable for its security, Your Majesty enjoined her to have it done without delay, so that it [[the aid]] might without fail go with the Governor (whom Your Majesty had then already appointed, Francisco de Melo e Castro), and Your Majesty should also be informed whether any aid had gone escorting the *naos*[1316] of the said year.

And Her Ladyship the Princess having written to Your Majesty, in a letter dated the 25th of that same month, informing you that Francisco de Melo had excused himself from the said governorship, which excusal Your Majesty was served to accept; [[and]] Her Ladyship the Princess having said that the Council of the Treasury had considered that some of the things which had been prepared to be sent as aid to the said garrison were perishing, which aid it was considered convenient to send together with the Governor, both because if it were not delayed there would be no need for other vessels and because there was no one there of recognized reliability, and it was to be feared that anything that should go earlier might go astray; [[and]] Her Ladyship the Princess having reminded Your Majesty that you should take a resolution regarding the appointment of a person to govern that garrison with as much haste as possible, given the significance of its lacking a head which might govern it,

– Your Majesty had a reply sent to Her Ladyship the Princess on the 12th of October next, [[saying]] that you would very soon inform her of the person you should appoint, so that he might embark immediately; and because it was convenient not to lose the time gained in the preparation of what would be sent to that fortress, Your Majesty strongly enjoined her to have checked three or four ships of the ports [[from]] which they usually go to those parts, and that they be made ready to sail, gathering the cloth, black people and all other aid which ought to be sent according to the needs of that garrison, so that it be not detained for any reason whatsoever.

And Your Majesty having ordered Her Ladyship the Princess to be informed, by letter dated the 17th of that same month of October, that Your Majesty had appointed Jorge de Mendoza Pazaña as Governor of Mina, she was informed that, since Jorge de Mendoza was at this Court, the grant had been made public here and orders given that he should depart immediately, enjoining Her Ladyship

---

[1316] Given the specificity of this reference, the original Castilian word '*naos*' (usually a synonym for 'large vessels') will be used in the translation.

the Princess to have the corresponding letters patent given to him without delay, and that all the aid which he will take should be prepared and made ready, in accordance with what Your Majesty has ordered.

Therefore, it is the opinion of the Council that Jorge Mendoza Pazaña should go immediately to Lisbon to make his preparations, and that Her Ladyship the Princess should be sent a letter [[enjoining her]] to give all that she can, in view of the needs of that fortress, and that he [[Jorge Mendoza Pazaña]] should be given the six pieces he requests, and a smelter's assistant to fit the bushings he mentions, and that in any case he should sail during the ships' monsoon,[1317] with orders to send back the pieces which cannot be used there.

[Four initialed signatures]

[On the reverse]: 10th of January 1636

160 Representations about the Abuses of the Blacks of the Coast of Mina[1318] (29/01/1637)

ABSTRACT – *A set of letters with information from the Holy Office containing news about arrangements for the investigation of complaints. There is a letter from Gaspar Lopes with information about the customs of 'black people, brown people and behaviors of some white residents in the fortress of São Jorge da Mina.' The document is published for the first time.*

[cross]

Most Illustrious Lord,

N° 13644

The letters and the enclosed memorial which are acknowledged in the paper of the Secretary of the Council having been seen in this *Mesa*,[1319] it appears that the most effective way of remedying the matters mentioned in the said letters would be for Your Most Illustrious Lordship to send a Visitor to those places, and that meanwhile a commission could be sent to their Ordinaries, [..............][1320] an examination in the accustomed manner [...................], and because there is no evidence of the inquiry referred to in the letter of Manuel Correia, it should be ordered that it be remitted to this *Mesa*, after the witnesses have been ratified. And the person who presented the said memorial should declare the other

---

[1317] As in Portuguese ('*monção*'), '*monzón*' seems to also mean, by extension, the period of the year most favorable for sailing to certain places. In this context, this may refer specifically to the departure of the Indiamen.

[1318] ANTT, Tribunal do Santo Ofício, Inquisição de Lisboa, proc. 13644, ff. 1–7v.

[1319] *Mesa*: in this case, the assembly of the inquisitorial judges of the first instance, as opposed to the *Conselho Geral* (which judged the appeals).

[1320] Dots between square brackets indicate words which are illegible, due mainly to stains in the paper.

distinguishing marks he knows of Diogo Henriques Cardoso, because he, being the son-in-law of one Vasco Pires of Trás-os-Montes, has considerable evidence against him, unlike the other people included in the memorial, as mentioned in the attached report of this Inquisition's Prosecutor. May Your Most Illustrious Lordship order what is of service to you. *Mesa*, the 29th of January 1637.

[sign.] *Pantaleão Roiz [......]* Inquisitor   *Álvaro*

Pacheco   de Ataíde [...]

This morning His Most Illustrious [Lordship] delivered to me the three papers which I enclose in this [letter] to Your Graces. 1st, a letter of Doctor Gaspar Lopes, Vicar of Mina, [....] Your Graces to decide whether, in view of [.................] to take any course of action. 2nd, another which came from São Tomé, for the *Mesa* to confirm whether it received the inquiry [...........] order to be remitted. 3rd, a memorial similar to the one sent three days ago to Your Graces, which was submitted to the Council, about which Your Graces have already informed, for Your Graces to do the same in this case. To all of which I attend with this [letter], which has no other purpose. May God keep Your Graces. From the *Secreto*,[1321] Monday, the 29th of January 1637.

[sign.] *Diogo Velho*[?] [...]

[cross]

My Lord,

In order to unburden my conscience and to fulfill my obligations, I cannot but inform Your Lordship of the abuses and superstitions of the black people in this town and fortress of São Jorge da Mina and its district, without there being a means of eliminating them or submitting the black people to the knowledge of our Holy Catholic Faith.

Firstly, it is their custom, on given Fridays of the year, to kill a number of dogs and to throw their blood over what they call their saints; and they eat the dogs' meat on the said days; and the greater part of them are Christians, and when they are rebuked, they say that it is their custom and that His Majesty orders them to keep their customs.

For their saints or idols, they have stones and sticks which they take from the bush, and *valee's* [*sic*][1322] bones, and mud wallows for pigs, and other dirty and filthy things.

[1321] *Secreto*: a part of the Inquisition building, where files, books, and other documents were kept in secret.

[1322] '*Valee,*' or '*valé*' (the double 'e' usually means the vowel is accentuated), the meaning of which is obscure. Since in Portuguese the 'v' and the 'b' were often interchangeable, there are two possibilities. The first is that it should read '*balé,*' though the single (and uncommon) meaning attached to this word was head of the house, or the oldest man in the lineage; in this case, '*valé/balé*' could stand for 'ancestor,' thus 'ancestors' bones.' The second is that it should read '*baleia*' ('whale'), but this seems as unlikely in this context as the first.

They celebrate a feast that they call Tompós [?],[1323] which [consists of] four Saturdays and in which they throw into the sea a great amount of food, as well as of wine, so that the sea might give them many fish.

They marry according to the uses of this land, Christian man with gentile woman, and gentile man with Christian woman, and often Christian man with Christian woman, and they live in sin all their lives, without there being a remedy for it, because if they are urged to marry at the church door, they immediately reply that it is their custom; and when some of them do marry at the church door, if they get angry with their wives, they throw them out of the house and repudiate them according to their use, and they take other women as their concubines, and their wives other men as lovers.

They also have the custom of marrying five or many women, and they marry one of them at the church door and keep the rest according to their customs, and there is no way of taking these from them.

They also have the custom, as was the usage in the Old Law, that in marriages between a black man and a black woman, if she dies, the man immediately takes for his wife the nearest female relative of his dead wife, even if she is her sister; in the same way, if he dies, the woman takes for her husband the nearest male relative of her dead husband.

In matters of affinity, they have no scruples, whether the black or the mulatto people of this land, for they place no check on cohabiting with two relatives, and sisters, and often with mother and daughter.

When a black man dies, even if he is a Christian and is buried in church, they will make him a grave in the brush, where they perform his obsequies, and place there sheep and much wine and all his trophies and insignia of his titles; and in mourning they use up thirty and forty thousand *reais* of palm wine, which they offer to all the people, and not even a prayer for the dead[1324] is said for his soul.

As regards the observance of the Commandments of the Holy Mother Church, it is better not to speak about it, for they never or only seldom attend Mass, and they work on Sundays and on holy days, and they observe the Tuesday as a feast day, and every seven weeks they celebrate a feast which they call Mufina [?], when it is forbidden to make contracts, or to pay and receive money.

They never confess the truth, nor do they acknowledge any mortal sin, because they say that stealing is not a sin, for what they steal is given by God. Fornication is not reprehensible among them. They do not know what fasting is, nor do they abstain from eating meat on the days when it is forbidden or have scruples regarding any of these matters; they do not fear excommunication. If they are put in prison or sentenced to pay a fine, we risk having a riot and losing this fortress, because these people are untamable and without reason. This as regards black people.

[1323] The handwriting here is not clear; it might also read '*Sompós.*'
[1324] In the manuscript, '*responso.*'

As regards the mulatto people of this land, men as well as women, it is almost the same, but I cannot see any remedy as they are more influenced by the evil customs of the black people than by the virtues of the white people of Portugal (admitting that any virtue can last long in this land); since neither through excommunications which I have imposed on them, nor through any warning on my part, have I been able to make them Christians, to come to Mass, to keep Sunday and holy days, and not to live in sin, for many of them are married and have their concubines living in their houses, without there being any remedy for it; because when I want to take action against these, the Governor tells me that this is a garrison and that he does not want any riot that would put the fortress at risk, and thus everything remains unpunished.

These black and mulatto people, and I gather that even some white people, also have the custom of giving oath to one another, and to their own wives, according to the uses of this land. And wishing to remedy it, I imposed an excommunication, which I published in the station of the Mass[1325] on a Sunday. The result of this was that a married mulatto man, who seemed to be included in this case, sent word for me to go to his house, saying that there was a sick woman in his house who needed me to hear her confession. And when he caught me inside, he started asking me why I had imposed excommunications for matters such as those, and other foolish things of the kind, so much so that I found myself in dire straits and ran away as fast as I could.

As regards mulatto women, I am informed that they use the same ceremonies and superstitions as the black women; and once, when someone rebuked a mulatto woman for certain things which in this land are called *feitiços*[1326] (even though they are not such and should rather be called superstitions, for these people have no pact with the devil, nor does he have much to bother with them), she replied that the white people of Portugal also showed their *feitiço*, saying it by the Holy Sacrament.[1327]

Regarding all these matters, I will receive much pleasure if Your Lordship should seek information from certain persons who have lived in this land, in particular from Pedro Sardinha, who used to be Factor of this fortress, born in Palmela, and Diogo Correia, born in Santarém, first scribe of this fortress, and in particular from the bearer of this [letter], who may inform Your Lordship of the bad Christianity that there is in this land, so much so that, apart from the innocent children who die baptized before they can use their reason, I do not know of any other person who is saved. This is what is going on in this fortress regarding

---

[1325] In the manuscript, *'estação da Missa,'* i.e. the address the priest made to the faithful (from the Latin *'statio'*).
[1326] *Feitiços*: in Portuguese, this applies both to so-called African 'fetishes' and to European witchcraft.
[1327] Literal translation of '[...] *mostrauão o seu feitiço dizendo-o pello Santissimo Sacrament'* ('[...] *mostravam o seu feitiço, dizendo-o pelo Santíssimo Sacramento'*); another possible translation of the last section might be '[...] saying it for the Holy Sacrament.' This is possibly a reference to the practice of Eucharistic adoration and/or the sacrifice of the sacrament of the Eucharist during the mass, when transubstantiation is said to take place.

the Christian religion. I will be very much obliged if Your Lordship sends me some order, so that I and the Vicars who shall come after me may unburden our consciences. May God keep Your Lordship for the defense of the Catholic Faith and the extirpation of heresies.

São Jorge da Mina, on the 5ᵗʰ of December 1635 years.

[sign.] *Doctor Gaspar Lopes*

Vicar Administrator

161 Petition of Jorge De Almeida[1328] (13/11/1638)

ABSTRACT – *Services Pascoal de Almeida in Mina rendered. He established good relations with the local people and their leaders to attract and then withdraw them from the influence of the Dutch, in both political and religious terms. The Portuguese had lost São Jorge da Mina to the Dutch in 1637.*

+

[My Lord],

Pascoal de Almeida, Captain and Factor of the Castle of Akyem,[1329] in the district of Mina, through his procurator and father Jorge de Almeida, declares that, for his services, Your Majesty granted him, the Petitioner, the said post for a period of six years, and [[that]] the Petitioner has been serving in it for nine [[years]] with notoriously great satisfaction, spending there a greater part of his wealth with the black people of those settlements, with a view to keeping them under the obligation of not rebelling against Your Majesty in favor of the Dutch rebels, who, by every means, and many expedients and endeavors, tried to entice the said black people and have them on their side: because they believe that without them they cannot seize or attack the said castle, which is their entire purpose, in order to extinguish definitively the Catholic arms and the name of Portugal in those parts.

And the Petitioner, in order to serve Your Majesty in the said post, which Your Majesty was served to entrust to him, and to prevent so great a damage and discredit to this Monarchy, has, with great expenditure of his own wealth, been maintaining the said castle and the said black people in the Faith and in the service of Your Majesty, by keeping them under obligation with offerings, which he gave them, and with promises, which he made them in Your Majesty's name, and, these last four years, meeting the great need of providing for the said castle with all necessities, because of which [[situation]] it is in great danger of being lost if Your

---

[1328] AHU, S. Tomé, cx. 1, doc. 163; cf. MMA vol. 8, doc. 112, pp. 405–7.
[1329] Pascoal de Almeida was appointed factor of the castle of Akyem ('Axim'), for six years, by writ dated 13-9-1628. See ANTT, *Chancelaria de D. Filipe III*, liv. 31, fol. 326.

Majesty should fail to send aid, with all haste, in men and in everything else of which it is greatly in need, and some capes, hats and fascine knives,[1330] which it is customary to send to the said black people and which the Petitioner has promised them in Your Majesty's name, so that they do not go to the enemy, as they would have done were it not for the said offerings which the Petitioner made from his own wealth, and for the promises made in Your Majesty's name through which he is bound. And because the abovementioned is of great importance, and a matter which Your Majesty should order to be provided for most carefully, so as not to lose definitively the dominion of Mina, which used to be so honorable and so useful for this Crown; and also because the Petitioner completed three years ago the six-year [[term]] for which Your Majesty appointed him to the said post, since he has been serving in it for these last nine [[years]],

– [[the Petitioner]] asks that Your Majesty may grant him the favor of sending someone to succeed him, to whom he may entrust the said castle, and that you discharge him from the promises which he has made in Your Majesty's name to the said black people and their captains, by sending them capes, hats, [[and]] fascine knives; and also that Your Majesty may be served to have aid sent to the said endangered castle, providing it with men and everything else in which it is greatly lacking, & *R.M.*[1331]

+

a) Jorge de Almeida

[*In the margin*]: It seems very fair that Jorge de Almeida be granted what he requests in his letter.

[*Initialed signature*]

[*Vertically*]: To be seen by the Procurator of the Exchequer. Lisbon, the 13th of November 1638.

[*Three initialed signatures*]

162 Notes by Manuel Da Cunha Regarding the Aid for Akyem ('Axim')[1332] (04/06/1639)

ABSTRACT – *The former governor of Mina presents his comments and reservations regarding the aid suggested by Captain José Martins for the military defense of the castle of Akyem ('Axim'), having already lost São Jorge da Mina to the Dutch two years earlier.*

[1330] In Brásio's transcription, '*treçados*' ('*terçados*'), a kind of short broad sword. See Antonio Luiz M.C. Costa, *Armas Brancas: Lanças, espadas, maças e flechas: Como lutar sem pólvora da pré-história ao século XXI* (São Paulo: Editora Draco, 2015).
[1331] & *R.M.* (or *E.R.M.*): an abbreviation for '*Espera receber mercê*,' i.e. 'Hopes to be granted the favor.'
[1332] AHU, S. Tomé, cx. 1, doc. 176; cf. MMA vol. 8, doc. 116, pp. 416–19.

The aid which José Martins[1333] indicates as necessary for
the provision of the castle of Akyem, to which a reply is given
in the margin as appropriate, is as follows.

Two hundred iron bars. – Only a few of these iron bars were sent at Your Majesty's
expense in my time, while I was Governor in Mina, for the blacksmith of the
fortress to use in repairing it, since the rebels used to take them in great
numbers and sell them cheaply, while the monopoly was in the hands of
Count Mauricio,[1334] to whom it had been given by the estates; and today the
same must happen with the person who succeeded him. In spite of this, it is
my opinion that a hundred [[iron bars]] should be sent, since, as the black
people of Akyem are far from the Dutch commerce, I do not doubt that they
will be sold there easily.

Four thousand brass manillas. – The four thousand manillas which are mentioned
did not use to be sent to Mina while I was there, nor do I know what use this
merchandise could have apart from buying from the black Alande[1335] (!) a
kind of strips which they call *bandas*,[1336] which is not the type of cloth usually given as payment to the soldiers, and therefore it is my opinion that they
should not be sent.

Four thousand rods[1337] *of* almafega.[1338] – Two thousand rods of *almafega* will be
enough, because even though this is a fabric which is quite profitable, it is
not sold rapidly.

Forty score caudel[1339] *and* mantaz[1340] *cloths.* – All forty score should go, but
the *mantaz* cloths should be black and large, rather than white, which sell
poorly; and should there be no black *mantaz* cloth (which would necessarily
come in this ship) to be found, there could go [[in their place]] *especes*[1341] or
gandares.[1342] But I declare that black *mantazes* and *caudéis* are what is there
most common and most easily sold.

Six carmine[1343] *capes, with six hats and golden fascine knives.* – It is sufficient
to send three of each of these items, which is the maximum [[quantity]] we,

[1333] See MMA vol. 8, docs. 117–18.
[1334] Portuguese for 'Maurits'; reference to Count Johan Maurits van Nassau-Siegen. See MMA vol.
6, doc. 138.
[1335] In Brásio's transcription, '*alans*.'
[1336] A definition of these '*bandas*' may be found in MMA, vol. 3, doc. 15: 'two strips of cotton one or
two palms wide' which 'the natives [[use]] for covering themselves.'
[1337] In Portuguese, '*vara*' (sing.): see Glossary.
[1338] *Almafega* (also written '*almáfega*' or '*almárfega*'): see Glossary.
[1339] *Caudel* (or '*chaudel*'; pl. '*caudéis*'/'*chaudéis*'): a kind of calico used for bedcovers.
[1340] *Mantaz*: a sort of cloth which comes from Cambaya.
[1341] Unidentified type of cloth.
[1342] *Gandar* was a kind of coarse cotton cloth, which was exported from India to Africa.
[1343] In Brásio's transcription, '*grã*,' i.e. 'carmine,' hence 'carmine fabric.'

the Governors, used to take when we went to Mina; and we used to give them to the three black Captains who are in that town of São Jorge as soon as we arrived there. As regards the capes, they should be of cochineal[1344] remnants and not of carmine, as indicated, which is much more expensive.

Gunpowder, [[cannon-]] balls, and fuses. – All these three items should go, though with the proviso that the balls should fit the artillery of that castle, [[which]] is ^made up of small falconets, as I remember. And I nevertheless [[recommend]] that two good 12- to 16-pounder pieces should be sent there, even if they are made of iron, as they will be useful should an occasion present itself. And there should go a couple of bombardiers, since I believe there are none there.

A pharmacopeia. – Of this very little will be sufficient, as it soon spoils there.

A clergyman. – It is indispensable that this clergyman should go unfailingly to remedy the state of abandonment of the Christians, both white and black, who are in that castle and village.[1345]

Ten soldiers. – I do not think that these ten soldiers are necessary, because I have heard that José Martins used to say that, when he arrived in that castle, there were twenty-five there, which is sufficient, nor will it bear any more. And this may be confirmed with him.

Biscuit,[1346] *vegetables, and flour.* – Of these three items, only flour is needed for holy wafers, and for these two barrels of six *almudes*[1347] each are enough.

Oil and wine for the soldiers. – There could go one pipe of oil, and twelve to fifteen pipes of wine, of which it should be ordered that three be immediately given on the part of Your Majesty to the black people, since this is what pleases and satisfies them most. And, after this, they should be given the capes, hats, and swords. And I am also of the opinion that they should be given a score of cloth, as the Factor may think appropriate, so that they can be divided between them all, and with this – [[and]] telling them that Your Majesty will send much aid and restore Mina soon – they will be very happy and propitious.

One hundred dozen wood-handled knives. – These knives are not necessary, since the rebels bring many with them and sell them very cheaply, which they can do, and the black people buy them from them for that reason.

Brandy[1348] *for the black captains.* – These spirits are dispensable if wine, which is less costly, is given.

[Manuel da Cunha]

[1344] Cloth dyed with cochineal.
[1345] The village of Adena.
[1346] In Portuguese, '*biscoito*': see Glossary.
[1347] *Almude*: see Glossary.
[1348] In Brásio's transcription, '*aguardente*,' a strong distilled beverage.

163 Petition of Captain José Martins[1349] (16/06/1639)

ABSTRACT – *A petition by Captain José Martins for services rendered on the coast of Mina.*

+

My Lord,

Captain José Martins[1350] says that about a year ago he departed from the island of São Tomé with a message for Your Majesty, of importance for your royal service, requesting aid for that garrison and for the castle of Akyem, which is on the coast of Mina, and [[that]] he arrived in this city at the end of the month of September of last year. And he, the Petitioner, having made all the appeals he could to Your Majesty's officials in charge of this affair, has not yet seen any of them approved as regards the said aid, with the argument that they were expecting a vessel from England, of an English merchant named Guilherme Roles[1351] – which he will send to the said island, since he has a license from Your Majesty – in which [[vessel]] it has been determined that the said aid will be sent.

And given that, in the said garrisons, there is no news of this Petitioner or of his arrival here, and because of the delay in receiving the said aid, it must be assumed that he was either drowned or seized by the enemy, and their [[the garrisons']] residents will have lost any hope of receiving assistance, for which very reason it is necessary that Your Majesty should give the necessary orders so that he, the Petitioner, may be given due dispatch and sent for the said purpose, especially since the vessel of the said Englishman, which was being expected, has already arrived.

[[The Petitioner]] requests that Your Majesty be served to order that the said vessel be made ready as soon as possible, and that the said aid be sent, and that [[the vessel]] should take it to the said garrisons, before they are definitely lost and in the hands of the enemy, bearing in mind the great expense Your Majesty's Exchequer would incur in recovering them. *E. R. M.*

164 Consultation of the Council of State[1352] (16/06/1639)

ABSTRACT – *Favor granted to Captain José Martins for services rendered on the coast of Mina. The council is of the opinion he should be sent as commander of the ship with aid for Mina.*

[1349] AHU, *S. Tomé*, cx. 1, doc. 165; cf. MMA vol. 8, doc. 117, pp. 420–21. The document is undated. I have given it the same date as the following document because its contents suggest it belongs in June 1639, though it might have been written at an earlier date.

[1350] See MMA vol. 8, doc. 116 and doc. 118.

[1351] Portuguese for 'William Rawls' or 'Rowls.'

[1352] AHU, S. Tomé, cx. 1, doc. 15; cf. MMA vol. 8, doc. 118, pp. 422–3.

+

My Lord,

A petition and papers of Captain José Martins[1353] were remitted to this Council, with orders from the Government that they should be examined, and a consultation made. In which petition he [[the Petitioner]] says that he came from the island of São Tomé with a message for Your Majesty by order of the Governor of the said island, with great danger to his person and expenditure of his own resources, since he came at his own expense, as is shown in the certificates which he presented. And for eight months now he has been going around in this city, making requests, and trying to obtain aid for that island and for the castle of Akyem, which is on the coast of Mina. And since presently Your Majesty has a ship in this city's port by which you are sending the said aid, and because he has knowledge of the said parts and last year, by order of the Governor, there seized two ships of Dutch pirates, he, José Martins, being the commander[1354] of the vessels which assailed them,

– he asks that, in consideration of the above, Your Majesty may grant him the favor of sending him as commander of the said aid with the title of Captain, giving him the customary payment, considering also the fact that he has served Your Majesty, as attested in the certificates which he presented.

With the abovementioned petition and certificates, the Provider of the Depot[1355] was ordered to give information [[on the matter]], which he did, saying that what the said José Martins reports in his petition is attested in his papers, and that, in accordance with this, he is deserving that Your Majesty should grant him every honor and favor which he requests, considering both his valor and the long time he has been away from his home[[?]].[1356]

And all this having been examined by Your Majesty's Procurator of the Exchequer, he replied that this is not a legal matter but a favor, and that Your Majesty should grant it to him as you might think fit for your service.

It was the opinion of the Council that, considering the valor with which Captain José Martins has been serving in those parts, having through his endeavor and industry seized two Dutch ships, and that he came to this Kingdom with a message from the Governor of São Tomé asking that aid be sent to that garrison and the castle of Akyem, Your Majesty should grant him the favor that he requests, giving him only three payments on account of the salary he earns there, [[and]] for that purpose issuing the necessary orders.

Lisbon, the 16th of June 1639.

[1353] See MMA vol. 8, docs. 116–17.
[1354] In the transcription, '*cabo*,' the head person in charge.
[1355] In Brásio's transcription, '*Prouedor dos Almazês*' ('*Provedor dos Almazéns*'): see Glossary.
[1356] In Brásio's transcription, '*Caza*' ('*Casa*'), which might also be translated as '(the) House.'

a) Tomás de Ibio *a)* Rodrigo Francisco de Carvalho Calderón

Doctor António das Póvoas also voted in this consultation, and he did not sign because he was not present.

[*Ruling, in the margin*]: Letters patent will be issued for him as appropriate, and he should receive the payments in the island of São Tomé, where he is going, to which effect orders should be issued. Lisbon, the 24th of June '639.

(Initialed signature)

165 Consultation of the Overseas Council[1357] (26/11/1649)

ABSTRACT – *The situation of the Dutch, both on land and sea, gives Portuguese officials, especially King João IV, hope of recovering the coast of Mina. Since 1640, Portugal has been independent of Spanish rule. By 1649, their principal fortresses were lost to the Dutch.*

Since it is to be assumed that Your Majesty will have seen and considered what the Governor of the island of São Tomé, among other things, has written in his letters, which recently arrived, about the state in which the Dutch had been left on the coast of Mina and the limited power they had there, both on land and sea,

– it was the opinion of the Council that Your Majesty should be sent a copy of what he states, separately from the other affairs, so that, once Your Majesty has communicated the matter to the Council of State and considered the importance of returning that fortress, commerce and trade to Your Majesty's obedience, and of the enemies of the Crown not benefiting from the gains[1358] that they obtain, since the occasion and the discord between them and the Gentiles give good hope that it may be so, it may be decided what would be best for Your Majesty's service.

Lisbon, on the 26th of November '649.

Marquis / Figueira / Pereira

[*Ruling, in the margin*]: I stand informed of what is reported by the Governor of São Tomé, and represented to me by the Council, so that I may have this matter dealt with when the occasion arises, which I hope will be soon. Lisbon, the 24th of December '649.

The King

[1357] AHU, Cod. 14, fols. 200v.-201; cf. MMA vol. 8, doc. 152.
[1358] In Brásio's transcription, '*prouimentos*' ('*provimentos*'), literally 'provisions'; it should read '*proveitos*' ('gains'/'profits').

166 Consultation of the Overseas Council[1359] (19/04/1655)

ABSTRACT – *The council address the evolving situation in Mina, observing that European nations which trade on the Mina (Gold) Coast do so to the detriment of the Portuguese Crown.*

Cristóvão de Barros Rego,[1360] Governor of the island of São Tomé, informs Your Majesty in a letter dated the 29th of October of last year that, through the *nau* Suécia, which went to that island, and through her Purser,[1361] the conflict between the black people of Mina and the Dutch came to an end, [[to which he adds]] the other circumstances which are mentioned in the report that he sent to Your Majesty on the 20th of September '653; and that the Dutch are in such straits that they eventually surrendered at the stronghold on the hill, which is called Santiago, where their throats were cut by the black men; and that this affair would have gone even further if the great offer they made them had not put a brake on their fury, after which they retreated to a place where it is said that they fortified themselves with a palisade; and that the King of Akatakyi ('Komenda')[1362] and [[Butri]][1363] did not want to accept the said offer, and even opposed offers which the Dutch had made to other kings from further away; and that everyone assures him of the memory and remembrance which those Gentiles keep of the Portuguese.

And [[he also adds]] that today there will hardly be one hundred soldiers in the castle of São Jorge, and in that of Boure thirty; [[and]] that the English lay claim to be[1364] lords of that commerce, for which reason General Jorge Militão went to England; and [[that]] the Swedes, who have few people and little strength, are those, nevertheless, who take most gold, since, as he was told, from five factories which they have on that coast, they obtain over three thousand pounds[1365] of gold each year; and that it was a great pity that another nation should enjoy such wealth, while this Kingdom takes no benefit from it.

It was the opinion of the Council to inform Your Majesty (as has been done on other occasions) of what the Governor of São Tomé reports about the state of affairs in Mina and the nations which trade there, so that Your Majesty, in view of the importance of this matter, may order that it be examined and decided upon in the Council of State, as you may think best for your service.

In Lisbon, on the 19th of April '655.

Vasconcelos / Pinto / Pereira

[1359] AHU, Cod. 15, fol. 163; cf. MMA vol. 11, doc. 150, pp. 479–80.
[1360] See MMA vol. 15, doc. 233.
[1361] In Brásio's transcription, '*Comissario*' ('*Comissário*'); another possible, though less likely, translation would be '*Commissioner.*'
[1362] In Brásio's transcription, '*Cumane.*'
[1363] In Brásio's transcription, 'Fatri.'
[1364] In Brásio's transcription, '*soliçitão*' ('*solicitam*'), literally '(they) solicit.'
[1365] In Brásio's transcription, '*liuras*' ('*libras*'), a unit of weight equivalent to 12 to 16 ounces, but also a unit of currency.

[*In the margin*]: I shall bear this matter very much in mind. In Lisbon, on the 7th of July '655.

The King

167 *Consultation of the Overseas Council*[1366] *(12/02/1656)*

ABSTRACT – *Considerations regarding Brazil and its mines, Mina, and Angola. Only the Mina excerpts are presented here.*

[[…]]
Mina is in the state which Your Majesty knows, and which this Council has on occasions presented to you. It is [[the Council's]] opinion that it should also be taken care of in the manner indicated,[1367] and that there should not be so much delay.
[[…]]
In Lisbon, on the 12th of February '656.

Salvador Correia de Sá, José Pinto Pereira, Francisco
de Vasconcelos da Cunha, Diogo Lobo Pereira.

168 *Letter from Brito Freire to the King*[1368] *(29/11/1657)*

ABSTRACT – *Preparation of the fleet to reconquer the town and fortress of São Jorge da Mina.*

My Lord,

On the coast of Mina, which extends from Cape Palms inwards, there is a beach which received the name of Formosa from being very pleasant, [[and which has]] various rivers that flow into a [[…]][1369] called The Sete Aldeias,[1370] where there are permanently to be found two Dutch ships that take great quantities of gold in exchange for European goods.

Twelve leagues leeward used to lie our old castle of Akyem, which gave this Kingdom the celebrated gold of the Portuguese *dobrões*,[1371] since it was the finest gold of those parts. The black people bring it by River Ogueira [[*sic*]], which we

---

[1366] AHU, Moçambique, cx. 2 – Copy; cf. MMA vol. 12, doc. 2, pp. 7, 10.
[1367] Presumably, and according to the opinion of the council concerning Brazil stated earlier in the document, as regards fortification of the garrisons and mining.
[1368] BNL, CP, Ms. 738, fols. 345–346v; cf. MMA vol. 12, doc. 61, pp. 147–53.
[1369] A word seems to be missing in Brásio's transcription.
[1370] Literally, 'Seven Villages.'
[1371] The *dobrão* was an old Portuguese gold coin, which was worth 24,000 *reis*.

may call the *morgado*[1372] of the riches of Mina, since on its margins were located those large [[mines]] which His Lordship the King Dom Sebastião ordered to be opened by Martim Afonso de Sousa,[1373] and then covered, so that the news of such an important treasure would not awaken the ambition of foreign nations.

From this castle of Akyem to the fortress of São Jorge (which is the largest and most important of all) is twenty-eight leagues, inhabited by many Gentile black people [[and with]] much trade of gold, above all in a port called Esma, where we used to have a House assisted by a Portuguese garrison, both because of this and because it was close to a river from where a great quantity of gold and *malagueta* is taken. This House has now been turned into a factory or a fortress by the Dutch, which is permanently garrisoned with men and artillery.

Three leagues leeward from the Port of Esma lies that of Aldeia do Torto,[1374] which is well known in that coast because it belongs to the King of Akatakyi ('Komenda'),[1375] a most mighty black man due to the fertility of the people and the abundance of gold which is produced by his lands. And thus there are usually five or six ships anchored at this latitude, Dutch as well as from other nations.

Four leagues immediately below can be seen the fortress of São Jorge, which is situated on the best part of the entire coast, between Fetu[1376] and Akatakyi ('Komenda'), the two largest kingdoms of those Gentiles, which extend along the sea beaches, in such a manner that other peoples from inland have to cross their lands, in order to go on board the ships to get the goods which they need in exchange for the customary commerce.

This fortress is erected upon bare rock beaten by the sea which, with one of its arms entering alongside that same fortress, surrounds it so that it looks like an island. It was composed of three bulwarks: two towards the river, and one towards land with a cavalier overlooking the river, which faces a large elevation.[1377] For this reason (among many other works done by the Dutch to improve it [[the fortress]]), a royal fort was built on that elevation, with many good defense walls and artillery. And anticipating future contingencies, they have raised the cavalier higher, so that they might have a better view of the elevation, in case it should be seized. Already in our time this fortress had, dug out of that same rock with pickaxes, two considerable ditches and two cisterns with so much water that there could be no lack of it, however extensive the place might be.

[[Oguaa ('Cape Coast')]],[1378] Moure/Mori and Kormantin are located within the first seven leagues leeward from Mina; on [[Oguaa ('Cape Coast')]] the

---

[1372] *Morgado*: in Portugal, the first-born male descendant who inherited a family's entailed property, according to the institution of the *morgadio*.

[1373] *Fidalgo* of the Royal Household, son of Gaspar de Sousa, Martim Afonso de Sousa was given the post of captain of São Jorge da Mina for two years, starting when he took office. Lisbon, dated 22-12-1563, ANTT, *Chancelaria de D. Sebastião, Ofícios*, liv. 13, fol. 5.

[1374] Known in English as 'Komenda,' but properly as Akatakyi.

[1375] In Brásio's transcription, '*Comane.*'

[1376] In Brásio's transcription, '*Afuto.*'

[1377] In Brásio's transcription, '*padrasto*,' a rise overlooking a town or fortress.

[1378] In Portuguese, '*Cabo Corso.*'

Swedes have a fortress; in Boure the Dutch have another fortress; and the English have another one in Kormantin – all of them of considerable importance, above all that of Kormantin, frequented by the Akan, [[who are]] most wealthy merchants and among the most industrious people of those parts.

Further down the Dutch have a fort at the Port of Nkrãn,[1379] and then there extends the coast of Allada,[1380] Bèneiabu [[*sic*]], and Còere [[*sic*]], whence, apart from gold, a great quantity of slaves, ivory, civet and *malagueta* is taken.

Once the Dutch became lords of all the fortresses we used to have on the coast of Mina, because of the state of negligence in which they found them [[and]] learning from our very losses, they repaired the ruins, adding larger defense walls and new fortifications in the most appropriate places. Then, with the news of the restoration of Angola and, lately, with that of Pernambuco (whence, as soon as we had achieved it, we should have carried out this undertaking, for which I offered myself when pointing it out to the Generals while still in Recife), informed about these victories and fearful lest the fortune of the Portuguese arms should leave no place for Holland's flag to be flown north of the Cape of Good Hope, they endeavored most diligently to reinforce with great improvements all their fortifications, which today they maintain much better provided with people, artillery and supplies.

Thus we should surmise from such clear reasons, even if there were no news as certain as that which we have received from people who came from those parts three or four years ago. Therefore everything that might make the occasion appear easier is to lose sight of it, and likewise to make it appear much more difficult than it might seem like not wanting to seize it. A mid-point between these two extremes could be found by providing what is needed, even though part of what is necessary might be cut, taking at least 1,200 men to disembark on land, an engineer, 400 pistols, 400 bucklers, 3 hand petards, 500 grenades, 100 hatchets, 50 large axes, 600 mattocks, 600 spades, 4 mantlets, 50 pickaxes, 50 handspikes, 50 pick hammers, [[and]] some miners used to quarrying, because of the soil of the fortress of São Jorge, which is bare rock.

The armada[1381] must be composed of ten ships and four rowing pataches which will be very useful on the coast of Mina, where there is almost always a permanent calm. On these ships, in addition to the men who will disembark, there should remain those necessary to man them, since there will always be large ships from Holland cruising along those seas.

The armada should take not only the supplies which will be needed, but also goods to buy them from the black people, with affability, ingenuity, and generosity, as they will act on our behalf, distributing between them some coarse cloth

---

[1379] In Brásio's transcription, '*Cará.*'

[1380] In Brásio's transcription, '*Costa de Arda*,' on the so-called 'Slave Coast.' Cf. Robin Law, ed., *The English in West Africa, 1681-1683: The local correspondence of the Royal African Company of England, 1681-1699*, part 1 (Oxford: Oxford University Press, 1997), 216.

[1381] The Portuguese term '*armada*' usually refers to a fleet of military vessels of any size.

from India, brandy,[1382] wine, and iron. And since war will make the Dutch increasingly alert, with the strength that we have just detailed Mina will be restored in this first year; in the second [[year]] as much again will be necessary; and much more will probably not be sufficient in the third [[year]].

If we consider the great importance of this undertaking, we will conclude that no other could be of greater credit, more utility, and less expenditure, to this Kingdom than this one.

Of greater credit since, war gaining all its repute from the first victories,[1383] when the Dutch start to feel encouraged by the prospect of greater progress, for having seized from us ships [[loaded]] with sugar, if we seize gold mines from them the world will acknowledge the difference, should divine mercy allow the good fortune of this undertaking to equal the success we have achieved in Angola and Pernambuco.

More utility because every year, in the month of March, the Dutch obtain from that trade above six hundred thousand *cruzados*, the English above four hundred, and the Swedes hardly less; [[and]] still fresh in our mind is our coffer from Mina, whose government was exercised by the *fidalgos* of higher rank and greater worthiness, through which a most rich treasure came to Portugal.

Less expenditure since, without the royal Exchequer spending as much as Mina formerly used to yield in three months, it will be possible to restore it. It may seem an exaggeration, but the reason is evident: because, since I am told that we will not go straight from this city to this undertaking, but we will first make port in Brazil, so as to keep the secret, which is the soul of every military action, and in particular of this one (as was shown by the good fortune with which we have restored Pernambuco), we may organize the journey as follows.

The armada of the Company,[1384] war against Holland having already been declared, should sail in a different manner. Usually, one [[armada]] departs [[?]][1385] when another one arrives, and each of them is composed of ten ships. These (joining the two convoys) should be reduced to twenty, or to less than ten[[*sic*]]. Because they are too few to face the enemy armada, and too many to fight against pirates, which ordinarily are not more than one or two.

By joining the two convoys, there will be no increase in expenditure on the part of the Company, since, if until now it used to launch ten ships every year, from now on it will launch twenty every two years; because, if the delay of one harvest damages Brazil, much more is endangered if a fleet is put at risk. But assistance to that State with products of the Kingdom should always be carried out by isolated ships, which will then return escorted by the armada.

[1382] In Brásio's transcription, '*agoardente*' ('*aguardente*'), a strong distilled beverage.
[1383] Literal translation of '*tomando a guerra toda a reputação dos primeiros sucessos*'; an alternative translation would be 'with all repute in war coming from the first victories.'
[1384] The General Company of the Commerce of Brazil, founded in 1649.
[1385] In Brásio's transcription, '*parar*' ('to stop'), which does not seem to make sense; it should probably read '*partir*' ('to depart').

And as the merchant ships which used to be divided between the two journeys will add up to two hundred sails in all, and thirty of the best and better armed being selected and men taken from the others to man these (as I have done in the fleets of which I was a General and as may be seen from the regulations [[that were given to me]], which Your Majesty was served to have printed), their number will increase, with the galleys of the convoy, to fifty men-of-war, which, commanded with industrious valor and an anticipatory disposition, bringing them always as alert as if they were already facing the enemy, when they fight against any other armada, no matter how large, they may aspire not only to defend themselves but to achieve victory. From all other means I dare to assert – and not only do I assert, but I also assure – that the greatest discredit and most certain perdition will stem, should we desire (all hope in our forces being lost) to rely only on caution and fortunate success.

And as regards the port of this city being left less protected for want of the Company's ships which usually wait there for those which go to Brazil, one fleet leaving after the other has arrived, it is certain that the Company, given that it has only thirteen ships which belong to it, sends back again the best of them and hires [[ships]] from other nations, as a result of which not less than two or three vessels remain unrigged, which are left with any sailors or soldiers at this bar because they require the most difficult repairs, so much so that, when they have been concluded, those [[ships]] which had gone to Brazil have already returned to the Kingdom.

Even if the [[number of the]] said ships were higher and their want greatly felt, one should consider where it would be greater, whether in this city's port – which, from Cascais as far as the Terreiro do Paço,[1386] looks like an uninterrupted fortress with artillery, garrisons and bulwarks, where are to be found the galleys of the royal armada, the Indiamen, so many ships belonging to both natives and foreigners – or in the America fleet, which in the direst straits will find itself left only with what it may have brought with it. And to consider anything else is a manifest mistake, as we have seen and experienced in previous examples.

At present the security of the armadas and garrisons in Brazil is the matter which deserves most attention, given that the preservation of this Kingdom depends totally on its commerce, against which I can hear the echo of Dutch cannons; which Dutch, with very different forces, became formidable to the whole Monarchy of Spain.

I have not written at length in order to deal only with the reasons indicated for joining both convoys of the Company, but also with those for organizing the conquest of Mina with less expenditure and more secretly, killing two birds with

---

[1386] Today known as 'Praça do Comércio,' Lisbon's main square, where one of the royal palaces, administrative buildings, and a port were built.

one stone[1387] – without any further effort on Your Majesty's part than that of, on the day prior to the departure, adding to the fleet soldiers a *tercio*[1388] of infantry as aid for reinforcing the armada or to assist Brazil, taking advantage of the war against Holland, which is the best disguise for the undertaking.

After arriving in Pernambuco, and there not being any enemy armada on the coast of Brazil, the ships of its [[Pernambuco's]] *repartição*[1389] should be sent to Bahia and Rio de Janeiro, and those most appropriate for the journey should return, together with the necessary men and implements, and the black men of Henrique Dias's *tercio* should depart as quickly as possible to carry out the enterprise, because thus it will be more easily concluded. Thus there will be time left for returning to Pernambuco, where the entire armada should be reunited; because, as part of it goes to Rio de Janeiro, it takes at the least six months to return to that latitude; and even if it takes one or two [[months]] more, this is not so great a delay for a matter of such importance.

As regards both the manner we have pointed out to undertake the journey of Mina and the ways we have indicated to sail the armada of the Board,[1390] with experience giving me the confidence which my talent lacks, I am obliged by zeal in Your Majesty's service, free from the ordinary vainglory with which one rewards oneself for one's own opinion, considering [[as I do]] that the future successes will prove these arguments of mine to be infallible, because even if they are disregarded now, they will later be ratified by time.

I oblige myself to present them to Your Majesty, so that you may know the honor and favor you bestow upon me by intending to charge me with the conquest of Mina. For which [[conquest]] all I wish is to have my strength intact, since the poor health which I endured while in the army of Alentejo, the injury I suffered in the scaling of Badajoz, and then in the armada of the coast in which Your Majesty ordered me to make sail, with rain and tempest, not resting for nights on end while I was sailing on the unmasted flagship with such manifest danger, being unable to sail close to the wind[1391] because it was crosswind and close to the shore – caused me, as soon as I disembarked, to suffer a perilous accident of apoplexy, by whose effects I am still afflicted, [[even]] after having gone to the baths, where I am being sent again: which will not be sufficient to prevent me from committing my life, as long as it may last and up to its last breath, to Your Majesty's service.

Lisbon, on the 29th of November '657.

Francisco de Brito Freire

[1387] In the document, *'fazendo duas jornadas de um caminho'* ('making two days' journey in one').
[1388] In Portuguese, *'terço.'*
[1389] *Repartição*: a colonial administrative division.
[1390] In Brásio's transcription, *'junta'*; here probably as a synonym of 'company' (for 'General Company of the Commerce of Brazil').

169 Letter from Paulo Freire De Noronha to the Prince Regent Dom Pedro[1392] (07/12/1672)

ABSTRACT – *Paulo Freire de Noronha recommends the castle of São Jorge da Mina, which is in the hands of the Dutch, should be seized. He lays out a set of ambitious reasons in favor of Portuguese occupation.*

+

My Lord,

During the government of the islands of São Tomé I have come to learn from experience how much it would be to the interest of Your Highness's Crown that the restoration of the garrison of Mina should be carried out. There is sufficient reason for Your Highness to order that it be affected, and the means for Your Highness to achieve it are readily at hand. And I am sure that, should they be very difficult, they would all be overcome by Your Highness's piety towards God since Heaven is losing many souls with the separation of Mina from Your Highness's Crown. And let this be the first reason I present to Your Highness.

My Lord, the inhabitants of the whole of that coast's mainland anxiously wish to trade with the Portuguese, because they sigh for the water of baptism; and as they have so many dealings with the neighbors of the garrisons occupied by the Nations,[1393] they want to expel all of them [[the Nations]], only in order to gain Heaven through Your Highness's subjects. The King of Fetu[1394] and Dom Nuno, his chief *Mestre de Campo*,[1395] have so endeavored and declared it many times, and there is no reason for there to be any neglect on our part when the inhabitants themselves open their doors to receive us, only in order that we may teach them the road to their salvation. In the past, the Kings of Portugal, Your Highness's ancestors, were led for this same reason to search for new lands with great expenditure for their Exchequer, so as to spread the Catholic religion in all of them; and, judging by the zeal for the honor of God which I see in Your Highness, I trust that you will assist in the remedy of so many souls, who so anxiously beg for Your Highness's gentle yoke so that through it they may escape from Hell.

The second reason is grounded on the temporal advantages for Your Highness's estate, given that this Kingdom shares [[?]][1396] the profit of over twenty million

---

[1392] In Portuguese, '*bolinar*,' i.e. to sail with the bowlines hauled.
[1392] BNP, Fonds Portugais, vol. 25, fols. 89–91; cf. MMA vol. 13, doc. 65, pp. 153–9. Document is undated, but evidence from MMA vol. 13, doc. 190 points to the date provided. Paulo Freire de Noronha (and not Ferreira, as Lopes de Lima has it) was appointed governor of São Tomé, for three years, by royal writ dated 20-2-1668, in which post he succeeded Pedro da Silva. See ANTT, *Chancelaria de D. Afonso VI*, liv. 22, fol. 243v.
[1393] The nations from Northern Europe, above all Holland and England.
[1394] In Brásio's transcription, '*Afuto.*'
[1395] *Mestre de Campo*: literally, 'Field Master'; a former military rank, equivalent today to that of colonel.
[1396] In Brásio's transcription, '*parte*' (from '*partir*,' i.e. 'to share,' 'to divide'), though it could also read '*perde*' (that, is, 'loses'), which makes more sense in this context.

in gold which the Nations obtain each year, not including ivory, and slaves, and other goods which abound in those kingdoms, taking from there over fifteen thousand souls to work in their sugar plantations in Barbados and other parts, greatly increasing their yield with this supply, and reducing that of Brazil, because today the [[supply of]] slaves of the Angola trade is very restricted, and it is presently so difficult to trade there that it is necessary to penetrate many leagues inland, which would not be the case if Brazil was provided [[with slaves]] not only from Angola but also from that coast. It is not only Portugal, however, which suffers losses with these shipments [[?]],[1397] but Heaven also loses many souls, since the heretics indoctrinate and instruct them in the dogmas of their depraved sects, making large shipments of those Gentiles to sell to the Castilians, depriving us of the gains which we would make if they came to our conquests to make them [[the shipments]]. Such a great resource for Portugal as this can be recovered with few means, since, without altering the peace with the Dutch, we may devise them in such a way that it would look as though they had been chosen by the Gentiles rather than negotiated by us.

For this purpose a ship should be sent from the island of São Tomé to sell supplies in Kormantin, an English Factory which is not far from the castle of São Jorge da Mina; and on this ship there may go either Miguel Pais or João Moreira, persons who are fit for this negotiation – the one because I have sent him to go from Pernambuco to São Tomé, and the other to meet Dom Nuno. Any of the abovementioned who may go on the ship with the pretext of selling supplies will meet either the King of Fetu or Dom Nuno, informing them that, if they still have the will, as they have made manifest so many times, to free themselves from the heretical yoke which is oppressing them, Your Highness is willing to assist them, and that when they return with confirmation of what they promise, the time and appropriate occasion being indicated by them, the aforesaid ship will go a second time to Kormantin with the same pretext of selling supplies, so that she may be there at the time chosen by them for the attack (or the number of times needed to arrange it) which will be carried out against the castle of São Jorge da Mina, since without this garrison as the head it will be difficult to keep the others. And once the undertaking has succeeded the ship will come to São Tomé to collect the inhabitants who were expelled from Mina to garrison the castle, because, if the stronghold is [[occupied]] by the same men who were expelled from Mina, the affair will be better concealed, since it will signify that it was caused by that first wrong committed against them by the Dutch, rather than by any encouragement or design on our part. And because there are only a few [[men from Mina]] in São Tomé, they will be joined by some others who will also be called sons of Mina.

This same purpose has already been intended by His Lordship the King of Portugal Dom João IV, Your Highness's glorious father, when he planned to send Henrique Dias, who served in Pernambuco, with his *tercio*,[1398] to that coast to see

---

[1397] In Brásio's transcription, '*levas*,' literally 'groups'/'bunches.'
[1398] In Portuguese, '*terço*': see Glossary.

whether he might conquer this resource for the Crown of Portugal, unmindful of the expenditure with it, at a time when he was occupied with the war against Castile and without having clear information or anyone to offer him a calculation of expenditure with this enterprise, such as I here lay at Your Highness's royal feet, offering to Your Highness my person and my property, with the sole purpose of being able to see Your Highness's estate further increased, since to this same effect I have already prepared all that is needed for this enterprise, all of which I left in São Tomé[1399] to be offered to the King of Fetu, in order to encourage his resolve to expel the heretics, without expecting for myself any other payment for this expenditure than Your Highness's glory, because loyal vassals are motivated for these enterprises by the nobility of their blood and not by any increase of their profits.

I conclude this appeal by reminding Your Highness that the restoration of Mina does not allow much delay, because it is entirely dependent on the will of the King of Fetu and of Dom Nuno. These, since they are human, may easily change; and even if change of will does not hamper this affair, it may well be cut off by Death taking the lives of these two [[men]], since they are already advanced in years. And the present state in which Holland manifestly finds herself seems to be the most appropriate time. And Your Highness should take a resolution, since in this affair greater diligence will be the mother of the best fortune.

The reasons for the Gentiles to carry out this enterprise are: that they have at present a considerable army, which consists of eighteen thousand men, twelve thousand with firearms and the other six [[thousand]] with assegais and adargas, and artillery, with which they have already seized the castle of [[Oguaa ('Cape Coast')]][1400] from the Swedes, and sold it, together with many lands from the surrounding Gentiles, for this King of Fetu is the most warlike [[king]] and lives solely from waging war.

The 2nd reason [[is]] the great hatred that the Dutch feel for them, since they offer a considerable reward for the heads of either the King or Dom Nuno, as they are certain that either of them is capable of defeating them and, by taking their lives, not only would they save their own, but also the many interests they possess [[there]]. And the desire [[to kill them]] of other nations, which have garrisons and factories there, is not weaker, even though they may conceal it, by continuing to have relations with them.

The 3rd [[reason is]] that most of the gold and other goods which are taken from that coast, and bought from them, is in the hands of the Company of Holland, and it is certain that they will covet the great plunder which they [[the Dutch]] take from it. And furthermore the offer that will be made to them of eight or ten thousand *cruzados* in goods, which in their estimation are worth over twenty

---

[1399] Noronha was ordered to return to Portugal in 1671.
[1400] In Brásio's transcription, '*Cabbocorço*' ('*Cabo Corso*').

[[thousand]], will raise their spirits. Which [[gift]] I have already prepared in iron, Indian cloth and other goods, together with shipping and the persons of João Moreira and Miguel Pais to carry out this affair, because without this arrangement we will not be able to oblige these men [[the 'Gentiles']]; and I was given to understand [[by them]] that they would give their children as hostages as a pledge of greater security, which is a common practice among them.

The 4th [[reason is]] that, to guard the castle, they [[the Dutch]] frequently place black men and native mulattos, who have commerce with the King and Dom Nuno and who may, since they are descended from the Portuguese (and in the absence of a garrison, which is today certain, since Holland has been unable to send men as before[1401]), assist in this enterprise, [[also]] because of their eagerness to become Catholics. And I understand that there is so little care that it often happens that the castle is left with only the sentries.

The 5th [[reason]] is to consider that war will continue between the English and the Dutch in the garrisons they have on that coast, and the Gentiles will more easily help the English in order to get rid of their greater enemy; and even more so when they are told that Your Highness has given them that coast. And should this happen (which is the strong desire of the English), since they will want to have its trade for themselves, it could hardly ever be taken out of their hands.

The 6th [[reason is]] that the King of Fetu, seeing that Your Highness does not reply to his advice, will avail himself of whomsoever may want to favor him. And as France planned three years ago to build a factory close to Mina and the Nations did not consent to it, and she now wants to build it in Ardra, which borders on that coast, and the King of Ardra has an envoy in France[1402] – the French may gather forces to oppose the garrisons occupied by the Nations and overrun them [[?]].[1403]

The 7th [[reason]] is that there are many horses in Ardra and Benin, which are feared by the Gentiles and which the French may make use of for everything they may plan. But those Gentiles are so fond of the Portuguese that a resident of Mina once went to its castle to say to the General Falcambourg, the predecessor of this Rodrigo[1404] Viltre, that that land belonged to Your Highness and that they [[the French]] could only stay there as long as he and the other inhabitants allowed.

The 8th [[reason is]] that the fortress has an elevation[1405] that the Dutch wanted to fortify (after they had done likewise in the case of another [[elevation]], with the fort which they call Santiago[1406]), which the black people did not allow, and it is certain that they intend to recover it. Furthermore there is water only outside

---

[1401] In Brásio's transcription, '*como ategora*' ('*como até agora*'), which could also be translated as 'as until now.'

[1402] Dom Mateus Lopes was sent as envoy to Louis XIV's Court in 1670. See Henri Labouret, *Le Royaume d'Arda et son evangélisation au XVIIᵉ siècle* (Paris: Institut d'ethnologie, 1929), and J.B. Labat, *Voyage du Chevalier des Marchais en Guinée, isles voisines, et à Cayenne* (Paris: Pierre Prault, 1730), 2: 337–64.

[1403] Tentative translation of '*pasar a mais*' ('*passar a mais*'), literally, 'become more.'

[1404] Portuguese for the French 'Rodéric.'

[1405] In Brásio's transcription, '*padrasto*,' a rise overlooking a town or fortress.

[1406] Portuguese for unknown Dutch name.

[[the fortress]] and, according to what I am told by a French engineer, it can be very easily cut off. In addition there is a fair that takes place every week, in which the black people sell them the supplies with which they maintain themselves, since those that they take from those islands are never sufficient because they spend them with the shipment of black people that they embark. And if the Gentiles take up arms, and one or other [[of the abovementioned]] fails, it will be difficult [[for them]] to keep it [[the fortress]].

The 9th [[reason is]] that, once Your Highness has gained control over Mina, you will not only possess one of the greatest things in the world, but you will not need to pay heed to any of its nations, since with what it has of least value, which are the slaves,[1407] and with the additional people to be found in the islands, Your Highness will be able to proceed with [[building]] an empire in Brazil. And for its conservation there is no need for any other expenditure than paying each ship which may go to those [[places of]] trade per ton, as may seem best, and collecting what the black people pay to the Nations, which, if my information is correct, is a tenth of everything. And the garrison can be paid from the payment made by the vessels.

Your Highness is the most zealous of all Princes as regards the interests of your subjects, so much so that, despite having sent such magnificent aid to India, with which, because of the very long journey, you spend so much wealth, you today allow private persons to sail there. And this navigation, though very short, is no less profitable, and not taking advantage of it would be cause for greater regret, because the more the Nations control it, the more opulent they become, as lords of the commerce and trade from Guasquas [[*sic*]] to Akyem, Mina, Ardra, Calabar, Oribó [[*sic*]], and Benin, Jabù, Owerri [[?]],[1408] Rio Real, and Lago,[1409] Gabon, Cape Lopez [[?]],[1410] Mayombe, and Cabinda, and Loango, where they have many factories.

For this occasion instructions are necessary to bring 60 or 80 soldiers from Angola, if need be, since the journey is a shorter one, or to send them from here on the pretext of going to the fortress of São Tomé, together with two or three commanders[1411] who are capable and accustomed to that climate – so that, should one of them fail, the occasion may not be lost – and some other persons, the most important among them, at least, being a responsible[1412] person, and a good Portuguese, experienced and valorous. And in this undertaking great secrecy will be the most important cause for achieving the intended purpose, as I have observed in other papers. João Moreira and Miguel Pais are now in São Tomé, and everything is ready for the enterprise, since I have thus arranged, as I have reported above.

[1407] Tentative translation of '*com o menos que della se fas estimasaõ saõ os escrauos*' ('*com o menos que dela se faz estimação [que] são os escravos*').
[1408] In Brásio's transcription, '*Oheri.*'
[1409] '*Lagos.*'
[1410] In Brásio's transcription, '*Cabo Lope*,' probably from '*Cabo de Lopo Gonçalves*.'
[1411] In Brásio's transcription, '*cabo(s),*' the person who is the local ruler or leading figure.
[1412] In Brásio's transcription, '*de obrigações*,' which refers to a person with responsibilities, familial or otherwise.

a) Paulo Freire de Noronha[1413]
List of the garrisons occupied by the Nations on the coast of Mina

The Dutch:		
The castle of São Jorge	60 soldiers — Artillery	28 pieces
The Fort of Santiago	60 soldiers — Artillery	15 pieces
The castle of Akyem	60 soldiers — Artillery	17 pieces
Akatakyi ('Komenda')[1414]	40 soldiers — Artillery	14 pieces
Botura [[*sic*]]	15 soldiers — Artillery	04 pieces
	____	____
Soldiers Total 335	Artillery 78	
English:		
The castle of Kormantin	60 soldiers Artillery	28 pieces
Atacará [[*sic*]]	30 soldiers — Artillery	08 pieces
Annacha [[*sic*]]	20 soldiers — Artillery	08 pieces
Uniba [[*sic*]]	15 soldiers — Artillery	06 pieces
	____	____
Soldiers Total 125	Artillery 50	
Denmark:		
Cape and Mountain of Numberg [[*sic*]]	60 soldiers — Artillery	24 pieces
Chumá [[*sic*]][1415]	30 soldiers — Artillery	19 pieces
	____	____
Soldiers Total 90	Artillery 43	

170 Letter from a Jesuit to the King[1416] *(17/10/1678)*

ABSTRACT – *The Jesuit father writes about São Tomé and the coast of Mina, Calabar, Ardra, Owerri, and Benin. Only excerpts relevant to Mina are included here.*

[...] I went to the aid of the island of São Tomé, for I had learned through the same Dutchmen that our [[men]] had there killed people of theirs and that they were a little uneasy. We arrived in good time, since they were shooting[1417] against our

---

[1413] See MMA vol. 13, doc. 190.
[1414] In Brásio's transcription, '*Cumane*.'
[1415] Possibly Esma ('Shama').
[1416] BADE, Cod. 103/2/16, fols. 4–8; cf. MMA vol. 13, doc. 190, pp. 447–52.
[1417] In Brásio's transcription, '*apelouradas*,' which should read '*a pelouradas*'; '*pelourada*,' of course, being a shot with an iron bullet.

people and there were not many [[men]] in that garrison experienced in warfare, for which they were immediately taught and drilled by the men from Brazil. Were it not for their being so experienced in warfare and labors, they would all have died, as did some seventy [[men]] who were taken by Filipe de Moura, out of which only seven or eight escaped.

With two armed ships it is possible to restore that fortress, since they would prevent any aid from the sea, and [[the fortress]] has none from land. For lack of [[aid]], some eighty Dutch came over to us; but with the arrival of Filipe de Moura a truce was made, and supplies sold to them, with which they did better than before.

In October the Dutch were feeling so secure in our castle of São Jorge da Mina that there were no more than thirty soldiers there. And that fortress has a great elevation,[1418] whence we can fulfill our wishes and regain the first fortress we had in those parts. In this land I travelled through the backwoods, and it is certain that the Dutch take more gold from that coast than the Castilians from the Indies. And these backwoods, which are the healthy part of the land, should be populated.

From the castle of Akyem ('Axim'), which was seized after the acclamation of Your Royal Majesty, I met two men, who had been castrated[1419] there; and these were brought by the Dutch as forced laborers,[1420] making use of them in Angola. They told me of their miseries, and of there being little or no fortification in Akyem.

The English and the Dutch go to Calabar, Ardra, Benin, to load ships with slaves; and, passing themselves all off as Englishmen, they take them [[the slaves]] to be sold in the Indies.

The Guinea Coast, and especially that of Mina, used to be Portugal's India as long as India was not discovered; and when it was discovered, it continued to be so, with a chest full of gold arriving every year from the castle of São Jorge, which can still today be seen at the Mint; and it was carried by a galleon which was called 'of Mina' and which would wait in the Azores islands for the men-of-war to escort her securely to this port, as can be seen in the instructions which His Lordship Dom Sebastião gave to Jorge de Sousa, chief Sea Captain.

On this coast, from the shallows of Saint Anne, which are not distant from land, in front of Sierra Leone, as far as Cape Baxas,[1421] there is trade of ivory; and from here [[Cape Baxas]] as far as[1422] Cape Palms, in addition to ivory, there is trade of *malagueta*, which is a kind of pepper that was used in Portugal

---

[1418] In Brásio's transcription, *'padrasto'*: see Glossary.
[1419] In Brásio's transcription, *'capados'* ('castrated'), though this is probably an abbreviation for *'cap(tur)ados'* ('captured').
[1420] In Brásio's transcription, *'forçados,'* a term usually applied to 'galley-slaves,' but also to those forced to work as captives without receiving any payment.
[1421] 'Cape Baixos'; also known as 'Noti Cornu,' 'Southern Horn,' or 'Cape Shallows.'
[1422] In Brásio's transcription, *'á ré'* ('behind'), which makes no sense in this context; it should thus read *'até'* ('as far as').

before the arrival of the one from India, and for this reason it is called Malagueta Coast; after which, as far as[1423] the Kingdom of Owerri,there is trade of gold and slaves, [[sometimes]] more and [[sometimes]] less,[1424] and here are to be found the kingdoms of Fetu, Ardra, Judá [[*sic*]], Jabù, and Benin, with all of which there was communication in the time of Their Lordships the Kings of Portugal, bringing from there the abovementioned commerce.

Once His Lordship the King [[Dom João IV]] was acclaimed, Manuel Carvalho Falcão went to that coast on an English ship, and informed those kings that Portugal had a king of her own, after which the Portuguese started to proclaim His Lordship King Dom João and to persuade Manuel de Carvalho to seize the fortresses there which were in the hands of the Dutch, since they would help him, because they wanted to restore to the King of Portugal what belonged to him and take revenge for all the treachery committed against them by the Dutch, persuading them that there were no more Portuguese left in the world, as can be seen from a letter of the said Manuel Carvalho Falcão, sent to Pedro Fernandes Monteiro, and dated the 15th of May 1653.

In the office of the Secretary of State there is a letter from Paulo Freire de Noronha, dated the 7th of December 1672, in which he insists on the benefits derived from the commerce of this coast, and the wish of the native black people to see it inhabited and to trade with the Portuguese.

There is another [[letter]] of Julião de Campos,[1425] who succeeded him [[Paulo Freire de Noronha]] in the Governorship, about what had happened between the Canon Jerónimo de Andrade, nephew of Nuno Vaz, and the kings of that coast, with whom he had communication when he went there by order of the Governor, and about how much they wished and longed for the Portuguese, and the recommendation which their[[?]] parents had made them[[?]][1426] in this regard.

In addition to this, there is a letter from the King of Owerri, called Dom Matias, written in October '673, in which he signs as vassal and brother of Your Majesty; and in it he complains that the Chapter of the island of São Tomé was not sending them priests to preach the Faith and to teach them the Doctrine of the Holy Mother Church, and that without this many of them had returned to the adoration of false idols, as Father Friar Sebastião dos Reis, religious of St Francis, was to declare, wishing, for his part, to represent [[to Your Majesty]] the abovementioned and the miserable state in which that kingdom was left for lack of trade with the Portuguese. [...]

[1423] In Brásio's transcription, '*á ré*': see previous note.

[1424] Tentative translation of '*maez e menos*' ('*mais e menos*'), literally 'more and less.'

[1425] Julião de Campos Barreto was appointed as governor of São Tomé by writ dated 8-3-1673, ANTT, *Chancelaria de D. Afonso VI*, liv. 41, fols. 269–269v.

[1426] It is not clear whether '*seus*' and '*lhe(s)*' should be translated as 'their'/'them' or 'his'/'him.'

171 Commerce of the Coast of Mina[1427]
(06/05/1680)

ABSTRACT – *The Prince Regent entrusts the commerce of the 'coast of Mina' to the Board of Commerce of Brazil, in order that it may administer and direct it, as it does the commerce of that State, in the manner declared below. By 1680, with São Jorge da Mina lost decades ago to the Dutch, 'Mina' morphed from a reference to said fortress and its relative surroundings to the 'coast of Mina,' which now included places east of the Volta River, into the Bight of Benin.*

I, the Prince, as Successor, Regent, [[and]] Governor of the Kingdoms of Portugal and the Algarves and their Dominions, make known to all those who may see this writ of mine that, considering what has several times been represented to me as to the great advantage which could be derived from continuing the commerce of Mina, which has been introduced by my subjects a short time ago, and that with this navigation it would be possible, with little expenditure, to achieve the great profits which are obtained, and much more so should there be a fortress and factories on that coast, given the favorable disposition of its black people towards the Portuguese, their first conquerors; and having had the papers and other documents examined by various commissions and officials, who gave their full attention to the relevance of this matter,

– I have been served to decide that the Governor of São Tomé, Bernardino Freire,[1428] should put it into practice, to that effect sending the frigate Madre de Deus, carrying the person of Jacinto de Figueiredo de Abreu to stay as Governor of the fortress he should build, and the patache São João Baptista, [[under]] Captain Lourenço Fernandes Lima, with the goods which may seem convenient for opening up the commerce, which should be run, as Factor, by the said Lourenço Fernandes Lima, [[as]] a man who is experienced in that coast, [[and]] with all the appropriate instructions and regulations to this effect.

And in order that he may obtain the intended success, from which to derive the profit which the nations of Europe achieve, it is advisable to endeavor in such a way that, at the same time as those Gentiles engage in our commerce, that of those nations may diminish. And because the permanent assistance with supplies and ships cannot be continued, and [[so that]] the effort and expenditure which I ordered should not be wasted, for all these considerations, it is my wish to entrust [[the commerce of the coast of Mina]] to the Board of the General Commerce of Brazil[1429] – given the judicious way in which it proceeds in the administration of

---

[1427] ACL, Colecção de Legislação Trigoso, liv. 9, doc. 64; cf. MMA vol. 15, doc. 236, pp. 645–7.
[1428] Also known as 'Bernardim Freire.' See MMA vol. 13, doc. 190.
[1429] In Portuguese, *'Junta do Comércio Geral do Brasil.'*

the Exchequer, and the fitting out of its fleets, and whatever it[1430] was brought to do by this commerce of the coast of Mina – so that it may administer it with the same power, jurisdiction [[and]] direction with which it administers that of Brazil, benefiting from all the profits, duties and appurtenances which it may obtain from it, for which it shall be obliged to have the said commerce carried on, in the manner it may find best and as it administers that of Brazil. And for this purpose, it may appoint factors to the factories which shall be established, to whom it may send the goods which they may be entitled to receive,[1431] and they [[the factors]] shall give account of their consignments and follow their instructions and regulations, as the other administrators do. With a declaration that, for the military posts of the fortresses which are built, the Board, after consultation, shall name three persons; and once I receive the consultation, I will have it examined in the Overseas Council, so that it may propose the person whom it may think best from among those named, in the manner done by the donataries[1432] of land overseas, when choosing and appointing the most fit. And I shall have the Board informed that the person appointed will be issued [[?]][1433] letters patent by the Overseas Council, since in this way no prejudice to or conflict between these tribunals[1434] will arise, and because it is thus in accordance with the good management of this matter.

And furthermore it is my wish that the subjects of the island of São Tomé, [[and]] adjacent ones, and all other [[subjects]] of this Kingdom and its conquests, may not go to trade in the fortresses and factories which may be built on the said coast of Mina, nor even take goods such as iron, brandy, smoking tobacco, cloth from Cape Verde, or cotton from São Tomé, Allada [[and]] Benin, ocher, sabers [[?]],[1435] weapons and gunpowder. And should they take them to the said fortresses and factories, they shall present them to the factors so that they may buy them for their real price, which they will pay in slaves, and never in gold, since this will be reserved for the trades which the Board of Commerce will make on its own account.

The said subjects will be allowed to take other goods, but not to sell them in the said fortresses and factories, or in the villages of the Gentiles, [[or]] where there might be a trade vessel of the Board, because it will harm [[the trade]]; and they will only be able to do it through the factors, and with their intervention,

---

[1430] In Brásio's transcription, the article 'o' (masculine); it should probably read 'a' (feminine), as it seems to refer to the 'Junta' (here translated as 'Board').
[1431] Tentative translation of 'que ouuerem de beneficiar' ('que houverem de beneficiar'), literally 'from which they may benefit.'
[1432] Anglicized form of 'donatários,' which may also be translated as 'beneficiaries': the title given to someone who was granted a piece of land of considerable extent in the overseas territories, to populate, explore and administer on behalf of the Portuguese king.
[1433] In Brásio's transcription, 'cassará,' from the verb 'cassar,' i.e. 'to revoke,' which does not make sense here; instead, it should probably read 'passará' (from 'passar,' 'to issue').
[1434] In Brásio's transcription, 'Tribunaes' ('tribunais'), which here refers to the Board of Commerce and the Overseas Council.
[1435] Literal translation of 'sabre' (sing.).

and on board their ships, where the said Gentiles will go to buy them. And in all other ports they shall be allowed to trade in all kinds of goods, under the obligation of paying for each item, on leaving, one dram of gold, for the repair of any of the said fortresses and factories by which clearance is given, or in the deposit which they might make in São Tomé prior to their departure for the coast. And the same shall apply to the ships which depart from the Kingdom, or Brazil, or the islands, and do not make port in that [[island]] of São Tomé, and that for this reason go on trust, a document being issued to that effect by the said Board and signed by me.

And should they not pay the dram of gold on these goods [[?]],[1436] they will pay[1437] seven hundred and fifty *reais*, all of it applied to the expenses of the said fortresses and factories. And the persons who should go with their ships in a manner other than the abovementioned shall incur the penalties established in the Regulations of the Governor and of the Factor of the said fortress, chapter 19.15., for as long as the Board does not advise me as regards an alternative, according to experience with this commerce. Which Board shall be obliged to cover the costs and expenses of the said fortresses and factories, whether they are newly erected or rebuilt, and to garrison them with artillery, and weapons, and respective ammunition, as well as with soldiers, all of which should be paid through the Exchequer it administers.

Therefore I order and command all the governors of my conquests, and the military and treasury officials, the Justice, and the subjects of my kingdoms and dominions, to obey and observe what is stated in this writ, without any impediment or doubt whatsoever, and notwithstanding the regulations, laws and orders which may exist to the contrary, even if everything is referred and declared explicitly, since it is convenient for my service and my *motu proprio* and royal power, and even though it may not pass through the Chancery, even if it should last more than a year, and notwithstanding the ordinance of book 2, titles 39 and 40 to the contrary. And I order that this writ be printed, and sent to the conquests, giving full authority and credit to the printed copies signed by the President of the Board.

Issued in the city of Lisbon, on the sixth day of the month of May – Aires Monteiro wrote it – year of the birth of Our Lord Jesus Christ of one thousand six hundred and eighty. Francisco Correia de Lacerda had it written down.

Prince

Writ in which it is Your Highness's wish to entrust the commerce and administration of the coast of Mina to the Board of Commerce of Brazil, so that it may administer them with the same power, jurisdiction and direction, with which it administers that of Brazil, in the manner declared above.

To be examined by Your Highness.

[1436] In Brásio's transcription, in the singular: '*neste genero*' ('*neste género*'), literally 'on this kind.'
[1437] Tentative translation of '*erá a respeito de*' (probably '*será a respeito de*'), which could also possibly be translated as 'at the rate of.'

APPENDIX

Governors at São Jorge da Mina[1]

1. Diogo de Azambuja (1482–84)

2. Pero/Pedro da Silva (1484–86)[2]

3. João Fernandes de Abreu (1486–87; died)

---

[1] Appointments for captain-governor were usually three years and granted as a reward for loyalty and services rendered to the Crown, whereas the tenure for a factor (*feitor*) varied. The factor was in charge of buying and selling goods as well as deal with matters concerning navigation and shipping (e.g. provisioning ships, [un]loading ships, repair of ships, etc.). Several dates of appointments do not match when appointees actually assumed their post in Mina, and so the dates above match, as close as possible, the time in which appointees served in Mina. Sources: ANTT, *Gavatas*, no. 14, maço 3, doc. 2, 29 Dec. 1531; ANTT, Tribunal do Santo Ofício, Inquisição de Lisboa, Processo 12431; ANTT, *Chancelaria de D. João III*, liv. 13, fol. 42; liv. 21, fol. 160; liv. 22, fols. 98v, 133; liv. 22, fol. 133; liv. 25, fol. 4; liv. 26, fol. 262v; liv. 33, fol. 82; liv. 45, fols. 37v-38, 158v; liv. 63, fol. 106; liv. 67, fols. 55v-56; liv. 70, fols. 42v-43; *Chancelaria de D. João III, Privilégios*, liv. 1, fols. 115-115v, 220-220v, 305-305v; liv. 5, fols. 289-289v, 336; *Chancelaria de D. Manuel*, liv. 2, fol. 55; liv. 3, fol. 9v; liv. 5, fol. 20; *Chancelaria de D. Sebastião*, liv. 13, fol. 5; liv. 19, fol. 19; liv. 27, fol. 100v; *Chancelaria de D. Sebastião e D. Henrique, Privilégios*, liv. 3, fol. 223; liv. 4, fols. 206v, 271, 276v; liv. 5, fols. 105, 137v, 150v; liv. 8, fols. 193v-194; liv. 9, fols. 57-57v; liv. 12, fol. 26; *Chancelaria de Filipe I*, liv. 15, fol. 287; *Chancelaria de Filipe I, Privilégios*, liv. 2, fols. 205v-206; *Chancelaria de Filipe II*, liv. 23, fols. 15-15v; liv. 31, fol. 231; liv. 32, fols. 88v-89; *Colecção de Cartas, Núcleo Antigo 878*, n. 180; *Corpo Cronológico*, pt. 1, maço 112, doc. 3, fols. 1, 3; pt. 2, maço 85, doc. 85, fol. 2; pt. 2, maço 8, doc. 98; pt. 2, maço 16, docs. 123, 161; pt. 2, maço 85, doc. 85; pt. 2, maço 109, doc. 129; pt. 2, maço 231, docs. 27, 36, 42-43, 55, 77; pt. 2, maço 233, docs. 83, 85, 133; pt. 2, maço 234, docs. 23, 86; pt. 2, maço 235, docs. 6, 167; pt. 2, maço 238, doc. 32; *Mesa da Consciência e Ordens, Consultas*, liv. 16, fols. 28-29; MMA, 15: 82, 89; MMA, 4: apêndice III (pp. 649-61); PMA, 1: 375-76, 385-86; 2: 48-49, 85, 185, 257, 331, 438-72; PMA, 3: 272-3, 343-5; PMA, 5: 11, 490-94, 504-9, 654-5; João Cordeiro Pereira, *Le Troc de l'or à Mina pendant les Règnes du roi Jean III et du roi Sébastien* (Paris: Foudation Calouste Gulbenkian, 1990), 182–83, 193; John Vogt, *Portuguese Rule on the Gold Coast* (Athens: University of Georgia Press, 1979), 214–16; John T. Furley and J. Cremona, 'Notes on Some Portuguese Governors of the Captaincy da Mina,' *Transactions of the Historical Society of Ghana* 3, no. 3 (1958): 194–214; John T. Furley and J. D. Fage 'Provisional List of Some Portuguese Governors of the Captaincy da Mina,' *Transactions of the Gold Coast & Togoland Historical Society* 2, no. 2 (1956): 53-62; Alberto Iria, 'Da fundação e governo do castelo ou fortaleza de São Jorge da Mina pelos portugueses e da sua acão missionária após o descobrimento desta costa,' *Studia* 1 (1958): 55–62; Anselmo Braamcamp Freire, 'Cartas de quitação del rei D. Manuel,' *Archivo Historico Portuguez* vols. 1-11 (1903-16).

[2] Some think Azambuja was succeed by Álvaro Vaz Pestana as new governor of São Jorge da Mina. See Vogt's list.

4. João Fogaça (1487–89)

5. Afonso de Bobadilha (1489–92)?[3]

6. Fernando Pereira (1492–95)?

7. Lopo Soares de Albergaria (1495–99)[4]

8. Fernão Lopes Correia (1499–1502)

9. Nuno Vaz de Castelo Branco (1502–3)

10. António de Miranda de Azevedo (1503–4)

11. Diogo Lopes de Sequeira (1504–5)

12. D. Martinho da Silva (1505–8)

13. Afonso de Bobadilha (1508–9)

14. Manuel de Góis (1509–11)

15. Nuno Vaz de Castelo Branco (1512–16)[5]

16. Afonso Caldeira (1513; died)

17. Fernão Lopes Correia (1517–19)

18. Duarte Pacheco Pereira (1519–22)

19. Afonso de Albuquerque (1522–24)

20. João Vaz de Almada (1525–29)?[6]

21. Estêvão da Gama (1529–32)[7]

22. Francisco Pereira (1532–36)?[8]

23. Manuel de Albuquerque (1536–40)

24. Lopo de Sousa Coutinho (1541–43)

25. João Gomes Souro/Fernão Gomes (1543–45)

---

[3] Possibly Alvaro Mascarenhas was governor before 1490 but left or was recalled at an unstated date (Hair, *Founding*, 96). One 1496 source (PMA, 2: 257) says Bobadilha was Mina captain, which could mean he stayed there longer in that role. He was also mentioned in the 1495–99 inquiry.

[4] The 1495–99 inquiry noted one 'Estêvão Fernandes, who came here as Captain,' but there is no other evidence of when, if at all.

[5] Nuno Vaz is possibly there for 1515–16, but this is not certain.

[6] João de Barros sailed to Mina in 1522/23 and assumed the post of treasurer of the Casa da India e Mina in 1525. His official role is uncertain. G. R. Crone, *The Voyages of Cadamosto*, p. 103, thinks he served as Mina caption, 1522–25. This is doubtful.

[7] Captain of Arguim castle in 1514–15 and perhaps more.

[8] 1533: The unnamed captain is reported as ill; hence, the factor wrote to the king. That factor was either Lopo de Pina or Fernão Cardoso, which have led some to believe Cardoso was Mina captain. See the articles by Furley in note 1.

26. António de Brito (1545–46; died)

27. D. Martim de Castro (1546–48)

28. Filipe Lobo (1548, vacated)

29. Lopo de Sousa Coutinho (1548–50)?[9]

30. Diogo Soares de Albergaria (1550–52)

31. Jorge Rui de Melo (1552–56)[10]

32. Afonso Gonçalves Botafogo (1556–57)

33. Rui Gomes de Azevedo (1558–62; died)

34. Manuel Mesquita de Perestrelo (1562–63)[11]

35. Martim Afonso de Sousa (1563–67)?[12]

36. Francisco de Barros de Paiva (1567–70)?[13]

37. António de Sá (1570–73)

38. Martim Afonso de Sousa (1573; died)

39. Vasco Fernandes Pimentel (1579–83)

40. João Roiz/Rodrigues Pessanha (1583–86)

41. João Roiz/Rodrigues Coutinho (1586–95)

42. D. Cristóvão de Melo (1596–1608)

43. D. Duarte de Lima (1609–13; died)[14]

44. João de Castro (1613)

45. Pedro da Silva (1613–16)

46. Manuel da Cunha (d)e Teive (1616–24)

47. D. Francisco Souto Maior (1624–26)

48. João da Serra de Morais (1626–29; died)

---

[9] Father of Frei Luís de Sousa, who came to write a (famous) chronicle on the life of D. João III, during which reign his father lived.

[10] Jorge Rui de Melo definitely served as Mina captain, starting on 13-9-1552; Francisco Pereira was also a caption before this time but when?

[11] Perestrelo was only in post as Mina captain for a year, then arrested and brought to trial then prison in Lisbon.

[12] Served as governor of India before coming to Mina.

[13] Crown monopoly abandoned and Mina and its trade handed over to a consortium of merchants (Vogt, *Portuguese Rule*, 122–3).

[14] Appointed April 1606 but royal writ was in April 1607; he did not arrive until February 1609. He was in 'poor health' for over a year.

49. Vacant, 1629–31[15]

50. D. Pedro de Mascarenhas (1631–34; died)

51. Frei Duarte Borges (1634; died in 3 mos.)

52. André da Rocha Magalhães (1634–36)[16]

53. Jorge de Mendonça Pessanha (1636–?)[17]

Factors at São Jorge da Mina

1. Gil Velho (1491–95)?

2. Gil Matoso (1495–99)

3. João Fernandes (1499–1502)

4. Barnabé Henriques (1502–04)?

5. Estêvão Barradas (1504–07)

6. Aires de Sequeira (1507–09)

7. Manuel de Góis (1509–11)[18]

8. Afonso Mexia (1511–13)

9. Francisco Fróis (1513–14)

10. Paulo da Mota (1514–17?)

11. Vasco de Pina (?–1517)[19]

12. Manuel de Sande (1517–19)

13. João de Figueiredo (1519–22)

14. João Coelho (1522–23)

15. Paio Rodrigues (1525–28)

16. Gonçalo de Campos (1528–31)

---

[15] A few yeas after de Lima's death, a note: 'and so it [i.e. the fortress] is presently without a governor, because no successor has been sent to the one who died two years ago' (APF-SRCG, v. 99, fols. 14–14v).

[16] Francisco de Melo e Castro was appointed governor in 1635 but he 'excused himself from the said governorship.'

[17] Jorge de Mendonça Pessanha was appointed in 1636. There is no evidence he made it, a moot point since the Dutch captured Sao Jorge da Mina in 1637.

[18] Manuel de Góis signed a 1510 letter, like Francisco Fróis, stating he was the king's servant and factor.

[19] See MMA vol. 4, doc. 32.

17. Fernão/Fernando Cardoso (1531–2)[20]

18. Lopo de Pina (1532–34)

19. Sebastião Pestana (1534–36)

20. Fernão/Fernando Cardoso (1536–?)?

21. Lopo de Pina (1539)

22. Jorge Velho (1539–40)

23. Lourenço Costa (1541)

24. Barnabé Henriques (1541–43)[21]

25. João Leitão (1541–43)?

26. Jorge Tenreiro (1543–45)

27. Gonçalo de Freitas (1546)

28. Fernão Gomes (1547)

29. Ambrósio Roiz (1548; renounced)

30. Jorge da Costa (1548–50)

31. Belchior Leitão (1550)

32. Estêvão Limpo (1550–51)?

33. Diogo Vaz (1551–52)

34. Simão Roiz (?–1557)?

35. Jorge Murzelo (1558–59)

36. Pero/Pedro Rodrigues (1559)

37. Simão Pires Cotão (1559–60)

38. Diogo Vaz (1561–62)

39. Gaspar de Magalhães (1562–64)

40. ?

41. ?

42. ?

[20] Fernão (Fernando) Cardoso granted factorship on 29-12-1531. João Pereira, in *Le Troc de l'or*, says Lopo de Pina was factor from 1531–34 and does not have Cardoso on his list. Pina was appointed factor on 29-9-1539, though he served also as factor previously.
[21] Henriques is mentioned in an October 1542 letter as factor of Mina. See MMA vol. 15, doc. 59.

43. ?

44. Lourenço Carvalho (1580–85)

45. João Marques da Costa (1585–90?)

46. Mateus Gonçalves (1590–93)?

47. Gaspar da Rosa de Meira (1593–96)?

48. ?

49. ?

50. Afonso Martins Albernãs (1603–08)?

51. Francisco Soares (1616–23)?

52. Pedro Sardinha (1626–37)

Clergy at São Jorge da Mina[22]

1. No vicar (V)/chaplain (C) named (1495–99)

2. Vicar mentioned but unnamed (1503)

3. Cristóvão/Estêvão Lopes (V), Duarte Rodrigues (C), Friar Diogo Zagala, Álvaro Fernandes (1509)

4. Luís Henriques (V), Rui Carvalho (1510)[23]

5. Brás Goncalves (V), João Alvares (1509–11)

6. João André (V), João de Barros (C), Fernão Lourenço (clergy) (1514)

7. Rui Pires (V) (1518)

8. Friar Amaro (V) (1521–24)

9. Cristóvão Cortes (1523)

10. Luís Alvares (V) (1524–27)

11. Vicar /chaplain mentioned but unnamed (1529)

12. Miguel de Valadares (C) (1538)

13. Pedro Lopes (V) (1540)

14. Gonçalo Toscano de Almeida (V) (1546–48)

[22] Later regulations, perhaps in 1529–31, required one vicar and three chaplains serving at all times, and usually for 3-year terms.
[23] Enslaved females were given to each on appointment or arrival.

15. António Loureiro (1548)

16. Francisco da Costa (1556)

17. Gaspar Gonçalves (V) (1559)

18. Gaspar Lopes (1566–69)

19. Domingos Barbosa (1569)[24]

20. Luís Godinho (1571–74)

21. Domingos Barbosa (treasurer), Martim Gonçalves (V),[25] Jerónimo Dias (C) (1571)

22. Valentim de Barros (treasurer) (1574 & 1578)

23. Dr. Fr. Dionísio (V), Fr. Agostinho, Fr. Bernardo de Chaves (1579)

24. Fr. Máximo das Chagas (C),[26] Fr. Sebastião das Chagas (V)[27](1584)

25. Pedro Moreira (treasurer) (1584–87; 1592–95)

26. André de Sousa (V) (1589)

27. Fr. Clemente (15??)

28. Sebastião Lopes (V), Hector Dias (1591)

29. Miguel Fernandes Rebelo (V) (1592)

30. Gaspar Rebelo (treasurer; replaced P. Moreira; 1593)

31. Diogo Roiz Vale (V), Francisco Ribeiro (C), Bento da Fonseca Figueira (treasurer) (1594)

32. João Vaz [treasurer; replaced Figueira] (1597–1600)

33. Estevão Gomes, Gaspar Soares (V) (1598)

34. Pedro Álvares de Fontes (V), Fr. Agostinho de Cristo, Fr. Boaventura (1606–?)

35. Fr. Duarte Borges (V) (1619–34)

36. Gaspar Lopes (V) (1634–37)

---

[24] Named vicar of the Nossa Senhora da Conceição and administrator of ordinary and ecclesiastical justice in the city of São Jorge da Mina, after Gaspar Lopes was called back to Portugal after serving three years. His term as vicar started in 1579. I think this should be 1569, if the years for Gaspar Lopes is accurate.

[25] Named chaplain of the church of Nossa Senhora da Conceição and administrator of ecclesiastical justice of São Jorge da Mina.

[26] Appointed chaplain to one of Infante D. Henrique's chaplains in the church of São Jorge da Mina. He was professed from Tomar on 28-7-1584.

[27] Professed friar of Christ, vicar of Nossa Senhora da Conceição da Mina and administrator of the ordinary and ecclesiastical jurisdiction of the same city. Frei Sebastião would receive another estate as much as the factor. For the license of 3-8-1584, 80,000 réis would be paid annually to Friar Sebastião das Chagas from the estate of Mina. See MMA, vol. 4: appendix 3, p. 656.

Captains of Akyem ('Axim')

1. Vasco Gil (1532)?

2. Gaspar de Almeida (1635)?

3. Pascoal de Almeida (1628–37)

4. Pascoal de Almeida (1637–42?)[28]

5. José Martins ((1639–42?)

Factors of Akyem ('Axim')

1. Diogo de Alvarenga (1503–5)

2. Aires Botelho (1505–6)

3. Francisco de Brito/Rui Lobo (1509)

4. João Franco (1517–19)?

5. Soeiro da Gama (1519-)?

6. Lourenço Velho (?–1540)

7. Lourenço Correia (1540–42)

8. Cristóvão Soares (1549–51)

9. Diogo Lobo (1552–54)

10. Lopo Fernandes (1554–56)

11. Pero/Pedro Vaz Henriques (1558–61)

12. Miguel de Montarroio (1561–63)

13. Luís Mendes Quaresma (1572–75)

14. Luís Soares (1607–)?

15. Pascoal de Almeida (1628–42?)

---

[28] Pascoal de Almeida was appointed captain and factor of Akyem ('Axim') in 1628 for a six year term. He said he served for nine years in November 1638, and appeared to have continued in that capacity, more by circumstance than by choice. Almeida shared the captaincy of São António with José Martins from 1639 until (possibly) when the Dutch seized the fort in 1642.

Clergy of Akyem ('Axim')

1. Garcia Lourenço (1529–32)

2. Vasco Gil (1532–35)

3. Leonel Fernandes (C) (1533–36)

4. Francisco da Costa (V) (1570–73)

5. Fr. Isidro (1579–82)

6. Fr. António de Brito (1584)

7. Fr. Maurício (replaced Brito) (1584)

8. Manuel Dias (C; filled vacancy left by Mauricio) (1593)

9. Licenciado Francisco Luís (V) (1598)

BIBLIOGRAPHY

Archival Sources (other than those listed in the Abbreviations)

University of Liverpool, Special Collections and Archives, Papers of Professor Paul Hair

GB141 HAI/1/1/4, item 8, 'Sources for English and French Voyages to Guinea in the Mid Sixteenth Century.'

GB141 HAI/1/3/6/6, item 19, Memorandum from Dr. Hair to Mr. Lamb, Mr. Varley and Dr. Rowe, 10 September 1969.

GB141 HAI/1/3/6/6, item 26, Memorandum from P. E. H. Hair, 29 October 1969.

GB141 HAI/1/1/4, item 1, P. E. H. Hair, 'The Guinea Texts Project: A further note,' 14 June 1987.

University of Ghana, Legon, Balme Library, The Furley Collection

P3 1529, 'Regimento da Mina'

Bibliotheque Municipale de Valenciennes, France

MS 493, ff.134v-137r

Algemeen Rijksarchief (The Hague), Leupe-collectie 743

Map of the Gold Coast dated 25 December 1629

Houghton Library, Harvard University

Fernando Palha Collection of Portuguese Historical Autographs, 1523–1890 (MS Port 19)

Secondary Sources

Albuquerque, Luís de, Maria Emília Madeira Santos, and Maria Luísa Esteves, *Portugaliae Monumenta Africana*, vol. 3 (Lisboa: Comissão Nacional para as Comemorações dos Decobrimentos Portugueses, 2000).

Alpern, Stanley B., 'What Africans Got for Their Slaves: A Master List of European Trade Goods,' *History in Africa* 22 (1995): 5–43.

Ardener, Edwin, *Kingdom on Mount Cameroon: Studies in the History of the Cameroon Coast, 1500–1970* (New York: Berghahn Books, 1996).

Austen, Ralph A., *Trans-Saharan Africa in World History* (New York: Oxford University Press, 2010).

Azevedo Pedro A. de, and António Baião, *O Archivo da Torre do Tombo, sua historia, corpos que o compõem e organisação* (Lisboa: Annaes da Academia de Estudos Livres, 1905).

Ballong-Wen-Mewuda, Joseph B., *São Jorge da Mina, 1482– 1637: A vie d'un Comptoir Portugais en Afrique Occidentale, 2 vols.* (Lisbon: Fondation Calouste Gulbenkian, 1993).

Ballong-Wen-Mewuda, Joseph B., '"Africains et Portugais: tous des négriers": Aux XVe et XVIe siècles dans le Golfe de Guinée,' *Cahiers des Anneaux de la Mémoire: La Traite et l'esclavage dans le monde lusophone*, Nantes, 3 (2001): 19–38.

Baretti Giuseppe Marco Antonio, *A Dictionary, Spanish and English, and English and Spanish: Containing, the Signification of Words, and their Different Uses, together with the Terms of Arts, Sciences, and Trades...*, *vol. 1* (London: F. Wingrave, 1809).

Barros, João de, *Chronica de Emperador Clarimundo, donde os Reys de Portugal descendem...* (Lisboa: na Officina de Francisco da Sylva, Livreiro da Academia Real, 1742).

Barros, João de, *Da Asia de João de Barros e de Diogo do Couto* [new edition] (Lisbon: Na Regia Officina Typografica, 1777–88).

Bellefond, Nicolas Villault de, *Relation des costes d'Afrique appelées Guinée* (Paris: D. Thierry, 1669).

Biaudet, Henry, *Les nonciatures apostoliques permanentes jusqu'en 1648* (Helsinki: Suomalainen Tiedeakatemia, 1910).

Birmingham, David, *Trade and Conquest in Angola* (New York: Oxford University Press, 1966).

Birmingham, David, 'The Regimento da Mina,' *Transactions of the Historical Society of Ghana* 11 (1970): 1–7.

Blake, John W., *Europeans in West Africa, 1450–1560, 2 vols.* (London: The Hakluyt Society, 1941–2).

Blanchard, Ian, *Mining, Metallurgy, and Minting in the Middle Ages, vols. 2–3* (Stuttgart: F. Steiner, 2001).

Bluteau, Rafael, *Supplemento ao Vocabulario Portuguez, e Latino...* (Lisboa: Na Patriarcal Oficina da Música, 1728).

Boerio, Giuseppe, *Dizionario del Dialetto Veneziano* (Venezia: Reale Tipografia di Giovanni Cecchini Edit., 1867).

Boxer, Charles R., *The Portuguese Seaborne Empire, 1415–1825* (New York: A. A. Knopf, 1969).

Brásio, António, 'Os Proto-Missionários do Congo,' *Portugal em África* 1 (1944): 99–112.

Brásio, António, 'A Política do Espírito no Ultramar Português,' *Portugal em África* 31–34 (1949): 20–29, 75–85, and 209–223.

Brásio, António, *História e missiologia: inéditos e esparsos* (Luanda: Instituto de Investigação Científica de Angola, 1973).

Brasio, António, ed., *Monumenta Missionaria Africana. Africa Occidental, 15 vols.* (Lisbon: Agência Geral do Ultramar, Divisão de Publicações e Biblioteca, 1952–88).

Brito, Pedro de, 'The Stillbirth of a Portuguese Bourgeoisie: Leading Families of Porto (1500–1580),' *Mediterranean Studies* 5 (1995): 7–29.

Bruscoli, Francesco Guidi, *Bartolomeo Marchionni 'homem de grossa fazenda' (ca. 1450–1530): Un mercante fiorentino a Lisbona e l'impero portoghese* (Florence: Casa editrice Leo S. Olschki, 2014).

Cardoso, George [Jorge], *Agiológio Lusitano dos sanctos e varoens illustres em virtude do reino de Portugal e suas conquistas...* (Lisboa: na officina de Henrique Valente d'Oliveira, 1657).

Carreira, António, *Panaria Cabo-Verdiana Guineense: Aspectos históricos e sócio-económicos* (Lisboa: Museu de Etnologia do Ultramar/Junta de Investigações do Ultramar, 1968).

Chouin, Gérard, *Eguafo: Un Royaume Africain 'au coeur francois (1637–1688)* (Paris: Aftra, 1998).

Chouin, Gérard, 'The "Big Bang" Theory Reconsidered: Framing Early Ghanaian History,' *Transactions of the Historical Society of Ghana* 14 (2012): 13–40.

Collet, Hadrien, 'Landmark Empires: Searching for Medieval Empires and Imperial Tradition in Historiographies of West Africa,' *The Journal of African History* 61, no. 3 (2020): 341–357.

Costa, A. Fontoura da, *Uma Carta Náutica Portuguesa, Anonima, de circa 1471* (Lisbon: Agencia Gêral das Colónias, 1940).

Costa, Antonio Luiz M. C., *Armas Brancas: Lanças, espadas, maças e flechas: Como lutar sem pólvora da pré-história ao século XXI* (São Paulo: Editora Draco, 2015).

Costa, Teresa Manuela Camacha José da, 'Umbundismos no Portugês de Angola: Proposta de um Dicionário de Umbundismos.' PhD thesis, Universidade Nova de Lisboa, 2015.

Crone G. R., ed. and trans., *The Voyages of Cadamosto and other Documents on Western Africa in the Second Half of the Fifteenth Century* (London: Hakluyt Society, 1937).

Curtis, Thomas, *The London Encyclopaedia, or Universal Dictionary of Science, Art, Literature, and Practical Mechanics, Comprising a Popular View of the Present State of Knowledge, vol. 3* (London: Thomas Tegg, 1829).

Daaku, Kwame Yeboa, *Trade and Politics on the Gold Coast, 1600–1720: A Study of the African Reaction to European Trade* (London: The Clarendon Press, 1970).

Dantzig, Albert van, ed., *The Dutch and the Guinea Coast, 1674–1742: A Collection of Documents from the General State Archive at the Hague* (Accra: Ghana Academy of Arts and Sciences, 1978).

Dantzig, Albert van, 'The Furley Collection. Its Value and Limitations for the Study of Ghana's History in European Sources for Sub-Saharan Africa before 1900: Use and Abuse,' *Paideuma* 33 (1987): 423–32.

Dantzig, Albert van, 'The Akanists: A West Africa Hansa,' in *West African Economic and Social History: Studies in Memory of Marion Johnson*, eds. David Henige and T.C. McCaskie (Madison: University of Wisconsin, African Studies Program, 1990).

Dapper, Olfert, *Naukeurige Beschrijvinge der Afrikaensche Gewesten* (Amsterdam: Jacob van Meurs, 1668).

Day, John, 'The Great Bullion Famine of the Fifteenth Century,' *Past & Present* 79 (1978): 3–54.

Deffontaine, Yann, *Guerre et Société au Royaume de Fetu (Efutu): Des débuts du commerce atlantique à la constitution de la Fédération Fanti: Ghana, Côte de l'or, 1471–1720* (Ibadan: IFRA, 1993).

Dickinson, R. W., 'Sofala and the Rivers of Cuama: Crusade and commerce in S. E. Africa, 1505–1595' (Unpublished PhD thesis, University of Cape Town, South Africa, 1971).

Diffie, Bailey W., and George D. Winius, *Foundations of the Portuguese Empire, 1415–1580* (Minneapolis: University of Minnesota Press, 1977).

Disney, A. R. A., *History of Portugal and the Portuguese Empire, Vol. 1: From Beginnings to 1807* (New York: Cambridge University Press, 2009).

Elbl, Ivana, 'The Portuguese Trade with West Africa, 1440–1521' (PhD thesis, University of Toronto, 1986).

Elbl, Ivana, 'Archival Evidence of the Portuguese Expansion in Africa, 1440–1521,' in Lawrence J. McCrank, ed., *Discovery in the Archives of Spain and Portugal: Quincentenary essays, 1492–1992* (New York: Haworth Press, 1994), 335–55.

Enciso, Martín Fernándes de, *Suma de geographia que trata de todas las partidas y provincias del mundo* (Seville: Jacobo Cronberger, 1519).

Escudier, Denis, *Voyage d'Eustache Delafosse sur la cÙte de GuinÈe, au Portugal et en Espagne, 1479–1481* (Paris: Chandeigne, 1992).

Faria, Francisco Leite de, and Avelino Teixeira da Mota, 'Novidades Náuticas e Ultramarinas numa Informação dada em Veneza em 1517,' *Memórias da Academia das Ciências de Lisboa: Classe de Ciências* 20 (1977): 7–75.

Ford, Jeremiah D. M., ed., *Letters of John III, King of Portugal, 1521–1557* (Cambridge, MA: Harvard University Press, 1931).

Fosse, Eustache de la, *Voyage a la Cote occidentale d'Afrique, en Portugal et en Espagne (1479–1480)*, ed. R. Foulche-Delbosc (Paris: Alfonse Picard et Fils, 1897).

Fynn, John Kofi, *Asante and its Neighbors 1700–1807* (London: Longman, 1971).

Fynn, John Kofi, *Oral Traditions of Fante States* (Legon: Institute of African Studies, University of Ghana, 1974).

Fromont, Cecile, *The Art of Conversion: Christian Visual Culture in the Kingdom of Kongo* (Chapel Hill: University of North Carolina Press, 2014).

Garfield, Robert, 'Sources for Portuguese West African History in the Vatican and Related Collections,' in Lawrence J. McCrank, ed., *Discovery in the Archives of Spain and Portugal: Quincentenary essays, 1492–1992* (New York: Haworth Press, 1994).

Godinho, Vitorino Magalhães, *Documentos sobre a Expansão Portuguesa, 3 vols.* (Lisbon: Edições Cosmos, 1956).

Gomez, Michael A., *African Dominion: A New History of Empire in Early and Medieval West Africa* (Princeton: Princeton University Press, 2018).

Good, John Mason, *Pantologia: A New Cabinet Cyclopaedia, Comprehending a Complete Series of Essays, Treatises, and Systems...*, vol. 4 (London: J. Walker, 1819).

Grande Enciclopédia Portuguesa e Brasileira, vol. 14 (Lisboa: Editorial Enciclopédia, 1936–60).

Gray, Richard, 'A Kongo Princess, the Kongo Ambassadors and the Papacy,' *Journal of Religion in Africa* 29, no. 2 (1999): 140–54.

Green, Monica H., 'The Four Black Deaths,' *The American Historical Review* 125, no. 5 (2020): 1601–31.

Green, Toby, *A Fistful of Shells: West Africa from the Rise of the Slave Trade to the Age of Revolution* (Chicago: University of Chicago Press, 2021).

Greenlee, William B., 'The Captaincy of the Second Portuguese Voyage to Brazil, 1501–1502,' *The Americas* 2, no. 1 (1945): 3–12.

Hagan, George P., 'A Note on Akan Colour Symbolism,' *Research Review* 7, no. 1 (1970): 8–13.

Hair, P. E. H., 'An Ethnolinguistic Inventory of the Upper Guinea Coast before 1700,' *African Language Review* 6 (1967): 47–73.

Hair, P. E. H., 'The Teixeira da Mota Archives and the Guinea Texts Project,' *History in Africa* 10 (1983): 387–394.

Hair, P. E. H., 'The Task Ahead: The Editing of Early European-Language Texts on Black Africa,' *Paideuma* 33 (1987): 29–51.

Hair, P. E. H., *The Founding of the Castelo de São Jorge da Mina: An Analysis of Sources* (Madison: African Studies Program, University of Wisconsin, 1994).

Hair, P. E. H., 'The Early Sources on Guinea,' *History in Africa* 21 (1994): 87–126.

Hair, P. E. H., 'Portuguese Documents on Africa and Some Problems of Translation,' *History in Africa* 27 (2000): 91–97.

Hakluyt, Richard, *The Principal Navigations, Voyages, Traffiques and Discoveries of the English Nation*, 12 vols. (Glasgow: James MacLehose & Sons, 1903–05).

Handler, Jerome S., and Matthew C. Reilly, 'Contesting "White Slavery" in the Caribbean,' *New West Indian Guide / Nieuwe West-Indische Gids* 91, 1–2 (2017): 30–55.

Herbert, Eugenia W., *Red Gold of Africa: Copper in Precolonial History and Culture* (Madison: University of Wisconsin Press, 2003).

Hespanha, António Manuel, 'As Finanças Portuguesas nos Séculos XVII e XVIII,' *Cadernos do Programa de Pós-Graduação em Direito/UFRGS* 8, no. 2 (2013): 79–132.

Hilário, Ana Teresa, 'Capitães das fortalezas do Índico no tempo do Conselho da Índia: Continuidades e rupturas da vertente social do Estado da Índia,' *Revista de História da Sociedade e da Cultura* 17 (2017): 79–101.

Hilton, Ann, *The Kingdom of Kongo* (New York: Oxford University Press, 1982).

Hogendorn, J. S., and H. A. Gemery, 'Continuity in West African Monetary History? An Outline of Monetary Development,' *African Economic History* no. 17 (1988): 127–46.

Inikori, Joseph E., 'Africa and the Globalization Process: Western Africa, 1450–1850,' *Journal of Global History* 2, no. 1 (2007): 63–86.

Jones, Adam, *German Sources for West African History 1599–1669* (Wiesbaden: Franz Steiner Verlag, 1983).

Jacobi, Lauren, 'Reconsidering the World-System: The Agency and Material Geography of Gold,' in *The Globalization of Renaissance Art*, ed., Daniel Savoy (Leiden: Brill, 2017), 131–57.

Justesen, Ole, ed., *Danish Sources for the History of Ghana, 1657–1754*, 2 vols., trans. James Manley (Copenhagen: Det Kongelige Danske Videnskabernes Selskab, 2005).

Kalous, Milan, 'A Contribution to the Problem of Akori Beads,' *The Journal of African History* 7, no. 1 (1966): 61–66.

Konadu, Kwasi, *The Akan Diaspora in the Americas* (New York: Oxford University Press, 2012).

Konadu, Kwasi, *Akan Pioneers: African Histories, Diasporic Experiences* (New York: Diasporic Africa Press, 2018).

Konadu, Kwasi, and Clifford Campbell, eds., *The Ghana Reader: History, Culture, Politics* (Durham: Duke University Press, 2016).

Kea, Ray A., *Settlements, Trade, and Politics in the Seventeenth Century Gold Coast* (Baltimore: The Johns Hopkins University Press, 1982).

Kea, Ray, 'The Local and the Global: Historiographical Reflections on West Africa in the Atlantic Age,' in *Power and Landscape in Atlantic West Africa: Archaeological Perspectives*, eds. J. Cameron Monroe and Akinwumi Ogundiran (New York: Cambridge University Press, 2011), 339–75.

Kea, Ray, 'The Mediterranean and Africa,' in *A Companion to Mediterranean History*, eds. Peregrine Horden and Sharon Kinoshita (West Sussex: Wiley Blackwell, 2014), 426–40.

La Fleur, James D., *Fusion Foodways of Africa's Gold Coast in the Atlantic Era* (Leiden: Brill, 2012).

Labat, Jean Baptiste, *Voyage du Chevalier des Marchais en Guinée, isles voisines, et à Cayenne fait en 1725, 1726 & 1727, vol. 2* (Paris: Guillaume Saugrain, 1730).

Labouret, Henri, *Le Royaume d'Arda et son evangélisation au XVIIe siècle* (Paris: Institut d'Ethnologie VII, 1929).

Lange, Jacob de, *Demonomanie of Der Mooren Wonderheden...* (Amsterdam: Bartholomeus Schouwers, 1658).

Law, Robin, 'Trade and Politics behind the Slave Coast: The Lagoon Traffic and the Rise of Lagos, 1500–1800,' *The Journal of African History* 24, no. 3 (1983): 321–48.

Law, Robin, 'Early European Sources Relating to the Kingdom of Ijebu (1500–1700): A Critical Survey,' *History in Africa* 13 (1986): 245–60.

Law, Robin, ed., *The English in West Africa, 1681–1699: The local correspondence of the Royal African Company of England, 3 parts* (Oxford: Oxford University Press, 1997–2007).

Law, Robin, 'The Komenda Wars, 1694–1700: A Revised Narrative,' *History in Africa* 34 (2007): 133–68.

Law, Robin, 'The Akani War of 1693–6,' *Transactions of the Historical Society of Ghana* 11 (2008): 89–111.

Law, Robin, 'Fante Expansion Reconsidered: Seventeenth-Century Origins,' *Transactions of the Historical Society of Ghana* 14 (2012): 41–78.

Law, Robin, ' "There's Nothing Grows in the West Indies but Will Grow Here": Dutch and English Projects of Plantation Agriculture on the Gold Coast, 1650s–1780s,' in *Commercial Agriculture, the Slave Trade and Slavery in Atlantic Africa*, eds. Robin Law et al. (London: Boydell & Brewer, 2013), 116–37.

Law, Robin, 'The Government of Fante in the Seventeenth Century,' *The Journal of African History* 54, no. 1 (2013): 31–51.

Law, Robin, 'The "Golden Age" in the History of the Pre-Colonial Gold Coast.' *Transactions of the Historical Society of Ghana* 17 (2015): 109–36.

Lobato, A., *A Expansão Portuguesa em Moçambique de 1458 a 1530, 3 vols.* (Lisboa: Agencia Geral do Ultramar – Centro de Estudos Histórico Ultramarinos, 1954–1960).

Lopes, Nei, and José Rivair Macedo, eds., *Dicionário de História da África: séculos VII a XVI* (Belo Horizonte: Autêntica, 2017).

Lovejoy, Paul E., and David Richardson, 'The Business of Slaving: Pawnship in Western Africa, C. 1600–1810,' *The Journal of African History* 42, no. 1 (2001): 67–89.

Lovejoy, Paul E., 'Pawnship, Debt, and "Freedom" in Atlantic Africa During the Era Of The Slave Trade: A Reassessment,' *The Journal of African History* 55, no. 1 (2014): 55–78.

Lowe, Kate J. P., *Cultural Links between Portugal and Italy in the Renaissance* (New York: Oxford University Press, 2000).

Lydon, Ghislaine, *On Trans-Saharan Trails: Islamic Law, Trade Networks, and Cross-Cultural Exchange in Nineteenth-Century Western Africa* (New York: Cambridge University Press, 2009).

Magasich-Airola, Jorge, and Jean-Marc de Beer, *America Magica: When Renaissance Europe Thought it had Conquered Paradise*, trans. Monica Sandor (New York: Anthem Press, 2007).

Marees, Pieter de, *Beschrijvinghe ende historische verhael van het Gout Koninckrijck van Gunea* (Amsterdam: Corn. Claesz, 1602).

Marees, Pieter de, *Description and Historical Account of the Gold Kingdom of Guinea (1602)*, eds. and trans., Albert van Dantzig and Adam Jones (New York: Oxford University Press, 1987).

Massing, Andreas, 'Mapping the Malagueta Coast: a History of the Lower Guinea Coast, 1460–1510 through Portuguese Maps and Accounts,' *History in Africa* 36 (2009): 331–365.

Mattingly, David. J. et al., eds, *Trade in the Ancient Sahara and Beyond: Trans-Saharan Archaeology* (New York: Cambridge University Press, 2017).

McCaskie, T. C., *State and Society in Pre-colonial Asante* (New York: Cambridge University Press, 1995).

Monumenta historica Societatis Iesu, *Epistolae mixtae ex variis Europae locis ab anno 1537 ad 1556 scriptae: Nunc primum a patribus Societatis Jesu in lucem editae*, vol. 4 (Madrid: A. Avrial, 1900).

Montefiore, Joshua, *Commercial Dictionary: Containing the Present State of Mercantile Law, Practice, and Custom...* (London: The Author, 1803).

Mota, Avelino Teixeira da, and P. E. H. Hair, *East of Mina: Afro-European relations on the Gold Coast in the 1550s and 1560s: An Essay with Supporting Documents* (Madison: University of Wisconsin, African Studies Program, 1988).

Mota, Avelino Teixeira da, 'The Mande Trade in Costa da Mina according to Portuguese documents until the mid-sixteenth century,' unpublished paper presented to the Conference on Manding Studies, SOAS, London, 1972.

Mudenge, S. I. G., *A Political History of Munhumutapa c. 1400–1902* (Harare: Zimbabwe Publishing House, 1988).

Newitt, Malyn, *História de Moçambique* (Lisboa: Europa-América, 1995).

Newitt, Malyn, ed., *The Portuguese in West Africa, 1415–1670: A Documentary History* (New York: Cambridge University Press, 2010).

Oliveira, Maria Inês Côrtes de, 'Quem eram os 'negros da Guiné'? A origem dos africanos na Bahia,' *Afro-Ásia* 19–20 (1997): 37–73.

Pappafava, Giovanni, *Vocabolario Veneziano e Padovano co'termini e modi corrispondenti toscani* (Padova: Nella stamperia Conzatti, 1796).

Pavanello, Mariano, 'Foragers or Cultivators? A Discussion of Wilks's "Big Bang" Theory of Akan History,' *Journal of West African History* 1, no. 2 (2015): 1–26.

Pietz, William, 'The Problem of the Fetish, I,' *RES: Anthropology and Esthetics* 9 (1985): 5–17.

Pietz, William, 'The Problem of the Fetish, II: The Origin of the Fetish,' *RES: Anthropology and Esthetics* 13 (1987): 23–45.

Pietz, William, 'The Problem of the Fetish, IIIa: Bosman's Guinea and the Enlightenment Theory of Fetichism,' *RES: Anthropology and Esthetics* 16 (1988): 106–23.

Pereira, Duarte Pacheco, *Esmeraldo de Situ Orbis* (Lisbon: Imprensa Nacional, 1892).

Pereira, João Cordeiro, *Le Troc de l'or à Mina Pendant les Règnes du roi Jean III et du roi Sébastien* (Paris: Fondation Calouste Gulbenkian/Centre Culturel Portugais, 1990).

Peres, Damião, *História dos Descobrimentos Portugueses* (Porto: Portucalense Editora, 1943).

Peres, Damião, *Regimento Das Cazas Das Indias E Mina* (Coimbra: Faculdade de Letras da Universidade de Coimbra, Instituto de Estudos Historicos Dr. Antonio de Vasconcelos, 1947).

Pinto, Pedro, and Robin Law, 'New Evidence on Relations between Portugal and the Kingdom of Allada in the Sixteenth Century,' *History in Africa* 47 (2020): 37–49.

Pissarra, José Virgílio Amaro, 'Livros de armação,' in *Navegações Portuguesas* (Lisboa: Instituto Camões, 2002–2006).

Popplau, Nicolas von, *Reisebeschreibung Niclas von Popplau, Ritters, bürtig von Breslau*, ed. Piotr Radzikowski (Kraków: Trans-Krak, 1998).

Pulgar, Hernando del, *Crónica de los senores reyes católicos Don Fernando y Dona Isabel de Castilla y de Aragón*, ed., Juan de Mata Carriazo, 2 vols. (Madrid: Espasa-Calpe, 1943).

Ratelband, Klass, ed., *Vijf dagregisters van het kasteel São Jorge da Mina (Elmina) aan de Goutkust (1645–1647)* (The Hague: Martinus Nijhoff, 1953).

Rego, Antonio da Silva, 'Ghana and the Portuguese: A Synthetical Survey of Relations,' *Ultramar* I, no. 4 (1973): 7–27.

Remedios, Mendes dos, 'Inéditos da Bibliotheca da Universidade de Coimbra,' *Archivo Bibliographico* 9, no. 8 (1908): 123–25.

Rocca, Sandra Vasco, and Natália Correia Guedes, eds., *Thesaurus: Vocabulário de Objectos do Culto Católico* (Lisboa: Universidade Católica Portuguesa/ Fundação da Casa de Bragança, 2004).

Rodney, Walter, *How Europe Underdeveloped Africa* (London: Bogle-L'Ouverture Publications, 1972).

Rogers, Francis M., *The Obedience of a King of Portugal* (Minneapolis: University of Minnesota Press, 1958).

Ruiters, Dierick, *Toortse der Zee-Vaert (1623)*, ed., S. P. l'Honoré Naber (The Hague: Martinus Nijhoff, 1913).

Russell, Peter E., 'Novos apontamentos sobre os problemas textuais do *Voiaige à la Guinée* de Eustáquio de la Fosse (1479–1480),' *Revista Portuguesa de História* 16 (1976): 209–21.

Russell-Wood, A. J. R., 'Iberian Expansion and the Issue of Black Slavery: Changing Portuguese Attitudes, 1440–1770,' *The American Historical Review* 83, no. 1 (1978): 16–42.

Russell-Wood, A. J. R., *The Portuguese Empire, 1415–1808: A World on the Move* (Baltimore: The Johns Hopkins University Press, 1998).

Ryder, A. F. C., 'An Early Portuguese Trading Voyage to the Forcados River,' *Journal of the Historical Society of Nigeria* 1, no. 4 (1959): 294–321.

Ryder, A. F. C., *Material for West Africa History in Portuguese Archives* (London: The Athlone Press, 1965).

Ryder, A. F. C., *Benin and the Europeans: 1485–1897* (London: Longmans, 1969).

Saccardo, Graziano, *Congo e Angola con la storia dell'antica missione dei Cappuccini, 3 vols.* (Venice: Curia provinciale dei Cappuccini, 1982–83).

Sansi-Roca, Roger, 'The Fetish in the Lusophone Atlantic,' in *Cultures of the Lusophone Black Atlantic: Studies of the Americas*, eds. N. P. Naro, R. Sansi-Roca, D. H. Treece (New York: Palgrave, 2007).

Saunders, A. C. De C. M., *A Social History of Black Slaves and Freedmen in Portugal, 1441–1555* (New York: Cambridge University Press, 1982).

Santarém, Visconde de, *Quadro elementar das relações politicas e diplomaticas de Portugal, 18 vols.* (Paris: J. P. Aillaud, 1842–76).

Santos, Father Angél, S. J., 'Francisco Ros S.J., Arzobispo de Cranganor, primer Obispo Jesuíta de la India,' *Missionalia Hispanica* 6, no. 16 (1949): 79–142.

Santos, Maria Emília Madeira, 'Rotas Atlânticas: O caso da carreira de S. Tomé,' in *Actas do II Colóquio Internacional de História da Madeira* (Lisboa, Instituto de Investigação Científica e Tropical, 1989).

Schwarz, George Robert, 'The History and Development of Caravels.' Master's Thesis, Texas A&M University, 2008.

Silva, António de Morais, *Diccionario da Lingua Portugueza composto pelo Padre D. Rafael Bluteau, reformado, e accrescentado por...*, 2 vols. (Lisboa: Na Oficina de Simão Tadeu Ferreira, 1789).

Silva, Filipa Ribeiro da, *Dutch and Portuguese in Western Africa: Empires, Merchants and the Atlantic System, 1580–1674* (Leiden: Brill, 2011).

Spicksley, Judith, 'Pawns on The Gold Coast: The Rise of Asante and Shifts in Security for Debt, 1680–1750,' *The Journal of African History* 54, no. 2 (2013): 147–175.

Spiers, Sam, 'The Eguafo Polity: Between the Traders and Raiders,' in *Power and Landscape in Atlantic West Africa: Archaeological Perspectives*, eds. J. Cameron Monroe and Akinwumi Ogundiran (New York: Cambridge University Press, 2012).

Sweet, James H., 'The Iberian Roots of American Racist Thought,' *The William and Mary Quarterly* 54, no. 1 (1997): 143–66.

Tattersfield, Nigel, *The Forgotten Trade: Comprising the Log of the Daniel and Henry of 1700 and Accounts of the Slave Trade from the Minor Ports of England, 1698–1725* (London: Pimlico, 1998).

Thornton, John K., *The Kongolese Saint Anthony: Dona Beatriz Kimpa Vita and the Antonian Movement, 1683–1706* (New York: Cambridge University Press, 1998).

Thornton, John K., The Origins and Early History of the Kingdom of Kongo,' *International Journal of African Historical Studies* 34, no. 1 (2001): 89–120.

Vieira, António, *A Dictionary of the English and Portuguese Languages...*, pt. 2 (Lisbon: Printed for Rolland, 1861 [1st ed. 1773]).

Viterbo, Sousa, *Trabalhos Náuticos Dos Portuguezes nos Seculos XVI e XVII*, 2 vols. (Lisboa: Typ. da Academia Real das Sciencias, 1898–1900).

Vogt, John L., 'Fernão De Loronha and the Rental of Brazil in 1502: A New Chronology,' *The Americas* 24, no. 2 (1967): 153–59.

Vogt, John L., *Portuguese Rule on the Gold Coast, 1469–1682* (Athens: University of Georgia Press, 1979).

Vogt, Olgário Paulo, and Roberto Radünz, 'Condenados à morte natural: o rito processual contra os escravos Leopoldo e Rodolpho em 1828/1829,' *Revista Brasileira de História & Ciências Sociais* 5, no. 10 (2013): 84–103.

Wilks, Ivor, 'The State of the Akan and the Akan states: A Discursion,' *Cahiers d'Etudes Africaines* 22, 3–4 (1987–88): 232–35.

Wilks, Ivor, *Forests of Gold: Essays on the Akan and the Kingdom of Asante* (Athens: Ohio University Press, 1993).

Wilks, Ivor, *Akwamu 1640–1750: A Study of the Rise and Fall of a West African Empire* (Trondheim: Norwegian University of Science and Technology, 2001).

INDEX